JEFFERSON COLLEGE
3 6021 00026 8551

P9-DHC-552

Contemporary Drama

ELEVEN PLAYS

AMERICAN · ENGLISH · EUROPEAN

Selected and Edited by

E. Bradlee Watson

DARTMOUTH COLLEGE

and

Benfield Pressey

DARTMOUTH COLLEGE

CHARLES SCRIBNER'S SONS

NEW YORK

23 25 27 29 V/P 30 28 26 24 22
Printed in the United States of America

Library of Congress Catalog Card Number 56-6149
SBN 684-41477-5

FOREWORD

This eleven-play anthology of contemporary drama, which, with the single exception of *Pygmalion,* includes only plays of the last quarter-century, is issued in the present inexpensive form to make it available for freshman, sophomore, or other college courses that combine the study of current drama with that of different forms of literature.

The brief prefaces that precede the plays are designed to place each dramatist and his work in the context of his time. Not to overburden these comments with routine detail, the complete date lists of each author's activities and his plays are printed separately. Pertinent bibliographies are appended for the period as a whole and for each dramatist, whose own important comments and essays on drama are listed with the other prefatory matter before his play. In short, we have tried to put every facility for extensive study within easy reach of the thorough student, including detailed references to available prints showing scenes from the productions of all the plays—a listing to be found nowhere else and a convenience indispensable to a complete understanding of the theatre art of the present or any other theatre period.

Except for Bernard Shaw and Jean Giraudoux, all the playwrights included are still alive and potently influential in the world theatre of today—and, perhaps, of tomorrow. Although Shaw's *Pygmalion* is from an earlier period we are including it now because we were barred from making use of that outstanding author's plays in our first collection on account of his refusal to permit the editing of them for classroom study ("See what it has done for Shakespeare!"). From the limited number released for the purpose since Shaw's death we have chosen this ingenious comedy not merely because of its immense success on stage and screen, but rather as an illustration of the free adaptation of the realistic "drama of discussion" inherited from Ibsen. The present-day dramatist, with even fewer inhibitions than Shaw, has little choice but to intensify such reflecting of life, or to adopt some ancient theatre pattern—for which purpose the Greek seems increasingly popular at the moment,—or to free the stage completely from the confinement of the "well-made" play and even its logic. The first of these tendencies is apparent in the work of a Lillian Hellman with its frank and almost brutal analysis of a human situation; the second, in the modernizing of classic plays by a Sartre or an Anouilh; and the last, or complete abandonment of traditional form, is sometimes perplexingly evident in the wide-ranging fantasies of a Christopher Fry or a Giraudoux.

Clearly the theatre of today, like most human institutions in the wake of war, is in process of transition not easy to define. The process, so far, seems to be rather the adaptation of all preceding dramatic invention to a new outlook on existence than a clearly observable progress towards a new dramatic creation. The new outlook—a dim one at best—discerns past errors rather than new victories. Its devoted dramatists have fewer certainties on which to rely than their predecessors of a not very remote past. And so in the present plays we are more affected by their defiance and boldness than by their originality or form of their dramatic substance. Confident "messages," like those of Shaw or O'Neill, are rarely to be heard in the present theatres of free nations. In their stead have come upon our stage an intense and microscopic penetration into life as it is and a free, almost nonchalant display of fantasy and satire. But these are excellencies in themselves, and, to say the least, they are giving to the theatre a forthright sincerity that we clearly recognize in the plays of Arthur Miller, William Saroyan, Thornton Wilder, Lillian Hellman, and Tennessee Williams; and, only less distinctly, in the fantastic vagaries of a Marc Connelly, a Giraudoux, an Anouilh, or a Christopher Fry. And from the freer imaginings of these last and more exuberant visionaries of the new outlook, has come into our theatre a fresh poetic fascination of rare beauty and significance to enrich and delight all who find the highest possible form of entertainment in the many facets of imaginative drama such as this volume presents.

We ourselves were surprised to note, for instance, as we reread these texts in their present arrangement, the wide variations of form, technique, and verbal style with which five of these dramatists had treated, more or less directly, the ancient theme of Chaucer's *Pardoner's Tale: Radix malorum est cupiditas.* Such refreshing variations are, indeed, the penetrating realism of *Another Part of the Forest;* the expressionistic liberties of *Death of a Salesman;* the haunting poetic fantasy of *The Madwoman of Chaillot;* the down-to-earth but scintillating satire of *Ways and Means;* and the hypnotic poetry and symbolism of *Venus Observed.*

The same striving for newness and variety in matters external that has marked the present state of the world—which has still to discover its own inner meaning —seems also to have set its stamp on world drama. In this sense, our plays are still very significantly "the abstract and brief chronicles of the time."

E. B. W.
B. P.

CONTENTS

CONTEMPORARY DRAMA
ELEVEN PLAYS

PYGMALION*

[*A Romance in Five Acts*]

By

BERNARD SHAW

EDITORS' NOTE

IN COMPLIANCE WITH MR. SHAW'S strongly expressed desire that his plays be read for enjoyment without annotation or explanation other than his own, we are presenting below passages from his *Preface to Pygmalion* that are essential to a complete appreciation of his theme and characters.

Following the intentionally inconclusive ending of the play text, we are also reprinting excerpts from Shaw's appended note to explain why the expected happy ending of comedy would be irrational as the outcome of the action of this particular play, and to present the dramatist's own version of a probable, if unromantic, sequence of events that might follow in real life. Shaw's intention in this note is not so much to challenge as to stimulate the reader's own reasoning as to what might happen after the final curtain.

The production of *Pygmalion* in 1913 at His Majesty's Theatre, famous for its sumptuous mountings of Shakespeare, was more widely acclaimed and far more profitable financially than any previous staging of a Shaw play. In a German version it had been acted a few months earlier in Berlin, and the following year it was produced in New York with similar acclaim. In these years just preceding the World War, which culminated what Shaw called his "middle period," *Pygmalion* confirmed, from the theatre point of view, his already wide reputation as a world dramatist of a high order. In the London production, Sir Herbert Beerbohm Tree, England's leading actor-manager, created Higgins; and the most glamorous actress of the day in socialite rôles, Mrs. Beatrice Stella Tanner Patrick Campbell, for whom Shaw wrote the part, *was* Eliza.

It should also be noted that the subject material dealt with in the play, in Shaw's frankly didactic manner, featured two of Shaw's most personal interests: practical phonetics that had made it possible for him to convert his own Irish brogue into the standard pronunciation of London and the universities, giving his most devastating repartee a conversational charm that was quite disarming; and, more essential, his persistent belief that sex should be secondary to mental compatibility and companionship in marriage. So consistent was his devotion to these interests that he willed his large fortune to be spent on a strictly phonetic reform of English spelling; and he exemplified in his own unbroken and, for a genius, uncommonly happy marriage, the desirability of rational wedlock.

CONDENSATION OF SHAW'S

PREFACE TO PYGMALION

A PROFESSOR OF PHONETICS

AS WILL BE SEEN LATER ON, PYGMALION needs, not a preface, but a sequel, which I have supplied in its due place.

The English have no respect for their language, and will not teach their children to speak it. They cannot spell it because they have nothing to spell it with but an old foreign alphabet of which only the consonants—and not all of them—have any agreed speech value. Consequently no man can teach himself what it should sound like from reading it; and it is impossible for an Englishman to open his mouth without making some other Englishman despise him. Most European languages are now accessible in black and white to foreigners: English and French are not thus accessible even to Englishmen and Frenchmen. The reformer we need most today is an energetic phonetic enthusiast: that is why I have made such a one the hero of a popular play.

There have been heroes of that kind crying in the wilderness for many years past. When I became interested in the subject towards the end of the eighteen-seventies, the illustrious Alexander Melville Bell, the inventor of Visible Speech, had emigrated to Canada, where his son invented the telephone; but Alexander J. Ellis was still a London Patriarch, with an impressive head always covered by a velvet skull cap, for which he would apologize to public meetings in a very courtly manner. He and Tito Pagliardini, another phonetic veteran, were men whom it was impossible to dislike. Henry Sweet, then a young man, lacked their sweetness of character: he was about as conciliatory to conventional mortals as Ibsen or Samuel Butler. His great ability as a phonetician (he was, I think, the best of them all at his job) would have entitled him to high official recognition, and perhaps enabled him to popularize his subject, but for his Satanic contempt for all academic dignitaries and persons in general who thought more of Greek than of phonetics. He was, I believe, not in the least an ill-natured man: very much the opposite, I should say; but he would not suffer fools gladly; and to him all scholars who were not rabid phoneticians were fools.

Those who knew him will recognize in my third act the allusion to the Current Shorthand in which he used to write postcards. The postcards which Mrs Higgins describes are such as I have received from Sweet.

Pygmalion Higgins is not a portrait of Sweet, to whom the adventure of Eliza Doolittle would have been impossible; still, as will be seen, there are touches of Sweet in the play. With Higgins's physique and temperament Sweet might have set the Thames on fire.

Of the later generations of phoneticians I know little. Among them towered Robert Bridges, to whom perhaps Higgins may owe his Miltonic sympathies, though here again I must disclaim all portraiture. But if the play makes the public aware that there are such people as phoneticians, and that they are among the most important people in England at present, it will serve its turn.

It is so intensely and deliberately didactic, and its subject is esteemed so dry, that I delight in throwing it at the heads of the wiseacres who repeat the parrot cry that art should never be didactic. It goes to prove my contention that great art can never be anything else.

I may add that the change wrought by Professor Higgins in the flower-girl is neither impossible nor uncommon. The modern concierge's daughter who fulfills her ambition by playing the Queen of Spain in *Ruy Blas* at the Théâtre Français is only one of many thousands of men and women who have sloughed off their native dialects and acquired a new tongue. But the thing has to be done scientifically, or the last state of the aspirant may be worse than the first. An honest slum dialect is more tolerable than the attempts of phonetically untaught persons to imitate the plutocracy. Ambitious flower-girls who read this play must not imagine that they can pass themselves off as fine ladies by untutored imitation. They must learn their alphabet over again, and differently, from a phonetic expert. Imitation will only make them ridiculous.

GEORGE BERNARD SHAW

Born 1856, Dublin. Parents, poor but genteel Protestants: George Carr Shaw, an alcoholic and wit; Elizabeth Gurly, a singer with strong Celtic imagination.
Education: irregular, with governess and clerical uncle, and in three schools. ("I learned nothing from the curriculum.")

1871–1876, Clerk in Dublin Land Agency.

1876, Moved to London with mother; lived on her earnings as singing teacher. He himself earned "a total of £6 in nine years." Read incessantly in the British Museum and practiced on the piano. Joined debating societies and attended lectures.

1882, At lecture by Henry George on Land Nationalization and the Single Tax, he was converted to socialism, which he made his life mission.

1884–1888, Wrote four novels.

1884, Joined the Fabian Society and was elected as Executive.

1885, William Archer, whom with Sidney Webb he met in the Zetetical Debating

Society, obtained for him regular employment as book reviewer to *The Pall Mall Gazette* and art critic to *The World.*

1888–1890, Music critic to *The Star,* signing himself "Corno di Bassetto."

1890–1894, Music critic to *The World.*

1892, Completed his first play, *Widower's Houses,* begun six years earlier in collaboration with William Archer, inspired by their interest in Ibsen; produced the same year by J. T. Grein in The Independent Theatre he had founded in 1891 to introduce Ibsen and encourage young playwrights. A partial success convinced Shaw that the theatre was his most effective medium.

1894, *Arms and the Man,* his third play, but the second produced, was staged by Miss A. E. F. Horniman and Miss Florence Farr. Ran 11 weeks at a loss. It was produced the same year in New York by Richard Mansfield with little better results.

1895–1898, Dramatic critic to *The Saturday Review.* Selected reviews were republished later (1904) under the title: *Dramatic Opinions and Essays* and republished (1932 and 1948) as *Our Theatre in the Nineties.*

1897, *The Devil's Disciple,* produced in New York by actor-manager Richard Mansfield, was a brilliant success, the first to bring its author a considerable return (£3000). His dramatic ambition was confirmed. He resigned from his ill-paid work as critic.

1897–1903, Borough Councillor of St. Pancras, London. As candidate for London City Council, defeated the following year.

1898, *Plays Pleasant and Unpleasant,* the first published collection of Shaw's works. Followed by *Three Plays for Puritans* (1901).

1898, A serious breakdown in health led to his civil marriage with Miss Charlotte Frances Payne-Townshend, a wealthy Irish heiress and fellow Fabian, who offered him companionate marriage to make proper care of his health possible. They were mutually attracted apart from sex, and the marriage was typical of Shaw's treatment of the subject in the plays: although a Marxian, he insisted on marriage, because in the present state of society he believed that no woman should pay the penalty of notoriety for defiance of the marriage convention.

1903, Arnold Daly produced *Candida* in New York, making it a hit of the season. He followed with *Mrs. Warren's Profession* (closed by the censor) and *Arms and the Man,* adding greatly to American interest in Shaw.

1904–1907, The Court Theatre management by Harley Granville-Barker and J. E. Vedrenne as actors and producers gave Shaw his first completely successful London hearing, artistically as well as financially, in their lavish repertory experiment. Hesketh Pearson, Shaw's official English biographer, called it: "The most noteworthy episode in English theatrical history since Shakespeare and Burbage ran the Globe on the Bankside," and he added: "Shaw was at last creating the plays, actors and audiences of his dreams!" For this management Shaw completed and staged under his own direction: *John Bull's Other Island, How He Lied to Her Husband, Major Barbara,* and *The Doctor's Dilemma,* besides reviving earlier plays.

1905, *Man and Superman* (Acts I, II, and IV), superbly mounted and acted by Robert Loraine, gave New York and other American cities their first strong realization of Shaw's depth and power. Loraine was the most perfect embodiment in physique and voice of Tanner ever to appear in the part. In 1907 he was the first to enact Don Juan of Act III (in Hell) at a Court Theatre production in London.

1906, *Candida* in translation by Siegfried Trebitsch given in Dresden, followed by much of the Shaw repertory throughout Germany and Europe. *Candida* was his first play produced in French at Brussels, 1907, and in Paris the following year.

1911, Elected to the Academic Committee of the Royal Society of Literature.

1913, *Pygmalion* a brilliant success at His Majesty's with Sir Herbert Beerbohm Tree and Mrs. Patrick Campbell as Higgins and Eliza, netting £13000.

1914, *Common Sense about the War,* the first of Shaw's polemics against the government's entry into and conduct of World War I, winning him much unpopularity throughout the Empire.

1922, The New York Theatre Guild becomes Shaw's American sponsor, producing among others *Back to Methuselah* (1922) and *St. Joan* (1923).

1925, Awarded the Nobel Prize for Literature. Refused it. ("The money is a lifebelt thrown to a swimmer who has already reached the shore in safety.") Pressed to accept, he deeded the £7000 to The Anglo-Swedish Literary Foundation.

1928, Made Ayot St. Lawrence his permanent place of residence.

1929, Sir Barry Jackson inaugurated the Malvern Festival, a summer theatre enterprise of the highest order, devoted primarily to producing Shaw's work. Shaw wrote for it: *The Apple Cart, The Simpleton of the Unexpected Isles, Geneva,* and *In Good King Charles's Golden Days*. Many earlier plays were revived.

1931, Toured Russia with Lord and Lady Astor.

1950, Died November 1, age 94. Willed the residue of a large fortune in trust for the reform of English spelling on phonetic principles.

PLAYS

(Date of completion precedes title; date of production is in italics; date of publication follows in roman.) 1892 *Widowers' Houses, 1892,* 1893. 1893 *The Philanderer, 1898,* 1898. 1893 *Mrs. Warren's Profession, 1902,* 1898. 1894 *Arms and the Man, 1894,* 1898. 1894 *Candida, 1895,* 1898. 1895 *The Man of Destiny, 1897,* 1898. 1896 *You Never Can Tell, 1898,* 1898. 1896 *The Devil's Disciple, 1897,* 1901. 1898 *Caesar and Cleopatra, 1899,* 1901. 1899 *Captain Brassbound's Conversion, 1899,* 1901. 1901 *The Admirable Bashville, 1902,* 1909 (dramatization in verse of Shaw's novel *Cashel Byron's Profession.* Productions under the title *Cashel Byron's Profession* are of dramatizations not made by Shaw). 1903 *Man and Superman, 1903,* 1903. 1904 *John Bull's Other Island, 1904,* 1907. 1904 *How He Lied to Her Husband, 1904,* 1907 (one act). 1905 *Major Barbara, 1905,* 1907. 1905 *Passion, Poison, and Petrifaction, or, The Fatal Gazogene, 1905,* 1926 (one act). 1906 *The Doctor's Dilemma, 1906,* 1911. 1907 *The Interlude at the Playhouse, 1907,* 1907 (one act). 1908 *Getting Married, 1908,* 1911. 1909 *The Shewing-up of Blanco Posnet, 1909,* 1911 (one act). 1909 *Press Cuttings, 1909,* 1926 (one act). 1909 *The Fascinating Foundling, 1909,* 1926 (one act). 1909 *The Glimpse of Reality, 1927,* 1926 (one act). 1910 *Misalliance, 1910,* 1914. 1910 *The Dark Lady of the Sonnets, 1910,* 1914 (one act). 1911 *Fanny's First Play, 1911,* 1914. 1912 *Androcles and the Lion, 1912,* 1916. 1912 *Overruled, 1912,* 1916 (one act). 1912 *Pygmalion, 1913,* 1916. 1913 *Great Catherine, 1913,* 1919. 1913 *The Music Cure, 1914,* 1926 (one act). 1915 *O'Flaherty, V.C., 1917,* 1919 (one act). 1916 *The Inca of Perusalem, 1916,* 1919 (one act). 1916 *Augustus Does His Bit, 1917,* 1919 (one act). 1917 *Annajanska, the Bolshevik Empress, 1918,* 1919 (one act). 1919 *Heartbreak House, 1920,* 1919. 1920 *Back to Methuselah, 1922,* 1921 (a play cycle in five parts: I, *In the Beginning,* B.C. 4004. II, *The Gospel of the Brothers Barnabas,* A.D. 1920. III, *The Thing Happens,* A.D. 2170. IV, *The Tragedy of an Elderly Gentleman,* A.D. 3000. V, *As Far as Thought Can Reach,* A.D. 31920). 1922 *Jitta's Atonement, 1923,* 1926 ("translation" of *Frau Gitta's Sühne,* by Siegfried Trebitsch). 1923 *Saint Joan, 1923,* 1924. 1929 *The Apple Cart, 1929,* 1931. 1931 *Too True to Be Good, 1932,* 1934. 1933 *Village Wooing, 1934,* 1934. 1933 *On the Rocks, 1933,* 1934. 1934 *The Simpleton of the Unexpected Isles, 1935,* 1936. 1934 *The Six of Calais, 1934,* 1936 (one act). 1935 *The Millionairess, 1936,* 1936. 1937 *Cymbeline Refinished, 1937,* 1947 (Shaw's substitute for the fifth act of Shakespeare's *Cymbeline,* in verse). 1938 *Geneva, 1938,* 1939 (This play was much rewritten after first publication, and subsequent editions differ). 1939 *In Good King Charles's Golden Days, 1939,* 1939. 1948 *Buoyant Billions, 1948,* 1950. 1949 *Shakes versus Shav, 1949,* 1951 (A puppet play, one act). 1950 *Farfetched Fables, 1950,* 1951. 1950 *Why She Would Not* (unfinished, unpublished, unproduced).

SCREENWRITING

1938 *Pygmalion.* 1941 *Major Barbara.* 1945 *Caesar and Cleopatra.*

WRITINGS ON DRAMA

Extensive prefaces printed with Shaw's plays, as published individually or in collections; many are carefully composed essays of great interest, containing much that is essential to the understanding and appreciation of the dramatist's work, and the critical conceptions on which it is based. *The Quintessence of Ibsenism,* a lecture before the Fabian Society (1890), first published in 1891, enlarged in later editions, 1913, 1922. *Dramatic Opinions and Essays,* a collection of Shaw's reviews written while critic to *The Saturday Review* (January 5, 1895 to May 21, 1898), 1906; re-edited by Shaw as *Our Theatre in the Nineties,* 1932, 1948. "Stage Censorship in England," in *North American Review,* August, 1899. Verbatim report of Shaw's testimony before the Joint Select Committee of Inquiry (*re.* censorship) published in *The Stage,* 1910. (See also Preface to *Blanco Posnet.*) "Mr. Trench's Dramatic Values," *Saturday Review,* July, 1910. "A Dramatic Realist to His Critics" (*re. Arms and the Man*) in *The New Review,* July, 1910; also in *The Eclectic Magazine,* September, 1894. "The Theatre of the Future," in *The Grand Magazine,* 1905. "Solution of the Censorship Problem," in *The Academy,* June, 1907. "Censorship of Plays," in *The Nation* (London), November 16, 1907. Preface to *Three Plays of Brieux,* 1911. "On Cutting Shakespeare," in *The Fortnightly Review,* August, 1919. "Make Them Do It Well" (on play production), *Collier's,* June 22, 1922, published separately as *The Art of Rehearsal,* 1928. "Drama and Films" (a dialogue), *Fortnightly Review* and *Harper's,* September, 1924. "Theatre Reviews Then and Now," *Saturday Review,* November 7, 1925. "Censorship of the Drama," *Spectator,* September 12, 1925. *Ellen Terry and Bernard Shaw: a Correspondence,* 1931. *Sixteen Self Sketches,* 1949; although mostly personal, these throw light on Shaw's dramatic aims, especially in Chapter 14 ("Biographers' Blunders Corrected"—note refutation of claim that he was "better than Shakespeare," page 153) and in Chapter 16 on his attitude towards sex and marriage, reflected in his plays. *Bernard Shaw and Mrs. Patrick Campbell, Their Correspondence,* 1952.

PYGMALION

ACT I

Covent Garden at 11.15 p.m. Torrents of heavy summer rain. Cab whistles blowing frantically in all directions. Pedestrians running for shelter into the portico of St Paul's church (not Wren's cathedral but Inigo Jones's church in Covent Garden vegetable market), among them a lady and her daughter in evening dress. All are peering out gloomily at the rain, except one man with his back turned to the rest, wholly preoccupied with a notebook in which he is writing.

The church clock strikes the first quarter.

The Daughter. [*In the space between the central pillars, close to the one on her left.*] I'm getting chilled to the bone. What can Freddy be doing all this time? He's been gone twenty minutes.

The Mother. [*On her* DAUGHTER'S *right.*] Not so long. But he ought to have got us a cab by this.

A Bystander. [*On the* LADY'S *right.*] He wont get no cab not until half-past eleven, missus, when they come back after dropping their theatre fares.

The Mother. But we must have a cab. We cant stand here until half-past eleven. It's too bad.

The Bystander. Well, it ain't my fault, missus.

The Daughter. If Freddy had a bit of gumption he would have got one at the theatre door.

The Mother. What could he have done, poor boy?

The Daughter. Other people got cabs. Why couldnt he?

[FREDDY *rushes in out of the rain from the Southampton Street side, and comes between them closing a dripping umbrella. He is a young man of twenty, in evening dress, very wet round the ankles.*]

The Daughter. Well, havnt you got a cab?

Freddy. Theres not one to be had for love or money.

The Mother. Oh, Freddy, there must be one. You cant have tried.

The Daughter. It's too tiresome. Do you expect us to go and get one ourselves?

Freddy. I tell you theyre all engaged. The rain was so sudden: nobody was prepared; and everybody had to take a cab. I've been to Charing Cross one way and nearly to Ludgate Circus the other; and they were all engaged.

The Mother. Did you try Trafalgar Square?

Freddy. There wasn't one at Trafalgar Square.

The Daughter. Did you try?

Freddy. I tried as far as Charing Cross Station. Did you expect me to walk to Hammersmith?

The Daughter. You havnt tried at all.

The Mother. You really are very helpless, Freddy. Go again; and dont come back until you have found a cab.

Freddy. I shall simply get soaked for nothing.

The Daughter. And what about us? Are we to stay here all night in this draught, with next to nothing on? You selfish pig——

Freddy. Oh, very well: I'll go, I'll go.

[*He opens his umbrella and dashes off Strandwards, but comes into collision with a* FLOWER GIRL *who is hurrying in for shelter, knocking her basket out of her hands. A blinding flash of lightning, followed instantly by a rattling peal of thunder, orchestrates the incident.*]

The Flower Girl. Nah then, Freddy: look wh' y' gowin, deah.

Freddy. Sorry. [*He rushes off.*]

The Flower Girl. [*Picking up her scattered flowers and replacing them in the basket.*] Theres menners f' yer! Te-oo banches o voylets trod into the mad.

[*She sits down on the plinth of the column, sorting her flowers, on the lady's right. She is not at all a romantic figure. She is perhaps eighteen, perhaps twenty, hardly older. She wears a little sailor hat of black straw that has long been exposed to the dust and soot of London and has seldom if ever been brushed. Her hair needs washing rather badly: its mousy color can hardly be natural. She wears a shoddy black coat that reaches nearly to her knees and is shaped to her waist. She has a brown skirt with a coarse apron. Her boots are much the worse for wear. She is no doubt as clean as she can afford to be; but compared to the ladies she is very dirty. Her features are no worse than theirs; but their condition leaves something to be desired; and she needs the services of a dentist.*]

The Mother. How do you know that my son's name is Freddy, pray?

The Flower Girl. Ow, eez ye-ooa san, is e? Wal, fewd dan y' de-ooty bawmz a mather should, eed now bettern to spawl a pore gel's flahrzn than ran awy athaht pyin. Will ye-oo py me f'them?

[*Here, with apologies, this desperate attempt to represent her dialect without a phonetic alphabet must be abandoned as unintelligible outside London.*]

The Daughter. Do nothing of the sort, mother. The idea!

The Mother. Please allow me, Clara. Have you any pennies?

The Daughter. No. Ive nothing smaller than sixpence.

The Flower Girl. [*Hopefully.*] I can give you change for a tanner,* kind lady.

The Mother. [*To* CLARA.] Give it to me. [CLARA *parts reluctantly.*] Now. [*To the girl.*] This is for your flowers.

The Flower Girl. Thank you kindly, lady.

The Daughter. Make her give you the change. These things are only a penny a bunch.

The Mother. Do hold your tongue, Clara. [*To the girl.*] You can keep the change.

The Flower Girl. Oh, thank you, lady.

The Mother. Now tell me how you know that young gentleman's name.

The Flower Girl. I didnt.

The Mother. I heard you call him by it. Dont try to deceive me.

The Flower Girl. [*Protesting.*] Who's trying to deceive you? I called him Freddy or Charlie same as you might yourself if you was talking to a stranger and wished to be pleasant.

The Daughter. Sixpence thrown away! Really, mamma, you might have spared Freddy that.

[*She retreats in disgust behind the pillar.*]

[*An elderly* GENTLEMAN *of the amiable military type rushes into the shelter, and closes a dripping umbrella. He is in the same plight as* FREDDY, *very wet about the ankles. He is in evening dress, with a light overcoat. He takes the place left vacant by the* DAUGHTER.]

The Gentleman. Phew!

The Mother. [*To the* GENTLEMAN.] Oh, sir, is there any sign of its stopping?

The Gentleman. I'm afraid not. It started worse than ever about two minutes ago.

* Sixpence.

[*He goes to the plinth beside the* FLOWER GIRL; *puts up his foot on it; and stoops to turn down his trouser ends.*]

The Mother. Oh dear!

[*She retires sadly and joins her* DAUGHTER.]

The Flower Girl. [*Taking advantage of the military* GENTLEMAN'S *proximity to establish friendly relations with him.*] If it's worse, it's a sign it's nearly over. So cheer up, Captain; and buy a flower off a poor girl.

The Gentleman. I'm sorry. I havnt any change.

The Flower Girl. I can give you change, Captain.

The Gentleman. For a sovereign? Ive nothing less.

The Flower Girl. Garn! Oh do buy a flower off me, Captain. I can change half-a-crown. Take this for tuppence.

The Gentleman. Now dont be troublesome: theres a good girl. [*Trying his pockets.*] I really havnt any change— Stop: heres three hapence, if thats any use to you.

[*He retreats to the other pillar.*]

The Flower Girl. [*Disappointed, but thinking three halfpence better than nothing.*] Thank you, sir.

The Bystander. [*To the girl.*] You be careful: give him a flower for it. Theres a bloke here behind taking down every blessed word youre saying.

[*All turn to the man who is taking notes.*]

The Flower Girl. [*Springing up terrified.*] I aint done nothing wrong by speaking to the gentleman. Ive a right to sell flowers if I keep off the kerb. [*Hysterically.*] I'm a respectable girl: so help me, I never spoke to him except to ask him to buy a flower off me.

[*General hubbub, mostly sympathetic to the* FLOWER GIRL, *but deprecating her excessive sensibility. Cries of* Dont start hollerin. Who's hurting you? Nobody's going to touch you. Whats the good of fussing? Steady on. Easy easy, etc., *come from the elderly staid spectators, who pat her comfortingly. Less patient ones bid her shut her head, or ask her roughly what is wrong with her. A remoter group, not knowing what the matter is, crowd in and increase the noise with question and answer:* Whats the row? What she do? Where is he? A tec taking her down. What! him? Yes: him over there: Took money off the gentleman, etc.]

The Flower Girl. [*Breaking through them to the* GENTLEMAN, *crying wildly.*] Oh, sir, dont let him charge me. You dunno what it means to me. Theyll take away my character and drive me on the streets for speaking to gentlemen. They——

The Note Taker. [*Coming forward on her right, the rest crowding after him.*] There! there! there! there! who's hurting you, you silly girl? What do you take me for?

The Bystander. It's aw rawt: e's a genleman: look at his be-oots. [*Explaining to the* Note Taker.] She thought you was a copper's nark, sir.

The Note Taker. [*With quick interest.*] Whats a copper's nark?

The Bystander. [*Inapt at definition.*] It's a—well, it's a copper's nark, as you might say. What else would you call it? A sort of informer.

The Flower Girl. [*Still hysterical.*] I take my Bible oath I never said a word——

The Note Taker. [*Overbearing but good-humored.*] Oh, shut up, shut up. Do I look like a policeman?

The Flower Girl. [*Far from reassured.*] Then what did you take down my words for? How do I know whether you took me down right? You just shew me what youve wrote about me. [*The* Note Taker *opens his book and holds it steadily under her nose, though the pressure of the mob trying to read it over his shoulders would upset a weaker man.*] Whats that? That aint proper writing. I cant read that.

The Note Taker. I can. [*Reads, reproducing her pronunciation exactly.*] "Cheer ap, Keptin; n' baw ya flahr orf a pore gel."

The Flower Girl. [*Much distressed.*] It's because I called him Captain. I meant no harm. [*To the* Gentleman.] Oh, sir, dont let him lay a charge agen me for a word like that. You——

The Gentleman. Charge! I make no charge. [*To the* Note Taker.] Really, sir, if you are a detective, you need not begin protecting me against molestation by young women until I ask you. Anybody could see that the girl meant no harm.

The Bystanders Generally. [*Demonstrating against police espionage.*] Course they could. What business is it of yours? You mind your own affairs. He wants promotion, he does. Taking down people's words! Girl never said a word to him. What harm if she did? Nice thing a girl cant shelter from the rain without being insulted, etc., etc., etc.,

[*She is conducted by the more sympathetic demonstrators back to her plinth, where she resumes her seat and struggles with her emotion.*]

The Bystander. He aint a tec. He's a blooming busybody: thats what he is. I tell you, look at his be-oots.

The Note Taker. [*Turning on him genially.*] And how are all your people down at Selsey?

The Bystander. [*Suspiciously.*] Who told you my people come from Selsey?

The Note Taker. Never you mind. They did. [*To the girl.*] How do you come to be up so far east? You were born in Lisson Grove.

The Flower Girl. [*Appalled.*] Oh, what harm is there in my leaving Lisson Grove? It wasnt fit for a pig to live in; and I had to pay four-and-six a week. [*In tears.*] Oh, boo —hoo—oo——

The Note Taker. Live where you like; but stop that noise.

The Gentleman. [*To the girl.*] Come, come! he cant touch you: you have a right to live where you please.

A Sarcastic Bystander. [*Thrusting himself between the* Note Taker *and the* Gentleman.] Park Lane, for instance. I'd like to go into the Housing Question with you, I would.

The Flower Girl. [*Subsiding into a brooding melancholy over her basket, and talking very low-spiritedly to herself.*] I'm a good girl, I am.

The Sarcastic Bystander. [*Not attending to her.*] Do you know where *I* come from?

The Note Taker. [*Promptly.*] Hoxton.

[*Titterings. Popular interest in the* Note Taker's *performance increases.*]

The Sarcastic One. [*Amazed.*] Well, who said I didnt? Bly me! you know everything, you do.

The Flower Girl. [*Still nursing her sense of injury.*] Aint no call to meddle with me, he aint.

The Bystander. [*To her.*] Of course he aint. Dont you stand it from him. [*To the* Note Taker.] See here: what call have you to know about people what never offered to meddle with you?

The Flower Girl. Let him say what he likes. I dont want to have no truck with him.

The Bystander. You take us for dirt under your feet, dont you? Catch you taking liberties with a gentleman!

The Sarcastic Bystander. Yes: tell him where he come from if you want to go fortune-telling.

The Note Taker. Cheltenham, Harrow, Cambridge, and India.

The Gentleman. Quite right.

[*Great laughter. Reaction in the* Note Taker's *favor. Exclamations of* He knows all about it. Told him proper.

Hear him tell the toff where he come from? etc.]

The Gentleman. May I ask, sir, do you do this for your living at a music hall?

The Note Taker. I've thought of that. Perhaps I shall some day.

[*The rain has stopped; and the persons on the outside of the crowd begin to drop off.*]

The Flower Girl. [*Resenting the reaction.*] He's no gentleman, he aint, to interfere with a poor girl.

The Daughter. [*Out of patience, pushing her way rudely to the front and displacing the* GENTLEMAN, *who politely retires to the other side of the pillar.*] What on earth is Freddy doing? I shall get pneumownia if I stay in this draught any longer.

The Note Taker. [*To himself, hastily making a note of her pronunciation of "monia."*] Earlscourt.

The Daughter. [*Violently.*] Will you please keep your impertinent remarks to yourself?

The Note Taker. Did I say that out loud? I didnt mean to. I beg your pardon. Your mother's Epsom, unmistakeably.

The Mother. [*Advancing between the* DAUGHTER *and the* NOTE TAKER.] How very curious! I was brought up in Largelady Park, near Epsom.

The Note Taker. [*Uproariously amused.*] Ha! ha! What a devil of a name! Excuse me. [*To the* DAUGHTER.] You want a cab, do you?

The Daughter. Dont dare speak to me.

The Mother. Oh please, please, Clara. [*Her* DAUGHTER *repudiates her with an angry shrug and retires haughtily.*] We should be so grateful to you, sir, if you found us a cab. [*The* NOTE TAKER *produces a whistle.*] Oh, thank you. [*She joins her* DAUGHTER.]

[*The* NOTE TAKER *blows a piercing blast.*]

The Sarcastic Bystander. There! I knowed he was a plain-clothes copper.

The Bystander. That aint a police whistle: thats a sporting whistle.

The Flower Girl. [*Still preoccupied with her wounded feelings.*] He's no right to take away my character. My character is the same to me as any lady's.

The Note Taker. I dont know whether youve noticed it; but the rain stopped about two minutes ago.

The Bystander. So it has. Why didn't you say so before? and us losing our time listening to your silliness!

[*He walks off towards the Strand.*]

The Sarcastic Bystander. I can tell where you come from. You come from Anwell. Go back there.

The Note Taker. [*Helpfully.*] *H*anwell.*

The Sarcastic Bystander. [*Affecting great distinction of speech.*] Thenk you, teacher. Haw haw! So long.

[*He touches his hat with mock respect and strolls off.*]

The Flower Girl. Frightening people like that! How would he like it himself?

The Mother. It's quite fine now, Clara. We can walk to a motor bus. Come.

[*She gathers her skirts above her ankles and hurries off towards the Strand.*]

The Daughter. But the cab— [*Her mother is out of hearing.*] Oh, how tiresome!

[*She follows angrily.*]

[*All the rest have gone except the* NOTE TAKER, *the* GENTLEMAN, *and the* FLOWER GIRL, *who sits arranging her basket, and still pitying herself in murmurs.*]

The Flower Girl. Poor girl! Hard enough for her to live without being worrited and chivied.

The Gentleman. [*Returning to his former place on the* NOTE TAKER's *left.*] How do you do it, if I may ask?

The Note Taker. Simply phonetics. The science of speech. Thats my profession: also my hobby. Happy is the man who can make a living by his hobby! You can spot an Irishman or a Yorkshire man by his brogue. *I* can place any man within six miles. I can place him within two miles in London. Sometimes within two streets.

The Flower Girl. Ought to be ashamed of himself, unmanly coward!

The Gentleman. But is there a living in that?

The Note Taker. Oh yes. Quite a fat one. This is an age of upstarts. Men begin in Kentish Town with £80 a year, and end in Park Lane with a hundred thousand. They want to drop Kentish Town; but they give themselves away every time they open their mouths. Now I can teach them——

The Flower Girl. Let him mind his own business and leave a poor girl——

The Note Taker. [*Explosively.*] Woman: cease this detestable boohooing instantly; or else seek the shelter of some other place of worship.

The Flower Girl. [*With feeble defiance.*] Ive a right to be here if I like, same as you.

The Note Taker. A woman who utters such depressing and disgusting sounds has no right

* Location of a large insane asylum.

to be anywhere—no right to live. Remember that you are a human being with a soul and the divine gift of articulate speech: that your native language is the language of Shakespear and Milton and The Bible; and dont sit there crooning like a bilious pigeon.

The Flower Girl. [*Quite overwhelmed, looking up at him in mingled wonder and deprecation without daring to raise her head.*] Ah-ah-ah-ow-ow-ow-oo!

The Note Taker. [*Whipping out his book.*] Heavens! what a sound! [*He writes; then holds out the book and reads, reproducing her vowels exactly.*] Ah-ah-ah-ow-ow-ow-oo!

The Flower Girl. [*Tickled by the performance, and laughing in spite of herself.*] Garn!

The Note Taker. You see this creature with her kerbstone English: the English that will keep her in the gutter to the end of her days. Well, sir, in three months I could pass that girl off as a duchess at an ambassador's garden party. I could even get her a place as lady's maid or shop assistant, which requires better English.

The Flower Girl. What's that you say?

The Note Taker. Yes, you squashed cabbage leaf, you disgrace to the noble architecture of these columns, you incarnate insult to the English language: I could pass you off as the Queen of Sheba. [*To the* GENTLEMAN.] Can you believe that?

The Gentleman. Of course I can. I am myself a student of Indian dialects; and——

The Note Taker. [*Eagerly.*] Are you? Do you know Colonel Pickering, the author of Spoken Sanscrit?

The Gentleman. I am Colonel Pickering. Who are you?

The Note Taker. Henry Higgins, author of Higgins's Universal Alphabet.

Pickering. [*With enthusiasm.*] I came from India to meet you.

Higgins. I was going to India to meet you.

Pickering. Where do you live?

Higgins. 27A Wimpole Street. Come and see me tomorrow.

Pickering. I'm at the Carlton. Come with me now and lets have a jaw over some supper.

Higgins. Right you are.

The Flower Girl. [*To* PICKERING, *as he passes her.*] Buy a flower, kind gentleman. I'm short for my lodging.

Pickering. I really havnt any change. I'm sorry. [*He goes away.*]

Higgins. [*Shocked at the girl's mendacity.*] Liar. You said you could change half-a-crown.

The Flower Girl. [*Rising in desperation.*] You ought to be stuffed with nails, you ought. [*Flinging the basket at his feet.*] Take the whole blooming basket for sixpence.

[*The church clock strikes the second quarter.*]

Higgins. [*Hearing in it the voice of God, rebuking him for his Pharisaic want of charity to the poor girl.*] A reminder.

[*He raises his hat solemnly; then throws a handful of money into the basket and follows* PICKERING.]

The Flower Girl. [*Picking up a half-crown.*] Ah-ow-ooh! [*Picking up a couple of florins.*] Aaah-ow-ooh! [*Picking up several coins.*] Aaaaah-ow-ooh! [*Picking up a half-sovereign.*] Aaaaaaaaaaaah-ow-ooh!!!

Freddy. [*Springing out of a taxicab.*] Got one at last. Hallo! [*To the girl.*] Where are the two ladies that were here?

The Flower Girl. They walked to the bus when the rain stopped.

Freddy. And left me with a cab on my hands! Damnation!

The Flower Girl. [*With grandeur.*] Never mind, young man. *I'm* going home in a taxi. [*She sails off to the cab. The driver puts his hand behind him and holds the door firmly shut against her. Quite understanding his mistrust, she shews him her handful of money.*] A taxi fare aint no object to me, Charlie. [*He grins and opens the door.*] Angel Court, Drury Lane, next Meiklejohn's oil shop. Let's see how fast you can make her hop it.

[*She gets in and pulls the door to with a slam as the taxicab starts.*]

Freddy. Well, I'm dashed!

ACT II

Next day at 11 a.m. HIGGINS's *laboratory in Wimpole Street. It is a room on the first floor, looking on the street, and was meant for the drawing room. The double doors are in the middle of the back wall; and persons entering find in the corner to their right two tall file cabinets at right angles to one another against the walls. In this corner stands a flat writing-table, on which are a phonograph, a laryngoscope, a row of tiny organ pipes with a bellows, a set of lamp chimneys for singing flames with burners attached to a gas plug in the wall by an indiarubber tube, several tuning-forks of different sizes, a life-size image of half a human head, shewing in section the vocal organs, and a box containing a supply of wax cylinders for the phonograph.*

Further down the room, on the same side, is a fireplace, with a comfortable leather-covered easy-chair at the side of the hearth nearest the door, and a coal-scuttle. There is a clock on the mantelpiece. Between the fireplace and the phonograph table is a stand for newspapers.

On the other side of the central door, to the left of the visitor, is a cabinet of shallow drawers. On it is a telephone and the telephone directory. The corner beyond, and most of the side wall, is occupied by a grand piano, with the keyboard at the end furthest from the door, and a bench for the players extending the full length of the keyboard. On the piano is a dessert dish heaped with fruit and sweets, mostly chocolates.

The middle of the room is clear. Besides the easy-chair, the piano bench, and two chairs at the phonograph table, there is one stray chair. It stands near the fireplace. On the walls, engravings: mostly Piranesis and mezzotint portraits. No paintings.

[PICKERING *is seated at the table, putting down some cards and a tuning-fork which he has been using.* HIGGINS *is standing up near him, closing two or three file drawers which are hanging out. He appears in the morning light as a robust, vital, appetizing sort of man of forty or thereabouts, dressed in a professional-looking black frock-coat with a white linen collar and black silk tie. He is of energetic, scientific type, heartily, even violently interested in everything that can be studied as a scientific subject, and careless about himself and other people, including their feelings. He is, in fact, but for his years and size, rather like a very impetuous baby "taking notice" eagerly and loudly, and requiring almost as much watching to keep him out of unintended mischief. His manner varies from genial bullying when he is in a good humor to stormy petulance when anything goes wrong; but he is so entirely frank and void of malice that he remains likeable even in his least reasonable moments.*]

Higgins. [*As he shuts the last drawer.*] Well, I think thats the whole show.

Pickering. It's really amazing. I havnt taken half of it in, you know.

Higgins. Would you like to go over any of it again?

Pickering. [*Rising and coming to the fireplace, where he plants himself with his back to the fire.*] No, thank you: not now. I'm quite done up for this morning.

Higgins. [*Following him, and standing beside him on his left.*] Tired of listening to sounds?

Pickering. Yes. It's a fearful strain. I rather fancied myself because I can pronounce twenty-four distinct vowel sounds; but your hundred and thirty beat me. I cant hear a bit of difference between most of them.

Higgins. [*Chuckling, and going over to the piano to eat sweets.*] Oh, that comes with practice. You hear no difference at first; but you keep on listening, and presently you find theyre all as different as A from B. [MRS PEARCE *looks in: she is* HIGGINS's *housekeeper.*] Whats the matter?

Mrs Pearce. [*Hesitating, evidently perplexed.*] A young woman asks to see you, sir.

Higgins. A young woman! What does she want?

Mrs Pearce. Well, sir, she says youll be glad to see her when you know what she's come about. She's quite a common girl, sir. Very common indeed. I should have sent her away, only I thought perhaps you wanted her to talk into your machines. I hope Ive not done wrong; but really you see such queer people sometimes—youll excuse me, I'm sure, sir——

Higgins. Oh, thats all right, Mrs Pearce. Has she an interesting accent?

Mrs Pearce. Oh, something dreadful, sir, really. I dont know how you can take an interest in it.

Higgins. [*To* PICKERING.] Lets have her up. Shew her up, Mrs Pearce.

[*He rushes across to his working table and picks out a cylinder to use on the phonograph.*]

Mrs Pearce. [*Only half resigned to it.*] Very well, sir. It's for you to say.

[*She goes downstairs.*]

Higgins. This is rather a bit of luck. I'll shew you how I make records. We'll set her talking; and I'll take it down first in Bell's Visible Speech; then in broad Romic; and then we'll get her on the phonograph so that you can turn her on as often as you like with the written transcript before you.

Mrs Pearce. [*Returning.*] This is the young woman, sir.

[*The* FLOWER GIRL *enters in state. She has a hat with three ostrich feathers, orange, sky-blue, and red. She has a nearly clean apron, and the shoddy coat has been tidied a little. The pathos of this deplorable figure, with its innocent vanity and consequential air, touches* PICKERING, *who has already straightened himself in the presence of* MRS PEARCE. *But as to* HIGGINS, *the only distinction he makes between men and women is that when he is neither bullying nor exclaiming to the heavens against some feather-weight cross, he coaxes women as a child coaxes its nurse when it wants to get anything out of her.*]

Higgins. [*Brusquely, recognizing her with unconcealed disappointment, and at once, babylike, making an intolerable grievance of it.*] Why, this is the girl I jotted down last night. She's no use: I've got all the records I want of the Lisson Grove lingo; and I'm not going to waste another cylinder on it. [*To the girl.*] Be off with you: I dont want you.

The Flower Girl. Dont you be so saucy. You aint heard what I come for yet. [*To* MRS PEARCE, *who is waiting at the door for further instructions.*] Did you tell him I come in a taxi?

Mrs Pearce. Nonsense, girl! what do you think a gentleman like Mr Higgins cares what you came in?

The Flower Girl. Oh, we are proud! He aint above giving lessons, not him: I heard him say so. Well, I aint come here to ask for any compliment; and if my money's not good enough I can go elsewhere.

Higgins. Good enough for what?

The Flower Girl. Good enough for ye-oo. Now you know, dont you? I've come to have lessons, I am. And to pay for em te-oo: make no mistake.

Higgins. [*Stupent.*] Well!!! [*Recovering his breath with a gasp.*] What do you expect me to say to you?

The Flower Girl. Well, if you was a gentleman, you might ask me to sit down, I think. Dont I tell you I'm bringing you business?

Higgins. Pickering: shall we ask this baggage to sit down, or shall we throw her out of the window?

The Flower Girl. [*Running away in terror to the piano, where she turns at bay.*] Ah-ah-oh-ow-ow-ow-oo! [*Wounded and whimpering.*] I wont be called a baggage when Ive offered to pay like any lady.

[*Motionless, the two men stare at her from the other side of the room, amazed.*]

Pickering. [*Gently.*] But what is it you want?

The Flower Girl. I want to be a lady in a flower shop stead of sellin at the corner of Tottenham Court Road. But they wont take me unless I can talk more genteel. He said he could teach me. Well, here I am ready to pay him—not asking any favor—and he treats me zif I was dirt.

Mrs Pearce. How can you be such a foolish ignorant girl as to think you could afford to pay Mr Higgins?

The Flower Girl. Why shouldnt I? I know what lessons cost as well as you do; and I'm ready to pay.

Higgins. How much?

The Flower Girl. [*Coming back to him, triumphant.*] Now youre talking! I thought youd come off it when you saw a chance of getting back a bit of what you chucked at me last night. [*Confidentially.*] Youd had a drop in, hadnt you?

Higgins. [*Peremptorily.*] Sit down.

The Flower Girl. Oh, if youre going to make a compliment of it——

Higgins. [*Thundering at her.*] Sit down.

Mrs Pearce. [*Severely.*] Sit down, girl. Do as youre told.

The Flower Girl. Ah-ah-ah-ow-ow-oo!

[*She stands, half rebellious, half bewildered.*]

Pickering. [*Very courteous.*] Wont you sit down?

[*He places the stray chair near the hearthrug between himself and* HIGGINS.]

Liza. [*Coyly.*] Dont mind if I do.

[*She sits down.* PICKERING *returns to the hearthrug.*]

Higgins. Whats your name?

The Flower Girl. Liza Doolittle.

Higgins. [*Declaiming gravely.*]

Eliza, Elizabeth, Betsy and Bess,
They went to the woods to get a bird's nes':

Pickering. They found a nest with four eggs in it:

Higgins. They took one apiece, and left three in it.

[*They laugh heartily at their own fun.*]

Liza. Oh, dont be silly.

Mrs Pearce. [*Placing herself behind* ELIZA'S *chair.*] You mustnt speak to the gentleman like that.

Liza. Well, why wont he speak sensible to me?

Higgins. Come back to business. How much do you propose to pay me for the lessons?

Liza. Oh, I know whats right. A lady friend of mine gets French lessons for eighteenpence an hour from a real French gentleman. Well, you wouldnt have the face to ask me the same for teaching me my own language as you would for French; so I wont give more than a shilling. Take it or leave it.

Higgins. [*Walking up and down the room, rattling his keys and his cash in his pockets.*]

You know, Pickering, if you consider a shilling, not as a simple shilling, but as a percentage of this girl's income, it works out as fully equivalent to sixty or seventy guineas from a millionaire.

Pickering. How so?

Higgins. Figure it out. A millionaire has about £150 a day. She earns about half-a-crown.

Liza. [*Haughtily.*] Who told you I only——

Higgins. [*Continuing.*] She offers me two-fifths of her day's income for a lesson. Two-fifths of a millionaire's income for a day would be somewhere about £60. It's handsome. By George, it's enormous! it's the biggest offer I ever had.

Liza. [*Rising, terrified.*] Sixty pounds! What are you talking about? I never offered you sixty pounds. Where would I get——

Higgins. Hold your tongue.

Liza. [*Weeping.*] But I aint got sixty pounds. Oh——

Mrs Pearce. Dont cry, you silly girl. Sit down. Nobody is going to touch your money.

Higgins. Somebody is going to touch you, with a broomstick, if you dont stop snivelling. Sit down.

Liza. [*Obeying slowly.*] Ah-ah-ah-ow-oo-o! One would think you was my father.

Higgins. If I decide to teach you, I'll be worse than two fathers to you. Here!

[*He offers her his silk handkerchief.*]

Liza. Whats this for?

Higgins. To wipe your eyes. To wipe any part of your face that feels moist. Remember: thats your handkerchief; and thats your sleeve. Dont mistake the one for the other if you wish to become a lady in a shop.

[LIZA, *utterly bewildered, stares helplessly at him.*]

Mrs Pearce. It's no use talking to her like that, Mr Higgins: she doesnt understand you. Besides, youre quite wrong: she doesnt do it that way at all.

[*She takes the handkerchief.*]

Liza. [*Snatching it.*] Here! You give me that handkerchief. He gev it to me, not to you.

Pickering. [*Laughing.*] He did. I think it must be regarded as her property, Mrs Pearce.

Mrs Pearce. [*Resigning herself.*] Serve you right, Mr Higgins.

Pickering. Higgins: I'm interested. What about the ambassador's garden party? I'll say youre the greatest teacher alive if you make that good. I'll bet you all the expenses of the experiment you cant do it. And I'll pay for the lessons.

Liza. Oh, you are real good. Thank you, Captain.

Higgins. [*Tempted, looking at her.*] It's almost irresistible. She's so deliciously low—so horribly dirty——

Liza. [*Protesting extremely.*] Ah-ah-ah-ah-ow-ow-oo-oo!!! I aint dirty: I washed my face and hands afore I come, I did.

Pickering. Youre certainly not going to turn her head with flattery, Higgins.

Mrs Pearce. [*Uneasy.*] Oh, dont say that, sir: theres more ways than one of turning a girl's head; and nobody can do it better than Mr Higgins, though he may not always mean it. I do hope, sir, you wont encourage him to do anything foolish.

Higgins. [*Becoming excited as the idea grows on him.*] What is life but a series of inspired follies? The difficulty is to find them to do. Never lose a chance: it doesnt come every day. I shall make a duchess of this draggletailed guttersnipe.

Liza. [*Strongly deprecating this view of her.*] Ah-ah-ah-ow-ow-oo!

Higgins. [*Carried away.*] Yes: in six months—in three if she has a good ear and a quick tongue—I'll take her anywhere and pass her off as anything. We'll start today: now! this moment! Take her away and clean her, Mrs Pearce. Monkey Brand,* if it wont come off any other way. Is there a good fire in the kitchen?

Mrs Pearce. [*Protesting.*] Yes; but——

Higgins. [*Storming on.*] Take all her clothes off and burn them. Ring up Whitely † or somebody for new ones. Wrap her up in brown paper til they come.

Liza. Youre no gentleman, youre not, to talk of such things. I'm a good girl, I am; and I know what the like of you are, I do.

Higgins. We want none of your Lisson Grove prudery here, young woman. Youve got to learn to behave like a duchess. Take her away, Mrs Pearce. If she gives you any trouble, wallop her.

Liza. [*Springing up and running between* PICKERING *and* MRS PEARCE *for protection.*] No! I'll call the police, I will.

Mrs Pearce. But Ive no place to put her.

Higgins. Put her in the dustbin.

Liza. Ah-ah-ah-ow-ow-oo!

Pickering. Oh come, Higgins! be reasonable.

Mrs Pearce. [*Resolutely.*] You must be reasonable, Mr Higgins: really you must. You cant walk over everybody like this.

[HIGGINS, *thus scolded, subsides. The*

* A pumice or sand soap.

† Well-known London department store.

hurricane is succeeded by a zephyr of amiable surprise.]

Higgins. [*With professional exquisiteness of modulation.*] *I* walk over everybody! My dear Mrs Pearce, my dear Pickering, I never had the slightest intention of walking over anyone. All I propose is that we should be kind to this poor girl. We must help her to prepare and fit herself for her new station in life. If I did not express myself clearly it was because I did not wish to hurt her delicacy, or yours.

[LIZA, *reassured, steals back to her chair.*]

Mrs Pearce. [*To* PICKERING.] Well, did you ever hear anything like that, sir?

Pickering. [*Laughing heartily.*] Never, Mrs Pearce: never.

Higgins. [*Patiently.*] Whats the matter?

Mrs Pearce. Well, the matter is, sir, that you cant take a girl up like that as if you were picking up a pebble on the beach.

Higgins. Why not?

Mrs Pearce. Why not! But you dont know anything about her. What about her parents? She may be married.

Liza. Garn!

Higgins. There! As the girl very properly says, Garn! Married indeed! Dont you know that a woman of that class looks a worn out drudge of fifty a year after she's married?

Liza. Whood marry me?

Higgins. [*Suddenly resorting to the most thrillingly beautiful low tones in his best elocutionary style.*] By George, Eliza, the streets will be strewn with the bodies of men shooting themselves for your sake before Ive done with you.

Mrs Pearce. Nonsense, sir. You mustnt talk like that to her.

Liza. [*Rising and squaring herself determinedly.*] I'm going away. He's off his chump, he is. I dont want no balmies teaching me.

Higgins. [*Wounded in his tenderest point by her insensibility to his elocution.*] Oh, indeed! I'm mad, am I? Very well, Mrs Pearce: you neednt order the new clothes for her. Throw her out.

Liza. [*Whimpering.*] Nah-ow. You got no right to touch me.

Mrs Pearce. You see now what comes of being saucy. [*Indicating the door.*] This way, please.

Liza. [*Almost in tears.*] I didnt want no clothes. I wouldnt have taken them. [*She throws away the handkerchief.*] I can buy my own clothes.

Higgins. [*Deftly retrieving the handkerchief and intercepting her on her reluctant way to the door.*] Youre an ungrateful wicked girl. This is my return for offering to take you out of the gutter and dress you beautifully and make a lady of you.

Mrs Pearce. Stop, Mr Higgins. I wont allow it. It's you that are wicked. Go home to your parents, girl; and tell them to take better care of you.

Liza. I aint got no parents. They told me I was big enough to earn my own living and turned me out.

Mrs Pearce. Wheres your mother?

Liza. I aint got no mother. Her that turned me out was my sixth stepmother. But I done without them. And I'm a good girl, I am.

Higgins. Very well, then, what on earth is all this fuss about? The girl doesnt belong to anybody—is no use to anybody but me. [*He goes to* MRS PEARCE *and begins coaxing.*] You can adopt her, Mrs Pearce: I'm sure a daughter would be a great amusement to you. Now dont make any more fuss. Take her downstairs; and——

Mrs Pearce. But whats to become of her? Is she to be paid anything? Do be sensible, sir.

Higgins. Oh, pay her whatever is necessary: put it down in the housekeeping book. [*Impatiently.*] What on earth will she want with money? She'll have her food and her clothes. She'll only drink if you give her money.

Liza. [*Turning on him.*] Oh you are a brute. It's a lie: nobody ever saw the sign of liquor on me.

[*She goes back to her chair and plants herself there defiantly.*]

Pickering. [*In good-humored remonstrance.*] Does it occur to you, Higgins, that the girl has some feelings?

Higgins. [*Looking critically at her.*] Oh no, I dont think so. Not any feelings that we need bother about. [*Cheerily.*] Have you, Eliza?

Liza. I got my feelings same as anyone else.

Higgins. [*To* PICKERING, *reflectively.*] You see the difficulty?

Pickering. Eh? What difficulty?

Higgins. To get her to talk grammar. The mere pronunciation is easy enough.

Liza. I dont want to talk grammar. I want to talk like a lady in a flower-shop.

Mrs Pearce. Will you please keep to the point, Mr Higgins? I want to know on what terms the girl is to be here. Is she to have any wages? And what is to become of her when youve finished your teaching? You must look ahead a little.

Higgins. [*Impatiently.*] Whats to become of her if I leave her in the gutter? Tell me that, Mrs Pearce.

Mrs Pearce. Thats her own business, not yours, Mr Higgins.

Higgins. Well, when Ive done with her, we can throw her back into the gutter; and then it will be her own business again; so thats all right.

Liza. Oh, youve no feeling heart in you: you dont care for nothing but yourself. [*She rises and takes the floor resolutely.*] Here! I've had enough of this. I'm going. [*Making for the door.*] You ought to be ashamed of yourself, you ought.

Higgins. [*Snatching a chocolate cream from the piano, his eyes suddenly beginning to twinkle with mischief.*] Have some chocolates, Eliza.

Liza. [*Halting, tempted.*] How do I know what might be in them? Ive heard of girls being drugged by the like of you.

[HIGGINS *whips out his penknife; cuts a chocolate in two; puts one half into his mouth and bolts it; and offers her the other half.*]

Higgins. Pledge of good faith, Eliza. I eat one half: you eat the other. [LIZA *opens her mouth to retort: he pops the half chocolate into it.*] You shall have boxes of them, barrels of them, every day. You shall live on them. Eh?

Liza. [*Who has disposed of the chocolate after being nearly choked by it.*] I wouldnt have ate it, only I'm too ladylike to take it out of my mouth.

Higgins. Listen, Eliza. I think you said you came in a taxi.

Liza. Well, what if I did? Ive as good a right to take a taxi as anyone else.

Higgins. You have, Eliza; and in future you shall have as many taxis as you want. You shall go up and down and round the town in a taxi every day. Think of that, Eliza.

Mrs Pearce. Mr Higgins: youre tempting the girl. It's not right. She should think of the future.

Higgins. At her age! Nonsense! Time enough to think of the future when you havnt any future to think of. No, Eliza: do as this lady does: think of other people's futures; but never think of your own. Think of chocolates, and taxis, and gold, and diamonds.

Liza. No: I dont want no gold and no diamonds. I'm a good girl, I am. [*She sits down again, with an attempt at dignity.*]

Higgins. You shall remain so, Eliza, under the care of Mrs Pearce. And you shall marry an officer in the Guards, with a beautiful moustache: the son of a marquis, who will disinherit him for marrying you, but will relent when he sees your beauty and goodness——

Pickering. Excuse me, Higgins; but I really must interfere. Mrs Pearce is quite right. If this girl is to put herself in your hands for six months for an experiment in teaching, she must understand thoroughly what she's doing.

Higgins. How can she? She's incapable of understanding anything. Besides, do any of us understand what we are doing? If we did, would we ever do it?

Pickering. Very clever, Higgins; but not to the present point. [*To* ELIZA.] Miss Doolittle——

Liza. [*Overwhelmed.*] Ah-ah-ow-oo!

Higgins. There! Thats all youll get out of Eliza. Ah-ah-ow-oo! No use explaining. As a military man you ought to know that. Give her her orders: thats enough for her. Eliza: you are to live here for the next six months, learning how to speak beautifully, like a lady in a florist's shop. If youre good and do whatever youre told, you shall sleep in a proper bedroom, and have lots to eat, and money to buy chocolates and take rides in taxis. If youre naughty and idle you will sleep in the back kitchen among the black beetles, and be walloped by Mrs Pearce with a broomstick. At the end of six months you shall go to Buckingham Palace in a carriage, beautifully dressed. If the King finds out youre not a lady, you will be taken by the police to the Tower of London, where your head will be cut off as a warning to other presumptuous flower girls. If you are not found out, you shall have a present of seven-and-sixpence to start life with as a lady in a shop. If you refuse this offer you will be a most ungrateful wicked girl; and the angels will weep for you. [*To* PICKERING.] Now are you satisfied, Pickering? [*To* MRS PEARCE.] Can I put it more plainly and fairly, Mrs Pearce?

Mrs Pearce. [*Patiently.*] I think youd better let me speak to the girl properly in private. I dont know that I can take charge of her or consent to the arrangement at all. Of course I know you dont mean her any harm; but when you get what you call interested in people's accents, you never think or care what may happen to them or you. Come with me, Eliza.

Higgins. Thats all right. Thank you, Mrs Pearce. Bundle her off to the bath-room.

Liza. [*Rising reluctantly and suspiciously.*] Youre a great bully, you are. I wont stay here if I dont like. I wont let nobody wallop me.

I never asked to go to Bucknam Palace, I didnt. I was never in trouble with the police, not me. I'm a good girl——

Mrs Pearce. Dont answer back, girl. You dont understand the gentleman. Come with me. [*She leads the way to the door, and holds it open for* ELIZA.]

Liza. [*As she goes out.*] Well, what I say is right. I wont go near the King, not if I'm going to have my head cut off. If I'd known what I was letting myself in for, I wouldnt have come here. I always been a good girl; and I never offered to say a word to him; and I dont owe him nothing; and I dont care; and I wont be put upon; and I have my feelings the same as anyone else——

[MRS PEARCE *shuts the door; and* ELIZA'S *plaints are no longer audible.* PICKERING *comes from the hearth to the chair and seats himself astride it with his arms on the back.*]

Pickering. Excuse the straight question, Higgins. Are you a man of good character where women are concerned?

Higgins. [*Moodily.*] Have you ever met a man of good character where women are concerned?

Pickering. Yes: very frequently.

Higgins. [*Dogmatically, lifting himself on his hands to the level of the piano, and sitting on it with a bounce.*] Well, I havnt. I find that the moment I let a woman make friends with me, she becomes jealous, exacting, suspicious, and a damned nuisance. I find that the moment I let myself make friends with a woman, I become selfish and tyrannical. Women upset everything. When you let them into your life, you find that the woman is driving at one thing and youre driving at another.

Pickering. At what, for example?

Higgins. [*Coming off the piano restlessly.*] Oh, Lord knows! I suppose the woman wants to live her own life; and the man wants to live his; and each tries to drag the other on to the wrong track. One wants to go north and the other south; and the result is that both have to go east, though they both hate the east wind. [*He sits down on the bench at the keyboard.*] So here I am, a confirmed old bachelor, and likely to remain so.

Pickering. [*Rising and standing over him gravely.*] Come, Higgins! You know what I mean. If I'm to be in this business I shall feel responsible for that girl. I hope it's understood that no advantage is to be taken of her position.

Higgins. What! That thing! Sacred, I assure you. [*Rising to explain.*] You see, she'll be a pupil; and teaching would be impossible unless pupils were sacred. Ive taught scores of American millionairesses how to speak English: the best looking women in the world. I'm seasoned. They might as well be blocks of wood. *I* might as well be a block of wood. It's——

[MRS PEARCE *opens the door. She has* ELIZA'S *hat in her hand.* PICKERING *retires to the easy-chair at the hearth and sits down.*]

Higgins. [*Eagerly.*] Well, Mrs Pearce: is it all right?

Mrs Pearce. [*At the door.*] I just wish to trouble you with a word, if I may, Mr Higgins.

Higgins. Yes, certainly. Come in. [*She comes forward.*] Dont burn that, Mrs Pearce. I'll keep it as a curiosity. [*He takes the hat.*]

Mrs Pearce. Handle it carefully, sir, please. I had to promise her not to burn it; but I had better put it in the oven for a while.

Higgins. [*Putting it down hastily on the piano.*] Oh! thank you. Well, what have you to say to me?

Pickering. Am I in the way?

Mrs Pearce. Not in the least, sir. Mr. Higgins: will you please be very particular what you say before the girl?

Higgins. [*Sternly.*] Of course. I'm always particular about what I say. Why do you say this to me?

Mrs Pearce. [*Unmoved.*] No, sir: youre not at all particular when youve mislaid anything or when you get a little impatient. Now it doesnt matter before me: I'm used to it. But you really must not swear before the girl.

Higgins. [*Indignantly.*] *I* swear! [*Most emphatically.*] I never swear. I detest the habit. What the devil do you mean?

Mrs Pearce. [*Stolidly.*] Thats what I mean, sir. You swear a great deal too much. I dont mind your damning and blasting, and what the devil and where the devil and who the devil——

Higgins. Mrs Pearce: this language from your lips! Really!

Mrs Pearce. [*Not to be put off.*]—but there is a certain word I must ask you not to use. The girl used it herself when she began to enjoy the bath. It begins with the same letter as bath. She knows no better: she learnt it at her mother's knee. But she must not hear it from your lips.

Higgins. [*Loftily.*] I cannot charge myself with having ever uttered it, Mrs Pearce. [*She looks at him steadfastly. He adds, hiding an uneasy conscience with a judicial air.*] Except perhaps in a moment of extreme and justifiable excitement.

Mrs Pearce. Only this morning, sir, you applied it to your boots, to the butter, and to the brown bread.

Higgins. Oh, that! Mere alliteration, Mrs Pearce, natural to a poet.

Mrs Pearce. Well, sir, whatever you choose to call it, I beg you not let the girl hear you repeat it.

Higgins. Oh, very well, very well. Is that all?

Mrs Pearce. No, sir. We shall have to be very particular with this girl as to personal cleanliness.

Higgins. Certainly. Quite right. Most important.

Mrs Pearce. I mean not to be slovenly about her dress or untidy in leaving things about.

Higgins. [*Going to her solemnly.*] Just so. I intended to call your attention to that. [*He passes on to* PICKERING, *who is enjoying the conversation immensely.*] It is these little things that matter, Pickering. Take care of the pence and the pounds will take care of themselves is as true of personal habits as of money. [*He comes to anchor on the hearthrug, with the air of a man in an unassailable position.*]

Mrs Pearce. Yes, sir. Then might I ask you not to come down to breakfast in your dressing-gown, or at any rate not to use it as a napkin to the extent you do, sir. And if you would be so good as not to eat everything off the same plate, and to remember not to put the porridge saucepan out of your hand on the clean tablecloth, it would be a better example to the girl. You know you nearly choked yourself with a fishbone in the jam only last week.

Higgins. [*Routed from the hearthrug and drifting back to the piano.*] I may do these things sometimes in absence of mind; but surely I dont do them habitually. [*Angrily.*] By the way: my dressing-gown smells most damnably of benzine.

Mrs Pearce. No doubt it does, Mr Higgins. But if you will wipe your fingers——

Higgins. [*Yelling.*] Oh very well, very well: I'll wipe them in my hair in future.

Mrs Pearce. I hope youre not offended, Mr Higgins.

Higgins. [*Shocked at finding himself thought capable of an unamiable sentiment.*] Not at all, not at all. Youre quite right, Mrs Pearce: I shall be particularly careful before the girl. Is that all?

Mrs Pearce. No, sir. Might she use some of those Japanese dresses you brought from abroad? I really cant put her back into her old things.

Higgins. Certainly. Anything you like. Is that all?

Mrs Pearce. Thank you, sir. Thats all. [*She goes out.*]

Higgins. You know, Pickering, that woman has the most extraordinary ideas about me. Here I am, a shy, diffident sort of man. Ive never been able to feel really grown-up and tremendous, like other chaps. And yet she's firmly persuaded that I'm an arbitrary overbearing bossing kind of person. I cant account for it. [MRS PEARCE *returns.*]

Mrs Pearce. If you please, sir, the trouble's beginning already. Theres a dustman downstairs, Alfred Doolittle, wants to see you. He says you have his daughter here.

Pickering. [*Rising.*] Phew! I say!

Higgins. [*Promptly.*] Send the blackguard up.

Mrs Pearce. Oh, very well, sir. [*She goes out.*]

Pickering. He may not be a blackguard, Higgins.

Higgins. Nonsense. Of course he's a blackguard.

Pickering. Whether he is or not, I'm afraid we shall have some trouble with him.

Higgins. [*Confidently.*] Oh no: I think not. If theres any trouble he shall have it with me, not I with him. And we are sure to get something interesting out of him.

Pickering. About the girl?

Higgins. No. I mean his dialect.

Pickering. Oh!

Mrs Pearce. [*At the door.*] Doolittle, sir. [*She admits* DOOLITTLE *and retires.*]

[ALFRED DOOLITTLE *is an elderly but vigorous dustman, clad in the costume of his profession, including a hat with a back brim covering his neck and shoulders. He has well marked and rather interesting features, and seems equally free from fear and conscience. He has a remarkably expressive voice, the result of a habit of giving vent to his feelings without reserve. His present pose is that of wounded honor and stern resolution.*]

Doolittle. [*At the door, uncertain which of the two gentlemen is his man.*] Professor Iggins?

Higgins. Here. Good morning. Sit down.

Doolitle. Morning, Governor. [*He sits down magisterially.*] I come about a very serious matter, Governor.

Higgins. [*To* PICKERING.] Brought up in Hounslow. Mother Welsh, I should think.

[DOOLITTLE *opens his mouth, amazed.* HIGGINS *continues.*] What do you want, Doolittle?

Doolittle. [*Menacingly.*] I want my daughter: thats what I want. See?

Higgins. Of course you do. Youre her father, arnt you? You dont suppose anyone else wants her, do you? I'm glad to see you have some spark of family feeling left. She's upstairs. Take her away at once.

Doolittle. [*Rising, fearfully taken aback.*] What!

Higgins. Take her away. Do you suppose I'm going to keep your daughter for you?

Doolittle. [*Remonstrating.*] Now, now, look here, Governor. Is this reasonable? Is it fairity to take advantage of a man like this? The girl belongs to me. You got her. Where do I come in? [*He sits down again.*]

Higgins. Your daughter had the audacity to come to my house and ask me to teach her how to speak properly so that she could get a place in a flower-shop. This gentleman and my housekeeper have been here all the time. [*Bullying him.*] How dare you come here and attempt to blackmail me? You sent her here on purpose.

Doolittle. [*Protesting.*] No, Governor.

Higgins. You must have. How else could you possibly know that she is here?

Doolittle. Don't take a man up like that, Governor.

Higgins. The police shall take you up. This is a plant—a plot to extort money by threats. I shall telephone for the police.

[*He goes resolutely to the telephone and opens the directory.*]

Doolittle. Have I asked you for a brass farthing? I leave it to the gentleman here: have I said a word about money?

Higgins. [*Throwing the book aside and marching down on* DOOLITTLE *with a poser.*] What else did you come for?

Doolittle. [*Sweetly.*] Well, what would a man come for? Be human, Governor.

Higgins. [*Disarmed.*] Alfred: did you put her up to it?

Doolittle. So help me, Governor, I never did. I take my Bible oath I aint seen the girl these two months past.

Higgins. Then how did you know she was here?

Doolittle. [*"Most musical, most melancholy."*] I'll tell you, Governor, if youll only let me get a word in. I'm willing to tell you. I'm wanting to tell you. I'm waiting to tell you.

Higgins. Pickering: this chap has a certain natural gift of rhetoric. Observe the rhythm of his native woodnotes wild. "I'm willing to tell you: I'm wanting to tell you: I'm waiting to tell you." Sentimental rhetoric! thats the Welsh strain in him. It also accounts for his mendacity and dishonesty.

Pickering. Oh, please, Higgins: I'm west country myself. [*To* DOOLITTLE.] How did you know the girl was here if you didnt send her?

Doolittle. It was like this, Governor. The girl took a boy in the taxi to give him a jaunt. Son of her landlady, he is. He hung about on the chance of her giving him another ride home. Well, she sent him back for her luggage when she heard you was willing for her to stop here. I met the boy at the corner of Long Acre and Endell Street.

Higgins. Public house. Yes?

Doolittle. The poor man's club, Governor: why shouldnt I?

Pickering. Do let him tell his story, Higgins.

Doolittle. He told me what was up. And I ask you, what was my feelings and my duty as a father? I says to the boy, "You bring me the luggage," I says——

Pickering. Why didnt you go for it yourself?

Doolittle. Landlady wouldnt have trusted me with it, Governor. She's that kind of woman: you know. I had to give the boy a penny afore he trusted me with it, the little swine. I brought it to her just to oblige you like, and make myself agreeable. Thats all.

Higgins. How much luggage?

Doolittle. Musical instrument, Governor. A few pictures, a trifle of jewelry, and a bird-cage. She said she didnt want no clothes. What was I to think from that, Governor? I ask you as a parent what was I to think?

Higgins. So you came to rescue her from worse than death, eh?

Doolittle. [*Appreciatively: relieved at being so well understood.*] Just so, Governor. Thats right.

Pickering. But why did you bring her luggage if you intended to take her away?

Doolittle. Have I said a word about taking her away? Have I now?

Higgins. [*Determinedly.*] Youre going to take her away, double quick.

[*He crosses to the hearth and rings the bell.*]

Doolittle. [*Rising.*] No, Governor. Dont say that. I'm not the man to stand in my girl's light. Heres a career opening for her, as you might say; and——

[MRS PEARCE *opens the door and awaits orders.*]

Higgins. Mrs Pearce: this is Eliza's father. He has come to take her away. Give her to him. [*He goes back to the piano, with an air of washing his hands of the whole affair.*]

Doolittle. No. This is a misunderstanding. Listen here——

Mrs Pearce. He cant take her away, Mr Higgins: how can he? You told me to burn her clothes.

Doolittle. Thats right. I cant carry the girl through the streets like a blooming monkey, can I? I put it to you.

Higgins. You have put it to me that you want your daughter. Take your daughter. If she has no clothes go out and buy her some.

Doolittle. [*Desperate.*] Wheres the clothes she come in? Did I burn them or did your missus here?

Mrs Pearce. I am the housekeeper, if you please. I have sent for some clothes for your girl. When they come you can take her away. You can wait in the kitchen. This way, please.

[DOOLITTLE, *much troubled, accompanies her to the door; then hesitates; finally turns confidentially to* HIGGINS.]

Doolittle. Listen here, Governor. You and me is men of the world, aint we?

Higgins. Oh! Men of the world, are we? Youd better go, Mrs Pearce.

Mrs Pearce. I think so, indeed, sir.

[*She goes, with dignity.*]

Pickering. The floor is yours, Mr Doolittle.

Doolittle. [*To* PICKERING.] I thank you, Governor. [*To* HIGGINS, *who takes refuge on the piano bench, a little overwhelmed by the proximity of his visitor; for* DOOLITTLE *has a professional flavor of dust about him.*] Well, the truth is, I've taken a sort of fancy to you, Governor; and if you want the girl, I'm not so set on having her back home again but what I might be open to an arrangement. Regarded in the light of a young woman, she's a fine handsome girl. As a daughter she's not worth her keep; and so I tell you straight. All I ask is my rights as a father; and youre the last man alive to expect me to let her go for nothing; for I can see youre one of the straight sort, Governor. Well, whats a five-pound note to you? and whats Eliza to me?

[*He turns to his chair and sits down judicially.*]

Pickering. I think you ought to know, Doolittle, that Mr Higgins's intentions are entirely honorable.

Doolittle. Course they are, Governor. If I thought they wasn't, I'd ask fifty.

Higgins. [*Revolted.*] Do you mean to say that you would sell your daughter for £50?

Doolittle. Not in a general way I wouldn't; but to oblige a gentleman like you I'd do a good deal, I do assure you.

Pickering. Have you no morals, man?

Doolittle. [*Unabashed.*] Cant afford them, Governor. Neither could you if you was as poor as me. Not that I mean any harm, you know. But if Liza is going to have a bit out of this, why not me too?

Higgins. [*Troubled.*] I dont know what to do, Pickering. There can be no question that as a matter of morals it's a positive crime to give this chap a farthing. And yet I feel a sort of rough justice in his claim.

Doolittle. Thats it, Governor. Thats all I say. A father's heart, as it were.

Pickering. Well, I know the feeling; but really it seems hardly right——

Doolittle. Dont say that, Governor. Dont look at it that way. What am I, Governors both? I ask you, what am I? I'm one of the undeserving poor: thats what I am. Think of what that means to a man. It means that he's up agen middle class morality all the time. If theres anything going, and I put in for a bit of it, it's always the same story: "Youre undeserving; so you cant have it." But my needs is as great as the most deserving widow's that ever got money out of six different charities in one week for the death of the same husband. I dont need less than a deserving man: I need more. I dont eat less hearty than him; and I drink a lot more. I want a bit of amusement, cause I'm a thinking man. I want cheerfulness and a song and a band when I feel low. Well, they charge me just the same for everything as they charge the deserving. What is middle class morality? Just an excuse for never giving me anything. Therefore, I ask you, as two gentlemen, not to play that game on me. I'm playing straight with you. I aint pretending to be deserving. I'm undeserving; and I mean to go on being undeserving. I like it; and thats the truth. Will you take advantage of a man's nature to do him out of the price of his own daughter what he's brought up and fed and clothed by the sweat of his brow until she's growed big enough to be interesting to you two gentlemen? Is five pounds unreasonable? I put it to you; and I leave it to you.

Higgins. [*Rising, and going over to* PICKERING.] Pickering: if we were to take this man in hand for three months, he could choose between a seat in the Cabinet and a popular pulpit in Wales.

Pickering. What do you say to that, Doolittle?

Doolittle. Not me, Governor, thank you kindly. Ive heard all the preachers and all the prime ministers—for I'm a thinking man and game for politics or religion or social reform same as all the other amusements—and I tell you it's a dog's life any way you look at it. Undeserving poverty is my line. Taking one station in society with another, it's—it's—well, it's the only one that has any ginger in it, to my taste.

Higgins. I suppose we must give him a fiver.

Pickering. He'll make a bad use of it, I'm afraid.

Doolittle. Not me, Governor, so help me I wont. Dont you be afraid that I'll save it and spare it and live idle on it. There wont be a penny of it left by Monday: I'll have to go to work same as if I'd never had it. It wont pauperize me, you bet. Just one good spree for myself and the missus, giving pleasure to ourselves and employment to others, and satisfaction to you to think it's not been throwed away. You couldnt spend it better.

Higgins. [*Taking out his pocket book and coming between* DOOLITTLE *and the piano.*] This is irresistible. Lets give him ten.

[*He offers two notes to the dustman.*]

Doolittle. No, Governor. She wouldnt have the heart to spend ten; and perhaps I shouldnt neither. Ten pounds is a lot of money: it makes a man feel prudent like; and then goodbye to happiness. You give me what I ask you, Governor: not a penny more, and not a penny less.

Pickering. Why dont you marry that missus of yours? I rather draw the line at encouraging that sort of immorality.

Doolittle. Tell her so, Governor: tell her so. *I*'m willing. It's me that suffers by it. Ive no hold on her. I got to be agreeable to her. I got to give her presents. I got to buy her clothes something sinful. I'm a slave to that woman, Governor, just because I'm not her lawful husband. And she knows it too. Catch her marrying me! Take my advice, Governor: marry Eliza while she's young and dont know no better. If you dont you'll be sorry for it after. If you do, she'll be sorry for it after; but better her than you, because youre a man, and she's only a woman and dont know how to be happy anyhow.

Higgins. Pickering: if we listen to this man another minute, we shall have no convictions left. [*To* DOOLITTLE.] Five pounds I think you said.

Doolittle. Thank you kindly, Governor.

Higgins. Youre sure you wont take ten?

Doolittle. Not now. Another time, Governor.

Higgins. [*Handing him a five-pound note.*] Here you are.

Doolittle. Thank you, Governor. Good morning. [*He hurries to the door, anxious to get away with his booty. When he opens it he is confronted with a dainty and exquisitely clean young* JAPANESE LADY *in a simple blue cotton kimono printed cunningly with small white jasmine blossoms.* MRS PEARCE *is with her. He gets out of her way deferentially and apologizes.*] Beg pardon, miss.

The Japanese Lady. Garn! Dont you know your own daughter?

Doolittle. } *Exclaiming* { Bly me! it's Eliza!
Higgins. } *simul-* { What's that? This!
Pickering. } *taneously.* { By Jove!

Liza. Dont I look silly?

Higgins. Silly?

Mrs Pearce. [*At the door.*] Now, Mr Higgins, please dont say anything to make the girl conceited about herself.

Higgins. [*Conscientiously.*] Oh! Quite right, Mrs Pearce. [*To* ELIZA.] Yes: damned silly.

Mrs Pearce. Please, sir.

Higgins. [*Correcting himself.*] I mean extremely silly.

Liza. I should look all right with my hat on.

[*She takes up her hat; puts it on; and walks across the room to the fireplace with a fashionable air.*]

Higgins. A new fashion, by George! And it ought to look horrible!

Doolittle. [*With fatherly pride.*] Well, I never thought she'd clean up as good looking as that, Governor. She's a credit to me, aint she?

Liza. I tell you, it's easy to clean up here. Hot and cold water on tap, just as much as you like, there is. Woolly towels, there is; and a towel horse so hot, it burns your fingers. Soft brushes to scrub yourself, and a wooden bowl of soap smelling like primroses. Now I know why ladies is so clean. Washing's a treat for them. Wish they could see what it is for the like of me!

Higgins. I'm glad the bathroom met with your approval.

Liza. It didnt: not all of it; and I dont care who hears me say it. Mrs Pearce knows.

Higgins. What was wrong, Mrs Pearce?

Mrs Pearce. [*Blandly.*] Oh, nothing sir. It doesnt matter.

Liza. I had a good mind to break it. I didnt know which way to look. But I hung a towel over it, I did.

Higgins. Over what?

Mrs Pearce. Over the looking-glass, sir.

Higgins. Doolittle: you have brought your daughter up too strictly.

Doolittle. Me! I never brought her up at all, except to give her a lick of a strap now and again. Dont put it on me, Governor. She aint accustomed to it, you see: thats all. But she'll soon pick up your free-and-easy ways.

Liza. I'm a good girl, I am; and I wont pick up no free-and-easy ways.

Higgins. Eliza: if you say again that youre a good girl, your father shall take you home.

Liza. Not him. You dont know my father. All he come here for was to touch you for some money to get drunk on.

Doolittle. Well, what else would I want money for? To put into the plate in church, I suppose. [*She puts out her tongue at him. He is so incensed by this that* PICKERING *presently finds it necessary to step between them.*] Dont you give me none of your lip; and dont let me hear you giving this gentleman any of it neither, or youll hear from me about it. See?

Higgins. Have you any further advice to give her before you go, Doolittle? Your blessing, for instance.

Doolittle. No, Governor: I aint such a mug as to put up my children to all I know myself. Hard enough to hold them in without that. If you want Eliza's mind improved, Governor, you do it yourself with a strap. So long, gentlemen. [*He turns to go.*]

Higgins. [*Impressively.*] Stop. Youll come regularly to see your daughter. It's your duty, you know. My brother is a clergyman; and he could help you in your talks with her.

Doolittle. [*Evasively.*] Certainly, I'll come, Governor. Not just this week, because I have a job at a distance. But later on you may depend on me. Afternoon, gentlemen. Afternoon, maam.

[*He touches his hat to* MRS PEARCE, *who disdains the salutation and goes out. He winks at* HIGGINS, *thinking him probably a fellow-sufferer from* MRS PEARCE'S *difficult disposition, and follows her.*]

Liza. Dont you believe the old liar. He'd as soon you set a bulldog on him as a clergyman. You wont see him again in a hurry.

Higgins. I dont want to, Eliza. Do you?

Liza. Not me. I dont want never to see him again, I dont. He's a disgrace to me, he is, collecting dust, instead of working at his trade.

Pickering. What is his trade, Eliza?

Liza. Talking money out of other people's pockets into his own. His proper trade's a navvy; and he works at it sometimes too—for exercise—and earns good money at it. Aint you going to call me Miss Doolittle any more?

Pickering. I beg you pardon, Miss Doolittle. It was a slip of the tongue.

Liza. Oh, I dont mind; only it sounded so genteel. I should just like to take a taxi to the corner of Tottenham Court Road and get out there and tell it to wait for me, just to put the girls in their place a bit. I wouldnt speak to them, you know.

Pickering. Better wait til we get you something really fashionable.

Higgins. Besides, you shouldnt cut your old friends now that you have risen in the world. Thats what we call snobbery.

Liza. You dont call the like of them my friends now, I should hope. Theyve took it out of me often enough with their ridicule when they had the chance; and now I mean to get a bit of my own back. But if I'm to have fashionable clothes, I'll wait. I should like to have some. Mrs Pearce says youre going to give me some to wear in bed at night different to what I wear in the daytime; but it do seem a waste of money when you could get something to shew. Besides, I never could fancy changing into cold things on a winter night.

Mrs Pearce. [*Coming back.*] Now, Eliza. The new things have come for you to try on.

Liza. Ah-ow-oo-ooh! [*She rushes out.*]

Mrs Pearce. [*Following her.*] Oh, dont rush about like that, girl.

[*She shuts the door behind her.*]

Higgins. Pickering: we have taken on a stiff job.

Pickering. [*With conviction.*] Higgins: we have.

ACT III

It is MRS HIGGINS'S *at-home day. Nobody has yet arrived. Her drawing room, in a flat on Chelsea Embankment, has three windows looking on the river; and the ceiling is not so lofty as it would be in an older house of the same pretension. The windows are open, giving access to a balcony with flowers in pots. If you stand with your face to the windows, you have the fireplace on your left and the door in the righthand wall close to the corner nearest the windows.*

MRS HIGGINS *was brought up on Morris and Burne Jones; and her room, which* *is very unlike her son's room in Wimpole Street, is not crowded with furniture and little tables and nicknacks. In the middle of the room there is a big ottoman; and this, with the carpet, the Morris wall-papers, and the Morris chintz window curtains and brocade covers of the ottoman and its cushions, supply all the ornament, and are much too handsome to be hidden by odds and ends of useless things. A few good oil-paintings from the exhibitions in the Grosvenor Gallery thirty years ago (the Burne Jones, not the Whistler side of them) are on the walls. The only landscape is a Cecil Lawson* on the scale of a Rubens. There is a portrait of* MRS HIGGINS *as she was when she defied the fashion in her youth in one of the beautiful Rossettian costumes which, when caricatured by people who did not understand, led to the absurdities of popular estheticism in the eighteen-seventies.*

In the corner diagonally opposite the door MRS HIGGINS, *now over sixty and long past taking the trouble to dress out of the fashion, sits writing at an elegantly simple writing-table with a bell button within reach of her hand. There is a Chippendale chair further back in the room between her and the window nearest her side. At the other side of the room, further forward, is an Elizabethan chair roughly carved in the taste of Inigo Jones. On the same side a piano in a decorated case. The corner between the fireplace and the window is occupied by a divan cushioned in Morris chintz.*

It is between four and five in the afternoon.

[*The door is opened violently; and* HIGGINS *enters with his hat on.*]

Mrs Higgins. [*Dismayed.*] Henry! [*Scolding him.*] What are you doing here today? It is my at-home day: you promised not to come.

[*As he bends to kiss her, she takes his hat off, and presents it to him.*]

Higgins. Oh bother!

[*He throws the hat down on the writing-table.*]

Mrs Higgins. Go home at once.

Higgins. [*Kissing her.*] I know, mother. I came on purpose.

Mrs Higgins. But you mustnt. I'm serious, Henry. You offend all my friends: they stop coming whenever they meet you.

* A now forgotten painter, who befriended Shaw when he first came to London in 1876.

Higgins. Nonsense! I know I have no small talk; but people dont mind.

[*He sits on the ottoman.*]

Mrs Higgins. Oh! dont they? Small talk indeed! What about your large talk? Really, dear, you mustnt stay.

Higgins. I must. Ive a job for you. A phonetic job.

Mrs Higgins. No use, dear. I'm sorry; but I cant get round your vowels; and though I like to get pretty postcards in your patent shorthand, I always have to read the copies in ordinary writing you so thoughtfully send me.

Higgins. Well, this isnt a phonetic job.

Mrs Higgins. You said it was.

Higgins. Not your part of it. Ive picked up a girl.

Mrs Higgins. Does that mean that some girl has picked you up?

Higgins. Not at all. I dont mean a love affair.

Mrs Higgins. What a pity!

Higgins. Why?

Mrs Higgins. Well, you never fall in love with anyone under forty-five. When will you discover that there are some rather nice-looking young women about?

Higgins. Oh, I cant be bothered with young women. My idea of a lovable woman is somebody as like you as possible. I shall never get into the way of seriously liking young women: some habits lie too deep to be changed. [*Rising abruptly and walking about, jingling his money and his keys in his trouser pockets.*] Besides, theyre all idiots.

Mrs Higgins. Do you know what you would do if you really loved me, Henry?

Higgins. Oh bother! What? Marry, I suppose.

Mrs Higgins. No. Stop fidgeting and take your hands out of your pockets. [*With a gesture of despair, he obeys and sits down again.*] Thats a good boy. Now tell me about the girl.

Higgins. She's coming to see you.

Mrs Higgins. I dont remember asking her.

Higgins. You didnt. *I* asked her. If youd known her you wouldnt have asked her.

Mrs Higgins. Indeed! Why?

Higgins. Well, it's like this. She's a common flower girl. I picked her off the kerbstone.

Mrs Higgins. And invited her to my at-home!

Higgins. [*Rising and coming to her to coax her.*] Oh, thatll be all right. Ive taught her to speak properly; and she has strict orders as to her behavior. She's to keep to two subjects: the weather and everybody's health—

Fine day and How do you do, you know—and not to let herself go on things in general. That will be safe.

Mrs Higgins. Safe! To talk about our health! about our insides! perhaps about our outsides! How could you be so silly, Henry?

Higgins. [*Impatiently.*] Well, she must talk about something. [*He controls himself and sits down again.*] Oh, she'll be all right: dont you fuss. Pickering is in it with me. Ive a sort of bet on that I'll pass her off as a duchess in six months. I started on her some months ago; and she's getting on like a house on fire. I shall win my bet. She has a quick ear; and she's easier to teach than my middle-class pupils because she's had to learn a complete new language. She talks English almost as you talk French.

Mrs Higgins. Thats satisfactory, at all events.

Higgins. Well, it is and it isnt.

Mrs Higgins. What does that mean?

Higgins. You see, Ive got her pronunciation all right; but you have to consider not only how a girl pronounces, but what she pronounces; and that's where——

[*They are interrupted by the* PARLOR-MAID, *announcing guests.*]

The Parlor-Maid. Mrs and Miss Eynsford Hill. [*She withdraws*].

Higgins. Oh Lord!

[*He rises; snatches his hat from the table; and makes for the door; but before he reaches it his mother introduces him.*]

[MRS *and* MISS EYNSFORD HILL *are the mother and daughter who sheltered from the rain in Covent Garden. The mother is well bred, quiet, and has the habitual anxiety of straitened means. The daughter has acquired a gay air of being very much at home in society: the bravado of genteel poverty.*]

Mrs Eynsford Hill. [*To* MRS HIGGINS.] How do you do? [*They shake hands.*]

Miss Eynsford Hill. How d'you do? [*She shakes.*]

Mrs Higgins. [*Introducing.*] My son Henry.

Mrs Eynsford Hill. Your celebrated son! I have so longed to meet you, Professor Higgins.

Higgins. [*Glumly, making no movement in her direction.*] Delighted.

[*He backs against the piano and bows brusquely.*]

Miss Eynsford Hill. [*Going to him with confident familiarity.*] How do you do?

Higgins. [*Staring at her.*] Ive seen you before somewhere. I havnt the ghost of a notion where; but Ive heard your voice. [*Drearily.*] It doesnt matter. Youd better sit down.

Mrs Higgins. I'm sorry to say that my celebrated son has no manners. You mustnt mind him.

Miss Eynsford Hill. [*Gaily.*] I don't.

[*She sits in the Elizabethan chair.*]

Mrs Eynsford Hill. [*A little bewildered.*] Not at all.

[*She sits on the ottoman between her daughter and* MRS HIGGINS, *who has turned her chair away from the writing-table.*]

Higgins. Oh, have I been rude? I didnt mean to be.

[*He goes to the central window, through which, with his back to the company, he contemplates the river and the flowers in Battersea Park on the opposite bank as if they were a frozen desert. The* PARLOR-MAID *returns, ushering in* PICKERING.]

The Parlor-Maid. Colonel Pickering.

[*She withdraws.*]

Pickering. How do you do, Mrs Higgins?

Mrs Higgins. So glad youve come. Do you know Mrs Eynsford Hill—Miss Eynsford Hill?

[*Exchange of bows. The* COLONEL *brings the Chippendale chair a little forward between* MRS HILL *and* MRS HIGGINS, *and sits down.*]

Pickering. Has Henry told you what weve come for?

Higgins. [*Over his shoulder.*] We were interrupted: damn it!

Mrs Higgins. Oh Henry, Henry, really!

Mrs Eynsford Hill. [*Half rising.*] Are we in the way?

Mrs Higgins. [*Rising and making her sit down again.*] No, no. You couldnt have come more fortunately: we want you to meet a friend of ours.

Higgins. [*Turning hopefully.*] Yes, by George! We want two or three people. You'll do as well as anybody else.

[*The* PARLOR-MAID *returns, ushering* FREDDY.]

The Parlor-Maid. Mr Eynsford Hill.

Higgins. [*Almost audibly, past endurance.*] God of Heaven! another of them.

Freddy. [*Shaking hands with* MRS HIGGINS.] Ahdedo?

Mrs Higgins. Very good of you to come. [*Introducing.*] Colonel Pickering.

Freddy. [*Bowing.*] Ahdedo?

Mrs Higgins. I dont think you know my son, Professor Higgins.

Freddy. [*Going to* HIGGINS.] Ahdedo?

Higgins. [*Looking at him much as if he

were a pickpocket.] I'll take my oath Ive met you before somewhere. Where was it?

Freddy. I dont think so.

Higgins. [*Resignedly.*] It dont matter, anyhow. Sit down.

[*He shakes* FREDDY's *hand, and almost slings him on to the ottoman with his face to the window; then comes round to the other side of it.*]

Higgins. Well, here we are, anyhow! [*He sits down on the ottoman next* MRS EYNSFORD HILL, *on her left.*] And now, what the devil are we going to talk about until Eliza comes?

Mrs Higgins. Henry: you are the life and soul of the Royal Society soirées; but really youre rather trying on more commonplace occasions.

Higgins. Am I? Very sorry. [*Beaming suddenly.*] I suppose I am, you know. [*Uproariously.*] Ha, ha!

Miss Eynsford Hill. [*Who considers* HIGGINS *quite eligible matrimonially.*] I sympathize. *I* havnt any small talk. If people would only be frank and say what they really think!

Higgins. [*Relapsing into gloom.*] Lord forbid!

Mrs Eynsford Hill. [*Taking up her daughter's cue.*] But why?

Higgins. What they think they ought to think is bad enough, Lord knows; but what they really think would break up the whole show. Do you suppose it would be really agreeable if I were to come out now with what *I* really think?

Miss Eynsford Hill. [*Gaily.*] Is it so very cynical?

Higgins. Cynical! Who the dickens said it was cynical? I mean it wouldnt be decent.

Mrs Eynsford Hill. [*Seriously.*] Oh! I'm sure you dont mean that, Mr Higgins.

Higgins. You see, we're all savages, more or less. We're supposed to be civilized and cultured—to know all about poetry and philosophy and art and science, and so on; but how many of us know even the meanings of these names? [*To* MISS HILL.] What do you know of poetry? [*To* MRS. HILL.] What do you know of science? [*Indicating* FREDDY.] What does he know of art or science or anything else? What the devil do you imagine I know of philosophy?

Mrs Higgins. [*Warningly.*] Or of manners, Henry?

The Parlor-Maid. [*Opening the door.*] Miss Doolittle. [*She withdraws.*]

Higgins. [*Rising hastily and running to* MRS HIGGINS.] Here she is, mother.

[*He stands on tiptoe and makes signs over his mother's head to* ELIZA *to indicate to her which lady is her hostess.* ELIZA, *who is exquisitely dressed, produces an impression of such remarkable distinction and beauty as she enters that they all rise, quite fluttered. Guided by* HIGGINS's *signals, she comes to* MRS HIGGINS *with studied grace.*]

Liza. [*Speaking with pedantic correctness of pronunciation and great beauty of tone.*] How do you do, Mrs. Higgins? [*She gasps slightly in making sure of the H in* HIGGINS, *but is quite successful.*] Mr. Higgins told me I might come.

Mrs Higgins. [*Cordially.*] Quite right: I'm very glad indeed to see you.

Pickering. How do you do, Miss Doolittle?

Liza. [*Shaking hands with him.*] Colonel Pickering, is it not?

Mrs Eynsford Hill. I feel sure we have met before, Miss Doolittle. I remember your eyes.

Liza. How do you do?

[*She sits down on the ottoman gracefully in the place just left vacant by* HIGGINS.]

Mrs Eynsford Hill. [*Introducing.*] My daughter Clara.

Liza. How do you do?

Clara. [*Impulsively.*] How do you do?

[*She sits down on the ottoman beside* ELIZA, *devouring her with her eyes.*]

Freddy. [*Coming to their side of the ottoman.*] Ive certainly had the pleasure.

Mrs Eynsford Hill. [*Introducing.*] My son Freddy.

Liza. How do you do?

[FREDDY *bows and sits down in the Elizabethan chair, infatuated.*]

Higgins. [*Suddenly.*] By George, yes: it all comes back to me! [*They stare at him.*] Covent Garden! [*Lamentably.*] What a damned thing!

Mrs Higgins. Henry, please! [*He is about to sit on the edge of the table.*] Dont sit on my writing-table: youll break it.

Higgins. [*Sulkily.*] Sorry.

[*He goes to the divan, stumbling into the fender and over the fire-irons on his way; extricating himself with muttered imprecations; and finishing his disastrous journey by throwing himself so impatiently on the divan that he almost breaks it.* MRS HIGGINS *looks at him, but controls herself and says nothing. A long and painful pause ensues.*]

Mrs Higgins. [*At last, conversationally.*] Will it rain, do you think?

Liza. The shallow depression in the west of these islands is likely to move slowly in an easterly direction. There are no indications of any great change in the barometrical situation.

Freddy. Ha! ha! how awfully funny!

Liza. What is wrong with that, young man? I bet I got it right.

Freddy. Killing!

Mrs Eynsford Hill. I'm sure I hope it wont turn cold. Theres so much influenza about. It runs right through our whole family regularly every spring.

Liza. [*Darkly.*] My aunt died of influenza: so they said.

Mrs Eynsford Hill. [*Clicks her tongue sympathetically*!!!]

Liza. [*In the same tragic tone.*] But it's my belief they done the old woman in.

Mrs Higgins. [*Puzzled.*] Done her in?

Liza. Y-e-e-e-es, Lord love you! Why should she die of influenza? She come through diphtheria right enough the year before. I saw her with my own eyes. Fairly blue with it, she was. They all thought she was dead; but my father he kept ladling gin down her throat til she came to so sudden that she bit the bowl off the spoon.

Mrs Eynsford Hill. [*Startled.*] Dear me!

Liza. [*Piling up the indictment.*] What call would a woman with that strength in her have to die of influenza? What become of her new straw hat that should have come to me? Somebody pinched it; and what I say is, them as pinched it done her in.

Mrs Eynsford Hill. What does doing her in mean?

Higgins. [*Hastily.*] Oh, thats the new small talk. To do a person in means to kill them.

Mrs Eynsford Hill. [*To* ELIZA, *horrified.*] You surely dont believe that your aunt was killed?

Liza. Do I not! Them she lived with would have killed her for a hat-pin, let alone a hat.

Mrs Eynsford Hill. But it cant have been right for your father to pour spirits down her throat like that. It might have killed her.

Liza. Not her. Gin was mother's milk to her. Besides, he'd poured so much down his own throat that he knew the good of it.

Mrs Eynsford Hill. Do you mean that he drank?

Liza. Drank! My word! Something chronic.

Mrs Eynsford Hill. How dreadful for you!

Liza. Not a bit. It never did him no harm what I could see. But then he did not keep it up regular. [*Cheerfully.*] On the burst, as you might say, from time to time. And always more agreeable when he had a drop in. When he was out of work, my mother used to give him fourpence and tell him to go out and not come back until he'd drunk himself cheerful and loving-like. Theres lots of women has to make their husbands drunk to make them fit to live with. [*Now quite at her ease.*] You see, it's like this. If a man has a bit of conscience, it always takes him when he's sober; and then it makes him low-spirited. A drop of booze just takes that off and makes him happy. [*To* FREDDY, *who is in convulsions of suppressed laughter.*] Here! what are you sniggering at?

Freddy. The new small talk. You do it so awfully well.

Liza. If I was doing it proper, what was you laughing at? [*To* HIGGINS.] Have I said anything I oughtnt?

Mrs Higgins. [*Interposing.*] Not at all, Miss Doolittle.

Liza. Well, thats a mercy, anyhow. [*Expansively.*] What I always say is——

Higgins. [*Rising and looking at his watch.*] Ahem!

Liza. [*Looking round at him; taking the hint; and rising.*] Well: I must go. [*They all rise.* FREDDY *goes to the door.*] So pleased to have met you. Goodbye.

[*She shakes hands with* MRS HIGGINS.]

Mrs Higgins. Goodbye.

Liza. Goodbye, Colonel Pickering.

Pickering. Goodbye, Miss Doolittle.

[*They shake hands.*]

Liza. [*Nodding to the others.*] Goodbye, all.

Freddy. [*Opening the door for her.*] Are you walking across the Park, Miss Doolittle? If so——

Liza. [*With perfectly elegant diction.*] Walk! Not bloody likely. [*Sensation.*] I am going in a taxi. [*She goes out.*]

[PICKERING *gasps and sits down.* FREDDY *goes out on the balcony to catch another glimpse of* ELIZA.]

Mrs Eynsford Hill. [*Suffering from shock.*] Well, I really cant get used to the new ways.

Clara. [*Throwing herself discontentedly into the Elizabethan chair.*] Oh, it's all right, mamma, quite right. People will think we never go anywhere or see anybody if you are so old-fashioned.

Mrs Eynsford Hill. I daresay I am very old-fashioned; but I do hope you wont begin using that expression, Clara. I have got accustomed to hear you talking about men as rotters, and calling everything filthy and beastly; though I do think it horrible and unladylike. But this last is really too much. Dont you think so, Colonel Pickering?

Pickering. Dont ask me. Ive been away in India for several years; and manners have changed so much that I sometimes dont know whether I'm at a respectable dinnertable or in a ship's forecastle.

Clara. It's all a matter of habit. Theres no

right or wrong in it. Nobody means anything by it. And it's so quaint, and gives such a smart emphasis to things that are not in themselves very witty. I find the new small talk delightful and quite innocent.

Mrs Eynsford Hill. [*Rising.*] Well, after that, I think it's time for us to go.

[PICKERING *and* HIGGINS *rise.*]

Clara. [*Rising.*] Oh yes: we have three at-homes to go to still. Goodbye, Mrs Higgins. Goodbye, Colonel Pickering. Goodbye, Professor Higgins.

Higgins. [*Coming grimly at her from the ottoman, and accompanying her to the door.*] Goodbye. Be sure you try on that small talk at the three at-homes. Dont be nervous about it. Pitch it in strong.

Clara. [*All smiles.*] I will. Goodbye. Such nonsense, all this early Victorian prudery!

Higgins. [*Tempting her.*] Such damned nonsense!

Clara. Such bloody nonsense!

Mrs Eynsford Hill. [*Convulsively.*] Clara!

Clara. Ha! ha!

[*She goes out radiant, conscious of being thoroughly up to date, and is heard descending the stairs in a stream of silvery laughter.*]

Freddy. [*To the heavens at large.*] Well, I ask you—— [*He gives it up, and comes to* MRS HIGGINS.] Goodbye.

Mrs Higgins. [*Shaking hands.*] Goodbye. Would you like to meet Miss Doolittle again?

Freddy. [*Eagerly.*] Yes, I should, most awfully.

Mrs Higgins. Well, you know my days.

Freddy. Yes. Thanks awfully. Goodbye.

[*He goes out.*]

Mrs Eynsford Hill. Goodbye, Mr Higgins.

Higgins. Goodbye. Goodbye.

Mrs Eynsford Hill. [*To* PICKERING.] It's no use. I shall never be able to bring myself to use that word.

Pickering. Dont. It's not compulsory, you know. Youll get on quite well without it.

Mrs Eynsford Hill. Only, Clara is so down on me if I am not positively reeking with the latest slang. Goodbye.

Pickering. Goodbye. [*They shake hands.*]

Mrs Eynsford Hill. [*To* MRS HIGGINS.] You mustnt mind Clara. [PICKERING, *catching from her lowered tone that this is not meant for him to hear, discreetly joins* HIGGINS *at the window.*] We're so poor! and she gets so few parties, poor child! She doesnt quite know. [MRS HIGGINS, *seeing that her eyes are moist, takes her hand sympathetically and goes with her to the door.*] But the boy is nice. Dont you think so?

Mrs Higgins. Oh, quite nice. I shall always be delighted to see him.

Mrs Eynsford Hill. Thank you, dear. Goodbye. [*She goes out.*]

Higgins. [*Eagerly.*] Well? Is Eliza presentable?

[*He swoops on his mother and drags her to the ottoman, where she sits down in* ELIZA'S *place with her son on her left.* PICKERING *returns to his chair on her right.*]

Mrs Higgins. You silly boy, of course she's not presentable. She's a triumph of your art and of her dressmaker's; but if you suppose for a moment that she doesn't give herself away in every sentence she utters, you must be perfectly cracked about her.

Pickering. But dont you think something might be done? I mean something to eliminate the sanguinary element from her conversation.

Mrs Higgins. Not as long as she is in Henry's hands.

Higgins. [*Aggrieved.*] Do you mean that my language is improper?

Mrs Higgins. No, dearest: it would be quite proper—say on a canal barge; but it would not be proper for her at a garden party.

Higgins. [*Deeply injured.*] Well I must say——

Pickering. [*Interrupting him.*] Come, Higgins: you must learn to know yourself. I havent heard such language as yours since we used to review the volunteers in Hyde Park twenty years ago.

Higgins. [*Sulkily.*] Oh, well, if you say so, I suppose I dont always talk like a bishop.

Mrs Higgins. [*Quieting* HENRY *with a touch.*] Colonel Pickering: will you tell me what is the exact state of things in Wimpole Street?

Pickering. [*Cheerfully: as if this completely changed the subject.*] Well, I have come to live there with Henry. We work together at my Indian Dialects; and we think it more convenient——

Mrs Higgins. Quite so. I know all about that: it's an excellent arrangement. But where does this girl live?

Higgins. With us, of course. Where should she live?

Mrs Higgins. But on what terms? Is she a servant? If not, what is she?

Pickering. [*Slowly.*] I think I know what you mean, Mrs Higgins.

Higgins. Well, dash me if *I* do! Ive had to work at the girl every day for months to get her to her present pitch. Besides, she's useful. She knows where my things are, and remembers my appointments and so forth.

Mrs Higgins. How does your housekeeper get on with her?

Higgins. Mrs Pearce? Oh, she's jolly glad to get so much taken off her hands; for before Eliza came, she used to have to find things and remind me of my appointments. But she's got some silly bee in her bonnet about Eliza. She keeps saying "You dont think, sir": doesnt she, Pick?

Pickering. Yes: thats the formula. "You dont think, sir." Thats the end of every conversation about Eliza.

Higgins. As if I ever stop thinking about the girl and her confounded vowels and consonants. I'm worn out, thinking about her, and watching her lips and her teeth and her tongue, not to mention her soul, which is the quaintest of the lot.

Mrs Higgins. You certainly are a pretty pair of babies, playing with your live doll.

Higgins. Playing! The hardest job I ever tackled: make no mistake about that, mother. But you have no idea how frightfully interesting it is to take a human being and change her into a quite different human being by creating a new speech for her. It's filling up the deepest gulf that separates class from class and soul from soul.

Pickering. [*Drawing his chair closer to* Mrs Higgins *and bending over to her eagerly.*] Yes: it's enormously interesting. I assure you, Mrs Higgins, we take Eliza very seriously. Every week—every day almost—there is some new change. [*Closer again.*] We keep records of every stage—dozens of gramophone disks and photographs——

Higgins. [*Assailing her at the other ear.*] Yes, by George: it's the most absorbing experiment I ever tackled. She regularly fills our lives up: doesnt she, Pick?

Pickering. We're always talking Eliza.

Higgins. Teaching Eliza.

Pickering. Dressing Eliza.

Mrs Higgins. What!

Higgins. Inventing new Elizas.

Higgins.	[*Speaking together.*]	You know, she has the most extraordinary quickness of ear:
Pickering.		I assure you, my dear Mrs Higgins, that girl
Higgins.		just like a parrot. Ive tried her with every
Pickering.		is a genius. She can play the piano quite beautifully.
Higgins.	[*Speaking together.*]	possible sort of sound that a human being can make——
Pickering.		We have taken her to classical concerts and to music
Higgins.		Continental dialects, African dialects, Hottentot
Pickering.		halls; and it's all the same to her: she plays everything
Higgins.		clicks, things it took me years to get hold of; and
Pickering.		she hears right off when she comes home, whether it's
Higgins.		she picks them up like a shot, right away, as if she had
Pickering.		Beethoven and Brahms or Lehar and Lionel Monckton;
Higgins.		been at it all her life.
Pickering.		though six months ago, she'd never as much as touched a piano——

Mrs Higgins. [*Putting her fingers in her ears, as they are by this time shouting one another down with an intolerable noise.*] Sh-sh-sh—sh! [*They stop.*]

Pickering. I beg your pardon.

[*He draws his chair back apologetically.*]

Higgins. Sorry. When Pickering starts shouting nobody can get a word in edgeways.

Mrs Higgins. Be quiet, Henry. Colonel Pickering: dont you realize that when Eliza walked in Wimpole Street, something walked in with her?

Pickering. Her father did. But Henry soon got rid of him.

Mrs Higgins. It would have been more to the point if her mother had. But as her mother didnt something else did.

Pickering. But what?

Mrs Higgins. [*Unconsciously dating herself by the word.*] A problem.

Pickering. Oh, I see. The problem of how to pass her off as a lady.

Higgins. I'll solve that problem. Ive half solved it already.

Mrs Higgins. No, you two infinitely stupid male creatures: the problem of what is to be done with her afterwards.

Higgins. I dont see anything in that. She can go her own way, with all the advantages I have given her.

Mrs Higgins. The advantages of that poor woman who was here just now! The manners and habits that disqualify a fine lady from earning her own living without giving her a fine lady's income! Is that what you mean?

Pickering. [*Indulgently, being rather bored.*] Oh, that will be all right, Mrs Higgins. [*He rises to go.*]

Higgins. [*Rising also.*] We'll find her some light employment.

Pickering. She's happy enough. Dont you worry about her. Goodbye.

[*He shakes hands as if he were consoling a frightened child, and makes for the door.*]

Higgins. Anyhow, theres no good bothering now. The thing's done. Goodbye, mother.

[*He kisses her, and follows* PICKERING.]

Pickering. [*Turning for a final consolation.*] There are plenty of openings. We'll do whats right. Goodbye.

Higgins. [*To* PICKERING *as they go out together.*] Lets take her to the Shakespear exhibition at Earls Court.

Pickering. Yes: lets. Her remarks will be delicious.

Higgins. She'll mimic all the people for us when we get home.

Pickering. Ripping.

[*Both are heard laughing as they go downstairs.*]

Mrs Higgins. [*Rises with an impatient bounce, and returns to her work at the writing-table. She sweeps a litter of disarranged papers out of the way; snatches a sheet of paper from her stationery case; and tries resolutely to write. At the third line she gives it up; flings down her pen; grips the table angrily and exclaims.*] Oh, men! men!! men!!!

ACT IV

The Wimpole Street laboratory. Midnight. Nobody in the room. The clock on the mantelpiece strikes twelve. The fire is not alight: it is a summer night.

[*Presently* HIGGINS *and* PICKERING *are heard on the stairs.*]

Higgins. [*Calling down to* PICKERING.] I say, Pick: lock up, will you? I shant be going out again.

Pickering. Right. Can Mrs Pearce go to bed? We dont want anything more, do we?

Higgins. Lord, no!

[ELIZA *opens the door and is seen on the lighted landing in all the finery in which she has just won* HIGGINS's *bet for him. She comes to the hearth, and switches on the electric lights there. She is tired: her pallor contrasts strongly with her dark eyes and hair; and her expression is almost tragic. She takes off her cloak; puts her fan and gloves on the piano; and sits down on the bench, brooding and silent.* HIGGINS, *in evening dress, with overcoat and hat, comes in, carrying a smoking jacket which he has picked up downstairs. He takes off the hat and overcoat; throws them carelessly on the newspaper stand; disposes of his coat in the same way; puts on the smoking jacket; and throws himself wearily into the easychair at the hearth.* PICKERING, *similarly attired, comes in. He also takes off his hat and overcoat, and is about to throw them on* HIGGINS's *when he hesitates.*]

Pickering. I say: Mrs Pearce will row if we leave these things lying about in the drawing room.

Higgins. Oh, chuck them over the banisters into the hall. She'll find them there in the morning and put them away all right. She'll think we were drunk.

Pickering. We are, slightly. Are there any letters?

Higgins. I didnt look. [PICKERING *takes the overcoats and hats and goes downstairs.* HIGGINS *begins half singing half yawning an air from La Fanciulla del Golden West. Suddenly he stops and exclaims.*] I wonder where the devil my slippers are!

[ELIZA *looks at him darkly; then rises suddenly and leaves the room.* HIGGINS *yawns again, and resumes his song.* PICKERING *returns, with the contents of the letter-box in his hand.*]

Pickering. Only circulars, and this coroneted billet-doux for you.

[*He throws the circulars into the fender, and posts himself on the hearth-rug, with his back to the grate.*]

Higgins. [*Glancing at the billet-doux.*] Money-lender.

[*He throws the letter after the circulars.* ELIZA *returns with a pair of large down-at-heel slippers. She places them on the carpet before* HIGGINS, *and sits as before without a word.*]

Higgins. [*Yawning again.*] Oh Lord! What an evening! What a crew! What a silly tomfoolery! [*He raises his shoe to unlace it, and catches sight of the slippers. He stops unlacing and looks at them as if they had appeared there of their own accord.*] Oh! theyre there, are they?

Pickering. [*Stretching himself.*] Well, I feel a bit tired. It's been a long day. The garden party, a dinner party, and the reception! Rather too much of a good thing. But youve won your bet, Higgins. Eliza did the trick, and something to spare, eh?

Higgins. [*Fervently.*] Thank God it's over!

[ELIZA *flinches violently; but they take no notice of her; and she recovers herself and sits stonily as before.*]

Pickering. Were you nervous at the garden party? *I* was. Eliza didnt seem a bit nervous.

Higgins. Oh, she wasnt nervous. I knew she'd be all right. No: it's the strain of putting the job through all these months that has told on me. It was interesting enough at first, while we were at the phonetics; but after that I got deadly sick of it. If I hadnt backed myself to do it I should have chucked the whole thing up two months ago. It was a silly notion: the whole thing has been a bore.

Pickering. Oh come! the garden party was frightfully exciting. My heart began beating like anything.

Higgins. Yes, for the first three minutes. But when I saw we were going to win hands down, I felt like a bear in a cage, hanging about doing nothing. The dinner was worse: sitting gorging there for over an hour, with nobody but a damned fool of a fashionable woman to talk to! I tell you, Pickering, never again for me. No more artificial duchesses. The whole thing has been simple purgatory.

Pickering. Youve never been broken in properly to the social routine. [*Strolling over to the piano.*] I rather enjoy dipping into it occasionally myself: it makes me feel young again. Anyhow, it was a great success: an immense success. I was quite frightened once or twice because Eliza was doing it so well. You see, lots of the real people cant do it at all: theyre such fools that they think style comes by nature to people in their position; and so they never learn. Theres always something professional about doing a thing superlatively well.

Higgins. Yes: thats what drives me mad: the silly people dont know their own silly business. [*Rising.*] However, it's over and done with; and now I can go to bed at last without dreading tomorrow.

[ELIZA'S *beauty becomes murderous.*]

Pickering. I think I shall turn in too. Still, it's been a great occasion: a triumph for you. Goodnight. [*He goes.*]

Higgins. [*Following him.*] Goodnight. [*Over his shoulder, at the door.*] Put out the lights, Eliza; and tell Mrs Pearce not to make coffee for me in the morning: I'll take tea. [*He goes out.*]

[ELIZA *tries to control herself and feel indifferent as she rises and walks across to the hearth to switch off the lights. By the time she gets there she is on the point of screaming. She sits down in* HIGGINS'S *chair and holds on hard to the arms. Finally she gives way and flings herself furiously on the floor, raging.*]

Higgins. [*In despairing wrath outside.*] What the devil have I done with my slippers? [*He appears at the door.*]

Liza. [*Snatching up the slippers, and hurling them at him one after the other with all her force.*] There are your slippers. And there. Take your slippers; and may you never have a day's luck with them!

Higgins. [*Astounded.*] What on earth——! [*He comes to her.*] Whats the matter? Get up. [*He pulls her up.*] Anything wrong?

Liza. [*Breathless.*] Nothing wrong—with you. Ive won your bet for you, havnt I? Thats enough for you. *I* dont matter, I suppose.

Higgins. You won my bet! You! Presumptuous insect! *I* won it. What did you throw those slippers at me for?

Liza. Because I wanted to smash your face. I'd like to kill you, you selfish brute. Why didnt you leave me where you picked me out of—in the gutter? You thank God it's all over, and that now you can throw me back again there, do you?

[*She crisps her fingers frantically.*]

Higgins. [*Looking at her in cool wonder.*] The creature is nervous, after all.

Liza. [*Gives a suffocated scream of fury, and instinctively darts her nails at his face!!*]

Higgins. [*Catching her wrists.*] Ah! would you? Claws in, you cat. How dare you shew your temper to me? Sit down and be quiet.

[*He throws her roughly into the easy-chair.*]

Liza. [*Crushed by superior strength and weight.*] Whats to become of me? Whats to become of me?

Higgins. How the devil do I know whats to become of you? What does it matter what becomes of you?

Liza. You dont care. I know you dont care. You wouldnt care if I was dead. I'm nothing to you—not so much as them slippers.

Higgins. [*Thundering.*] Those slippers.

Liza. [*With bitter submission.*] Those slippers. I didnt think it made any difference now.

[*A pause.* Eliza *hopeless and crushed.* Higgins *a little uneasy.*]

Higgins. [*In his loftiest manner.*] Why have you begun going on like this? May I ask whether you complain of your treatment here?

Liza. No.

Higgins. Has anybody behaved badly to you? Colonel Pickering? Mrs Pearce? Any of the servants?

Liza. No.

Higgins. I presume you dont pretend that *I* have treated you badly?

Liza. No.

Higgins. I am glad to hear it. [*He moderates his tone.*] Perhaps youre tired after the strain of the day. Will you have a glass of champagne? [*He moves towards the door.*]

Liza. No. [*Recollecting her manners.*] Thank you.

Higgins. [*Good-humored again.*] This has been coming on you for some days. I suppose it was natural for you to be anxious about the garden party. But thats all over now. [*He pats her kindly on the shoulder. She writhes.*] Theres nothing more to worry about.

Liza. No. Nothing more for you to worry about. [*She suddenly rises and gets away from him by going to the piano bench, where she sits and hides her face.*] Oh God! I wish I was dead.

Higgins. [*Staring after her in sincere surprise.*] Why? In heaven's name, why? [*Reasonably, going to her.*] Listen to me, Eliza. All this irritation is purely subjective.

Liza. I dont understand. I'm too ignorant.

Higgins. It's only imagination. Low spirits and nothing else. Nobody's hurting you. Nothing's wrong. You go to bed like a good girl and sleep it off. Have a little cry and say your prayers: that will make you comfortable.

Liza. I heard your prayers. "Thank God it's all over!"

Higgins. [*Impatiently.*] Well, dont you thank God it's all over? Now you are free and can do what you like.

Liza. [*Pulling herself together in desperation.*] What am I fit for? What have you left me fit for? Where am I to go? What am I to do? Whats to become of me?

Higgins. [*Enlightened, but not at all impressed.*] Oh, thats whats worrying you, is it? [*He thrusts his hands into his pockets, and walks about in his usual manner, rattling the contents of his pockets, as if condescending to a trivial subject out of pure kindness.*] I shouldnt bother about it if I were you. I should imagine you wont have much difficulty in settling yourself somewhere or other, though I hadnt quite realized that you were going away. [*She looks quickly at him: he does not look at her, but examines the dessert stand on the piano and decides that he will eat an apple.*] You might marry, you know. [*He bites a large piece out of the apple and munches it noisily.*] You see, Eliza, all men are not confirmed old bachelors like me and the Colonel. Most men are the marrying sort (poor devils!); and youre not badlooking: it's quite a pleasure to look at you sometimes—not now, of course, because youre crying and looking as ugly as the very devil; but when youre all right and quite yourself, youre what I should call attractive. That is, to the people in the marrying line, you understand. You go to bed and have a good nice rest; and then get up and look at yourself in the glass; and you wont feel so cheap.

[Eliza *again looks at him, speechless, and does not stir. The look is quite lost on him: he eats his apple with a dreamy expression of happiness, as it is quite a good one.*]

Higgins. [*A genial afterthought occurring to him.*] I daresay my mother could find some chap or other who would do very well.

Liza. We were above that at the corner of Tottenham Court Road.

Higgins. [*Waking up.*] What do you mean?

Liza. I sold flowers. I didnt sell myself. Now youve made a lady of me I'm not fit to sell anything else. I wish youd left me where you found me.

Higgins. [*Slinging the core of the apple decisively into the grate.*] Tosh, Eliza. Dont you insult human relations by dragging all this cant about buying and selling into it.

You neednt marry the fellow if you dont like him.

Liza. What else am I do?

Higgins. Oh, lots of things. What about your old idea of a florist's shop? Pickering could set you up in one: he has lots of money. [*Chuckling.*] He'll have to pay for all those togs you have been wearing today; and that, with the hire of the jewellery, will make a big hole in two hundred pounds. Why, six months ago you would have thought it the millennium to have a flower shop of your own. Come! youll be all right. I must clear off to bed: I'm devilish sleepy. By the way, I came down for something: I forget what it was.

Liza. Your slippers.

Higgins. Oh yes, of course. You shied them at me.

[*He picks them up, and is going out when she rises and speaks to him.*]

Liza. Before you go, sir——

Higgins. [*Dropping the slippers in his surprise at her calling him Sir.*] Eh?

Liza. Do my clothes belong to me or to Colonel Pickering?

Higgins. [*Coming back into the room as if her question were the very climax of unreason.*] What the devil use would they be to Pickering?

Liza. He might want them for the next girl you pick up to experiment on.

Higgins. [*Shocked and hurt.*] Is that the way you feel towards us?

Liza. I dont want to hear anything more about that. All I want to know is whether anything belongs to me. My own clothes were burnt.

Higgins. But what does it matter? Why need you start bothering about that in the middle of the night?

Liza. I want to know what I may take away with me. I dont want to be accused of stealing.

Higgins. [*Now deeply wounded.*] Stealing! You shouldnt have said that, Eliza. That shews a want of feeling.

Liza. I'm sorry. I'm only a common ignorant girl; and in my station I have to be careful. There cant be any feelings between the like of you and the like of me. Please will you tell me what belongs to me and what doesnt?

Higgins. [*Very sulky.*] You may take the whole damned houseful if you like. Except the jewels. Theyre hired. Will that satisfy you?

[*He turns on his heel and is about to go in extreme dudgeon.*]

Liza. [*Drinking in his emotion like nectar, and nagging him to provoke a further supply.*] Stop, please. [*She takes off her jewels.*] Will you take these to your room and keep them safe? I dont want to run the risk of their being missing.

Higgins. [*Furious.*] Hand them over. [*She puts them into his hands.*] If these belonged to me instead of to the jeweller, I'd ram them down your ungrateful throat.

[*He perfunctorily thrusts them into his pockets, unconsciously decorating himself with the protruding ends of the chains.*]

Liza. [*Taking a ring off.*] This ring isnt the jeweller's: it's the one you bought me in Brighton. I dont want it now. [HIGGINS *dashes the ring violently into the fireplace, and turns on her so threateningly that she crouches over the piano with her hands over her face, and exclaims.*] Dont you hit me.

Higgins. Hit you! You infamous creature, how dare you accuse me of such a thing? It is you who have hit me. You have wounded me to the heart.

Liza. [*Thrilling with hidden joy.*] I'm glad. Ive got a little of my own back, anyhow.

Higgins. [*With dignity, in his finest professional style.*] You have caused me to lose my temper: a thing that has hardly ever happened to me before. I prefer to say nothing more tonight. I am going to bed.

Liza. [*Pertly.*] Youd better leave a note for Mrs Pearce about the coffee; for she wont be told by me.

Higgins. [*Formally.*] Damn Mrs Pearce; and damn the coffee; and damn you; and [*Wildly.*] damn my own folly in having lavished my hard-earned knowledge and the treasure of my regard and intimacy on a heartless guttersnipe.

[*He goes out with impressive decorum, and spoils it by slamming the door savagely.*]

[ELIZA *goes down on her knees on the hearthrug to look for the ring. When she finds it she considers for a moment what to do with it. Finally she flings it down on the dessert stand and goes upstairs in a tearing rage.*]

ACT V

MRS. HIGGINS's *drawing room. She is at her writing-table as before. The* PARLOR-MAID *comes in.*

The Parlor-maid. [*At the door.*] Mr Henry, maam, is downstairs with Colonel Pickering.

Mrs Higgins. Well, shew them up.

The Parlor-maid. Theyre using the telephone, maam. Telephoning to the police, I think.

Mrs Higgins. What!

The Parlor-maid. [*Coming further in and lowering her voice.*] Mr Henry is in a state, maam. I thought I'd better tell you.

Mrs Higgins. If you had told me that Mr Henry was not in a state it would have been more surprising. Tell them to come up when theyve finished with the police. I suppose he's lost something.

The Parlor-maid. Yes, maam. [*Going.*]

Mrs Higgins. Go upstairs and tell Miss Doolittle that Mr Henry and the Colonel are here. Ask her not to come down till I send for her.

The Parlor-maid. Yes, maam.

[HIGGINS *bursts in. He is, as the* PARLOR-MAID *has said, in a state.*]

Higgins. Look here, mother: heres a confounded thing!

Mrs Higgins. Yes, dear. Good morning. [*He checks his impatience and kisses her, whilst the* PARLOR-MAID *goes out.*] What is it?

Higgins. Eliza's bolted.

Mrs Higgins. [*Calmly continuing her writing.*] You must have frightened her.

Higgins. Frightened her! nonsense! She was left last night, as usual, to turn out the lights and all that; and instead of going to bed she changed her clothes and went right off: her bed wasnt slept in. She came in a cab for her things before seven this morning; and that fool Mrs Pearce let her have them without telling me a word about it. What am I to do?

Mrs Higgins. Do without, I'm afraid, Henry. The girl has a perfect right to leave if she chooses.

Higgins. [*Wandering distractedly across the room.*] But I cant find anything. I dont know what appointments Ive got. I'm——

[PICKERING *comes in.* MRS HIGGINS *puts down her pen and turns away from the writing-table.*]

Pickering. [*Shaking hands.*] Good morning, Mrs Higgins. Has Henry told you? [*He sits down on the ottoman.*]

Higgins. What does that ass of an inspector say? Have you offered a reward?

Mrs Higgins. [*Rising in indignant amazement.*] You dont mean to say you have set the police after Eliza.

Higgins. Of course. What are the police for? What else could we do?

[*He sits in the Elizabethan chair.*]

Pickering. The inspector made a lot of difficulties. I really think he suspected us of some improper purpose.

Mrs Higgins. Well, of course he did. What right have you to go to the police and give the girl's name as if she were a thief, or a lost umbrella, or something? Really!

[*She sits down again, deeply vexed.*]

Higgins. But we want to find her.

Pickering. We cant let her go like this, you know, Mrs Higgins. What were we to do?

Mrs Higgins. You have no more sense, either of you, than two children. Why——

[*The* PARLOR-MAID *comes in and breaks off the conversation.*]

The Parlor-maid. Mr Henry: a gentleman wants to see you very particular. He's been sent on from Wimpole Street.

Higgins. Oh, bother! I cant see anyone now. Who is it?

The Parlor-maid. A Mr Doolittle, sir.

Pickering. Doolittle! Do you mean the dustman?

The Parlor-maid. Dustman! Oh no, sir: a gentleman.

Higgins. [*Springing up excitedly.*] By George, Pick, it's some relative of hers that she's gone to. Somebody we know nothing about. [*To the* PARLOR-MAID.] Send him up, quick.

The Parlor-maid. Yes, sir. [*She goes.*]

Higgins. [*Eagerly, going to his mother.*] Genteel relatives! now we shall hear something.

[*He sits down in the Chippendale chair.*]

Mrs Higgins. Do you know any of her people?

Pickering. Only her father: the fellow we told you about.

The Parlor-maid. [*Announcing.*] Mr Doolittle. [*She withdraws.*]

[DOOLITTLE *enters. He is resplendently dressed as for a fashionable wedding, and might, in fact, be the bridegroom. A flower in his buttonhole, a dazzling silk hat, and patent leather shoes complete the effect. He is too concerned with the business he has come on to notice* MRS HIGGINS. *He walks straight to* HIGGINS, *and accosts him with vehement reproach.*]

Doolittle. [*Indicating his own person.*] See here! Do you see this? You done this.

Higgins. Done what, man?

Doolittle. This, I tell you. Look at it. Look at this hat. Look at this coat.

Pickering. Has Eliza been buying you clothes?

Doolittle. Eliza! not she. Why would she buy me clothes?

Mrs Higgins. Good morning, Mr Doolittle. Wont you sit down?

Doolittle. [*Taken aback as he becomes conscious that he has forgotten his hostess.*] Asking your pardon, maam. [*He approaches her and shakes her proffered hand.*] Thank you. [*He sits down on the ottoman, on* PICKERING'S *right.*] I am that full of what has happened to me that I cant think of anything else.

Higgins. What the dickens has happened to you?

Doolittle. I shouldnt mind if it had only happened to me: anything might happen to anybody and nobody to blame but Providence, as you might say. But this is something that you done to me: yes, you, Enry Iggins.

Higgins. Have you found Eliza?

Doolittle. Have you lost her?

Higgins. Yes.

Doolittle. You have all the luck, you have. I aint found her; but she'll find me quick enough now after what you done to me.

Mrs Higgins. But what has my son done to you, Mr Doolittle?

Doolittle. Done to me! Ruined me. Destroyed my happiness. Tied me up and delivered me into the hands of middle class morality.

Higgins. [*Rising intolerantly and standing over* DOOLITTLE.] Youre raving. Youre drunk. Youre mad. I gave you five pounds. After that I had two conversations with you, at half-a-crown an hour. Ive never seen you since.

Doolittle. Oh! Drunk am I? Mad am I? Tell me this. Did you or did you not write a letter to an old blighter in America that was giving five millions to found Moral Reform Societies all over the world, and that wanted you to invent a universal language for him?

Higgins. What! Ezra D. Wannafeller! He's dead.

[*He sits down again carelessly.*]

Doolittle. Yes: he's dead; and I'm done for. Now did you or did you not write a letter to him to say that the most original moralist at present in England, to the best of your knowledge, was Alfred Doolittle, a common dustman?

Higgins. Oh, after your first visit I remember making some silly joke of the kind.

Doolittle. Ah! you may well call it a silly joke. It put the lid on me right enough. Just give him the chance he wanted to shew that Americans is not like us: that they reckonize and respect merit in every class of life, however humble. Them words is in his blooming will, in which, Henry Higgins, thanks to your silly joking, he leaves me a share in his Predigested Cheese Trust worth four thousand a year on condition that I lecture for his Wannafeller Moral Reform World League as often as they ask me up to six times a year.

Higgins. The devil he does! Whew! [*Brightening suddenly.*] What a lark!

Pickering. A safe thing for you, Doolittle. They wont ask you twice.

Doolittle. It aint the lecturing I mind. I'll lecture them blue in the face, I will, and not turn a hair. It's making a gentleman of me that I object to. Who asked him to make a gentleman of me? I was happy. I was free. I touched pretty nigh everybody for money when I wanted it, same as I touched you, Enry Iggins. Now I am worrited; tied neck and heels; and everybody touches me for money. It's a fine thing for you, says my solicitor. Is it? says I. You mean it's a good thing for you, I says. When I was a poor man and had a solicitor once when they found a pram in the dust cart, he got me off, and got shut of me and got me shut of him as quick as he could. Same with the doctors: used to shove me out of the hospital before I could hardly stand on my legs, and nothing to pay. Now they finds out that I'm not a healthy man and cant live unless they looks after me twice a day. In the house I'm not let do a hand's turn for myself: somebody else must do it and touch me for it. A year ago I hadnt a relative in the world except two or three that wouldnt speak to me. Now Ive fifty, and not a decent week's wages among the lot of them. I have to live for others and not for myself: thats middle class morality. You talk of losing Eliza. Dont you be anxious: I bet she's on my doorstep by this: she that could support herself easy by selling flowers if I wasnt respectable. And the next one to touch me will be you, Enry Iggins. I'll have to learn to speak middle class language from you, instead of speaking proper English. Thats where youll come in; and I daresay thats what you done it for.

Mrs Higgins. But, my dear Mr Doolittle, you need not suffer all this if you are really in earnest. Nobody can force you to accept this bequest. You can repudiate it. Isnt that so, Colonel Pickering?

Pickering. I believe so.

Doolittle. [*Softening his manner in deference to her sex.*] Thats the tragedy of it, maam. It's easy to say chuck it; but I havnt the nerve. Which of us has? We're all intimidated. Intimidated, maam: thats what we are. What is there for me if I chuck it but the workhouse in my old age? I have to dye my hair already to keep my job as a dustman. If I was one of the deserving poor, and had put by a bit, I could chuck it; but then why should I, acause the deserving poor might as well be millionaires for all the happiness they ever has. They dont know what happiness is. But I, as one of the undeserving poor, have nothing between me and the pauper's uniform but this here blasted four thousand a year that shoves me into the middle class. (Excuse the expression, maam; youd use it yourself if you had my provocation.) Theyve got you every way you turn: it's a choice between the Skilly of the workhouse and the Char Bydis of the middle class; and I havnt the nerve for the workhouse. Intimidated: thats what I am. Broke. Bought up. Happier men than me will call for my dust, and touch me for their tip; and I'll look on helpless, and envy them. And thats what your son has brought me to.

[*He is overcome by emotion.*]

Mrs Higgins. Well, I'm very glad youre not going to do anything foolish, Mr Doolittle. For this solves the problem of Eliza's future. You can provide for her now.

Doolittle. [*With melancholy resignation.*] Yes, maam: I'm expected to provide for everyone now, out of four thousand a year.

Higgins. [*Jumping up.*] Nonsense! he cant provide for her. He shant provide for her. She doesnt belong to him. I paid him five pounds for her. Doolittle: either youre an honest man or a rogue.

Doolittle. [*Tolerantly.*] A little of both, Henry, like the rest of us: a little of both.

Higgins. Well, you took that money for the girl; and you have no right to take her as well.

Mrs Higgins. Henry: dont be absurd. If you want to know where Eliza is, she is upstairs.

Higgins. [*Amazed.*] Upstairs!!! Then I shall jolly soon fetch her downstairs.

[*He makes resolutely for the door.*]

Mrs Higgins. [*Rising and following him.*] Be quiet, Henry. Sit down.

Higgins. I——

Mrs Higgins. Sit down, dear; and listen to me.

Higgins. Oh very well, very well, very well. [*He throws himself ungraciously on the ottoman, with his face towards the windows.*] But I think you might have told us this half an hour ago.

Mrs Higgins. Eliza came to me this morning. She told me of the brutal way you two treated her.

Higgins. [*Bounding up again.*] What!

Pickering. [*Rising also.*] My dear Mrs Higgins, she's been telling you stories. We didnt treat her brutally. We hardly said a word to her; and we parted on particularly good terms. [*Turning on* HIGGINS.] Higgins: did you bully her after I went to bed?

Higgins. Just the other way about. She threw my slippers in my face. She behaved in the most outrageous way. I never gave her the slightest provocation. The slippers came bang into my face the moment I entered the room—before I had uttered a word. And used perfectly awful language.

Pickering. [*Astonished.*] But why? What did we do to her?

Mrs Higgins. I think I know pretty well what you did. The girl is naturally rather affectionate, I think. Isnt she, Mr Doolittle?

Doolittle. Very tender-hearted, maam. Takes after me.

Mrs Higgins. Just so. She had become attached to you both. She worked very hard for you, Henry. I dont think you quite realize what anything in the nature of brain work means to a girl of her class. Well, it seems that when the great day of trial came, and she did this wonderful thing for you without making a single mistake, you two sat there and never said a word to her, but talked together of how glad you were that it was all over and how you had been bored with the whole thing. And then you were surprised because she threw your slippers at you! *I* should have thrown the fire-irons at you.

Higgins. We said nothing except that we were tired and wanted to go to bed. Did we, Pick?

Pickering. [*Shrugging his shoulders.*] That was all.

Mrs Higgins. [*Ironically.*] Quite sure?

Pickering. Absolutely. Really, that was all.

Mrs Higgins. You didnt thank her, or pet

her, or admire her, or tell her how splendid she'd been.

Higgins. [*Impatiently.*] But she knew all about that. We didnt make speeches to her, if thats what you mean.

Pickering. [*Conscience stricken.*] Perhaps we were a little inconsiderate. Is she very angry?

Mrs Higgins. [*Returning to her place at the writing-table.*] Well, I'm afraid she wont go back to Wimpole Street, especially now that Mr Doolittle is able to keep up the position you have thrust on her; but she says she is quite willing to meet you on friendly terms and to let bygones be bygones.

Higgins. [*Furious.*] Is she, by George? Ho!

Mrs Higgins. If you promise to behave yourself, Henry, I'll ask her to come down. If not, go home; for you have taken up quite enough of my time.

Higgins. Oh, all right. Very well. Pick: you behave yourself. Let us put on our best Sunday manners for this creature that we picked out of the mud.

[*He flings himself sulkily into the Elizabethan chair.*]

Doolittle. [*Remonstrating.*] Now, now, Enry Iggins! Have some consideration for my feelings as a middle class man.

Mrs Higgins. Remember your promise, Henry. [*She presses the bell-button on the writing-table.*] Mr Doolittle: will you be so good as to step out on the balcony for a moment. I dont want Eliza to have the shock of your news until she has made it up with these two gentlemen. Would you mind?

Doolittle. As you wish, lady. Anything to help Henry to keep her off my hands.

[*He disappears through the window. The* PARLOR-MAID *answers the bell.* PICKERING *sits down in* DOOLITTLE'S *place.*]

Mrs Higgins. Ask Miss Doolittle to come down, please.

The Parlor-maid. Yes, maam.

[*She goes out.*]

Mrs Higgins. Now, Henry: be good.

Higgins. I am behaving myself perfectly.

Pickering. He is doing his best, Mrs Higgins.

[*A pause.* HIGGINS *throws back his head; stretches out his legs; and begins to whistle.*]

Mrs Higgins. Henry, dearest, you dont look at all nice in that attitude.

Higgins. [*Pulling himself together.*] I was not trying to look nice, mother.

Mrs Higgins. It doesnt matter, dear. I only wanted to make you speak.

Higgins. Why?

Mrs Higgins. Because you cant speak and whistle at the same time.

[HIGGINS *groans. Another very trying pause.*]

Higgins. [*Springing up, out of patience.*] Where the devil is that girl? Are we to wait here all day?

[ELIZA *enters, sunny, self-possessed, and giving a staggeringly convincing exhibition of ease of manner. She carries a little workbasket, and is very much at home.* PICKERING *is too much taken aback to rise.*]

Liza. How do you do, Professor Higgins? Are you quite well?

Higgins. [*Choking.*] Am I——

[*He can say no more.*]

Liza. But of course you are: you are never ill. So glad to see you again, Colonel Pickering. [*He rises hastily; and they shake hands.*] Quite chilly this morning, isnt it?

[*She sits down on his left. He sits beside her.*]

Higgins. Dont you dare try this game on me. I taught it to you; and it doesnt take me in. Get up and come home; and dont be a fool.

[ELIZA *takes a piece of needlework from her basket, and begins to stitch at it, without taking the least notice of this outburst.*]

Mrs Higgins. Very nicely put, indeed, Henry. No woman could resist such an invitation.

Higgins. You let her alone, mother. Let her speak for herself. You will jolly soon see whether she has an idea that I havnt put into her head or a word that I havnt put into her mouth. I tell you I have created this thing out of the squashed cabbage leaves of Covent Garden; and now she pretends to play the fine lady with me.

Mrs Higgins. [*Placidly.*] Yes, dear; but youll sit down, wont you?

[HIGGINS *sits down again, savagely.*]

Liza. [*To* PICKERING, *taking no apparent notice of* HIGGINS, *and working away deftly.*] Will you drop me altogether now that the experiment is over, Colonel Pickering?

Pickering. Oh dont. You mustnt think of it as an experiment. It shocks me, somehow.

Liza. Oh, I'm only a squashed cabbage leaf——

Pickering. [*Impulsively.*] No.

Liza. [*Continuing quietly.*] —but I owe so much to you that I should be very unhappy if you forgot me.

Pickering. It's very kind of you to say so, Miss Doolittle.

Liza. It's not because you paid for my

dresses. I know you are generous to everybody with money. But it was from you that I learnt really nice manners; and that is what makes one a lady, isnt it? You see it was so very difficult for me with the example of Professor Higgins always before me. I was brought up to be just like him, unable to control myself, and using bad language on the slightest provocation. And I should never have known that ladies and gentlemen didnt behave like that if you hadnt been there.

Higgins. Well!!

Pickering. Oh, thats only his way, you know. He doesnt mean it.

Liza. Oh, *I* didnt mean it either, when I was a flower girl. It was only my way. But you see I did it; and thats what makes the difference after all.

Pickering. No doubt. Still, he taught you to speak; and I couldnt have done that, you know.

Liza. [*Trivially.*] Of course: that is his profession.

Higgins. Damnation!

Liza. [*Continuing.*] It was just like learning to dance in the fashionable way: there was nothing more than that in it. But do you know what began my real education?

Pickering. What?

Liza. [*Stopping her work for a moment.*] Your calling me Miss Doolittle that day when I first came to Wimpole Street. That was the beginning of self-respect for me. [*She resumes her stitching.*] And there were a hundred little things you never noticed, because they came naturally to you. Things about standing up and taking off your hat and opening doors——

Pickering. Oh, that was nothing.

Liza. Yes: things that shewed you thought and felt about me as if I were something better than a scullery-maid; though of course I know you would have been just the same to a scullery-maid if she had been let into the drawing room. You never took off your boots in the dining room when I was there.

Pickering. You mustnt mind that. Higgins takes off his boots all over the place.

Liza. I know. I am not blaming him. It is his way, isnt it? But it made such a difference to me that you didnt do it. You see, really and truly, apart from the things anyone can pick up (the dressing and the proper way of speaking, and so on), the difference between a lady and a flower girl is not how she behaves, but how she's treated. I shall always be a flower girl to Professor Higgins, because he always treats me as a flower girl, and always will; but I know I can be a lady to you, because you always treat me as a lady, and always will.

Mrs Higgins. Please dont grind your teeth, Henry.

Pickering. Well, this is really very nice of you, Miss Doolittle.

Liza. I should like you to call me Eliza, now, if you would.

Pickering. Thank you. Eliza, of course.

Liza. And I should like Professor Higgins to call me Miss Doolittle.

Higgins. I'll see you damned first.

Mrs Higgins. Henry! Henry!

Pickering. [*Laughing.*] Why dont you slang back at him? Dont stand it. It would do him a lot of good.

Liza. I cant. I could have done it once; but now I cant go back to it. You told me, you know, that when a child is brought to a foreign country, it picks up the language in a few weeks, and forgets its own. Well, I am a child in your country. I have forgotten my own language, and can speak nothing but yours. Thats the real break-off with the corner of Tottenham Court Road. Leaving Wimpole Street finishes it.

Pickering. [*Much alarmed.*] Oh! but youre coming back to Wimpole Street, arnt you? You'll forgive Higgins?

Higgins. [*Rising.*] Forgive! Will she, by George! Let her go. Let her find out how she can get on without us. She will relapse into the gutter in three weeks without me at her elbow.

[DOOLITTLE *appears at the centre window. With a look of dignified reproach at* HIGGINS, *he comes slowly and silently to his daughter, who, with her back to the window, is unconscious of his approach.*]

Pickering. He's incorrigible, Eliza. You wont relapse, will you?

Liza. No: not now. Never again. I have learnt my lesson. I dont believe I could utter one of the old sounds if I tried. [DOOLITTLE *touches her on the left shoulder. She drops her work, losing her self-possession utterly at the spectacle of her father's splendor.*] A-a-a-a-ah-ow-ooh!

Higgins. [*With a crow of triumph.*] Aha! Just so. A-a-a-a-ahowooh! A-a-a-a-ahowooh! A-a-a-a-ahowooh! Victory! Victory!

[*He throws himself on the divan, folding his arms, and spraddling arrogantly.*]

Doolittle. Can you blame the girl? Dont look at me like that, Eliza. It aint my fault. Ive come into some money.

Liza. You must have touched a millionaire this time, dad.

Doolittle. I have. But I'm dressed something special today. I'm going to St George's, Hanover Square. Your stepmother is going to marry me.

Liza. [*Angrily.*] Youre going to let yourself down to marry that low common woman!

Pickering. [*Quietly.*] He ought to, Eliza. [*To* DOOLITTLE.] Why has she changed her mind?

Doolittle. [*Sadly.*] Intimidated, Governor. Intimidated. Middle class morality claims its victim. Wont you put on your hat, Liza, and come and see me turned off?

Liza. If the Colonel says I must, I—I'll [*Almost sobbing.*] I'll demean myself. And get insulted for my pains, like enough.

Doolittle. Dont be afraid: she never comes to words with anyone now, poor woman! respectability has broke all the spirit out of her.

Pickering. [*Squeezing* ELIZA's *elbow gently.*] Be kind to them, Eliza. Make the best of it.

Liza. [*Forcing a little smile for him through her vexation.*] Oh well, just to shew theres no ill feeling. I'll be back in a moment. [*She goes out.*]

Doolittle. [*Sitting down beside* PICKERING.] I feel uncommon nervous about the ceremony, Colonel. I wish youd come and see me through it.

Pickering. But youve been through it before, man. You were married to Eliza's mother.

Doolittle. Who told you that, Colonel?

Pickering. Well, nobody told me. But I concluded—naturally——

Doolittle. No: that aint the natural way, Colonel: it's only the middle class way. My way was always the undeserving way. But dont say nothing to Eliza. She dont know: I always had a delicacy about telling her.

Pickering. Quite right. We'll leave it so, if you dont mind.

Doolittle. And youll come to the church, Colonel, and put me through straight?

Pickering. With pleasure. As far as a bachelor can.

Mrs Higgins. May I come, Mr Doolittle? I should be very sorry to miss your wedding.

Doolittle. I should indeed be honored by your condescension, maam; and my poor old woman would take it as a tremenjous compliment. She's been very low, thinking of the happy days that are no more.

Mrs Higgins. [*Rising.*] I'll order the carriage and get ready. [*The men rise, except* HIGGINS]. I shant be more than fifteen minutes. [*As she goes to the door* ELIZA *comes in, hatted and buttoning her gloves.*] I'm going to the church to see your father married, Eliza. You had better come in the brougham with me. Colonel Pickering can go on with the bridegroom.

[MRS HIGGINS *goes out.* ELIZA *comes to the middle of the room between the centre window and the ottoman.* PICKERING *joins her.*]

Doolittle. Bridegroom. What a word! It makes a man realize his position, somehow.

[*He takes up his hat and goes towards the door.*]

Pickering. Before I go, Eliza, do forgive Higgins and come back to us.

Liza. I dont think dad would allow me. Would you, dad?

Doolittle. [*Sad but magnanimous.*] They played you off very cunning, Eliza, them two sportsmen. If it had been only one of them, you could have nailed him. But you see, there was two; and one of them chaperoned the other, as you might say. [*To* PICKERING.] It was artful of you, Colonel; but I bear no malice: I should have done the same myself. I been the victim of one woman after another all my life, and I dont grudge you two getting the better of Liza. I shant interfere. It's time for us to go, Colonel. So long, Henry. See you in St George's, Eliza. [*He goes out.*]

Pickering. [*Coaxing.*] Do stay with us, Eliza. [*He follows* DOOLITTLE.]

[ELIZA *goes out on the balcony to avoid being alone with* HIGGINS. *He rises and joins her there. She immediately comes back into the room and makes for the door; but he goes along the balcony and gets his back to the door before she reaches it.*]

Higgins. Well, Eliza, youve had a bit of your own back, as you call it. Have you had enough? and are you going to be reasonable? Or do you want any more?

Liza. You want me back only to pick up your slippers and put up with your tempers and fetch and carry for you.

Higgins. I havnt said I wanted you back at all.

Liza. Oh, indeed. Then what are we talking about?

Higgins. About you, not about me. If you come back I shall treat you just as I have always treated you. I cant change my nature; and I dont intend to change my manners. My manners are exactly the same as Colonel Pickering's.

Liza. Thats not true. He treats a flower girl as if she was a duchess.

Higgins. And I treat a duchess as if she was a flower girl.

Liza. I see. [*She turns away composedly,*

and sits on the ottoman, facing the window.] The same to everybody.

Higgins. Just so.

Liza. Like father.

Higgins. [*Grinning, a little taken down.*] Without accepting the comparison at all points, Eliza, it's quite true that your father is not a snob, and that he will be quite at home in any station of life to which his eccentric destiny may call him. [*Seriously.*] The great secret, Eliza, is not having bad manners or good manners or any other particular sort of manners, but having the same manner for all human souls: in short, behaving as if you were in Heaven, where there are no third-class carriages, and one soul is as good as another.

Liza. Amen. You are a born preacher.

Higgins. [*Irritated.*] The question is not whether I treat you rudely, but whether you ever heard me treat anyone else better.

Liza. [*With sudden sincerity.*] I dont care how you treat me. I dont mind your swearing at me. I shouldnt mind a black eye: Ive had one before this. But [*Standing up and facing him.*] I wont be passed over.

Higgins. Then get out of my way; for I wont stop for you. You talk about me as if I were a motor bus.

Liza. So you are a motor bus: all bounce and go, and no consideration for anyone. But I can do without you: dont think I cant.

Higgins. I know you can. I told you you could.

Liza. [*Wounded, getting away from him to the other side of the ottoman with her face to the hearth.*] I know you did, you brute. You wanted to get rid of me.

Higgins. Liar.

Liza. Thank you.

[*She sits down with dignity.*]

Higgins. You never asked yourself, I suppose, whether *I* could do without you.

Liza. [*Earnestly.*] Dont you try to get round me. Youll have to do without me.

Higgins. [*Arrogant.*] I can do without anybody. I have my own soul: my own spark of divine fire. But [*With sudden humility.*] I shall miss you, Eliza. [*He sits down near her on the ottoman.*] I have learnt something from your idiotic notions: I confess that humbly and gratefully. And I have grown accustomed to your voice and appearance. I like them, rather.

Liza. Well, you have both of them on your gramophone and in your book of photographs. When you feel lonely without me, you can turn the machine on. It's got no feelings to hurt.

Higgins. I cant turn your soul on. Leave me those feelings; and you can take away the voice and the face. They are not you.

Liza. Oh, you are a devil. You can twist the heart in a girl as easy as some could twist her arms to hurt her. Mrs Pearce warned me. Time and again she has wanted to leave you; and you always got round her at the last minute. And you dont care a bit for her. And you dont care a bit for me.

Higgins. I care for life, for humanity; and you are a part of it that has come my way and been built into my house. What more can you or anyone ask?

Liza. I wont care for anybody that doesnt care for me.

Higgins. Commercial principles, Eliza. Like [*Reproducing her Covent Garden pronunciation with professional exactness.*] s'yollin voylets [selling violets], isnt it?

Liza. Dont sneer at me. It's mean to sneer at me.

Higgins. I have never sneered in my life. Sneering doesnt become either the human face or the human soul. I am expressing my righteous contempt for Commercialism. I dont and wont trade in affection. You call me a brute because you couldnt buy a claim on me by fetching my slippers and finding my spectacles. You were a fool: I think a woman fetching a man's slippers is a disgusting sight: did I ever fetch your slippers? I think a good deal more of you for throwing them in my face. No use slaving for me and then saying you want to be cared for: who cares for a slave? If you come back, come back for the sake of good fellowship; for youll get nothing else. Youve had a thousand times as much out of me as I have out of you; and if you dare to set up your little dog's tricks of fetching and carrying slippers against my creation of a Duchess Eliza, I'll slam the door in your silly face.

Liza. What did you do it for if you didnt care for me?

Higgins. [*Heartily.*] Why, because it was my job.

Liza. You never thought of the trouble it would make for me.

Higgins. Would the world ever have been made if its maker had been afraid of making trouble? Making life means making trouble. Theres only one way of escaping trouble; and thats killing things. Cowards, you notice, are always shrieking to have troublesome people killed.

Liza. I'm no preacher: I dont notice things like that. I notice that you dont notice me.

Higgins. [*Jumping up and walking about intolerantly.*] Eliza: youre an idiot. I waste the treasures of my Miltonic mind by spreading them before you. Once for all, understand that I go my way and do my work without caring twopence what happens to either of us. I am not intimidated, like your father and your stepmother. So you can come back or go to the devil: which you please.

Liza. What am I to come back for?

Higgins. [*Bouncing up on his knees on the ottoman and leaning over it to her.*] For the fun of it. Thats why I took you on.

Liza. [*With averted face.*] And you may throw me out tomorrow if I dont do everything you want me to?

Higgins. Yes; and you may walk out tomorrow if I dont do everything you want me to.

Liza. And live with my stepmother?

Higgins. Yes, or sell flowers.

Liza. Oh! if I only could go back to my flower basket! I should be independent of both you and father and all the world! Why did you take my independence from me? Why did I give it up? I'm a slave now, for all my fine clothes.

Higgins. Not a bit. I'll adopt you as my daughter and settle money on you if you like. Or would you rather marry Pickering?

Liza. [*Looking fiercely round at him.*] I wouldnt marry you if you asked me; and youre nearer my age than what he is.

Higgins. [*Gently.*] Than he is: not "than what he is."

Liza. [*Losing her temper and rising.*] I'll talk as I like. Youre not my teacher now.

Higgins. [*Reflectively.*] I dont suppose Pickering would, though. He's as confirmed an old bachelor as I am.

Liza. Thats not what I want; and dont you think it. I've always had chaps enough wanting me that way. Freddy Hill writes to me twice and three times a day, sheets and sheets.

Higgins. [*Disagreeably surprised.*] Damn his impudence!

[*He recoils and finds himself sitting on his heels.*]

Liza. He has a right to if he likes, poor lad. And he does love me.

Higgins. [*Getting off the ottoman.*] You have no right to encourage him.

Liza. Every girl has a right to be loved.

Higgins. What! By fools like that?

Liza. Freddy's not a fool. And if he's weak and poor and wants me, maybe he'd make me happier than my betters that bully me and dont want me.

Higgins. Can he make anything of you? Thats the point.

Liza. Perhaps I could make something of him. But I never thought of us making anything of one another; and you never think of anything else. I only want to be natural.

Higgins. In short you want me to be as infatuated about you as Freddy? Is that it?

Liza. No I dont. Thats not the sort of feeling I want from you. And dont you be too sure of yourself or of me. I could have been a bad girl if I'd liked. Ive seen more of some things than you, for all your learning. Girls like me can drag gentlemen down to make love to them easy enough. And they wish each other dead the next minute.

Higgins. Of course they do. Then what in thunder are we quarrelling about?

Liza. [*Much troubled.*] I want a little kindness. I know I'm a common ignorant girl, and you a book-learned gentleman; but I'm not dirt under your feet. What I done [*Correcting herself.*] what I did was not for the dresses and the taxis: I did it because we were pleasant together and I come—came—to care for you; not to want you to make love to me, and not forgetting the difference between us, but more friendly like.

Higgins. Well, of course. Thats just how I feel. And how Pickering feels. Eliza: youre a fool.

Liza. Thats not a proper answer to give me.

[*She sinks on the chair at the writing-table in tears.*]

Higgins. It's all youll get until you stop being a common idiot. If youre going to be a lady, youll have to give up feeling neglected if the men you know dont spend half their time snivelling over you and the other half giving you black eyes. If you cant stand the coldness of my sort of life, and the strain of it, go back to the gutter. Work til youre more a brute than a human being; and then cuddle and squabble and drink til you fall asleep. Oh, it's a fine life, the life of the gutter. It's real: it's warm: it's violent: you can feel it through the thickest skin: you can taste it and smell it without any training or any work. Not like Science and Literature and Classical Music and Philosophy and Art. You find me cold, unfeeling, selfish, dont you? Very well: be off with you to the sort of people you like. Marry some sentimental hog or other with lots of money, and a thick pair of lips to kiss you with and a thick pair of boots to kick you with. If you cant appreciate what youve got, youd better get what you can appreciate.

Liza. [*Desperate.*] Oh you are a cruel tyrant. I cant talk to you: you turn everything against me: I'm always in the wrong. But you know very well all the time that youre nothing but a bully. You know I cant go back to the gutter, as you call it, and that I have no real friends in the world but you and the Colonel. You know well I couldnt bear to live with a low common man after you two; and it's wicked and cruel of you to insult me by pretending I could. You think I must go back to Wimpole Street because I have nowhere else to go but father's. But dont you be too sure that you have me under your feet to be trampled on and talked down. I'll marry Freddy, I will, as soon as I'm able to support him.

Higgins. [*Thunderstruck.*] Freddy!!! that young fool! That poor devil who couldnt get a job as an errand boy even if he had the guts to try for it! Woman: do you not understand that I have made you a consort for a king?

Liza. Freddy loves me: that makes him king enough for me. I dont want him to work: he wasnt brought up to it as I was. I'll go and be a teacher.

Higgins. Whatll you teach, in heaven's name?

Liza. What you taught me. I'll teach phonetics.

Higgins. Ha! ha! ha!

Liza. I'll offer myself as an assistant to that hairyfaced Hungarian.

Higgins. [*Rising in a fury.*] What! That imposter! that humbug! that toadying ignoramous! Teach him my methods! my discoveries! You take one step in his direction and I'll wring your neck. [*He lays hands on her.*] Do you hear?

Liza. [*Defiantly non-resistant.*] Wring away. What do I care? I knew youd strike me some day. [*He lets her go, stamping with rage at having forgotten himself, and recoils so hastily that he stumbles back into his seat on the ottoman.*] Aha! Now I know how to deal with you. What a fool I was not to think of it before! You cant take away the knowledge you gave me. You said I had a finer ear than you. And I can be civil and kind to people, which is more than you can. Aha! [*Purposely dropping her aitches to annoy him.*] Thats done you, Enry Iggins, it az. Now I dont care that [*Snapping her fingers.*] for your bullying and your big talk. I'll advertize it in the papers that your duchess is only a flower girl that you taught, and that she'll teach anybody to be a duchess just the same in six months for a thousand guineas. Oh, when I think of myself crawling under your feet and being trampled on and called names, when all the time I had only to lift up my finger to be as good as you, I could just kick myself.

Higgins. [*Wondering at her.*] You damned impudent slut, you! But it's better than snivelling; better than fetching slippers and finding spectacles, isnt it? [*Rising.*] By George, Eliza, I said I'd make a woman of you; and I have. I like you like this.

Liza. Yes: you turn round and make up to me now that I'm not afraid of you, and can do without you.

Higgins. Of course I do, you little fool. Five minutes ago you were like a millstone round my neck. Now you're a tower of strength: a consort battleship. You and I and Pickering will be three old bachelors instead of only two men and a silly girl.

[MRS HIGGINS *returns, dressed for the wedding.* ELIZA *instantly becomes cool and elegant.*]

Mrs Higgins. The carriage is waiting, Eliza. Are you ready?

Liza. Quite. Is the Professor coming?

Mrs Higgins. Certainly not. He cant behave himself in church. He makes remarks out loud all the time on the clergyman's pronunciation.

Liza. Then I shall not see you again, Professor. Goodbye. [*She goes to the door.*]

Mrs Higgins. [*Coming to* HIGGINS.] Goodbye, dear.

Higgins. Goodbye, mother. [*He is about to kiss her, when he recollects something.*] Oh, by the way, Eliza, order a ham and a Stilton cheese, will you? And buy me a pair of reindeer gloves, number eights, and a tie to match that new suit of mine. You can choose the color.

[*His cheerful, careless, vigorous voice shews that he is incorrigible.*]

Liza. [*Disdainfully.*] Number eights are too small for you if you want them lined with lamb's wool. You have three new ties that you have forgotten in the drawer of your washstand. Colonel Pickering prefers double Gloucester to Stilton; and you dont notice the difference. I telephoned Mrs Pearce this morning not to forget the ham. What you are to do without me I cannot imagine. [*She sweeps out.*]

Mrs Higgins. I'm afraid youve spoilt that girl, Henry. I should be uneasy about you and her if she were less fond of Colonel Pickering.

Higgins. Pickering! Nonsense: she's going to marry Freddy. Ha ha! Freddy! Freddy!! Ha ha ha ha ha!!!!!

[*He roars with laughter as the play ends.*]

*The rest of the story need not be shewn in action, and indeed, would hardly need telling if our imaginations were not so enfeebled by their lazy dependence on the ready-mades and reach-me-downs of the ragshop in which Romance keeps its stock of "happy endings" to misfit all stories. Now,

* Like the *Preface,* the author's concluding passage is condensed.

the history of Eliza Doolittle, though called a romance because the transfiguration it records seems exceedingly improbable, is common enough. Such transfigurations have been achieved by hundreds of resolutely ambitious young women since Nell Gwynne set them the example by playing queens and fascinating kings in the theatre in which she began by selling oranges. Nevertheless, people in all directions have assumed, for no other reason than that she [Eliza] became the heroine of a romance, that she must have married the hero of it. This is unbearable, not only because her little drama, if acted on such a thoughtless assumption, must be spoiled, but because the true sequel is patent to anyone with a sense of human nature in general, and of feminine instinct in particular.

Eliza, in telling Higgins she would not marry him if he asked her, was not coquetting: she was announcing a well-considered decision. When a bachelor interests, and dominates, and teaches, and becomes important to a spinster, as Higgins with Eliza, she always, if she has character enough to be capable of it, considers very seriously indeed whether she will play for becoming that bachelor's wife, especially if he is so little interested in marriage that a determined and devoted woman might capture him if she set herself resolutely to do it. If she is at the end of her youth, and has no security for her livelihood, she will marry him because she must marry anybody who will provide for her. But at Eliza's age a good-looking girl does not feel that pressure: she feels free to pick and choose. She is therefore guided by her instinct in the matter. Eliza's instinct tells her not to marry Higgins. It does not tell her to give him up. It is not in the slightest doubt as to his remaining one of the strongest personal interests in her life.

As our own instincts are not appealed to by her conclusion, let us see whether we cannot discover some reason in it. When Higgins excused his indifference to young women on the ground that they had an irresistible rival in his mother, he gave the clue to his inveterate old-bachelordom. The case is uncommon only to the extent that remarkable mothers are uncommon. If an imaginative boy has a sufficiently rich mother who has intelligence, personal grace, dignity of character without harshness, and a cultivated sense of the best art of her time to enable her to make her house beautiful, she sets a standard for him against which very few women can struggle, besides effecting for him a disengagement of his affections, his sense of beauty, and his idealism from his specifically sexual impulses. This makes him a standing puzzle to the huge number of uncultivated people who have been brought up in tasteless homes by commonplace or disagreeable parents, and to whom, consequently, literature, painting, sculpture, music, and affectionate personal relations come as modes of sex if they come at all. The word passion means nothing else to them; and that Higgins could have a passion for phonetics and idealize his mother instead of Eliza, would seem to them absurd and unnatural.

Now, though Eliza was incapable of thus explaining to herself Higgins's formidable powers of resistance to the charm that prostrated Freddy at the first glance, she was instinctively aware that she could never obtain a complete grip of him, or come between him and his mother (the first necessity of the married woman). Even had there been no mother-rival, she would still have refused to accept an interest in herself that was secondary to philosophic interests. Had Mrs Higgins died, there would still have been Milton and the Universal Alphabet. Put that along with her resentment of Higgins's domineering superiority, and her mistrust of his coaxing cleverness in getting round her and evading her wrath when he had gone too far with his impetuous bullying, and you will see that Eliza's instinct had good grounds for warning her not to marry her Pygmalion.

And now, whom did Eliza marry? For if Higgins was a predestinate old bachelor, she was most certainly not a predestinate old maid. Well, that can be told very shortly to those who have not guessed it from the indications she has herself given them.

Almost immediately after Eliza is stung into proclaiming her considered determination not to marry Higgins, she mentions the fact that young Mr Frederick Eynsford Hill is pouring out his love for her daily through the post. Now Freddy is young, practically twenty years younger than Higgins: he is a gentleman (or, as Eliza would qualify him, a toff), and speaks like one. He is nicely dressed, is treated by the Colonel as an equal, loves her unaffectedly, and is not her master, nor ever likely to dominate her in spite of his advantage of social standing. Will she look forward to a lifetime of fetching Higgins's slippers or to a lifetime of Freddy fetching hers? There can be no doubt about the answer. Unless Freddy is biologically repulsive to her, and Higgins biologically attractive to a degree that overwhelms all her other instincts, she will, if she marries either of them, marry Freddy.

And that is just what Eliza did.

Complications ensued; but they were economic, not romantic. Freddy had no money and no occupation.

Thus Freddy and Eliza, now Mr and Mrs Eynsford Hill, would have spent a penniless honeymoon but for a wedding present of £500 from the Colonel to Eliza. Her desire to have Freddy in the house with her seemed of no more importance [to Higgins] than if she had wanted an extra piece of bedroom furniture.

It was the Colonel who finally solved the problem, which had cost him much perplexed cogitation. He one day asked Eliza, rather shyly, whether she had quite given up her notion of keeping a flower shop. She replied that she had thought of it, but had put it out of her head. They broke the matter to Higgins that evening. The sole comment vouchsafed by him very nearly led to a serious quarrel with Eliza. It was to the effect that she would have in Freddy an ideal errand boy.

Colonel Pickering had to explain to him what a cheque book and a bank account meant. The pair were by no means easily teachable. Freddy backed up Eliza in her obstinate refusal to believe that they could save money by engaging a bookkeeper with some knowledge of the business. How, they argued, could you possibly save money by going to extra expense when you already could not make both ends meet? But the Colonel, after making the ends meet over and over again, at last gently insisted; and Eliza, humbled to the dust by having to beg from him so often, and stung by the uproarious derision of Higgins, to whom the notion of Freddy succeeding at anything was a joke that never palled, grasped the fact that business, like phonetics, has to be learned.

Mr F. Hill, florist and green grocer (they soon discovered that there was money in asparagus; and asparagus led to other vegetables), had an air which stamped the business as classy; and in private life he was still Frederick Eynsford Hill, Esquire. Not that there was any swank about him: nobody but Eliza knew that he had been christened Frederick Challoner. Eliza herself swanked like anything.

That is all. That is how it has turned out. It is astonishing how much Eliza still manages to meddle in the housekeeping at Wimpole Street in spite of the shop and her own family. But when it comes to business, to the life that she really leads as distinguished from the life of dreams and fancies, she likes Freddy and she likes the Colonel; and she does not like Higgins and Mr Doolittle. Galatea never does quite like Pygmalion: his relation to her is too godlike to be altogether agreeable.

THE GREEN PASTURES*

[*A Fable*]

SUGGESTED BY ROARK BRADFORD'S SOUTHERN SKETCHES, "OL' MAN ADAM AN' HIS CHILLUN"

By

MARC CONNELLY

A FRIEND SUGGESTED TO MARC CONNELLY in 1928 that he read Roark Bradford's *Ol' Man Adam and His Chillun,* a newly published collection of Bible-story retellings in negro dialect. These stories were not genuine folk tales, but Mr. Bradford's own reworking of Biblical material, and their tone and point of view were distinctly twentieth-century, sophisticated, and at bottom skeptical rather than religious. Nobody's faith was ever strengthened by Mr. Bradford's book, it is safe to guess, but if unbelievers were converted to faith by the play Mr. Connelly based on that book, it would not be surprising.

For Mr. Connelly saw how some of the material in *Ol' Man Adam and His Chillun* could be brought closer both to true folk feeling and true religious belief in a play. To accomplish this the audience must be made to adopt not only the innocent negro approach to the Old Testament stories, it must be made doubly innocent, like a negro child. Therefore the Sunday-School scenes. And to be carried along in this delicate balance between the familiar and the unfamiliar, between knowledge and innocence, the scenes must be bridged with music. And the music should be negro, folksy, and religious. The spirituals which connect the scenes in *The Green Pastures* and which even at times are used to advance the action were ready to be fitted into the texture of the play as they were selected by Mr. Connelly and Mr. Hall Johnson, the trainer and director of the choir. Mr. Johnson also wrote the final spiritual, "Hallelujah King Jesus," since a suitable parallel for it could not be found in the traditional negro-spiritual literature.

Altogether, *The Green Pastures,* telling of so many miracles, seems itself both miraculous and inevitable—miraculous because it arose out of such unpredictable comings-together; inevitable because by 1930 the theatre in America was ripe and overripe for a great negro play and a great religious play. In the seventy years since the Civil War the Negro had made tremendous advances to nearly full position as American like any other, nowhere more visibly than in the theatre. Also 1930 marked the end of the feverish decade of the Twenties, the decade of prohibition, sports champions, stock-market boom, flappers, gangsters, and bathtub gin. Since World War I America had pursued the pleasures of this world; the "morning-after" decade of the Thirties was about to dawn. In literature the satires of Sinclair Lewis, the gropings of Eugene O'Neill, the sardonic analyses of Dos Passos and Dreiser, the nihilism of Hemingway, the pervasive disillusionment among all kinds of creative talents, which showed America as the land where despair ought to reign if it didn't, all these made Americans ready for a reminder of hope and faith. Unconsciously, of course, but truly, America needed *The Green Pastures.*

But the standard and even the most advanced producers viewed the play askance when Mr. Connelly offered it to them. No religious play had succeeded on Broadway for many years. Besides, the play's enormous cast, its many scenes, its elaborate machinery (treadmills, magic effects, rainbows, and so forth) called for a very large pre-curtain investment. Somehow, again miraculously, a producer was found, a Wall-Street "angel," inexperienced in theatrical production but ready to back his judgment with his money —and he judged *The Green Pastures* good.

He won his money back, for the play ran for five years, 1642 performances, 640 on Broadway and the rest in the country at large.

Naturally enough, however, *The Green Pastures* is a difficult play to export. It has been forbidden in Great Britain because it shows God on stage, though the British were allowed to see the motion-picture version in 1936. It was performed in Sweden, however, and revived on Broadway in 1951 for a brief run.

The part of The Lord in the first production was taken by Richard B. Harrison, an unknown actor, who never missed a performance until he died just before the play finally closed. The perfection of Mr. Harrison's combined authority and sweetness has lingered in the memories of the many thousands who were deeply moved by that production. The delightful settings were by Robert Edmund Jones.

The Green Pastures' impact may be difficult to gauge when the play is read and not seen, and it is not likely to be often available in revival, but it remains a monumental attainment of the American theatre.

MARC CONNELLY

Born 1890, McKeesport, Penna.
Educated at Trinity Hall, Washington, Penna.
Journalist and free-lance magazine writer.
1930, awarded Pulitzer Prize for *The Green Pastures.*
1953– , President of The National Institute of Arts and Letters.
Member of the United States Commission for UNESCO.
Proponent of international copyright.

PLAYS

1916 *The Amber Empress,* musical comedy. 1920 *Erminie,* musical comedy (with others). 1921 *Dulcy* (with George S. Kaufman). 1922 *Merton of the Movies* (with George S. Kaufman, from story by Harry Leon Wilson). 1923 *Helen of Troy, New York,* musical comedy (with George S. Kaufman). 1923 *The Deep Tangled Wildwood* (with George S. Kaufman). 1924 *Be Yourself,* musical comedy (with George S. Kaufman). 1924 *Beggar on Horseback* (with George S. Kaufman). 1926 *The Wisdom Tooth.* 1927 *The Wild Man of Borneo* (with Herman J. Mankiewicz). 1930 *The Green Pastures.* 1930 *Little David,* one act. 1934 *The Farmer Takes a Wife* (with Frank B. Elser from novel *Rome Haul* by Walter D. Edmunds). 1938 *Everywhere I Roam* (with Arnold Sundgaard). 1939 *The Traveler,* one act. 1941 *The Mole on Lincoln's Cheek,* one act. 1942 *The Flowers of Virtue.* 1948 *A Story for Strangers.*

SCREENWRITING

1933 *Cradle Song.* 1936 *The Green Pastures.* 1937 *Captains Courageous.* 1942 *I Married a Witch.* 1942 *Reunion.*

WRITINGS ON THE THEATRE

"We're Going to Have Better Plays," *Theatre Magazine,* LII (December 1930), 16f. "Fantasies and Their Audience," *The New York Times,* Sept. 19, 1948, II.1.5. "The Totalitarian Theatre," *U.S. Department of State Bulletin,* XXVII (Oct. 6, 1952), 542f. "The Curtain Rises," *The New Yorker,* XXX (Dec. 18, 1954), 120ff.

THE GREEN PASTURES

Characters

Mr. Deshee, *the Preacher.*
Myrtle.
First Boy.
Second Boy.
First Cook.
A Voice.
Second Cook.
First Man Angel.
First Mammy Angel.
A Stout Angel.
A Slender Angel.
Archangel.
Gabriel.
God.
Choir Leader.
Custard Maker.
Adam.
Eve.
Cain.
Cain's Girl.
Zeba.
Cain the Sixth.
Boy Gambler.
First Gambler.
Second Gambler.
Voice in Shanty.
Noah.
Noah's Wife.
Shem.
First Woman.
Second Woman.
Third Woman.
First Man.
Flatfoot.
Ham.
Japheth.
First Cleaner.
Second Cleaner.
Abraham.
Isaac.
Jacob.
Moses.
Zipporah.
Aaron.
A Candidate Magician.
Pharaoh.
General.
Head Magician.
First Wizard.
Second Wizard.
Joshua.
First Scout.
Master of Ceremonies.
King of Babylon.
Prophet.
High Priest.
Corporal.
Hezdrel.
Second Officer.

AUTHOR'S NOTE

The Green Pastures is an attempt to present certain aspects of a living religion in the terms of its believers. The religion is that of thousands of Negroes in the deep South. With terrific spiritual hunger and the greatest humility these untutored black Christians—many of whom cannot even read the book which is the treasure house of their faith—have adapted the contents of the Bible to the consistencies of their everyday lives.

Unburdened by the differences of more educated theologians they accept the Old Testament as a chronicle of wonders which happened to people like themselves in vague but actual places, and of rules of conduct, true acceptance of which will lead them to a tangible, three-dimensional Heaven. In this Heaven, if one has been born in a district where fish frys are popular, the angels do have magnificent fish frys through an eternity somewhat resembling a series of earthly holidays. The Lord Jehovah will be the promised comforter, a just but compassionate patriarch, the summation of all the virtues His follower has observed in the human beings about him. The Lord may look like the Reverend Mr. Dubois as our Sunday School teacher speculates in the play, or he may resemble another believer's own grandfather. In any event, His face will be familiar to the one who has come for his reward.

The author is indebted to Mr. Roark Bradford, whose retelling of several of the Old Testament stories in "Ol' Man Adam an' His

Chillun" first stimulated his interest in this point of view.

One need not blame a hazy memory of the Bible for the failure to recall the characters of Hezdrel, Zeba and others in the play. They are the author's apocrypha, but he believes persons much like them have figured in the meditations of some of the old Negro preachers, whose simple faith he has tried to translate into a play.

PART ONE

SCENE I

A corner in a Negro church.

Ten children and an elderly preacher.

The costumes are those that might be seen in any lower Louisiana town at Sunday-School time. As the curtain rises, MR. DESHEE, *the preacher, is reading from a Bible. The* CHILDREN *are listening with varied degrees of interest. Three or four are wide-eyed in their attention. Two or three are obviously puzzled, but interested, and the smallest ones are engaged in more physical concerns. One is playing with a little doll, and another runs his finger on all the angles of his chair.*

Deshee. "An' Adam lived a hundred and thirty years, an' begat a son in his own likeness, after his image; an' called his name Seth. An' de days of Adam, after he had begotten Seth, were eight hundred years; an' he begat sons an' daughters; an' all de days dat Adam lived were nine hundred an' thirty years; an' he died. An' Seth lived a hundred an' five years an' begat Enos; an' Seth lived after he begat Enos eight hundred an' seven years and begat sons and daughters. An' all de days of Seth were nine hundred and twelve years; an' he died." An' it go on like dat till we come to Enoch an' de book say: "An' Enoch lived sixty an' five years and begat Methuselah." Den it say: "An' all de days of Methuselah were nine hund'ed an' sixty an' nine years an' he died." An' dat was de oldest man dat ever was. Dat's why we call ol' Mr. Gurney's mammy ol' Mrs. Methuselah, caize she's so ol'. Den a little later it tell about another member of de fam'ly. His name was Noah. Maybe some of you know about him already. I'm gonter tell you all about him next Sunday. Anyway dat's de meat an' substance of de first five chapters of Genesis. Now, how you think you gonter like de Bible?

Myrtle. I think it's jest wonderful, Mr. Deshee. I cain't understand any of it.

First Boy. Why did dey live so long, Mr. Deshee?

Deshee. Why? Caize dat was de way God felt.

Second Boy. Dat made Adam a way back.

Deshee. Yes, he certainly 'way back by de time Noah come along. Want to ask me any mo' questions?

Second Boy. What de worl' look like when de Lawd begin, Mr. Deshee?

Deshee. How yo' mean what it look like?

Myrtle. Carlisle mean who was in N'Orleans den.

Deshee. Dey wasn't nobody in N'Orleans on 'count dey wasn't any N'Orleans. Dat's de whole idea I tol' you at de end of de first Chapter. Yo' got to get yo' minds fixed. Dey wasn't any Rampart Street. Dey wasn't any Canal Street. Dey wasn't any Louisiana. Dey wasn't nothin' on de earth at all caize fo' de reason dey wasn't any earth.

Myrtle. Yes, but what Carlisle wanter know is——

Deshee. [*Interrupting and addressing* LITTLE BOY *who has been playing with his chair and paying no attention.*] Now Randolph, if you don't listen, how yo' gonter grow up and be a good man? Yo' wanter grow up an' be a transgressor?

Little Boy. [*Frightened.*] No.

Deshee. You tell yo' mammy yo' sister got to come wid you next time. She kin git de things done in time to bring you to de school. You content yo'self. [*The* LITTLE BOY *straightens up in his chair.*] Now, what do Carlisle want to know?

Carlisle. How he decide he want de worl' to be right yere and how he git de idea he wanted it?

Myrtle. Caize de Book say, don't it, Mr. Deshee?

Deshee. De Book say, but at de same time dat's a good question. I remember when I was a little boy de same thing recurred to me. An' ol' Mr. Dubois, he was a wonderful preacher at New Hope Chapel over in East Gretna, he said: "De answer is dat de Book ain't got time to go into all de details." And he was right. You know sometimes I think de Lawd expects us to figure out a few things for ourselves. We know that at one time dey wasn't anything except Heaven; we don't know jest where it was but we know it was dere. Maybe it was everywhere. Den one day de Lawd got the idea he'd like to make some places. He made de sun and de moon, de stars. An' he made de earth.

Myrtle. Who was aroun' den, nothin' but angels?

Deshee. I suppose so.

First Boy. What was de angels doin' up dere?

Deshee. I suppose dey jest flew aroun' and had a good time. Dey wasn't no sin, so dey musta had a good time.

First Boy. Did dey have picnics?

Deshee. Sho, dey had the nicest kind of picnics. Dey probably had fish frys, wid b'iled custard and ten cent seegars for de adults. God gives us humans lotsa ideas about havin' good times. Maybe dey were things he'd seen de angels do. Yes, sir, I bet dey had a fish fry every week.

Myrtle. Did dey have Sunday School, too?

Deshee. Yes, dey musta had Sunday School for de cherubs.

Myrtle. What did God look like, Mr. Deshee?

Deshee. Well, nobody knows exactly what God looked like. But when I was a little boy I used to imagine dat he looked like de Reverend Dubois. He was de finest looking ol' man I ever knew. Yes, I used to bet de Lawd looked exactly like Mr. Dubois in de days when he walked de earth in de shape of a natchel man.

Myrtle. When was dat, Mr. Deshee?

Deshee. Why, when he was gettin' things started down heah. When He talked to Adam and Eve and Noah and Moses and all dem. He made mighty men in dem days. But aldo they was awful mighty dey always knew dat He was beyond dem all. Pretty near one o'clock, time fo' you chillun to go home to dinner, but before I let you go I wan' you to go over wid me de main facts of de first lesson. What's de name of de book?

Children. Genesis.

Deshee. Dat's right. And what's de other name?

Children. First Book of Moses.

Deshee. Dat's right. And dis yere's Chapter One. [*The lights begin to dim.*] "In de beginnin' God created de heaven an' de earth. An' de earth was widout form an' void. An' de darkness was upon de face of de deep."

SCENE II

In the darkness many voices are heard singing "Rise, Shine, Give God The Glory." They sing it gayly and rapidly. The lights go up as the second verse ends. The chorus is being sung diminuendo by a mixed company of angels. That is, they are angels in that they wear brightly colored robes and have wings protruding from their backs. Otherwise they look and act like a company of happy negroes at a fish fry. The scene itself is a pre-Creation Heaven with compromises. In the distance is an unbroken stretch of blue sky. Companionable varicolored clouds billow down to the floor of the stage and roll overhead to the branches of a live oak tree which is up left. The tree is leafy and dripping with Spanish moss, and with the clouds makes a frame for the scene. In the cool shade of the tree are the usual appurtenances of a fish fry: a large kettle of hot fat set on two small parallel logs, with a fire going underneath, and a large rustic table formed by driving four stakes into the ground and placing planks on top of the small connecting boards. On the table are piles of biscuits and corn bread and the cooked fish in dish pans. There are one or two fairly large cedar or crock "churns" containing boiled custard, which looks like milk. There is a gourd dipper beside the churns and several glasses and cups of various sizes and shapes from which the custard is drunk. The principal singers are marching two by two in a small area at the R. *of the stage. Two* MAMMY ANGELS *are attending to the frying beside the kettle. Behind the table a* MAN ANGEL *is skinning fish and passing them to the cooks. Another is ladling out the custard. A* MAMMY ANGEL *is putting fish on bread for a brood of* CHERUBS, *and during the first scene they seat themselves on a grassy bank upstage. Another* MAMMY ANGEL *is clapping her hands disapprovingly and beckoning a laughing* BOY CHERUB *down from a cloud a little out of her reach. Another* MAMMY ANGEL *is solicitously slapping the back of a* GIRL CHERUB *who has a large fish sandwich in her hand and a bone in her throat. There is much movement about the table, and during the first few minutes several individuals go up to the table to help themselves to the food and drink. Many of the women angels wear hats and a few of the men are smoking cigars. A large boxful is on the table. There is much laughter and chatter, as the music softens but continues, during the early part of the action. The following short scenes are played almost simultaneously.*

First Cook. [*At kettle. Calling off.*] Hurry up, Cajey. Dis yere fat's cryin' fo' mo' feesh.

A Voice. [*Off stage.*] We comin', fas' we kin. Dey got to be ketched, ain't dey? We cain't say, "C'm'on little fish. C'm'on an' git fried," kin we?

Second Cook. [*At table.*] De trouble is de mens is all worm fishin'.

First Man Angel. [*At table.*] Whut dif'runce do it make? Yo' all de time got to make out like somebody's doin' somethin' de wrong way.

Second Cook. [*Near table.*] I s'pose you got de per'fec' way fo' makin' bait.

First Man Angel. I ain't sayin' dat. I is sayin' whut's wrong wid worm fishin'.

Second Cook. Whut's wrong wid worm fishin'? Ever'thing, dat's all. Dey's only one good way fo' catfishin', an' dat's minny fishin'. Anybody know dat.

First Man Angel. Well, it jest so happen dat minny fishin' is de doggondest fool way of fishin' dey is. You kin try minny fishin' to de cows come home an' all you catch'll be de backache. De trouble wid you, sister, is you jest got minny fishin' on de brain.

Second Cook. Go right on, loud mouf. You tell me de news. My, my! You jest de wisest person in de worl'. First you, den de Lawd God.

First Man Angel. [*To the* CUSTARD LADLER.] You cain't tell dem nothin'. [*Walks away to the custard churn.*] Does you try to 'splain some simple fac' dey git man-deaf.

First Mammy Angel. [*To* CHERUB *on the cloud.*] Now, you heerd me. [*The* CHERUB *assumes several mocking poses, as she speaks.*] You fly down yere. You wanter be put down in de sin book? [*She goes to the table, gets a drink for herself and points out the* CHERUB *to one of the men behind the table.*] Dat baby must got imp blood in him he so vexin'. [*She returns to her position under the cloud.*] You want me to fly up dere an' slap you down? Now, I tol' you.

[*The* CHERUB *starts to come down.*]

Stout Angel. [*To the* CHERUB *with a bone in her throat.*] I tol' you you was too little fo' cat fish. What you wanter git a bone in yo' froat fo'? [*She slaps the* CHERUB'*s back.*]

Slender Angel. [*Liesurely eating a sandwich as she watches the backslapping.*] What de trouble wid Leonetta?

Stout Angel. She got a catfish bone down her froat. [*To the* CHERUB.] Doggone, I tol' you to eat grinnel instead.

Slender Angel. Ef'n she do git all dat et, she gonter have de bellyache.

Stout Angel. Ain't I tol' her dat? [*To* CHERUB.] Come on now; let go dat bone. [*She slaps* CHERUB'*s back again. The bone is dislodged and the* CHERUB *grins her relief.*] Dat's good.

Slender Angel. [*Comfortingly.*] Now she all right.

Stout Angel. Go on an' play wid yo' cousins. [*The* CHERUB *joins the* CHERUBS *sitting on the embankment. The concurrency of scenes ends here.*] I ain't seen you lately, Lily. How you been?

Slender Angel. Me, I'm fine. I been visitin' my mammy. She waitin' on de welcome table over by de throne of grace.

Stout Angel. She always was pretty holy.

Slender Angel. Yes, ma'am. She like it dere. I guess de Lawd's took quite a fancy to her.

Stout Angel. Well, dat's natural. I declare yo' mammy one of de finest lady angels I know.

Slender Angel. She claim you de best one she know.

Stout Angel. Well, when you come right down to it, I suppose we is all pretty near perfec'.

Slender Angel. Yes, ma'am. Why is dat, Mis' Jenny?

Stout Angel. I s'pose it's caize de Lawd he don' 'low us 'sociatin' wid de devil any mo' so dat dey cain' be no mo' sinnin'.

Slender Angel. Po' ol' Satan. Whutevah become of him?

Stout Angel. De Lawd put him some place I s'pose.

Slender Angel. But dey ain't any place but Heaven, is dey?

Stout Angel. De Lawd could make a place, couldn't he?

Slender Angel. Dat's de truth. Dey's one thing confuses me though.

Stout Angel. What's dat?

Slender Angel. I do a great deal of travelin' an' I ain't never come across any place but Heaven anywhere. So if de Lawd kick Satan out of Heaven jest whereat did he go? Dat's my question.

Stout Angel. You bettah let de Lawd keep his own secrets, Lily. De way things is goin' now dey ain't been no sinnin' since dey give dat scamp a kick in de pants. Nowadays Heaven's free of sin an' if a lady wants a little constitutional she kin fly 'til she wing-weary widout gittin' insulted.

Slender Angel. I was jest a baby when Satan lef'. I don't even 'member what he look like.

Stout Angel. He was jest right fo' a devil.

[*An* ARCHANGEL *enters. He is older than the others and wears a white beard. His clothing is much darker than that of the others and his wings a trifle more imposing.*] Good mo'-nin', Archangel. [*Others say good morning.*]

Archangel. Good mo'nin', folks. I wonder kin I interrup' de fish fry an' give out de Sunday school cyards? [*Cries of "Suttingly!" "Mah goodness, yes"—etc. The marching* CHOIR *stops.*] You kin keep singin' if you want to. Why don' you sing "When de Saints Come Marchin' In?" Seem to me I ain' heard dat lately. [*The* CHOIR *begins "When the Saints Come Marching In," rather softly, but does not resume marching. The* ARCHANGEL *looks off left.*] All right, bring 'em yere. [*A prim looking* WOMAN TEACHER-ANGEL *enters, shepherding ten* BOY *and* GIRL CHERUBS. *The* TEACHER *carries ten beribboned diplomas, which she gives to the* ARCHANGEL. *The* CHERUBS *are dressed in stiffly starched white suits and dresses, the little* GIRLS *having enormous ribbons at the backs of their dresses and smaller ones on their hair and on the tips of their wings. They line up in front of the* ARCHANGEL *and receive the attention of the rest of the company. The* CHOIR *sings through the ceremony.*] Now den, cherubs, why is you yere?

Children. Because we so good.

Archangel. Dat's right. Now who de big boss?

Children. Our dear Lawd.

Archangel. Dat's right. When you all grow up what you gonter be?

Children. Holy angels at de throne of grace.

Archangel. Dat's right. Now, you passed yo' 'xaminations and it gives me great pleasure to hand out de cyards for de whole class. Gineeva Chaproe. [*The* FIRST GIRL CHERUB *goes to him and gets her diploma. The* CHOIR *sings loudly and resumes marching, as the* ARCHANGEL *calls out another name—and presents diplomas.*] Corey Moulter. [SECOND GIRL CHERUB *gets her diploma.*] Nootzie Winebush. [THIRD GIRL CHERUB.] Harriet Prancy. [FOURTH GIRL CHERUB.] I guess you is Brozain Stew't. [*He gives the* FIFTH GIRL CHERUB *the paper. Each of the presentations has been accompanied by hand-clapping from the bystanders.*] Now you boys know yo' own names. Suppose you come yere and help me git dese 'sorted right.

[BOY CHERUBS *gather about him and receive their diplomas. The little* GIRLS *have scattered about the stage, joining groups of the adult angels. The angel* GABRIEL *enters. He is bigger and more elaborately winged than even the* ARCHANGEL, *but he is also much younger and beardless. His costume is less conventional than that of the other men, resembling more the Gabriel of the Doré drawings. His appearance causes a flutter among the others. They stop their chattering with the children. The* CHOIR *stops as three or four audible whispers of "Gabriel!" are heard. In a moment the heavenly company is all attention.*]

Gabriel. [*Lifting his hand.*] Gangway! Gangway for de Lawd God Jehovah!

[*There is a reverent hush and* GOD *enters. He is the tallest and biggest of them all. He wears a white shirt with a white bow tie, a long Prince Albert coat of black alpaca, black trousers and congress gaiters. He looks at the assemblage. There is a pause. He speaks in a rich, bass voice.*]

God. Is you been baptized?

Others. [*Chanting.*] Certainly, Lawd.

God. Is you been baptized?

Others. Certainly, Lawd.

God. [*With the beginning of musical notation.*] Is you been baptized?

Others. [*Now half-singing.*] Certainly Lawd. Certainly, certainly, certainly, Lawd.

[*They sing the last two verses with equivalent part division.*]

Is you been redeemed?
  Certainly, Lawd.
Is you been redeemed?
  Certainly, Lawd.
Is you been redeemed?
  Certainly, Lawd. Certainly, certainly,
    certainly, Lawd.

Do you bow mighty low?
  Certainly, Lawd.
Do you bow mighty low?
  Certainly, Lawd.
Do you bow mighty low?
  Certainly, Lawd. Certainly, certainly,
    certainly, Lawd.

[*As the last response ends all heads are bowed.* GOD *looks at them for a moment; then lifts His hand.*]

God. Let de fish fry proceed.

[EVERYONE *rises. The* ANGELS *relax and resume their inaudible conversations. The activity behind the table and about the cauldron is resumed. Some of the choir members cross to the table and get sandwiches and cups of the boiled custard. Three or four of the children in the Sunday School class and the little* GIRL *who had the bone in her throat affectionately group themselves about* GOD *as he speaks with the* ARCHANGEL. *He pats their heads, they hang to his coat-tails, etc.*]

Archangel. Good mo'nin', Lawd.

God. Good mo'nin', Deacon. You lookin' pretty spry.

Archangel. I cain' complain. We just been givin' our cyards to de chillun.

God. Dat's good.

[*A small* CHERUB, *his feet braced against one of* GOD'S *shoes, is using* GOD'S *coat tail as a trapeze. One of the* COOKS *offers a fish sandwich which* GOD *politely declines.*]

First Mammy Angel. Now, you leave go de Lawd's coat, Herman. You heah me?

God. Dat's all right, sister. He jest playin'.

First Mammy Angel. He playin' too rough.

[GOD *picks up the* CHERUB *and spanks him goodnaturedly. The* CHERUB *squeals with delight and runs to his mother.* GABRIEL *advances to* GOD *with a glass of the custard.*]

Gabriel. Little b'iled custud, Lawd?

God. Thank you very kindly. Dis looks nice.

Custard Maker. [*Offering a box.*] Ten cent seegar, Lawd?

God. [*Taking it.*] Thank you, thank you. How de fish fry goin'? [*Ad lib. cries of "O. K. Lawd," "Fine an' dandy, Lawd," "De best one yit, Lawd," etc. To the choir.*] How you shouters gittin' on?

Choir Leader. We been marchin' and singin' de whole mo'nin'.

God. I heerd you. You gittin' better all de time. You gittin' as good as de one at de throne. Why don' you give us one dem ol' time jump-ups?

Choir Leader. Anythin' you say, Lawd. [*To the others.*] "So High!"

[*The* CHOIR *begins to sing "So High You Can't Get Over It." They sing softly, but do not march. An* ANGEL *offers his cigar to* GOD *from which He can light His own.*]

God. No, thanks. I'm gonter save dis a bit.

[*He puts the cigar in his pocket and listens to the singers a moment. Then he sips his custard. After the second sip, a look of displeasure comes on his face.*]

Gabriel. What's de matter, Lawd?

God. [*Sipping again.*] I ain't jest sure, yit. Dey's something 'bout dis custahd.

[*Takes another sip.*]

Custard Maker. Ain't it all right, Lawd?

God. It don't seem seasoned jest right. You make it?

Custard Maker. Yes, Lawd. I put everythin' in it like I allus do. It's supposed to be perfec'.

God. Yeah. I kin taste de eggs and de cream and de sugar. [*Suddenly.*] I know what it is. It needs jest a little bit mo' firmament.

Custard Maker. Dey's firmament in it, Lawd.

God. Maybe, but it ain' enough.

Custard Maker. It's all we had, Lawd. Dey ain't a drap in de jug.

God. Dat's all right. I'll jest r'ar back an' pass a miracle. [CHOIR *stops singing.*] Let it be some firmament! An' when I say let it be some firmament, I don't want jest a little bitty dab o' firmament caize I'm sick an' tired of runnin' out of it when we need it. Let it be a whole mess of firmament! [*The stage has become misty until* GOD *and the heavenly company are obscured. As he finishes the speech there is a burst of thunder. As the stage grows darker.*] Dat's de way I like it.

[*Murmurs from the others; "Dat's a lot of firmament." "My, dat is firmament!" "Look to me like he's created rain," etc.*]

First Mammy Angel. [*When the stage is dark.*] Now look, Lawd, dat's too much firmament. De Cherubs is gettin' all wet.

Second Mammy Angel. Look at my Carlotta, Lawd. She's soaked to de skin. Dat's *plenty* too much firmament.

God. Well, 'co'se we don't want de chillun to ketch cold. Can't you dreen it off?

Gabriel. Dey's no place to dreen it, Lawd.

First Mammy Angel. Why don't we jest take de babies home, Lawd?

God. No, I don' wanta bust up de fish fry. You angels keep quiet an I'll pass another miracle. Dat's always de trouble wid miracles. When you pass one you always gotta r'ar back an' pass another. [*There is a hush.*] Let dere be a place to dreen off dis firmament. Let dere be mountains and valleys an' let dere be oceans an' lakes. An' let dere be rivers and bayous to dreen it off in, too. As a matter of fac' let dere be de earth. An' when dat's done let dere be de sun, an' let it come out and dry my Cherubs' wings.

[*The lights go up until the stage is bathed in sunlight. On the embankment upstage there is now a waist-high wrought iron railing such as one sees on the galleries of houses in the French quarter of New Orleans. The* CHERUBS *are being examined by their parents and there is an ad lib. murmur of, "You all right, honey?" "You feel better now, Albert?" "Now you all dry, Vangy?" until the* ARCHANGEL, *who has been gazing in awe at the railing, drowns them out.*]

Archangel. Look yere!

[*There is a rush to the embankment accompanied by exclamations, "My goodness!" "What's dis?" "I declah!" etc.* GABRIEL *towers above the group on the middle of the embankment.* GOD *is wrapped in thought, facing the audience. The* CHOIR *resumes singing "So High You Can't Get Over It" softly. The babbling at the balustrade dies away as the people lean over the railing.* GABRIEL *turns and faces* GOD, *indicating the earth below the railing with his left hand.*]

Gabriel. Do you see it, Lawd?

God. [*Quietly, without turning his head upstage.*] Yes, Gabriel.

Gabriel. Looks mighty nice, Lawd.

God. Yes.

[GABRIEL *turns and looks over the railing.*]

Gabriel. [*Gazing down.*] Yes, suh. Dat'd make mighty nice farming country. Jest look at dat South forty over dere. You ain't going to let dat go to waste is you, Lawd? Dat would be a pity an' a shame.

God. [*Not turning.*] It's a good earth. [GOD *turns, room is made for him beside* GABRIEL *on the embankment.*] Yes. I ought to have somebody to enjoy it. [*He turns, facing the audience. The others, save for the* CHOIR *who are lined up in two rows of six on an angle up right, continue to look over the embankment.*] Gabriel!

[GOD *steps down from the embankment two paces.*]

Gabriel. [*Joining him.*] Yes, Lawd.

God. Gabriel, I'm goin' down dere.

Gabriel. Yes, Lawd.

God. I want you to be my working boss yere while I'm gone.

Gabriel. Yes, Lawd.

God. You know dat matter of dem two stars?

Gabriel. Yes, Lawd.

God. Git dat fixed up! You know dat sparrow dat fell a little while ago? 'Tend to dat, too.

Gabriel. Yes, Lawd.

God. I guess dat's about all. I'll be back Saddy. [*To the* CHOIR.] Quiet, angels. [*The* CHOIR *stops singing. Those on the embankment circle down stage.* GOD *goes to embankment. Turns and faces the company.*] I'm gonter pass one more miracle. You all gonter help me an' not make a soun' caize it's one of de most impo'tant miracles of all. [*Nobody moves.* GOD *turns, facing the sky and raises his arms above his head.*] Let there be man.

[*There is growing roll of thunder as stage grows dark. The* CHOIR *bursts into "Hallelujah," and continues until the lights go up on the next scene.*]

SCENE III

Enclosing the stage is a heterogeneous cluster of cottonwood, camphor, live oak and sycamore trees, youpon and turkey-berry bushes, with their purple and red berries, sprays of fern-like indigo fiera and splashes of various Louisiana flowers. In the middle of the stage, disclosed when the mistiness at rise grows into warm sunlight, stands ADAM. *He is a puzzled man of 30, of medium height, dressed in the clothing of the average field hand. He is bare-headed. In the distance can be heard the choir continuing, "Bright Mansions Above." A bird begins to sing.* ADAM *smiles and turns to look at the source of this novel sound. He senses his strength and raises his forearms, his fists clenched. With his left hand he carefully touches the muscles of his upper right arm. He smiles again, realizing his power. He looks at his feet which are stretched wide apart. He stamps once or twice and now almost laughs in his enjoyment. Other birds begin trilling and* ADAM *glances up joyfully toward the foliage.* GOD *enters.*

God. Good mo'nin', Son.

Adam. [*With a little awe.*] Good mo'nin', Lawd.

God. What's yo' name, Son?

Adam. Adam.

God. Adam which?

Adam. [*Frankly, after a moment's puzzled groping.*] Jest Adam, Lawd.

God. Well, Adam, how dey treatin' you? How things goin'?

Adam. Well, Lawd, you know it's kind of a new line of wukk.

God. You'll soon get de hang of it. You know yo' kind of a new style with me.

Adam. Oh, I guess I'm gonter make out all right soon as I learn de ropes.

God. Yes, I guess you will. Yo' a nice job.

Adam. Yes, Lawd.

God. Dey's jest one little thing de matter with you. Did you notice it?

Adam. Well, now you mentioned it, Lawd, I kind of thought dey was somethin' wrong.

God. Yes suh, you ain't quite right. Adam, you need a family. De reason for dat is in yo' heart you is a family man. [*Flicking the ash off his cigar.*] I'd say dat was de main trouble at de moment.

Adam. [*Smiling.*] Yes, sir. [*His smile*

fades and he is puzzled again.] At de same time—dey's one thing puzzlin' me, Lawd. Could I ask you a question?

God. Why, certainly, Adam.

Adam. Lawd, jest what *is* a family?

God. I'm gonter show you. [*Indicates a spot.*] Jest lie down dere, Adam. Make out like you was goin' to slumber.

Adam. [*Gently.*] Yes, Lawd.

[*He lies down.* GOD *stands beside him and as he raises his arms above his head the lights go down. In the darkness* GOD *speaks.*]

God. Eve. [*Lights go up.* EVE *is standing beside* ADAM. *She is about twenty-six, and quite pretty. She is dressed like a country girl. Her gingham dress is quite new and clean.* GOD *is now at the other side of the stage, looking at them critically.* EVE *looks at* ADAM *in timid wonder and slowly turns her head until she meets the glance of* GOD. ADAM *stands beside* EVE. *They gaze at each other for a moment.* GOD *smiles.*] Now you all right, Eve. [ADAM *and* EVE *face him.*] Now I'll tell you what I'm gonter do. I'm gonter put you in charge here. I'm gonter give you de run of dis whole garden. Eve, you take care of dis man an' Adam you take care of dis woman. You belong to each other. I don' want you to try to do too much caize yo' both kind of experiment wid me an' I ain't sho' whether you could make it. You two jest enjoy yo'self. Drink de water from de little brooks an' de wine from de grapes an' de berries, an' eat de food dat's hangin' for you in de trees. [*He pauses, startled by a painful thought.*] Dat is, in all but one tree. [*He pauses. Then, not looking at them.*] You know what I mean, my children?

Adam and Eve. Yes, Lawd.

[*They slowly turn their heads left, toward the branches of an offstage tree. Then they look back at* GOD.]

Adam. Thank you, Lawd.

Eve. Thank you, Lawd.

God. I gotter be gittin' along now. I got a hund'ed thousan' things to do 'fo' you take yo' nex' breath. Enjoy yo'selves——

[GOD *exits.* ADAM *and* EVE *stand looking after Him for a moment, then each looks down and watches their hands meet and clasp. After a moment they lift their heads slowly until they are again gazing at the tree.*]

Eve. Adam.

Adam. [*Looking at the tree, almost in terror.*] What?

Eve. [*Softly as she too continues to look at the tree.*] Adam.

[*The* CHOIR *begins singing "Turn You Round" and as the lights go down the* CHOIR *continues until there is blackness. The* CHOIR *suddenly stops. The following scene is played in the darkness.*]

Mr. Deshee's Voice. Now, I s'pose you chillun know what happened after God made Adam 'n' Eve. Do you?

First Girl's Voice. I know, Mr. Deshee.

Mr. Deshee's Voice. Jest a minute, Randolph. Didn't I tell you you gotta tell yo' mammy let yo' sister bring you. Carlisle, take way dat truck he's eatin'. You sit by him, see kin you keep him quiet. Now den, Myrtle, what happened?

First Girl's Voice. Why, den dey ate de fo'bidden fruit and den dey got driv' out de garden.

Mr. Deshee's Voice. An' den what happened?

First Girl's Voice. Den dey felt ver bad.

Mr. Deshee's Voice. I don' mean how dey feel, I mean how dey do. Do dey have any children or anything like dat?

First Girl's Voice. Oh yes, suh, dey have Cain 'n' Abel.

Mr. Deshee's Voice. Dat's right, dey have Cain an' Abel.

Boy's Voice. Dat was a long time after dey got married, wasn't it, Mr. Deshee? My mammy say it was a hund'ed years.

Mr. Deshee's Voice. Well, nobody kin be so sure. As I tol' you befo', dey was jest beginnin' to be able to tell de time an' nobody was any too sure 'bout anythin' even den. So de bes' thing to do is jest realize dat de thing happened an' don't bother 'bout how many years it was. Jest remember what I told you about it gittin' dark when you go to sleep an' it bein' light when you wake up. Dat's de way time went by in dem days. One thing we do know an' dat was dis boy Cain was a mean rascal.

[*The lights go up on the next scene.*]

SCENE IV

A roadside.

CAIN, *a husky young Negro, stands over the body of the dead* ABEL. *Both are dressed as laborers.* CAIN *is looking at the body in awe, a rock in his right hand.* [GOD *enters.*]

God. Cain, look what you done to Abel.

Cain. Lawd, I was min'in' my own business and he come monkeyin' aroun' wit' me. I was wukkin' in de fiel' an' he was sittin' in de shade of de tree. He say, "Me, I'd be skeered to git out in dis hot sun. I be 'fraid my brains git cooked. Co'se you ain't got no brains so you ain' in no danger." An' so I up and flang de rock. If it miss 'im all right, an' if it hit 'im, all right. Dat's de way I feel.

God. All right, but I'm yere to tell you dat's called a crime. When de new Judge is done talkin' to you, you'll be draggin' a ball and chain de rest of yo' life.

Cain. Well, what'd he want to come monkeyin' aroun' me fo' den? I was jest plowin', min'in' my own business, and not payin' him no min', and yere he come makin' me de fool. I'd bust anybody what make me de fool.

God. Well, I ain't sayin' you right an' I ain't sayin' you wrong. But I do say was I you I'd jest git myself down de road 'til I was clean out of de county. An' you better take an' git married an' settle down an' raise some chillun. Dey ain't nothin' to make a man fo'git his troubles like raisin' a family. Now, you better git.

Cain. Yessuh.

[CAIN *walks off.* GOD *watches him from the forestage and as the lights begin to dim looks off. The* CHOIR *begins "Run, Sinner, Run."*]

God. Adam an' Eve, you better try again. You better have Seth an' a lot mo' chillun.

[*There is darkness. The* CHOIR *continues until the lights go up on the next scene.*]

SCENE V

CAIN *is discovered walking on an unseen treadmill. A middle distance of trees, hillsides and shrubbery passes him on an upper treadmill. Behind is the blue sky. He stops under the branches of a tree to look at a sign on a fence railing. Only half the tree is visible on the stage. The sign reads,* "NOD PARISH. COUNTY LINE."

Cain. [*Sitting down with a sigh of relief under the tree.*] At las'! Phew! [*Wipes his forehead with a handkerchief.*] Feels like I been walkin' fo'ty years. [*He looks back.*] Well, dey cain' git me now. Now I kin raise a fam'ly. [*An idea occurs to him, and suddenly he begins looking right and left.*] Well, I'll be hit by a mule! Knock me down for a trustin' baby! Where I gonter git dat fam'ly? Dat preacher fooled me. [*He is quite dejected.*] Doggone!

Cain's Girl. [*Off stage.*] Hello, Country Boy!

[CAIN *glances up to the offstage branches of the tree.*]

Cain. Hey-ho, Good lookin'! Which way is it to town?

Cain's Girl. [*Off stage.*] What you tryin' to do? You tryin' to mash me? I be doggone if it ain't gittin' so a gal cain't hardly leave de house 'out some of dese fast men ain' passin' remarks at her.

Cain. I ain' passin' remarks.

Cain's Girl. [*Off stage.*] If I thought you was tryin' to mash me, I'd call de police an' git you tooken to de first precinct.

Cain. Look yere, gal, I ast you a question, an' if you don' answer me I'm gonter bend you 'cross my pants an' burn you up.

Cain's Girl. [*Off stage.*] I'm comin' down.

[CAIN *takes his eyes from the tree.*]

Cain. Yes, an' you better hurry.

[CAIN'S GIRL *enters. She is as large as* CAIN, *wickedly pretty, and somewhat flashily dressed. She smiles at* CAIN.]

Cain's Girl. I bet you kin handle a gal mean wid dem big stout arms of yourn. I sho' would hate to git you mad at me, Country Boy.

Cain. [*Smiling.*] Come yere. [*She goes a little closer to him.*] Don't be 'fraid, I ain' so mean.

Cain's Girl. You got two bad lookin' eyes. I bet yo' hot coffee 'mong de women folks.

Cain. I ain' never find out. What was you doin' in dat tree?

Cain's Girl. Jest coolin' myself in de element.

Cain. Is you a Nod Parish gal?

Cain's Girl. Bo'n an' bred.

Cain. You know yo' kinda pretty.

Cain's Girl. Who tol' you dat?

Cain. Dese yere two bad eyes of mine.

Cain's Girl. I bet you say dat to everybody all de way down de road.

Cain. Comin' down dat road I didn't talk to nobody.

Cain's Girl. Where you boun' for, Beautiful?

Cain. I'm jest seein' de country. I thought I might settle down yere fo' a spell. You live wit' yo' people?

Cain's Girl. Co'se I does.

Cain. 'Spose dey'd like to take in a boarder?

Cain's Girl. Be nice if dey would, wouldn' it?

Cain. I think so. You got a beau?

Cain's Girl. Huh-uh!

Cain. [*Smiling.*] You has *now.*

Cain's Girl. I guess—I guess if you wanted to kiss me an' I tried to stop you, you could pretty nearly crush me wit' dem stout arms.

Cain. You wouldn't try too much, would you?

Cain's Girl. Maybe for a little while.

Cain. An' den what?

Cain's Girl. Why don' we wait an' see?

Cain. When would dat be?

Cain's Girl. Tonight. After supper. Think you kin walk a little further now, City Boy?

Cain. Yeh, I ain't so weary now.

[*She takes his hand.*]

Cain's Girl. What yo' name?

[*Takes his arm.*]

Cain. Cain.

Cain's Girl. Then I'm Cain's Gal. Come on, honey, an' meet de folks.

[*They exit. The* CHOIR *is heard singing "You Better Mind," as* GOD *enters.* GOD *watches the vanished* CAIN *and his* GIRL.]

God. [*After shaking his head.*] Bad business. I don' like de way things is goin' atall.

[*The stage is darkened. The* CHOIR *continues singing until the lights go up on the next scene.*]

SCENE VI

GOD'S *private office in Heaven. It is a small room, framed by tableau curtains. A large window up center looks out on the sky. There is a battered roll-top desk. On the wall next to the window is a framed religious oleograph with a calendar attached to it underneath. A door is at the left. A hat rack is on the wall above the door. There are two or three cheap pine chairs beside the window and beyond the door. In front of the desk is an old swivel armchair which creaks every time* GOD *leans back in it. The desk is open and various papers are stuck in the pigeonholes. Writing implements, etc., are on the desk. On a shelf above the desk is a row of law books. A cuspidor is near the desk, and a waste basket by it. The general atmosphere is that of the office of a Negro lawyer in a Louisiana town. As the lights go up* GOD *takes a fresh cigar from a box on the desk and begins puffing it without bothering to light it. There is no comment on this minor miracle from* GABRIEL, *who is sitting in one of the chairs with a pencil and several papers in his hand. The singing becomes pianissimo.*

Gabriel. [*Looking at the papers.*] Well, I guess dat's about all de impo'tant business this mornin', Lawd.

God. How 'bout dat Cherub over to Archangel Montgomery's house?

Gabriel. Where do dey live, Lawd?

[*The singing stops.*]

God. Dat little two story gold house, over by de pearly gates.

Gabriel. Oh, *dat* Montgomery. I thought you was referrin' to de ol' gentleman. Oh, yeh. [*He sorts through the papers and finds one he is looking for.*] Yere it 'tis. [*Reads.*] "Cherub Christina Montgomery; wings is moltin' out of season an' nobody knows what to do."

God. Well now, take keer of dat. You gotter be more careful, Gabe.

Gabriel. Yes, Lawd.

[*Folds the papers and puts them in a pocket.* GOD *turns to his desk, takes another puff or two of the cigar, and with a pencil, begins checking off items on a sheet of paper before him. His back is turned toward* GABRIEL. GABRIEL *takes his trumpet from the hat rack and burnishes it with his robe. He then wets his lips and puts the mouthpiece to his mouth.*]

God. [*Without turning around.*] Now, watch yo'self, Gabriel.

Gabriel. I wasn't goin' to blow, Lawd. I jest do dat every now an' den so I can keep de feel of it.

[*He leans trumpet against the wall.* GOD *picks up the papers and swings his chair around toward* GABRIEL.]

God. What's dis yere about de moon?

Gabriel. [*Suddenly remembering.*] Oh! De moon people say it's beginnin' to melt a little, on 'count caize de sun's so hot.

God. It's goin' roun' 'cordin' to schedule, ain't it?

Gabriel. Yes, Lawd.

God. Well, tell 'em to stop groanin'. Dere's nothin' de matter wid dat moon. Trouble is so many angels is flyin' over dere on Saddy night. Dey git to beatin' dere wings when dey dancin' an' dat makes de heat. Tell dem dat from now on dancin' 'roun' de moon is sinnin'. Dey got to stop it. Dat'll cool off de moon. [*He swings back and puts the paper on the desk. He leans back in the chair comfortably, his hands clasped behind his head.*] Is dere anythin' else you ought to remin' me of?

Gabriel. De prayers, Lawd.

God. [*Puzzled, slowly swinging chair around again.*] De prayers?

Gabriel. From mankind. You know, down on de earth.

God. Oh, yeh, de poor little earth. Bless my soul, I almos' forgot about dat. Mus' be three or four hund'ed years since I been down dere. I wasn't any too pleased wid dat job.

Gabriel. [*Laughing.*] You know you don' make mistakes, Lawd.

God. [*Soberly, with introspective detachment.*] So dey tell me. [*He looks at* GA-

BRIEL, *then through the window again.*] So dey tell me. I fin' I kin be displeased though, an' I was displeased wid de mankind I las' seen. Maybe I ought to go down dere agin—I need a little holiday.

Gabriel. Might do you good, Lawd.

God. I think I will. I'll go down an' walk de earth agin an' see how dem poor humans is makin' out. What time is it, by de sun an' de stars?

Gabriel. [*Glancing out of the window.*] Jest exactly halfpast, Lawd.

[GOD *is taking his hat and stick from the hat rack.*]

God. [*Opening the door.*] Well, take keer o' yo'self. I'll be back Saddy. [*He exits.*]

[*The stage is darkened. The* CHOIR *begins "Dere's no Hidin' Place," and continues until the lights go up on the next scene.*]

SCENE VII

GOD *is walking along a country road. He stops to listen. Church bells are heard in the distance.*

God. Dat's nice. Nice an' quiet. Dat's de way I like Sunday to be. [*The sound is broken by a shrill voice of a girl. It is* ZEBA *singing a "blues."*] Now, dat ain't so good. [GOD *resumes his walk and the upper treadmill brings on a tree stump on which* ZEBA *is sitting. She is accompanying her song with a ukulele.* GOD *and the treadmills stop. When the stump reaches the center of the stage, it is seen that* ZEBA *is a rouged and extremely flashily dressed chippy of about eighteen.*] Stop dat!

Zeba. What's de matter wid you, Country Boy? Pull up yo' pants.

[*She resumes singing.*]

God. Stop dat!

Zeba. [*Stops again.*] Say, listen to me, Banjo Eyes. What right you got to stop a lady enjoyin' herself?

God. Don't you know dis is de Sabbath? Da's no kin' o' song to sing on de Lawd's day.

Zeba. Who care 'bout de Lawd's day, anymo'? People jest use Sunday now to git over Saddy.

God. You a awful sassy little girl.

Zeba. I come fum sassy people! We even speak mean of de dead.

God. What's yo' name?

Zeba. [*Flirtatiously.*] "What's my name?" Ain't you de ol'-time gal hunter! Fust, "What's my name?" den I s'pose, what would it be like if you tried to kiss me? You preachers' is de debbils.

God. I ain't aimin' to touch you, daughter. [*A sudden sternness frightens* ZEBA. *She looks at him sharply.*] What is yo' name?

Zeba. Zeba.

God. Who's yo' fam'ly?

Zeba. I'm de great-great gran' daughter of Seth.

God. Of Seth? But Seth was a good man.

Zeba. Yeh, he too good, he die of holiness.

God. An' yere's his little gran' daughter reekin' wid cologne. Ain't nobody ever tol' you yo' on de road to Hell?

Zeba. [*Smiling.*] Sho' dat's what de preacher say. Exceptin' of course, I happens to know dat I'm on de road to de picnic groun's, an' at de present time I'm waitin' to keep a engagement wid my sweet papa. He don' like people talkin' to me.

[CAIN THE SIXTH *enters. He is a young buck, wearing a "box" coat and the other flashy garments of a Rampart Street swell.*]

Cain the Sixth. Hello, sugah! [*He crosses in front of* GOD *and faces* ZEBA.] Hello, mamma! Sorry I'm late, baby, but de gals in de barrel-house jest wouldn't let me go. Doggone, one little wirehead swore she'd tear me down.

[ZEBA *smiles and takes his hand.*]

God. What's yo' name, son?

Cain the Sixth. [*Contemptuously, without turning.*] Soap 'n water, Country Boy.

God. [*Sternly.*] What's yo' name, son?

Cain the Sixth. [*Slowly turns and for a moment his manner is civil.*] Cain the Sixth.

God. I was afraid so.

Cain the Sixth. [*His impudence returning.*] You a new preacher?

God. Where you live?

Cain the Sixth. Me, I live mos' any place.

God. Yes, an' you gonter see dem all. Is de udder young men all like you?

Cain the Sixth. [*Smiling.*] De gals don' think so.

[*He turns towards* ZEBA *again, picks her up and sits on the stump with the laughing* ZEBA *on his lap.*]

ZEBA. Dey ain't nobody in de worl' like my honey-cake.

[CAIN *kisses her and she resumes her song.* GOD *watches them.* ZEBA *finishes a verse of the song and begins another softly.* CAIN THE SIXTH'S *eyes have been closed during the singing.*]

Cain the Sixth. [*His eyes closed.*] Is de preacher gone?

[ZEBA *looks quickly at* GOD *without seeing him, and then looks off. She stops the song.*]

Zeba. Yeh, I guess he walks fast.

[CAIN *pushes her off his lap and rises.*]

Cain the Sixth. [*With acid sweetness.*] Dey tell me las' night you was talkin' to a creeper man, baby.

Zeba. Why, you know dey ain't nobody in de world fo' me but you.

Cain the Sixth. [*Smiling.*] I know dey ain't. I even got dat guaranteed. [*Takes a revolver from his pocket.*] See dat, baby?

Zeba. Sho' I see it, honey.

Cain the Sixth. Dat jest makes me positive. [*Puts the gun back.*]

Zeba. [*Pushing him back on the stump.*] You don' wanter believe dem stories, papa.

Cain the Sixth. [*With sinister lightness.*] No, I didn't believe dem, baby. Co'se dat big gorilla, Flatfoot, from de other side of de river *is* in town ag'in.

Zeba. Dat don' mean nothin'. Flatfoot ain't nothin' to me.

Cain the Sixth. [*Sitting again.*] Co'se he ain't. Go 'head, sing some mo', baby.

[ZEBA *resumes singing.*]

God. Bad business. [*The treadmills start turning.* GOD *resumes his walk.* ZEBA, *still singing, and* CAIN THE SIXTH *recede with the landscape.* GOD *is again alone on the country road. There is a twitter of birds.* GOD *looks up and smiles.*] De birds is goin' 'bout dere business, all right. [*A patch of flowers goes by, black-eyed Susans, conspicuously.*] How you flowers makin' out? [*Children's voices answer, "We O. K., Lawd."*] Yes, an' you looks very pretty. [*Children's voices: "Thank you, Lawd." The flowers pass out of sight.*] It's only de human bein's makes me downhearted. Yere's as nice a Sunday as dey is turnin' out anywhere, an' nobody makin' de right use of it. [*Something ahead of him attracts his attention. His face brightens.*] Well, now dis is mo' like it. Now dat's nice to see people prayin'. It's a wonder dey don' do it in de church. But I fin' I don' min' it if dey do it outdoors.

[*A group of five adult* NEGROES *and a* BOY *on their knees in a semicircle appears. The treadmills stop. The* BOY, *his head bent, swings his hands rhythmically up to his head three or four times. There is a hush.*]

Boy Gambler. Oh, Lawd, de smoke-house is empty. Oh, Lawd, lemme git dem groceries. Oh, Lawd, lemme see dat little *six.* [*He casts the dice.*] Wham! Dere she is, frien's.

[*Exclamations from the others: "Well damn my eyes!" "Doggone, dat's de eighth pass he make." "For God's sake, can't you ever crap?" etc. The* BOY *is picking up the money.*]

God. Gamblin'! [*Looks over the group's shoulders.*] An' wid frozen dice!

Boy Gambler. Dey's a dolla' 'n' a half talkin' fo' me. How much you want of it, Riney?

First Gambler. I take fo' bits. Wait a minute. Mebbe I take a little mo'.

[*He counts some money in his hand.*]

Second Gambler. [*Glancing up at* GOD.] Hello, Liver Lips. [*To the others.*] Looka ol' Liver Lips.

[*The others look up and laugh good-naturedly, repeating "Liver Lips."*]

First Gambler. Ain't his pockets high from de groun'? Ol' High-Pockets.

[*The others keep saying "Ole Liver Lips." "Ol' Liver Lips don't like to see people dicin'." "Dats a good name, 'High Pockets.'"*]

Boy Gambler. [*To others.*] Come on, you gonter fade me or not?

[GOD *seizes the* BOY'S *ears and drags him to his feet. The others do not move, but watch, amused.*]

God. Come yere, son. Why, yo' jest a little boy. Gamblin' an' sinnin'. [GOD *looks at the* BOY'S *face.*] You been chewin' tobacco, too, like you was yo' daddy. [GOD *sniffs.*] An' you been drinkin' sonny-kick-mammy wine. You oughta be 'shamed. [*To the others.*] An' you gamblers oughta be 'shamed, leadin' dis boy to sin.

First Gambler. He de bes' crap shooter in town, mister.

God. I'm gonter tell his mammy. I bet she don' know 'bout dis.

First Gambler. No, she don' know. [*The others laugh.*] She don' know anythin'.

Second Gambler. Das de God's truth.

First Gambler. See kin you beat 'im, High Pockets. Dey's a dolla' open yere.

God. I ain't gonter beat 'im. I'm gonter teach 'im. I may have to teach you all.

[*He starts walking from them. The* BOY *sticks out his tongue the moment* GOD'S *back is turned.*]

Boy Gambler. If you fin' my mammy you do mo'n I kin. Come on, gamblers, see kin you gimme a little action. Who wants any part of dat dollar?

[*The treadmill carries them off. The* FIRST GAMBLER *is heard saying: "I'll take anoder two bits," and the others, "Gimme a dime's wo'th," "I ain't only got fifteen cents left," etc., as they disappear.*]

God. [*Walking.*] Where's dat little boy's home? [*The front of a shanty appears and* GOD *stops in front of the door.*] Yere's de place. It ain't any too clean, either.

[*Knocks on the door with his cane.*]

Voice in Shanty. Who dar?

God. Never you min' who's yere. Open de door.

Voice in Shanty. You gotta search warrant?

God. I don' need one.

Voice in Shanty. Who you wanter see?

God. I wanter see de mammy of de little gamblin' boy.

Voice in Shanty. You mean little Johnny Rucker?

God. Dat may be his name.

Voice in Shanty. Well, Mrs. Rucker ain't home.

God. Where's she at?

Voice in Shanty. Who, Mrs. Rucker?

God. You heerd me.

Voice in Shanty. Oh, she run away las' night wid a railroad man. She's *e*loped.

God. Where's Rucker?

Voice in Shanty. He's flat under de table. He so drunk he cain't move.

God. Who are you?

Voice in Shanty. I'se jest a fren' an' neighbor. I come in las' night to de party, an' everybody in yere's dead drunk but me. De only reason I kin talk is I drank some new white mule I made myself, an' it burn my throat so I cain't drink no mo'. You got any mo' questions?

God. Not for you.

[*The shanty begins to move off as* GOD *starts walking again.*]

Voice in Shanty. Good riddance, I say.

[*Shanty disappears.*]

God. Dis ain't gittin' me nowheres. All I gotta say dis yere mankind I been peoplin' my earth wid sho' ain't much. [*He stops and looks back.*] I got good min' to wipe 'em all off an' people de earth wid angels. No. Angels is all right, singin' an' playin' an' flyin' around, but dey ain't much on workin' de crops and buildin' de levees. No, suh, mankind's jest right for my earth, if he wasn't so doggone sinful. I'd rather have my earth peopled wit' a bunch of channel catfish, dan I would mankin' an' his sin. I jest cain't stan' sin.

[*He is about to resume his walk when* NOAH *enters.* NOAH *is dressed like a country preacher. His coat is of the "Hammer-tail" variety. He carries a prayer book under his arm.*]

Noah. Mo'nin', brother.

God. Mo'nin', brother. I declare you look like a good man.

Noah. I try to be, brother. I'm de preacher yere. I don't think I seen you to de meetin'. [*They resume walking.*]

God. I jest come to town a little while ago an' I been pretty busy.

Noah. Yes, mos' everybody say dey's pretty busy dese days. Dey so busy dey cain't come to meetin'. It seem like de mo' I preaches de mo' people ain't got time to come to church. I ain't hardly got enough members to fill up de choir. I gotta do de preachin' an' de bassin' too.

God. Is dat a fac'?

Noah. Yes, suh, brother. Everybody is mighty busy, gamblin', good-timin', an' goin' on. You jest wait, though. When Gabriel blow de horn you gonter fin' dey got plenty of time to punch chunks down in Hell. Yes, suh.

God. Seems a pity. Dey all perfec'ly healthy?

Noah. Oh, dey healthy, all right. Dey jest all lazy, and mean, and full of sin. You look like a preacher, too, brother.

God. Well, I am, in a way.

Noah. You jest passin' through de neighborhood?

God. Yes. I wanted to see how things was goin' in yo' part of de country, an' I been feelin' jest 'bout de way you do. It's enough to discourage you.

Noah. Yes, but I gotta keep wres'lin' wid 'em. Where you boun' for right now, brother?

God. I was jest walkin' along. I thought I might stroll on to de nex' town.

Noah. Well, dat's a pretty good distance. I live right yere. [*He stops walking.*] Why don' you stop an' give us de pleasure of yo' comp'ny for dinner? I believe my ol' woman has kilt a chicken.

God. Why, dat's mighty nice of you, brother. I don' believe I caught yo' name.

Noah. Noah, jest brother Noah. Dis is my home, brother. Come right in.

[GOD *and* NOAH *start walking towards* NOAH'S *house, which is just coming into view on the treadmill. The stage darkens, the* CHOIR *sings "Feastin' Table," and when the lights go up again, the next scene is disclosed.*]

SCENE VIII

Interior of NOAH'S *house. The ensemble suggests the combination living-dining room in a fairly prosperous Negro's cabin. Clean white curtains hang at the window. A table and chairs are in the center of the room. There is a cheerful checked tablecloth on the table, and on the wall a framed, highly colored picture reading "God Bless Our Home."*

[NOAH'S WIFE, *an elderly Negress, simply and neatly dressed,* GOD, *and* NOAH *are discovered grouped about the table.*]

Noah. Company, darlin'. [NOAH'S WIFE *takes* NOAH'S *and* GOD'S *hats.*] Dis gemman's a preacher, too. He's jest passin' through de country.

God. Good mo'nin', sister.

Noah's Wife. Good mo'nin'. You jest ketch me when I'm gittin' dinner ready. You gonter stay with us?

God. If I ain't intrudin'. Brother Noah suggested——

Noah's Wife. You set right down yere. I got a chicken in de pot an' it'll be ready in 'bout five minutes. I'll go out de back an' call Shem, Ham 'n' Japheth. [*To* GOD.] Dey's our sons. Dey live right acrost de way but always have Sunday dinner wid us. You mens make yo'selves comf'table.

God. Thank you, thank you very kindly.

Noah. You run along, we all right.

[GOD *and* NOAH *seat themselves.* NOAH'S WIFE *exits.*]

God. You got a fine wife, Brother Noah.

Noah. She pretty good woman.

God. Yes, suh, an' you got a nice little home. Have a ten cent seegar?

[GOD *offers him one.*]

Noah. Thank you, much obliged.

[*Both men lean back restfully in their chairs.*]

God. Jest what seems to be de main trouble 'mong mankind, Noah?

Noah. Well, it seems to me de main trouble is dat de whol' distric' is wide open. Now you know dat makes fo' loose livin'. Men folks spen's all dere time fightin', loafin' an' gamblin', an' makin' bad likker.

God. What about de women?

Noah. De women is worse dan de men. If dey ain't makin' love powder dey out beg, borrow an' stealin' money for policy tickets. Doggone, I come in de church Sunday 'fo' las' 'bout an' hour befo' de meetin' was to start, and dere was a woman stealin' de altar cloth. She was goin' to hock it. Dey ain't got no moral sense. Now you take dat case las' month, over in East Putney. Case of dat young Willy Roback.

God. What about him?

Noah. Dere is a boy sebenteen years old. Doggone, if he didn't *e*lope with his aunt. Now, you know, dat kin' of goin' on is bad fo' a neighborhood.

God. Terrible, terrible.

Noah. Yes, suh. Dis use' to be a nice, decent community. I been doin' my best to preach de Word, but seems like every time I preach, de place jest goes a little mo' to de dogs. De good Lawd only knows what's gonter happen.

God. Dat is de truth.

[*There is a pause. Each puffs his cigar. Suddenly* NOAH *grasps his knee, as if it were paining him, and twists his foot.*]

Noah. Huh!

God. What's de matter?

Noah. I jest got a twitch. My buck-aguer I guess. Every now and den I gets a twitch in de knee. Might be a sign of rain.

God. That's just what it is. Noah, what's de mos' rain you ever had 'round dese parts?

Noah. Well, de water come down fo' six days steady last April an' de ribber got so swole it bust down de levee up 'bove Freeport. Raise cain all de way down to de delta.

God. What would you say was it to rain for forty days and forty nights?

Noah. I'd say dat was a *complete* rain!

God. Noah, you don't know who I is, do you?

Noah. [*Puzzled.*] Yo' face looks easy, but I don' think I recall de name.

[GOD *rises slowly, and as he reaches his full height there is a crash of lightning, a moment's darkness, and a roll of thunder. It grows light again.* NOAH *is on his knees in front of* GOD.]

I should have known you. I should have seen de glory.

God. Dat's all right, Noah. You didn' know who I was.

Noah. I'm jes' ol' preacher Noah, Lawd, an' I'm yo' servant. I ain' very much, but I'se all I got.

God. Sit down, Noah. Don' let me hear you shamin' yo'se'f, caize yo' a good man. [*Timidly* NOAH *waits until* GOD *is seated, and then sits, himself.*] I jest wanted to fin' out if you was good, Noah. Dat's why I'm walkin' de earth in de shape of a natchel man. I wish dey was mo' people like you. But far as I kin see, you and yo' fam'ly is de only respectable people in de worl'.

Noah. Dey jest all poor sinners, Lawd.

God. I know. I am your Lawd. I am a god of wrath and vengeance an' dat's why I'm gonter destroy dis worl'.

Noah. [*Almost in a whisper. Drawing back.*] Jest as you say, Lawd.

God. I ain't gonter destroy you, Noah. You and yo' fam'ly, yo' sheep an' cattle, an' all de udder things dat ain't human I'm gonter preserve. But de rest is gotta go. [*Takes a pencil and a sheet of paper from his pocket.*] Look yere, Noah. [NOAH *comes over and looks over his shoulder.*] I want you to build me a boat. I want you to call it de "Ark," and I want it to look like dis. [*He is drawing on the paper. Continues to write as he speaks.*] I want you to take two of every kind of animal and bird dat's in de country. I want you to take seeds an' sprouts an' everythin' like dat an' put dem on dat Ark, because dere is gonter be all dat rain. Dey's gonter to be a deluge, Noah, an' dey's goin' to be a flood. De levees is gonter bust an' everything dat's fastened down is comin' loose, but it ain't gonter float long, caize I'm gonter make a storm dat'll sink everythin' from a hencoop to a barn. Dey ain't a ship on de sea dat'll be able to fight dat tempest. Dey all got to go. Everythin'. Everythin' in dis pretty worl' I made, except one thing, Noah. You an' yo' fam'ly an' de things I said are going to ride dat storm in de Ark. Yere's de way it's to be.

[*He hands* NOAH *the paper.* NOAH *takes it and reads.*]

Noah. [*Pause. Looks at paper again.*] Yes, suh, dis seems to be complete. Now 'bout the animals, Lawd, you say you want everythin'?

God. Two of everythin'.

Noah. Dat would include jayraffes an' hippopotamusses?

God. Everythin' dat is.

Noah. Dey was a circus in town las' week. I guess I kin fin' dem. Co'se I kin git all de rabbits an' possums an' wil' turkeys easy. I'll sen' de boys out. Hum, I'm jest wonderin'——

God. 'Bout what?

Noah. 'Bout snakes. Think you'd like snakes, too?

God. Certainly, I want snakes.

Noah. Oh, I kin git snakes, lots of 'em. Co'se, some of 'em's a little dangerous. Maybe I better take a kag of likker, too?

God. You kin have a kag of likker.

Noah. [*Musingly.*] Yes, suh, dey's a awful lot of differ'nt kin's of snakes, come to think about it. Dey's water moccasins, cotton-moufs, rattlers—mus' be a hund'ed kin's of other snakes down in de swamps. Maybe I better take two kags of likker.

God. [*Mildly.*] I think de one kag's enough.

Noah. No. I better take two kags. Besides I kin put one on each side of de boat, an' balance de ship wid dem as well as havin' dem fo' medicinal use.

God. You kin put one kag in de middle of de ship.

Noah. [*Buoyantly.*] Jest as easy to take de two kags, Lawd.

God. I think one kag's enough.

Noah. Yes, Lawd, but you see forty days an' forty nights——

[*There is a distant roll of thunder.*]

God. [*Firmly.*] One kag, Noah.

Noah. Yes, Lawd. One kag.

[*The door in the back opens and* NOAH'S WIFE *enters with a tray of dishes and food.*]

Noah's Wife. Now den, gen'lemen, if you'll jest draw up cheers.

[*The stage is darkened. The* CHOIR *is heard singing "I Want to Be Ready." They continue in the darkness until the lights go up on the next scene.*]

SCENE IX

In the middle of the stage is the Ark. On the hillside, below the Ark, a dozen or more men and women, townspeople, are watching NOAH, SHEM, HAM *and* JAPHETH *on the deck of the Ark. The three sons are busily nailing boards on the cabin.* NOAH *is smoking a pipe. He wears a silk hat, captain's uniform and a "slicker."*

Noah. [*To* SHEM.] You, Shem, tote up some ol' rough lumber; don' bring up any planed up lumber, caize dat ain't fo' de main deck.

Shem. Pretty near suppertime, daddy.

Noah. Maybe tis, but I got de feelin' we ought to keep goin'.

First Woman. You gonter work all night, Noah, maybe, huh?

Noah. [*Without looking at her.*] If de sperrit move me.

Second Woman. Look yere, Noah, whyn't you give up all dis damn foolishness? Don' you know people sayin' yo crazy? What you think you doin' anyway?

Noah. I'se buildin' a Ark. [*Other men and women join those in the foreground.*] Ham, you better stop for a while 'n see whether dey bringin' de animals up all right. [*He looks at his watch.*] Dey ought to be pretty near de foot o' de hill by dis time; if dey ain't you wait fo' dem and bring 'em yo'se'f.

[HAM *goes down a ladder at the side of the ship and exits during the following scene. The newcomers in group have been speaking to some of the early arrivals.*]

Second Woman. [*To* THIRD WOMAN, *one of the newcomers.*] No, you don't mean it!

Third Woman. I do so. Dat's what de talk is in de town.

First Man. You hear dat, Noah? Dey say yo' ol' lady is tellin' everybody it's gonter rain fo' fo'ty days and fo'ty nights. You know people soon gonter git de idea you *all* crazy.

Noah. Lot I keer what you think. [*To* JAPHETH.] Straighten up dem boards down dere, Japheth.

[*Indicates floor of deck.*]

First Man. [*To* THIRD WOMAN.] Was I you, I wouldn' go 'round with Mrs. Noah anymore, lady. Fust thing you know you'll be gittin' a hard name, too.

Third Woman. Don' I know?

Second Woman. A lady cain't be too partic'lar dese days.

[ZEBA *and* FLATFOOT, *a tall, black, wicked-looking buck, enter, their arms around each other's waist.*]

Zeba. Dere it is, baby. Was I lyin'?

Flatfoot. Well, I'll be split in two!

First Man. What you think of it, Flatfoot?

Flatfoot. I must say! Look like a house wit' a warpin' cellar.

Noah. Dis yere vessel is a boat.

Flatfoot. When I was a little boy, dey used to build boats down near de ribber, where de water was. [*The others laugh.*]

Noah. Dis time it's been arranged to have de water come up to de boat. [JAPHETH *looks belligerently over the rail of the Ark at* FLATFOOT. *To* JAPHETH.] Keep yo' shirt on, son.

Second Woman. [*To* THIRD WOMAN.] Now, you see de whole fam'ly's crazy.

Third Woman. Listen, dey ain't gonter 'taminate me. It was me dat started resolvin' dem both out o' de buryin' society.

Zeba. When all dis water due up yere, Noah?

Noah. You won't know when it gits yere, daughter.

Zeba. Is she goin' to be a side-wheeler, like de Bessy-Belle?

Flatfoot. No! If she was a side-wheeler she'd get her wheels all clogged wid sharks. She gonter have jus' one great big stern wheel, like de Commodore. Den if dey ain't 'nuf water why de big wheel kin stir some up.

[*General laughter. Two or three of the* GAMBLERS *enter and join the group, followed by* CAIN THE SIXTH.]

Cain the Sixth. Dere's de fool an' his monument, jest like I said!

[*The* GAMBLERS *and* CAIN THE SIXTH *roar with laughter, slap their legs, etc., the members of the main group talk sotto voce to each other as* CAIN THE SIXTH *catches* ZEBA'S *eye.* FLATFOOT *is on her right and is not aware of* CAIN THE SIXTH'S *presence.*]

Noah. See how dey makin' out inside, son.

[*Stops hammering.* JAPHETH *exits into Ark.* NOAH *turns and gazes towards the east.*]

Cain the Sixth. Hello, honey.

Zeba. [*Frightened but smiling.*] Hello, sugah.

Cain the Sixth. [*Pleasantly.*] Ain' dat my ol' frien' Flatfoot wid you?

Zeba. Why, so 'tis! [FLATFOOT *is now listening. To* FLATFOOT.] He's got a gun.

Cain the Sixth. No, I ain't.

[*He lifts his hands over his head.* ZEBA *quickly advances and runs her hands lightly over his pockets.*]

Zeba. [*Relieved.*] I guess he ain't.

Cain the Sixth. No, I ain't got no gun for my ol' friend Flatfoot.

[*He walks up to him.*]

Flatfoot. [*Smiling.*] Hi, Cain. How's de boy?

[CAIN *quickly presses his chest against* FLATFOOT'S, *his downstage arm sweeps around* FLATFOOT'S *body and his hand goes up to the small of* FLATFOOT'S *back.*]

Cain the Sixth. [*Quietly, but triumphantly.*] I got a little *knife* fo' him.

[FLATFOOT *falls dead. The laughter of the others stops and they look at the scene.* ZEBA *for a moment is terrified, her clenched hand pressed to her mouth. She looks at* CAIN THE SIXTH, *who is smiling at her. He tosses the knife on the ground and holds his hands out to her. She goes to him, smiling.*]

Zeba. You sho' take keer of me, honey.

Cain the Sixth. Dat's caize I think yo' wo'th takin' keer of. [*To the others.*] It's all right, folks. I jest had to do a little cleanin' up.

First Woman. [*Smiling.*] You is de quickes' scoundrel.

First Gambler. It was a nice quick killin'. Who was he?

Second Woman. [*Casually.*] Dey called him Flatfoot. From over de river. He wa'nt any good. He owed me for washin' for over a year.

Third Woman. Used to peddle muggles. Said it had a kick like reg'lar snow. Wasn't no good.

Second Gambler. Think we ought to bury him?

First Man. No, just leave him dere. Nobody comes up yere, 'cept ol' Manatee.

[*Indicates* NOAH. *Cries of "Ol' Manatee! Ol' Manatee, dat's good!"*]

Noah. [*Still looking off.*] You bettah

pray, you po' chillun. [*They all laugh.*]

First Woman. We bettah pray? You bettah pray, Ol' Manatee.

Zeba. You bettah pray for rain.

[*Laughter again.*]

Noah. Dat's what I ain't doin', sinners. Shem! Japheth! [*To others, as he points off. Patter of rain.*] Listen!

Cain the Sixth. [*Casually.*] Doggone, I believe it *is* gonter shower a little.

First Gambler. It do looks like rain.

First Woman. I think I'll git on home. I got a new dress on.

Zeba. Me, too. I wants to keep lookin' nice fo' my sweet papa.

[*She pats* CAIN THE SIXTH'S *cheek.* CAIN THE SIXTH *hugs her.*]

Noah. [*Almost frantically.*] Ham! Is de animals dere?

Ham. [*Off stage.*] Yes, sir, dere yere. We're comin'.

Noah. Den bring 'em on.

[SHEM *and* JAPHETH *come on deck with their hammers. The stage begins to darken.*]

Third Woman. I guess we all might go home 'til de shower's over. Come on, papa.

Second Gambler. See you after supper, Noah. [*Crowd starts moving off* R.]

Noah. God's gittin' ready to start, my sons. Let's git dis plankin' done.

Zeba. Put a big Texas on it, Noah, an' we'll use it fo' excursions.

[*There is a distant roll of thunder; there are cries of "Good night, Admiral," "See you later," "So long, Manatee," as the crowd goes off. The thunder rumbles again. There is the sound of increasing rain. The hammers of* SHEM *and* JAPHETH *sound louder and are joined by the sounds of other hammerers. There is a flash of lightning. The* CHOIR *begins "De Ol' Ark's a-Movering," the sounds on the Ark become faster and louder. The rush of rain grows heavier.*]

Noah. Hurry! Hurry! Where are you, Ham?

Ham. [*Just off stage.*] Yere I am, father, wid de animals.

Noah. God's give us his sign. Send 'em up de gangplank.

[*An inclined plane is thrown against the Ark from the side of the stage by* HAM, *who cracks a whip.*]

Ham. Get on, dere.

[*The heads of two elephants are seen.*]

Noah. Bring 'em on board! De Lawd is strikin' down de worl'!

[*The singing and the noises reach fortissimo as* HAM *cracks his whip again, and the rain falls on the stage. The stage is darkened. The* CHOIR *continues singing in the darkness.*]

SCENE X

When the lights go up on scene, the Ark is at sea. Stationary waves run in front of it. The hillside has disappeared. The Ark is in the only lighted area.

SHEM *is smoking a pipe on the deck, leaning on the rail. A steamboat whistle blows three short and one long blast.* SHEM *is surprised.* [*In a moment* HAM *appears, also with a pipe, and joins* SHEM *at the rail.*]

Shem. Who'd you think you was signallin'?

Ham. Dat wasn't me, dat was daddy

Shem. He think he gonter git a reply?

Ham. I don' know. He's been gittin' a heap of comfort out of dat likker.

Shem. De kag's nearly empty, ain't it?

Ham. Pretty nearly almos'. [*They look over the rail. A pause.*] Seen anythin'?

Shem. Dis mornin' I seen somethin' over dere migh'a' been a fish.

Ham. Dat's de big news of de week.

Shem. How long you think dis trip's gonter las'?

Ham. I don' know! Rain fo'ty days 'n' fo'ty nights an' when dat stop' I thought sho' we'd come up ag'inst a san' bar o' somethin'. Looks now like all dat rain was jest a little incident of de trip. [*The whistle blows again.*] Doggone! I wish he wouldn't do dat. Fust thing we know he'll wake up dem animals ag'in. [JAPHETH *appears.*]

Shem. What de matter wit' de ol' man, Jape?

Japheth. Doggone, he say he had a dream dat we're nearly dere. Dat's why he pullin' de whistle cord. See kin he git a' answer. [*He looks over the rail.*] Look to me like de same ol' territory. [MRS. NOAH *appears on deck.*]

Noah's Wife. You boys go stop yo' paw pullin' dat cord. He so full of likker he think he's in a race.

Japheth. He claim he know what he's doin'.

Noah's Wife. I claim he gittin' to be a perfec' nuisance. Me an' yo' wives cain't hardly heah ou'sel'es think. [NOAH *appears, his hat rakishly tilted on his head. He goes to the railing and looks out.*] You 'spectin' company?

Noah. Leave me be, woman. De watah don' look so rough today. De ol' boat's ridin' easier.

Noah's Wife. Ridin' like a ol' mule!

Noah. Yes, suh, de air don't feel so wet. Shem! 'Spose you sen' out 'nother dove. [SHEM *goes into the Ark.*] Ham, go git de soundin' line. Jape, keep yo' eye on de East.

[JAPHETH *goes to the end of the boat.*]

Noah's Wife. As fo' you, I s'pose you'll help things along by takin' a little drink.

Noah. Look yere, who's de pilot of dis vessel?

Noah's Wife. Ol' Mister Dumb Luck.

Noah. Well see, dat's where you don' know anythin'.

Noah's Wife. I s'pose you ain't drunk as a fool?

Noah. [*Cordially.*] I feel congenial.

Noah's Wife. An' you look it. You look jest wonderful. I wonder if you'd feel so congenial if de Lawd was to show up?

Noah. De Lawd knows what I'm doin', don' you worry 'bout dat.

Noah's Wife. I wouldn't say anythin' ag'inst de Lawd. He suttinly let us know dey'd be a change in de weather. But I bet even de Lawd wonders sometimes why he ever put you in charge.

Noah. Well, you let de Lawd worry 'bout dat. [SHEM *appears with the dove.*]

Shem. Will I leave her go, Paw?

Noah. Leave 'er go. [*There is a chorus of "Good Luck, Dove," from the group as the dove flies off stage.* HAM *appears with the sounding line.*] Throw 'er over, Boy.

[HAM *proceeds to do so.*]

Noah's Wife. An' another thing——

Ham. Hey!

Noah. [*Rushing to his side.*] What is it?

Ham. Only 'bout a inch! Look!

[*They lean over.*]

Japheth. It's gettin' light in de East.

[*As* HAM *works the cord up and down,* NOAH *and* NOAH'S WIFE *turn toward* JAPHETH. *The* CHOIR *begins "My Soul Is a Witness for the Lord."*]

Noah. Praise de Lawd, so it is.

Noah's Wife. Oh, dat's pretty.

Noah. [*To* HAM.] An' de boat's stopped. We've landed. Shem, go down n' drag de fires an' dreen de boiler. You go help 'im, Ham.

Japheth. Look, Paw.

[*The dove wings back to the Ark with an olive branch in its mouth.*]

Noah. 'N' yere's de little dove wid greenery in its mouth! Take 'er down, Jape, so she kin tell de animals. [JAPHETH *exits after* SHEM *and* HAM *carrying the dove. To* MRS. NOAH.] Now, maybe you feel little different.

Noah's Wife. [*Contritely.*] It was jes' gittin' to be so tiresome. I'm sorry, Noah.

Noah. Dat's all right, ol' woman. [NOAH'S WIFE *exits.* NOAH *looks about him. The lights have changed and the water piece is gone and the ark is again on the hillside. Two mountains can be seen in the distance and a rainbow slowly appears over the Ark. The singing has grown louder.*] Thank you, Lawd, thank you very much indeed. Amen.

[*The singing stops with the "Amen."* GOD *appears on the deck.*]

God. Yo' welcome, Noah.

[NOAH *turns and sees him.*]

Noah. O, Lawd, it's wonderful.

God. [*Looking about him.*] I sort of like it. I like de way you handled de ship, too, Noah.

Noah. Was you watchin', Lawd?

God. Every minute. [*He smiles.*] Didn't de ol' lady light into you?

Noah. [*Apologetically.*] She was kinda restless.

God. That's all right. I ain't blamin' nobody. I don' even min' you' cussin' an drinkin'. I figure a steamboat cap'n on a long trip like you had has a right to a little redeye, jest so he don' go crazy.

Noah. Thank you, Lawd. What's de orders now?

God. All de animals safe?

Noah. Dey all fin'n' dandy, Lawd.

God. Den I want you to open dat starboard door, an' leave 'em all out. Let 'em go down de hill. Den you an' de family take all de seeds 'n de sprouts an' begin plantin' ag'in. I'm startin' all over, Noah.

[NOAH *exits.* GOD *looks around.*]

God. Well, now we'll see what happens. [GOD *listens with a smile, as noises accompanying the debarking of the animals are heard. There are the cracks of whips, the voices of the men on the Ark, shouting: "Git along dere." "Whoa, take it easy." "Duck yo' head." "Keep in line dere," etc. Over the Ark there is a burst of centrifugal shadows, and the sound of a myriad of wings.* GOD *smiles at the shadows.*] Dat's right, birds, fin' yo' new homes. [*Bird twitters are heard again.* GOD *listens a moment and rests an arm on the railing. He speaks softly.*] Gabriel, kin you spare a minute?

[GABRIEL *appears.*]

Gabriel. Yes, Lawd?

[*The sounds from the other side of the Ark are by now almost hushed. The* LORD *indicates the new world with a wave of the hand.*]

God. Well, it's did.

Gabriel. [*Respectfully, but with no enthusiasm.*] So I take notice.

God. Yes, suh, startin' all over again.

Gabriel. So I see.

God. [*Looking at him suddenly.*] Don' seem to set you up much.

Gabriel. Well, Lawd, you see—— [*He hesitates.*] 'Tain't none of my business.

God. What?

Gabriel. I say, I don' know very much about it.

God. I know you don'. I jest wanted you to see it. [*A thought strikes him.*] Co'se, it ain' yo' business, Gabe. It's my business. 'Twas my idea. De whole thing was my idea. An' every bit of it's my business 'n nobody else's. De whole thing rests on my shoulders. I declare, I guess *dat's* why I feel so solemn an' serious, at dis particklar time. You know *dis* thing's turned into quite a proposition.

Gabriel. [*Tenderly.*] But it's all right, Lawd; as you say, it's did.

God. Yes, suh, it's did. [*Sighs deeply. Looks slowly to the right and the left. Then softly.*] I only hope it's goin' to work out all right.

CURTAIN

PART TWO

SCENE I

GOD'S *Office again.*

Somewhere the CHOIR *is singing: "A City Called Heaven." In the office are* TWO WOMEN CLEANERS. *One is scrubbing the floor, the other dusting the furniture. The one dusting stops and looks out the window. There is a whirr and a distant faint Boom. The* CHOIR *stops.*

First Cleaner. Dat was a long way off.

Second Cleaner. [*At window.*] Yes, ma'am. An' dat must a' been a big one. Doggone, de Lawd mus' be mad fo' sho', dis mo'nin'. Dat's de fo'ty-six' thunde'-bolt since breakfast.

First Cleaner. I wonder where at He's pitchin' dem.

Second Cleaner. My goodness, don' you know?

First Cleaner. [*A little hurt.*] Did I know I wouldn't ask de question.

Second Cleaner. Every one of dem's bound fo' de earth.

First Cleaner. De earth? You mean dat little ol' dreenin' place?

Second Cleaner. Dat's de planet. [*Another faint whirr and boom.*] Dere goes another.

First Cleaner. Well, bless me. *I* didn't know dey was thunde'bolts.

Second Cleaner. Wha'd you think dey was?

First Cleaner. [*Above desk.*] I wasn't sho', but I thought maybe He might be whittlin' a new star o' two, an' de noise was jest de chips fallin'.

Second Cleaner. Carrie, where you been? Don' you know de earth is de new scandal? Ever'body's talkin' 'bout it.

First Cleaner. Dey kep' it from me.

Second Cleaner. Ain't you noticed de Lawd's been unhappy lately?

First Cleaner. [*Thoughtfully.*] Yeah, He ain't been his old self.

Second Cleaner. What did you think was de matteh? Lumbago?

First Cleaner. [*Petulantly.*] I didn't know. I didn't think it was fo' me t'inquieh.

Second Cleaner. Well, it jest so happens dat de Lawd is riled as kin be by dat measly little earth. Or I should say de scum dat's on it.

First Cleaner. Dat's mankind down dere.

Second Cleaner. Dey mus' be scum, too, to git de Lawd so wukked up.

First Cleaner. I s'pose so. [*Another whirr and boom.*] Looks like He's lettin' dem feel de wrath. Ain' dat a shame to plague de Lawd dat way?

Second Cleaner. From what I hear dey been beggin' fo' what dey're gittin'. My brother flew down to bring up a saint de other day and he say from what he see mos' of de population down dere has made de debbil king an' dey wukkin' in three shifts fo' him.

First Cleaner. You cain't blame de Lawd.

Second Cleaner. Co'se you cain't. Dem human bein's 'd make anybody bile oveh. Ev'rytime de Lawd try to do sompin' fo' dem, doggone if dey don't staht some new ruckus.

First Cleaner. I take notice He's been wukkin' in yere mo' dan usual.

Second Cleaner. I wish He'd let us ladies fix it up. Wouldn't take a minute to make dis desk gold-plated.

First Cleaner. I 'spose He likes it dis way. De Lawd's kind o' ol' fashioned in some ways. I s'pose He keeps dis office plain an' simple on purpose.

Second Cleaner. [*Finishing her work.*] I don' see why.

First Cleaner. [*Looking off.*] Well, it's kind of a nice place to come to when He's studyin' somethin' impo'tant. 'Most evahthin' else in heaven's so fin' 'n' gran', maybe ev'ry now and den He jest gits sick an' tired of de glory. [*She is also collecting her utensils.*]

Second Cleaner. Maybe so. Jest de same I'd like to have a free hand wid dis place for a while, so's I could gold it up.

[GOD *appears in the doorway.*]

God. Good mo'nin', daughters.

First and Second Cleaners. Good mo'nin', Lawd. We was jest finishin'.

God. Go ahead den, daughters.

[*Goes to the window.*]

First and Second Cleaners. Yes, Lawd. [*They exeunt. Off stage.*] Good mo'nin', Gabriel.

[*Off stage* GABRIEL *says, "Good mo'nin', sisters," and enters immediately. He stands in the doorway for a moment watching* GOD—*a notebook and pencil in his hand.*]

God. What's de total?

Gabriel. [*Consulting the book.*] Eighteen thousand nine hund'ed an' sixty for de mo'-nin'. Dat's includin' de village wid de fo'tune tellers. Dey certainly kin breed fast.

God. [*Solemnly.*] Dey displease me. Dey displease me greatly.

Gabriel. Want some more bolts, Lawd?

God. [*Looking through window.*] Look at 'em dere. Squirmin' an' fightin' an' bearin' false witness. Listen to dat liar, dere. He don' intend to marry dat little gal. He don' even love her. What did you say?

Gabriel. Should I git mo' bolts?

God. Wait a minute. [*He carefully points his finger down through the window.*] I'm goin' to git dat wicked man myself. [*From a great distance comes an agonized cry: "Oh, Lawd!"* GOD *turns from the window.*] No use gittin' mo' thunde'bolts. Dey don' do de trick. [*He goes to the swivel chair and sits.*] It's got to be somethin' else.

Gabriel. How would it be if you was to doom 'em all ag'in, like dat time you sent down de flood? I bet dat would make dem mind.

God. You see how much good de flood did. Dere dey is, jest as bad as ever.

Gabriel. How about cleanin' up de whole mess of 'em and sta'tin' all over ag'in wid some new kind of animal?

God. An' admit I'm licked?

Gabriel. [*Ashamedly.*] No, of co'se not, Lawd.

God. No, suh. No, suh. Man is a kind of pet of mine and it ain't right fo' me to give up tryin' to do somethin' wid him. Doggone, mankin' *mus'* be all right at de core or else why did I ever bother wid him in de first place? [*Sits at desk.*]

Gabriel. It's jest dat I hates to see you worryin' about it, Lawd.

God. Gabe, dere ain't anythin' worth while anywheres dat didn't 'cause somebody some worryin'. I ain't never tol' you de trouble I had gittin' things started up yere. Dat's a story in itself. No, suh, de more I keep on bein' de Lawd de more I know I got to keep improvin' things. An' dat takes time and worry. De main trouble wid mankin' is he takes up so much of my time. He ought to be able to help hisself a little. [*He stops suddenly and cogitates.*] Hey, dere! I think I got it!

Gabriel. [*Eagerly.*] What's de news?

God. [*Still cogitating.*] Yes, suh, dat seems like an awful good idea.

Gabriel. Tell me, Lawd.

God. Gabriel, have you noticed dat every now an' den, mankin' turns out some pretty good specimens?

Gabriel. Dat's de truth.

God. Yes, suh. Dey's ol' Abraham and Isaac an' Jacob an' all dat family.

Gabriel. Dat's so, Lawd.

God. An' everyone of dem boys was a hard wukker an' a good citizen. We got to admit dat.

Gabriel. Dey wouldn't be up yere flyin' wid us if dey hadn't been.

God. No, suh. An' I don' know but what de answer to de whole trouble is right dere.

Gabriel. How you mean, Lawd?

God. Why, doggone it, de good man is de man dat keeps busy. I mean I been goin' along on de principle dat he was something like you angels—dat you ought to be able to give him somethin' an' den jest let him sit back an' enjoy it. Dat ain't so. Now dat I recollec' I put de first one down dere to take keer o' dat garden an' den I let him go ahead an' do nothin' but git into mischief. [*He rises.*] Sure, *dat's* it. He ain't *built* jest to fool 'roun' an' not do nothin'. Gabe, I'm gonter try a new scheme.

Gabriel. [*Eagerly.*] What's de scheme, Lawd?

God. I'll tell you later. Send in Abraham, Isaac an' Jacob. [*A voice outside calls: "Right away, Lawd."*] You go tell dem to put dem bolts back in de boxes. I ain' gonter use dem ag'in a while.

Gabriel. O. K., Lawd.

God. Was you goin' anywhere near de Big Pit?

Gabriel. I could go.

God. Lean over de brink and tell Satan he's

jest a plain fool if he thinks he kin beat anybody as big as me.

Gabriel. Yes, suh, Lawd. Den I'll spit right in his eye.

[GABRIEL *exits.* GOD *looks down through the window again to the earth below.*]

God. Dat new polish on de sun makes it powerful hot. [*He "r'ar back."*] Let it be jest a little bit cooler. [*He feels the air.*] Dat's nice. [*Goes to His desk. A knock on the door.*] Come in.

[ABRAHAM, ISAAC *and* JACOB *enter. All are very old men, but the beard of* ABRAHAM *is the longest and whitest, and they suggest their three generations. They have wings that are not quite so big as those of the native angels.*]

Isaac. Sorry we so long comin', Lawd. But Pappy and me had to take de boy [*Pointing to* JACOB.] over to git him a can of wing ointment.

God. What was de matter, son?

Jacob. Dey was chafin' me a little. Dey fine now, thank you, Lawd.

God. Dat's good. Sit down an' make yo'-selves comf'table. [*The three sit.* MEN: *"Thank you, Lawd."*] Men, I'm goin' to talk about a little scheme I got. It's one dat's goin' to affec' yo' fam'lies an' dat's why I 'cided I'd talk it over wid you, 'fo' it goes into ee-fect. I don' know whether you boys know it or not, but you is about de three best men of one fam'ly dat's come up yere since I made little apples. Now I tell you what I'm gonter do. Seein' dat you human bein's cain't 'preciate anythin' lessen you fust wukk to git it and den keep strugglin' to hold it, why I'm gonter turn over a very valuable piece of property to yo' fam'ly, and den see what kin dey do with it. De rest of de worl' kin go jump in de river fo' all I keer. I'm gonter be lookin' out fo' yo' descendants only. Now den, seein' dat you boys know de country pretty tho'ly, where at does you think is de choice piece of property in de whole worl'? Think it over for a minute. I'm gonter let you make de s'lection.

Abraham. If you was to ask me, Lawd, I don't think dey come any better dan de Land of Canaan.

God. [*To* ISAAC *and* JACOB.] What's yo' feelin' in de matter?

Jacob. [*After a nod from* ISAAC.] Pappy an' me think do we get a pick, dat would be it.

God. [*Goes to window again; looks out.*] De Land of Canaan. Yes, I guess dat's a likely neighborhood. It's all run over wid Philistines and things right now, but we kin clean dat up. [*He turns from the window and resumes his seat.*] All right. Now who do you boys think is de best of yo' men to put in charge down dere? You see I ain't been payin' much attention to anybody in partic'lar lately.

Isaac. Does you want de brainiest or de holiest, Lawd? [MEN *look up.*]

God. I want de holiest. I'll make him brainy. [MEN *appreciate the miracle.*]

Isaac. [*As* ABRAHAM *and* JACOB *nod to him.*] Well, if you want A Number One goodness, Lawd, I don't know where you'll git more satisfaction dan in a great-great-great-great grandson of mine.

God. Where's he at?

Isaac. At de moment I b'lieve he's in de sheep business over in Midian County. He got in a little trouble down in Egypt, but t'wan't his doin'. He killed a man dat was abusin' one of our boys in de brick works. Of co'se you know old King Pharaoh's got all our people in bondage.

God. I heard of it. [*With some ire.*] Who did you think put them dere? [*The visitors lower their heads.*] It's all right, boys. [*All rise.*] I'm gonter take dem out of it. An' I'm gonter turn over de whole Land of Canaan to dem. An' do you know whose gonter lead dem dere? Yo' great, great, great, great grandson. Moses, ain't it?

Isaac. Yes, Lawd.

God. [*Smiling.*] Yes. I been noticin' *him.*

Abraham. It's quite a favor fo' de fam'ly, Lawd.

God. Dat's why I tol' you. You see, it so happens I love yo' fam'ly, an' I delight to honor it. Dat's all, gen'lemen. [*The three others rise and cross to the door, murmuring, "Yes, Lawd," "Thank you, Lawd," "Much obliged, Lawd." etc. The* CHOIR *begins, "My Lord's A-Writin' All De Time" pianissimo.* GOD *stands watching the men leave.*] Enjoy yo' selves. [*He goes to the window. The singing grows softer. He speaks through the window to the earth.*] I'm comin' down to see you, Moses, an' dis time my scheme's *got* to wukk.

[*The stage is darkened. The singing grows louder and continues until the lights go up on the next scene.*]

SCENE II

The tableau curtains frame the opening of a cave, which is dimly lighted. A large turkey-berry bush is somewhere near the foreground. MOSES *is seated on the grass eating his lunch from a basket in his lap.* ZIPPORAH, *his wife, stands watching him. He is about forty,* ZIP-

ZIPPORAH *somewhat younger. They are dressed inconspicuously.* MOSES *stutters slightly when he speaks. He looks up to see* ZIPPORAH *smiling.*

Moses. What you smilin' at, Zipporah?

Zipporah. Caize you enjoyin' yo'self.

Moses. You is a good wife, Zipporah.

Zipporah. You is a good husband, Moses. [MOSES *wipes his mouth with a handkerchief and begins putting into the basket the various implements of the meal which had been on the ground about him.*] Why you suppose it's so dark yere today? Dey's no rain in de air.

Moses. Seems like it's jest aroun' dis cave. Yo' father's house is got de sun on it. [*He looks in another direction.*] Looks all clear down toward Egypt.

Zipporah. Co'se it *would* be fine weather in Egypt. De sky looks all right. Maybe it's gonter rain jest right yere. Why don't you move de sheep over to de other pasture?

Moses. [*A bit puzzled.*] I don' know. It got dark like dis befo' you come along wid de dinner an' I was gonter stop you on de top of de hill. Den somethin' kep' me yere.

Zipporah. S'pose it could be de Lawd warnin' you dat dey's 'Gyptians hangin' 'roun'?

Moses. Dey may have fo'gotten all about dat killin' by now. Dey got a new Pharaoh down dere.

Zipporah. An' I hear he's jest as mean to yo' people as his pappy was. I wouldn't put it pas' him to send soljahs all the way up yere fo' you.

Moses. Dat's all right. De Lawd's looked after me so far, I don't 'spect him to fall down on me now. You better be gittin' home.

Zipporah. [*Taking the basket.*] I'll be worryin' about you.

Moses. [*Kissing her and then smiling.*] 'Parently de Lawd ain't. He knows I'm safe as kin be. Lemme see you feel dat way.

Zipporah. You is a good man, Moses.

Moses. I's a lucky man. [ZIPPORAH *exits with the basket.* MOSES *looks up at the sky.*] Dat's funny. De sun seems to be shinin' everyplace but right yere. It's shinin' on de sheep. Why ain't dey no cloud dere?

God. [*Off stage.*] Caize I want it to be like dat, Moses.

Moses. [*Looking about him.*] Who's dat?

God. [*Off stage again.*] I'm de Lawd, Moses.

Moses. [*Smiling.*] Dat's what you say. Dis yere shadow may be de Lawd's wukk, but dat voice soun' pretty much to me like my ol' brother Aaron.

God. [*Off stage.*] Den keep yo' eyes open, son. [*The turkey-berry bush begins to glow and then turns completely red.* MOSES *looks at it fascinated.*] Maybe you notice de bush ain't burnin' up.

Moses. Dat's de truth.

[MOSES *is full of awe but not frightened.*]

God. [*Off stage.*] Now you believe me?

Moses. Co'se I does. It's wonderful.

[*The light in the bush dies and* GOD *appears from behind it.*]

God. No, it ain't, Moses. It was jest a trick.

Moses. 'Scuse me doubtin' you, Lawd. I always had de feelin' you wuz takin' keer of me, but I never 'spected you'd fin' de time to talk wid me pussunly. [*He laughs.*] Dat was a good trick, Lawd. I'se seen some good ones, but dat was de beatenest.

God. Yo' gonter see lots bigger tricks dan dat, Moses. In fac', yo' gonter perfo'm dem.

Moses. [*Incredulously.*] Me? I'm gonter be a tricker?

God. Yes, suh.

Moses. An' do magic? Lawd, my mouth ain't got de quick talk to go wid it.

God. It'll come to you now.

Moses. [*Now cured of stuttering.*] Is I goin' wid a circus?

God. [*Slowly and solemnly.*] Yo' is goin' down into Egypt, Moses, and lead my people out of bondage. To do dat I'm gonter make you de bes' tricker in de worl'.

Moses. [*A little frightened.*] Egypt! You know I killed a man dere, Lawd. Won't dey kill me?

God. Not when dey see yo' tricks. You ain't skeered, is you?

Moses. [*Simply and bravely.*] No, suh, Lawd.

God. Den yere's what I'm gonter do. Yo' people is my chillun, Moses. I'm sick and tired o' de way ol' King Pharaoh is treatin' dem, so I'se gonter take dem away, and yo' gonter lead dem. You gonter lead 'em out of Egypt an' across de river Jordan. It's gonter take a long time, and you ain't goin' on no excursion train. Yo' gonter wukk awful hard for somethin' yo' goin' to fin' when de trip's over.

Moses. What's dat, Lawd?

God. It's de Land of Canaan. It's de bes' land I got. I've promised it to yo' people, an' I'm gonter give it to dem.

Moses. Co'se, ol' King Pharaoh will do everything he kin to stop it.

God. Yes, an' dat's where de tricks come in. Dey tell me he's awful fond of tricks.

Moses. I hear dat's *all* he's fon' of. Dey

say if you can't take a rabbit out of a hat you cain't even git in to see him.

God. Wait'll you see de tricks you an' me's goin' to show him.

Moses. [*Delightedly.*] Doggone! Huh, Lawd?

God. Yes, suh. Now de first trick——

[GOD *is lifting a stick which he carries.*]

Moses. Jest a minute, Lawd. [GOD *halts the demonstration.*] I'm gonter learn de tricks and do just like you tell me, but I *know* it's gonter take me a little time to learn all dat quick talkin'. Cain't I have my brother Aaron go wid me? He's a good man.

God. I was gonter have him help you wid de Exodus. I guess he can watch, too.

Moses. I'll call 'im.

[*He turns as if to shout.*]

God. Wait. [MOSES *turns and looks at* GOD.] I'll *bring* him. [*Softly.*] Aaron!

[AARON *appears between* GOD *and* MOSES *in the mouth of the cave. He is a little taller than* MOSES *and slightly older. He, too, is dressed like a field hand.*]

Aaron. [*Blankly.*] Hey!

[MOSES *goes to him, takes his hand and leads him, bewildered, down to where* MOSES *had been standing alone.* AARON *then sees* GOD.]

Moses. [*Almost in a whisper.*] It's all right.

God. Don't worry, son, I'm jest showin' some tricks. Bringin' you yere was one of dem. [AARON *stares at* GOD *as if hypnotized.*] Now den, you see dis yere rod? Looks like a ordinary walking stick, don' it?

Moses. Yes, Lawd.

God. Well, it ain't no ordinary walkin' stick, caize look. [MOSES *leans forward.*] When I lays it down on de groun'——

[*The stage is darkened. The* CHOIR *begins, "Go Down, Moses," and continues until the lights go up on the next scene.*]

SCENE III

The throne room of PHARAOH. *It suggests a Negro lodge room. The plain board walls are colored by several large parade banners of varying sizes, colors and materials, bordered with gold fringe and tassels on them. Some of the inscriptions on them read:*

SUBLIME ORDER OF PRINCES OF THE HOUSE OF PHARAOH———HOME CHAPTER

MYSTIC BROTHERS OF THE EGYPTIAN HOME GUARD———LADIES AUXILIARY, NO. 1

SUPREME MAGICIANS AND WIZARDS OF THE UNIVERSE

PRIVATE FLAG OF HIS HONOR OLD KING PHARAOH

ROYAL YOUNG PEOPLE'S PLEASURE CLUB

ENCHANTED AND INVISIBLE CADETS OF EGYPT BOY'S BRIGADE

There is one door up right and a window. The throne, an ordinary armchair with a drapery over its back, is on a dais. PHARAOH *is seated on the throne. His crown and garments might be those worn by a high officer in a Negro lodge during a ritual. About the throne itself are high officials, several of them with plumed hats, clothing that suggests military uniforms, and rather elaborate sword belts, swords, and scabbards. A few* SOLDIERS *carrying spears are also in his neighborhood and one or two bearded* ANCIENTS *in brightly colored robes with the word "Wizard" on their conical hats. In the general group of men and women scattered elsewhere in the room Sunday finery is noticeable everywhere. Most of the civilians have bright "parade" ribbons and wear medals. In a cleared space immediately before the throne a* CANDIDATE MAGICIAN *is performing a sleight-of-hand trick with cards.* PHARAOH *watches him apathetically. He is receiving earnest attention from a few of the others, but the majority of the men and women are talking quietly among themselves. Beside the* CANDIDATE MAGICIAN *are several paraphernalia of previously demonstrated tricks.*

Candidate Magician. [*Holding up some cards.*] Now den, ol' King Pharaoh, watch dis. [*He completes a trick. There is a murmur of "Not bad," "Pretty good," etc., from a few of the watchers.* PHARAOH *makes no comment.*] Now, I believe de cyard I ast you to keep sittin' on was de trey of diamonds, wasn't it?

Pharaoh. Yeah.

Candidate Magician. Den kin I trouble you to take a look at it now? [PHARAOH *half rises to pick up a card he has been sitting on, and looks at it.*] I believe you'll now notice dat it's de King of Clubs? [PHARAOH *nods and shows the card to those nearest him. The* CANDIDATE MAGICIAN *waits for an audible approval and gets practically none.*] An' dat, ol' King Pharaoh, completes de puffohmance.

[*An elderly* MAN *in a uniform steps forward.*]

General. On behalf of my nephew I beg

Yo' Honor to let him jine de ranks of de royal trickers and magicians.

Pharaoh. [*To the two* WIZARDS.] What do de committee think? [*The* WIZARDS *shake their heads.*] Dat's what I thought. He ain't good enough. I'd like to help you out, General, but you know a man's got to be a awful good tricker to git in de royal society dese days. You better go back an' steddy some mo', son. [*He lifts his voice and directs two* SOLDIERS *guarding the door.*] Is de head magician reached de royal waitin' room yit? [*One of the* SOLDIERS *opens the door to look out.*] If he is, send him in.

[*The* SOLDIER *beckons to some one off stage, throws the door open, and announces to the court.*]

Soldier. De Head Magician of de land of Egypt.

[*A very old and villainous* MAN *enters. His costume is covered with cabalistic and zodiacal signs. He advances to the* KING, *the other* MAGICIAN *and his* UNCLE *making way for him. He bows curtly to* PHARAOH.]

Head Magician. Good mo'nin', ol' King Pharaoh.

Pharaoh. Mo'nin', Professor. What's de news?

Head Magician. Evahthing's bein' carried out like you said.

Pharaoh. How's de killin' of de babies 'mongst de Hebrews comin' 'long?

Head Magician. Jes' like you ordered.

Pharaoh. [*Genially.*] Dey killed all of 'em, huh?

Head Magician. Do dey see one, dey kill 'im. You teachin' 'em a great lesson. Dey don' like it a-tall.

Pharaoh. [*Smiling.*] What do dey say?

Head Magician. [*Pawing the air inarticulately.*] I hates to tell in front of de ladies.

Pharaoh. Dey feels pretty bad, huh?

Head Magician. Dat's jest de beginnin' of it. Betwixt de poleece and de soljahs we killed about a thousan' of 'em las' night. Dat's purty good.

Pharaoh. [*Thoughtfully.*] Yeh, it's fair. I guess you boys is doin' all you kin. But I fin' I ain't satisfied, though.

Head Magician. How you mean, Yo' Honor?

Pharaoh. I mean I'd like to make dose Hebrew chillun realize dat I kin be even mo' of a pest. I mean I hates dem chillun. An' I'm gonter think of a way of makin' 'em even mo' mizzable.

Head Magician. But dey *ain't* anythin' meaner dan killin' de babies, King.

Pharaoh. Dey must be sump'n. Doggone, you is my head tricker, you put yo' brains on it. [*To the others.*] Quiet, whilst de Head Magician go into de silence.

Head Magician. [*After turning completely around twice, and a moment's cogitation.*] I tell you what I kin do. All de Hebrews dat ain't out to de buryin' grounds or in de hospitals is laborin' in de brick wukks.

Pharaoh. Yeh?

Head Magician. [*After a cackling laugh.*] How would it be to take de straw away from 'em and tell 'em dey's got to turn out jest as many bricks as usual? Ain't dat nasty?

Pharaoh. Purty triflin', but I s'pose it'll have to do for de time bein'. Where's de extreme inner guard? [*One of the military* ATTENDANTS *comes forward.*] Go on out an' tell de sup'intendent to put dat into e-ffect. [*The* ATTENDANT *bows and starts for the door. He stops as* PHARAOH *calls to him.*] Wait a minute! Tell 'im to chop off de hands of anybody dat say he cain't make de bricks dat way. [*The* ATTENDANT *salutes and exits, the door being opened and closed by one of the* SOLDIERS.] Now what's de news in de magic line?

Head Magician. I ain't got very many novelties today, King; I bin wukkin' too hard on de killin's. I'm so tired I don' believe I could lift a wand.

[*There are murmurs of protest from the assemblage.*]

Pharaoh. Doggone, you was to 'a been de chief feature o' de meetin' dis mawnin'. Look at de turn-out you got account of me tellin' 'em you was comin'.

Head Magician. Well, dat's de way it is, King. Why don' you git de wizards to do some spell castin'?

Pharaoh. Dey say it's in de cyards dat dey cain't wukk till high noon. [*He glances at the* WIZARDS.] Think mebbe you kin cheat a little?

First Wizard. Oh dat cain't be done, King.

Pharaoh. Well, we might as well adjourn, den. Looks to me like de whole program's shot to pieces. [*He starts to rise, when there is a furious banging on the door.*] What's de idea dere? See who dat is. [*The* SOLDIERS *open the door.* MOSES *and* AARON *enter, pushing the two* SOLDIERS *aside and coming down in front of* PHARAOH. *The* SOLDIERS *are bewildered and* PHARAOH *is angry.*] Say, who tol' you two baboons you could come in yere?

Moses. Is you ol' King Pharaoh?

Pharaoh. Dat's me. Did you heah what I asked you?

Moses. My name is Moses, and dis is my brother Aaron.

[*Murmur of "Hebrews" spreads through the room.*]

Pharaoh. [*In a rage.*] Is you Hebrews?

Moses. Yes, suh.

Pharaoh. [*Almost screaming.*] Put 'em to de sword!

[*As the* COURTIERS *approach,* AARON *suddenly discloses the rod, which he swings once over his head. The* COURTIERS *draw back as if their hands had been stung. Cries of "Hey!" "Lookout," etc.*]

Moses. Keep outside dat circle.

[*The* COURTIERS *nearest* MOSES *and* AARON *look at each other, exclaiming ad lib., "Did you feel dat?" "What is dat?" "What's goin' on, heah?" "My hands is stingin'!" etc.*]

Pharaoh. [*Puzzled but threatening.*] What's de idea yere?

Moses. We is magicians, ol' King Pharaoh.

Pharaoh. [*To the* HEAD MAGICIAN.] Put a spell on 'em. [*The* HEAD MAGICIAN *stands looking at them bewildered. To* MOSES.] I got some magicians, too. We'll see who's got de bes' magic. [MOSES *and* AARON *laugh. Most of the* COURTIERS *are cowering. To the* HEAD MAGICIAN.] Go ahead, give 'em gri-gri.

Moses. Sure, go ahead.

Pharaoh. Hurry up, dey's laughin' at you. What's de matter?

Head Magician. I cain't think of de right spell.

Pharaoh. [*Now frightened himself.*] You mean dey got even *you* whupped?

Head Magician. Dey's got a new kind of magic.

Pharaoh. [*Gazes at* HEAD MAGICIAN *a moment, bewildered. To the* WIZARDS.] I s'pose if de Professor cain't, you cain't.

First Wizard. Dat's a new trick, King.

Head Magician. [*Rubbing his fingers along his palms.*] It's got 'lectricity in it!

Pharaoh. Hm, well dat may make it a little diff'rent. So you boys is magicians, too?

Moses. Yes, suh.

Pharaoh. Well, we's always glad to see some new trickers in de co't, dat is if dey good. [*He glances about him.*] You look like you is O. K.

Moses. Dat's what we claims, ol' King Pharaoh. We think we's de best in de worl'.

Pharaoh. You certainly kin talk big. Jest what is it you boys would like?

Moses. We came to show you some tricks. Den we's goin' to ask you to do somethin' for us.

Pharaoh. Well, I s'pose you know I'm a fool for conjurin'. If a man kin show me some tricks I ain't seen, I goes out of my way to do him a favor.

Moses. Dat's good. Want to see de first trick?

Pharaoh. It ain't goin' to hurt nobody?

Moses. Dis one won't.

Pharaoh. Go ahead.

Moses. Dis yere rod my brother has looks jes' like a walkin' stick, don't it?

[*The* COURTIERS *now join the* KING *in interest.*]

Pharaoh. Uh huh. Le's see.

[AARON *hands him the rod, which* PHARAOH *inspects and returns.*]

Moses. Well, look what happens when he lays it on de groun'.

[AARON *places the rod on the second step of the throne. It turns into a lifelike snake. There are exclamations from the assemblage.*]

Pharaoh. Dat's a good trick! Now turn it back into a walkin' stick again. [AARON *picks it up and it is again a rod. Exclamations of "Purty good!" "Dat's all right!" "What do you think of that!" etc.*] Say, you is good trickers!

Moses. You ain't never seen de beat of us. Now I'm goin' to ask de favor.

Pharaoh. Sure, what is it?

Moses. [*Solemnly.*] Let de Hebrew chillun go!

Pharaoh. [*Rises and stares at them. There is a murmur of "Listen to 'im!" "He's got nerve!" "I never in my life!" "My goodness!" etc.*] What did you say?

Moses. Let de Hebrew chillun go.

[PHARAOH *seats himself again.*]

Pharaoh. [*Slowly.*] Don' you know de Hebrews is my slaves?

Moses. Yes, suh.

Pharaoh. Yes, suh, my slaves. [*There is a distant groaning.*] Listen, and you kin hear 'em bein' treated like slaves. [*He calls toward the window.*] What was dey doin' den?

Man Near the Window. Dey's jest gettin' de news down in de brick-yard.

Pharaoh. I won't let them go. [*He snorts contemptuously.*] Let's see another trick.

Moses. Yes, suh, yere's a better one. [*He lowers his head.*] Let's have a plague of de flies.

[AARON *raises the rod. The room grows dark and a great buzzing of flies is heard. The* COURTIERS *break out in cries of "Get away fum me!" "Take 'em away!" "De place is filled with flies!" "Dis is terrible!" "Do sump'n, Pharaoh!"*]

Pharaoh. [*Topping the others.*] All right —stop de trick!

Moses. Will you let de Hebrews go?

Pharaoh. Sho' I will. Go ahead, stop it!

Moses. [*Also above the others.*] Begone!

[*The buzzing stops and the room is filled with light again, as* AARON *lowers the rod. All except* MOSES AND AARON *are brushing the flies from their persons.*]

Pharaoh. [*Laughing.*] Doggone, dat was a good trick! [*The others, seeing they are uninjured, join in the laughter, with exclamations of "Doggone!" "You all right?" "Sho' I'm all right." "Didn' hurt me," etc.*] You *is* good trickers.

Moses. Will you let de Hebrew chillun go?

Pharaoh. [*Sitting down again.*] Well, I'll tell you, boys. I'll tell you sump'n you didn' know. You take me, *I'm* a pretty good tricker, an' I jest outtricked you. So, bein' de bes' tricker, I don' think I will let 'em go. You got any mo' tricks yo'self?

Moses. Yes, suh. Dis is a little harder one. [AARON *lifts the rod.*] Gnats in de mill pon', gnats in de clover, gnats in de tater patch, stingin' all over.

[*The stage grows dark again. There is the humming of gnats and the slapping of hands against faces and arms, and the same protests as were heard with the flies, but with more feeling, "I'm gittin' stung to death!" "I'm all stung!" "Dey're like hornets!" "Dey's on my face!" etc.*]

Pharaoh. Take 'em away, Moses!

Moses. [*His voice drowning the others.*] If I do, will you let 'em go?

Pharaoh. Sho' I will, dis time.

Moses. Do you mean it?

Pharaoh. Co'se I mean it! Doggone, one just stang me on de nose.

Moses. Begone! [*Lights come up as* AARON *lowers the rod. There is a moment of general recovery again.* PHARAOH *rubs his nose, looks at his hands, etc., as do the others.*] Now, how about it?

Pharaoh. [*Smiling.*] Well, I'll tell you, Moses. Now dat de trick's over——

[MOSES *takes a step toward* PHARAOH.]

Moses. Listen, Pharaoh. You been lyin' to me, and I'm gittin' tired of it.

Pharaoh. I ain't lyin'; I'm trickin', too. You been trickin' me and I been trickin' you.

Moses. I see. Well, I got one mo' trick up my sleeve which I didn't aim to wukk unless I had to. Caize when I does it, I cain't undo it.

Pharaoh. Wukk it an' I'll trick you right back. I don' say you ain't a good tricker, Moses. You is one of de best I ever seen. But I kin outtrick you. Dat's all.

Moses. It ain't only me dat's goin' to wukk dis trick. It's me an' de Lawd.

Pharaoh. Who?

Moses. De Lawd God of Israel.

Pharaoh. I kin outtrick you an' de Lawd too!

Moses. [*Angrily.*] Now you done it, ol' King Pharaoh. You been mean to de Lawd's people, and de Lawd's been easy on you caize you didn' know no better. You been givin' me a lot of say-so and no do-so, and I didn' min' dat. But now you've got to braggin' dat you's better dan de Lawd, and dat's too many.

Pharaoh. You talk like a preacher, an' I never did like to hear preachers talk.

Moses. You ain't goin' to like it any better, when I strikes down de oldes' boy in every one of yo' people's houses.

Pharaoh. Now you've given up trickin' and is jest lyin'. [*He rises.*] Listen, I'm Pharaoh. I do de strikin' down yere. I strike down my enemies, and dere's no one in all Egypt kin kill who he wants to, 'ceptin' me.

Moses. I'm sorry, Pharaoh. Will you let de Hebrews go?

Pharaoh. You heard my word. [AARON *is lifting his rod again at a signal from* MOSES.] Now, no more tricks or I'll——

Moses. Oh, Lawd, you'll have to do it, I guess. Aaron, lift de rod.

[*There is a thunderclap, darkness, and screams. The lights go up. Several of the younger* MEN *on the stage have fallen to the ground or are being held in the arms of the horrified elders.*]

Pharaoh. What have you done yere? Where's my boy?

[*Through the door come four* MEN *bearing a young man's body.*]

First of the Four Men. King Pharaoh.

[PHARAOH *drops into his chair, stunned, as the dead boy is brought to the throne.*]

Pharaoh. [*Grief-stricken.*] Oh, my son, my fine son.

[*The* COURTIERS *look at him with mute appeal.*]

Moses. I'm sorry, Pharaoh, but you cain't fight de Lawd. Will you let his people go?

Pharaoh. Let them go.

[*The lights go out. The* CHOIR *begins "Mary Don't You Weep," and continues until it is broken by the strains of "I'm Noways Weary and I'm Noways Tired." The latter is sung by many more voices than the former, and the cacophony ends as the latter grows in volume and the lights go up on the next scene.*]

SCENE IV

The CHILDREN OF ISRAEL *are marching on the treadmill and now singing fortissimo. They are of all ages and most of them are ragged. The men have packs on their shoulders, one or two have hand carts. The line stretches across the stage. It is nearing twilight, and the faces of the assemblage are illumined by the rays of the late afternoon sun. The upper tread-mill carries a gradually rising and falling middle distance past the marchers. The foot of a mountain appears; a trumpet call is heard as the foot of the mountain reaches stage center. The marchers halt. The picture now shows the mountain running up out of sight off right. The singing stops. A babel of "What's de matter?" "Why do we stop?" "Tain't sundown yet!" "What's happened?" "What's goin' on?" "What are they blowin' for?" etc. Those looking ahead begin to murmur. "It's Moses." "Moses." "What's happened to him?" The others take up the repetition of "Moses," and* MOSES *enters, on the arm of* AARON. *He is now an old man, as is his brother, and he totters toward the center of the stage. Cries of "What's de matter, Moses?" "You ain't hurt, is you?" "Ain't that too bad?" etc. He slowly seats himself on the rock at the foot of the mountain.*

Aaron. How you feelin' now, brother?

Moses. I'm so weary, Aaron. Seems like I was took all of a sudden.

Aaron. Do we camp yere?

Moses. [*Pathetically.*] No, you got to keep goin'.

Aaron. But you cain't go no further to-night, brother.

Moses. Dis never happened to me befo'.

A Young Woman. But you's a ol' man, now, Father Moses. You cain't expect to go as fas' as we kin.

Moses. But de Lawd said I'd do it. He said I was to show you de Promised Land. Fo'ty years I bin leadin' you. I led you out o' Egypt. I led you past Sinai, and through de wilderness. Oh, I cain't fall down on you now!

Aaron. Le's res' yere fo' de night. Den we'll see how you feel in de mo'nin'.

Moses. We tol' de scouts we'd meet 'em three miles furder on. I hate fo' 'em to come back all dis way to report. 'Tis gettin' a little dark, ain't it?

Aaron. It ain't dark, Brother.

Moses. No, it's my eyes.

Aaron. Maybe it's de dust.

Moses. No, I jest cain't seem to see. Oh, Lawd, dey cain't have a blind man leadin' 'em! Where is you, Aaron?

Aaron. I'se right yere, Moses.

Moses. Do you think—— [*Pause.*] Oh! Do you think it's de time He said?

Aaron. How you mean, Moses?

[*Crowd look from one to another in wonder.*]

Moses. He said I could lead 'em to de Jordan, dat I'd *see* de Promised Land, and dat's all de further I could go, on account I broke de laws. Little while back I thought *I did* see a river ahead, and a pretty land on de other side. [*Distant shouts "Hooray!" "Yere dey are!" "Dey travelled quick." etc.*] Where's de young leader of de troops? Where's Joshua?

[*The call "Joshua" is taken up by those on the right of the stage, followed almost immediately by "Yere he is!" "Moses wants you!" etc.* JOSHUA *enters. He is a fine-looking Negro of about thirty.*]

Joshua. [*Going to* MOSES' *side.*] Yes, suh.

Moses. What's de shoutin' 'bout, Joshua?

Joshua. De scouts is back wid de news. De Jordan is right ahead of us, and Jericho is jest on de other side. Moses, we're dere! [*There are cries of "Hallelujah!" "De Lawd be praised!" "Hooray!" "De Kingdom's comin'!" etc. With a considerable stir among the marchers, several new arrivals crowd in from right, shouting "Moses, we're dere!"* JOSHUA *seeing the newcomers.*] Yere's de scouts!

[*Three very ragged and dusty young* MEN *advance to* MOSES.]

Moses. [*As the shouting dies.*] So it's de River Jordan?

First Scout. Yes, suh.

Moses. All we got to take is de city of Jericho.

First Scout. Yes, suh.

Moses. Joshua, you got to take charge of de fightin' men, an' Aaron's gotta stay by de priests.

Joshua. What about you?

Moses. You are leavin' me behind. Joshua, you gonter get de fightin' men to-gether and take dat city befo' sundown.

Joshua. It's a big city, Moses, wid walls all 'round it. We ain't got enough men.

Moses. You'll take it, Joshua.

Joshua. Yes, suh, but how?

Moses. Move up to de walls wid our people. Tell de priests to go wid you with de rams' horns. You start marchin' 'roun' dem walls, and den——

Joshua. Yes, suh.

Moses. De Lawd'll take charge, jest as he's took charge ev'y time I've led you against a city. He ain't never failed. has he?

Several Voices. No, Moses.

[*All raise their heads.*]

Moses. And he ain't goin' to fail us now. [*He prays. All bow.*] Oh, Lawd, I'm turnin' over our brave young men to you, caize I know you don' want me to lead 'em any further. [*Rises.*] Jest like you said, I've got to de Jordan but I cain't git over it. An' yere dey goin' now to take de city of Jericho. In a little while dey'll be marchin' 'roun' it. An' would you please be so good as to tell 'em what to do? Amen. [*To* JOSHUA.] Go ahead. Ev'ybody follows Joshua now. Give de signal to move on wid e'vything. [*A trumpet is heard.*] You camp fo' de night in de City of Jericho.

[MOSES *seats himself on the rock.*]

Joshua. Cain't we help you, Moses?

Moses. You go ahead. De Lawd's got his plans fo' me. Soun' de signal to march. [*Another trumpet call is heard. The company starts marching off.* AARON *lingers a moment.*] Take care of de Ark of de Covenant, Aaron.

Aaron. Yes, Brother. Good-bye.

Moses. Good-bye, Aaron. [*The singing is resumed softly and dies away. The last of the marchers has disappeared.*] Yere I is, Lawd. De chillun is goin' into de Promised Land. [GOD *enters from behind the hill. He walks to* MOSES, *puts his hands on his shoulders.*] You's with me, ain't you, Lawd?

God. Co'se I is.

Moses. Guess I'm through, Lawd. Jest like you said I'd be, when I broke de tablets of de law. De ol' machine's broke down.

God. Jest what was it I said to you, Moses? Do you remember?

Moses. You said I couldn't go into de Promised Land.

God. Dat's so. But dat ain't all dey was to it.

Moses. How you mean, Lawd?

God. Moses, you been a good man. You been a good leader of my people. You got me angry once, dat's true. And when you anger me I'm a God of Wrath. But I never meant you wasn't gonter have what was comin' to you. An' I ain't goin' to do you out of it, Moses. It's jest de country acrost de River dat you ain't gonter enter. You gonter have a Promised Land. I been gettin' it ready fo' you, fo' a long time. Kin you stand up?

Moses. [*Rising, with* GOD'S *help.*] Yes, suh, Lawd.

God. Come on, I'm goin' to show it to you. We goin' up dis hill to see it. Moses, it's a million times nicer dan de Land of Canaan.

[*They start up the hill.*]

Moses. I cain't hardly see.

God. Don't worry. Dat's jest caize you so old.

[*They take a step or two up the hill, when* MOSES *stops suddenly.*]

Moses. Oh!

God. What's de matter?

Moses. We cain't be doin' dis!

God. Co'se we kin!

Moses. But I fo'got! I fo'got about Joshua and de fightin' men!

God. How about 'em?

Moses. Dey're marchin' on Jericho. I tol' 'em to march aroun' de walls and den de Lawd would be dere to tell 'em what to do.

God. Dat's all right. He's dere.

Moses. Den who's dis helpin' me up de hill?

God. Yo' faith, yo' God.

Moses. And is you over dere helpin' them too, Lawd? Is you goin' to tell dem poor chillun what to do?

God. Co'se I is. Listen, Moses. I'll show you how I'm helpin' dem.

[*From the distance comes the blast of the rams' horns, the sound of crumbling walls, a roar, and a moment's silence. The* CHOIR *begins "Joshua Fit De Battle of Jericho" and continues through the rest of the scene.*]

Moses. You did it, Lawd! You've tooken it! Listen to de chillun'—dey's in de Land of Canaan at last! You's de only God dey ever was, ain't you, Lawd?

God. [*Quietly.*] Come on, ol' man.

[*They continue up the hill. The stage is darkened.*]

Mr. Deshee. [*In the dark.*] But even dat scheme didn' work. Caize after dey got into the Land of Canaan dey went to de dogs again. And dey went into bondage again. Only dis time it was in de City of Babylon.

[*The* CHOIR, *which has been singing "Cain't Stay Away," stops as the next scene begins.*]

SCENE V

Under a low ceiling is a room vaguely resembling a Negro night club in New Orleans. Two or three long tables run across the room, and on the left is a table on a dais with a gaudy canopy above it. The table bears a card marked "Reserved for King and guests."

Flashy young MEN *and* WOMEN *are seated at the tables. About a dozen couples are dancing in the foreground to the tune of a jazz orchestra. The costumes are what would be worn at a Negro masquerade to represent the debauchees of Babylon.*

First Man. When did yuh git to Babylon?

Second Man. I jes' got in yesterday.

Third Man. [*Dancing.*] How do you like dis baby, Joe?

Fourth Man. Hot damn! She could be de King's pet!

A Woman. Anybody seen my papa?

Third Man. Don' fo'git de dance at de High Priest's house tomorrow.

[*The dance stops as a bugle call is heard. Enter* MASTER OF CEREMONIES.]

Master of Ceremonies. Stop! Tonight's guest of honor, de King of Babylon an' party of five.

[*Enter the* KING *and five* GIRLS. *The* KING *has on an imitation ermine cloak over his conventional evening clothes and wears a diamond tiara. All rise as the* KING *enters, and sing, "Hail, de King of Bab—Bab—Babylon."*]

King. Wait till you see de swell table I got. [*He crosses the stage to his table. The* GIRLS *are jabbering.*] Remind me to send you a peck of rubies in de mo'nin'.

Master of Ceremonies. Ev'nin', King!

King. Good ev'nin'. How's de party goin'?

Master of Ceremonies. Bes' one we ever had in Babylon, King.

King. Any Jew boys yere?

Master of Ceremonies. [*Indicating some of the others.*] Lot o' dem yere. I kin go git mo' if you want 'em.

King. I was really referrin' to de High Priest. He's a 'ticlar frien' o' mine an' he might drop in. You know what he look like?

Master of Ceremonies. No, suh, but I'll be on de look-out fo' him.

King. O.K. Now le's have a li'l good time.

Master of Ceremonies. Yes, suh. [*To the orchestra.*] Let 'er go, boys.

[*The music begins.* WAITERS *appear with food and great urns painted gold and silver, from which they pour out wine for the guests. The* MASTER OF CEREMONIES *exits. The* KING'S DANCING-GIRLS *go to the middle of the floor, and start to dance. The* KING *puts his arms about the waists of two* GIRLS *and draws them to him.*]

King. Hot damn! Da's de way! Let de Jew boys see our gals kin dance better'n dere's. [*There is an ad lib. babel of "Da's de truth, King!" "I don' know—we got some good gals, too!" etc.*] Dey ain' nobody in de worl' like de Babylon gals.

[*The dancing grows faster; the watchers keep time with hand-claps. The door at the left opens suddenly, and the* PROPHET, *a patriarchal, ragged figure enters. He looks belligerently about the room, and is followed almost immediately by the* MASTER OF CEREMONIES.]

Prophet. Stop!

[*The music and the* DANCERS *halt.*]

King. What's the idea, bustin' up my party?

Master of Ceremonies. He said he was expected, King. I thought mebbe he was de——

King. Did you think he was de High Priest of de Hebrews? Why, he's jest an ol' bum! De High Priest is a fashion plate. T'row dis ole bum out o' yere!

Prophet. Stop!

[*Those who have been advancing to seize him stop, somewhat amused.*]

King. Wait a minute. Don't throw him out. Let's see what he has to say.

Prophet. Listen to me, King of Babylon! I've been sent yere by de Lawd God Jehovah. Don't you dare lay a hand on de Prophet!

King. Oh, you're a prophet, is yuh? Well, you know we don' keer much fo' prophets in dis part of de country.

Prophet. Listen to me, sons and daughters of Babylon! Listen, you children of Israel dat's given yo'selves over to de evil ways of yo' oppressors! You're all wallowin' like hogs in sin, an' de wrath of Gawd ain' goin' to be held back much longer! I'm tellin' you, repent befo' it's too late. Repent befo' Jehovah casts down de same fire dat burned up Sodom and Gomorrah. Repent befo' de——

[*During this scene yells increase as the* PROPHET *continues. The* HIGH PRIEST *enters left. He is a fat voluptuary, elaborately clothed in brightly colored robes. He walks in hand in hand with a gaudily dressed "chippy."*]

High Priest. [*Noise stops.*] Whoa, dere! What you botherin' the King fo'?

Prophet. [*Wheeling.*] And you, de High Priest of all Israel, walkin' de town wid a dirty li'l tramp.

King. Seems to be a frien' o' yours, Jake.

High Priest. [*Crossing to the* KING *with his* GIRL.] Ah, he's one of dem wild men, like Jeremiah and Isaiah. Don' let him bother you none.

[*Pushes* PROPHET *aside and goes to* KING'S *table.*]

Prophet. You consort with harlots, an' yo'

pollution in the sight of de Lawd. De Lawd God's goin' to smite you down, jest as he's goin' to smite down all dis wicked world!

[*Grabs* HIGH PRIEST *and turns him around.*]

King. [*Angrily against the last part of the preceding speech.*] Wait a minute. I'm getting tired of this. Don' throw him out. Jest kill him!

[*There is the sound of a shot. The* PROPHET *falls.*]

Prophet. Smite 'em down, Lawd, like you said. Dey ain't a decent person left in de whole world.

[*He dies.* MASTER OF CEREMONIES, *revolver in hand, looks down at the* PROPHET.]

Master of Ceremonies. He's dead, King.

King. Some of you boys take him out.

[*A couple of young* MEN *come from the background and walk off with the body.*]

High Priest. Don' know whether you should'a done that, King.

King. Why not?

High Priest. I don' know whether de Lawd would like it.

King. Now, listen, Jake. You know yo' Lawd ain't payin' much attention to dis man's town. Except fo' you boys, it's tho'ly protected by de Gods o' Babylon.

High Priest. I know, but jest de same——

King. Look yere, s'pose I give you a couple hund'ed pieces of silver. Don' you s'pose you kin arrange to persuade yo' Gawd to keep his hands off?

High Priest. [*Oilily.*] Well of co'se we could try. I dunno how well it would work.

[*As the* HIGH PRIEST *speaks, the* KING *claps his hands.* MASTER OF CEREMONIES *enters with bag of money.*]

King. Yere it is.

High Priest. [*Smiling.*] I guess we kin square things up. [*He prays—whiningly.*] Oh Lawd, please forgive my po' frien' de King o' Babylon. He didn't know what he was doin' an'——

[*There is a clap of thunder, darkness for a second. The lights go up and* GOD *is standing in the center of the room.*]

God. [*In a voice of doom.*] Dat's about enough. [*The guests are horrified.*] I's stood all I kin from you. I tried to make dis a good earth. I helped Adam, I helped Noah, I helped Moses, an' I helped David. What's de grain dat grew out of de seed? Sin! Nothin' but sin throughout de whole world. I've given you ev'y chance. I sent you warriors and prophets. I've given you laws and commandments, an' you betrayed my trust. Ev'ything I've given you, you've defiled. Ev'y time I've fo'given you, you've mocked me. An' now de High Priest of Israel tries to trifle wid my name. Listen, you chillun of darkness, yo' Lawd is tried. I'm tired of de struggle to make you worthy of de breath I gave you. I put you in bondage ag'in to cure you, an' yo' worse dan you was amongst de flesh pots of Egypt. So I renounce you. Listen to the words of yo' Lawd God Jehovah, for dey is de last words yo' ever hear from me. I repent of dese people dat I have made and I will deliver dem no more.

[*There is darkness and cries of "Mercy!" "Have pity, Lawd!" "We didn' mean it, Lawd!" "Forgive us, Lawd!" etc. The* CHOIR *sings "Death's Gwinter Lay His Cold Icy Hands On Me" until the lights go up on the next scene.*]

SCENE VI

GOD *is writing at his desk. Outside, past the door, goes* HOSEA, *a dignified old man, with wings like* JACOB'S. GOD, *sensing his presence, looks up from the paper he is examining, and follows him out of the corner of his eye. Angrily he resumes his work as soon as* HOSEA *is out of sight.* [*There is a knock on the door.*]

God. Who is it? [GABRIEL *enters.*]

Gabriel. It's de delegation, Lawd.

God. [*Wearily.*] Tell 'em to come in.

[ABRAHAM, ISAAC, JACOB, *and* MOSES *enter.*] Good mo'nin', gen'lemen.

The Visitors. Good mo'nin', Lawd.

God. What kin I do for you?

Moses. You know, Lawd. Go back to our people.

God. [*Shaking his head.*] Ev'ry day fo' hund'ed's of years you boys have come in to ask dat same thing. De answer is still de same. I repented of de people I made. I said I would deliver dem no more. Good mo'nin', gen'lemen. [*The four* VISITORS *rise and exeunt.* GABRIEL *remains.*] Gabe, why do dey do it?

Gabriel. I 'spect dey think you gonter change yo' mind.

God. [*Sadly.*] Dey don' know me. [HOSEA *again passes the door. His shadow shows on wall.* GABRIEL *is perplexed, as he watches.* GOD *again looks surreptitiously over His shoulder at the passing figure.*] I don' like dat, either.

Gabriel. What, Lawd?

God. Dat man.

Gabriel. He's jest a prophet, Lawd. Dat's

jest old Hosea. He jest come up the other day.

God. I know. He's one of de few dat's come up yere since I was on de earth last time.

Gabriel. Ain' been annoyin' you, has he?

God. I don' like him walkin' past de door.

Gabriel. All you got to do is tell him to stop, Lawd.

God. Yes, I know. I don' want to tell him. He's got a right up yere or he wouldn' be yere.

Gabriel. You needn' be bothered by him hangin' aroun' de office all de time. I'll tell 'im. Who's he think he——

God. No, Gabe. I find it ain't in me to stop him. I sometimes jest wonder why he don' come in and say hello.

Gabriel. You want him to do dat?

[*He moves as if to go to the door.*]

God. He never has spoke to me, and if he don' wanta come in, I ain't gonter make him. But dat ain't de worst of it, Gabriel.

Gabriel. What is, Lawd?

God. Ev'y time he goes past de door I hears a voice.

Gabriel. One of de angels?

God. [*Shaking his head.*] It's from de earth. It's a man.

Gabriel. You mean he's prayin'?

God. No, he ain't exactly prayin'. He's jest talkin' in such a way dat I got to lissen. His name is Hezdrel.

Gabriel. Is he on de books?

God. No, not yet. But ev'y time dat Hosea goes past I hear dat voice.

Gabriel. Den tell *it* to stop.

God. I find I don' want to do that, either. Dey's gettin' ready to take Jerusalem down dere. Dat was my big fine city. Dis Hezdrel, he's jest one of de defenders. [*Suddenly and passionately, almost wildly.*] I ain't comin' down. You hear me? I ain't comin' down. [*He looks at* GABRIEL.] Go ahead, Gabriel. 'Tend to yo' chores. I'm gonter keep wukkin' yere.

Gabriel. I hates to see you feelin' like dis, Lawd.

God. Dat's all right. Even bein' Gawd ain't a bed of roses. [GABRIEL *exits.* HOSEA'S *shadow is on the wall. For a second* HOSEA *hesitates.* GOD *looks at the wall. Goes to window.*] I hear you. I know yo' fightin' bravely, but I ain't comin' down. Oh, why don' you leave me alone? You know you ain't talkin' to me. *Is* you talkin' to me? I cain't stand yo' talkin' dat way. I kin only hear part of what you' sayin', and it puzzles me. Don' you know you cain't puzzle God? [*A pause. Then tenderly.*] Do you want me to come down dere ve'y much? You know I said I wouldn't come down? [*Fiercely.*] Why don' he answer me a little? [*With clenched fists, looks down through the window.*] Listen! I'll tell you what I'll do. I ain't goin' to promise you anythin', and I ain't goin' to do nothin' to help you. I'm jest feelin' a little low, an' I'm only comin' down to make myself feel a little better, dat's all.

[*The stage is darkened.* CHOIR *begins "A Blind Man Stood In De Middle of De Road," and continues until the lights go up on the next scene.*]

SCENE VII

It is a shadowed corner beside the walls of the temple in Jerusalem. The light of camp fires flickers on the figure of HEZDREL, *who was* ADAM *in Part I. He stands in the same position* ADAM *held when first discovered but in his right hand is a sword, and his left is in a sling. Around him are several prostrate bodies. Pistol and cannon shots, then a trumpet call. Six young* MEN *enter from left in command of a* CORPORAL. *They are all armed.*

Corporal. De fightin's stopped fo' de night, Hezdrel.

Hezdrel. Yes?

Corporal. Dey're goin' to begin ag'in at cockcrow. [MAN *enters, crosses the stage and exits.*] Herod say he's goin' to take de temple tomorrow, burn de books and de Ark of de Covenant, and put us all to de sword.

Hezdrel. Yo' ready, ain't you?

Everybody. Yes, Hezdrel.

Hezdrel. Did de food get in through de hole in de city wall?

[*Two* SOLDIERS *enter, cross the stage and exit.*]

Corporal. Yessuh, we's goin' back to pass it out now.

Hezdrel. Good. Any mo' of our people escape today?

Corporal. Ol' Herod's got de ol' hole covered up now, but fifteen of our people got out a new one we made.

[*Other* SOLDIERS *enter, cross the stage and exit.*]

Hezdrel. Good. Take dese yere wounded men back and git 'em took care of.

Corporal. Yes, suh.

[*They pick up the bodies on the ground and carry them offstage as* HEZDREL *speaks.*]

Hezdrel. So dey gonter take de temple

in de mo'nin'? We'll be waitin' for 'em. Jest remember, boys, when dey kill us we leap out of our skins, right into de lap of God.

[*The* MEN *disappear with the wounded; from the deep shadow upstage comes* GOD.]

God. Hello, Hezdrel—Adam.

Hezdrel. [*Rubbing his forehead.*] Who is you?

God. Me? I'm jest an ol' preacher, from back in de hills.

Hezdrel. What you doin' yere?

God. I heard you boys was fightin'. I jest wanted to see how it was goin'.

Hezdrel. Well, it ain't goin' so well.

God. Dey got you skeered, huh?

Hezdrel. Look yere, who is you, a spy in my brain?

God. Cain't you see I's one of yo' people?

Hezdrel. Listen, Preacher, we ain't skeered. We's gonter be killed, but we ain't skeered.

God. I's glad to hear dat. Kin I ask you a question, Hezdrel?

Hezdrel. What is it?

God. How is it you is so brave?

Hezdrel. Caize we got faith, dat's why!

God. Faith? In who?

Hezdrel. In our dear Lawd God.

God. But God say he abandoned ev' one down yere.

Hezdrel. Who say dat? Who dare say dat of de Lawd God of Hosea?

God. De God of Hosea?

Hezdrel. You heard me. Look yere, you *is* a spy in my brain!

God. No, I ain't, Hezdrel. I'm jest puzzled. You ought to know dat.

Hezdrel. How come you so puzzled 'bout de God of Hosea?

God. I don' know. Maybe I jest don' hear things. You see, I live 'way back in de hills.

Hezdrel. What you wanter find out?

God. Ain't de God of Hosea de same Jehovah dat was de God of Moses?

Hezdrel. [*Contemptuously.*] No. Dat ol' God of wrath and vengeance? We have de God dat Hosea preached to us. He's de one God.

God. Who's he?

Hezdrel. [*Reverently.*] De God of mercy.

God. Hezdrel, don' you think dey must be de same God?

Hezdrel. I don' know. I ain't bothered to think much about it. Maybe dey is. Maybe our God is de same ol' God. I guess we jest got tired of his appearance dat ol' way.

God. What you mean, Hezdrel?

Hezdrel. Oh, dat ol' God dat walked de earth in de shape of a man. I guess he lived wid man so much dat all he seen was de sins in man. Dat's what made him de God of wrath and vengeance. Co'se he made Hosea. An' Hosea never would a found what mercy was unless dere was a little of it in God, too. Anyway, he ain't a fearsome God no mo'. Hosea showed us dat.

God. How you s'pose Hosea found dat mercy?

Hezdrel. De only way he could find it. De only way I found it. De only way anyone kin find it.

God. How's dat?

Hezdrel. Through sufferin'.

God. [*After a pause.*] What if dey kill you in de mo'nin', Hezdrel?

Hezdrel. If dey do, dey do. Dat's all.

God. Herod say he's goin' to burn de temple——

Hezdrel. So he say.

God. And burn de Ark an' de books. Den dat's de end of de books, ain't it?

Hezdrel. [*Buoyantly.*] What you mean? If he burns dem things in dere? Naw. Dem's jest copies.

God. Where is de others?

Hezdrel. [*Tapping his head.*] Dey's a set in yere. Fifteen got out through de hole in the city wall today. A hundred and fifty got out durin' de week. Each of 'em is a set of de books. Dey's scattered safe all over de countryside now, jest waitin' to git pen and paper fo' to put 'em down agin.

God. [*Proudly.*] Dey cain't lick you, kin dey, Hezdrel?

Hezdrel. [*Smiling.*] I know dey cain't. [*Trumpet.*] You better get out o' yere, Preacher, if you wanter carry de news to yo' people. It'll soon be daylight.

God. I'm goin'. [*He takes a step upstage and stops.*] Want me to take any message?

Hezdrel. Tell de people in de hills dey ain't nobody like de Lawd God of Hosea.

God. I will. If dey kill you tomorrow I'll bet dat God of Hosea'll be waitin' for you.

Hezdrel. I *know* he will.

God. [*Quietly.*] Thank you, Hezdrel.

Hezdrel. Fo' what?

God. Fo' tellin' me so much. You see I been so far away, I guess I was jest way behin' de times.

[*He exits. Pause, then trumpet sounds.* HEZDREL *paces back and forth once or twice. Another young* SOLDIER *appears. Other* MEN *enter and stand grouped about* HEZDREL.]

Second Officer. [*Excitedly.*] De cock's jest crowed, Hezdrel. Dey started de fightin' ag'in.

Hezdrel. We's ready for 'em. Come on,

boys. [*From the darkness upstage comes another group of* SOLDIERS.] Dis is de day dey say dey'll git us. Le's fight till de last man goes. What d'you say?

Corporal. Le's go, Hezdrel!

Hezdrel. [*Calling left.*] Give 'em ev'ything, boys!

[*There is a movement toward the left, a bugle call and the sound of distant battle. The lights go out. The* CHOIR *is heard singing, "March On," triumphantly. They continue to sing after the lights go up on the next scene.*]

SCENE VIII

It is the same setting as the Fish Fry Scene in Part I. The same ANGELS *are present but the* CHOIR, *instead of marching, is standing in a double row on an angle upstage right.* GOD *is seated in an armchair near center. He faces the audience. As the* CHOIR *continues to sing,* GABRIEL *enters, unnoticed by the chattering angels. He looks at* GOD *who is staring thoughtfully toward the audience.*

Gabriel. You look a little pensive, Lawd. [GOD *nods his head.*] Have a seegar, Lawd?

God. No thanks, Gabriel.

[GABRIEL *goes to the table, accepts a cup of custard; chats with the* ANGEL *behind the table for a moment as he sips, puts the cup down and returns to the side of* GOD.]

Gabriel. You look awful pensive, Lawd. You been sittin' yere, lookin' dis way, an awful long time. Is it somethin' serious, Lawd?

God. Very serious, Gabriel.

Gabriel. [*Awed by His tone.*] Lawd, is de time come for me to blow?

God. Not yet, Gabriel. I'm just thinkin'.

Gabriel. What about, Lawd?

[*Puts up hand. Singing stops.*]

God. 'Bout somethin' de boy tol' me. Somethin' 'bout Hosea, and himself. How dey foun' somethin'.

Gabriel. What, Lawd?

God. Mercy. [*A pause.*] Through *sufferin'*, he said.

Gabriel. Yes, Lawd.

God. I'm tryin' to find it, too. It's awful impo'tant. It's awful impo'tant to all de people on my earth. Did he mean dat even God must suffer?

[GOD *continues to look out over the audience for a moment and then a look of surprise comes into his face. He sighs. In the distance a* VOICE *cries.*]

The Voice. Oh, look at him! Oh, look, dey goin' to make him carry it up dat high hill! Dey goin' to nail him to it! Oh, dat's a terrible burden for one man to carry!

[GOD *rises and murmurs "Yes!" as if in recognition. The heavenly beings have been watching him closely, and now, seeing him smile gently, draw back, relieved. All the* ANGELS *burst into "Hallelujah, King Jesus."* GOD *continues to smile as the lights fade away. The singing becomes fortissimo.*]

CURTAIN

THE HAPPY JOURNEY TO TRENTON AND CAMDEN*

By

THORNTON WILDER

FEW DRAMATISTS HAVE HAD SO NOTABLE and enviable a success in the theatre with so few major plays as Thornton Wilder has written. *Our Town,* in fact, has become a classic of its type; and *The Skin of Our Teeth,* with its ingenious and amusing telescoping of the ages of human existence, has been enthusiastically enjoyed on American, French, and British stages. Both have received the highest American award for dramatic excellence—the Pulitzer Prize. Both have done much to encourage the freer use of experimental devices in playwriting and in staging. We regret that neither is available for reprinting in this anthology.

As creative dramatist, Mr. Wilder, like Mr. Saroyan, is unalterably committed to the unconventional approach, and seems even more determined to break through the confinement of the "picture-frame stage" and its "four-walled room." Besides their unconventionality, however, they have little in common. Mr. Saroyan is bluntly scornful of the academic attitude of mind and draws exclusively on personal observation and inspiration for characters, situation, and message. Mr. Wilder, on the contrary, brings to his novels and plays the mind of a scholar, but a freely imaginative one. He writes with the conscious restraint of a painstaking teacher and deeply read man of culture, but fortunately not in the pedantic and unrealistic style that the term scholar too often implies. Nor does he belittle the theatre and its audiences as men of letters sometimes do; he has been a frequent playgoer and has occasionally acted himself, notably as the Narrator in *Our Town.*

If his style lacks the exuberance and directness of a Saroyan, it has all the simplicity of common speech without its vulgarities; and he pictures life with a contagious warmth of sympathy for the ordinary and humble—a sympathy that is more convincing to an auditor than would be possible from so unselective and doctrinary a sympathizer as Saroyan. Wilder's satiric humor is subtler and more genial, but is none the less penetrating. His characters are from the highways of life and not the byways and dead ends, and his message is of ageless truth and is conveyed by implication and not driven home by forceful statement. If the effect is less stirring it is none the less profound and significant. It has the haunting charm of simplicity.

The little playlet we are here permitted to present is a telling example of Wilder's ingenuity in stimulating the imagination to supply both scenery and properties on a bare stage with nothing but chairs to suggest an automobile; and a cot bed for all furnishings indoors. The frequent productions of *The Happy Journey to Trenton and Camden* as delightful entertainment have amply proved its success in creating illusion, despite the fact that Wilder carries this practice of ancient sceneless theatres to greater extremes than many others who have used it as a means of disparaging our theatre's claptrap extravagance.

One may reasonably ask, however, whether such seemingly novel experimentation, however successful, can long establish itself as a satisfying medium of theatre expression, especially after its freshness as novelty has worn off. It has the obvious advantage, like the similar practice of Shakespeare's theatre, of focusing attention on speech and action with no distracting competition from scenic artist or mechanician, a distraction often found to lessen, if not ruin, the effect of the Bard's lines. The sceneless stage has the further advantage, well illustrated in

The Happy Journey, of permitting imagined movement over such long distances as would be absurdly incongruous in a pictorial setting.

For the present, at least, such novelty itself is a diversion. But the dramatist has cleverly harmonized its naively amusing values with those of the dialogue and action. Certainly they add a charm of their own to an otherwise delicately satirical little comedy, which presents, both as reality and symbol, father, mother, son, daughter, trying their best to have a happy journey and to pay a happy visit. As we watch, our convictions suffer no shocks, but the glimpse we have had is perhaps as amiable a sermon as any.

THORNTON NIVEN WILDER

Born 1897, Madison, Wisconsin. Elementary education at Berkeley and Ojai, California.

1906, Went with family to China, where his father served eight years as Consul General in Hong Kong and Shanghai. Attended school in Chefoo.

1915, Two years at Oberlin.

1918, Corporal in Coast Artillery.

1920, A.B., Yale, followed by a year of study in the American Academy in Rome.

1921, Began seven years as housemaster and teacher of French at The Lawrenceville School.

1925, M.A., Princeton. (Litt.D. later conferred by seven colleges and universities.)

1926, First novel, *The Cabala,* published.

1926, First play, *The Trumpet Shall Sound,* produced by the American Laboratory Theatre. (Written while its author was at Yale, in 1919 it had appeared serially in *The Yale Literary Magazine,* of which he was editor. It clearly foreshadowed the dramatist's experimental techniques.)

1927, Internationally acclaimed upon the publication of his second novel, *The Bridge of San Luis Rey.* (A successful film version soon followed.)

1928, Toured the eastern Mediterranean for material for his *Woman of Andros.* The following year, visited the continental theatres.

1930, Began seven years of teaching on the English faculty of the University of Chicago, during which time he produced his translation and adaptation of Obey's *Lucrèce* (1932), with Katharine Cornell in the title role, and his revision of Ibsen's *A Doll's House* (1937).

1938, Pulitzer Prize awarded for *Our Town,* and again in 1942 for *The Skin of Our Teeth.*

1942, Enlisted in Air Corps Intelligence; Lt. Colonel in 1944.

1950, Appointed Charles Eliot Norton Professor of Poetry at Harvard.

Mr. Wilder has been awarded national honors by England, France, and Spain, and elected to membership in several leading literary organizations including the American Academy of Arts and Letters.

PLAYS

1919 *The Trumpet Shall Sound.* 1928 *The Bridge of San Luis Rey* (film script). 1928 *The Angel That Troubled the Waters,* a collection of sixteen brief plays begun in 1915 "as three-minute plays for three persons." 1931 *The Long Christmas Dinner,* title play of a collection of short pieces including: *Queens of France, Pullman Car Hiawatha, Such Things Happen Only in Books, The Happy Journey to Trenton and Camden, Love and How to Cure It.* 1932 *Lucrece,* translated and adapted from *Lucrèce* by Obey. 1938 *Our Town.* 1938 *The Merchant of Yonkers,* translated and adapted from *Einen Jux will er sich machen,* a comedy by Nestroy based on a Victorian farce, *A Well Spent Day* by John Oxenford. 1942 *The Skin of Our Teeth.* 1947 *Our Century.* 1948 *The Victors,* translated and adapted from Jean Paul Sartre's *Morts sans sépulture.* 1954 *The Matchmaker,* a revision of *The Merchant of Yonkers.* 1955 *A Life in the Sun.*

WRITING ON DRAMA

"Some Thoughts on Playwriting," in *The Intent of the Artist,* edited by Augusto Centeno, 1941.

THE HAPPY JOURNEY TO TRENTON AND CAMDEN

No scenery is required for this play. Perhaps a few dusty flats may be seen leaning against the brick wall at the back of the stage.

The five members of the Kirby family and THE STAGE MANAGER *compose the cast.*

THE STAGE MANAGER *not only moves forward and withdraws the few properties that are required, but he reads from a typescript the lines of all the minor characters. He reads them clearly, but with little attempt at characterization, scarcely troubling himself to alter his voice, even when he responds in the person of a child or a woman.*

As the curtain rises THE STAGE MANAGER *is leaning lazily against the proscenium pillar at the audience's left. He is smoking.*

ARTHUR *is playing marbles in the center of the stage.*

CAROLINE *is at the remote back right talking to some girls who are invisible to us.*

MA KIRBY *is anxiously putting on her hat before an imaginary mirror.*

Ma. Where's your pa? Why isn't he here? I declare we'll never get started.

Arthur. Ma, where's my hat? I guess I don't go if I can't find my hat.

Ma. Go out into the hall and see if it isn't there. Where's Caroline gone to now, the plagued child?

Arthur. She's out waitin' in the street talkin' to the Jones girls.—I just looked in the hall a thousand times, ma, and it isn't there. [*He spits for good luck before a difficult shot and mutters:*] Come on, baby.

Ma. Go and look again, I say. Look carefully.

[ARTHUR *rises, runs to the right, turns around swiftly, returns to his game, flinging himself on the floor with a terrible impact and starts shooting an aggie.*]

Arthur. No, ma, it's not there.

Ma. [*Serenely.*] Well, you don't leave Newark without that hat, make up your mind to that. I don't go no journeys with a hoodlum.

Arthur. Aw, ma!

[MA *comes down to the footlights and talks toward the audience as through a window.*]

Ma. Oh, Mrs. Schwartz!

The Stage Manager. [*Consulting his script.*] Here I am, Mrs. Kirby. Are you going yet?

Ma. I guess we're going in just a minute. How's the baby?

The Stage Manager. She's all right now. We slapped her on the back and she spat it up.

Ma. Isn't that fine!—Well now, if you'll be good enough to give the cat a saucer of milk in the morning and the evening, Mrs. Schwartz, I'll be ever so grateful to you.—Oh, good afternoon, Mrs. Hobmeyer!

The Stage Manager. Good afternoon, Mrs. Kirby, I hear you're going away.

Ma. [*Modest.*] Oh, just for three days, Mrs. Hobmeyer, to see my married daughter, Beulah, in Camden. Elmer's got his vacation week from the laundry early this year, and he's just the best driver in the world.

[CAROLINE *comes "into the house" and stands by her mother.*]

The Stage Manager. Is the whole family going?

Ma. Yes, all four of us that's here. The change ought to be good for the children. My married daughter was downright sick a while ago——

The Stage Manager. Tchk—Tchk—Tchk! Yes. I remember you tellin' us.

Ma. And I just want to go down and see the child. I ain't seen her since then. I just won't rest easy in my mind without I see her. [*To* CAROLINE.] Can't you say good afternoon to Mrs. Hobmeyer?

Caroline. [*Blushes and lowers her eyes and says woodenly.*] Good afternoon, Mrs. Hobmeyer.

The Stage Manager. Good afternoon, dear. —Well, I'll wait and beat these rugs until after you're gone, because I don't want to choke you. I hope you have a good time and find everything all right.

Ma. Thank you, Mrs. Hobmeyer, I hope I will.—Well, I guess that milk for the cat is all, Mrs. Schwartz, if you're sure you don't mind. If anything should come up, the key to the back door is hanging by the ice box.

Arthur and Caroline. Ma! Not so loud. Everybody can hear yuh.

Ma. Stop pullin' my dress, children. [*In a loud whisper.*] The key to the back door I'll leave hangin' by the ice box and I'll leave the screen door unhooked.

The Stage Manager. Now have a good trip, dear, and give my love to Loolie.

Ma. I will, and thank you a thousand times. [*She returns "into the room."*] What can be keeping your pa?

Arthur. I can't find my hat, ma.

[*Enter* ELMER *holding a hat.*]

Elmer. Here's Arthur's hat. He musta left it in the car Sunday.

Ma. That's a mercy. Now we can start. —Caroline Kirby, what you done to your cheeks?

Caroline. [*Defiant-abashed.*] Nothin'.

Ma. If you've put anything on 'em, I'll slap you.

Caroline. No, ma, of course I haven't. [*Hanging her head.*] I just rubbed'm to make'm red. All the girls do that at High School when they're goin' places.

Ma. Such silliness I never saw. Elmer, what kep' you?

Elmer. [*Always even-voiced and always looking out a little anxiously through his spectacles.*] I just went to the garage and had Charlie give a last look at it, Kate.

Ma. I'm glad you did. I wouldn't like to have no breakdown miles from anywhere. Now we can start. Arthur, put those marbles away. Anybody'd think you didn't want to go on a journey, to look at yuh.

[*They go out through the "hall," take the short steps that denote going downstairs, and find themselves in the street.*]

Elmer. Here, you boys, you keep away from that car.

Ma. Those Sullivan boys put their heads into everything.

[THE STAGE MANAGER *has moved forward four chairs and a low platform. This is the automobile. It is in the center of the stage and faces the audience. The platform slightly raises the two chairs in the rear.* PA'S *hands hold an imaginary steering wheel and continually shift gears.* CAROLINE *sits beside him.* ARTHUR *is behind him and* MA *behind* CAROLINE.]

Caroline. [*Self-consciously.*] Goodbye, Mildred. Goodbye, Helen.

The Stage Manager. Goodbye, Caroline. Goodbye, Mrs. Kirby. I hope y'have a good time.

Ma. Goodbye, girls.

The Stage Manager. Goodbye, Kate. The car looks fine.

Ma. [*Looking upward toward a window.*] Oh, goodbye, Emma! [*Modestly.*] We think it's the best little Chevrolet in the world. —Oh, goodbye, Mrs. Adler!

The Stage Manager. What, are you going away, Mrs. Kirby?

Ma. Just for three days, Mrs. Adler, to see my married daughter in Camden.

The Stage Manager. Have a good time.

[*Now* MA, CAROLINE, *and* THE STAGE MANAGER *break out into a tremendous chorus of goodbyes. The whole street is saying goodbye.* ARTHUR *takes out his pea shooter and lets fly happily into the air. There is a lurch or two and they are off.*]

Arthur. [*In sudden fright.*] Pa! Pa! Don't go by the school. Mr. Biedenbach might see us!

Ma. I don't care if he does see us. I guess I can take my children out of school for one day without having to hide down back streets about it. [ELMER *nods to a passerby.* MA *asks without sharpness:*] Who was that you spoke to, Elmer?

Elmer. That was the fellow who arranges our banquets down to the Lodge, Kate.

Ma. Is he the one who had to buy four hundred steaks? [PA *nods.*] I declare, I'm glad I'm not him.

Elmer. The air's getting better already. Take deep breaths, children.

[*They inhale noisily.*]

Arthur. Gee, it's almost open fields already. "*Weber and Heilbronner Suits for Well-dressed Men.*" Ma, can I have one of them some day?

Ma. If you graduate with good marks perhaps your father'll let you have one for graduation.

Caroline. [*Whining.*] Oh, Pa! do we have to wait while that whole funeral goes by?

[PA *takes off his hat.* MA *cranes forward with absorbed curiosity.*]

Ma. Take off your hat, Arthur. Look at your father.—Why, Elmer, I do believe that's a lodge-brother of yours. See the banner? I suppose this is the Elizabeth branch. [ELMER *nods.* MA *sighs: Tchk—tchk—tchk. They all lean forward and watch the funeral in silence, growing momentarily more solemnized. After a pause,* MA *continues almost dreamily:*] Well, we haven't forgotten the one that we went on, have we? We haven't forgotten our good Harold. He gave his life for his country, we musn't forget that. [*She passes her finger from the corner of her eye across her cheek. There is another pause.*] Well, we'll all hold up the traffic for a few minutes some day.

The Children. [*Very uncomfortable.*] Ma!

Ma. [*Without self-pity.*] Well I'm "ready," children. I hope everybody in this car is "ready." [*She puts her hand on* PA's *shoulder.*] And I pray to go first, Elmer. Yes. [PA *touches her hand.*]

The Children. Ma, everybody's looking at you. Everybody's laughing at you.

Ma. Oh, hold your tongues! I don't care what a lot of silly people in Elizabeth, New Jersey, think of me.—Now we can go on. That's the last.

[*There is another lurch and the car goes on.*]

Caroline. "*Fit-Rite Suspenders. The Working Man's Choice.*" Pa, why do they spell Rite that way?

Elmer. So that it'll make you stop and ask about it, Missy.

Caroline. Papa, you're teasing me.—Ma, why do they say "*Three Hundred Rooms Three Hundred Baths?*"

Arthur. "*Miller's Spaghetti: The Family's Favorite Dish.*" Ma, why don't you ever have spaghetti?

Ma. Go along, you'd never eat it.

Arthur. Ma, I like it now.

Caroline. [*With gesture.*] Yum-yum. It looks wonderful up there. Ma, make some when we get home?

Ma. [*Dryly.*] "The management is always happy to receive suggestions. We aim to please."

[*The whole family finds this exquisitely funny. The* CHILDREN *scream with laughter. Even* ELMER *smiles.* MA *remains modest.*]

Elmer. Well, I guess no one's complaining, Kate. Everybody knows you're a good cook.

Ma. I don't know whether I'm a good cook or not, but I know I've had practice. At least I've cooked three meals a day for twenty-five years.

Arthur. Aw, ma, you went out to eat once in a while.

Ma. Yes. That made it a leap year.

[*This joke is no less successful than its predecessor. When the laughter dies down,* CAROLINE *turns around in an ecstasy of well-being and kneeling on the cushions says:*]

Caroline. Ma, I love going out in the country like this. Let's do it often, ma.

Ma. Goodness, smell that air will you! It's got the whole ocean in it.—Elmer, drive careful over that bridge. This must be New Brunswick we're coming to.

Arthur. [*Jealous of his mother's successes.*] Ma, when is the next comfort station?

Ma. [*Unruffled.*] You don't want one. You just said that to be awful.

Caroline. [*Shrilly.*] Yes, he did, ma. He's terrible. He says that kind of thing right out in school and I want to sink through the floor, ma. He's terrible.

Ma. Oh, don't get so excited about nothing, Miss Proper! I guess we're all yewman-beings in this car, at least as far as I know. And, Arthur, you try and be a gentleman. —Elmer, don't run over that collie dog. [*She follows the dog with her eyes.*] Looked kinda peakèd to me. Needs a good honest bowl of leavings. Pretty dog, too. [*Her eyes fall on a billboard.*] That's a pretty advertisement for Chesterfield cigarettes, isn't it? Looks like Beulah, a little.

Arthur. Ma?

Ma. Yes.

Arthur. [*"Route" rhymes with "out".*] Can't I take a paper route with the Newark *Daily Post?*

Ma. No, you cannot. No, sir. I hear they make the paper boys get up at four-thirty in the morning. No son of mine is going to get up at four-thirty every morning, not if it's to make a million dollars. Your *Saturday Evening Post* route on Thursday mornings is enough.

Arthur. Aw, ma.

Ma. No, sir. No son of mine is going to get up at four-thirty and miss the sleep God meant him to have.

Arthur. [*Sullenly.*] Hhm! Ma's always talking about God. I guess she got a letter from him this morning. [MA *rises, outraged.*]

Ma. Elmer, stop that automobile this minute. I don't go another step with anybody that says things like that. Arthur, you get out of this car. Elmer, you give him another dollar bill. He can go back to Newark, by himself. I don't want him.

Arthur. What did I say? There wasn't anything terrible about that.

Elmer. I didn't hear what he said, Kate.

Ma. God has done a lot of things for me and I won't have him made fun of by anybody. Go away. Go away from me.

Caroline. Aw, Ma,—don't spoil the ride.

Ma. No.

Elmer. We might as well go on, Kate, since we've got started. I'll talk to the boy tonight.

Ma. [*Slowly conceding.*] All right, if you say so, Elmer. But I won't sit beside him. Caroline, you come, and sit by me.

Arthur. [*Frightened.*] Aw, ma, that wasn't so terrible.

Ma. I don't want to talk about it. I hope your father washes your mouth out with soap and water.—Where'd we all be if I started talking about God like that, I'd like to know! We'd be in the speak-easies and night-clubs and places like that, that's where we'd be.—All right, Elmer, you can go on now.

Caroline. What did he say, ma? I didn't hear what he said.

Ma. I don't want to talk about it.

[*They drive on in silence for a moment, the shocked silence after a scandal.*]

Elmer. I'm going to stop and give the car a little water, I guess.

Ma. All right, Elmer. You know best.

Elmer. [*To a garage hand.*] Could I have a little water in the radiator—to make sure?

The Stage Manager. [*In this scene alone he lays aside his script and enters into a rôle seriously.*] You sure can. [*He punches the tires.*] Air, all right? Do you need any oil or gas?

Elmer. No, I think not. I just got fixed up in Newark.

Ma. We're on the right road for Camden, are we?

The Stage Manager. Yes, keep straight ahead. You can't miss it. You'll be in Trenton in a few minutes. [*He carefully pours some water into the hood.*] Camden's a great town, lady, believe me.

Ma. My daughter likes it fine,—my married daughter.

The Stage Manager. Ye'? It's a great burg all right. I guess I think so because I was born near there.

Ma. Well, well. Your folks still live there?

The Stage Manager. No, my old man sold the farm and they built a factory on it. So the folks moved to Philadelphia.

Ma. My married daughter Beulah lives there because her husband works in the telephone company.—Stop pokin' me, Caroline! —We're all going down to see her for a few days.

The Stage Manager. Ye'?

Ma. She's been sick, you see, and I just felt I had to go and see her. My husband and my boy are going to stay at the Y.M.C.A. I hear they've got a dormitory on the top floor that's real clean and comfortable. Had you ever been there?

The Stage Manager. No. I'm Knights of Columbus myself.

Ma. Oh.

The Stage Manager. I used to play basketball at the Y though. It looked all right to me. [*He has been standing with one foot on the rung of* MA'S *chair. They have taken a great fancy to one another. He reluctantly shakes himself out of it and pretends to examine the car again, whistling.*] Well, I guess you're all set now, lady. I hope you have a good trip; you can't miss it.

Everybody. Thanks. Thanks a lot. Good luck to you. [*Jolts and lurches.*]

Ma. [*With a sigh.*] The world's full of nice people.—That's what I call a nice young man.

Caroline. [*Earnestly.*] Ma, you oughtn't to tell'm all everything about yourself.

Ma. Well, Caroline, you do your way and I'll do mine.—He looked kinda thin to me. I'd like to feed him up for a few days. His mother lives in Philadelphia and I expect he eats at those dreadful Greek places.

Caroline. I'm hungry. Pa, there's a hot dog stand. K'n I have one?

Elmer. We'll all have one, eh, Kate? We had such an early lunch.

Ma. Just as you think best, Elmer.

Elmer. Arthur, here's half a dollar.—Run over and see what they have. Not too much mustard either. [ARTHUR *descends from the car and goes off stage right.* MA *and* CAROLINE *get out and walk a bit.*]

Ma. What's that flower over there?—I'll take some of those to Beulah.

Caroline. It's just a weed, ma.

Ma. I like it.—My, look at the sky, wouldya! I'm glad I was born in New Jersey. I've always said it was the best state in the Union. Every state has something no other state has got.

[*They stroll about humming. Presently* ARTHUR *returns with his hands full of imaginary hot dogs which he distributes. He is still very much cast down by the recent scandal. He finally approaches his mother and says falteringly:*]

Arthur. Ma, I'm sorry. I'm sorry for what I said.

[*He bursts into tears and puts his forehead against her elbow.*]

Ma. There. There. We all say wicked things at times. I know you didn't mean it like it sounded. [*He weeps still more violently than before.*] Why, now, now! I forgive you, Arthur, and tonight before you go to bed you . . . [*She whispers.*] You're a good boy at heart, Arthur, and we all know it. [CAROLINE *starts to cry too.* MA *is suddenly joyously alive and happy.*] Sakes alive, it's too nice a day for us all to be cryin'. Come now, get in. You go up in front with your father, Caroline. Ma wants to sit with her beau. I never saw such children. Your hot dogs are all getting wet. Now chew them fine, everybody.—All right, Elmer, forward march.—Caroline, whatever are you doing?

Caroline. I'm spitting out the leather, ma.

Ma. Then say: Excuse me.

Caroline. Excuse me, please.

Ma. What's this place? Arthur, did you see the post office?

Arthur. It said Lawrenceville.

Ma. Hhn. School kinda. Nice. I wonder what that big yellow house set back was. —Now it's beginning to be Trenton.

Caroline. Papa, it was near here that George Washington crossed the Delaware. It was near Trenton, mama. He was first in war and first in peace, and first in the hearts of his countrymen.

Ma. [*Surveying the passing world, serene and didactic.*] Well, the thing I like about him best was that he never told a lie. [*The* CHILDREN *are duly cast down. There is a pause.*] There's a sunset for you. There's nothing like a good sunset.

Arthur. There's an Ohio license in front of us. Ma, have you ever been to Ohio?

Ma. No.

[*A dreamy silence descends upon them.* CAROLINE *sits closer to her father.* MA *puts her arm around* ARTHUR.]

Arthur. Ma, what a lotta people there are in the world, ma. There must be thousands and thousands in the United States. Ma, how many are there?

Ma. I don't know. Ask your father.

Arthur. Pa, how many are there?

Elmer. There are a hundred and twenty-six million, Kate.

Ma. [*Giving a pressure about* ARTHUR'S *shoulder.*] And they all like to drive out in the evening with their children beside'm. [*Another pause.*] Why doesn't somebody sing something? Arthur, you're always singing something; what's the matter with you?

Arthur. All right. What'll we sing? [*He sketches:*]

"In the Blue Ridge mountains of Virginia,
On the trail of the lonesome pine . . ."

No, I don't like that any more. Let's do:

"I been workin on de railroad
All de liblong day.
I been workin' on de railroad
Just to pass de time away."

[CAROLINE *joins in at once. Finally even* MA *is singing. Even* PA *is singing.* MA *suddenly jumps up with a wild cry:*]

Ma. Elmer, that signpost said Camden, I saw it.

Elmer. All right, Kate, if you're sure.

[*Much shifting of gears, backing, and jolting.*]

Ma. Yes, there it is. Camden—five miles. Dear old Beulah.—Now, children, you be good and quiet during dinner. She's just got out of bed after a big sorta operation, and we must all move around kinda quiet. First you drop me and Caroline at the door and just say hello, and then you men-folk go over to the Y.M.C.A. and come back for dinner in about an hour.

Caroline. [*Shutting her eyes and pressing her fists passionately against her nose.*] I see the first star. Everybody make a wish.

Star light, star bright,
First star I seen tonight.
I wish I may, I wish I might
Have the wish I wish tonight.

[*Then solemnly.*] Pins. Mama, you say "needles."

[*She interlocks little fingers with her mother.*]

Ma. Needles.

Caroline. Shakespeare. Ma, you say "Longfellow."

Ma. Longfellow.

Caroline. Now it's a secret and I can't tell it to anybody. Ma, you make a wish.

Ma. [*With almost grim humor.*] No, I can make wishes without waiting for no star. And I can tell my wishes right out loud too. Do you want to hear them?

Caroline. [*Resignedly.*] No, ma, we know'm already. We've heard'm. [*She hangs her head affectedly on her left shoulder and says with unmalicious mimicry:*] You want me to be a good girl and you want Arthur to be honest-in-word-and-deed.

Ma. [*Majestically.*] Yes. So mind yourself.

Elmer. Caroline, take out that letter from Beulah in my coat pocket by you and read aloud the places I marked with red pencil.

Caroline. [*Working.*] *"A few blocks after you pass the two big oil tanks on your left . . ."*

Everybody. [*Pointing backward.*] There they are!

Caroline. *". . . you come to a corner where there's an A and P store on the left and a firehouse kitty-corner to it . . ."* [*They all jubilantly identify these landmarks.*] *". . . turn right, go two blocks, and our house is Weyerhauser St. Number 471."*

Ma. It's an even nicer street than they used to live in. And right handy to an A and P.

Caroline. [*Whispering.*] Ma, it's better than our street. It's richer than our street. —Ma, isn't Beulah richer than we are?

Ma. [*Looking at her with a firm and glassy eye.*] Mind yourself, missy. I don't want to hear anybody talking about rich or not rich when I'm around. If people aren't nice I don't care how rich they are. I live in the best street in the world because my husband and children live there. [*She glares impres-*

sively at CAROLINE *a moment to let this lesson sink in, then looks up, sees* BEULAH *and waves.*] There's Beulah standing on the steps lookin' for us.

[BEULAH *has appeared and is waving. They all call out:*] Hello, Beulah—Hello. [*Presently they are all getting out of the car.* BEULAH *kisses her father long and affectionately.*]

Beulah. Hello, papa. Good old papa. You look tired, pa.—Hello, mama.—Lookit how Arthur and Caroline are growing!

Ma. They're bursting all their clothes! —Yes, your pa needs a rest. Thank Heaven, his vacation has come just now. We'll feed him up and let him sleep late. Pa has a present for you, Loolie. He would go and buy it.

Beulah. Why, pa, you're terrible to go and buy anything for me. Isn't he terrible?

Ma. Well, it's a secret. You can open it at dinner.

Elmer. Where's Horace, Loolie?

Beulah. He was kep' over a little at the office. He'll be here any minute. He's crazy to see you all.

Ma. All right. You men go over to the Y and come back in about an hour.

Beulah. [*As her father returns to the wheel, stands out in the street beside him.*] Go straight along, pa, you can't miss it. It just stares at yuh. [*She puts her arm around his neck and rubs her nose against his temple.*] Crazy old pa, goin' buyin' things! It's me that ought to be buyin' things for you, pa.

Elmer. Oh, no! There's only one Loolie in the world.

Beulah. [*Whispering, as her eyes fill with tears.*] Are you glad I'm still alive, pa? [*She kisses him abruptly and goes back to the house steps.* THE STAGE MANAGER *removes the automobile with the help of* ELMER *and* ARTHUR *who go off waving their goodbyes.*] Well, come on upstairs, ma, and take off your things. Caroline, there's a surprise for you in the back yard.

Caroline. Rabbits?

Beulah. No.

Caroline. Chickins?

Beulah. No. Go and see. [CAROLINE *runs off stage.* BEULAH *and* MA *gradually go upstairs.*] There are two new puppies. You be thinking over whether you can keep one in Newark.

Ma. I guess we can. It's a nice house, Beulah. You just got a *lovely* home.

Beulah. When I got back from the hospital, Horace had moved everything into it, and there wasn't anything for me to do.

Ma. It's lovely.

[THE STAGE MANAGER *pushes out a bed from the left. Its foot is toward the right.* BEULAH *sits on it, testing the springs.*]

Beulah. I think you'll find the bed comfortable, ma.

Ma. [*Taking off her hat.*] Oh, I could sleep on a heapa shoes, Loolie! I don't have no trouble sleepin'. [*She sits down beside her.*] Now let me look at my girl. Well, well, when I last saw you, you didn't know me. You kep' saying: *When's mama comin'? When's mama comin'?* But the doctor sent me away.

Beulah. [*Puts her head on her mother's shoulder and weeps.*] It was awful, mama. It was awful. She didn't even live a few minutes, mama. It was awful.

Ma. [*Looking far away.*] God thought best, dear. God thought best. We don't understand why. We just go on, honey, doin' our business. [*Then almost abruptly—passing the back of her hand across her cheek.*] Well, now, what are we giving the men to eat tonight?

Beulah. There's a chicken in the oven.

Ma. What time didya put it in?

Beulah. [*Restraining her.*] Aw, ma, don't go yet. I like to sit here with you this way. You always get the fidgets when we try and pet yuh, mama.

Ma. [*Ruefully, laughing.*] Yes, it's kinda foolish. I'm just an old Newark bag-a-bones.

[*She glances at the backs of her hands.*]

Beulah. [*Indignantly.*] Why, ma, you're good-lookin'! We always said you were good-lookin'.—And besides, you're the best ma we could ever have.

Ma. [*Uncomfortable.*] Well, I hope you like me. There's nothin' like being liked by your family.—Now I'm going downstairs to look at the chicken. You stretch out here for a minute and shut your eyes.—Have you got everything laid in for breakfast before the shops close?

Beulah. Oh, you know! Ham and eggs.

[*They both laugh.*]

Ma. I declare I never could understand what men see in ham and eggs. I think they're horrible.—What time did you put the chicken in?

Beulah. Five o'clock.

Ma. Well, now, you shut your eyes for ten minutes. [BEULAH *stretches out and shuts her eyes.* MA *descends the stairs absentmindedly singing:*]

"There were ninety and nine that safely lay
In the shelter of the fold,
But one was out on the hills away,
Far off from the gates of gold. . . ."

AND THE CURTAIN FALLS

WAYS AND MEANS*

[*A Light Comedy in Three Scenes*]

By

NOEL COWARD

EVEN IF "WAYS AND MEANS" WERE NOT signed, anyone faintly familiar with the modern theatre would recognize it as by Noël Coward. It shows "high-life" people engaged in distinctly low-life activities; it has characteristic little risqué touches; it is very actable, amusing, quick; it has his characteristic racy verbal agility. When one knows that it was written by Noël Coward to be acted by himself and Gertrude Lawrence, and has seen those two either together or apart, one cannot help seeing them imaginatively as the play is read. They two could give the play a verve that probably no other two players could, quite, yet the play has been repeatedly performed with success by players of less distinction or even of no distinction at all. The situation Mr. Coward uses in *Ways and Means* may not be a universal one; his characters may not be taken from your or my circle of acquaintances; the conclusion may defy probability, but the play is nevertheless good drama and good theatre, in that it excites, amuses, entertains, and, unless you wish to spend your time exclusively with worthy people, satisfies.

Ways and Means was among the group of nine short plays which Mr. Coward called *Tonight at 8:30*. These plays were performed by him and Miss Lawrence in groups of threes, each group consisting of one musical play or play with music, and two dramatic pieces of differing mood. Each group of three made a theatre evening. After six had been written in 1935, Mr. Coward and Miss Lawrence toured the English provinces with them, playing the first three for three evenings and the second three for the next three evenings. At matinees the title was changed to *This Afternoon at 2:30*. When the tour established that the program was successful, Mr. Coward added the final three plays, including *Ways and Means*, and brought the whole bill into London in January 1936 and to New York in November of the same year.

Mr. Coward said of them:

> The idea of presenting three short plays in an evening instead of one long one is far from original. The 'triple bill' has been used with varying success since the early days of the theatre. A curtain raiser still appears occasionally, wearing a hang-dog expression, because it knows only too well, poor thing, that it would not be there at all were the main attraction of the evening long enough.
>
> A short play, having great advantage over a long one in that it can sustain a mood without technical creaking or overpadding, deserves a better fate. If by careful writing, acting, and producing, I can do a little toward reinstating it in its rightful pride, I shall have achieved one of my more sentimental ambitions.

Mr. Coward likes to act in his own plays, but he does not like acting in long runs. Since his plays are almost invariably successful, he confronts a dilemma. Perhaps Mr. Coward felt that the variety the short plays of *Tonight at 8:30* provided took a good deal of the drudgery out of acting in a success.

Intellectual critics in the theatre tend to look down their noses at Noël Coward because he never writes tragedy and because his comedy is not profound. But unquestionably the theatre needs the kind of play Mr. Coward writes as much as it needs Shakespeare. Few dramatists in all dramatic history are more skilful in getting the effects intended. Those effects are no doubt often enough theatrical and thin, but they usually delight audiences. And Mr. Coward is inclined to think the kind of dramatist the intellectuals admire is pompous, and he is sometimes not unjustified. Mr. Coward's devotion to the theatre, and to its perfection in presen tation, is unquestionable. His plays have more vitality than those of many prodigies proclaimed by the highbrows and they keep the stage better. They remind the detached critic of Restoration comedies: their very identification with the period in which they appeared preserves them; they rapidly become period pieces and escape dating, while the play with a solemn message to its age often decays.

NOEL COWARD

Born 1899, Teddington, England.

Educated at Croydon School and privately.

1911, First appearance as an actor.

1911–1917, Somewhat irregularly employed in theatres and music-halls.

1917–1918, War service; afterwards resumed acting career.

1920, Appeared in his own *I'll Leave It to You,* and thereafter tried to write good parts for himself into his plays.

1924, First big success as author and actor in *The Vortex,* London and New York.

1928, First complete revue, book, lyrics, music: *This Year of Grace.*

1940–1944, Information and propaganda service for Great Britain in World War II.

1941–1946, *Blithe Spirit,* with 1997 performances, establishes the longest-run record in the London theatre for a non-musical play.

Traveler, short-story writer, parodist.

PLAYS

1920 *I'll Leave It to You.* 1923 *The Young Idea.* 1923 *London Calling,* revue, (with others). 1924 *The Rat Trap* (earliest written play). 1924 *The Vortex.* 1924 *Charlot's Revue* (with others). 1925 *Fallen Angels.* 1925 *On with the Dance,* revue, (music with others). 1925 *Hay Fever.* 1925 *Easy Virtue.* 1926 *The Queen Was in the Parlor.* 1926 *This Was a Man.* 1927 *The Marquise.* 1927 *Home Chat.* 1927 *Sirocco.* 1928 *This Year of Grace,* revue, book, lyrics, and music. 1929 *Bitter Sweet,* operette, book, lyrics, and music. 1930 *Private Lives,* with music. 1931 *Cochran's 1931 Revue,* book, lyrics, and music. 1931 *Cavalcade,* with music. 1931 *Post Mortem* (not produced). 1932 *Words and Music,* revue, book, lyrics, and music, called *Set to Music* in New York, 1939. 1932 *Design for Living.* 1934 *Conversation Piece,* operette, book, lyrics, and music. 1934 *Point Valaine.* 1935, 1936 *Tonight at 8:30,* nine short plays: *We Were Dancing* (musical); *The Astonished Heart; "Red Peppers"; Hands Across the Sea; Fumed Oak; The Shadow Play* (musical); *Ways and Means; Still Life; Family Album* (musical). 1938 *Operette,* operette, book, lyrics, and music. 1941 *Blithe Spirit.* 1943 *Present Laughter.* 1943 *This Happy Breed.* 1945 *Sigh No More,* revue, (with others). 1946 *Pacific 1860,* operette, book, lyrics, and music. 1947 *Peace in Our Time.* 1950 *Ace of Clubs,* musical comedy, book, lyrics, and music. 1951 *Relative Values.* 1952 *Quadrille.* 1954 *After the Ball,* musical comedy, book, lyrics, and music, based on Oscar Wilde's *Lady Windermere's Fan.*

SCREENWRITING

1942 *In Which We Serve.* 1944 *This Happy Breed.* 1945 *Brief Encounter* (*Still Life*). 1945 *Blithe Spirit.* 1950 *The Astonished Heart.*

WRITINGS ON DRAMA

Preface to *Three Plays,* 1924. Preface to *Collected Sketches and Lyrics,* 1932. Preface to *Play Parade,* 1934. *Present Indicative,* 1937, *passim. Future Indefinite,* 1954, *passim.*

WAYS AND MEANS

Characters

STELLA CARTWRIGHT.
TOBY CARTWRIGHT.
OLIVE LLOYD-RANSOME.
LORD CHAPWORTH (*Chaps*).
NANNY.
MURDOCH.
STEVENS.
PRINCESS ELÈNA KRASSILOFF.
GASTON.

The action of the play takes place in a bedroom in the LLOYD-RANSOMES' *house, Villa Zephyre, on the Côte d'Azur.*

The time is the present (1936).

SCENE I. *11.30 a.m. on an April morning.*
SCENE II. *1.30 a.m. the following morning.*
SCENE III. *Two hours later.*

SCENE I

The Scene is a bedroom in the Villa Zephyre on the Côte d'Azur. The Villa Zephyre belongs to MRS. LLOYD-RANSOME, *who is excessively rich, comparatively pleasant and entirely idle; the bedroom therefore is luxurious and tastefully appointed. On the right there is a dressing-table with, above it, a door leading to the bathroom. On the left there is a French window leading on to a small verandah, above that, in the back wall, is a door leading to the passage and the rest of the house. There is a slight recess in the back wall containing a very wide and comfortable bed.*

This is occupied at the rise of the curtain by STELLA *and* TOBY CARTWRIGHT. *They are an attractive couple in the thirties. Between them there is a breakfast tray.* STELLA *is opening and reading letters,* TOBY *is scanning the* Continental Daily Mail. *A certain amount of pale sunshine is coming through the window, but this fails to banish from either of their faces an expression of gloomy dissatisfaction. After a considerable silence,* STELLA *speaks.*

Stella. Here's a letter from Aunt Hester.

Toby. Is she well and hearty?

Stella. Apparently.

Toby. To hell with her!

[*There is a further silence.*]

Stella. [*Pensively eating a brioche.*] Why do other people's breakfasts always taste much nicer than one's own?

Toby. Probably because they are.

[*There is another silence.*]

Stella. I knew marrying you was a mistake at least seven years ago, but I never realised the thoroughness of the mistake until now——

Toby. [*Reading his paper.*] You will be interested to hear that Mrs. S. J. Pendleton gave a small dinner party for Mr. and Mrs. Hubert Weir at the Hotel Normandie in Le Touquet last night——

Stella. How thrilling.

Toby. Among the guests were Lord and Lady Haven, Mrs. George Durlap, the Countess Pantulucci, Mr. Henry Bird, Mr. and Mrs. Harvey Lincoln, Miss Styles——

Stella. Shut up!

Toby. I beg your pardon?

Stella. I said shut up.

Toby. [*Continuing.*] —Mr. and Mrs. Sidney Alford have returned from Vichy and are staying at the Crillon——

Stella. Toby——

Toby. They are to be joined in a few days by Mrs. Alford's sister, Lady Croker——

Stella. Toby, please——

Toby. Prince and Princess Jean Marie de Larichon have left the Hotel George Cinq en route for the Riviera——

[STELLA *snatches the paper from him.*]

Stella. [*Angrily.*] Mr. and Mrs. Toby Cartwright have left the Villa Zephyre under a cloud——

Toby. [*Complacently taking some coffee.*] Not yet they haven't——

Stella. Owing to the idiocy of Mr. Toby

Cartwright losing his shirt at the Casino——

Toby. Oh, God, must we go back over that again?

Stella. Yes, we must—don't you see—we've got to do something——

Toby. Darling, what's the use——?

Stella. Give me the pad and pencil—they're just by you——

Toby. [*Taking a pencil and pad from the bedside table.*] So what?

Stella. Give it to me.

Toby. [*Giving it to her.*] Toby lost fifty pounds—Toby lost fifty pounds—Toby lost fifty pounds—write it down quickly, it would be awful if you happened to forget it——

Stella. [*Near tears.*] Oh, Toby!

Toby. [*Relenting.*] All right, darling—I am sorry—really I am.

[*He leans towards her, nearly upsetting the breakfast-tray.*]

Stella. Look out!

Toby. Damn——

Stella. It isn't that I want to rub in about the fifty pounds—really it isn't—but we are in the most awful jam, and we've got to concentrate.

Toby. We concentrated up until four-thirty this morning and nothing came of it——

Stella. Will you promise not to take offense at anything I say for ten minutes?

Toby. That means you're going to be absolutely bloody.

Stella. Promise.

Toby. All right—I promise.

Stella. We must face facts. Now then. Our combined incomes amount to seven hundred and fifty pounds a year——

Toby. Until Aunt Hester dies.

Stella. Aunt Hester will not die—she's outwitted life for seventy years and is now determined to outwit death.

Toby. It's indecent.

Stella. Never mind about that now—our combined overdrafts amount to roughly thirteen hundred pounds—in addition to which, you owe about three thousand——

Toby. What about you?

Stella. [*Writing.*] Two thousand.

Toby. I can't understand why you don't get a job of some sort—look at Liza Herrick—she at least made some effort—she opened a hat shop.

Stella. And shut it again.

Toby. No talent—that's what's wrong with you—no marketable talent whatsoever.

Stella. You seem to forget that on a certain bleak day in 1928 I gave my life into your keeping.

Toby. Marriage is a sacrament, a mystic rite, and you persist in regarding it as a sort of plumber's estimate.

Stella. Be quiet. Where was I?

Toby. Wandering along the paths of memory, dear, with a singularly nasty expression.

Stella. You will admit, I suppose, that we live beyond our income?

Toby. You have a genius for understatement.

Stella. Having managed to rake up seventy-two pounds in order to stay—God knows why—in this over-elaborate house——

Toby. I don't agree. I think Olive, considering her innate vulgarity, has done this house with remarkable restraint.

Stella. Olive is not vulgar—she's one of my oldest friends. She was at school with me, and——

Toby. Well, let's just say that she was at school with you.

Stella. Now look here, Toby——

Toby. Go on—concentrate.

Stella. You're maddening.

Toby. Go on, write—write down the truth—face facts—put down our congenital idiocy in black and white—write down that we were brought up merely to be amiable and pleasant and socially attractive—that we have no ambition and no talent—except for playing games.

Stella. [*Sharply.*] And not enough of that.

Toby. Toby lost fifty pounds—Toby lost fifty pounds——

Stella. I wrote that down first—but what I didn't write down was that you were a silly, selfish, careless, bloody fool to do it——

Toby. [*Furiously.*] Look here, Stella——

[*He makes a violent movement.*]

Stella. Look out!

Toby. Damn!

Stella. It's no use quarrelling. The fifty pounds has gone—we've already stayed over our time here—the Lorings are expecting us in Venice—we have, at the moment, one hundred and fourteen francs—and we are down two thousand four hundred francs in the Bridge Book.

Toby. That's entirely your fault—you play Bridge too merrily, Stella.

Stella. My merriment is entirely a social gesture. I loathe Bridge.

Toby. That is no excuse for playing it as though it were lacrosse.

Stella. I don't know what you mean.

Toby. Your bids have a certain girlish devil-may-care abandon—you whoop through every rubber like a games' mistress.

Stella. What do you mean, whoop?

Toby. What I say—whoop—W-H-O-O-P.

Stella. Oh, do be quiet! What was I saying?

Toby. You were saying that we were down two thousand four hundred francs in the

Bridge Book. What you should have said was, that owing to your——

Stella. Never mind about that now—within the next week we shall be asked definitely to leave—Olive was dropping hints all over the dinner-table last night.

Toby. We can't leave.

Stella. We'll have to.

Toby. Chaps owes you some money, doesn't he?

Stella. Yes. Backgammon—seven thousand francs.

Toby. Thank God for that!

Stella. If we travel to Venice second-class and send Nanny home——

Toby. I can't think why you had to bring her in the first place; I don't have to have a valet, why should you have a maid?

Stella. Nanny's not a maid—Nanny's saved our lives a million times.

Toby. Wrongly.

Stella. Anyhow——

[*There is a knock on the door and* GASTON *enters. He is a neatly dressed French valet.*]

Gaston. Bon jour, monsieur.

Toby. Bon jour, Gaston.

Gaston. Bon jour, madame.

Stella. Bon jour.

Gaston. Lord Chapworth wish to speak to you.

Toby. Is he there?

Stella. Tell him to come in. [*She calls.*] Come in, Chaps!

[GASTON *stands aside to let* LORD CHAPWORTH *enter.* LORD CHAPWORTH *is an amiable-looking young man.* GASTON *goes out.*]

Chaps. Good morning—how d'you feel?

Toby. Frightful.

Chaps. So do I.

Toby. Good!

Stella. You look very sweet, Chaps darling, and very dapper—why are you up so early?

Chaps. It's after eleven. I came to say good-bye——

Stella. Of course, you're leaving to-day—I'd forgotten. Are you going to May Bainbridge?

Chaps. Yes—Guy's picking me up.

Stella. You must find out all about the chauffeur scandal and wire us immediately.

Chaps. What chauffeur scandal?

Stella. Don't be silly, darling, the whole coast is buzzing with it.

Chaps. Oh, that!—I always thought it was a valet.

Toby. Chauffeur-valet—a combined occupation rife, apparently, with the most delirious opportunities——

Chaps. Do you think it's true?—I mean, do you think May really did——?

Stella. Certainly—you only have to look at her.

Toby. Don't be catty, Stella.

Stella. As May Bainbridge has been consistently odious to me for years I really don't see why I shouldn't be as catty as I like.

Toby. After all, Chaps is going to stay with them.

Stella. Serve him right.

Chaps. Oh, old May's not bad—she just has an unfortunate manner.

Stella. To be not bad with an unfortunate manner is not enough——

Chaps. You seem a bit scratchy this morning.

Toby. Compared with what took place in the night, this is purring.

Chaps. Well, it's a nice sunny day, anyhow.

Stella. It had better be.

Chaps. I had an awful evening—I got stuck with Pearl Brandt—she insisted on playing at the big table and I lost a packet.

Toby. You what?

Chaps. Just dropped about four hundred pounds—cleaned myself out.

Stella. Oh, Chaps!

Chaps. She kept on asking me to go in with her, she never ran a hand more than two coups except once, then she passed it after the fourth and it ran eleven times.

Toby. Did it occur to you to strike her in the face?

Chaps. So I wondered if you'd mind waiting for that seven thousand francs I owe you, Stella, until I get my allowance?

Toby. When do you get your allowance?

Chaps. First of May.

Stella. [*Hurriedly.*] Of course I don't mind, Chaps—it doesn't matter a bit.

Toby. God is love, there is no pain.

Chaps. It's awfully sweet of you.

Stella. Don't be silly.

[OLIVE LLOYD-RANSOME'S *voice is heard, outside.*]

Olive. [*Outside.*] Can we come in?

Stella. [*Calling.*] Of course!

Toby. Send for a Bridge table and the Corinthian Bagatelle—don't let's waste a moment.

[OLIVE LLOYD-RANSOME *and* PRINCESS ELÈNA KRASSILOFF *enter.* OLIVE *is smartly dressed and dark.* ELÈNA *is fair and rather vague.*]

Olive. Good morning, everybody—I'm suicidal.

Stella. Why—what's the matter?

Olive. Everything's the matter. I went down twenty mille last night, Precious Bane's got distemper and I had to send him off to the vet. at seven o'clock this morning, and on the top of that I've had a telegram from Nicky and Vera to say they're arriving to-morrow.

Toby. To-morrow!

Olive. It's the most awful bore—it means that I shall have to turn you out, which I absolutely loathe—it also means that I shall have to put off Dolly, because she and Vera aren't speaking and——

Stella. Why don't you put off Nicky and Vera?

Olive. Bob would never forgive me—he worships Nicky. They talk about international finance—also I've already put them off once—I feel absolutely dreadful about the whole business.

Toby. Don't worry about us—we've got to go to the Lorings anyhow.

Olive. But I do—I adore you being here—you're the nicest guests I've ever had in my life.

Elèna. [*Scrutinising the breakfast-tray.*] Do you mind if I take one of your lumps of sugar?

Toby. Not at all—take the whole bowl.

Elèna. Angel!

[*She sits down quietly with the bowl of sugar and devours several lumps.*]

Olive. And to-night we've got the Brandt dinner party—nobody wants to go—I tried to hint that we'd all rather stay in, but they're absolutely set on it—it's something to do with being American, I think, that passion for entertaining in restaurants.

Toby. That means the Casino again.

Stella. Yes, dear, that's what that means.

Chaps. Have you got any messages for May, Olive?

Olive. [*Laughing.*] None that I could possibly send her.

Elèna. He was lovely, that chauffeur—he wore his cap bravely as though he wasn't afraid.

Olive. Wasn't afraid of what, darling?

Toby. George Bainbridge.

Elèna. Anything—anything in the world. I remember he drove me to the station once, and I knew the back of his neck reminded me of someone, and who do you think it was?

Stella. [*Wearily.*] Who?

Elèna. [*Triumphantly.*] Dimitri.

Olive. Everybody reminds you of Dimitri, darling.

Elèna. I loved him dreadfully. [*At the dressing-table.*] Do you mind if I take a little of your scent?

Stella. [*With false enthusiasm.*] Do, dear!

[ELÈNA *sprays herself lavishly.*]

Olive. We're going up to Vence to lunch—do you want to come?

Stella. We shan't be ready in time.

Olive. I'll leave the small car for you—Irving and Pearl want to buy some of that awful pottery.

[MURDOCH *enters through the open door. He is a very correct English butler.*]

Murdoch. Excuse me, madame.

Olive. What is it, Murdoch?

Murdoch. Mr. Guy Forster has arrived, madame, for Lord Chapworth.

Chaps. I must go.

Olive. Has his lordship's luggage gone down?

Murdoch. Yes, madame.

Elèna. I love Guy, he's an angel. Where is he, Murdoch?

Murdoch. In the bar, madame.

Elèna. I'll come down. [MURDOCH *exits.*]

Chaps. Good-bye, Stella—— Good-bye, Toby.

Stella. Good-bye.

Toby. Good-bye.

Chaps. It's awfully sweet of you to hold that over. Good-bye, Olive.

Olive. I'll see you off—don't forget to write in the book—give Guy a drink.

Chaps. He's probably had three already—come on, Elèna.

[ELÈNA *and* CHAPS *go out.*]

Olive. I do feel so horrid about turning you out.

Stella. Don't be silly, darling—we've overstayed frightfully, but we were having such a lovely time.

Olive. If it were anyone else but Vera and Nicky I'd tell them to go to hell, but Bob really has to discuss business with Nicky and—oh, well, I know you understand perfectly.

Toby. Of course we do—when are they arriving?

Olive. To-morrow afternoon—I must pop down and see Chaps off. The car will be waiting for you at twelve-thirty; we'd better meet in the main square.

Stella. All right.

Olive. You *do* understand, don't you?

[*She kisses her hand to them and goes out. There is silence for a moment.*]

Stella. Dear Olive!

Toby. She's done everything but throw us into the drive!

Stella. We must think—we must think.

Toby. What's the use of thinking—we haven't even enough to tip the servants.

Stella. Oh, don't!

Toby. If we asked Olive to lend us five thousand francs, do you think she would?

Stella. Of course she would, and she'd dine out on it for a week—I'd rather die than ask her. Anyway, five thousand francs wouldn't be enough—not nearly enough. We've got to pay our train fares—Nanny's fare home—our Bridge debts—the servants—— Oh, God! [*There is a knock on the door.*] Yes, who is it?

Murdoch. Murdoch, madame.

Toby. Come in! [MURDOCH *enters.*]

Murdoch. Mrs. Lloyd-Ransome asked me to come and see you, madame, about your reservations.

Stella. Reservations?

Murdoch. On the afternoon train to-morrow. I took the liberty of telephoning in to the hall porter of the Majestic about them.

Toby. How thoughtful of you, Murdoch.

Stella. Why the hall porter at the Majestic?

Murdoch. He happens to be a personal friend of mine, madame—he does a lot of odd jobs.

Toby. This one may be odder than he bargained for.

Murdoch. I beg your pardon, sir?

Stella. [*Hurriedly.*] When did you order these reservations, Murdoch?

Murdoch. Last night, madame, directly Mrs. Lloyd-Ransome told me.

Stella. [*With an attempt at lighthearted naturalness.*] What have you got for us?

Murdoch. Two single sleepers and one for your maid—that is what Mrs. Lloyd-Ransome told me you required.

Toby. It's a pity they don't have sitting-rooms on Continental trains.

Stella. I'm afraid you'll have to change them, Murdoch. You see, we're not going back to London—we're going to Venice.

Murdoch. That's all right, madame, Mrs. Lloyd-Ransome told me that, too.

Stella. She didn't happen to mention in passing that my sister was going to have a baby in July?

Murdoch. I'll send the tickets up to you the moment they arrive; there's a small laundry bill as well—I've given that to your maid.

Toby. You think of everything, Murdoch.

Murdoch. Thank you, sir.

Stella. Thank *you,* Murdoch.

[MURDOCH *bows and goes out.*]

Toby. Dear Olive!

Stella. Last night—she had it all arranged last night.

Toby. [*Pensively.*] I think I should like something quite dreadful to happen to Olive, you know—something really humiliating, like being sick at a Court Ball.

Stella. How dare she!

Toby. It's unsufferable.

Stella. After all, she badgered us to come.

Toby. Now she's badgering us to go.

Stella. Isn't there anyone we could cable to?

Toby. Don't be silly, dear—we've exhausted every possible telegraphic saviour years ago. . . . Think—think—there must be some way out.

Stella. There isn't—it's no use—nothing's any use.

Toby. Listen, darling, this is desperate—we've got to take a chance.

Stella. What do you mean?

Toby. Your bracelet.

Stella. Don't be so absurd—it wouldn't fetch fifteen pounds.

Toby. [*Ringing the bell.*] We'll send Nanny into Cannes with it this afternoon.

Stella. But I tell you——

Toby. Shut up. Listen, at worst we can get a couple of thousand francs on it.

Stella. I bet we couldn't.

Toby. With my waistcoat buttons we could.

Stella. Even then—what's the use?

Toby. This is the use—listen—I'll gamble to-night.

Stella. Oh, no, Toby—no!

Toby. It's our only chance. I'll be careful, I promise. We'll have enough for three goes of the minimum at the big table——

Stella. Oh, not the big table!

Toby. The biggest——

[*He springs out of bed and goes over to the dressing-table.* NANNY *enters. She is a capable-looking, middle-aged woman.*]

Stella. Nanny, we're in the most awful trouble!

Nanny. I don't wonder—lying about in bed on a lovely morning like this.

Toby. [*Springing at her with the bracelet and buttons.*] Here, Nanny——

Nanny. What's this?

Toby. Go into Cannes this afternoon and pop them.

Nanny. Oh, I couldn't—I really couldn't!

Toby. You must.

Nanny. That lovely bracelet your Aunt Agnes left you.

Stella. Listen, Nanny, we've got to leave to-morrow and we haven't got any money at all—we owe a lot as well—you must do this for us—go in by the twelve o'clock bus—please, Nanny.

Nanny. I could let you have a little, you know.

Toby. We wouldn't hear of it, Nanny.

Stella. Anyhow, a little's no good—we've got to have a lot.

Nanny. I shan't get much on these.

Stella. Get what you can—promise you will, Nanny.

Nanny. That man in the pawnshop will split his sides when he sees me again.

Toby. Never mind, Nanny—please!

Nanny. Won't you let me advance you a little?—I could go up to seven pounds.

Toby. I tell you, Nanny, we couldn't possibly dream of such a thing.

Nanny. Oh, very well.

Stella. How much do we owe you already?

Nanny. Three hundred and forty-two pounds all told.

Stella. Oh, dear!

[*She collapses on to the bed in helpless laughter.*]

Toby. Go on, Nanny—go like the wind.

[*He pushes her out of the room.* GASTON *enters and crosses over to run the bath —he disappears into the bathroom.* TOBY *gets into bed again.*]

Stella. It's madness—stark, staring madness! [TOBY *casually starts to read the paper again.*] You'll lose it, I know you will. Oh, God, I wish I could play the damned game—— [*There is a pause.*]

Toby. [*Reading.*] Mr. and Mrs. Eugene B. Oglander arrived yesterday at the Hotel Maurice with their daughters Margaret and Helen——

Stella. It's too humiliating—I wish I were dead!

Toby. I wonder what the B stands for?

Stella. [*Bitterly.*] I *know!*

THE LIGHTS FADE

SCENE II

The Scene is the same. TOBY *is lying on the bed, smoking. He is in his dressing-gown and pyjamas.* STELLA, *in a negligee, is doing her face at the dressing-table. The time is about 1.30 a.m.*

Toby. Is there no justice in the universe? No decency?

Stella. Absolutely none, dear. I remember remarking that to Nanny only the other day when the stopper came out of my nail varnish and made the inside of my handbag look like Borsch.*

Toby. There was no reason in what happened—it had nothing to do with the law of logic or the law of compensation or the law of anything—it was just low, senseless bad luck.

Stella. Never mind, darling.

Toby. Mind! I shall mind to the end of my days. The whole beastly scene is etched on to my brain in blood. [*Reconstructing his despair.*] I went up to the table—seven, my lucky number, was miraculously vacant—I sat down and waited for the shoe to come round—just as it was two away from me that New Jersey hag tapped me on the shoulder. "It's terrible," she said. "I can't find a place anywheres—will you be a dear and let me have yours just for a little while? I'm feeling so lucky to-night."

Stella. She was right.

Toby. Right! She ran the bank seventeen times—collected one hundred and seventy thousand francs with all the delicacy of a starving jaguar let loose in a butcher's shop —and graciously gave me back my place.

Stella. Whereupon you proceeded to lose our two thousand francs in the brief space of four minutes, borrow five hundred francs from Bertie Gifford, who will never let us forget it, lose that too, and join me in the bar wearing what might be moderately described as a 'set look.'

Toby. Correct. Have you anything more to say?

Stella. Not for the moment.

Toby. Good! Then we might talk of something else.

Stella. I can't see any necessity to talk at all.

Toby. That is only because you are temporarily exhausted by your own verbosity. Your natural flow will return in a minute.

Stella. I was fond of Aunt Agnes and she was fond of me.

Toby. That rather cloying relationship belongs mercifully to the days before I met you.

Stella. She left me that bracelet in her will.

Toby. It seems odd that she should symbolize her almost incestuous love for you by such an undistinguished little trinket.

Stella. You have a disgusting mind, Toby.

Toby. I said almost.

Stella. Aunt Agnes was the most generous woman in the world.

Toby. I suspect that your memory of her

* A popular Russian soup colored with beet juice.

has been softened by time. To the impartial observer she appears to have been a mean old bitch.

Stella. Toby!

Toby. If it's all the same to you, I would prefer to leave Aunt Agnes where she rightly belongs, warbling through eternity with the Feathered Choir.

Stella. It seems a pity that you can't turn your devastating wit to a more commercial advantage—you should write a gossip column.

Toby. I haven't got a title.

Stella. Oh, shut up!

Toby. That was merely rude.

Stella. There's no sense in going on like this—snapping at each other—we've got to face facts——

Toby. [*Rolling over.*] Oh, God!

Stella. [*Turning round.*] Toby, don't you see——

Toby. Your passion for facing facts is rapidly becoming pathological. You'll go mad, that's what you'll do, and spend your declining years being led about some awful institute by a keeper—facing the fact that you're the Empress Eugènie.

Stella. Don't be so idiotic.

Toby. I'm sick of facing facts; in future I shall cut every fact I meet stone dead—I intend to relax, to live in a lovely dream world of my own where everything is hilariously untrue. After all, at least three-quarters of the civilised world do it, why shouldn't I?

Stella. Why shouldn't you what?

Toby. Delude myself! I'm going to start deluding myself this very minute. I'm going to begin with the Old Testament and believe every word of it—I'm going to believe in Jehovah and Buddha and Krishna and Mahomet and Luther and Mary Baker Eddy and Aimèe Semple Macpherson—I'm even going to believe in Aunt Agnes!

Stella. Will you shut up about Aunt Agnes!

Toby. It is possible, in my present state of splendid detachment, that I might go off into a Yogi trance and stay upside down for several days—in that case all our troubles would be over—even Olive's social conscience would jib at one of her guests being carried out of the house in a sort of sailor's knot.

Stella. Darling, darling Toby!

[*She rushes to him and flings her arms round his neck.*]

Toby. Look out—you're strangling me.

Stella. I've been wanting to strangle you for hours and now I'm doing it—it's heaven!

Toby. This might lead to almost anything.

Stella. [*In his arms.*] Fiddling while Rome's burning—that's what we're doing.

Toby. In the present circumstances fiddling sounds singularly offensive.

Stella. I didn't mean that sort of fiddling.

Toby. Really, Stella——

Stella. Oh, darling, what are we to do?

Toby. Let's go quietly but firmly along the passage and murder Pearl Brandt.

Stella. We should be hanged.

Toby. It would be worth it.

Stella. She sleeps alone, you know—Irving is separated from her by the bathroom—it would be deliciously easy.

Toby. [*Wistfully.*] I hate her so. There's a certain austere scientific beauty about my hatred for that shrill harpy—like higher mathematics.

Stella. I'd like to fasten that wad of thousand franc notes to her nose with a safety-pin.

Toby. I had other plans for them.

Stella. Hush, darling.

Toby. [*Jumping up and striding about the room.*] I can't bear it—I really can't!

Stella. Well, now let's talk about something else. I consider this particular topic exhausted and I don't want to get angry again.

Toby. Angry!—Again! I shall never stop being angry until the end of my days.

Stella. Being angry is very bad for you—I believe that when you are angry all the red corpuscles in your blood fight with the white ones.

Toby. If that's so, my circulation at the moment would make the battle of Mons look like a Morris dance.

Stella. It's dreadfully late, we'd better go to sleep.

Toby. I shall never sleep again.

Stella. Nonsense!—go and brush your teeth.

Toby. We must think of something.

Stella. No, we mustn't—we're worn out—go on.

Toby. But, darling——

Stella. Go on—leave the door open—the noise of your gargling will give me a sense of security, as though everything was all right. [TOBY *goes into the bathroom, leaving the door open.* STELLA *gives a few final pats to her face and tries to spray herself with scent, but there isn't any left.*] Toby!

Toby. What?

Stella. Were Russians always predatory—even before the Revolution, I mean?

Toby. I expect so. Why?

Stella. Elèna's splashed herself from head to foot with the last precious drops of my scent this morning.

Toby. Personally, I'm very glad—I never cared for it.

Stella. That's beside the point.

Toby. It smells like bad salad dressing.

Stella. Smelt, dear—you can use the past tense now.

Toby. Good—from now onwards I intend to live in the past anyhow—the present is too unbearable. I intend to go back to the happy scenes of my boyhood. . . . [*After a pause, during which the sound of gargling is heard.*] Stella!

Stella. [*Getting into bed.*] What?

Toby. What are we going to do?

Stella. I told you just now—I refuse to discuss it—I'm too tired.

Toby. If you broke your leg we should have to stay, shouldn't we?

Stella. I have no intention of breaking my leg.

Toby. Modern women have no courage—in olden times women did brave things for their menfolk every day of the week.

Stella. I don't look upon you as my menfolk.

Toby. Think of the girl who put her arm through the latches of the door to save Bonnie Prince Charlie.

Stella. In my opinion a misguided ass.

Toby. I won't hear a word against Flora Macdonald.

Stella. It wasn't Flora Macdonald.

Toby. Don't be so ignorant, of course it was. Flora Macdonald never stopped doing things like that.

Stella. It was not.

Toby. Who was it, then?

Stella. I don't know who it was, but it was *not* Flora Macdonald.

Toby. [*Appearing with a toothbrush.*] I suppose you'll tell me it was Grace Darling in a minute.

Stella. I see no reason for you to suppose any such thing.

Toby. It was Flora Macdonald.

Stella. It's a matter of supreme indifference to me whether it was Nell Gwynn or Marie Antoinette.

Toby. Well, we're getting on—by a process of tedious elimination—we might ultimately arrive at who you think it was.

Stella. I tell you I don't know who it was, I only know who it wasn't, and it wasn't Flora Macdonald.

Toby. Oh, God.

[*He slams into the bathroom in a rage. There is a moment's pause then a crash. Then* Toby *gives a wail of pain.*]

Stella. What's happened?

Toby. I'm hurt.

Stella. What sort of hurt?

Toby. Badly hurt.

Stella. Oh, darling!

[*She jumps out of bed and rushes into the bathroom. The following dialogue takes place off stage.*]

Toby. [*Groaning.*] It was the door of that blasted little cupboard——

Stella. My poor sweet!

Toby. Do something—it's bleeding.

Stella. Where's the iodine?

Toby. How do I know?

Stella. Wait a minute—no, that's eye-drops—here——

Toby. It's agony.

Stella. Stand still.

Toby. I don't want to stand still—I want to jump out of the window. This is the end——

Stella. Don't be so silly!

Toby. Cotton-wool.

Stella. There isn't any.

Toby. There ought to be.

Stella. Wait a minute—I've got some. [*She comes running in and goes to the dressing-table. She rummages in the drawers for a moment and produces some cotton-wool.* Toby *comes in carrying a bottle of iodine. There is an enormous bruise on his forehead which is bleeding slightly.*] Here we are.

Toby. God, what a crack!

Stella. Stand still.

Toby. Do stop telling me to stand still.

Stella. Don't be so irritable.

Toby. [*As she dabs him with iodine.*] Ow!—hell!—ow!——

Stella. Stand still.

Toby. Shut up!

Stella. I'm doing my best—don't be so childish. There!

Toby. [*Looking in the glass.*] For this to happen—on top of everything else—it's too much.

Stella. Never mind, darling.

Toby. It's not even bad enough to keep us here.

Stella. You might pretend it had given you concussion and behave very peculiarly to-morrow morning.

Toby. I couldn't carry it through—I'm too depressed.

Stella. Get into bed, darling.

Toby. The light's on in the bathroom.

Stella. I'll turn it out.

[*She goes into the bathroom and does so, while he takes off his dressing-gown and gets into bed.* Stella *returns.*]

Toby. You don't think we ought to bandage it?

Stella. No—let the air get to it.

Toby. Open the window.

Stella. All right—I was just going to.

Toby. If you're beastly to me I swear to God I'll yell the place down.

[STELLA *opens the window, switches out all lights except one by the bed, and gets into bed.*]

Stella. Does it hurt?

Toby. Was that question merely rhetorical or do you really care?

Stella. Of course I care—it's horrid for you.

Toby. It does hurt, Stella—it hurts dreadfully.

Stella. Try to forget about it.

Toby. That remark was just plain silly.

Stella. Do you want to read?

Toby. Read! I doubt if I shall ever be able to read again.

Stella. I'll turn out the light then.

Toby. It would make no appreciable difference to me if the light of the world went out. My mind is a trackless waste of impenetrable darkness.

Stella. That's right, dear.

[*There is a pause.* STELLA *switches out the bed light.*]

Toby. Stella—what *are* we to do?

Stella. We'll deliver ourselves over to Olive bound and gagged in the morning. We'll meet her delighted, patronising contempt with fortitude—we'll humiliate ourselves without flinching—we'll add up how much we need and borrow it from her gaily, as though we enjoyed it—no matter how broken we are we'll never let her see——

Toby. [*Drowsily.*] Like Flora Macdonald.

Stella. It was *not* Flora Macdonald!

THE LIGHTS FADE

SCENE III

The scene is the same about two hours later. Moonlight is streaming into the room. TOBY *and* STELLA *are fast asleep. There is a slight noise on the verandah, a shadow falls across the moonlight. A man steps softly into the room. His face is muffled. He tiptoes across and trips over the stool in front of the dressing-table.*

Toby. [*Switching on the light.*] Who's there?

Stella. [*Waking.*] Oh, dear!

Stevens. [*Covering them with a revolver.*] Keep quiet.

Toby. Scream, dear, he wouldn't dare to shoot.

Stella. Scream yourself.

Stevens. Oh yes, I would.

Toby. What do you want?

Stevens. I want you to keep quiet.

Toby. Naturally you do—I meant apart from that.

Stevens. Where's your jewellery?

Toby. Number 18, Rue Mirabeau, Cannes.

Stella. We haven't a thing here—you've chosen probably the worst room to burgle in the whole world.

Stevens. Come on—tell me where it is.

[STELLA *makes a sudden movement; he switches his gun towards her.* TOBY *throws a pillow and knocks it out of his hand—he leaps out of bed, there is a scuffle and* TOBY *gets the revolver—he covers the man with it.*]

Toby. Now then!

Stevens. Look out—it's loaded!

Toby. I should damn well hope it was.

Stella. Why aren't you French? We're in France—you ought to be French.

Toby. Take off his muffler, Stella. [*To* STEVENS.] Keep your hands up.

Stella. [*Approaching.*] Excuse me.

Toby. Keep them up.

[STELLA *undoes the scarf from round his mouth.*]

Stella. There now!

Toby. Turn on the other lights, Stella.

Stella. [*Doing so.*] It's a very expensive scarf. [*She looks at the man.*] My God, it's Stevens!

Stevens. Oh, madame!

Stella. Stevens, how *could* you!

Toby. You ought to be ashamed of yourself.

Stevens. I had no idea, sir—madame—I didn't realise you was staying here.

Stella. Did you really mean to burgle this house?

Stevens. Yes, madame.

Stella. But why? You can't suddenly become a burglar all in a minute—you were a respectable chauffeur last week.

Stevens. That was before the crash came, madame.

Toby. You mean it was before George Bainbridge threw you out.

Stevens. Yes, sir.

Stella. [*Reproachfully.*] Oh, Stevens!

Stevens. He sacked me straight away—without even a reference.

Stella. You should have applied to Mrs. Bainbridge.

Toby. Stella!

Stevens. I'm desperate, madame—I haven't got a bob.

Stella. That's no excuse for becoming a criminal.

Stevens. It's the usual excuse—begging your pardon, madame.

Stella. Do you mean to tell me Mrs. Bainbridge didn't give you so much as a——

Toby. Stella, be quiet—your behaviour is in the worst possible taste.

Stella. I think it's a dirty shame—you have my sympathy, Stevens.

Stevens. Thank you, madame.

Toby. You'd better get out, Stevens—I'll keep the gun, if you don't mind.

Stevens. It belongs to Meadows, sir—Mr. Bainbridge's butler—I pinched it. If you wouldn't mind returning it to him I should be much obliged.

Toby. We ought to hand you over to the police.

Stevens. Oh, please don't do that, sir. I've had an awful time. I've got a wife and child in Walthamstow, I've got to get back somehow.

Stella. We can't help you—we would if we could, but——

Toby. Be quiet, Stella.

Stevens. Thank you, madame—you're very kind.

Toby. Go on—get out as quickly as you can.

Stevens. Yes, sir. Thank you, sir.

Toby. Go on.

[STEVENS *goes to the window.*]

Stella. Stop!

Toby. Stella!

Stella. Come back a minute.

Toby. Don't be an idiot, Stella.

Stella. Leave this to me—I know what I'm doing.

Toby. What are you talking about?

Stella. Sit down, Stevens.

Toby. Have you gone mad?

Stella. Shut up—sit down, Stevens.

Stevens. [*Bewildered.*] Yes, madame.

[*He sits down.*]

Stella. Now then——

Toby. Look here——

Stella. Put that gun down, Toby, and don't keep on waving it about like pampas grass—Stevens may be a potential thief, but he isn't a murderer and even if he were, he wouldn't murder us; he likes us, don't you, Stevens?

Stevens. Very much, madame.

Stella. You seem to forget, Toby, that when we were staying with the Bainbridges in Scotland last September, Stevens lent you seven pounds.

Toby. I paid it back.

Stevens. You certainly did, sir; within the month.

Stella. Do you trust us, Stevens?

Stevens. Trust you, madame?

Stella. Yes—I mean will you trust us if we trust you?

Stevens. I don't understand, madame.

Stella. I'll explain. We're broke—cleaned out.

Stevens. Yes, madame.

Stella. You're broke, too—in addition to which you've involved yourself in one of the juiciest scandals the Riviera has known for years.

Stevens. It wasn't my fault, madame—I——

Stella. I never imagined for one moment that it was.

Toby. Look here, Stella—what is the use——?

Stella. Toby, don't be such a fool—don't you see?

Toby. See what?

Stella. God sent Stevens to us to-night, Toby—or it may have been Buddha, or Mahomet or Mary Baker Eddy, but whoever it was he's here hale and hearty and ready to help us—you are ready to help us, aren't you, Stevens?

Stevens. Help you, madame?

Stella. If you can help yourself at the same time.

Stevens. Anything you say, madame—you can rely on me.

Toby. [*At last realising what she means.*] Stella—we can't!

Stella. We can—and we will.

Toby. You're raving.

Stella I'd rather face prison than Olive's patronising sneer to-morrow morning.

Stevens. [*Noticing* TOBY's *wound.*] Oh, sir, what have you done to your head?

Toby. Never mind about that now.

Stella. Mind about it—it's the most important thing in the world. You did it, Stevens—you knocked him out——

Stevens. Oh, madame, I'd never do such a thing.

Stella. Yes, you would—if you were an intelligent professional burglar you would—you'd knock him out; then you'd bind and gag us both—then you'd burgle the house and get away with the swag.

Stevens. Swag, madame?

Stella. That's what it's called.

Stevens. What what's called, madame?

Stella. The money that you're going to take from this house to-night.

Stevens. [*Rising.*] Oh, madame!

Stella. Sit down and listen. [STEVENS *sinks back again.*] A few yards away from this room there is wrapped in plebeian slumber a lady from New Jersey called Mrs. Irving Brandt——

Toby. Go on, darling—I'm with you.

Stella. In the top right-hand drawer of her dressing-table, just to the left of the door, there is a bundle of one hundred and seventy thousand francs——

Stevens. Oh, dear!

Stella. Halves, Stevens, halves!

Stevens. Oh, madame—I don't think I dare.

Toby. Be a man, Stevens.

Stella. Go now—it's the last door on the right at the end of the passage.

Toby. The carpet is ostentatiously soft, so you won't be heard.

Stella. If by any chance she wakes up and screams, double back here and out of the window—I'll scream, too, and bathe my husband's head. If, on the other hand, you get away with it—come back here, give us half, tie us both up and get out.

Stevens. All right, madame—I'll do it.

Toby. Think of Walthamstow.

Stella. Go on—last door on the right—dressing-table on left of the door—top right-hand drawer.

Toby. [*Holding out his hand.*] Good luck.

[STEVENS *shakes it.*]

Stella. [*Also shaking his hand.*] Good luck, Stevens.

Toby. Turn out the lights.

Stella. [*Doing so.*] There.

[STEVENS *slips out of the room. They listen anxiously for a moment.*]

Stella. [*In a whisper.*] Quick—get the bedclothes off the bed—and your dressing-gown cord——

Toby. [*Also in a whisper.*] My feet are cold.

Stella. [*Wrestling with the bedclothes.*] Put on your slippers.

Toby. [*Doing so.*] Handkerchiefs for gags.

[*He rummages in the dressing-table drawers.*]

Stella. Don't make such a row.

Toby. My God!

Stella. What is it?

Toby. Stevens might bind and gag us and then take all the money.

Stella. Don't be so absurd—he's utterly honest—you only have to look at him. His moral values may wobble a bit on the sex side, but otherwise I'm certain his integrity is beyond question. Why, he was a valet before he was a chauffeur—he's been trained as a gentleman's gentleman—they're always much more reliable than gentlemen.

Toby. Hush!—did you hear anything?

Stella. He's coming back. [*They stand in silence for a moment.* STEVENS *creeps back into the room. He closes the door softly after him.*] Got it?

Stevens. Yes.

Stella. Switch on the bed-light, Toby.

Toby. [*Doing so.*] Was she asleep?

Stevens. Snoring, sir.

Stella. I'm *glad!*

Stevens. Here you are, madame.

[*He flings the wad of notes on the bed.*]

Toby. Come on—help divide them.

Stevens. I'd rather not, sir, if you don't mind—I'd rather you had the money. I happened to find these on the dressing-table—they'll do me nicely.

[*He produces several diamond bracelets, some rings and a jewelled cigarette-case.*]

Stella. Stevens, for shame!—take them back at once!

Toby. They can be traced.

Stevens. I'll manage all right, sir.

Stella. You must take half the money.

Stevens. I'd really rather not.

Toby. It's extraordinarily generous of you, Stevens.

Stevens. You and Madame have always been very nice to me, sir—it feels somehow as if we was old friends.

Stella. Thank you, Stevens.

Toby. [*Giving him some bills.*] Here, you must take these, for travelling expenses.

Stevens. Very well, sir—if you insist.

Toby. Where shall I put the rest?

Stella. Put eleven thousand in the drawer and the rest in the inside pocket of your dinner-jacket.

Stevens. Allow me, sir.

Toby. Thank you, Stevens.

[STEVENS *puts some notes in the dressing-table drawer and stuffs the rest into* TOBY'S *dinner-coat; he then proceeds to fold it neatly and lay it on the chair.*]

Stella. Never mind about that now, Stevens—bind and gag us.

[*The following dialogue takes place while they are being bound and gagged.*]

Toby. Do you intend to go direct to England?

Stevens. Yes, sir. I thought of going by boat from Marseilles. I've never seen Gibraltar.

Toby. It's very impressive.

Stella. The P. & O. boats always stop at

Marseilles, don't they? I remember Blanche came home on one.

Stevens. I think I shall try another Line this time, madame. I once went P. & O. as far as Egypt with Mr. Bainbridge—and I didn't fancy it.

Toby. Why not, Stevens?

Stevens. All them bugles got me down, sir —it was like being in the army all over again.

Stella. You must look us up when you come to London—we might be able to help you find a job.

Stevens. Thank you, madame.

Toby. We're in the book.

Stevens. As a matter of fact, I've been thinking for a long time of giving up domestic service—I'd rather get a job that was more steady—more respectable, if you know what I mean.

Stella. I couldn't know better.

Stevens. I think my brother will be able to help me.

Toby. Oh—what does he do?

Stevens. He's got a very nice position in Barclay's Bank, sir.

Toby. Oh, I see.

[*By this time they are both successfully tied to two chairs.*]

Stevens. Now for the gags.

Stella. They're on the dressing-table.

[STEVENS *politely gags them.*]

Stevens. Let me know if they're too tight.

Toby. They ought to be pretty tight.

Stevens. I think we might allow ourselves a little poetic license, don't you, sir?

Toby. Thank you, Stevens.

Stevens. [*Regarding them.*] Quite comfy? [*They both nod.*] Light on or off?—One nod for on—two nods for off. [*They both nod once.*] Well, I'll be getting along now—thank you very much, sir and madame—it's been a great pleasure meeting you again. Good night.

[*He bows politely and goes out of the window. They are left tied to the chairs. Behind their gags it is apparent that they are convulsed with laughter.* STELLA *loosens her gag enough to speak.*]

Stella. If I'd been May Bainbridge, I'd have married him!

CURTAIN

HELLO OUT THERE*

[*A One-Act Play*]

By

WILLIAM SAROYAN

"HELLO OUT THERE," ALTHOUGH A short play, holds a conspicuous place among Saroyan's extensive works for the theatre. It was fortunate in its first New York production. After two years of this dramatist's relative failures on Broadway, its hypnotic performance by Eddie Dowling and Julie Haydon in 1942 did much to reawaken the immense interest and the critical discussions that attended *My Heart's in the Highlands* and the author's prize-winning *The Time of Your Life* three years earlier. *Hello Out There* had the further advantage of appearing on a double bill with G. K. Chesterton's *Magic*, which, in comparison, seemed to all the critics inept and lifeless. Some of them who had previously voiced one or more of the *clichés* about Saroyan's earlier plays—"ununified," "vague," "whimsical," "sentimental," and "lacking action and emotional appeal"—were now surprised to discover in the new play "directness" and "great moving force." It was even called "one of the very best things Saroyan has written—compassionate, direct, throbbing with suspense, and lighting a sordid situation with beauty." Still more gratifying to Saroyan himself was its successful performance in Santa Barbara in 1941 as a curtain-raiser to *The Devil's Disciple* by the one dramatist that above all others he admired and acknowledged as an "influence."

At this distance, Stark Young's comment seems nearest to the truth: "There was a human feeling and a beat of intensity moving outward from the heart of the piece and there was a certain elusive but fine weaving and pressure of rhythm within the whole of it." These words convey the real meaning of Saroyan's contribution to the American theatre. It has been a unique one—purposefully his own. Luckily it was not in his nature to imitate or to follow; otherwise he might now be one of the thwarted Armenian editors or poets that he admired and pitied in Fresno. To do so would be to renounce the best in himself, a best that amounts to a personal religion. Its chief tenet is familiar to all who have read a story or seen a play of his: a compassionate tolerance of all, good or bad, that walk the earth. To many this seems at best an amiable sentimentality, and at worst a reflection of moral indifference. To Saroyan it is neither, but is the inevitable expression of a deeper faith in the rightness of creation.

In *Coming Through the Rye*, when murder-destined Steve describes Earth as filled up "with terrible unclean animals in clothes," the all-wise Carroll retorts, "Those *animals* have created several magnificent civilizations, and right now they are creating another one. It's a privilege to participate."

Saroyan has allured himself into a somewhat forbidding Arden of the mind, seeing "good in everything"; his Arden is not of woods and fields, but of streets, honky-tonks, raffish people, and seeming futilities. In *The Bicycle Rider of Beverly Hills* he speaks bluntly of his search begun in impoverished boyhood: "In the most commonplace, tiresome, ridiculous, malicious, coarse, crude, or even crooked people or events I had to seek out rare things, good things, comic things, and I did so. . . . At the same time certain failures seemed to me the greatest men in town."

He speaks as bluntly of his independence as a writer. In *My Name Is Aram*, he says of his hero, obviously himself: "He does not belong to any school of writing and does not believe that [his own] manner of writing is the way to get a message to go high-rolling down the ages, but, at the same time, for a less ambitious intention, he can find no fault with the method, other than, perhaps, that it tends to make the writer unqualified for membership in The Authors' League of America." One may have valid doubts of Saroyan's self-created Arden of kindliness, but not of his deep sincerity as its apostle.

He has, too, an almost mystic faith in the careless rapidity with which he tells us he writes, and in the unmistakable rhythms of his style, for they come spontaneously from a tireless, driving energy that made him, as a boy, love the hoof-beats of runaway horses and the tapping of dancers' feet, and that won him, as a messenger, the nickname "Speed." It is surely Saroyan's rhythmic gusto that makes prize-fighter Blackstone say to the deaf boy in *Talking to You* that the sounds he likes best are: "Good talk, I guess. Good loud singing. Good tap-dancing. Good bag-punching. I like to hear a crowd. But the best of all, I guess, is laughing." This egoistic intensity at its best has given freshness and lyric eloquence to his innumerable stories, novels, and plays; and in *Hello Out There* it is at its best. In semi-professional and college productions this play has re-created unfailingly its original spell. The dramatist's obvious intent—to present a fragment of spiritual reality at white heat before it is swept away by an unfeeling counter-reality—accounts for the seemingly conventional form that in this instance, as in few other Saroyan plays, happens to serve best the dramatist's purpose. The rhythms of life and speech, the compassion, the beauty of spirit are Saroyan's own. They lift this poignant tragedy well above what O'Neill called "the banality of surfaces."

WILLIAM SAROYAN

Born 1908, Fresno, California, of Armenian parents from Bitlis in Turkish Armenia. Father, a Presbyterian preacher and writer, educated in an American mission school at Bitlis.

1911, Entered an Oakland orphanage upon death of father.

1915, Attended Fresno public schools to the second grade of high school. Otherwise self-educated from extensive reading. Worked as newsboy, telegraph messenger, vineyard worker, postal employee, later becoming office manager of the San Francisco Postal Telegraph Company.

1921, Began story writing, inspired by Guy de Maupassant's *The Bell*.

1933, First publication, "The Broken Wheel," in a Boston Armenian Magazine (*Hairenik*). Reprinted in E. J. O'Brien's *Best Short Stories of 1934* (pseudonym: Sirak Goryan).

1934, First story collection: *The Daring Young Man on the Flying Trapeze*. (Before 1940, said to have written 400 stories, appearing in 9 volumes.)

1935, First play: *Subway Circus*. Published in *Razzle Dazzle*, 1942. Traveled in Armenia and Russia. Notes of the tour in *Inhale and Exhale*.

1939, First New York production: *My Heart's in the Highlands*, by The Group Theatre; followed the same year by *The Time of Your Life*, produced by actor-manager Eddie Dowling under the auspices of the New York Theatre Guild. The latter play filmed in 1948.

1939, Awarded the Drama Critics' Circle and the Pulitzer

prizes for *The Time of Your Life*. Declined the latter because of its commercial implications.

1939, *Love's Old Sweet Song* produced by the Theatre Guild with Walter Hampden in the cast.

1941, "The Saroyan Theatre," organized and directed by the dramatist himself, produced *Across the Board* and *Talking to You*. Closed after the first week for failure to attract.

1941, His first ballet, "The Great American Goof" produced by the New York Ballet Theatre.

1942, *Hello Out There* successfully produced and acted by Eddie Dowling with Julie Haydon.

1942, Directed the filming of script, "The Good Job."

1943, Elected to the Art Institute of America.

Since 1942 no new play by this dramatist has been given important production, although in the meantime he has completed eleven full-length plays and some two dozen short ones. Six of the latter have appeared on T.V. (See "Saroyan on Saroyan," *New York Times*, January 18, 1955.) He insists on directing his own plays and refuses to abandon his experimental methods for those of the "sure-fire hit."

PLAYS

1939 *My Heart's in the Highlands*, adapted from the author's story, "The Man with the Heart in the Highlands." A one-act version had been published in *Theatre Arts*, 1936. 1939 *Love's Old Sweet Song*. 1940 *The Hero of the World*. 1940 *Something about a Soldier*. 1941 *Three Plays: The Beautiful People, Sweeney in the Trees, Across the Board on Tomorrow Morning*. 1942 *Razzle Dazzle* ("being many kinds of short plays as well as the story of writing them"); its short plays: *Hello Out There, Coming Through the Rye, Talking to You, Opera, Opera* (a musical satire), *The Agony of Little Nations, The Hungerers, Elmer and Lily* (a revue), *Subway Circus* (a vaudeville; the author's first dramatic composition, 1935); Ballets: *The Great American Goof, The Poetic Situation in America, Bad Men in the West;* Radio Scripts: *Special Announcement, a Radio Poem, Radio Play, The People with Light Coming Out of Them, There's Something I Got to Tell You*. 1942 *Jim Dandy, a Fat Man in a Famine* (published 1947). 1942 *The Good Job* (a film script). 1942 *The Human Comedy* (a film script from the author's novel). 1943 *Get Away, Old Man*. Full-length plays written since 1943, not produced: 1949 *Once Around the Block*. 1951 *Don't Go Away Mad*, title play of volume with *Sam Ego's House, A Decent Birth, a Happy Funeral*. 1952 *The Slaughter of the Innocents* (published in *Theatre Arts*, November, 1952). 1954 *The Cave Dwellers*. The following are mentioned without dates by the dramatist, who also refers to "about two dozen shorter plays" written since 1943, six of which were televised on the "Omnibus" program: *The Violin Messiah. Mano's Depression. The Muscat Vineyard. The Lost Child's Fireflies. An Imaginary Character Named Saroyan.*

WRITINGS ON DRAMA

Prefaces and essays in the volumes of his published plays. See especially *The Time of Your Life*, 1939, p. 199 ff.; *Three Plays*, 1939, p. 13 f.; *Razzle Dazzle*, 1942 (mostly personal notes). "How to See," *Theatre Arts*, March, 1949. "The Theatre Takes Stock," *Theatre Arts*, May, 1940. "A Formula for the Theatre," *New York Times Magazine*, October 10, 1948. "Critical Comments," printed with *The Slaughter of the Innocents, Theatre Arts*, November, 1952. "Saroyan Speaks Up," *Theatre Arts*, March, 1954. "Time of My Life," *Theatre Arts*, January, 1954. "There Ought to Be More," *Nation*, February 27, 1954. "Saroyan on Saroyan," *New York Times*, January 18, 1955.

HELLO OUT THERE

There is a FELLOW *in a small-town prison cell, tapping slowly on the floor with a spoon. After tapping half a minute, as if he were trying to telegraph words, he gets up and begins walking around the cell. At last he stops, stands at the center of the cell, and doesn't move for a long time. He feels his head, as if it were wounded. Then he looks around. Then he calls out dramatically, kidding the world.*

Young Man. Hello—out there! [*Pause.*] Hello—out there! Hello—out there! [*Long pause.*] Nobody out there. [*Still more dramatically, but more comically, too.*] Hello—out there! Hello—out there!

[*A* GIRL'S *voice is heard, very sweet and soft.*]

The Voice. Hello.

Young Man. Hello—out there.

The Voice. Hello.

Young Man. Is that you, Katey?

The Voice. No—this here is Emily.

Young Man. Who? [*Swiftly.*] Hello out there.

The Voice. Emily.

Young Man. Emily who? I don't know anybody named Emily. Are you that girl I met at Sam's in Salinas about three years ago?

The Voice. No—I'm the girl who cooks here. I'm the cook. I've never been in Salinas. I don't even know where it is.

Young Man. Hello out there. You say you cook here?

The Voice. Yes.

Young Man. Well, why don't you study up and learn to cook? How come I don't get no jello or anything good?

The Voice. I just cook what they tell me to. [*Pause.*] You lonesome?

Young Man. Lonesome as a coyote. Hear me hollering? Hello out there!

The Voice. Who you hollering to?

Young Man. Well—nobody, I guess. I been trying to think of somebody to write a letter to, but I can't think of anybody.

The Voice. What about Katey?

Young Man. I don't know anybody named Katey.

The Voice. Then why did you say, Is that you, Katey?

Young Man. Katey's a good name. I always did like a name like Katey. I never *knew* anybody named Katey, though.

The Voice. I did.

Young Man. Yeah? What was she like? Tall girl, or little one?

The Voice. Kind of medium.

Young Man. Hello out there. What sort of a looking girl are you?

The Voice. Oh, I don't know.

Young Man. Didn't anybody ever tell you? Didn't anybody ever talk to you that way?

The Voice. What way?

Young Man. You know. Didn't they?

The Voice. No, they didn't.

Young Man. Ah, the fools—they should have. I can tell from your voice you're O.K.

The Voice. Maybe I am and maybe I ain't.

Young Man. I never missed yet.

The Voice. Yeah, I know. That's why you're in jail.

Young Man. The whole thing was a mistake.

The Voice. They claim it was rape.

Young Man. No—it wasn't.

The Voice. That's what they claim it was.

Young Man. They're a lot of fools.

The Voice. Well, you sure are in trouble. Are you scared?

Young Man. Scared to death. [*Suddenly.*] Hello out there!

The Voice. What do you keep saying that for all the time?

Young Man. I'm lonesome. I'm as lonesome as a coyote. [*A long one.*] Hello—out there!

[*The* GIRL *appears, over to one side. She is a plain girl in plain clothes.*]

The Girl. I'm kind of lonesome, too.

Young Man. [*Turning and looking at her.*] Hey—— No fooling? Are you?

The Girl. Yeah—— I'm almost as lonesome as a coyote myself.

Young Man. Who *you* lonesome for?

The Girl. I don't know.

Young Man. It's the same with me. The minute they put you in a place like this you remember all the girls you ever knew, and all the girls you didn't get to know, and it sure gets lonesome.

The Girl. I bet it does.

Young Man. Ah, it's awful. [*Pause.*] You're a pretty kid, you know that?

The Girl. You're just talking.

Young Man. No, I'm not just talking—you *are* pretty. Any fool could see that. You're just about the prettiest kid in the whole world.

The Girl. I'm not—and you know it.

Young Man. No—you are. I never saw anyone prettier in all my born days, in all my travels. I knew Texas would bring me luck.

The Girl. Luck? You're in jail, aren't you? You've got a whole gang of people all worked up, haven't you?

Young Man. Ah, that's nothing. I'll get out of this.

The Girl. Maybe.

Young Man. No, I'll be all right—*now.*

The Girl. What do you mean—now?

Young Man. I mean after seeing you. I got something now. You know for a while there I didn't care one way or another. Tired. [*Pause.*] Tired of trying for the best all the time and never getting it. [*Suddenly.*] Hello out there!

The Girl. Who you calling now?

Young Man. You.

The Girl. Why, I'm right here.

Young Man. I know. [*Calling.*] Hello out there!

The Girl. Hello.

Young Man. Ah, you're sweet. [*Pause.*] I'm going to marry *you.* I'm going away with *you.* I'm going to take you to San Francisco or some place like that. I *am,* now. I'm going to win myself some real money, too. I'm going to study 'em real careful and pick myself some winners, and we're going to have a lot of money.

The Girl. Yeah?

Young Man. Yeah. Tell me your name and all that stuff.

The Girl. Emily.

Young Man. I know that. What's the rest of it? Where were you born? Come on, tell me the whole thing.

The Girl. Emily Smith.

Young Man. Honest to God?

The Girl. Honest. That's my name—Emily Smith.

Young Man. Ah, you're the sweetest girl in the whole world.

The Girl. Why?

Young Man. I don't know why, but you are, that's all. Where were you born?

The Girl. Matador, Texas.

Young Man. Where's that?

The Girl. Right here.

Young Man. Is this Matador, Texas?

The Girl. Yeah, it's Matador. They brought you here from Wheeling.

Young Man. Is that where I was—Wheeling?

The Girl. Didn't you even know what town you were in?

Young Man. All towns are alike. You don't go up and ask somebody what town you're in. It doesn't make any difference. How far away is Wheeling?

The Girl. Sixteen or seventeen miles. Didn't you know they moved you?

Young Man. How could I know, when I was out—cold? Somebody hit me over the head with a lead pipe or something. What'd they hit me for?

The Girl. Rape—that's what they *said.*

Young Man. Ah, that's a lie. [*Amazed, almost to himself.*] She wanted me to give her money.

The Girl. Money?

Young Man. Yeah, if I'd have known she was a woman like that—well, by God, I'd have gone on down the street and stretched out in a park somewhere and gone to sleep.

The Girl. Is that what she wanted—money?

Young Man. Yeah. A fellow like me hopping freights all over the country, trying to break his bad luck, going from one poor little town to another, trying to get in on something good somewhere, and she asks for money. I thought she was lonesome. She *said* she was.

The Girl. Maybe she was.

Young Man. She was *something.*

The Girl. I guess I'd never see you, if it didn't happen, though.

Young Man. Oh, I don't know—maybe I'd just mosey along this way and see you in this town somewhere. I'd recognize you, too.

The Girl. Recognize me?

Young Man. Sure, I'd recognize you the minute I laid eyes on you.

The Girl. Well, who would I be?

Young Man. Mine, that's who.

The Girl. Honest?

Young Man. Honest to God.

The Girl. You just say that because you're in jail.

Young Man. No, I mean it. You just pack up and wait for me. We'll high-roll the hell out of here to Frisco.

The Girl. You're just lonesome.

Young Man. I been lonesome all my life—there's no cure for that—but you and me—we can have a lot of fun hanging around together. You'll bring me luck. I know it.

The Girl. What are you looking for luck for all the time?

Young Man. I'm a gambler. I don't work. I've *got* to have luck, or I'm a bum. I haven't had any decent luck in years. Two whole years now—one place to another. Bad luck all the time. That's why I got in trouble back there in Wheeling, too. That was no accident. That was my bad luck following me around. So here I am, with my head half busted. I guess it was her old man that did it.

The Girl. You mean her father?

Young Man. No, her husband. If I had an old lady like that, I'd throw her out.

The Girl. Do you think you'll have better luck, if I go with you?

Young Man. It's a cinch. I'm a good handicapper. All I need is somebody good like you with me. It's no good always walking around in the streets for anything that might be there at the time. You got to have somebody staying with you all the time—through winters when it's cold, and springtime when it's pretty, and summertime when it's nice and hot and you can go swimming—through *all* the times—rain and snow and all the different kinds of weather a man's got to go through before he dies. You got to have somebody who's right. Somebody who knows you, from away back. You got to have somebody who even knows you're wrong but likes you just the same. I know I'm wrong, but I just don't want anything the hard way, working like a dog, or the *easy* way, working like a dog—working's the hard way and the easy way both. All I got to do is beat the price, always—and then I don't feel lousy and don't hate anybody. If you go along with me, I'll be the finest guy anybody ever saw. I won't be wrong any more. You know when you get enough of that money, you *can't* be wrong any more—you're right because the money says so. I'll have a lot of money and you'll be just about the prettiest, most wonderful kid in the whole world. I'll be proud walking around Frisco with you on my arm and people turning around to look at us.

The Girl. Do you think they will?

Young Man. Sure they will. When I get back in some decent clothes, and you're on my arm—well, Katey, they'll turn around and look, and they'll see something, too.

The Girl. Katey?

Young Man. Yeah—that's your name from now on. You're the first girl I ever called Katey. I've been saving it for you. O.K.?

The Girl. O.K.

Young Man. How long have I been here?

The Girl. Since last night. You didn't wake up until late this morning, though.

Young Man. What time is it now? About nine?

The Girl. About ten.

Young Man. Have you got the key to this lousy cell?

The Girl. No. They don't let me fool with any keys.

Young Man. Well, can you get it?

The Girl. No.

Young Man. Can you *try?*

The Girl. They wouldn't let me get near any keys. I cook for this jail, when they've got somebody in it. I clean up and things like that.

Young Man. Well, I want to get out of here. Don't you know the guy that runs this joint?

The Girl. I know him, but he wouldn't let you out. They were talking of taking you to another jail in another town.

Young Man. Yeah? Why?

The Girl. Because they're afraid.

Young Man. What are they afraid of?

The Girl. They're afraid these people from Wheeling will come over in the middle of the night and break in.

Young Man. Yeah? What do they want to do that for?

The Girl. Don't *you* know what they want to do it for?

Young Man. Yeah, I know all right.

The Girl. Are you scared?

Young Man. Sure I'm scared. Nothing scares a man more than ignorance. You can argue with people who ain't fools, but you can't argue with fools—they just go to work and do what they're set on doing. Get me out of here.

The Girl. How?

Young Man. Well, go get the guy with the key, and let me talk to him.

The Girl. He's gone home. Everybody's gone home.

Young Man. You mean I'm in this little jail all alone?

The Girl. Well—yeah—except me.

Young Man. Well, what's the big idea—doesn't anybody stay here all the time?

The Girl. No, they go home every night. I clean up and then I go, too. I hung around tonight.

Young Man. What made you do that?

The Girl. I wanted to talk to you.

Young Man. Honest? What did you want to talk about?

The Girl. Oh, I don't know. I took care of you last night. You were talking in your sleep. You liked me, too. I didn't think you'd like me when you woke up, though.

Young Man. Yeah? Why not?

The Girl. I don't know.

Young Man. Yeah? Well, you're wonderful, see?

The Girl. Nobody ever talked to me that way. All the fellows in town—— [*Pause.*]

Young Man. What about 'em? [*Pause.*] Well, what about 'em? Come on—tell me.

The Girl. They laugh at me.

Young Man. Laugh at *you?* They're fools. What do they know about anything? You go get your things and come back here. I'll take you with me to Frisco. How old are you?

The Girl. Oh, I'm of age.

Young Man. How old are you?—Don't lie to me! Sixteen?

The Girl. I'm seventeen.

Young Man. Well, bring your father and mother. We'll get married before we go.

The Girl. They wouldn't let me go.

Young Man. Why not?

The Girl. I don't know, but they wouldn't. I know they wouldn't.

Young Man. You go tell your father not to be a fool, see? What is he, a farmer?

The Girl. No—nothing. He gets a little relief from the government because he's supposed to be hurt or something—his side hurts, he says. I don't know what it is.

Young Man. Ah, he's a liar. Well, I'm taking you with me, see?

The Girl. He takes the money I earn, too.

Young Man. He's got no right to do that.

The Girl. I know it, but he does it.

Young Man. [*Almost to himself.*] This world stinks. You shouldn't have been born in this town, anyway, and you shouldn't have had a man like that for a father, either.

The Girl. Sometimes I feel sorry for him.

Young Man. Never mind feeling sorry for him. [*Pointing a finger.*] I'm going to talk to your father some day. I've got a few things to tell that guy.

The Girl. I know you have.

Young Man. [*Suddenly.*] Hello—out there! See if you can get that fellow with the keys to come down and let me out.

The Girl. Oh, I couldn't.

Young Man. Why not?

The Girl. I'm nobody here—they give me fifty cents every day I work.

Young Man. How much?

The Girl. Fifty cents.

Young Man. [*To the world.*] You see? They ought to pay money to *look* at you. To breathe the *air* you breathe. I don't know. Sometimes I figure it never is going to make sense. Hello—out there! I'm scared. You try to get me out of here. I'm scared them fools are going to come here from Wheeling and go crazy, thinking they're heroes. Get me out of here, Katey.

The Girl. I don't know what to do. Maybe I could break the door down.

Young Man. No, you couldn't do that. Is there a hammer out there or anything?

The Girl. Only a broom. Maybe they've locked the broom up, too.

Young Man. Go see if you can find anything.

The Girl. All right. [*She goes.*]

Young Man. Hello—out there! Hello—out there! [*Pause.*] Hello—out there! Hello—out there! [*Pause.*] Putting me in jail. [*With contempt.*] Rape! Rape? *They* rape everything good that was ever born. His side hurts. They laugh at her. Fifty cents a day. Little punk people. Hurting the only good thing that ever came their way. [*Suddenly.*] Hello—out there!

The Girl. [*Returning.*] There isn't a thing out there. They've locked everything up for the night.

Young Man. Any cigarettes?

The Girl. Everything's locked up—all the drawers of the desk, all the closet doors—everything.

Young Man. I ought to have a cigarette.

The Girl. I could get you a package maybe, somewhere. I guess the drug store's open. It's about a mile.

Young Man. A mile? I don't want to be alone that long.

The Girl. I could run all the way, and all the way back.

Young Man. You're the sweetest girl that ever lived.

The Girl. What kind do you want?

Young Man. Oh, any kind—Chesterfields or Camels or Lucky Strikes—any kind at all.

The Girl. I'll go get a package. [*She turns to go.*]

Young Man. What about the money?

The Girl. I've got some money. I've got a quarter I been saving. I'll run all the way. [*She is about to go.*]

Young Man. Come here.

The Girl. [*Going to him.*] What?

Young Man. Give me your hand. [*He takes her hand and looks at it, smiling. He lifts it and kisses it.*] I'm scared to death.

The Girl. I am, too.

Young Man. I'm not lying—I don't care what happens to me, but I'm scared nobody will ever come out here to this God-forsaken broken-down town and find you. I'm scared you'll get used to it and not mind. I'm scared you'll never get to Frisco and have 'em all turning around to look at you. Listen—go get me a gun, because if they come, I'll kill 'em! They don't understand. Get me a gun!

The Girl. I could get my father's gun. I know where he hides it.

Young Man. Go get it. Never mind the cigarettes. Run all the way. [*Pause, smiling but seriously.*] Hello, Katey.

The Girl. Hello. What's *your* name?

Young Man. Photo-Finish is what they

call me. My races are always photo-finish races. You don't know what that means, but it means they're very close. So close the only way they can tell which horse wins is to look at a photograph after the race is over. Well, every race I bet turns out to be a photo-finish race, and my horse never wins. It's my bad luck, all the time. That's why they call me Photo-Finish. Say it before you go.

The Girl. Photo-Finish.

Young Man. Come here. [*The* GIRL *moves close and he kisses her.*] Now, hurry. Run all the way.

The Girl. I'll run. [*The* GIRL *turns and runs. The* YOUNG MAN *stands at the center of the cell a long time. The* GIRL *comes running back in. Almost crying.*] I'm afraid. I'm afraid I won't see you again. If I come back and you're not here, I——

Young Man. Hello—out there!

The Girl. It's so lonely in this town. Nothing here but the lonesome wind all the time, lifting the dirt and blowing out to the prairie. I'll stay *here.* I won't *let* them take you away.

Young Man. Listen, Katey. Do what I tell you. Go get that gun and come back. Maybe they won't come tonight. Maybe they won't come at all. I'll hide the gun and when they let me out you can take it back and put it where you found it. And then we'll go away. But if they come, I'll kill 'em! Now, hurry——

The Girl. All right. [*Pause.*] I want to tell you something.

Young Man. O.K.

The Girl. [*Very softly.*] If you're not here when I come back, well, I'll have the gun and I'll know what to do with it.

Young Man. You know how to handle a gun?

The Girl. I know how.

Young Man. Don't be a fool. [*Takes off his shoe, brings out some currency.*] Don't be a fool, see? Here's some money. Eighty dollars. Take it and go to Frisco. Look around and find somebody. Find somebody alive and halfway human, see? Promise me—if I'm not here when you come back, just throw the gun away and get the hell to Frisco. Look around and find somebody.

The Girl. I don't *want* to find anybody.

Young Man. [*Swiftly, desperately.*] Listen, if I'm not here when you come back, how do you know I haven't gotten away? Now, do what I tell you. I'll meet you in Frisco. I've got a couple of dollars in my other shoe. I'll see you in San Francisco.

The Girl. [*With wonder.*] San Francisco?

Young Man. That's right—San Francisco. That's where you and me belong.

The Girl. I've always wanted to go to *some* place like San Francisco—but how could I go alone?

Young Man. Well, you're not alone any more, see?

The Girl. Tell me a little what it's like.

Young Man. [*Very swiftly, almost impatiently at first, but gradually slower and with remembrance, smiling, and the* GIRL *moving closer to him as he speaks.*] Well, it's on the Pacific to begin with—ocean water all around. Cool fog and sea-gulls. Ships from all over the world. It's got seven hills. The little streets go up and down, around and all over. Every night the fog-horns bawl. But they won't be bawling for you and me.

The Girl. What else?

Young Man. That's about all, I guess.

The Girl. Are people different in San Francisco?

Young Man. People are the same everywhere. They're different only when they love somebody. That's the only thing that makes 'em different. More people in Frisco love somebody, that's all.

The Girl. Nobody anywhere loves anybody as much as I love you.

Young Man. [*Shouting, as if to the world.*] You see? Hearing you say that, a man could die and still be ahead of the game. Now, hurry. And don't forget, if I'm not here when you come back, get the hell to San Francisco where you'll have a chance. Do you hear me? [*The* GIRL *stands a moment looking at him, then backs away, turns and runs. The* YOUNG MAN *stares after her, troubled and smiling. Then he turns away from the image of her and walks about like a lion in a cage. After a while he sits down suddenly and buries his head in his hands. From a distance the sound of several automobiles approaching is heard. He listens a moment, then ignores the implications of the sound, whatever they may be. Several automobile doors are slammed. He ignores this also. A wooden door is opened with a key and closed, and footsteps are heard in a hall. Walking easily, almost casually and yet arrogantly, a* MAN *comes in. The* YOUNG MAN *jumps up suddenly and shouts at the* MAN, *almost scaring him.*] What the hell kind of a jail-keeper are you, anyway? Why don't you attend to your business? You get paid for it, don't you? Now, get me out of here.

The Man. But I'm *not* the jail-keeper.

Young Man. Yeah? Well, who are you, then?

The Man. I'm the husband.

Young Man. What husband you talking about?

The Man. You know what husband.

Young Man. Hey! [*Pause, looking at the* MAN.] Are *you* the guy that hit me over the head last night?

The Man. I am.

Young Man. [*With righteous indignation.*] What do you mean going around hitting people over the head?

The Man. Oh, I don't know. What do you *mean* going around—the way you do?

Young Man. [*Rubbing his head.*] You hurt my head. You got no right to hit anybody over the head.

The Man. [*Suddenly angry, shouting.*] Answer my question! What do you mean?

Young Man. Listen, you—don't be hollering at me just because I'm locked up.

The Man. [*With contempt, slowly.*] You're a dog!

Young Man. Yeah? Well, let me tell you something. You *think* you're the husband. You're the husband of nothing. [*Slowly.*] What's more, your wife—if you want to call her that—is a tramp. Why don't you throw her out in the street where she belongs?

The Man. [*Draws a pistol.*] Shut up!

Young Man. Yeah? Go ahead, shoot—[*Softly.*] and spoil the fun. What'll your pals think? They'll be disappointed, won't they? What's the fun hanging a man who's already dead? [*The* MAN *puts the gun away.*] That's right, because now you can have some fun yourself, telling me what you're going to do. That's what you came here for, isn't it? Well, you don't need to tell me. I *know* what you're going to do. I've read the papers and I know. They have fun. A mob of 'em fall on one man and beat him, don't they? They tear off his clothes and kick him, don't they? And women and little children stand around watching, don't they? Well, before you go on *this* picnic, I'm going to tell you a few things. Not that that's going to send you home with your pals—the other heroes. No. You've been outraged. A stranger has come to town and violated your women. Your pure, innocent, virtuous women. You fellows have got to set this thing right. You're men, not mice. You're home-makers, and you beat your children. [*Suddenly.*] Listen, you—I didn't know she was your wife. I didn't know she was anybody's wife.

The Man. You're a liar!

Young Man. Sometimes—when it'll do somebody good—but not this time. Do you want to hear about it? [*The* MAN *doesn't answer.*] All right, I'll tell you. I met her at a lunch counter. She came in and sat next to me. There was plenty of room, but she sat next to me. Somebody had put a nickel in the phonograph and a fellow was singing *New San Antonio Rose.* Well, she got to talking about the song. I thought she was talking to the waiter, but *he* didn't answer her, so after a while *I* answered her. That's how I met her. I didn't think anything of it. We left the place together and started walking. The first thing I knew she said, This is where I live.

The Man. You're a dirty liar!

Young Man. Do you want to hear it? Or not? [*The* MAN *does not answer.*] O.K. She asked me to come in. Maybe she had something in mind, maybe she didn't. Didn't make any difference to me, one way or the other. If she was lonely, all right. If not, all right.

The Man. You're telling a lot of dirty lies!

Young Man. I'm telling the truth. Maybe your wife's out there with your pals. Well, call her in. I got nothing against her, or you—or any of you. Call her in, and ask her a few questions. Are you in love with her? [*The* MAN *doesn't answer.*] Well, that's too bad.

The Man. What do you mean, too bad?

Young Man. I mean this may not be the first time something like this has happened.

The Man. [*Swiftly.*] Shut up!

Young Man. Oh, you know it. You've always known it. You're afraid of your pals, that's all. She asked me for money. That's all she wanted. I wouldn't be here now if I had given her the money.

The Man. [*Slowly.*] How much did she ask for?

Young Man. I didn't ask her how much. I told her I'd made a mistake. She said she would make trouble if I didn't give her money. Well, I don't like bargaining, and I don't like being threatened, either. I told her to get the hell away from me. The next thing I knew she'd run out of the house and was hollering. [*Pause.*] Now, why don't you go out there and tell 'em they took me to another jail—go home and pack up and leave her. You're a pretty good guy, you're just afraid of your pals. [*The* MAN *draws his gun again. He is very frightened. He moves a step toward the* YOUNG MAN, *then fires three times. The* YOUNG MAN *falls to his knees. The* MAN *turns and runs, horrified.*] Hello—out there!

[*He is bent forward. The* GIRL *comes running in, and halts suddenly, looking at him.*]

The Girl. There were some people in the

street, men and women and kids—so I came in through the back, through a window. I couldn't find the gun. I looked all over but I couldn't find it. What's the matter?

Young Man. Nothing—nothing. Everything's all right. Listen. Listen, kid. Get the hell out of here. Go out the same way you came in and run—run like hell—run all night. Get to another town and get on a train. Do you hear me?

The Girl. What's happened?

Young Man. Get away—just get away from here. Take any train that's going—you can get to Frisco later.

The Girl. [*Almost sobbing.*] I don't want to go any place without you.

Young Man. I can't go. Something's happened. [*He looks at her.*] But I'll be with you always—God damn it. Always!

[*He falls forward. The* GIRL *stands near him, then begins to sob softly, walking away. She stands over to one side, stops sobbing, and stares out. The excitement of the mob outside increases. The* MAN, *with two of his pals, comes running in. The* GIRL *watches, unseen.*]

The Man. Here's the son of a bitch!

Another Man. O.K. Open the cell, Harry.

[*The* THIRD MAN *goes to the cell door, unlocks it, and swings it open. A* WOMAN *comes running in.*]

The Woman. Where is he? I want to see him. Is he dead? [*Looking down at him, as the* MEN *pick him up.*] There he is. [*Pause.*] Yeah, that's him.

[*Her husband looks at her with contempt, then at the dead man.*]

The Man. [*Trying to laugh.*] All right—let's get it over with.

Third Man. Right you are, George. Give me a hand, Harry. [*They lift the body.*]

The Girl. [*Suddenly, fiercely.*] Put him down!

The Man. What's this?

Second Man. What are you doing here? Why aren't you out in the street?

The Girl. Put him down and go away.

[*She runs toward the* MEN. *The* WOMAN *grabs her.*]

The Woman. Here—where do you think *you're* going?

The Girl. Let me go. You've got no right to take him away.

The Woman. Well, listen to her, will you? [*She slaps the* GIRL *and pushes her to the floor.*] Listen to the little slut, will you?

[*They all go, carrying the* YOUNG MAN's *body. The* GIRL *gets up slowly, no longer sobbing. She looks around at everything, then looks straight out, and whispers.*]

The Girl. Hello—out—there! Hello—out there!

CURTAIN

ANTIGONE*

By

JEAN ANOUILH

Adapted and translated by LEWIS GALANTIERE

WHEN "ANTIGONE" WAS PRODUCED IN the Théâtre de l'Atelier, Paris, in February, 1944, Paris was occupied by the Nazis, and all plays had to have their approval before performance. Yet *Antigone* was an immediate and enduring success with the French audiences, because it seemed to blazon before Frenchmen the message of the Resistance—"Say No, even if you die." Audience sympathy was all on Antigone's side; Creon might deprive her No of all rational foundation; he might show clearly that she could accomplish nothing useful or noble or even intelligible; nevertheless, the French audiences recognized in the desperate finality of her No the spirit which was working in the fields and bushes against the oppressors of France.

When Katharine Cornell produced the play in New York in February 1946, however, some of the American critics found that Creon engaged their sympathies far more than Antigone. She seemed to them to have a martyr complex. Other critics, unable to respond to the play as French audiences had, and feeling that they should, blamed Mr. Galantiere, who exposed himself to attack by confessing in a program note that he had added to the parts of Antigone, Haemon, and the guards. For this he has been intemperately abused in some quarters. Whatever textual changes may have been made for Miss Cornell's production, the text as printed here shows no serious additions to Anouilh's, except when Antigone distinguishes between God and His priests. This distinction is not found in the French text. In the French *Antigone* the name of God is used only as an oath or simple intensifier.

But in relation to the stream of modern drama Mr. Galantiere's addition is perhaps not unjustified. Any reader familiar with Shaw, for instance, will recognize that Antigone is in the same spiritual state as Lavinia in *Androcles and the Lion*, or Blanco Posnet in *The Shewing-up*, or even Dick Dudgeon in *The Devil's Disciple*. That is, the hand of God is upon her, as Lavinia puts it. Anouilh would not say so; he carefully follows Sophocles' plot while removing all Sophocles' religion, but willy-nilly he describes a condition of soul known throughout humanity's history as arising from irrational faith. Only such faith could arm the heroes of the Resistance; Communist or Christian, they were equally irrational and equally believing; the desperation of France's state demanded the fierce, senseless, shouted No to the blandishments of Vichy and the force of the Nazis. But to untouched Americans, committed like Creon to the rightness of getting things done, Antigone's No is only morbid, unsympathetic, impossible. Probably that is why the Nazis approved the play's production.

In the original Paris production Monelle Valentin, Mme. Anouilh, played Antigone. In New York Sir Cedric Hardwicke played Creon opposite Miss Cornell. In London, in 1949, the Old Vic Company produced the play with Sir Laurence Olivier as the Chorus and Vivien Leigh as Antigone. Except in Paris, runs have not been long, but the play's distinction has been everywhere admired.

Anouilh (pronounced Ahn-oo-ee, accented evenly) has attracted attention by titling his published plays as *Pièces Noires, Pièces Roses, Pièces Brillantes,* that is, gloomy plays, light plays, and sparkling plays. Criticism unites, however, in finding his meanings always pessimistic, even in the most sparkling play. But he commands the theatre, knowing with ease and surety how to attain dramatic effect; he always writes with precision and style; his plays are very actable, both by men and women. Among living French dramatists he is rivaled in international prestige only by Sartre, who cannot be regarded as a man of the theatre so much as the leader of a philosophical party.

Antigone illustrates the habit of French dramatists—never so common in other nations, though not unknown—of rewriting a play from classical antiquity. In the great days of the 17th century the practice appeared, for instance in the work of Corneille and Racine. Modern instances include Giraudoux' *Amphitryon 38,* Cocteau's *The Infernal Machine,* Sartre's *The Flies.*

Similarly Anouilh's version of Sophocles' *Antigone* is in no sense a translation, but rather a brilliant reflection of the original and even of its theatrical form. Although Anouilh has dealt freely with incidents and characters, he has given the twentieth-century audience the values of Greek tragedy more directly and forcibly than any recent reviser of a classic play.

JEAN ANOUILH

Born 1910, Bordeaux, France.

Moved to Paris while still very young. Attended Colbert Primary School and Chaptal College.

Studied law one and one-half years at the University of Paris.

1929–1931, Employed by advertising firm.

1931–1935, Secretary to Louis Jouvet's company, at the Comédie des Champs Élysées.

1932, Married Monelle Valentin, actress.

1935, First theatrical success.

PLAYS

1931 *Mandarine* (with Jean Aurenche. Not translated). 1932 *L'Hermine* (not translated). 1935 *Y Avait un Prisonnier* (not translated). 1935 *Le Petit Bonheur* (not translated). 1937 *Le Voyageur sans Bagages* (translated as *Traveler without Baggage*). 1938 *Le Bal des Voleurs* (translated as *Thieves' Carnival*). 1938 *La Sauvage* (not translated). 1938 *Le Rendez-vous de Senlis* (not translated). 1939 *Léocadia* (translated as *Time Remembered*). 1940 *Humulus le Muet* (written 1929, with Jean Aurenche. Not translated). 1941 *Eurydice* (translated as *Eurydice,* as *Point of Departure,* and as *Legend of Lovers*). 1944 *Antigone* (translated). 1945 *Oreste* (one act, not translated). 1946 *Jézabel* (not translated). 1946 *Roméo et Jeannette* (translated as *Fading Mansions*). 1946 *Médée* (one act, not translated). 1947 *L'Invitation au Château* (translated as *Ring Round the Moon*). 1949 *Ardèle ou La Marguerite* (translated as *Ardèle,* and as *The Cry of the Peacock*). 1949 *Episode de la Vie d'un Auteur* (not translated). 1949 *Cécile ou L'École des Pères* (not translated). 1950 *La Répétition ou L'Amour Puni* (not translated). 1951 *Colombe* (translated as *Colombe* and as *Mlle. Colombe*). 1952 *La Valse des Toréadors* (not translated). 1952 Three adaptations from Shakespeare: *The Winter's Tale, Twelfth Night,* and *As You Like It* (with J. C. Vincent). 1953 *L'Alouette* (translated as *The Lark*). 1955 *Ornifle, ou le Courant d'Air.*

SCREENWRITING

1939 *Les Otages.* 1944 *Le Voyageur sans Bagages.* 1946 *Deux Sous de Violettes.* 1947 *Cavalcade d'Amour.* 1948 *Monsieur Vincent.* 1949 *Anna Karénine.* 1949 *Pattes Blanches.* 1950 *Caroline Chérie.*

ANTIGONE

THE SETTING

A gray cloth cyclorama, semi-circular, hangs at the back of the set. At the bottom of the cyclorama, a stair, of three steps, sweeps in a semi-circle. Downstage, right and left, two archways. The curtains part in the center for entrance and exit.

A table stands left of center-stage, with matching chairs set at either end. A small stool is placed right of the chair at the right of the table.

ANTIGONE, *her hands clasped round her knees, sits on the top step. The* THREE GUARDS *sit on the steps, in a small group, playing cards. The* CHORUS *stands up on the top step.* EURYDICE *sits on the top step, just left of center, knitting. The* NURSE *sits on the second step, left of* EURYDICE. ISMENE *stands in front of arch, left, facing* HAEMON, *who stands left of her.* CREON *sits in the chair at right end of the table, his arm over the shoulder of his* PAGE, *who sits on the stool beside his chair. The* MESSENGER *is leaning against the downstage portal of the right arch.*

[*The curtain rises slowly; then the* CHORUS *turns and moves downstage.*]

Chorus. Well, here we are.

These people that you see here are about to act out for you the story of Antigone.

That thin little creature sitting by herself, staring straight ahead, seeing nothing, is Antigone. She is thinking. She is thinking that the instant I finish telling you who's who and what's what in this play, she will burst forth as the tense, sallow, wilful girl who would never listen to reason and who is about to rise up alone against Creon, her uncle, the King.

Another thing that she is thinking is this: she is going to die. Antigone is only twenty years old. She would much rather live than die. But there is no help for it. When you are on the side of the gods against the tyrant, of Man against the State, of purity against corruption—when, in short, your name is Antigone, there is only one part you can play; and she will have to play hers through to the end.

Mind you, Antigone doesn't know all these things about herself. I know them because it is my business to know them. That's what a Greek Chorus is for. All that she knows is that Creon will not allow her dead brother to be buried; and that in spite of Creon, she must bury him. Antigone doesn't think, she acts; she doesn't reason, she feels. And from the moment the curtain went up, she began to feel that inhuman forces were whirling her out of this world, snatching her away from her sister, Ismene, whom you see smiling and chatting with that young man, making her an instrument of the gods in a way she cannot fathom but that she will faithfully pursue.

You have never seen inhuman forces at work? You will, tonight.

[CHORUS *turns and indicates* HAEMON.]

The young man talking to Ismene—to the pliant and reasonable Ismene—is Haemon. He is the King's son, Creon's son. Antigone and he are engaged to be married. You wouldn't have thought she was his type. He likes dancing, sports, competition; he likes women, too. Now look at Ismene again. She is certainly more beautiful than Antigone. She is the girl you'd think he'd go for. Well . . . There was a ball one night. Ismene wore a new evening dress. She was radiant. Haemon danced every dance with her; he wouldn't look at any other girl. And yet, that same night, before the dance was over, suddenly he went in search of Antigone, found her sitting alone—like that, with her arms clasped round her knees—and asked her to marry him. It didn't seem to surprise Antigone in the least. She looked up at him out of those solemn eyes of hers, then smiled sort of sadly; and she said "yes." That was all. Well, here is Haemon expecting to marry Antigone. He won't, of course. He didn't know, when he asked her, that the earth wasn't made to hold a husband of Antigone, and that this princely distinction was to earn him no more than the right to die sooner than he might otherwise have done.

[CHORUS *turns toward* CREON.]

That gray-haired, powerfully built man sitting lost in thought, with his little page at his side, is Creon, the King. His face is lined. He is tired. He practices the difficult art of a leader of men. When he was younger, when

Oedipus was King and Creon was no more than the King's brother-in-law, he was different. He loved music, bought rare manuscripts, was a kind of art patron. He used to while away whole afternoons in the antique shops of this city of Thebes. But Oedipus died. Oedipus' sons died. Creon's moment had come. He took over the kingdom.

[CHORUS *moves downstage. Reflects a moment.*]

I'll tell you something about Creon. He has a tendency to fool himself. This leader of men, this brilliant debater and logician, likes to believe that if it were not for his sense of responsibility, he would step down from the throne and go back to collecting manuscripts. But the fact is, he loves being King. He's an artist who has always believed that he could govern just as well as any man of action could; and he's quite sure that no god nor any man can tell him anything about what is best for the common people.

Creon has a wife, a Queen. Her name is Eurydice. There she sits, the gentle old lady with the knitting, next to the Nurse who brought up the two girls. She will go on knitting all through the play, till the time comes for her to go to her room and die. She is a good woman, a worthy, loving soul. But she is no help to her husband. Creon has to face the music alone. Alone with his Page, who is too young to be of any help.

The others? Well, let's see.

[*He points toward the* MESSENGER.]

That pale young man leaning against the wall is the Messenger. Later on, he will come running in to announce that Haemon is dead. He has a premonition of catastrophe. That's what he is brooding over. That's why he won't mingle with the others.

As for those three pasty-faced card players—they are the guards, members of Creon's police force. They chew tobacco; one smells of garlic, another of beer; but they're not a bad lot. They have wives they are afraid of, kids who are afraid of them; they're bothered by the little day-to-day worries that beset us all. At the same time—they are policemen: eternally innocent, no matter what crimes are committed; eternally indifferent, for nothing that happens can matter to them. They are quite prepared to arrest anybody at all, including Creon himself, should the order be given by a new leader.

That's the lot. Now for the play.

Oedipus, who was the father of the two girls, Antigone and Ismene, had also two sons, Eteocles and Polynices. After Oedipus died, it was agreed that the two sons should share his throne, each to reign over Thebes in alternate years.

[*Gradually, the lights on the stage have been dimmed.*]

But when Eteocles, the elder son, had reigned a full year, and time had come for him to step down, he refused to yield up the throne to his younger brother. There was civil war. Polynices brought up allies—six foreign princes; and in the course of the war he and his foreigners were defeated, each in front of one of the seven gates of the city. The two brothers fought, and they killed one another in single combat just outside the city walls. Now Creon is King.

[CHORUS *is leaning, at this point, against the left proscenium arch. By now the stage is dark, with only the cyclorama bathed in dark blue. A single spot lights up the face of* CHORUS.]

Creon has issued a solemn edict that Eteocles, with whom he had sided, is to be buried with pomp and honors, and that Polynices is to be left to rot. The vultures and the dogs are to bloat themselves on his carcass. Nobody is to go into mourning for him. No gravestone is to be set up in his memory. And above all, any person who attempts to give him religious burial will himself be put to death.

It is against this blasphemy that Antigone rebels. What is for Creon merely the climax of a political purge, is for her an outrage against her dead brother which swells and grows until she perceives that it is an offense against God and against all men.

[*The light on* CHORUS *vanishes and* CHORUS *disappears through the left arch. It is dawn, gray and ashen, in a house asleep.* ANTIGONE *steals in from out-of-doors, through the arch right. She is carrying her sandals in her hand. She pauses, looking off through the arch, taut, listening, then turns and moves across downstage. As she reaches the table, she sees the* NURSE *approaching through the arch left. She runs quickly towards the exit. As she reaches the steps, the* NURSE *enters through arch and stands still when she sees* ANTIGONE.]

Nurse. Where have you been?

Antigone. Nowhere. It was beautiful. The whole world was gray when I went out. And now—you wouldn't recognize it. It's like a post card: all pink, and green and yellow. You'll have to get up earlier, Nurse, if you want to see a world without color.

Nurse. It was still pitch black when I got up. I went to your room, for I thought you might have flung off your blanket in the night. You weren't there.

Antigone. [*Comes down the steps.*] The garden was lovely. It was still asleep.

Nurse. You hadn't slept in your bed. I couldn't find you. I went to the back door. You'd left it half open.

Antigone. The fields were wet. They were waiting for something to happen. The whole world was breathless, waiting. I can't tell you what a roaring noise I seemed to make as I went up the road. I took off my sandals and slipped into a field.

[*She moves down to the stool and sits.*]

Nurse. [*Kneels at* ANTIGONE'S *feet to chafe them and put on the sandals.*] You'll do well to wash your feet before you go back to bed, Miss.

Antigone. I'm not going back to bed.

Nurse. Don't be a fool! You get some sleep! And me, getting up to see if she hasn't flung off her blanket; and I find her bed cold and nobody in it!

Antigone. Do you think that if a person got up every morning like this, it would be just as thrilling every morning to be the first girl out-of-doors?

[NURSE *puts* ANTIGONE'S *left foot down, lifts her other foot and chafes it.*]

Nurse. Morning my grandmother! It was night. It still is. And now, my girl, you'll stop trying to squirm out of this and tell me what you were up to. Where've you been?

Antigone. That's true. It was still night. There wasn't a soul out-of-doors but me who thought that it was morning.

Nurse. Oh, my little flibberty-gibbet! Just can't imagine what I'm talking about, can she? Go on with you! I know that game. Where have you been, wicked girl?

Antigone. [*Soberly.*] No. Not wicked.

Nurse. You went out to meet someone, didn't you? Deny it if you can.

Antigone. Yes. I went out to meet someone.

Nurse. A lover?

Antigone. Yes, Nurse. Yes, the poor dear. I have a lover.

Nurse. [*Stands up; bursting out.*] Ah, that's very nice now, isn't it? Such goings-on! You, the daughter of a king, running out to meet lovers. And we work our fingers to the bone for you, we slave to bring you up like young ladies! [*She sits on chair right of table.*] You're all alike, all of you. Even you —who never used to stop to primp in front of a looking-glass, or smear your mouth with rouge, or dindle and dandle to make the boys ogle you, and you ogle back. How many times I'd say to myself, "Now that one, now: I wish she was a little more of a coquette—always wearing the same dress, her hair tumbling round her face. One thing's sure," I'd say to myself, "none of the boys will look at her while Ismene's around, all curled and cute and tidy and trim. I'll have this one on my hands the rest of my life." And now, you see? Just like your sister, after all. Only worse: a hypocrite. Who is the lad? Some little scamp, eh? Somebody you can't bring home and show to your family, and say, "Well, this is him, and I mean to marry him and no other." That's how it is, is it? Answer me!

Antigone. [*Smiling faintly.*] That's how it is. Yes, Nurse.

Nurse. Yes, says she! God save us! I took her when she wasn't that high. I promised her poor mother I'd make a lady of her. And look at her! But don't you go thinking this is the end of this, my young 'un. I'm only your nurse and you can play deaf and dumb with me; I don't count. But your uncle Creon will hear of this! That, I promise you.

Antigone. [*A little weary.*] Yes. Creon will hear of this.

Nurse. And we'll hear what he has to say when he finds out that you go wandering alone o' nights. Not to mention Haemon. For the girl's engaged! Going to be married! Going to be married, and she hops out of bed at four in the morning to meet somebody else in a field.

Antigone. Please, Nurse, I want to be alone.

Nurse. And if you so much as speak of it, she says she wants to be alone!

Antigone. Nanny, you shouldn't scold, dear. This isn't a day when you should be losing your temper.

Nurse. Not scold, indeed! Along with the rest of it, I'm to like it. Didn't I promise your mother? What would she say if she was here? "Old Stupid!" That's what she'd call me. "Old Stupid. Not to know how to keep my little girl pure! Spend your life making them behave, watching over them like a mother hen, running after them with mufflers and sweaters to keep them warm and eggnogs to make them strong; and then at four o'clock in the morning snoring in your bed and letting them slip out into the bushes." That's what she'd say, your mother. And I'd stand there, dying of shame if I wasn't dead already. And all I could do would be not to dare look her in the face; and "That's true," I'd say. "That's all true what you say, Your Majesty."

Antigone. Nanny, dear. Dear Nanny. Don't cry. You'll be able to look Mamma in the face when it's your time to see her. And she'll say, "Good morning, Nanny. Thank you for my little Antigone. You did look after her so well." She knows why I went out this morning.

Nurse. Not to meet a lover?

Antigone. No. Not to meet a lover.

Nurse. Well, you've a queer way of teasing

me, I must say! Not to know when she's teasing me! [*Rises to stand behind* ANTIGONE.] I must be getting awfully old, that's what it is. But if you loved me, you'd tell me the truth. You'd tell me why your bed was empty when I went along to tuck you in. Wouldn't you?

Antigone. Please, Nanny, don't cry any more. [ANTIGONE *turns partly towards* NURSE, *puts an arm up to* NURSE'S *shoulder. With her other hand,* ANTIGONE *caresses* NURSE'S *face.*] There, now, my sweet red apple. Do you remember how I used to rub your cheeks to make them shine? My dear, wrinkled red apple! I didn't do anything tonight that was worth sending tears down the little gullies of your dear face. I am pure, and I swear that I have no other lover than Haemon. If you like, I'll swear that I shall never have any other lover than Haemon. Save your tears, Nanny, save them, Nanny dear; you may still need them. When you cry like that, I become a little girl again; and I mustn't be a little girl today.

[ANTIGONE *rises and moves upstage.* ISMENE *enters through arch left. She pauses in front of arch.*]

Ismene. Antigone! What are you doing up at this hour? I've just been to your room.

Nurse. The two of you, now! You're both going mad, to be up before the kitchen fire has been started. Do you like running about without a mouthful of breakfast? Do you think it's decent for the daughters of a king? [*She turns to* ISMENE.] And look at you with no wraps on, and the sun not up! I'll have you both on my hands with colds before I know it.

Antigone. Nanny dear, go away now. It's not chilly, really. Summer's here. Go make us some coffee. Please, Nanny, I'd love some coffee. It would do me so much good.

Nurse. My poor baby! Her head's swimming, what with nothing on her stomach, and I stand here like an idiot when I could be getting her something hot to drink.

[NURSE *exits. A pause.*]

Ismene. Aren't you well?

Antigone. Of course I am. Just a little tired. I got up too early.

[ANTIGONE *sits on chair, suddenly tired.*]

Ismene. I couldn't sleep, either.

Antigone. Ismene, you ought not to go without your beauty sleep.

Ismene. Don't make fun of me.

Antigone. I'm not, Ismene, truly. This particular morning, seeing how beautiful you are makes everything easier for me. Wasn't I a miserable little beast when we were small? I used to fling mud at you, and put worms down your neck. I remember tying you to a tree and cutting off your hair. Your beautiful hair! How easy it must be never to be unreasonable with all that smooth silken hair so beautifully set round your head.

Ismene. [*Abruptly.*] Why do you insist upon talking about other things?

Antigone. [*Gently.*] I am not talking about other things.

Ismene. Antigone, I've thought about it a lot.

Antigone. Have you?

Ismene. I thought about it all night long. Antigone, you're mad.

Antigone. Am I?

Ismene. We cannot do it.

Antigone. Why not?

Ismene. Creon will have us put to death.

Antigone. Of course he will. That's what he's here for. He will do what he has to do, and we will do what we have to do. He is bound to put us to death. We are bound to go out and bury our brother. That's the way it is. What do you think we can do to change it?

Ismene. [*Releases* ANTIGONE'S *hand; draws back a step.*] I don't want to die.

Antigone. I'd prefer not to die, myself.

Ismene. Listen to me, Antigone. I thought about it all night. I always think things over, and you don't. You are impulsive. You get a notion in your head and you jump up and do the thing straight off. And if it's silly, well, so much the worse for you. Whereas, *I* think things out.

Antigone. Sometimes it is better not to think too much.

Ismene. I don't agree with you! [ANTIGONE *looks at* ISMENE, *then turns and moves to chair behind table.* ISMENE *leans on end of table top, toward* ANTIGONE.] Oh, I know it's horrible. And I pity Polynices just as much as you do. But all the same, I sort of see what Uncle Creon means.

Antigone. I don't want to "sort of see" anything.

Ismene. Uncle Creon is the king. He has to set an example!

Antigone. Example! Do you call that edict an example? Polynices is cheated out of his rights. He makes war. Creon sides against him, and he is killed. After which Creon insists that Polynices must rot and putrefy and be mangled by dogs and birds, with no priest to bury him. And you talk to me of examples!

Ismene. Oh, Antigone, you don't understand!

Antigone. What in God's name is there to understand? Except that a man's body lies rotting, unburied. And that he is my brother. And that I must bury him.

Ismene. But Creon won't let us bury him. And he is stronger than we are. He has made himself king.

Antigone. [*Sits on chair.*] I am not listening to you.

Ismene. [*Kneels on stool, facing* ANTIGONE.] You must! You know how Creon organizes things. His mob will come running, howling as it runs. A thousand arms will seize our arms. A thousand breaths will breathe into our faces. Like one single pair of eyes, a thousand eyes will stare at us. We'll be driven in a tumbrel through their hatred, through the smell of them and their cruel roaring laughter. We'll be dragged to the scaffold for torture, surrounded by guards with their idiot faces all bloated, their animal hands cleanwashed for the sacrifice, their beefy eyes squinting as they stare at us. And we'll know that no shrieking and no begging will make them understand that we want to live. And we shall suffer, we shall feel pain rising in us until it becomes so unbearable that we *know* it must stop. But it won't stop; it will go on rising and rising, like a screaming voice. Oh, I can't, I can't, Antigone! [*A pause.*]

Antigone. How well you have thought it all out.

Ismene. I thought of it all night long. Didn't you?

Antigone. Oh, yes.

Ismene. I'm an awful coward, Antigone.

Antigone. So am I. But what has that to do with it?

Ismene. But, Antigone! Don't you want to go on living?

Antigone. Go on living! Who was it that was always the first out of bed because she loved the touch of the cold morning air on her bare skin? Who was always the last to bed because nothing less than infinite weariness could wean her from the lingering night?

Ismene. [*Clasps* ANTIGONE'S *hands, in a sudden rush of tenderness.*] Antigone! Darling little sister!

Antigone. [*Repulsing her.*] No! For heaven's sake! Don't paw me! And stop sniveling! You say you've thought it all out. The howling mob—the torture—the fear of death . . . They've made up your mind for you. Is that it?

Ismene. Yes.

Antigone. All right. They're as good excuses as any.

Ismene. [*Turns to* ANTIGONE.] Antigone, be sensible. It's all very well for men to believe in ideas and die for them. But you are a girl!

Antigone. Don't I know I'm a girl? Haven't I spent my life cursing the fact that I was a girl?

Ismene. [*With spirit.*] Antigone! You have everything in the world to make you happy. All you have to do is reach out for it. You are going to be married; you are young; you are beautiful . . .

Antigone. I am not beautiful.

Ismene. Yes, you are! Not the way other girls are. But it's always you that the little tough boys turn to look back at when they pass us in the street. And when you go by, the little girls stop talking. They stare and stare at you, until we've turned a corner.

Antigone. [*A faint smile.*] "Little tough boys—little girls."

Ismene. [*Challengingly.*] And what about Haemon? [*A pause.*]

Antigone. I shall see Haemon this morning. I'll take care of Haemon. Go back to bed now, Ismene. The sun is coming up, and, as you can see, there is nothing I can do today. Our brother Polynices is as well guarded as if he had won the war and were sitting on his throne.

Ismene. What are you going to do?

Nurse. [*Calls from off-stage.*] Come along, my dove. Come to breakfast.

Antigone. I don't feel like going to bed. However, if you like, I'll promise not to leave the house till you wake up.

Ismene. And you will listen to reason, won't you? You'll let me talk to you about this again? Promise?

Antigone. I promise. I'll let you talk. I'll let all of you talk. Go to bed, now. You're white with weariness.

[ISMENE *goes to arch and exits.* NURSE *enters through arch, speaking as she enters.*]

Nurse. Come along, my dove. I've made you some coffee and toast and jam.

[*She turns toward arch as if to exit.*]

Antigone. I'm not really hungry, Nurse.

[NURSE *stops, looks at* ANTIGONE, *then moves behind her.*]

Nurse. [*Very tenderly.*] Where is your pain?

Antigone. Nowhere, Nanny dear. But you must keep me warm and safe, the way you used to do when I was little. Nanny! Stronger than all fever, stronger than any nightmare, stronger than the shadow of the cupboard that used to turn into a dragon on the bedroom wall. Give me your hand, Nanny, as if I were ill in bed, and you sitting beside me.

Nurse. My sparrow, my lamb! What is it that's eating your heart out?

Antigone. Oh, it's just that I'm a little young still for what I have to go through. But nobody but you must know that.

Nurse. [*Places her other arm round* ANTIGONE's *shoulder.*] A little young for what, my kitten?

Antigone. Nothing in particular, Nanny. Just—all this. Oh, it's so good that you are here. I can hold your callused hand, your hand that is so prompt to ward off evil. You are very powerful, Nanny.

Nurse. What is it you want me to do for you, my baby?

Antigone. There isn't anything to do, except put your hand like this against my cheek. [*She places the* NURSE's *hand against her cheek. A pause, then, as* ANTIGONE *leans back, her eyes shut.*] There! I'm not afraid any more. Not afraid of the wicked ogre, nor of the sandman, nor of the dwarf who steals little children. [*A pause.* ANTIGONE *resumes on another note.*] Nanny . . .

Nurse. Yes?

Antigone. My dog, Puff . . .

Nurse. [*Straightens up, draws her hand away.*] Well?

Antigone. Promise me that you will never scold her again.

Nurse. Dogs that dirty up a house with their filthy paws deserve to be scolded.

Antigone. And promise me that you will talk to her. That you will talk to her often.

Nurse. [*Turns and looks at* ANTIGONE.] Me, talk to a dog!

Antigone. Yes. But mind you: you are not to talk to her the way people usually talk to dogs. You're to talk to her the way I talk to her.

Nurse. I don't see why the both of us have to make fools of ourselves. So long as you're here, one ought to be enough.

Antigone. But if there was a reason why I couldn't go on talking to her . . .

Nurse. [*Interrupting.*] Couldn't go on talking to her? And why couldn't you go on talking to her? What kind of poppycock . . . ?

Antigone. And if she got too unhappy, if she moaned and moaned, waiting for me with her nose under the door the way she does when I'm out all day, then the best thing, Nanny, might be to have her mercifully put to sleep.

Nurse. Now what *has* got into you this morning? [HAEMON *enters through arch.*] Running round in the darkness, won't sleep, won't eat— [ANTIGONE *sees* HAEMON.] and now it's her dog she wants killed. I never . . .

Antigone. [*Interrupting.*] Nanny! Haemon is here. Go inside, please. And don't forget that you've promised me. [NURSE *goes to arch and exits.* ANTIGONE *rises.*] Haemon, Haemon! Forgive me for quarreling with you last night. [*She crosses quickly to* HAEMON *and they embrace.*] Forgive me for everything. It was all my fault. I beg you to forgive me.

Haemon. You know that I've forgiven you. You had hardly slammed the door, your perfume still hung in the room, when I had already forgiven you. [*He holds her in his arms and smiles at her. Then draws slightly back.*] You stole that perfume. From whom?

Antigone. Ismene.

Haemon. And the rouge? and the face powder? and the dress? Whom did you steal them from?

Antigone. Ismene.

Haemon. And in whose honor did you get yourself up so elegantly?

Antigone. I'll tell you everything. [*She draws him closer.*] Oh, darling, what a fool I was! To waste a whole evening! A whole, beautiful evening!

Haemon. We'll have other evenings, my sweet.

Antigone. Perhaps we won't.

Haemon. And other quarrels, too. A happy love is full of quarrels, you know.

Antigone. A happy love, yes. Haemon, listen to me.

Haemon. Yes?

Antigone. Don't laugh at me this morning. Be serious.

Haemon. I am serious.

Antigone. And hold me tight. Tighter than you have ever held me. I want all your strength to flow into me.

Haemon. There! With all my strength.

[*A pause.*]

Antigone. [*Breathless.*] That's good. [*They stand for a moment, silent and motionless.*] Haemon! I wanted to tell you. You know—the little boy we were going to have when we were married?

Haemon. Yes?

Antigone. I'd have protected him against everything in the world.

Haemon. Yes, dearest.

Antigone. Oh, you don't know how I should have held him in my arms and given him my strength. He wouldn't have been afraid of anything. Our little boy, Haemon! His mother wouldn't have been very imposing: her hair wouldn't always have been brushed; but she would have been strong where he was concerned, so much stronger than all those real mothers with their real bosoms and their aprons round their middle. You believe that, don't you, Haemon?

Haemon. [*Soothingly.*] Yes, yes, my darling.

Antigone. And you believe me when I say that you would have had a real wife?

Haemon. Darling, you are my real wife.

Antigone. [*Pressing against him and crying out.*] Haemon, you loved me! You did love me that night, didn't you? You're sure of it!

Haemon. [*Rocking her gently.*] What night, my sweet?

Antigone. And you are very sure, aren't you, that that night, at the dance, when you came to the corner where I was sitting, there was no mistake? It was me you were looking for? It wasn't another girl? And you're sure that never, not in your most secret heart of hearts, have you said to yourself that it was Ismene you ought to have asked to marry you?

Haemon. [*Reproachfully.*] Antigone, you are idiotic. You might give me credit for knowing my own mind. It's you I love, and no one else.

Antigone. But you love me as a woman—as a woman wants to be loved, don't you? Your arms round me aren't lying, are they? Your hands, so warm against my back—they're not lying? This warmth, this confidence, this sense that I am safe, secure, that flows through me as I stand here with my cheek in the hollow of your shoulder: they are not lies, are they?

Haemon. Antigone, darling, I love you exactly as you love me. With all of myself.

[*They kiss.*]

Antigone. I'm sallow, and I'm scrawny. Ismene is pink and golden. She's like a fruit.

Haemon. Look here, Antigone . . .

Antigone. Ah, dearest, I am ashamed of myself. But this morning, this special morning, I must know. Tell me the truth! I beg you to tell me the truth! When you think about me, when it strikes you suddenly that I am going to belong to you—do you have the feeling that—that a great empty space is being hollowed out inside you, that there is something inside you that is just—dying?

Haemon. Yes, I do, I do. [*A pause.*]

Antigone. That's the way I feel. And another thing. I wanted you to know that I should have been very proud to be your wife—the woman whose shoulder you would put your hand on as you sat down to table, absent-mindedly, as upon a thing that belonged to you. [*After a moment, draws away from him. Her tone changes.*] There! Now I have two things more to tell you. And when I have told them to you, you must go away instantly, without asking any questions. However strange they may seem to you. However much they may hurt you. Swear that you will!

Haemon. [*Beginning to be troubled.*] What are these things that you are going to tell me?

Antigone. Swear, first, that you will go away without one word. Without so much as looking at me. [*She looks at him, wretchedness in her face.*] You hear me, Haemon. Swear it, please. This is the last mad wish that you will ever have to grant me.

[*A pause.*]

Haemon. I swear it, since you insist. But I must tell you that I don't like this at all.

Antigone. Please, Haemon. It's very serious. You must listen to me and do as I ask. First, about last night, when I came to your house. You asked me a moment ago why I wore Ismene's dress and rouge. It was because I was stupid. I wasn't very sure that you loved me as a woman; and I did it—because I wanted you to take me. I wanted to be your wife before . . .

Haemon. Oh, my darling . . .

Antigone. [*Shuts him off.*] You swore you wouldn't ask any questions. You swore, Haemon. [*Turns her face away and goes on in a hard voice.*] As a matter of fact, I'll tell you why. I wanted to be your wife last night because I love you that way very—very strongly. And also because— Oh, my darling, my darling, forgive me; I'm going to cause you quite a lot of pain. [*She draws away from him.*] I wanted it also because I shall never, never be able to marry you, never! [HAEMON *is stupefied and mute; then he moves a step toward her.*] Haemon! You took a solemn oath! You swore! Leave me quickly. Tomorrow—tomorrow the whole thing will be clear to you. Even before tomorrow: this afternoon. If you please, Haemon, go now. It is the only thing left that you can do for me if you still love me. [*A pause as* HAEMON *stares at her. Then he turns and goes out through the arch.* ANTIGONE *stands motionless, then moves to chair at end of table and lets herself gently down on it. In a mild voice, as of calm after storm.*] Well, it's over for Haemon, Antigone.

[ISMENE *enters through arch, pauses for a moment in front of it when she sees* ANTIGONE, *then crosses behind table.*]

Ismene. I can't sleep. I'm terrified. I'm so afraid that even though it is daylight, you'll still try to bury Polynices. Antigone, you remember what Polynices was like. He was our brother, of course. But he's dead; and he never loved us. He was a bad brother. He was like an enemy in this house. He never thought of you. Why should you think of him? What if he does have to lie rotting in a field? It's Creon's doing, not ours. Don't try to change things. You can't bury Polynices. I'm older than you are and I won't let you!

Antigone. You are too late, Ismene. When you first saw me this morning, I had just come in from burying him.

[ANTIGONE *exits through arch. The lighting, which by this time has reached a point of early morning sun, is quickly dimmed out, leaving the stage bathed in a light-blue color.* ISMENE *runs out after* ANTIGONE. *On* ISMENE'S *exit the lights are brought up suddenly to suggest a later period of the day.* CREON *and* PAGE *enter through curtain upstage.* CREON *stands on the top step; his* PAGE *stands at his right side.*]

Creon. A private of the guards, you say? One of those standing watch over the body? Show him in.

[*The* PAGE *crosses to arch and exits.* CREON *moves down to end of table.* PAGE *re-enters, preceded by the* FIRST GUARD, *livid with fear.* PAGE *remains on upstage side of arch.* GUARD *salutes.*]

Guard. Private Jonas, Second Battalion.

Creon. What are you doing here?

Guard. It's like this, chief. Soon as it happened, we said: "Got to tell the chief about this before anybody else spills it. He'll want to know right away." So we tossed a coin to see which one would come up and tell you about it. You see, chief, we thought only one man better come because, after all, you don't want to leave the body without a guard. Right? I mean, there's three of us on duty, guarding the body.

Creon. What's wrong about the body?

Guard. Chief, I've been seventeen years in the service. Volunteer. Wounded three times. Two citations. My record's clean. I know my business and I know my place. I carry out orders. Sir, ask any officer in the battalion; they'll tell you. "Leave it to Jonas. Give him an order; he'll carry it out." That's what they'll tell you, chief. Jonas, that's me—that's my name.

Creon. What's the matter with you, man? What are you shaking for?

Guard. By rights it's the corporal's job, chief. I've been recommended for a corporal but they haven't put it through yet. June, it was supposed to go through.

Creon. [*Interrupts.*] Stop chattering and tell me why you are here. If anything has gone wrong I'll break all three of you.

Guard. Nobody can say we didn't keep our eye on that body. We had the two o'clock watch—the tough one. You know how it is, chief. It's nearly the end of the night. Your eyes are like lead. You've got a crick in the back of your neck. There's shadows, and the fog is beginning to roll in. A fine watch they give us! And me, seventeen years in the service. But we was doing our duty, all right. On our feet, all of us. Anybody says we were sleeping is a liar. First place, it was too cold. Second place . . . [CREON *makes a gesture of impatience.*] Yes, chief. Well, I turned round and looked at the body. We wasn't only ten feet away from it, but that's how I am. I was keeping my eye on it. [*Shouts.*] Listen, chief, I was the first man to see it! Me! They'll tell you. I was the one let out that yell!

Creon. What for? What was the matter?

Guard. Chief, the body! Somebody had been there and buried it. [CREON *comes down a step on the stair. The* GUARD *becomes more frightened.*] It wasn't much, you understand. With us three there, it couldn't have been. Just covered over with a little dirt, that's all. But enough to hide it from the buzzards.

Creon. By God, I'll . . . ! [*He looks intently at the* GUARD.] You are sure that it couldn't have been a dog, scratching up the earth?

Guard. Not a chance, chief. That's kind of what we hoped it was. But the earth was scattered over the body just like the priests tell you you should do it. Whoever did that job knew what he was doing, all right.

Creon. Who could have dared? [*He turns and looks at the* GUARD.] Was there anything to indicate who might have done it?

Guard. Not a thing, chief. Maybe we heard a footstep—I can't swear to it. Of course we started right in to search, and the corporal found a shovel, a kid's shovel no bigger than that, all rusty and everything. Corporal's got the shovel for you. We thought maybe a kid did it.

Creon. [*To himself.*] A kid! [*He looks away from the* GUARD.] I broke the back of the rebellion; but like a snake, it is coming together again. Polynices' friends, with their gold, blocked by my orders in the banks of Thebes. The leaders of the mob allied to envious princes. And the temple priests, always ready for a bit of fishing in troubled waters. A kid! I can imagine what he is like, their kid: a baby-faced killer, creeping in the night with a toy shovel under his jacket. [*He looks *at his* PAGE.] Though why shouldn't they have corrupted a real child? There is something, now, to soften the hearts and weaken the minds of the populace! Very touching! Very useful to them, an innocent child. A martyr. A real white-faced baby of fourteen who will spit with contempt at the guards who kill him. A free gift to their cause: the precious, innocent blood of a child on my hands. [*He turns to the* GUARD.] They must have accomplices in the Guard itself. Look here, you. Who knows about this?

Guard. Only us three, chief. We flipped a coin, and I came right over.

Creon. Right. Listen, now. You will continue on duty. When the relief squad comes up, you will tell them to return to barracks. You will uncover the body. If another attempt is made to bury it, I shall expect you to make an arrest and bring the person straight to me. And you will keep your mouths shut. Not one word of this to a human soul. You are all guilty of neglect of duty, and you will be punished; but if the rumor spreads through Thebes that the body received burial, you will be shot—all three of you.

Guard. [*Excitedly.*] Chief, we never told nobody, I swear we didn't! Anyhow, I've been up here. Suppose my pals spilled it to the relief; I couldn't have been with them and here, too. That wouldn't be my fault if they talked. Chief, I've got two kids. You're my witness, chief, it couldn't have been me. I was here with you. I've got a witness! If anybody talked, it couldn't have been me! I was . . .

Creon. [*Interrupting.*] Clear out! If the story doesn't get round, you won't be shot. [*The* GUARD *salutes, turns, and exits on the run.* CREON *turns and paces upstage, then comes down to the end of the table.*] A child! [*He looks at* PAGE.] Come here, my lad. [PAGE *crosses to side of* CREON. CREON *puts his hand on* PAGE's *shoulder.*] Would you defy me with your little shovel? [PAGE *looks up at* CREON.] Of course you would. You would do it, too. [*A pause.* CREON *looks away from* PAGE *and murmurs.*] A child!

[CREON *and* PAGE *go slowly upstage center to top step.* PAGE *draws aside the curtain, through which* CREON *exits with* PAGE *behind him. As soon as* CREON *and* PAGE *have disappeared,* CHORUS *enters and leans against the upstage portal of arch, left. The lighting is brought up to its brightest point to suggest mid-afternoon.* CHORUS *allows a pause to indicate that a crucial moment has been reached in the play, then moves slowly downstage center. He stands for a moment silent, reflecting, and then smiles faintly.*]

Chorus. The spring is wound up tight. It will uncoil of itself. That is what is so convenient in tragedy. The least little turn of the wrist will do the job. Anything will set it going: a glance at a girl who happens to be lifting her arms to her hair as you go by; a feeling when you wake up on a fine morning that you'd like a little respect paid to you today, as if it were as easy to order as a second cup of coffee; one question too many, idly thrown out over a friendly drink—and the tragedy is on.

The rest is automatic. You don't need to lift a finger. The machine is in perfect order; it has been oiled ever since time began, and it runs without friction. Death, treason, and sorrow are on the march; and they move in the wake of storm, of tears, of stillness. Every kind of stillness. The hush when the executioner's axe goes up at the end of the last act. The unbreathable silence when, at the beginning of the play, the two lovers, their hearts bared, their bodies naked, stand for the first time face to face in the darkened room, afraid to stir. The silence inside you when the roaring crowd acclaims the winner—so that you think of a film without a sound-track, mouths agape and no sound coming out of them, a clamor that is no more than a picture; and you, the victor, already vanquished, alone in the desert of your silence. That is tragedy.

Tragedy is clean, it is firm, it is flawless. It has nothing to do with melodrama—with wicked villains, persecuted maidens, avengers, sudden revelations and eleventh-hour repentances. Death, in a melodrama, is really horrible because it is never inevitable. The dear old father might so easily have been saved; the honest young man might so easily have brought in the police five minutes earlier.

In a tragedy, nothing is in doubt and everyone's destiny is known. That makes for tranquillity. There is a sort of fellow-feeling among characters in a tragedy: he who kills is as innocent as he who gets killed: it's all a matter of what part you are playing. Tragedy is restful; and the reason is that hope, that foul, deceitful thing, has no part in it. There isn't any hope. You're trapped. The whole sky has fallen on you, and all you can do about it is to shout.

Don't mistake me: I said "shout": I did not say groan, whimper, complain. That, you cannot do. But you can shout aloud; you can get all those things said that you never thought you'd be able to say—or never even knew you had it in you to say. And you don't say these things because it will do any good to say them: you know better than that. You say them for their own sake; you say them because you learn a lot from them.

In melodrama, you argue and struggle in the hope of escape. That is vulgar; it's practical. But in tragedy, where there is no temptation to try to escape, argument is gratuitous: it's kingly. [*Voices of the* GUARDS *and scuffling sounds heard through the archway.* CHORUS *looks in that direction, then in a changed tone.*] The play is on. Antigone has been caught. For the first time in her life, little Antigone is going to be able to be herself.

[CHORUS *exits through arch. A pause, while the off-stage voices rise in volume, then the* FIRST GUARD *enters, followed by* SECOND *and* THIRD GUARDS, *holding the arms of* ANTIGONE *and dragging her along. The* FIRST GUARD, *speaking as he enters, crosses swiftly to end of the table. The* TWO GUARDS *and* ANTIGONE *stop downstage.*]

First Guard. [*Recovered from his fright.*] Come on, now, Miss, give it a rest. The chief will be here in a minute and you can tell him about it. All I know is my orders. I don't want to know what you were doing there. People always have excuses; but I can't afford to listen to them, see. Say, if we had to listen to all the people who want to tell us what's the matter with this country, we'd never get our work done. [*To the* GUARDS.] You keep hold of her and I'll see that she keeps her face shut.

Antigone. They are hurting me. Tell them to take their dirty hands off me.

First Guard. Dirty hands, eh? The least you can do is try to be polite, Miss. Look at me: I'm polite.

Antigone. Tell them to let me go. I shan't run away. My father was King Oedipus. I am Antigone.

First Guard. King Oedipus' little girl! What do you know about that! Listen, Miss, the night watch never picks up a lady, but she says, you better be careful; I'm sleeping with the police commissioner.

[*The* GUARDS *laugh.*]

Antigone. I don't mind being killed, but I don't want them to touch me.

First Guard. Yeah? And what about stiffs, and dirt, and such like? You wasn't afraid to touch them, was you? "Their dirty hands!" Take a look at your own hands. [ANTIGONE, *handcuffed, smiles despite herself as she looks down at her hands. They are grubby.*] Guess you must have lost your shovel, didn't you? Had to go at it with your fingernails the second time, I guess. By God, I never saw such nerve! I turn my back for about five seconds; I ask a pal for a chew; I say "thanks"; I get the tobacco stowed away in my cheek—the whole thing don't take ten seconds; and there she is, clawing away like a hyena. Right out in broad daylight! And boy! did she scratch and kick when I grabbed her! Straight for my eyes with them nails she went. And yelling something fierce about, "I ain't finished yet; let me finish!" She ain't got all her marbles!

Second Guard. I pinched a nut like that the other day. Right on the main square, she was, histin' up her skirts and showing her behind to anybody wanted to take a look.

First Guard. Listen, we're going to get a bonus out of this. What do you say we throw a party, the three of us?

Second Guard. At the old woman's? Behind Market Street?

Third Guard. Suits me. Sunday would be a good day. We're off duty Sunday. What do you say we bring our wives?

First Guard. Nix. Let's have some fun this time. Bring your wife, there's always something goes wrong. First place, what do you do with the kids? Bring them, they always want to go to the can just when you're right in the middle of a game of cards or something. Say, listen. Who would have thought an hour ago that us three would be talking about throwing a party right now? The way I felt when the old man was interrogatin' me, we'd be lucky if we got off with being docked a month's pay. I want to tell you, I was scared.

Second Guard. You sure we're going to get a bonus?

First Guard. Yeah. Something tells me this is big stuff.

Third Guard. [*To* SECOND GUARD.] What's-his-name, you know—in the Third Battalion? He got an extra month's pay for catching a fire-bug.

Second Guard. If we get an extra month's pay, I vote we throw the party at the Arabian's.

First Guard. You're crazy! He charges twice as much for liquor as anybody else in town. Unless you want to go upstairs, of course. Can't do that at the old woman's.

Third Guard. Say, we can't keep this from our wives, no matter how you figure it. You get an extra month's pay, and what happens? Everybody in the battalion knows it, and your wife knows it too. They might even line up the battalion and give it to you in front of everybody, so how could you keep your wife from finding out?

First Guard. Well, we'll see about that. If they do the job out in the barracks-yard—of course that means women, kids, everything.

Antigone. I should like to sit down, if you please.

[*A pause, as the* First Guard *thinks it over.*]

First Guard. Let her sit down. But keep hold of her. [*The two* Guards *start to lead her towards the chair at end of table. The curtain upstage opens, and* Creon *enters, followed by his* Page. First Guard *turns and moves upstage a few steps, sees* Creon.] 'Tenshun!

[*The three* Guards *salute.* Creon, *seeing* Antigone *handcuffed to* Third Guard, *stops on the top step, astonished.*]

Creon. Antigone! [*To the* First Guard.] Take off those handcuffs! [First Guard *crosses above table to left of* Antigone.] What is this?

[Creon *and his* Page *come down off the steps.* First Guard *takes key from his pocket and unlocks the cuff on* Antigone's *hand.* Antigone *rubs her wrist as she crosses below table toward chair at end of table.* Second *and* Third Guards *step back to front of arch.* First Guard *turns upstage toward* Creon.]

First Guard. The watch, chief. We all came this time.

Creon. Who is guarding the body?

First Guard. We sent for the relief.

[Creon *comes down.*]

Creon. But I gave orders that the relief was to go back to barracks and stay there! [Antigone *sits on chair at left of table.*] I told you not to open your mouth about this!

First Guard. Nobody's said anything, chief. We made this arrest, and brought the party in, the way you said we should.

Creon. [*To* Antigone.] Where did these men find you?

First Guard. Right by the body.

Creon. What were you doing near your brother's body? You knew what my orders were.

First Guard. What was she doing? Chief, that's why we brought her in. She was digging up the dirt with her nails. She was trying to cover up the body all over again.

Creon. Do you realize what you are saying?

First Guard. Chief, ask these men here. After I reported to you, I went back, and first thing we did, we uncovered the body. The sun was coming up and it was beginning to smell, so we moved it up on a little rise to get him in the wind. Of course you wouldn't expect any trouble in broad daylight. But just the same, we decided one of us better keep his eye peeled all the time. About noon, what with the sun and the smell, being the wind dropped, and I wasn't feeling none too good, I went over to my pal to get a chew. I just had time to say "thanks" and stick it in my mouth, when I turned round and there she was, clawing away at the dirt with both hands. Right out in broad daylight! Wouldn't you think when she saw me come running, she'd quit and beat it out of there? Not her! She went right on digging as fast as she could, as if I wasn't there at all. And when I grabbed her, she scratched and bit and yelled to leave her alone, she hadn't finished yet, the body wasn't all covered yet, and the like of that.

Creon. [*To* Antigone.] Is this true?

Antigone. Yes, it is true.

First Guard. We scraped the dirt off as fast as we could, then we sent for the relief and we posted them. But we didn't tell them a thing, chief. And we brought in the party so's you could see her. And that's the truth, so help me God.

Creon. [*To* Antigone.] And was it you who covered the body the first time? In the night?

Antigone. Yes, it was. With a toy shovel we used to take to the seashore when we were children. It was Polynices' own shovel; he had cut his name in the handle. That was why I left it with him. But these men took it away; so the next time, I had to do it with my hands.

First Guard. Chief, she was clawing away like a wild animal. Matter of fact, first minute we saw her, what with the heat haze and everything, my pal says, "That must be a dog," he says. "Dog!" I says, "That's a girl, that is!" And it was.

Creon. Very well. [*Turns to the* Page.] Show these men to the ante-room. [*The* Page *crosses to the arch, stands there, waiting.* Creon *moves behind the table. To the* First Guard.] You three men will wait outside. I may want a report from you later.

First Guard. Do I put the cuffs back on her, chief?

Creon. No. [*The three* Guards *salute, do an about-face and exit through arch right.* Page *follows them out. A pause.*] Had you told anybody what you meant to do?

Antigone. No.

Creon. Did you meet anyone on your way—coming or going?

Antigone. No, nobody.

Creon. Sure of that, are you?

Antigone. Perfectly sure.

Creon. Very well. Now listen to me. You will go straight to your room. When you get there, you will go to bed. You will say that you are not well and that you have not been out since yesterday. Your nurse will tell the same story. [*He looks toward arch, through which the* GUARDS *have exited.*] And I'll dispose of those three men.

Antigone. Uncle Creon, you are going to a lot of trouble for no good reason. You must know that I'll do it all over again tonight.

[*A pause. They look one another in the eye.*]

Creon. Why did you try to bury your brother?

Antigone. I owed it to him.

Creon. I had forbidden it.

Antigone. I owed it to him. Those who are not buried wander eternally and find no rest. Everybody knows that. I owe it to my brother to unlock the house of the dead in which my father and my mother are waiting to welcome him. Polynices has earned his rest.

Creon. Polynices was a rebel and a traitor, and you know it.

Antigone. He was my brother, and he was a human being. Who, except you, wants my brother's body to rot in a field? Does God want that? Do the people want it?

Creon. God and the people of Thebes are not concerned in this. You heard my edict. It was proclaimed throughout Thebes. You read my edict. It was posted up on the city walls.

Antigone. Of course I did.

Creon. You knew the punishment I decreed for any person who attempted to give him burial.

Antigone. Yes, I knew the punishment.

Creon. Did you by any chance act on the assumption that a daughter of Oedipus, a daughter of Oedipus' stubborn pride, was above the law?

Antigone. No, I did not act on that assumption.

Creon. Because if you had acted on that assumption, Antigone, you would have been deeply wrong. Nobody has a more sacred obligation to obey the law than those who make the law. You are a daughter of lawmakers, a daughter of kings, Antigone. You must observe the law.

Antigone. Had I been a scullery maid washing my dishes when that law was read aloud to me, I should have scrubbed the greasy water from my arms and gone out in my apron to bury my brother.

Creon. What nonsense! If you had been a scullery maid, there would have been no doubt in your mind about the seriousness of that edict. You would have known that it meant death; and you would have been satisfied to weep for your brother in your kitchen. But you! You thought that because you come of the royal line, because you were my niece and were going to marry my son, I shouldn't dare have you killed.

Antigone. You are mistaken. Quite the contrary. I never doubted for an instant that you would have me put to death.

[*A pause, as* CREON *stares fixedly at her.*]

Creon. The pride of Oedipus! Oedipus and his headstrong pride all over again. I can see your father in you—and I believe you. Of course you thought that I should have you killed! Proud as you are, it seemed to you a natural climax in your existence. Your father was like that. For him as for you human happiness was meaningless; and mere human misery was not enough to satisfy his passion for torment. [*He sits on stool behind the table.*] You come of people for whom the human vestment is a kind of strait-jacket: it cracks at the seams. You spend your lives wriggling to get out of it. Nothing less than a cosy tea-party with death and destiny will quench your thirst. The happiest hour of your father's life came when he listened greedily to the story of how, unknown to himself, he had killed his own father and dishonored the bed of his own mother. Drop by drop, word by word, he drank in the dark story that the gods had destined him, first to live and then to hear. How avidly men and women drink the brew of such a tale when their names are Oedipus—and Antigone! And it is so simple, afterwards, to do what your father did, to put out one's eyes and take one's daughter begging on the highways.

Let me tell you, Antigone: those days are over for Thebes. Thebes has a right to a king without a past. My name, thank God, is only Creon. I stand here with both feet firm on the ground; with both hands in my pockets; and I have decided that so long as I am king—being less ambitious than your father was—I shall merely devote myself to introducing a little order into this absurd kingdom; if that is possible.

Don't think that being a king seems to me romantic. It is my trade; a trade a man has to work at every day; and like every other trade, it isn't all beer and skittles. But since it is my trade, I take it seriously. And if, tomorrow, some wild and bearded messenger walks in from some wild and distant valley—which is what happened to your dad—and tells me that he's not quite sure who my parents were, but thinks that my wife Eurydice is actually my mother, I shall ask him to do me the kindness to go back where he came from; and I shan't let a little matter like that persuade me to order my wife to take a blood test and the police to let me know whether or not my birth certificate was forged. Kings, my girl, have other things to do than to surrender themselves to their private feelings. [*He looks at her and smiles.*] Hand *you* over to be killed! [*He rises, moves to end of table and sits on the top of table.*] I have other plans for you. You're going to marry Haemon; and I want you to fatten up a bit so that you can give him a sturdy boy. Let me assure you that Thebes needs that boy a good deal more than it needs your death. You will go to your room, now, and do as you have been told; and you won't say a word about this to anybody. Don't fret about the guards; I'll see that their mouths are shut. And don't annihilate me with those eyes. I know that you think I am a brute, and I'm sure you must consider me very prosaic. But the fact is, I have always been fond of you, stubborn though you always were. Don't forget that the first doll you ever had came from me. [*A pause.* ANTIGONE *says nothing, rises and crosses slowly below the table toward the arch.* CREON *turns and watches her; then.*] Where are you going?

Antigone. [*Stops downstage. Without any show of rebellion.*] You know very well where I am going.

Creon. [*After a pause.*] What sort of game are you playing?

Antigone. I am not playing games.

Creon. Antigone, do you realize that if, apart from those three guards, a single soul finds out what you have tried to do, it will be impossible for me to avoid putting you to death? There is still a chance that I can save you; but only if you keep this to yourself and give up your crazy purpose. Five minutes more, and it will be too late. You understand that?

Antigone. I must go bury my brother. Those men uncovered him.

Creon. What good will it do? You know that there are other men standing guard over Polynices. And even if you did cover him over with earth again, the earth would again be removed.

Antigone. I know all that. I know it. But that much, at least, I can do. And what a person can do, a person should do. [*Pause.*]

Creon. Tell me, Antigone, do you believe all that flummery about religious burial? Do you really believe that a so-called shade of your brother is condemned to wander forever homeless if a little earth is not flung on his corpse to the accompaniment of some priestly abracadabra? Have you ever listened to the priests of Thebes when they were mumbling their formula? Have you ever watched their dreary sullen faces while they were preparing the dead for burial—skipping half the gestures required by the ritual, swallowing half their words, hustling the dead into their graves out of fear that they might be late for lunch?

Antigone. Yes, I have seen all that.

Creon. And did you never say to yourself as you watched them, that if someone you really loved lay dead under the shuffling, mumbling ministrations of the priests, you would scream aloud and beg the priests to leave the dead in peace?

Antigone. No, Creon. There is God and there are His priests. They are not the same things. You are not free to do with men as you wish—not even when they are dead.

Creon. And you are going to stop me, are you?

Antigone. Yes, I am going to stop you.

[*A pause as they stand looking at one another.*]

Creon. You must want very much to die. You look like a trapped animal.

Antigone. Stop feeling sorry for me. Do as I do. Do your job. But if you are a human being, do it quickly.

Creon. [*Takes a step toward her.*] I want to save you, Antigone.

Antigone. You are the King, and you are all-powerful. But that you cannot do.

Creon. You think not?

Antigone. Neither save me nor stop me.

Creon. Prideful Antigone!

Antigone. Only this can you do: have me put to death.

Creon. Have you tortured, perhaps?

Antigone. Why would you do that? To see me cry? To hear me beg for mercy? Or swear whatever you wish, and then begin over again? [*A pause.*]

Creon. You listen to me. You have cast me for the villain in this little play of yours, and yourself for the heroine. And you know it, you damned little mischief-maker! But don't you drive me too far! If I were one of your preposterous little tyrants that Greece is full of, you would be lying in a ditch this minute with your tongue pulled out and your body drawn and quartered. But you can see something in my face that makes me hesitate to send for the guards and turn you over to them. Instead, I let you go on arguing; and vou taunt me, you take the offensive. [*He grasps her left wrist.*] What are you driving at, you she-devil?

Antigone. Let me go. You are hurting my arm.

Creon. [*Gripping her tighter.*] I will not let you go.

Antigone. [*Moans.*] Oh!

Creon. I was a fool to waste words. I should have done this from the beginning. [*He looks at her.*] I may be your uncle; but we are not a particularly affectionate family. Are we, eh? [*Through his teeth as he twists.*] Are we? [CREON *propels* ANTIGONE *round below him to his side.*] What fun for you, eh? To be able to spit in the face of a King who has all the power in the world; a man who has done his own killing in his day; who has killed people just as pitiable as you are—and who is still soft enough to go to all this trouble in order to keep you from being killed.

[*A pause.*]

Antigone. Now you are squeezing my arm too tightly. It doesn't hurt any more.

[CREON *stares at her, then drops her arm.*]

Creon. I shall save you yet. [*He goes below the table to the chair at end of table, takes off his coat and places it on the chair.*] God knows, I have things enough to do today without wasting my time on an insect like you. But urgent things can wait. I am not going to let politics be the cause of your death. For it is a fact that this whole business is nothing but politics: the mournful shade of Polynices, the decomposing corpse, the sentimental weeping and the hysteria that you mistake for heroism, nothing but politics.

Look here. I may not be soft, but I'm fastidious. I like things clean, ship-shape, well scrubbed. Don't think that I am not just as offended as you are by the thought of that meat rotting in the sun. In the evening, when the breeze comes in off the sea, you can smell it in the palace, and it nauseates me. But I refuse even to shut my window. The people of Thebes have got to have their noses rubbed into it a little longer. My God! If it was up to me, I should have had them bury your brother long ago as a mere matter of public hygiene. I admit that what I am doing is childish. But it is by childish tricks like this that men are governed. And if the feather-headed rabble I govern are to understand what's what, that stench has got to fill the town for a month!

Antigone. [*Turns to him.*] You are a loathsome man!

Creon. I agree. My trade forces me to be. We could argue whether I ought or ought not to follow my trade; but once I take on the job, I must do it properly.

Antigone. Why do you do it at all?

Creon. My dear, I woke up one morning and found myself King of Thebes. God knows, there were other things I loved in life more than power.

Antigone. Then you should have said no.

Creon. Yes, I could have done that. Only, I felt that it would have been cowardly. I should have been like a workman who turns down a job that has to be done. So I said yes.

Antigone. So much the worse for you, then. I didn't say yes. I can say no to anything I think vile, and I don't have to count the cost. But because you said yes to your lust for power, all that you can do, for all of your crown, your trappings, and your guards—all that you can do is to have me killed.

Creon. Listen to me.

Antigone. If I want to. I don't have to listen to you if I don't want to. There is nothing you can tell me that I don't know. Whereas, I can tell you a thousand things that you don't know. You stand there, drinking in my words. [*She moves behind chair.*] Why is it that you don't call your guards? I'll tell you why. You want to hear me out to the end; that's why.

Creon. You amuse me.

Antigone. Oh, no, I don't. I frighten you. That is why you talk about saving me. Everything would be so much easier if you had a docile, tongue-tied little Antigone living in the palace. But you are going to have to bury Polynices or put me to death today—one of the two—and you know it. And that's what frightens you.

Creon. Very well. I am afraid, then. Does that satisfy you? I am afraid that if you insist upon it, I shall have to have you killed. And I don't want to.

Antigone. I don't have to do things that I think are wrong. If it comes to that, you didn't really want to leave my brother's body unburied, did you? Say it! Admit that you didn't.

Creon. I have said it already.

Antigone. But you did it just the same. And now, though you don't want to do it, you are going to have me killed. And you call that being a king!

Creon. Yes, I call that being a king.

Antigone. Poor Creon! My nails are broken, my fingers are bleeding, my arms are covered with the welts left by the paws of your guards—but I am a queen!

Creon. Then why not have pity on me, and live? Isn't your brother's corpse, rotting under my windows, payment enough for peace and order in Thebes?

Antigone. What have I to do with your slave's peace and your barbarian's order? No, Creon! You said yes, and made yourself king. Now you will never stop paying.

Creon. But God in Heaven! Won't you try to understand me! I'm trying hard enough to understand you! There had to be one man who said yes. Somebody had to agree to captain the ship. She had sprung a hundred leaks; she was loaded to the water-line with crime, ignorance, poverty. The wheel was swinging with the wind. The crew refused to work and were looting the cargo. The officers were building a raft, ready to slip overboard and desert the ship. The mast was splitting, the sails were beginning to rip. Every man-jack on board was about to drown—and only because the only thing they thought of was their own skins and their cheap little day-to-day traffic. Was that a time, do you think, for playing with words like yes and no? You grab the wheel, you right the ship in the face of a mountain of water. You shout an order, and if one man refuses to obey, you shoot straight into the mob. Into the mob, I say! The beast as nameless as the wave that crashes down upon your deck; as nameless as the whipping wind. The thing that drops when you shoot may be someone who poured you a drink the night before; but it has no name. And you, braced at the wheel, you have no name, either. Nothing has a name—except the ship, and the storm. [*A pause as he looks at her.*] Now do you understand?

Antigone. I am not here to understand. Not what you call understand. I am here to say no to you, and bury Polynices.

Creon. It is easy to say no.

Antigone. Not always.

Creon. It is easy to say no. To say yes, you have to sweat and roll up your sleeves and plunge both hands into life up to the elbows. It is easy to say no, even if saying no means death. All you have to do is to sit still and wait. Wait to go on living; wait to be killed. That is the coward's part. *No* is one of your man-made words. Can you imagine a world in which trees say *no* to the sap? In which beasts say *no* to hunger or to propagation? Animals are good, simple, tough. They move in droves, nudging one another onwards, all traveling the same road. Some of them keel over; but the rest go on; and no matter how many may fall by the wayside, there are always those few left who go on bringing their young into the world, traveling the same road with the same obstinate will, unchanged from those who went before.

Antigone. Animals, eh, Creon! What a king you could be if only men were animals!

[*A pause.* CREON *turns and looks at her.*]

Creon. You despise me, don't you? [ANTIGONE *is silent.* CREON *goes on, as if to himself.*] Strange. Again and again, I have imagined myself holding this conversation with a pale young man I have never seen in the flesh. He would have come to assassinate me, and would have failed. I would be trying to find out from him why he wanted to kill me. But with all my logic and all my powers of debate, the only thing I could get out of him would be that he despised me. Who would have thought that that white-faced boy would turn out to be you? And that the debate would arise out of something so meaningless as the burial of your brother?

Antigone. [*Repeats contemptuously.*] Meaningless!

Creon. [*Earnestly, almost desperately.*] And yet, you must hear me out. My part is not a heroic one, but I shall play my part. I shall have you put to death. Only before I do, I want to make one last appeal. I want to be sure that you know what you are doing as well as I know what I am doing. Antigone, do you know what you are dying for? Do you know the sordid story to which you are going to sign your name in blood, for all time to come?

Antigone. What story?

Creon. The story of Eteocles and Polynices, the story of your brothers. You think you know it, but you don't. Nobody in Thebes knows that story but me. And it seems to me, this afternoon, that you have a right to know it, too. [*A pause as* ANTIGONE *moves to chair and sits.*] It's not a pretty story. [*He turns, gets stool from behind the table and places it between the table and the chair.*] You'll see. [*He looks at her for a moment.*] Tell me, first. What do you remember about your brothers? They were older than you, so they must have looked down on you. And I imagine that they tormented you—pulled your pigtails, broke your dolls, whispered secrets to each other to put you in a rage.

Antigone. They were big and I was little.

Creon. And later on, when they came home wearing evening clothes, smoking cigarettes, they would have nothing to do with you; and you thought they were wonderful.

Antigone. They were boys and I was a girl.

Creon. You didn't know why, exactly, but you knew that they were making your mother unhappy. You saw her in tears over them; and your father would fly into a rage because of them. You heard them come in, slamming doors, laughing noisily in the corridors —insolent, spineless, unruly, smelling of drink.

Antigone. [*Staring outward.*] Once, it was very early and we had just got up. I saw them coming home, and hid behind a door. Polynices was very pale and his eyes were shining. He was so handsome in his evening clothes. He saw me, and said: "Here, this is for you"; and he gave me a big paper flower that he had brought home from his night out.

Creon. And of course you still have that flower. Last night, before you crept out, you opened a drawer and looked at it for a time, to give yourself courage.

Antigone. Who told you so?

Creon. Poor Antigone! With her night-club flower. Do you know what your brother was?

Antigone. Whatever he was, I know that you will say vile things about him.

Creon. A cheap, idiotic bounder, that is what he was. A cruel, vicious little voluptuary. A little beast with just wit enough to drive a car faster and throw more money away than any of his pals. I was with your father one day when Polynices, having lost a lot of money gambling, asked him to settle the debt; and when your father refused, the boy raised his hand against him and called him a vile name.

Antigone. That's a lie!

Creon. He struck your father in the face with his fist. It was pitiful. Your father sat at his desk with his head in his hands. His nose was bleeding. He was weeping with anguish. And in a corner of your father's study, Polynices stood sneering and lighting a cigarette.

Antigone. That's a lie. [*A pause.*]

Creon. When did you last see Polynices alive? When you were twelve years old. *That's* true, isn't it?

Antigone. Yes, that's true.

Creon. Now you know why. Oedipus was too chicken-hearted to have the boy locked up. Polynices was allowed to go off and join the Argive army. And as soon as he reached Argos, the attempts upon your father's life began—upon the life of an old man who couldn't make up his mind to die, couldn't bear to be parted from his kingship. One after another, men slipped into Thebes from Argos for the purpose of assassinating him, and every killer that we caught always ended by confessing who had put him up to it, who had paid him to try it. And it wasn't only Polynices. That is really what I am trying to tell you. I want you to know what went on in the back room, in the kitchen of politics; I want you to know what took place in the wings of this drama in which you are burning to play a part.

Yesterday, I gave Eteocles a State funeral, with pomp and honors. Today, Eteocles is a saint and a hero in the eyes of all Thebes. The whole city turned out to bury him. The schoolchildren emptied their piggy-banks to buy wreaths for him. Old men, orating in quavering, hypocritical voices, glorified the virtues of the great-hearted brother, the devoted son, the loyal prince. I made a speech myself; and every temple priest was present with an appropriate show of sorrow and solemnity in his stupid face. And military honors were accorded the dead hero.

Well, what else could I have done? People had taken sides in the civil war. Both sides couldn't be wrong; that would be too much. I couldn't have made them swallow the truth. Two gangsters were more of a luxury than I could afford. [*He pauses for a moment.*] And this is the whole point of my story. Eteocles, that virtuous brother, was just as rotten as Polynices. That great-hearted son had done his best, too, to procure the assassination of his father. That loyal prince had also offered to sell out Thebes to the highest bidder.

Funny, isn't it? Polynices lies rotting in the sun while Eteocles is given a hero's funeral and will be housed in a marble vault. Yet I have absolute proof that everything that Polynices did, Eteocles had plotted to do. They were a pair of blackguards—both engaged in selling out Thebes, and both engaged in selling out each other; and they died like the cheap gangsters they were, over a division of the spoils.

But, as I told you a moment ago, I had to make a martyr of one of them. I sent out to the holocaust for their bodies; they were found clasped in one another's arms—for the first time in their lives, I imagine. Each had been spitted on the other's sword, and the Argive cavalry had trampled them down. They were mashed to a pulp, Antigone. I had the prettier of the two carcasses brought in, and gave it a State funeral; and I left the other to rot. I didn't know which was which. And I assure you, I didn't care.

[*Long silence, neither looking at the other.*]

Antigone. [*In a mild voice.*] Why do you tell me all this? [*Another pause.*]

Creon. [*Relaxed in the belief that he has defeated her, speaks with pompous self-satisfaction.*] You hold a treasure in your hands, Antigone—life, I mean. [*He picks up his coat from the chair, puts it on.*] And you were about to throw it away. Would it have been better to let you die a victim to that obscene story? Don't think me fatuous if I say that I understand you; and that at your age I should have done the same thing. A moment ago, when we were quarreling, you said I was drinking in your words. I was. But it wasn't you I was listening to; it was a lad named Creon who lived here in Thebes many years ago. He was thin and pale, as you are. His mind, too, was filled with thoughts of self-sacrifice. Go find Haemon. And get married quickly, Antigone. Be happy. Life is not what you think it is.

Life is a child playing round your feet, a tool you hold firmly in your grip, a bench you sit down upon in the evening, in your garden. People will tell you that that's not life, that life is something else. They will tell you this because they need your strength and your fire, and they will want to make use of you. Don't listen to them. Believe me, the only poor consolation that we have in our old age is to discover that what I have just said to you is true. Life is nothing more than the happiness that you get out of it.

Antigone. [*Murmurs, lost in thought.*] Happiness . . .

Creon. [*Suddenly a little self-conscious.*] Not much of a word, is it?

Antigone. [*Quietly.*] What kind of happiness do you foresee for me? Paint me the picture of your happy Antigone. What are the unimportant little sins that I shall have to commit before I am allowed to sink my teeth into life and tear happiness from it? Tell me: to whom shall I have to lie? Upon whom shall I have to fawn? To whom must I sell myself? Whom do you want me to leave dying, while I turn away my eyes?

Creon. Antigone, be quiet.

Antigone. Why do you tell me to be quiet when all I want to know is what I have to do to be happy? You tell me that life is so wonderful. I want to know what I have to do in order to be able to say that myself.

Creon. Do you love Haemon?

Antigone. Yes, I love Haemon. The Haemon I love is hard and young, faithful and difficult to satisfy, the way I am. But if what I love in Haemon is to be worn away like a stone step by the tread of the thing you call life, the thing you call happiness; if Haemon reaches the point where he stops growing pale with fear when I grow pale, stops thinking that I must have been killed in an accident when I am five minutes late, stops feeling that he is alone on earth when I laugh and he doesn't know why—if he too has to learn to say yes to everything—why, no, then, no! I do not love Haemon!

Creon. You don't know what you are talking about!

Antigone. I do know what I am talking about! It is you who have lost your way and don't know what to say. I am too far away from you now, talking to you from a kingdom you can't get into, with your quick tongue and your hollow heart. [*Laughs.*] I laugh, Creon, because I see suddenly what a transparent hypocrite you are. Creon, the family man! Creon, the contented sitter on benches, in the evening, in his garden! Creon, desecrating the dead while he tries to fob me off with platitudes about happiness!

Creon. It is your happiness, too, Antigone!

Antigone. I spit on your happiness! I spit on your idea of life—that life that must go on, come what may. You are all like dogs that lick everything they smell. You with your promise of a humdrum happiness—provided a person doesn't ask too much of life. I want everything of life, I do; and I want it now! I want it total, complete: otherwise I reject it! If life must be a thing of fear and lying and compromise; if life cannot be free, gallant, incorruptible—then, Creon, I choose death!

Creon. Scream on, daughter of Oedipus! Scream on, in your father's own voice!

Antigone. In my father's own voice, yes! The voice of a king who died to purify his people, whereas you live to make them vile. You've told me that you'd like to bury Polynices, but that there are political reasons why—what was that horrible thing you said? —why that stench has got to fill the town for a month. I have nothing to do with your politics. Tell me why I can't bury him.

Creon. Because it's my order.

Antigone. The order of a coward King who makes war upon the dead!

Creon. Be quiet, I say!

Antigone. Why do you want me to be quiet? Because you know that I am right? Do you think I can't tell from your face that what I'm saying is true? Of course, it's true. But no, you can't admit it; because you have to growl and defend the bone that you call politics.

Creon. [*Grasps her by her arms.*] Shut up! If you could see how ugly you are, shrieking those words!

Antigone. Yes, I am ugly! Father was ugly, too. [CREON *releases her arms, turns and moves away. Stands with his back to* ANTIGONE.] But father became beautiful. And do you know when? [*She follows him to behind the table.*] At the very end. When all his questions had been answered. When he could no longer doubt that he *had* killed his own father; that he *had* gone to bed with his own mother. When he was absolutely certain that he had to die if the plague was to be lifted from his people. Then he was at peace; then he could smile, almost; then he became beautiful . . . Whereas you! Look at yourself, Creon! That never-extinguished glint of fear and suspicion in the corner of your eye—that ever-present crease in the corner of your power-loving mouth. Creon, you spoke the word a moment ago: the smelly kitchen of politics. That's where you were fathered and pupped—in a filthy kitchen!

Creon. [*Turns to her.*] I order you to shut up! Do you hear me!

Antigone. You order me? Cook! Do you really believe that you can give me orders?

Creon. Antigone! The ante-room is full of people! Do you want them to hear you?

Antigone. Open the doors! Let us make sure that they can hear me!

Creon. By God! You shut up, I tell you!

[ISMENE *enters through arch.*]

Ismene. [*Distraught.*] Antigone!

Antigone. [*Turns to* ISMENE.] You, too? What do you want?

Ismene. Oh, forgive me, Antigone. I've come back. I'll go with you now.

Antigone. Where will you go with me?

Ismene. [*To* CREON.] Creon! If you kill her, you'll have to kill me, too. I was with her. I helped her bury Polynices.

Antigone. Oh, no, Ismene! You had your chance to come with me in the black night, creeping on your hands and knees. You had your chance to claw up the earth with your nails, as I did; to get yourself caught like a thief, as I did. And you refused it.

Ismene. Not any more. If you die, I don't want to live. I'll do it alone tonight.

Antigone. You hear that, Creon? [*She turns round toward* CREON.] The thing is catching! Who knows but that lots of people will catch the disease from me! What are you waiting for? Call in your guards! Come on, Creon! Show a little courage! It only hurts for a minute! Come on, cook!

Creon. [*Turns toward arch and calls.*] Guards! [GUARDS *enter through arch.*]

Antigone. [*In a great cry of relief.*] At last, Creon!

[CHORUS *enters through left arch.*]

Creon. [*To the* GUARDS.] Take her away!

[CREON *goes up onto top step.* GUARDS *grasp* ANTIGONE *by her arms, turn and hustle her towards the arch right and exit.* ISMENE *mimes horror, backs away towards the arch left, then turns and runs out through the arch. A long pause, as* CREON *moves slowly downstage.*]

Chorus. [*Behind* CREON. *Speaks in a deliberate voice.*] You are out of your mind, Creon. What have you done?

Creon. [*His back to* CHORUS.] She had to die.

Chorus. You must not let Antigone die. We shall carry the scar of her death for centuries.

Creon. She insisted. No man on earth was strong enough to dissuade her. Polynices was a mere pretext. When she had to give up that pretext, she found another one—that life and happiness were tawdry things and not worth possessing. She was bent upon only one thing: to reject life and to die.

Chorus. You say so, Creon. But it is not the truth.

Creon. What do you want me to do for her? Condemn her to live?

Haemon. [*Calls from off-stage.*] Father!

[HAEMON *enters through arch right.* CREON *turns toward him.*]

Creon. Haemon, forget Antigone. Forget her, my dearest boy.

Haemon. How can you talk like that?

Creon. [*Grasps* HAEMON *by the hands.*] I did everything I could to save her, Haemon. I used every argument. I swear I did. The girl doesn't love you. She could have gone on living for you; but she refused. She wanted it this way; she wanted to die.

Haemon. Father! The Guards are dragging Antigone away! You've got to stop them! [*He breaks away from* CREON.]

Creon. [*Looks away from* HAEMON.] I can't stop them. It's too late. Antigone has spoken. The story is all over Thebes. I cannot save her now.

Chorus. Creon, you must find a way to keep Antigone from being put to death.

Creon. I cannot.

Chorus. You must recall your edict. You must order the burial of Polynices.

Creon. Too late. The law must be obeyed. I can do nothing.

Haemon. But, Father, you are master in Thebes!

Creon. I am master under the law. Not above the law.

Haemon. But you made that law yourself. What you ordained, you can repeal. You cannot let Antigone be taken from me.

Creon. I cannot do anything else, my poor boy. She must die and you must live.

Haemon. Live, you say! Live a life without Antigone? A life in which I am to go on admiring you as you busy yourself about your kingdom; go on admiring you as you make your persuasive speeches and strike your attitudes? Not without Antigone. I love Antigone. She never struck a pose and waited for me to admire her. Mirrors meant nothing to her. She never looked at herself. She looked at me, and expected me to be somebody. And I was—when I was with her. Do you think I am not going after her? I will not live without Antigone!

Creon. Haemon—you will have to resign yourself to life without Antigone. [*He moves to left of* HAEMON.] Sooner or later there comes a day of sorrow in each man's life when he must cease to be a child and take up the burden of being a man. That day has come for you.

Haemon. [*Backs away a step.*] That giant strength, that courage. That massive god who used to pick me up in his arms and shelter me from shadows and monsters—was that you, Father? Was it of you I stood in awe? Was that man you?

Creon. Yes, Haemon, that was me.

Haemon. Then you are not that man today. For if you were, you'd know that your enemies are abroad in every street. You'd know that the people are stirring and murmuring against you. You cannot put Antigone to death. She will not have been dead an hour before shame will sit on every Theban doorstep and horror will fill every Theban heart. Already the people are full of fear and anger because you have not buried Polynices. If you kill Antigone, they will hate you!

Creon. Silence! That edict stands!

Haemon. [*Stares at* CREON *for a moment.*] I tell you again that I will not live without Antigone.

[*Turns and goes quickly out through arch.*]

Chorus. Creon, the gods have a way of punishing injustice.

Creon. [*Contemptuously.*] The gods!

Chorus. Creon, that boy is wounded to death.

Creon. We are all wounded to death.

[FIRST GUARD *enters through arch right, followed by* SECOND *and* THIRD GUARDS *pulling* ANTIGONE *along with them.*]

First Guard. Chief, the people are crowding into the palace!

Antigone. Creon, you are going to kill me; let that be enough. I want to be alone until it is over.

Creon. Empty the palace! Guards at the gates!

[CREON *quickly crosses toward the arch and exits. Two* GUARDS *release* ANTIGONE *and exit behind* CREON. CHORUS *goes out through arch left. The lighting dims so that only the area about the table is lighted. The cyclorama is covered with a dark blue color. The scene is intended to suggest a prison cell, filled with shadows and dimly lit.* ANTIGONE *moves to stool and sits. The* FIRST GUARD *stands upstage. He watches* ANTIGONE, *and as she sits, he begins pacing slowly downstage, then upstage. A pause.*]

Antigone. [*Turns and looks at the* GUARD.] It's you, is it?

Guard. What do you mean, me?

Antigone. The last human face that I shall see. [*A pause as they look at one another; then* GUARD *paces upstage; turns and crosses behind table.*] Was it you that arrested me this morning?

Guard. Yes, that was me.

Antigone. You hurt me. There was no need for you to hurt me. Did I act as if I was trying to escape?

Guard. Come on now, Miss. It was my business to bring you in. I did it.

[*A pause. He paces to and fro upstage. Only the sound of his boots is heard.*]

Antigone. How old are you?

Guard. Thirty-nine.

Antigone. Have you any children?

Guard. Yeah. Two.

Antigone. Do you love your children?

Guard. What's that got to do with you?

[*A pause. He paces upstage and downstage.*]

Antigone. How long have you been in the Guards?

Guard. Since the war. I was in the army. Sergeant. Then I joined the Guards.

Antigone. Does one have to have been an army sergeant to get into the Guards?

Guard. Supposed to be. Either that or on special detail. But when they make you a guard, you lose your stripes.

Antigone. [*Murmurs.*] I see.

Guard. Yes. Of course, if you're a guard, everybody knows you're something special; they know you're an old non-com. Take pay, for instance. When you're a guard you get your pay, and on top of that you get six months' extra pay, to make sure you don't lose anything by not being a sergeant any more.

Antigone. [*Barely audible.*] I see.

Guard. That's what I'm telling you. That's why sergeants, now, they don't like guards. Maybe you noticed they try to make out they're better than us? Promotion, that's what it is. In the army, anybody can get promoted. All you need is good conduct

Now in the Guards, it's slow, and you have to know your business—like how to make out a report and the like of that. But when you're a non-com in the Guards, you've got something that even a sergeant-major ain't got. For instance . . .

Antigone. [*Breaking him off.*] Listen.

Guard. Yes, Miss.

Antigone. I'm going to die soon.

[*The* GUARD *looks at her a moment, then turns and moves away.*]

Guard. For instance, people have a lot of respect for guards, they have. A guard may be a soldier, but he's kind of in the civil service, too.

Antigone. Do you think it hurts to die?

Guard. How would I know? Of course, if somebody sticks a sabre in your gut and turns it round, it hurts.

Antigone. How are they going to put me to death?

Guard. Well, I'll tell you. I heard the proclamation, all right. There isn't much that gets away from me. It seems that they don't want to dirty up . . . Wait a minute. How did that go now? [*He stares into space and recites from memory.*] "In order that our fair city shall not be pol-luted with her sinful blood, she shall be im-mured—im-mured." That means, they shove you in a cave and wall up the cave.

Antigone. Alive?

Guard. Yes . . .

[*He moves away a few steps.*]

Antigone. [*Murmurs.*] O tomb! O bridal bed! Alone!

[ANTIGONE *sits there, a tiny figure in the middle of the stage. You would say she felt a little chilly. She wraps her arms around herself.*]

Guard. Yep! Outside the southeast gate of the town. In the Cave of Hades. In broad daylight. Some detail, eh, for them that's on the job! First they thought maybe it was a job for the army. Now it looks like it's going to be the Guards. There's an outfit for you! Nothing the Guards can't do. No wonder the army's jealous.

Antigone. A pair of animals.

Guard. What do you mean, a pair of animals?

Antigone. When the winds blow cold, all they need do is to press close against one another. I am all alone.

Guard. Say, is there anything you want? I can send out for it, you know.

Antigone. You are very kind. [*A pause.* ANTIGONE *looks up at the* GUARD.] Yes, there is something I want. I want you to give someone a letter from me, when I am dead.

Guard. How's that again? A letter?

Antigone. Yes, I want to write a letter; and I want you to give it to someone for me.

Guard. [*Straightens up.*] Hey, wait a minute. Take it easy. It's as much as my job is worth to go handing out letters from prisoners.

Antigone. [*Removes a ring from her finger and holds it out toward him.*] I'll give you this ring if you will do it.

Guard. Is it gold?

[*He takes the ring from her.*]

Antigone. Yes, it is gold.

Guard. [*Shakes his head.*] Uh-uh. No can do. Suppose they go through my pockets. I might get six months for a thing like that. [*He stares at the ring, then glances off right to make sure that he is not being watched.*] Listen, tell you what I'll do. You tell me what you want to say, and I'll write it down in my book. Then afterwards, I'll tear out the pages and give them to the party, see? If it's in my handwriting, it's all right.

Antigone. [*Winces.*] In your handwriting? [*She shudders slightly.*] No. That would be awful. The poor darling! In your handwriting.

Guard. [*Offers back the ring.*] O.K. It's no skin off my nose.

Antigone. [*Quickly.*] Of course, of course. No, keep the ring. But hurry. Time is getting short. Where is your notebook? [*The* GUARD *pockets the ring, takes his notebook and pencil from his pocket, puts his foot up on chair, and rests the notebook on his knee, licks his pencil.*] Ready? [*He nods.*] Write, now. "My darling . . ."

Guard. [*Writes as he mutters.*] The boy friend, eh?

Antigone. "My darling. I had to die, and perhaps you will not love me any more . . ."

Guard. [*Mutters as he writes.*] ". . . will not love me any more."

Antigone. "Perhaps it would have been simple to accept life . . ."

Guard. [*Repeats as he writes.*] ". . . to accept life . . ."

Antigone. "But it was not for myself. And now, it's so dreadful here alone. I am afraid . . . [*She glances wildly about.*] And these shadows . . ."

Guard. [*Looks at her.*] Wait a minute! How fast do you think I can write?

Antigone. [*Takes hold of herself.*] Where are you?

Guard. [*Reads from his notebook.*] ". . . dreadful here alone. I am afraid . . ."

Antigone. No. Scratch that out. Nobody must know that. They have no right to know. It's as if they saw me naked and touched me, after I was dead. Scratch it all out. Just write: "Forgive me."

Guard [*Looks at* ANTIGONE.] I cut out everything you said there at the end, and I put down, "Forgive me"?

Antigone. Yes. "Forgive me, my darling. But it wasn't for myself. I love you." [*She murmurs, as* GUARD *writes.*] No, it wasn't for myself.

Guard. [*Finishes the letter.*] ". . . I love you." [*He looks at her.*] Is that all?

Antigone. That's all.

Guard. [*Straightens up, looks at notebook.*] Damn funny letter.

Antigone. I know.

Guard. [*Looks at her.*] Who is it to? [*A sudden roll of drums begins and continues until after* ANTIGONE *exits. The* FIRST GUARD *pockets the notebook and shouts at* ANTIGONE.] O.K. That's enough out of you! Come on!

[*At the sound of the drum roll,* SECOND *and* THIRD GUARDS *enter through the right arch.* ANTIGONE *rises.* GUARDS *seize her and exit with her. The lighting moves up to suggest late afternoon.* CHORUS *enters.*]

Chorus. And now it is Creon's turn.

[MESSENGER *runs through the arch right.*]

Messenger. The Queen . . . the Queen! Where is the Queen?

Chorus. What do you want with the Queen? What have you to tell the Queen?

Messenger. News to break her heart. Antigone had just been thrust into the cave. They hadn't finished heaving the last blocks of stone into place when Creon and the rest heard a sudden moaning from the tomb. A hush fell over us all, for it was not the voice of Antigone. It was Haemon's voice that came forth from the tomb. Everybody looked at Creon; and he howled like a man demented: "Take away the stones! Take away the stones!" The slaves leaped at the wall of stones, and Creon worked with them, sweating and tearing at the blocks with his bleeding hands. Finally a narrow opening was forced, and into it slipped the smallest guard.

Antigone had hanged herself by the cord of her robe, by the red and golden twisted cord of her robe. The cord was round her neck like a child's collar. Haemon was on his knees, holding her in his arms and moaning, his face buried in her robe. More stones were removed, and Creon went into the tomb. He tried to raise Haemon to his feet. I could hear him begging Haemon to rise to his feet. Haemon was deaf to his father's voice, till suddenly he stood up of his own accord, his eyes dark and burning. Anguish was in his face, but it was the face of a little boy. He stared at his father. Then suddenly he struck him—hard; and he drew his sword. Creon leapt out of range. Haemon went on staring at him, his eyes full of contempt—a glance that was like a knife, and that Creon couldn't escape. The King stood trembling in the far corner of the tomb, and Haemon went on staring. Then, without a word, he stabbed himself and lay down beside Antigone, embracing her in a great pool of blood.

[*A pause as* CREON *and* PAGE *enter through arch on the* MESSENGER'S *last words.* CHORUS *and the* MESSENGER *both turn to look at* CREON, *then the* MESSENGER *exits through curtain.*]

Creon. I have had them laid out side by side. They are together at last, and at peace. Two lovers on the morrow of their bridal. Their work is done.

Chorus. But not yours, Creon. You have still one thing to learn. Eurydice, the Queen, your wife . . .

Creon. A good woman. Always busy with her garden, her preserves, her sweaters—those sweaters she never stopped knitting for the poor. Strange, how the poor never stop needing sweaters. One would almost think that was all they needed.

Chorus. The poor in Thebes are going to be cold this winter, Creon. When the Queen was told of her son's death, she waited carefully until she had finished her row, then put down her knitting calmly—as she did everything. She went up to her room, her lavender-scented room, with its embroidered doilies and its pictures framed in plush; and there, Creon, she cut her throat. She is laid out now in one of those two old-fashioned twin beds, exactly where you went to her one night when she was still a maiden. Her smile is still the same, scarcely a shade more melancholy. And if it were not for that great red blot on the bed linen by her neck, one might think she was asleep.

Creon. [*In a dull voice.*] She, too. They are all asleep. [*Pause.*] It must be good to sleep.

Chorus. Tomorrow they will sleep sweetly in the ground, Creon. You will bury them tomorrow. You who would not bury Polynices today will bury Eurydice and Haemon tomorrow. And Antigone, too. [*Pause.*] The gods take a hand in every game, Creon. Even politics.

Creon. [*Nodding soberly.*] The gods!

Chorus. And now you are alone, Creon.

Creon. Yes, all alone. [*He remains lost*

in thought as the hour strikes. To PAGE.] What time was that?

Page. Five o'clock, Sir.

Creon. What have we on at five o'clock?

Page. Cabinet meeting, Sir.

Creon. Cabinet meeting. Well, we might as well go along to it.

[CREON *and* PAGE *exit slowly through arch left and* CHORUS *moves downstage.*]

Chorus. And there we are. All those who were meant to die have died. Those who believed one thing, those who believed the contrary thing, and even those who believed nothing at all, yet were caught up in the web without knowing why. All dead: stiff, useless, rotting.

Creon was the most rational, the most plausible of tyrants. But like all tyrants, he refused to distinguish between the things that are Caesar's and the things that are God's. Now and again, in the three thousand years since the first Antigone was heard of, someone has had to come forward to remind men of this distinction. And whether we say that the result is Christianity, or popular revolution, or underground resistance, the cause is always the same—a passionate belief that moral law exists, and a passionate regard for the sanctity of human personality.

Well, Antigone is calm tonight. She has played her part.

[*Three* GUARDS *enter, resume their places on steps as at the rise of the curtain, and begin to play cards.*]

A great melancholy wave of unrest now settles down upon Thebes, upon the empty palace, upon Creon, who can now begin to long for his own death.

Only the guards are left, and none of this matters to them. It's no skin off their noses. They go on playing cards.

[CHORUS *walks toward the arch left as*]

THE CURTAIN FALLS

THE GLASS MENAGERIE*

By

TENNESSEE WILLIAMS

When "The Glass Menagerie" appeared in New York in 1945 after a run in Chicago, Tennessee Williams, though hitherto unknown to the public, was not unknown to the watchers for play-writing talent. He had received help and encouragement from the American Institute of Arts and Letters, from the Theatre Guild, and from others interested in the drama. He has so many writing talents that he can scarcely hide them if he writes at all. He can evoke moods of the most delicate sort, or stun with clamor and fury; he can make the commonest words in the most realistic speech seem to sing; he can articulate inarticulateness; he can charm with humor either dainty or robust; he can punch and roar most brutally in scenes of outrageous violence; he can be poetic without being fancy; he knows the theatre and how to use it. All this had been apparent to the discerning even before *The Glass Menagerie,* but *The Glass Menagerie's* New York success put Mr. Williams' talents before the public.

But *The Glass Menagerie* was in a way misleading. Mr. Williams said, "I put all the nice things I have to say about people into *The Glass Menagerie.* What I write hereafter will be harsher." And truly it has been harsher. For Mr. Williams' remarkable talents display a hopeless and hagridden view of mankind. Mr. Williams finds no God in Heaven, no Devil in Hell; the only reality is the phantasmagoric image in each man's or woman's lonely psyche. This psyche, since it differs from every other, is at war, but it yearns for an unattainable peace and unity. It seeks to impose itself on the whatever outside itself; it strives, as in *The Glass Menagerie,* for something it calls happiness: gentlemen callers or escape from the warehouse. Its weapons in its war are force or terror if it can use them, deceit and guile if it can't. But in all this it is unconsciously directed; man is automatically brutal, instinctively violent; an animal in his lusts, a beast in his savagery. He pretends to gentility or refinement or tenderness, but these are only pretences and they invariably are torn away from Mr. Williams' characters so that the carnivore appears in his primitive nakedness. Amanda in *The Glass Menagerie* has destroyed her daughter and would like to destroy her son—perhaps she did—though she "loves" them both. But she is not "guilty"; hers is the nature of mothers and of Southern ex-belles, and she cannot be blamed for behaving as she must behave. So Mr. Williams' attitude toward his characters can be compassionate and understanding, and is, for he does not write with contempt. He is the typical tragedian of modern times; his tragic hero cannot have nobility; there is no such thing as nobility in Mr. Williams' world unless it is pretence. But his tragic hero can suffer as we all suffer in a world which drives us hither and thither without our understanding either it or ourselves. And Mr. Williams' powerful plays catch us where we know we are weakest, where our wishes are the only horses we beggars may ride.

Clearly some of *The Glass Menagerie* is autobiographical, since Mr. Williams worked briefly in a shoe warehouse, and since his sister had a collection of glass animals. Of those animals he said, "By poetic association they came to represent in my memory all the softest emotions that belong to recollections of things past. They stood for all the tender things that relieve the austere pattern of life and make it endurable to the sensitive."

Some remarkable circumstances attended the first production of *The Glass Menagerie.* The play was submitted to Eddie Dowling, who was deeply engaged in preparing for another play. But after reading *The Glass Menagerie* he wanted so much to do it that he said to his backer, Louis J. Singer, "This I want to do first, but it won't make a cent." Mr. Singer said, "If you want to do it, count me in."

Laurette Taylor had not appeared on the stage in many years, though in her heyday she had been one of the brightest stars of the American theatre. In the meantime she had suffered from alcoholism and psychological disorder, but recovered, and then hunted and hunted, unsuccessfully, for a play she wished to do. None came until Mr. Dowling thought of her for Amanda. On first reading she fell in love with the play, and thereafter gave all her great powers to developing her performance, making a masterpiece of it. Mr. Dowling as Tom, Julie Haydon as Laura, and Anthony Ross as Jim completed a magnificent cast. The play ran for 563 performances in New York and many more on tour.

TENNESSEE WILLIAMS

Born 1914, Columbus, Mississippi. (Thomas Lanier Williams)

Attended University of Missouri and Washington University, St. Louis.

1936, Adopted pen name Tennessee.

1938, B.A., University of Iowa.

1943, Grant from American Institute of Arts and Letters.

1943, Script-writer for Metro-Goldwyn-Mayer.

1945, *The Glass Menagerie* wins the New York Drama Critics' Circle award as the year's best play.

1947, *A Streetcar Named Desire* wins the Pulitzer Prize and the New York Drama Critics' Circle award as the year's best play.

1955, *Cat on a Hot Tin Roof* wins the Pulitzer Prize and the New York Drama Critics' Circle award as the year's best play.

Poet, novelist, short-story writer.

PLAYS

1936 *Cairo, Shanghai, Bombay!* 1937 *Candles to the Sun.* 1937 *Fugitive Kind.* 1940 *Battle of Angels.* 1940 *Moony's Kid Don't Cry* (one act). 1944 *The Glass Menagerie.* 1944 *The Purification* (one act, also called *Dos Ranchos*). 1946 *You Touched Me!* (with Donald Windham). 1946 *27 Wagons Full of Cotton* (one act). 1946 *The Lady of Larkspur Lotion* (one act). 1946 *The Last of My Solid Gold Watches* (one act). 1946 *Portrait of a Madonna* (one act). 1946 *Auto-Da-Fé* (one act). 1946 *Lord Byron's Love Letter* (one act). 1946 *The Strangest Kind of Romance* (one act). 1946 *The Long Goodbye* (one act). 1946 *Hello from Bertha* (one act). 1946 *The Long Stay Cut Short, or, The Unsatisfactory Supper* (one act). 1947 *A Streetcar Named Desire.* 1948 *The Dark Room* (one act). 1948 *Ten Blocks on the Camino Real* (one act). 1948 *The Case of the Crushed Petunias* (one act). 1948 *Summer and Smoke.* 1949 *This Property Is Condemned* (one act). 1951 *The Rose Tattoo.* 1951 *I Rise in Flame, Cried the Phoenix* (one act). 1953 *Camino Real.* 1953 *Talk to Me Like the Rain* (one act). 1953 *Something Unspoken* (one act). 1955 *Cat on a Hot Tin Roof.*

SCREENWRITING

1950 *The Glass Menagerie.* 1955 *The Rose Tattoo.*

WRITINGS ON DRAMA

Preface to *27 Wagons Full of Cotton,* 1946. Introduction to Signet Book edition of *A Streetcar Named Desire,* 1952; reprinted from *The New York Times,* Nov. 30, 1947, II.1.3.

THE GLASS MENAGERIE

Characters

AMANDA WINGFIELD, *the mother.*
A little woman of great but confused vitality clinging frantically to another time and place. Her characterization must be carefully created, not copied from type. She is not paranoiac, but her life is paranoia. There is much to admire in AMANDA, *and as much to love and pity as there is to laugh at. Certainly she has endurance and a kind of heroism, and though her foolishness makes her unwittingly cruel at times, there is tenderness in her slight person.*

LAURA WINGFIELD, *her daughter.*
AMANDA, *having failed to establish contact with reality, continues to live vitally in her illusions, but* LAURA'S *situation is even graver. A childhood illness has left her crippled, one leg slightly shorter than the other, and held in a brace. This defect need not be more than suggested on the stage. Stemming from this,* LAURA'S *separation increases till she is like a piece of her own glass collection, too exquisitely fragile to move from the shelf.*

TOM WINGFIELD, *her son, and the narrator of the play. A poet with a job in a warehouse. His nature is not remorseless, but to escape from a trap he has to act without pity.*

JIM O'CONNOR, *the gentleman caller.*
A nice, ordinary, young man.

SCENE

An Alley in St. Louis

PART I. Preparation for a Gentleman Caller.
PART II. The Gentleman calls.
Time: Now and the Past.

PRODUCTION NOTES

Being a "memory play," *The Glass Menagerie* can be presented with unusual freedom of convention. Because of its considerably delicate or tenuous material, atmospheric touches and subtleties of direction play a particularly important part. Expressionism and all other unconventional techniques in drama have only one valid aim, and that is a closer approach to truth. When a play employs unconventional techniques, it is not, or certainly shouldn't be, trying to escape its responsibility of dealing with reality, or interpreting experience, but is actually or should be attempting to find a closer approach, a more penetrating and vivid expression of things as they are. The straight realistic play with its genuine frigidaire and authentic ice-cubes, its characters that speak exactly as its audience speaks, corresponds to the academic landscape and has the same virtue of a photographic likeness. Everyone should know nowadays the unimportance of the photographic in art: that truth, life, or reality is an organic thing which the poetic imagination can represent or suggest, in essence, only through transformation, through changing into other forms than those which were merely present in appearance.

These remarks are not meant as a preface only to this particular play. They have to do with a conception of a new, plastic theatre which must take the place of the exhausted theatre of realistic conventions if the theatre is to resume vitality as a part of our culture.

THE SCREEN DEVICE

There is *only one important difference between the original and acting versions of the play* and that is the *omission* in the latter of the device which I tentatively included in my *original* script. This device was the use of a screen on which were projected magic-lantern slides bearing images or titles. I do not regret the omission of this device from the Broadway production. The extraordinary power of Miss Taylor's performance made it suitable to have the utmost simplicity in the physical production. But I think it may be interesting to some readers to see how this device was conceived. So I am putting it into the published manuscript. These images and legends, projected from behind, were cast on a section of wall between the front-room and dining-room areas, which should be indistinguishable from the rest when not in use.

The purpose of this will probably be apparent. It is to give accent to certain values in each scene. Each scene contains a particular point (or several) which is structurally the most important. In an episodic play, such as this, the basic structure or narrative line may be obscured from the audience; the effect may seem fragmentary rather than architectural. This may not be the fault of the play so much as a lack of attention in the audience. The legend or image upon the screen will strengthen the effect of what is merely allusion in the writing and allow the primary point to be made more simply and lightly than if the entire responsibility were on the spoken lines. Aside from this structural value, I think the screen will have a definite emotional appeal, less definable but just as important. An imaginative producer or director may invent many other uses for this device than those indicated in the present script. In fact the possibilities of the device seem much larger to me than the instance of this play can possibly utilize.

The Music

Another extra-literary accent in this play is provided by the use of music. A single recurring tune, "The Glass Menagerie," is used to give emotional emphasis to suitable passages. This tune is like circus music, not when you are on the grounds or in the immediate vicinity of the parade, but when you are at some distance and very likely thinking of something else. It seems under those circumstances to continue almost interminably and it weaves in and out of your preoccupied consciousness; then it is the lightest, most delicate music in the world and perhaps the saddest. It expresses the surface vivacity of life with the underlying strain of immutable and inexpressible sorrow. When you look at a piece of delicately spun glass you think of two things: how beautiful it is and how easily it can be broken. Both of those ideas should be woven into the recurring tune, which dips in and out of the play as if it were carried on a wind that changes. It serves as a thread of connection and allusion between the narrator with his separate point in time and space and the subject of his story. Between each episode it returns as reference to the emotion, nostalgia, which is the first condition of the play. It is primarily Laura's music and therefore comes out most clearly when the play focuses upon her and the lovely fragility of glass which is her image.

The Lighting

The lighting in the play is not realistic. In keeping with the atmosphere of memory, the stage is dim. Shafts of light are focused on selected areas or actors, sometimes in contradistinction to what is the apparent center. For instance, in the quarrel scene between Tom and Amanda, in which Laura has no active part, the clearest pool of light is on her figure. This is also true of the supper scene, when her silent figure on the sofa should remain the visual center. The light upon Laura should be distinct from the others, having a peculiar pristine clarity such as light used in early religious portraits of female saints or madonnas. A certain correspondence to light in religious paintings, such as El Greco's, where the figures are radiant in atmosphere that is relatively dusky, could be effectively used throughout the play. (It will also permit a more effective use of the screen.) A free, imaginative use of light can be of enormous value in giving a mobile, plastic quality to plays of a more or less static nature.

T. W.

SCENE I

The Wingfield apartment is in the rear of the building, one of those vast hive-like conglomerations of cellular living-units that flower as warty growths in overcrowded urban centers of lower middle-class population and are symptomatic of the impulse of this largest and fundamentally enslaved section of American society to avoid fluidity and differentiation and to exist and function as one interfused mass of automatism.

The apartment faces an alley and is entered by a fire-escape, a structure whose name is a touch of accidental poetic truth, for all of these huge buildings are always burning with the slow and implacable fires of human desperation. The fire-escape is included in the set—that is, the landing of it and steps descending from it.

The scene is memory and is therefore nonrealistic. Memory takes a lot of poetic license. It omits some details; others are exaggerated, according to the emotional value of the articles it touches, for memory is seated predominantly in the heart. The interior is therefore rather dim and poetic.

At the rise of the curtain, the audience is faced with the dark, grim rear wall of the Wingfield tenement. This building, which runs parallel to the footlights, is flanked on both sides by dark, narrow alleys which run into murky canyons of tangled clotheslines, garbage cans, and the sinister lattice-work of neighboring fire-escapes. It is up and down these side alleys that exterior entrances and exits are made, during the play. At the end of TOM'S *opening commentary, the dark tenement wall slowly reveals (by means of a transparency) the interior of the ground floor Wingfield apartment.*

Downstage is the living room, which also serves as a sleeping room for LAURA, *the sofa unfolding to make her bed. Upstage, center, and divided by a wide arch or second proscenium with transparent faded portieres (or second curtain), is the dining room. In an old-fashioned what-not in the living room are seen scores of transparent glass animals. A blown-up photograph of the father hangs on the wall of the living room, facing the audience, to the left of the archway. It is the face of a very handsome young man in a doughboy's First World War cap. He is gallantly smiling, ineluctably smiling, as if to say, "I will be smiling forever."*

The audience hears and sees the opening scene in the dining room through both the transparent fourth wall of the building and the transparent gauze portiers of the dining-room arch. It is during this revealing scene that the fourth wall slowly ascends, out of sight. This transparent exterior wall is not brought down again until the very end of the play, during TOM'S *final speech.*

The narrator is an undisguised convention of the play. He takes whatever license with dramatic convention is convenient to his purposes.

[TOM *enters dressed as a merchant sailor from alley, stage left, and strolls across the front of the stage to the fire-escape. There he stops and lights a cigarette. He addresses the audience.*]

Tom. Yes, I have tricks in my pocket, I have things up my sleeve. But I am the opposite of a stage magician. He gives you illusion that has the appearance of truth. I give you truth in the pleasant disguise of illusion.

To begin with, I turn back time. I reverse it to that quaint period, the thirties, when the huge middle class of America was matriculating in a school for the blind. Their eyes had failed them, or they had failed their eyes, and so they were having their fingers pressed forcibly down on the fiery Braille alphabet of a dissolving economy.

In Spain there was revolution. Here there was only shouting and confusion.

In Spain there was Guernica. Here there were disturbances of labor, sometimes pretty violent, in otherwise peaceful cities such as Chicago, Cleveland, Saint Louis . . .

This is the social background of the play.

[*Music.*]

The play is memory.

Being a memory play, it is dimly lighted, it is sentimental, it is not realistic.

In memory everything seems to happen to music. That explains the fiddle in the wings.

I am the narrator of the play, and also a character in it.

The other characters are my mother, Amanda, my sister, Laura, and a gentleman caller who appears in the final scenes.

He is the most realistic character in the play, being an emissary from a world of reality that we were somehow set apart from.

But since I have a poet's weakness for symbols, I am using this character also as a symbol; he is the long delayed but always expected something that we live for.

There is a fifth character in the play who doesn't appear except in this larger-than-life-size photograph over the mantel.

This is our father who left us a long time ago.

He was a telephone man who fell in love with long distances; he gave up his job with the telephone company and skipped the light fantastic out of town . . .

The last we heard of him was a picture post-card from Mazatlan, on the Pacific coast of Mexico, containing a message of two words——

"Hello—— Good-bye!" and no address.

I think the rest of the play will explain itself. . . .

[AMANDA'S *voice becomes audible through the portieres.* LEGEND ON SCREEN: "OÙ SONT LES NEIGES?" *He divides the portieres and enters the upstage area.* AMANDA *and* LAURA *are seated at a drop-leaf table. Eating is indicated by gestures without food or utensils.* AMANDA *faces the audience.* TOM *and* LAURA *are seated in profile. The interior has lit up softly and through the scrim we see* AMANDA *and* LAURA *seated at the table in the upstage area.*]

Amanda. [*Calling.*] Tom?

Tom. Yes, Mother.

Amanda. We can't say grace until you come to the table!

Tom. Coming, Mother.

[*He bows slightly and withdraws, reappearing a few moments later in his place at the table.*]

Amanda. [*To her son.*] Honey, don't *push* with your *fingers.* If you have to push with something, the thing to push with is a crust of bread. And chew—chew! Animals have sections in their stomachs which enable them to digest food without mastication, but human beings are supposed to chew their food before they swallow it down. Eat food leisurely, son, and really enjoy it. A well-cooked meal has lots of delicate flavors that have to be held in the mouth for appreciation. So chew your food and give your salivary glands a chance to function!

[TOM *deliberately lays his imaginary fork down and pushes his chair back from the table.*]

Tom. I haven't enjoyed one bite of this dinner because of your constant directions on how to eat it. It's you that make me rush through meals with your hawk-like attention to every bite I take. Sickening—spoils my appetite—all this discussion of—animals' secretion—salivary glands—mastication!

Amanda. [*Lightly.*] Temperament like a Metropolitan star! [*He rises and crosses downstage.*] You're not excused from the table.

Tom. I'm getting a cigarette.

Amanda. You smoke too much.

[LAURA *rises.*]

Laura. I'll bring in the blanc mange.

[*He remains standing with his cigarette by the portieres during the following.*]

Amanda. [*Rising.*] No, sister, no, sister—you be the lady this time and I'll be the darky.

Laura. I'm already up.

Amanda. Resume your seat, little sister—I want you to stay fresh and pretty—for gentlemen callers!

Laura. I'm not expecting any gentlemen callers.

Amanda. [*Crossing out to kitchenette. Airily.*] Sometimes they come when they are least expected! Why, I remember one Sunday afternoon in Blue Mountain—

[*Enters kitchenette.*]

Tom. I know what's coming!

Laura. Yes. But let her tell it.

Tom. Again?

Laura. She loves to tell it.

[AMANDA *returns with bowl of dessert.*]

Amanda. One Sunday afternoon in Blue Mountain—your mother received—*seventeen!*—gentlemen callers! Why, sometimes there weren't chairs enough to accommodate them all. We had to send the nigger over to bring in folding chairs from the parish house.

Tom. [*Remaining at portieres.*] How did you entertain those gentlemen callers?

Amanda. I understood the art of conversation!

Tom. I bet you could talk.

Amanda. Girls in those days *knew* how to talk, I can tell you.

Tom. Yes?

[IMAGE: AMANDA AS A GIRL ON A PORCH, GREETING CALLERS.]

Amanda. They knew how to entertain their gentlemen callers. It wasn't enough for a girl to be possessed of a pretty face and a graceful figure—although I wasn't slighted in either respect. She also needed to have a nimble wit and a tongue to meet all occasions.

Tom. What did you talk about?

Amanda. Things of importance going on in the world! Never anything coarse or common or vulgar. [*She addresses* TOM *as though he were seated in the vacant chair at the table though he remains by portieres. He plays this scene as though he held the book.*] My callers were gentlemen—all! Among my callers were some of the most prominent young planters of the Mississippi Delta—planters and sons of planters! [TOM *motions for music and a spot of light on* AMANDA. *Her eyes lift, her face glows, her voice becomes rich and elegiac.* SCREEN LEGEND: "OÙ SONT LES NEIGES?"]

There was young Champ Laughlin, who later became vice-president of the Delta Planters Bank.

Hadley Stevenson, who was drowned in Moon Lake and left his widow one hundred and fifty thousand in Government bonds.

There were the Cutrere brothers, Wesley and Bates. Bates was one of my bright particular beaux! He got in a quarrel with that wild Wainwright boy. They shot it out on the floor of Moon Lake Casino. Bates was shot through the stomach. Died in the ambulance on his way to Memphis. His widow was also well-provided for, came into eight or ten thousand acres, that's all. She married him on the rebound—never loved her—carried my picture on him the night he died!

And there was that boy that every girl in the Delta had set her cap for! That beautiful, brilliant young Fitzhugh boy from Greene County!

Tom. What did he leave his widow?

Amanda. He never married! Gracious,

you talk as though all of my old admirers had turned up their toes to the daisies!

Tom. Isn't this the first you've mentioned that still survives?

Amanda. That Fitzhugh boy went North and made a fortune—came to be known as the Wolf of Wall Street! He had the Midas touch, whatever he touched turned to gold!

And I could have been Mrs. Duncan J. Fitzhugh, mind you! But—I picked your *father!*

Laura. [*Rising.*] Mother, let me clear the table.

Amanda. No, dear, you go in front and study your typewriter chart. Or practice your shorthand a little. Stay fresh and pretty!—It's almost time for our gentlemen callers to start arriving. [*She flounces girlishly toward the kitchenette*]. How many do you suppose we're going to entertain this afternoon?

[TOM *throws down the paper and jumps up with a groan.*]

Laura. [*Alone in the dining room.*] I don't believe we're going to receive any, Mother.

Amanda. [*Reappearing, airily.*] What? No one—not one? You must be joking! [LAURA *nervously echoes her laugh. She slips in a fugitive manner through the half-open portieres and draws them gently behind her. A shaft of very clear light is thrown on her face against the faded tapestry of the curtains.* MUSIC: "THE GLASS MENAGERIE" UNDER FAINTLY. *Lightly.*] Not one gentleman caller? It can't be true! There must be a flood, there must have been a tornado!

Laura. It isn't a flood, it's not a tornado, Mother. I'm just not popular like you were in Blue Mountain. . . . [TOM *utters another groan.* LAURA *glances at him with a faint, apologetic smile. Her voice catching a little.*] Mother's afraid I'm going to be an old maid.

THE SCENE DIMS OUT WITH "GLASS MENAGERIE" MUSIC.

SCENE II

LEGEND: "LAURA, HAVEN'T YOU EVER LIKED SOME BOY?"

On the dark stage the screen is lighted with the image of blue roses.

Gradually LAURA'S *figure becomes apparent and the screen goes out. The music subsides.*

LAURA *is seated in the delicate ivory chair at the small claw-foot table.*

She wears a dress of soft violet material for a kimono—her hair tied back from her forehead with a ribbon.

She is washing and polishing her collection of glass.

[AMANDA *appears on the fire-escape steps. At the sound of her ascent,* LAURA *catches her breath, thrusts the bowl of ornaments away and seats herself stiffly before the diagram of the typewriter keyboard as though it held her spellbound.*

Something has happened to AMANDA. *It is written in her face as she climbs to the landing: a look that is grim and hopeless and a little absurd.*

She has on one of those cheap or imitation velvety-looking cloth coats with imitation fur collar. Her hat is five or six years old, one of those dreadful cloche hats that were worn in the late twenties, and she is clasping an enormous black patent-leather pocketbook with nickel clasps and initials. This is her full-dress outfit, the one she usually wears to the D.A.R.

Before entering she looks through the door.

She purses her lips, opens her eyes very wide, rolls them upward and shakes her head.

Then she slowly lets herself in the door. Seeing her mother's expression LAURA *touches her lips with a nervous gesture.*]

Laura. Hello, Mother, I was——

[*She makes a nervous gesture toward the chart on the wall.* AMANDA *leans against the shut door and stares at* LAURA *with a martyred look.*]

Amanda. Deception? Deception?

[*She slowly removes her hat and gloves, continuing the sweet suffering stare. She lets the hat and gloves fall on the floor—a bit of acting.*]

Laura. [*Shakily.*] How was the D.A.R. meeting? [AMANDA *slowly opens her purse and removes a dainty white handkerchief which she shakes out delicately and delicately touches to her lips and nostrils.*] Didn't you go to the D.A.R. meeting, Mother?

Amanda. [*Faintly, almost inaudibly.*] —No.—No. [*Then more forcibly.*] I did not have the strength—to go to the D.A.R. In fact, I did not have the courage! I wanted to find a hole in the ground and hide myself in it forever!

[*She crosses slowly to the wall and removes the diagram of the typewriter keyboard. She holds it in front of her for a second, staring at it sweetly and sor-

rowfully—then bites her lips and tears it in two pieces.]

Laura. [*Faintly.*] Why did you do that, Mother? [AMANDA *repeats the same procedure with the chart of the Gregg Alphabet.*] Why are you——

Amanda. Why? Why? How old are you, Laura?

Laura. Mother, you know my age.

Amanda. I thought that you were an adult; it seems that I was mistaken.

[*She crosses slowly to the sofa and sinks down and stares at* LAURA.]

Laura. Please don't stare at me, Mother.

[AMANDA *closes her eyes and lowers her head. Count ten.*]

Amanda. What are we going to do, what is going to become of us, what is the future?

[*Count ten.*]

Laura. Has something happened, Mother? [AMANDA *draws a long breath and takes out the handkerchief again. Dabbing process.*] Mother, has—something happened?

Amanda. I'll be all right in a minute, I'm just bewildered— [*Count five.*] —by life. . . .

Laura. Mother, I wish that you would tell me what's happened!

Amanda. As you know, I was supposed to be inducted into my office at the D.A.R. this afternoon. [IMAGE: A SWARM OF TYPEWRITERS.] But I stopped off at Rubicam's Business College to speak to your teachers about your having a cold and ask them what progress they thought you were making down there.

Laura. Oh. . . .

Amanda. I went to the typing instructor and introduced myself as your mother. She didn't know who you were. Wingfield, she said. We don't have any such student enrolled at the school!

I assured her she did, that you had been going to classes since early in January.

"I wonder," she said, "if you could be talking about that terribly shy little girl who dropped out of school after only a few days' attendance?"

"No," I said, "Laura, my daughter, has been going to school every day for the past six weeks!"

"Excuse me," she said. She took the attendance book out and there was your name, unmistakably printed, and all the dates you were absent until they decided that you had dropped out of school.

I still said, "No, there must have been some mistake! There must have been some mix-up in the records!"

And she said, "No—I remember her perfectly now. Her hands shook so that she couldn't hit the right keys! The first time we gave a speed-test, she broke down completely —was sick at the stomach and almost had to be carried into the wash-room! After that morning she never showed up any more. We phoned the house but never got any answer" —while I was working at Famous and Barr, I suppose, demonstrating those—— Oh!

I felt so weak I could barely keep on my feet!

I had to sit down while they got me a glass of water!

Fifty dollars' tuition, all of our plans—my hopes and ambitions for you—just gone up the spout, just gone up the spout like that. [LAURA *draws a long breath and gets awkwardly to her feet. She crosses to the victrola and winds it up.*] What are you doing?

Laura. Oh!

[*She releases the handle and returns to her seat.*]

Amanda. Laura, where have you been going when you've gone out pretending that you were going to business college?

Laura. I've just been going out walking.

Amanda. That's not true.

Laura. It is. I just went walking.

Amanda. Walking? Walking? In winter? Deliberately courting pneumonia in that light coat? Where did you walk to, Laura?

Laura. All sorts of places—mostly in the park.

Amanda. Even after you'd started catching that cold?

Laura. It was the lesser of two evils, Mother. [IMAGE: WINTER SCENE IN PARK.] I couldn't go back up. I—threw up—on the floor!

Amanda. From half past seven till after five every day you mean to tell me you walked around the park, because you wanted to make me think that you were still going to Rubicam's Business College?

Laura. It wasn't as bad as it sounds. I went inside places to get warmed up.

Amanda. Inside where?

Laura. I went in the art museum and the bird-houses at the Zoo. I visited the penguins every day! Sometimes I did without lunch and went to the movies. Lately I've been spending most of my afternoons in the Jewel-box, that big glass house where they raise the tropical flowers.

Amanda. You did all this to deceive me, just for deception? [LAURA *looks down.*] Why?

Laura. Mother, when you're disappointed, you get that awful suffering look on your face, like the picture of Jesus' mother in the museum!

Amanda. Hush!

Laura. I couldn't face it.

[*Pause. A whisper of strings.* LEGEND: "THE CRUST OF HUMILITY."]

Amanda. [*Hopelessly fingering the huge pocketbook.*] So what are we going to do the rest of our lives? Stay home and watch the parades go by? Amuse ourselves with the glass menagerie, darling? Eternally play those worn-out phonograph records your father left as a painful reminder of him?

We won't have a business career—we've given that up because it gave us nervous indigestion! [*Laughs wearily.*] What is there left but dependency all our lives? I know so well what becomes of unmarried women who aren't prepared to occupy a position. I've seen such pitiful cases in the South—barely tolerated spinsters living upon the grudging patronage of sister's husband or brother's wife!—stuck away in some little mouse-trap of a room—encouraged by one in-law to visit another—little birdlike women without any nest—eating the crust of humility all their life!

Is that the future that we've mapped out for ourselves?

I swear it's the only alternative I can think of!

It isn't a very pleasant alternative, is it?

Of course—some girls *do marry.* [LAURA *twists her hands nervously.*]

Haven't you ever liked some boy?

Laura. Yes. I liked one once. [*Rises.*] I came across his picture a while ago.

Amanda. [*With some interest.*] He gave you his picture?

Laura. No, it's in the year-book.

Amanda. [*Disappointed.*] Oh—a high-school boy.

[SCREEN IMAGE: JIM AS HIGH-SCHOOL HERO BEARING A SILVER CUP.]

Laura. Yes. His name was Jim. [LAURA *lifts the heavy annual from the claw-foot table.*] Here he is in *The Pirates of Penzance.*

Amanda. [*Absently.*] The what?

Laura. The operetta the senior class put on. He had a wonderful voice and we sat across the aisle from each other Mondays, Wednesdays, and Fridays in the Aud. Here he is with the silver cup for debating! See his grin?

Amanda. [*Absently.*] He must have had a jolly disposition.

Laura. He used to call me—Blue Roses.

[IMAGE: BLUE ROSES.]

Amanda. Why did he call you such a name as that?

Laura. When I had that attack of pleurosis—he asked me what was the matter when I came back. I said pleurosis—he thought that I said Blue Roses! So that's what he always called me after that. Whenever he saw me, he'd holler, "Hello, Blue Roses!" I didn't care for the girl that he went out with. Emily Meisenbach. Emily was the best-dressed girl at Soldan. She never struck me, though, as being sincere . . . It says in the Personal Section—they're engaged. That's—six years ago! They must be married by now.

Amanda. Girls that aren't cut out for business careers usually wind up married to some nice man. [*Gets up with a spark of revival.*] Sister, that's what you'll do!

[LAURA *utters a startled, doubtful laugh. She reaches quickly for a piece of glass.*]

Laura. But, Mother——

Amanda. Yes? [*Crossing to photograph.*]

Laura. [*In a tone of frightened apology.*] I'm—crippled! [IMAGE: SCREEN.]

Amanda. Nonsense! Laura, I've told you never, never to use that word. Why, you're not crippled, you just have a little defect—hardly noticeable, even! When people have some slight disadvantage like that, they cultivate other things to make up for it—develop charm—and vivacity—and—*charm!* That's all you have to do! [*She turns again to the photograph.*] One thing your father had *plenty of*—was *charm!*

[TOM *motions to the fiddle in the wings.*]

THE SCENE FADES OUT WITH MUSIC

SCENE III

[LEGEND ON SCREEN: "AFTER THE FIASCO——" TOM *speaks from the fire-escape landing.*]

Tom. After the fiasco at Rubicam's Business College, the idea of getting a gentleman caller for Laura began to play a more and more important part in Mother's calculations.

It became an obsession. Like some archetype of the universal unconscious, the image of the gentleman caller haunted our small apartment. . . .

[IMAGE: YOUNG MAN AT DOOR WITH FLOWERS.]

An evening at home rarely passed without some allusion to this image, this spectre, this hope. . . .

Even when he wasn't mentioned, his presence hung in Mother's preoccupied look and in my sister's frightened, apologetic manner—hung like a sentence passed upon the Wingfields!

Mother was a woman of action as well as words.

She began to take logical steps in the planned direction.

Late that winter and in the early spring—realizing that extra money would be needed to properly feather the nest and plume the bird—she conducted a vigorous campaign on the telephone, roping in subscribers to one of those magazines for matrons called *The Home-maker's Companion,* the type of journal that features the serialized sublimations of ladies of letters who think in terms of delicate cup-like breasts, slim, tapering waists, rich, creamy thighs, eyes like wood-smoke in autumn, fingers that soothe and caress like strains of music, bodies as powerful as Etruscan sculpture.

[SCREEN IMAGE: GLAMOR MAGAZINE COVER. AMANDA *enters with phone on long extension cord. She is spotted in the dim stage.*]

Amanda. Ida Scott? This is Amanda Wingfield!

We *missed* you at the D.A.R. last Monday!

I said to myself: She's probably suffering with that sinus condition! How is that sinus condition?

Horrors! Heaven have mercy!—You're a Christian martyr, yes, that's what you are, a Christian martyr!

Well, I just now happened to notice that your subscription to the *Companion's* about to expire! Yes, it expires with the next issue, honey!—just when that wonderful new serial by Bessie Mae Hopper is getting off to such an exciting start. Oh, honey, it's something that you can't miss! You remember how *Gone With the Wind* took everybody by storm? You simply couldn't go out if you hadn't read it. All everybody *talked* was Scarlett O'Hara. Well, this is a book that critics already compare to *Gone With the Wind.* It's the *Gone With the Wind* of the post-World War generation!—What?—Burning?—Oh, honey, don't let them burn, go take a look in the oven and I'll hold the wire! Heavens—I think she's hung up!

DIM OUT

[LEGEND ON SCREEN: "YOU THINK I'M IN LOVE WITH CONTINENTAL SHOEMAKERS?" *Before the stage is lighted the violent voices of* TOM *and* AMANDA *are heard. They are quarreling behind the portieres. In front of them stands* LAURA *with clenched hands and panicky expression. A clear pool of light on her figure throughout this scene.*]

Tom. What in Christ's name am I——

Amanda. [*Shrilly.*] Don't you use that——

Tom. Supposed to do!

Amanda. Expression! Not in my——

Tom. Ohhh!

Amanda. Presence! Have you gone out of your senses?

Tom. I have, that's true, *driven* out!

Amanda. What is the matter with you, you—big—big—IDIOT!

Tom. Look!—I've got *no thing,* no single thing——

Amanda. Lower your voice!

Tom. In my life here that I can call my OWN! Everything is——

Amanda. Stop that shouting!

Tom. Yesterday you confiscated my books! You had the nerve to——

Amanda. I took that horrible novel back to the library—yes! That hideous book by that insane Mr. Lawrence. [TOM *laughs wildly.*] I cannot control the output of diseased minds or people who cater to them—[TOM *laughs still more wildly.*] BUT I WON'T ALLOW SUCH FILTH BROUGHT INTO MY HOUSE! No, no, no, no, no!

Tom. House, house! Who pays rent on it, who makes a slave of himself to——

Amanda. [*Fairly screeching.*] Don't you DARE to——

Tom. No, no, *I* mustn't say things! *I've* got to just——

Amanda. Let me tell you——

Tom. I don't want to hear any more!

[*He tears the portieres open. The upstage area is lit with a turgid smoky red glow.* AMANDA'S *hair is in metal curlers and she wears a very old bathrobe, much too large for her slight figure, a relic of the faithless Mr. Wingfield. An upright typewriter and a wild disarray of manuscripts is on the drop-leaf table. The quarrel was probably precipitated by* AMANDA'S *interruption of his creative labor. A chair lying overthrown on the floor. Their gesticulating shadows are cast on the ceiling by the fiery glow.*]

Amanda. You *will* hear more, you——

Tom. No, I won't hear more, I'm going out!

Amanda. You come right back in——

Tom. Out, out, out! Because I'm——

Amanda. Come back here, Tom Wingfield! I'm not through talking to you!

Tom. Oh go——

Laura. [*Desperately.*] —Tom!

Amanda. You're going to listen, and no more insolence from you! I'm at the end of my patience! [*He comes back toward her.*]

Tom. What do you think I'm at? Aren't I supposed to have any patience to reach the end of, Mother? I know, I know. It seems unimportant to you, what I'm *doing*—what I *want* to do—having a little *difference* between them! You don't think that——

Amanda. I think you've been doing things that you're ashamed of. That's why you act like this. I don't believe that you go every night to the movies. Nobody goes to the movies night after night. Nobody in their right minds goes to the movies as often as you pretend to. People don't go to the movies at nearly midnight, and movies don't let out at two A.M. Come in stumbling. Muttering to yourself like a maniac! You get three hours' sleep and then go to work. Oh, I can picture the way you're doing down there. Moping, doping, because you're in no condition.

Tom. [*Wildly.*] No, I'm in no condition!

Amanda. What right have you got to jeopardize your job? Jeopardize the security of us all? How do you think we'd manage if you were——

Tom. Listen! You think I'm crazy *about* the *warehouse?* [*He bends fiercely toward her slight figure.*] You think I'm in love with the Continental Shoemakers? You think I want to spend fifty-five *years* down there in that—*celotex interior!* with—*fluorescent—tubes!* Look! I'd rather somebody picked up a crowbar and battered out my brains—than go back mornings! I *go!* Every time you come in yelling that God damn *"Rise and Shine!" "Rise and Shine!"* I say to myself, "How *lucky dead* people are!" But I get up. I *go!* For sixty-five dollars a month I give up all that I dream of doing and being *ever!* And you say self—*self's* all I ever think of. Why, listen, if self is what I thought of, Mother, I'd be where he is—GONE! [*Pointing to father's picture.*] As far as the system of transportation reaches! [*He starts past her. She grabs his arm.*] Don't grab at me, Mother!

Amanda. Where are you going?

Tom. I'm going to the *movies!*

Amanda. I don't believe that lie!

Tom. [*Crouching toward her, overtowering her tiny figure. She backs away, gasping.*] I'm going to opium dens! Yes, opium dens, dens of vice and criminals' hang-outs, Mother. I've joined the Hogan gang, I'm a hired assassin, I carry a tommy-gun in a violin case! I run a string of cat-houses in the Valley! They call me Killer, Killer Wingfield, I'm leading a double-life: a simple, honest warehouse worker by day, by night a dynamic *czar* of the *underworld, Mother.* I go to gambling casinos, I spin away fortunes on the roulette table! I wear a patch over one eye and a false mustache; sometimes I put on green whiskers. On those occasions they call me—*El Diablo!* Oh, I could tell you things to make you sleepless! My enemies plan to dynamite this place. They're going to blow us all sky-high some night! I'll be glad, very happy, and so will you! You'll go up, up on a broomstick, over Blue Mountain with seventeen gentlemen callers! You ugly—babbling old—*witch.* . . .

[*He goes through a series of violent, clumsy movements, seizing his overcoat, lunging to the door, pulling it fiercely open. The* WOMEN *watch him, aghast. His arm catches in the sleeve of the coat as he struggles to pull it on. For a moment he is pinioned by the bulky garment. With an outraged groan he tears the coat off again, splitting the shoulder of it, and hurls it across the room. It strikes against the shelf of* LAURA'S *glass collection, there is a tinkle of shattering glass.* LAURA *cries out as if wounded.* MUSIC. LEGEND: "THE GLASS MENAGERIE."]

Laura. [*Shrilly.*] *My glass!*—menagerie. . . .

[*She covers her face and turns away. But* AMANDA *is still stunned and stupefied by the "ugly witch" so that she barely notices this occurrence. Now she recovers her speech.*]

Amanda. [*In an awful voice.*] I won't speak to you—until you apologize!

[*She crosses through portieres and draws them together behind her.* TOM *is left with* LAURA. LAURA *clings weakly to the mantel with her face averted.* TOM *stares at her stupidly for a moment. Then he crosses to shelf. Drops awkwardly on his knees to collect the fallen glass, glancing at* LAURA *as if he would speak but couldn't.*]

"THE GLASS MENAGERIE" *steals in as*

THE SCENE DIMS OUT

SCENE IV

The interior is dark. Faint light in the alley. A deep-voiced bell in a church is tolling the hour of five as the scene commences.

[TOM *appears at the top of the alley. After each solemn boom of the bell in the tower, he shakes a little noise-maker or rattle as if to express the tiny spasm of man in contrast to the sustained power*

and dignity of the Almighty. This and the unsteadiness of his advance make it evident that he has been drinking.
As he climbs the few steps to the fire-escape landing, light steals up inside. LAURA *appears in night-dress, observing* TOM's *empty bed in the front room.*
TOM *fishes in his pockets for door-key, removing a motley assortment of articles in the search, including a perfect shower of movie-ticket stubs and an empty bottle. At last he finds the key, but just as he is about to insert it, it slips from his fingers. He strikes a match and crouches below the door.*]

Tom. [*Bitterly.*] One crack—and it falls through! [LAURA *opens the door.*]

Laura. Tom! Tom, what are you doing?

Tom. Looking for a door-key.

Laura. Where have you been all this time?

Tom. I have been to the movies.

Laura. All this time at the movies?

Tom. There was a very long program. There was a Garbo picture and a Mickey Mouse and a travelogue and a newsreel and a preview of coming attractions. And there was an organ solo and a collection for the milk-fund—simultaneously—which ended up in a terrible fight between a fat lady and an usher!

Laura. [*Innocently.*] Did you have to stay through everything?

Tom. Of course! And, oh, I forgot! There was a big stage show! The headliner on this stage show was Malvolio the Magician. He performed wonderful tricks, many of them, such as pouring water back and forth between pitchers. First it turned to wine and then it turned to beer and then it turned to whiskey. I know it was whiskey it finally turned into because he needed somebody to come up out of the audience to help him, and I came up—both shows! It was Kentucky Straight Bourbon. A very generous fellow, he gave souvenirs. [*He pulls from his back pocket a shimmering rainbow-colored scarf.*] He gave me this. This is his magic scarf. You can have it, Laura. You wave it over a canary cage and you get a bowl of gold-fish. You wave it over the gold-fish bowl and they fly away canaries. . . . But the wonderfullest trick of all was the coffin trick. We nailed him into a coffin and he got out of the coffin without removing one nail. [*He has come inside.*] There is a trick that would come in handy for me—get me out of this 2 by 4 situation!

[*Flops onto bed and starts removing shoes.*]

Laura. Tom—Shhh!

Tom. What're you shushing me for?

Laura. You'll wake up Mother.

Tom. Goody, goody! Pay 'er back for all those "Rise an' Shines." [*Lies down, groaning.*] You know it don't take much intelligence to get yourself into a nailed-up coffin, Laura. But who in hell ever got himself out of one without removing one nail?

[*As if in answer, the father's grinning photograph lights up.*]

SCENE DIMS OUT

[*Immediately following: The church bell is heard striking six. At the sixth stroke the alarm clock goes off in* AMANDA's *room, and after a few moments we hear her calling: "Rise and Shine! Rise and Shine! Laura, go tell your brother to rise and shine!"*]

Tom. [*Sitting up slowly.*] I'll rise—but I won't shine. [*The light increases.*]

Amanda. Laura, tell your brother his coffee is ready. [LAURA *slips into front room.*]

Laura. Tom!—It's nearly seven. Don't make Mother nervous. [*He stares at her stupidly. Beseechingly.*] Tom, speak to Mother this morning. Make up with her, apologize, speak to her!

Tom. She won't to me. It's her that started not speaking.

Laura. If you just say you're sorry she'll start speaking.

Tom. Her not speaking—is that such a tragedy?

Laura. Please—please!

Amanda. [*Calling from kitchenette.*] Laura, are you going to do what I asked you to do, or do I have to get dressed and go out myself?

Laura. Going, going—soon as I get on my coat! [*She pulls on a shapeless felt hat with nervous, jerky movement, pleadingly glancing at* TOM. *Rushes awkwardly for coat. The coat is one of* AMANDA's, *inaccurately made-over, the sleeves too short for* LAURA.] Butter and what else?

Amanda. [*Entering upstage.*] Just butter. Tell them to charge it.

Laura. Mother, they make such faces when I do that.

Amanda. Sticks and stones can break our bones, but the expression on Mr. Garfinkel's face won't harm us! Tell your brother his coffee is getting cold.

Laura. [*At door.*] Do what I asked you, will you, will you, Tom?

[*He looks sullenly away.*]

Amanda. Laura, go now or just don't go at all!

Laura. [*Rushing out.*] Going—going!

[*A second later she cries out.* TOM *springs up and crosses to door.* AMANDA *rushes anxiously in.* TOM *opens the door.*]

Tom. Laura?

Laura. I'm all right. I slipped, but I'm all right.

Amanda. [*Peering anxiously after her.*] If anyone breaks a leg on those fire-escape steps, the landlord ought to be sued for every cent he possesses!

[*She shuts door. Remembers she isn't speaking and returns to other room. As* TOM *enters listlessly for his coffee, she turns her back to him and stands rigidly facing the window on the gloomy gray vault of the areaway. Its light on her face with its aged but childish features is cruelly sharp, satirical as a Daumier print.* MUSIC UNDER: "AVE MARIA." TOM *glances sheepishly but sullenly at her averted figure and slumps at the table. The coffee is scalding hot; he sips it and gasps and spits it back in the cup. At his gasp,* AMANDA *catches her breath and half turns. Then catches herself and turns back to window.* TOM *blows on his coffee, glancing sidewise at his mother. She clears her throat.* TOM *clears his. He starts to rise. Sinks back down again, scratches his head, clears his throat again.* AMANDA *coughs.* TOM *raises his cup in both hands to blow on it, his eyes staring over the rim of it at his mother for several moments. Then he slowly sets the cup down and awkwardly and hesitantly rises from the chair.*]

Tom. [*Hoarsely.*] Mother. I—I apologize, Mother. [AMANDA *draws a quick, shuddering breath. Her face works grotesquely. She breaks into childlike tears.*] I'm sorry for what I said, for everything that I said, I didn't mean it.

Amanda. [*Sobbingly.*] My devotion has made me a witch and so I make myself hateful to my children!

Tom. No, you *don't.*

Amanda. I worry so much, don't sleep, it makes me nervous!

Tom. [*Gently.*] I understand that.

Amanda. I've had to put up a solitary battle all these years. But you're my right-hand bower! Don't fall down, don't fail!

Tom. [*Gently.*] I'll try, Mother.

Amanda. [*With great enthusiasm.*] Try and you will SUCCEED! [*The notion makes her breathless.*] Why, you—you're just *full* of natural endowments! Both of my children—they're *unusual* children! Don't you think I know it? I'm so—*proud!* Happy and —feel I've—so much to be thankful for but—— Promise me one thing, Son!

Tom. What, Mother?

Amanda. Promise, son, you'll—never be a drunkard!

Tom. [*Turns to her, grinning.*] I will never be a drunkard, Mother.

Amanda. That's what frightened me so, that you'd be drinking! Eat a bowl of Purina!

Tom. Just coffee, Mother.

Amanda. Shredded wheat biscuit?

Tom. No. No, Mother, just coffee.

Amanda. You can't put in a day's work on an empty stomach. You've got ten minutes—don't gulp! Drinking too-hot liquids makes cancer of the stomach. . . . Put cream in.

Tom. No, thank you.

Amanda. To cool it.

Tom. No! No, thank you, I want it black.

Amanda. I know, but it's not good for you. We have to do all that we can to build ourselves up. In these trying times we live in, all that we have to cling to is—each other. . . . That's why it's so important to—— Tom, I—— I sent out your sister so I could discuss something with you. If you hadn't spoken I would have spoken to you. [*Sits down.*]

Tom. [*Gently.*] What is it, Mother, that you want to discuss?

Amanda. Laura!

[TOM *puts his cup down slowly.* LEGEND ON SCREEN: "LAURA." MUSIC: "THE GLASS MENAGERIE."]

Tom. —Oh.—Laura . . .

Amanda. [*Touching his sleeve.*] You know how Laura is. So quiet but—still water runs deep! She notices things and I think she—broods about them. [TOM *looks up.*] A few days ago I came in and she was crying.

Tom. What about?

Amanda. You.

Tom. Me?

Amanda. She has an idea that you're not happy here.

Tom. What gave her that idea?

Amanda. What gives her any idea? However, you do act strangely. I—I'm not criticizing, understand *that!* I know your ambitions do not lie in the warehouse, that like everybody in the whole wide world—you've had to—make sacrifices, but—Tom—Tom—life's not easy, it calls for—Spartan endurance! There's so many things in my heart that I cannot describe to you! I've never told you but I—*loved* your father. . . .

Tom. [*Gently.*] I know that, Mother.

Amanda. And you—when I see you taking after his ways! Staying out late—and—well, you *had* been drinking the night you were in that—terrifying condition! Laura says that you hate the apartment and that you go out nights to get away from it! Is that true, Tom?

Tom. No. You say there's so much in your heart that you can't describe to me. That's true of me, too. There's so much in my heart that I can't describe to *you!* So let's respect each other's——

Amanda. But, why—*why,* Tom—are you always so *restless?* Where do you *go* to, nights?

Tom. I—go to the movies.

Amanda. Why do you go to the movies so much, Tom?

Tom. I go to the movies because—I like adventure. Adventure is something I don't have much of at work, so I go to the movies.

Amanda. But, Tom, you go to the movies *entirely* too *much!*

Tom. I like a lot of adventure.

[AMANDA *looks baffled, then hurt. As the familiar inquisition resumes he becomes hard and impatient again.* AMANDA *slips back into her querulous attitude toward him.* IMAGE ON SCREEN: SAILING VESSEL WITH JOLLY ROGER.]

Amanda. Most young men find adventure in their careers.

Tom. Then most young men are not employed in a warehouse.

Amanda. The world is full of young men employed in warehouses and offices and factories.

Tom. Do all of them find adventure in their careers?

Amanda. They do or they do without it! Not everybody has a craze for adventure.

Tom. Man is by instinct a lover, a hunter, a fighter, and none of those instincts are given much play at the warehouse!

Amanda. Man is by instinct! Don't quote instinct to me! Instinct is something that people have got away from! It belongs to animals! Christian adults don't want it!

Tom. What do Christian adults want, then, Mother?

Amanda. Superior things! Things of the mind and the spirit! Only animals have to satisfy instincts! Surely your aims are somewhat higher than theirs! Than monkeys—pigs——

Tom. I reckon they're not.

Amanda. You're joking. However, that isn't what I wanted to discuss.

Tom. [*Rising.*] I haven't much time.

Amanda. [*Pushing his shoulders.*] Sit down.

Tom. You want me to punch in red at the warehouse, Mother?

Amanda. You have five minutes. I want to talk about Laura.

[LEGEND: "PLANS AND PROVISIONS."]

Tom. All right! What about Laura?

Amanda. We have to be making some plans and provisions for her. She's older than you, two years, and nothing has happened. She just drifts along doing nothing. It frightens me terribly how she just drifts along.

Tom. I guess she's the type that people call home girls.

Amanda. There's no such type, and if there is, it's a pity! That is unless the home is hers, with a husband!

Tom. What?

Amanda. Oh, I can see the handwriting on the wall as plain as I see the nose in front of my face! It's terrifying!

More and more you remind me of your father! He was out all hours without explanation!—Then *left! Good-bye!*

And me with the bag to hold. I saw that letter you got from the Merchant Marine. I know what you're dreaming of. I'm not standing here blindfolded.

Very well, then. Then *do* it!

But not till there's somebody to take your place.

Tom. What do you mean?

Amanda. I mean that as soon as Laura has got somebody to take care of her, married, a home of her own, independent—why, then you'll be free to go wherever you please, on land, on sea, whichever way the wind blows you!

But until that time you've got to look out for your sister. I don't say me because I'm old and don't matter! I say for your sister because she's young and dependent.

I put her in business college—a dismal failure! Frightened her so it made her sick at the stomach.

I took her over to the Young People's League at the church. Another fiasco. She spoke to nobody, nobody spoke to her. Now all she does is fool with those pieces of glass and play those worn-out records. What kind of a life is that for a girl to lead?

Tom. What can I do about it?

Amanda. Overcome selfishness!

Self, self, self is all that you ever think of! [TOM *springs up and crosses to get his coat. It is ugly and bulky. He pulls on a cap with earmuffs.*] Where is your muffler? Put your wool muffler on! [*He snatches it angrily from the closet and tosses it around his neck and pulls both ends tight.*] Tom! I haven't said what I had in mind to ask you.

Tom. I'm too late to——

Amanda. [*Catching his arm—very importunately. Then shyly.*] Down at the warehouse, aren't there some—nice young men?

Tom. No!

Amanda. There *must* be—*some* . . .

Tom. Mother—— [*Gesture.*]

Amanda. Find out one that's clean-living—doesn't drink and—ask him out for sister!

Tom. What?

Amanda. For *sister!* To *meet!* Get *acquainted!*

Tom. [*Stamping to door.*] Oh, my *go-osh!*

Amanda. Will you? [*He opens door. Imploringly.*] Will you? [*He starts down.*] Will you? *Will* you, dear?

Tom. [*Calling back.*] YES!

[AMANDA *closes the door hesitantly and with a troubled but faintly hopeful expression.* SCREEN IMAGE: GLAMOR MAGAZINE COVER. *Spot* AMANDA *at phone.*]

Amanda. Ella Cartwright? This is Amanda Wingfield!

How are you, honey?

How is that kidney condition?

[*Count five.*]

Horrors! [*Count five.*]

You're a Christian martyr, yes, honey, that's what you are, a Christian martyr!

Well, I just now happened to notice in my little red book that your subscription to the *Companion* has just run out! I knew that you wouldn't want to miss out on the wonderful serial starting in this new issue. It's by Bessie Mae Hopper, the first thing she's written since *Honeymoon for Three.*

Wasn't that a strange and interesting story? Well, this one is even lovelier, I believe. It has a sophisticated, society background. It's all about the horsey set on Long Island!

FADE OUT

SCENE V

LEGEND ON SCREEN: "ANNUNCIATION." *Fade with music.*

It is early dusk of a spring evening. Supper has just been finished in the Wingfield apartment. AMANDA *and* LAURA *in light-colored dresses are removing dishes from the table, in the upstage area, which is shadowy, their movements formalized almost as a dance or ritual, their moving forms as pale and silent as moths.*

[TOM, *in white shirt and trousers, rises from the table and crosses toward the fire-escape.*]

Amanda. [*As he passes her.*] Son, will you do me a favor?

Tom. What?

Amanda. Comb your hair! You look so pretty when your hair is combed! [TOM *slouches on sofa with evening paper. Enormous caption "Franco Triumphs."*] There is only one respect in which I would like you to emulate your father.

Tom. What respect is that?

Amanda. The care he always took of his appearance. He never allowed himself to look untidy. [*He throws down the paper and crosses to fire-escape.*] Where are you going?

Tom. I'm going out to smoke.

Amanda. You smoke too much. A pack a day at fifteen cents a pack. How much would that amount to in a month? Thirty times fifteen is how much, Tom? Figure it out and you will be astounded at what you could save. Enough to give you a night-school course in accounting at Washington U! Just think what a wonderful thing that would be for you, Son!

[TOM *is unmoved by the thought.*]

Tom. I'd rather smoke.

[*He steps out on landing, letting the screen door slam.*]

Amanda. [*Sharply.*] I know! That's the tragedy of it. . . .

[*Alone, she turns to look at her husband's picture.* DANCE MUSIC: "ALL THE WORLD IS WAITING FOR THE SUNRISE!"]

Tom. [*To the audience.*] Across the alley from us was the Paradise Dance Hall. On evenings in spring the windows and doors were open and the music came outdoors. Sometimes the lights were turned out except for a large glass sphere that hung from the ceiling. It would turn slowly about and filter the dusk with delicate rainbow colors. Then the orchestra played a waltz or a tango, something that had a slow and sensuous rhythm. Couples would come outside, to the relative privacy of the alley. You could see them kissing behind ash-pits and telephone poles.

This was the compensation for lives that passed like mine, without any change or adventure.

Adventure and change were imminent in this year. They were waiting around the corner for all these kids.

Suspended in the mist over Berchtesgaden, caught in the folds of Chamberlain's umbrella——

In Spain there was Guernica!

But here there was only hot swing music and liquor, dance halls, bars, and movies, and sex that hung in the gloom like a chandelier and flooded the world with brief, deceptive rainbows. . . .

All the world was waiting for bombardments!

[AMANDA *turns from the picture and comes outside.*]

Amanda. [*Sighing.*] A fire-escape landing's a poor excuse for a porch. [*She spreads a newspaper on a step and sits down, gracefully and demurely as if she were settling into a swing on a Mississippi veranda.*] What are you looking at?

Tom. The moon.

Amanda. Is there a moon this evening?

Tom. It's rising over Garfinkel's Delicatessen.

Amanda. So it is! A little silver slipper of a moon. Have you made a wish on it yet?

Tom. Um-hum.

Amanda. What did you wish for?

Tom. That's a secret.

Amanda. A secret, huh? Well, I won't tell mine either. I will be just as mysterious as you.

Tom. I bet I can guess what yours is.

Amanda. Is my head so transparent?

Tom. You're not a sphinx.

Amanda. No, I don't have secrets. I'll tell you what I wished for on the moon. Success and happiness for my precious children! I wish for that whenever there's a moon, and when there isn't a moon, I wish for it, too.

Tom. I thought perhaps you wished for a gentleman caller.

Amanda. Why do you say that?

Tom. Don't you remember asking me to fetch one?

Amanda. I remember suggesting that it would be nice for your sister if you brought home some nice young man from the warehouse. I think that I've made that suggestion more than once.

Tom. Yes, you have made it repeatedly.

Amanda. Well?

Tom. We are going to have one.

Amanda. *What?*

Tom. A gentleman caller!

[*The annunciation is celebrated with music.* AMANDA *rises.* IMAGE ON SCREEN: CALLER WITH BOUQUET.]

Amanda. You mean you have asked some nice young man to come over?

Tom. Yep. I've asked him to dinner.

Amanda. You really did?

Tom. I did!

Amanda. You did, and did he—*accept?*

Tom. He did!

Amanda. Well, well—well, well! That's—lovely!

Tom. I thought that you would be pleased.

Amanda. It's definite, then?

Tom. Very definite.

Amanda. Soon?

Tom. Very soon.

Amanda. For heaven's sake, stop putting on and tell me some things, will you?

Tom. What things do you want me to tell you?

Amanda. *Naturally* I would like to know when he's *coming!*

Tom. He's coming tomorrow.

Amanda. *Tomorrow?*

Tom. Yep. Tomorrow.

Amanda. But, Tom!

Tom. Yes, Mother?

Amanda. Tomorrow gives me no time!

Tom. Time for what?

Amanda. Preparations! Why didn't you phone me at once, as soon as you asked him, the minute that he accepted? Then, don't you see, I could have been getting ready!

Tom. You don't have to make any fuss.

Amanda. Oh, Tom, Tom, Tom, of course I have to make a fuss! I want things nice, not sloppy! Not thrown together. I'll certainly have to do some fast thinking, won't I?

Tom. I don't see why you have to think at all.

Amanda. You just don't know. We can't have a gentleman caller in a pig-sty! All my wedding silver has to be polished, the monogrammed table linen ought to be laundered! The windows have to be washed and fresh curtains put up. And how about clothes? We have to *wear* something, don't we?

Tom. Mother, this boy is no one to make a fuss over!

Amanda. Do you realize he's the first young man we've introduced to your sister?

It's terrible, dreadful, disgraceful that poor little sister has never received a single gentleman caller! Tom, come inside!

[*She opens the screen door.*]

Tom. What for?

Amanda. I want to ask you some things.

Tom. If you're going to make such a fuss, I'll call it off, I'll tell him not to come!

Amanda. You certainly won't do anything of the kind. Nothing offends people worse than broken engagements. It simply means I'll have to work like a Turk! We won't be brilliant, but we will pass inspection. Come on inside. [TOM *follows, groaning.*] Sit down.

Tom. Any particular place you would like me to sit?

Amanda. Thank heavens I've got that new sofa! I'm also making payments on a floor lamp I'll have sent out! And put the chintz covers on, they'll brighten things up! Of course I'd hoped to have these walls re-papered. . . . What is the young man's name?

Tom. His name is O'Connor.

Amanda. That, of course, means fish—tomorrow is Friday! I'll have that salmon loaf—with Durkee's dressing! What does he do? He works at the warehouse?

Tom. Of course! How else would I——

Amanda. Tom, he—doesn't drink?

Tom. Why do you ask me that?

Amanda. Your father *did!*

Tom. Don't get started on that!

Amanda. He *does* drink, then?

Tom. Not that I know of!

Amanda. Make sure, be certain! The last thing I want for my daughter's a boy who drinks!

Tom. Aren't you being a little bit premature? Mr. O'Connor has not yet appeared on the scene!

Amanda. But will tomorrow. To meet your sister, and what do I know about his character? Nothing! Old maids are better off than wives of drunkards!

Tom. Oh, my God!

Amanda. Be still!

Tom. [*Leaning forward to whisper.*] Lots of fellows meet girls whom they don't marry!

Amanda. Oh, talk sensibly, Tom—and don't be sarcastic!

[*She has gotten a hairbrush.*]

Tom. What are you doing?

Amanda. I'm brushing that cow-lick down! What is this young man's position at the warehouse?

Tom. [*Submitting grimly to the brush and the interrogation.*] This young man's position is that of a shipping clerk, Mother.

Amanda. Sounds to me like a fairly responsible job, the sort of a job *you* would be in if you just had more *get-up.*

What is his salary? Have you any idea?

Tom. I would judge it to be approximately eighty-five dollars a month.

Amanda. Well—not princely, but——

Tom. Twenty more than I make.

Amanda. Yes, how well I know! But for a family man, eighty-five dollars a month is not much more than you can just get by on. . . .

Tom. Yes, but Mr. O'Connor is not a family man.

Amanda. He might be, mightn't he? Some time in the future?

Tom. I see. Plans and provisions.

Amanda. You are the only young man that I know of who ignores the fact that the future becomes the present, the present the past, and the past turns into everlasting regret if you don't plan for it!

Tom. I will think that over and see what I can make of it.

Amanda. Don't be supercilious with your mother! Tell me some more about this—what do you call him?

Tom. James D. O'Connor. The D. is for Delaney.

Amanda. Irish on *both* sides! *Gracious!* And doesn't drink?

Tom. Shall I call him up and ask him right this minute?

Amanda. The only way to find out about those things is to make discreet inquiries at the proper moment. When I was a girl in Blue Mountain and it was suspected that a young man drank, the girl whose attentions he had been receiving, if any girl *was,* would sometimes speak to the minister of his church, or rather her father would if her father was living, and sort of feel him out on the young man's character. That is the way such things are discreetly handled to keep a young woman from making a tragic mistake!

Tom. Then how did you happen to make a tragic mistake?

Amanda. That innocent look of your father's had everyone fooled!

He *smiled*—the world was *enchanted!*

No girl can do worse than put herself at the mercy of a handsome appearance!

I hope that Mr. O'Connor is not too good-looking.

Tom. No, he's not too good-looking. He's covered with freckles and hasn't too much of a nose.

Amanda. He's not right-down homely, though?

Tom. Not right-down homely. Just medium homely, I'd say.

Amanda. Character's what to look for in a man.

Tom. That's what I've always said, Mother.

Amanda. You've never said anything of the kind and I suspect you would never give it a thought.

Tom. Don't be so suspicious of me.

Amanda. At least I hope he's the type that's up and coming.

Tom. I think he really goes in for self-improvement.

Amanda. What reason have you to think so?

Tom. He goes to night school.

Amanda. [*Beaming.*] Splendid! What does he do, I mean study?

Tom. Radio engineering and public speaking!

Amanda. Then he has visions of being advanced in the world!

Any young man who studies public speaking is aiming to have an executive job some day!

And radio engineering? A thing for the future!

Both of these facts are very illuminating. Those are the sort of things that a mother should know concerning any young man who comes to call on her daughter. Seriously or—not.

Tom. One little warning. He doesn't know about Laura. I didn't let on that we had dark ulterior motives. I just said, why don't you come and have dinner with us? He said okay and that was the whole conversation.

Amanda. I bet it was! You're eloquent as an oyster.

However, he'll know about Laura when he gets here. When he sees how lovely and sweet and pretty she is, he'll thank his lucky stars he was asked to dinner.

Tom. Mother, you mustn't expect too much of Laura.

Amanda. What do you mean?

Tom. Laura seems all those things to you and me because she's ours and we love her. We don't even notice she's crippled any more.

Amanda. Don't say crippled! You know that I never allow that word to be used!

Tom. But face facts, Mother. She is and—that's not all——

Amanda. What do you mean "not all"?

Tom. Laura is very different from other girls.

Amanda. I think the difference is all to her advantage.

Tom. Not quite all—in the eyes of others—strangers—she's terribly shy and lives in a world of her own and those things make her seem a little peculiar to people outside the house.

Amanda. Don't say peculiar.

Tom. Face the facts. She is.

[THE DANCE-HALL MUSIC CHANGES TO A TANGO THAT HAS A MINOR AND SOMEWHAT OMINOUS TONE.]

Amanda. In what way is she peculiar—may I ask?

Tom. [*Gently.*] She lives in a world of her own—a world of—little glass ornaments, Mother. . . . [*Gets up.* AMANDA *remains holding brush, looking at him, troubled.*] She plays old phonograph records and—that's about all——

[*He glances at himself in the mirror and crosses to door.*]

Amanda. [*Sharply.*] Where are you going?

Tom. I'm going to the movies.

[*Out screen door.*]

Amanda. Not to the movies, every night to the movies! [*Follows quickly to screen door.*] I don't believe you always go to the movies! [*He is gone.* AMANDA *looks worriedly after him for a moment. Then vitality and optimism return and she turns from the door. Crossing to portieres.*] Laura! Laura!

[LAURA *answers from kitchenette.*]

Laura. Yes, Mother.

Amanda. Let those dishes go and come in front! [LAURA *appears with dish towel. Gaily.*] Laura, come here and make a wish on the moon! [SCREEN IMAGE: MOON.]

Laura. [*Entering.*] Moon—moon?

Amanda. A little silver slipper of a moon.

Look over your left shoulder, Laura, and make a wish!

[LAURA *looks faintly puzzled as if called out of sleep.* AMANDA *seizes her shoulders and turns her at an angle by the door.*]

Now!

Now, darling, *wish!*

Laura. What shall I wish for, Mother?

Amanda. [*Her voice trembling and her eyes suddenly filling with tears.*] Happiness! Good fortune!

[*The violin rises and the stage dims out.*]

CURTAIN

SCENE VI

[IMAGE: HIGH-SCHOOL HERO.]

Tom. And so the following evening I brought Jim home to dinner. I had known Jim slightly in high school. In high school Jim was a hero. He had tremendous Irish good nature and vitality with the scrubbed and polished look of white chinaware. He seemed to move in a continual spotlight. He was a star in basketball, captain of the debating club, president of the senior class and the glee club and he sang the male lead in the annual light operas. He was always running or bounding, never just walking. He seemed always at the point of defeating the law of gravity. He was shooting with such velocity through his adolescence that you would logically expect him to arrive at nothing short of the White House by the time he was thirty. But Jim apparently ran into more interference after his graduation from Soldan. His speed had definitely slowed. Six years after he left high school he was holding a job that wasn't much better than mine.

[IMAGE: CLERK.]

He was the only one at the warehouse with whom I was on friendly terms. I was valuable to him as someone who could remember his former glory, who had seen him win basketball games and the silver cup in debating. He knew of my secret practice of retiring to a cabinet of the wash-room to work on poems when business was slack in the warehouse. He called me Shakespeare. And while the other boys in the warehouse regarded me with suspicious hostility, Jim took a humorous attitude toward me. Gradually his attitude affected the others; their hostility wore off and they also began to smile at me as people smile at an oddly fashioned dog who trots across their path at some distance.

I knew that Jim and Laura had known each other at Soldan, and I had heard Laura speak admiringly of his voice. I didn't know if Jim remembered her or not. In high school Laura had been as unobtrusive as Jim had been astonishing. If he did remember Laura, it was not as my sister, for when I asked him to dinner, he grinned and said, "You know, Shakespeare, I never thought of you as having folks!"

He was about to discover that I did. . . .

[LIGHT UP STAGE. LEGEND ON SCREEN: "THE ACCENT OF A COMING FOOT." *Friday evening. It is about five o'clock of a late spring evening which comes "scattering poems in the sky." A delicate lemony light is in the Wingfield apartment.* AMANDA *has worked like a Turk in preparation for the gentleman caller. The results are astonishing. The new floor lamp with its rose-silk shade is in place, a colored paper lantern conceals the broken light fixture in the ceiling, new billowing white curtains are at the windows, chintz covers are on chairs and sofa, a pair of new sofa pillows make their initial appearance. Open boxes and tissue paper are scattered on the floor.* LAURA *stands in the middle with lifted arms while* AMANDA *crouches before her, adjusting the hem of the new dress, devout and ritualistic. The dress is colored and designed by memory. The arrangement of* LAURA'S *hair is changed; it is softer and more becoming. A fragile, unearthly prettiness has come out in* LAURA: *she is like a piece of translucent glass touched by light, given a momentary radiance, not actual, not lasting.*]

Amanda. [*Impatiently.*] Why are you trembling?

Laura. Mother, you've made me so nervous!

Amanda. How have I made you nervous?

Laura. By all this fuss! You make it seem so important!

Amanda. I don't understand you, Laura. You couldn't be satisfied with just sitting home, and yet whenever I try to arrange something for you, you seem to resist it.

[*She gets up.*]

Now take a look at yourself.

No, wait! Wait just a moment—I have an idea!

Laura. What is it now?

[AMANDA *produces two powder puffs which she wraps in handkerchiefs and stuffs in* LAURA'S *bosom.*]

Laura. Mother, what are you doing?

Amanda. They call them "Gay Deceivers"!

Laura. I won't wear them!

Amanda. You will!

Laura. Why should I?

Amanda. Because, to be painfully honest, your chest is flat.

Laura. You make it seem like we were setting a trap.

Amanda. All pretty girls are a trap, a pretty trap, and men expect them to be.

[LEGEND: "A PRETTY TRAP."]

Now look at yourself, young lady. This is the prettiest you will ever be!

I've got to fix myself now! You're going to be surprised by your mother's appearance!

[*She crosses through portieres, humming gaily.* LAURA *moves slowly to the long mirror and stares solemnly at herself. A wind blows the white curtains inward in a slow, graceful motion and with a faint, sorrowful sighing.*]

Amanda. [*Off stage.*] It isn't dark enough yet.

[LAURA *turns slowly before the mirror with a troubled look.* LEGEND ON SCREEN: "THIS IS MY SISTER: CELEBRATE HER WITH STRINGS!" MUSIC.]

Amanda. [*Laughing, off.*] I'm going to show you something. I'm going to make a spectacular appearance!

Laura. What is it, Mother?

Amanda. Possess your soul in patience—you will see!

Something I've resurrected from that old trunk! Styles haven't changed so terribly much after all. . . .

[*She parts the portieres.*]

Now just look at your mother!

[*She wears a girlish frock of yellowed voile with a blue silk sash. She carries a bunch of jonquils—the legend of her youth is nearly revived. Feverishly.*]

This is the dress in which I led the cotillion. Won the cakewalk twice at Sunset Hill, wore one spring to the Governor's ball in Jackson!

See how I sashayed around the ballroom, Laura?

[*She raises her skirt and does a mincing step around the room.*]

I wore it on Sundays for my gentlemen callers! I had it on the day I met your father——

I had malaria fever all that spring. The change of climate from East Tennessee to the Delta—weakened resistance—I had a little temperature all the time—not enough to be serious—just enough to make me restless and giddy!—Invitations poured in—parties all over the Delta!—"Stay in bed," said Mother, "you have fever!"—but I just wouldn't.—I took quinine but kept on going, going!—Evenings, dances!—Afternoons, long, long rides! Picnics—lovely!—So lovely, that country in May.—All lacy with dogwood, literally flooded with jonquils! —That was the spring I had the craze for jonquils. Jonquils became an absolute obsession. Mother said, "Honey, there's no more room for jonquils." And still I kept on bringing in more jonquils. Whenever, wherever I saw them, I'd say, "Stop! Stop! I see jonquils!" I made the young men help me gather the jonquils! It was a joke, Amanda and her jonquils! Finally there were no more vases to hold them; every available space was filled with jonquils. No vases to hold them? All right, I'll hold them myself! And then I—— [*She stops in front of the picture.* MUSIC.] met your father!

Malaria fever and jonquils and then—this —boy. . . .

[*She switches on the rose-colored lamp.*]

I hope they get here before it starts to rain.

[*She crosses upstage and places the jonquils in bowl on table.*]

I gave your brother a little extra change so he and Mr. O'Connor could take the service car home.

Laura. [*With altered look.*] What did you say his name was?

Amanda. O'Connor.

Laura. What is his first name?

Amanda. I don't remember. Oh, yes, I do. It was—Jim.

[LAURA *sways slightly and catches hold of a chair.* LEGEND ON SCREEN: "NOT JIM!"]

Laura. [*Faintly.*] Not—Jim!

Amanda. Yes, that was it, it was Jim! I've never known a Jim that wasn't nice!

[MUSIC: OMINOUS.]

Laura. Are you sure his name is Jim O'Connor?

Amanda. Yes. Why?

Laura. Is he the one that Tom used to know in high school?

Amanda. He didn't say so. I think he just got to know him at the warehouse.

Laura. There was a Jim O'Connor we both knew in high school—— [*Then, with effort.*] If that is the one that Tom is bringing to dinner—you'll have to excuse me, I won't come to the table.

Amanda. What sort of nonsense is this?

Laura. You asked me once if I'd ever liked a boy. Don't you remember I showed you this boy's picture?

Amanda. You mean the boy you showed me in the year book?

Laura. Yes, that boy.

Amanda. Laura, Laura, were you in love with that boy?

Laura. I don't know, Mother. All I know is I couldn't sit at the table if it was him!

Amanda. It won't be him! It isn't the least bit likely. But whether it is or not, you will come to the table. You will not be excused.

Laura. I'll have to be, Mother.

Amanda. I don't intend to humor your silliness, Laura. I've had too much from you and your brother, both!

So just sit down and compose yourself till they come. Tom has forgotten his key so you'll have to let them in, when they arrive.

Laura. [*Panicky.*] Oh, Mother—*you* answer the door!

Amanda. [*Lightly.*] I'll be in the kitchen —busy!

Laura. Oh, Mother, please answer the door, don't make me do it!

Amanda. [*Crossing into kitchenette.*] I've got to fix the dressing for the salmon. Fuss, fuss—silliness!—over a gentleman caller!

[*Door swings shut.* LAURA *is left alone.* LEGEND: "TERROR!" *She utters a low moan and turns off the lamp—sits stiffly on the edge of the sofa, knotting her fingers together.* LEGEND ON SCREEN: "THE OPENING OF A DOOR!" TOM *and* JIM *appear on the fire-escape steps and climb to landing. Hearing their approach,* LAURA *rises with a panicky gesture. She retreats to the portieres. The doorbell.* LAURA *catches her breath and touches her throat. Low drums.*]

Amanda. [*Calling.*] Laura, sweetheart! The door!

[LAURA *stares at it without moving.*]

Jim. I think we just beat the rain.

Tom. Uh-huh.

[*He rings again, nervously.* JIM *whistles and fishes for a cigarette.*]

Amanda. [*Very, very gaily.*] Laura, that is your brother and Mr. O'Connor! Will you let them in, darling?

[LAURA *crosses toward kitchenette door.*]

Laura. [*Breathlessly.*] Mother—you go to the door!

[AMANDA *steps out of kitchenette and stares furiously at* LAURA. *She points imperiously at the door.*]

Laura. Please, please!

Amanda. [*In a fierce whisper.*] What is the matter with you, you silly thing?

Laura. [*Desperately.*] Please, you answer it, *please!*

Amanda. I told you I wasn't going to humor you, Laura. Why have you chosen this moment to lose your mind?

Laura. Please, please, please, you go!

Amanda. You'll have to go to the door because I can't!

Laura. [*Despairingly.*] I can't either!

Amanda. Why?

Laura. I'm *sick!*

Amanda. I'm sick, too—of your nonsense! Why can't you and your brother be normal people? Fantastic whims and behavior!

[TOM *gives a long ring.*]

Preposterous goings on! Can you give me one reason— [*Calls out lyrically.*] COMING! JUST ONE SECOND!—why you should be afraid to open a door? Now you answer it, Laura!

Laura. Oh, oh, oh . . .

[*She returns through the portieres. Darts to the victrola and winds it frantically and turns it on.*]

Amanda. Laura Wingfield, you march right to that door!

Laura. Yes—yes, Mother!

[*A faraway, scratchy rendition of "Dardanella" softens the air and gives her strength to move through it. She slips to the door and draws it cautiously open.* TOM *enters with the caller,* JIM O'CONNOR.]

Tom. Laura, this is Jim. Jim, this is my sister, Laura.

Jim. [*Stepping inside.*] I didn't know that Shakespeare had a sister!

Laura. [*Retreating stiff and trembling from the door.*] How—how do you do?

Jim. [*Heartily extending his hand.*] Okay!

[LAURA *touches it hesitantly with hers.*]

Jim. Your hand's *cold,* Laura!

Laura. Yes, well—I've been playing the victrola. . . .

Jim. Must have been playing classical music on it! You ought to play a little hot swing music to warm you up!

Laura. Excuse me—I haven't finished playing the victrola. . . .

[*She turns awkwardly and hurries into the front room. She pauses a second by the victrola. Then catches her breath and darts through the portieres like a frightened deer.*]

Jim. [*Grinning.*] What was the matter?

Tom. Oh—with Laura? Laura is—terribly shy.

Jim. Shy, huh? It's unusual to meet a shy girl nowadays. I don't believe you ever mentioned you had a sister.

Tom. Well, now you know. I have one. Here is the *Post Dispatch.* You want a piece of it?

Jim. Uh-huh.

Tom. What piece? The comics?

Jim. Sports! [*Glances at it.*] Ole Dizzy Dean is on his bad behavior.

Tom. [*Disinterest.*] Yeah?

[*Lights cigarette and crosses back to fire-escape door.*]

Jim. Where are *you* going?

Tom. I'm going out on the terrace.

Jim. [*Goes after him.*] You know, Shakespeare—I'm going to sell you a bill of goods!

Tom. What goods!

Jim. A course I'm taking.

Tom. Huh?

Jim. In public speaking! You and me, we're not the warehouse type.

Tom. Thanks—that's good news.

But what has public speaking got to do with it?

Jim. It fits you for—executive positions!

Tom. Awww.

Jim. I tell you it's done a helluva lot for me. [IMAGE: EXECUTIVE AT DESK.]

Tom. In what respect?

Jim. In every! Ask yourself what is the difference between you an' me and men in the office down front? Brains?—No!—Ability?—No! Then what? Just one little thing——

Tom. What is that one little thing?

Jim. Primarily it amounts to—social poise! Being able to square up to people and hold your own on any social level!

Amanda. [*Off stage.*] Tom?

Tom. Yes, Mother?

Amanda. Is that you and Mr. O'Connor?

Tom. Yes, Mother.

Amanda. Well, you just make yourselves comfortable in there.

Tom. Yes, Mother.

Amanda. Ask Mr. O'Connor if he would like to wash his hands.

Jim. Aw, no—no—thank you—I took care of that at the warehouse. Tom——

Tom. Yes?

Jim. Mr. Mendoza was speaking to me about you.

Tom. Favorably?

Jim. What do you think?

Tom. Well——

Jim. You're going to be out of a job if you don't wake up.

Tom. I am waking up——

Jim. You show no signs.

Tom. The signs are interior.

[IMAGE ON SCREEN: THE SAILING VESSEL WITH JOLLY ROGER AGAIN.]

Tom. I'm planning to change. [*He leans over the rail speaking with quiet exhilaration. The incandescent marquees and signs of the first-run movie houses light his face from across the alley. He looks like a voyager.*] I'm right at the point of committing myself to a future that doesn't include the warehouse and Mr. Mendoza or even a night-school course in public speaking.

Jim. What are you gassing about?

Tom. I'm tired of the movies.

Jim. Movies!

Tom. Yes, movies! Look at them—— [*A wave toward the marvels of Grand Avenue.*] All of those glamorous people—having adventures—hogging it all, gobbling the whole thing up! You know what happens? People go to the *movies* instead of *moving!* Hollywood characters are supposed to have all the adventures for everybody in America, while everybody in America sits in a dark room and watches them have them! Yes, until there's a war. That's when adventure becomes available to the masses! *Everyone's* dish, not only Gable's! Then the people in the dark room come out of the dark room to have some adventures themselves—Goody, goody!—It's our turn now, to go to the South Sea Islands—to make a safari —to be exotic, far-off!—But I'm not patient. I don't want to wait till then. I'm tired of the *movies* and I am *about* to *move!*

Jim. [*Incredulously.*] Move?

Tom. Yes.

Jim. When?

Tom. Soon!

Jim. Where? Where?

[THEME THREE MUSIC SEEMS TO ANSWER THE QUESTION, WHILE TOM THINKS IT OVER. HE SEARCHES AMONG HIS POCKETS.]

Tom. I'm starting to boil inside. I know I seem dreamy, but inside—well, I'm boiling! —Whenever I pick up a shoe, I shudder a little thinking how short life is and what I am doing!—Whatever that means, I know it doesn't mean shoes—except as something to wear on a traveler's feet! [*Finds paper.*] Look——

Jim. What?

Tom. I'm a member.

Jim. [*Reading.*] The Union of Merchant Seamen.

Tom. I paid my dues this month, instead of the light bill.

Jim. You will regret it when they turn the lights off.

Tom. I won't be here.

Jim. How about your mother?

Tom. I'm like my father. The bastard son of a bastard! See how he grins? And he's been absent going on sixteen years!

Jim. You're just talking, you drip. How does your mother feel about it?

Tom. Shhh!—Here comes Mother! Mother is not acquainted with my plans!

Amanda. [*Enters portieres.*] Where are you all?

Tom. On the terrace, Mother.

[*They start inside. She advances to them.* TOM *is distinctly shocked at her appearance. Even* JIM *blinks a little. He is making his first contact with girlish Southern vivacity and in spite of the night-school course in public speaking is somewhat thrown off the beam by the unexpected outlay of social charm. Certain responses are attempted by* JIM *but are swept aside by* AMANDA'S *gay laughter and chatter.* TOM *is embarrassed but after the first shock* JIM *reacts very warmly. Grins and chuckles, is altogether won over.* IMAGE: AMANDA AS A GIRL.]

Amanda. [*Coyly smiling, shaking her girlish ringlets.*] Well, well, well, so this is Mr O'Connor. Introductions entirely unnecessary. I've heard so much about you from my boy. I finally said to him, Tom—good gracious!—why don't you bring this paragon to supper? I'd like to meet this nice young man at the warehouse!—Instead of just hearing him sing your praises so much!

I don't know why my son is so standoffish—that's not Southern behavior!

Let's sit down and—I think we could stand a little more air in here! Tom, leave the door open. I felt a nice fresh breeze a moment ago. Where has it gone to?

Mmm, so warm already! And not quite summer, even. We're going to burn up when summer really gets started.

However, we're having—we're having a very light supper. I think light things are better fo' this time of year. The same as light clothes are. Light clothes an' light food are what warm weather calls fo'. You know our blood gets so thick during th' winter—it takes a while fo' us to *adjust* ou'selves!—when the season changes . . .

It's come so quick this year. I wasn't prepared. All of a sudden—heavens! Already summer!—I ran to the trunk an' pulled out this light dress— Terribly old! Historical almost! But feels so good—so good an' co-ol, y'know. . . .

Tom. Mother——

Amanda. Yes, honey?

Tom. How about—supper?

Amanda. Honey, you go ask Sister if supper is ready! You know that Sister is in full charge of supper!

Tell her you hungry boys are waiting for it. [*To* JIM.]

Have you met Laura?

Jim. She——

Amanda. Let you in? Oh, good, you've met already! It's rare for a girl as sweet an' pretty as Laura to be domestic! But Laura is, thank heavens, not only pretty but also very domestic. I'm not at all. I never was a bit. I never could make a thing but angel-food cake. Well, in the South we had so many servants. Gone, gone, gone. All vestige of gracious living! Gone completely! I wasn't prepared for what the future brought me. All of my gentlemen callers were sons of planters and so of course I assumed that I would be married to one and raise my family on a large piece of land with plenty of servants. But man proposes—and women accepts the proposal!—To vary that old, old saying a little bit—I married no planter! I married a man who worked for the telephone company!—That gallantly smiling gentleman over there! [*Points to the picture.*] A telephone man who—fell in love with long-distance!—Now he travels and I don't even know where!—But what am I going on for about my—tribulations?

Tell me yours—I hope you don't have any!

Tom?

Tom. [*Returning.*] Yes, Mother?

Amanda. Is supper nearly ready?

Tom. It looks to me like supper is on the table.

Amanda. Let me look—— [*She rises prettily and looks through portieres.*] Oh, lovely!—But where is Sister?

Tom. Laura is not feeling well and she says that she thinks she'd better not come to the table.

Amanda. What?—Nonsense!—Laura? Oh, Laura!

Laura. [*Off stage, faintly.*] Yes, Mother.

Amanda. You really must come to the table. We won't be seated until you come to the table!

Come in, Mr. O'Connor. You sit over there, and I'll——

Laura? Laura Wingfield!

You're keeping us waiting, honey! We can't say grace until you come to the table!

[*The back door is pushed weakly open and* LAURA *comes in. She is obviously quite faint, her lips trembling, her eyes wide and staring. She moves unsteadily toward the table.* LEGEND: "TERROR!" *Outside a summer storm is coming abruptly. The white curtains billow inward at the windows and there is a sorrowful murmur and deep blue dusk.* LAURA *suddenly stumbles—she catches at a chair with a faint moan.*]

Tom. Laura!

Amanda. Laura!

[*There is a clap of thunder.* LEGEND: "AH!" *Despairingly.*]

Why, Laura, you *are* sick, darling! Tom, help your sister into the living room, dear!

Sit in the living room, Laura—rest on the sofa.

Well! [*To the gentleman caller.*]

Standing over the hot stove made her ill!—I told her that it was just too warm this evening, but——

[TOM *comes back in.* LAURA *is on the sofa.*]

Is Laura all right now?

Tom. Yes.

Amanda. What *is* that? Rain? A nice cool rain has come up!

[*She gives the gentleman caller a frightened look.*]

I think we may—have grace—now . . .

[TOM *looks at her stupidly.*]

Tom, honey—you say grace!

Tom. Oh . . .

"For these and all thy mercies——

[*They bow their heads,* AMANDA *stealing a nervous glance at* JIM. *In the living room* LAURA, *stretched on the sofa, clenches her hand to her lips, to hold back a shuddering sob.*]

God's Holy Name be praised"——

THE SCENE DIMS OUT

SCENE VII

LEGEND: *A Souvenir.*

Half an hour later. Dinner is just being finished in the upstage area which is concealed by the drawn portieres.

As the curtain rises LAURA *is still huddled upon the sofa, her feet drawn under her, her head resting on a pale blue pillow, her eyes wide and mysteriously watchful. The new floor lamp with its shade of rose-colored silk gives a soft, becoming light to her face, bringing out the fragile, unearthly prettiness which usually escapes attention. There is a steady murmur of rain, but it is slackening and stops soon after the scene begins; the air outside becomes pale and luminous as the moon breaks out.*

A moment after the curtain rises, the lights in both rooms flicker and go out.

Jim. Hey, there, Mr. Light Bulb!

[AMANDA *laughs nervously.* LEGEND: "SUSPENSION OF A PUBLIC SERVICE."]

Amanda. Where was Moses when the lights went out? Ha-ha. Do you know the answer to that one, Mr. O'Connor?

Jim. No, Ma'am, what's the answer?

Amanda. In the dark!

[JIM *laughs appreciatively.*]

Everybody sit still. I'll light the candles. Isn't it lucky we have them on the table? Where's a match? Which of you gentlemen can provide a match?

Jim. Here.

Amanda. Thank you, sir.

Jim. Not at all, Ma'am!

Amanda. I guess the fuse has burnt out. Mr. O'Connor, can you tell a burnt-out fuse? I know I can't and Tom is a total loss when it comes to mechanics.

[SOUND: GETTING UP: VOICES RECEDE A LITTLE TO KITCHENETTE.]

Oh, be careful you don't bump into something. We don't want our gentleman caller to break his neck. Now wouldn't that be a fine howdy-do?

Jim. Ha-ha!

Where is the fuse-box?

Amanda. Right here next to the stove. Can you see anything?

Jim. Just a minute.

Amanda. Isn't electricity a mysterious thing?

Wasn't it Benjamin Franklin who tied a key to a kite?

We live in such a mysterious universe, don't we? Some people say that science clears up all the mysteries for us. In my opinion it only creates more!

Have you found it yet?

Jim. No, Ma'am. All these fuses look okay to me.

Amanda. Tom!

Tom. Yes, Mother?

Amanda. That light bill I gave you several days ago. The one I told you we got the notices about? [LEGEND: "HA!"]

Tom. Oh.—Yeah.

Amanda. You didn't neglect to pay it by any chance?

Tom. Why, I——

Amanda. Didn't! I might have known it!

Jim. Shakespeare probably wrote a poem on that light bill, Mrs. Wingfield.

Amanda. I might have known better than to trust him with it! There's such a high price for negligence in this world!

Jim. Maybe the poem will win a ten-dollar prize.

Amanda. We'll just have to spend the remainder of the evening in the nineteenth century, before Mr. Edison made the Mazda lamp!

Jim. Candlelight is my favorite kind of light.

Amanda. That shows you're romantic! But that's no excuse for Tom.

Well, we got through dinner. Very considerate of them to let us get through dinner before they plunged us into everlasting darkness, wasn't it, Mr. O'Connor?

Jim. Ha-ha!

Amanda. Tom, as a penalty for your carelessness you can help me with the dishes.

Jim. Let me give you a hand.

Amanda. Indeed you will not!

Jim. I ought to be good for something.

Amanda. Good for something?

[*Her tone is rhapsodic.*]

You? Why, Mr. O'Connor, nobody, *nobody's* given me this much entertainment in years—as you have!

Jim. Aw, now, Mrs. Wingfield!

Amanda. I'm not exaggerating, not one bit! But Sister is all by her lonesome. You go keep her company in the parlor!

I'll give you this lovely old candelabrum that used to be on the altar at the Church of the Heavenly Rest. It was melted a little out of shape when the church burnt down. Lightning struck it one spring. Gypsy Jones was holding a revival at the time and he intimated that the church was destroyed because the Episcopalians gave card parties.

Jim. Ha-ha.

Amanda. And how about you coaxing Sister to drink a little wine? I think it would be good for her! Can you carry both at once?

Jim. Sure. I'm Superman!

Amanda. Now, Thomas, get into this apron!

[*The door of kitchenette swings closed on* AMANDA'S *gay laughter; the flickering light approaches the portieres.* LAURA *sits up nervously as he enters. Her speech at first is low and breathless from the almost intolerable strain of being alone with a stranger.* [THE LEGEND: "I DON'T SUPPOSE YOU REMEMBER ME AT ALL!"] *In her first speeches in this scene, before* JIM'S *warmth overcomes her paralyzing shyness,* LAURA'S *voice is thin and breathless as though she has just run up a steep flight of stairs.* JIM'S *attitude is gently humorous. In playing this scene it should be stressed that while the incident is apparently unimportant, it is to* LAURA *the climax of her secret life.*]

Jim. Hello, there, Laura.

Laura. [*Faintly.*] Hello.

[*She clears her throat.*]

Jim. How are you feeling now? Better?

Laura. Yes. Yes, thank you.

Jim. This is for you. A little dandelion wine.

[*He extends it toward her with extravagant gallantry.*]

Laura. Thank you.

Jim. Drink it—but don't get drunk!

[*He laughs heartily.* LAURA *takes the glass uncertainly, laughs shyly.*]

Where shall I set the candles?

Laura. Oh—oh, anywhere . . .

Jim. How about here on the floor? Any objections?

Laura. No.

Jim. I'll spread a newspaper under to catch the drippings. I like to sit on the floor. Mind if I do?

Laura. Oh, no.

Jim. Give me a pillow?

Laura. What?

Jim. A pillow!

Laura. Oh . . . [*Hands him one quickly.*]

Jim. How about you? Don't you like to sit on the floor?

Laura. Oh—yes.

Jim. Why don't you, then?

Laura. I—will.

Jim. Take a pillow! [LAURA *does. Sits on the other side of the candelabrum.* JIM *crosses his legs and smiles engagingly at her.*] I can't hardly see you sitting way over there.

Laura. I can—see you.

Jim. I know, but that's not fair; I'm in the limelight. [LAURA *moves her pillow closer.*] Good! Now I can see you! Comfortable?

Laura. Yes.

Jim. So am I. Comfortable as a cow! Will you have some gum?

Laura. No, thank you.

Jim. I think that I will indulge, with your permission. [*Musingly unwraps it and holds it up.*] Think of the fortune made by the guy that invented the first piece of chewing gum. Amazing, huh? The Wrigley Building is one of the sights of Chicago.—I saw it summer before last when I went up to the Century of Progress. Did you take in the Century of Progress?

Laura. No, I didn't.

Jim. Well, it was quite a wonderful exposition. What impressed me most was the Hall of Science. Gives you an idea of what the future will be in America, even more wonderful than the present time is! [*Pause. Smiling at her.*] Your brother tells me you're shy. Is that right, Laura?

Laura. I—don't know.

Jim. I judge you to be an old-fashioned type of girl. Well, I think that's a pretty good type to be. Hope you don't think I'm being too personal—do you?

Laura. [*Hastily, out of embarrassment.*] I believe I *will* take a piece of gum, if you—don't mind. [*Clearing her throat.*] Mr. O'Connor, have you—kept up with your singing?

Jim. Singing? Me?

Laura. Yes. I remember what a beautiful voice you had.

Jim. When did you hear me sing?

[VOICE OFF STAGE IN THE PAUSE.]

Voice. [*Off stage.*]

O blow, ye winds, heigh-ho,
A-roving I will go!
I'm off to my love
With a boxing glove—
Ten thousand miles away!

Jim. You say you've heard me sing?

Laura. Oh, yes! Yes, very often . . . I—don't suppose—you remember me—at all?

Jim. [*Smiling doubtfully.*] You know I have an idea I've seen you before. I had that idea soon as you opened the door. It seemed almost like I was about to remember your name. But the name that I started to call you—wasn't a name! And so I stopped myself before I said it.

Laura. Wasn't it—Blue Roses?

Jim. [*Springs up. Grinning.*] Blue Roses!—My gosh, yes—Blue Roses!

That's what I had on my tongue when you opened the door!

Isn't it funny what tricks your memory plays? I didn't connect you with high school somehow or other.

But that's where it was; it was high school. I didn't even know you were Shakespeare's sister!

Gosh, I'm sorry.

Laura. I didn't expect you to. You—barely knew me!

Jim. But we did have a speaking acquaintance, huh?

Laura. Yes, we—spoke to each other.

Jim. When did you recognize me?

Laura. Oh, right away!

Jim. Soon as I came in the door?

Laura. When I heard your name I thought it was probably you. I knew that Tom used to know you a little in high school. So when you came in the door——

Well, then I was—sure.

Jim. Why didn't you *say* something, then?

Laura. [*Breathlessly.*] I didn't know what to say, I was—too surprised!

Jim. For goodness' sake! You know, this sure is funny!

Laura. Yes! Yes, isn't it, though . . .

Jim. Didn't we have a class in something together?

Laura. Yes, we did.

Jim. What class was that?

Laura. It was—singing—Chorus!

Jim. Aw!

Laura. I sat across the aisle from you in the Aud.

Jim. Aw.

Laura. Mondays, Wednesdays, and Fridays.

Jim. Now I remember—you always came in late.

Laura. Yes, it was so hard for me, getting upstairs. I had that brace on my leg—it clumped so loud!

Jim. I never heard any clumping.

Laura. [*Wincing at the recollection.*] To me it sounded like—thunder!

Jim. Well, well, well, I never even noticed.

Laura. And everybody was seated before I came in. I had to walk in front of all those people. My seat was in the back row. I had to go clumping all the way up the aisle with everyone watching!

Jim. You shouldn't have been self-conscious.

Laura. I know, but I was. It was always such a relief when the singing started.

Jim. Aw, yes, I've placed you now! I used to call you Blue Roses. How was it that I got started calling you that?

Laura. I was out of school a little while with pleurosis. When I came back you asked me what was the matter. I said I had pleurosis—you thought I said Blue Roses. That's what you always called me after that!

Jim. I hope you didn't mind.

Laura. Oh, no—I liked it. You see, I wasn't acquainted with many—people. . . .

Jim. As I remember you sort of stuck by yourself.

Laura. I—I—never have had much luck at—making friends.

Jim. I don't see why you wouldn't.

Laura. Well, I—started out badly.

Jim. You mean being——

Laura. Yes, it sort of—stood between me——

Jim. You shouldn't have let it!

Laura. I know, but it did, and——

Jim. You were shy with people!

Laura. I tried not to be but never could——

Jim. Overcome it?

Laura. No, I—I never could!

Jim. I guess being shy is something you have to work out of kind of gradually.

Laura. [*Sorrowfully.*] Yes—I guess it——

Jim. Takes time!

Laura. Yes——

Jim. People are not so dreadful when you know them. That's what you have to remember! And everybody has problems, not just you, but practically everybody has got some problems.

You think of yourself as having the only problems, as being the only one who is disappointed. But just look around you and you will see lots of people as disappointed as you are. For instance, I hoped when I was going to high school that I would be further along at this time, six years later, than I am now—— You remember that wonderful write-up I had in *The Torch?*

Laura. Yes!

[*She rises and crosses to table.*]

Jim. It said I was bound to succeed in anything I went into! [LAURA *returns with the annual.*] Holy Jeez! *The Torch!*

[*He accepts it reverently. They smile across it with mutual wonder.* LAURA *crouches beside him and they begin to turn through it.* LAURA'S *shyness is dissolving in his warmth.*]

Laura. Here you are in *The Pirates of Penzance!*

Jim. [*Wistfully.*] I sang the baritone lead in that operetta.

Laura. [*Raptly.*] So—*beautifully!*
Jim. [*Protesting.*] Aw——
Laura. Yes, yes—beautifully—beautifully!
Jim. You heard me?
Laura. All three times!
Jim. No!
Laura. Yes!
Jim. All three performances?
Laura. [*Looking down.*] Yes.
Jim. Why?
Laura. I—wanted to ask you to—autograph my program.
Jim. Why didn't you ask me to?
Laura. You were always surrounded by your own friends so much that I never had a chance to.
Jim. You should have just——
Laura. Well, I—thought you might think I was——
Jim. Thought I might think you was—what?
Laura. Oh——
Jim. [*With reflective relish.*] I was beleaguered by females in those days.
Laura. You were terribly popular!
Jim. Yeah——
Laura. You had such a—friendly way——
Jim. I was spoiled in high school.
Laura. Everybody—liked you!
Jim. Including you?
Laura. I—yes, I—I did, too——

[*She gently closes the book in her lap.*]

Jim. Well, well, well!—Give me that program, Laura. [*She hands it to him. He signs it with a flourish.*] There you are—better late than never!
Laura. Oh, I—what a—surprise!
Jim. My signature isn't worth very much right now.

But some day—maybe—it will increase in value!

Being disappointed is one thing and being discouraged is something else. I am disappointed but I am not discouraged.

I'm twenty-three years old.

How old are you?

Laura. I'll be twenty-four in June.
Jim. That's not old age!
Laura. No, but——
Jim. You finished high school?
Laura. [*With difficulty.*] I didn't go back.
Jim. You mean you dropped out?
Laura. I made bad grades in my final examinations. [*She rises and replaces the book and the program. Her voice strained.*] How is—Emily Meisenbach getting along?
Jim. Oh, that kraut-head!
Laura. Why do you call her that?
Jim. That's what she was.
Laura. You're not still—going with her?
Jim. I never see her.
Laura. It said in the Personal Section that you were—engaged!
Jim. I know, but I wasn't impressed by that—propaganda!
Laura. It wasn't—the truth?
Jim. Only in Emily's optimistic opinion!
Laura. Oh——

[LEGEND: "WHAT HAVE YOU DONE SINCE HIGH SCHOOL?" JIM *lights a cigarette and leans indolently back on his elbows smiling at* LAURA *with a warmth and charm which lights her inwardly with altar candles. She remains by the table and turns in her hands a piece of glass to cover her tumult.*]

Jim. [*After several reflective puffs on a cigarette.*] What have you done since high school? [*She seems not to hear him.*] Huh? [LAURA *looks up.*] I said what have you done since high school, Laura?
Laura. Nothing much.
Jim. You must have been doing something these six long years.
Laura. Yes.
Jim. Well, then, such as what?
Laura. I took a business course at business college——
Jim. How did that work out?
Laura. Well, not very—well—I had to drop out, it gave me—indigestion——

[JIM *laughs gently.*]

Jim. What are you doing now?
Laura. I don't do anything—much. Oh, please don't think I sit around doing nothing! My glass collection takes up a good deal of time. Glass is something you have to take good care of.
Jim. What did you say—about glass?
Laura. Collection I said—I have one——

[*She clears her throat and turns away again, acutely shy.*]

Jim. [*Abruptly.*] You know what I judge to be the trouble with you?

Inferiority complex! Know what that is? That's what they call it when someone low-rates himself!

I understand it because I had it, too. Although my case was not so aggravated as yours seems to be. I had it until I took up public speaking, developed my voice, and learned that I had an aptitude for science. Before that time I never thought of myself as being outstanding in any way whatsoever!

Now I've never made a regular study of it, but I have a friend who says I can analyze people better than doctors that make a profession of it. I don't claim that to be necessarily true, but I can sure guess a person's psychology, Laura! [*Takes out his gum.*] Excuse me, Laura. I always take it out when the flavor is gone. I'll use this scrap of paper to wrap it in. I know how it is to get it stuck on a shoe.

Yep—that's what I judge to be your principal trouble. A lack of confidence in yourself as a person. You don't have the proper amount of faith in yourself. I'm basing that fact on a number of your remarks and also on certain observations I've made. For instance that clumping you thought was so awful in high school. You say that you even dreaded to walk into class. You see what you did? You dropped out of school, you gave up an education because of a clump, which as far as I know was practically non-existent! A little physical defect is what you have. Hardly noticeable even! Magnified thousands of times by imagination!

You know what my strong advice to you is? Think of yourself as *superior* in some way!

Laura. In what way would I think?

Jim. Why, man alive, Laura! Just look about you a little. What do you see? A world full of common people! All of 'em born and all of 'em going to die!

Which of them has one-tenth of your good points? Or mine? Or anyone else's, as far as that goes——Gosh!

Everybody excels in some one thing. Some in many!

[*Unconsciously glances at himself in the mirror.*]

All you've got to do is discover in *what!*

Take me, for instance.

[*He adjusts his tie at the mirror.*]

My interest happens to lie in electro-dynamics. I'm taking a course in radio engineering at night school, Laura, on top of a fairly responsible job at the warehouse. I'm taking that course and studying public speaking.

Laura. Ohhhh.

Jim. Because I believe in the future of television! [*Turning back to her.*]

I wish to be ready to go up right along with it. Therefore I'm planning to get in on the ground floor. In fact I've already made the right connections and all that remains is for the industry itself to get under way! Full steam——

[*His eyes are starry.*]

Knowledge—Zzzzzp! *Money*—Zzzzzzp! —*Power!*

That's the cycle democracy is built on!

[*His attitude is convincingly dynamic.* LAURA *stares at him, even her shyness eclipsed in her absolute wonder. He suddenly grins.*]

I guess you think I think a lot of myself!

Laura. No—o-o-o, I——

Jim. Now how about you? Isn't there something you take more interest in than anything else?

Laura. Well, I do—as I said—have my —glass collection——

[*A peal of girlish laughter from the kitchen.*]

Jim. I'm not right sure I know what you're talking about.

What kind of glass is it?

Laura. Little articles of it, they're ornaments mostly!

Most of them are little animals made out of glass, the tiniest little animals in the world. Mother calls them a glass menagerie!

Here's an example of one, if you'd like to see it!

This one is one of the oldest. It's nearly thirteen.

[MUSIC: "THE GLASS MENAGERIE." *He stretches out his hand.*]

Oh, be careful—if you breathe, it breaks!

Jim. I'd better not take it. I'm pretty clumsy with things.

Laura. Go on, I trust you with him!

[*Places it in his palm.*]

There now—you're holding him gently!

Hold him over the light, he loves the light! You see how the light shines through him?

Jim. It sure does shine!

Laura. I shouldn't be partial, but he is my favorite one.

Jim. What kind of a thing is this one supposed to be?

Laura. Haven't you noticed the single horn on his forehead?

Jim. A unicorn, huh?

Laura. Mmm-hmmm!

Jim. Unicorns, aren't they extinct in the modern world?

Laura. I know!

Jim. Poor little fellow, he must feel sort of lonesome.

Laura. [*Smiling.*] Well, if he does he doesn't complain about it. He stays on a shelf with some horses that don't have horns and all of them seem to get along nicely together.

Jim. How do you know?

Laura. [*Lightly.*] I haven't heard any arguments among them!

Jim. [*Grinning.*] No arguments, huh? Well, that's a pretty good sign!

Where shall I set him?

Laura. Put him on the table. They all like a change of scenery once in a while!

Jim. [*Stretching.*] Well, well, well, well——

Look how big my shadow is when I stretch!

Laura. Oh, oh, yes—it stretches across the ceiling!

Jim. [*Crossing to door.*] I think it's stopped raining. [*Opens fire-escape door.*] Where does the music come from?

Laura. From the Paradise Dance Hall across the alley.

Jim. How about cutting the rug a little, Miss Wingfield?

Laura. Oh, I——

Jim. Or is your program filled up? Let me have a look at it. [*Grasps imaginary card.*] Why, every dance is taken! I'll just have to scratch some out. [WALTZ MUSIC: "LA GOLONDRINA."] Ahh, a waltz!

[*He executes some sweeping turns by himself then holds his arms toward* LAURA.]

Laura. [*Breathlessly*]. I—can't dance!

Jim. There you go, that inferiority stuff!

Laura. I've never danced in my life!

Jim. Come on, try!

Laura. Oh, but I'd step on you!

Jim. I'm not made out of glass.

Laura. How—how—how do we start?

Jim. Just leave it to me. You hold your arms out a little.

Laura. Like this?

Jim. A little bit higher. Right. Now don't tighten up, that's the main thing about it—relax.

Laura. [*Laughing breathlessly.*] It's hard not to.

Jim. Okay.

Laura. I'm afraid you can't budge me.

Jim. What do you bet I can't?

[*He swings her into motion.*]

Laura. Goodness, yes, you can!

Jim. Let yourself go, now, Laura, just let yourself go.

Laura. I'm——

Jim. Come on!

Laura. Trying!

Jim. Not so stiff—— Easy does it!

Laura. I know but I'm——

Jim. Loosen th' backbone! There now, that's a lot better.

Laura. Am I?

Jim. Lots, lots better!

[*He moves her about the room in a clumsy waltz.*]

Laura. Oh, my!

Jim. Ha-ha!

Laura. Oh, my goodness!

Jim. Ha-ha-ha! [*They suddenly bump into the table.* JIM *stops.*] What did we hit on?

Laura. Table.

Jim. Did something fall off it? I think——

Laura. Yes.

Jim. I hope that it wasn't the little glass horse with the horn!

Laura. Yes.

Jim. Aw, aw, aw. Is it broken?

Laura. Now it is just like all the other horses.

Jim. It's lost its——

Laura. Horn!

It doesn't matter. Maybe it's a blessing in disguise.

Jim. You'll never forgive me. I bet that that was your favorite piece of glass.

Laura. I don't have favorites much. It's no tragedy, Freckles. Glass breaks so easily. No matter how careful you are. The traffic jars the shelves and things fall off them.

Jim. Still I'm awfully sorry that I was the cause.

Laura. [*Smiling.*] I'll just imagine he had an operation.

The horn was removed to make him feel less—freakish! [*They both laugh.*]

Now he will feel more at home with the other horses, the ones that don't have horns . . .

Jim. Ha-ha, that's very funny!

[*Suddenly serious.*]

I'm glad to see that you have a sense of humor.

You know—you're—well—very different!

Surprisingly different from anyone else I know!

[*His voice becomes soft and hesitant with a genuine feeling.*]

Do you mind me telling you that?

[LAURA *is abashed beyond speech.*]

I mean it in a nice way . . .

[LAURA *nods shyly, looking away.*]

You make me feel sort of—I don't know how to put it!

I'm usually pretty good at expressing things, but——

This is something that I don't know how to say!

[LAURA *touches her throat and clears it—turns the broken unicorn in her hands. Even softer.*]

Has anyone ever told you that you were pretty?

[PAUSE: MUSIC. LAURA *looks up slowly, with wonder, and shakes her head.*]

Well, you are! In a very different way from anyone else.

And all the nicer because of the difference, too.

[*His voice becomes low and husky.* LAURA *turns away, nearly faint with the novelty of her emotions.*]

I wish that you were my sister. I'd teach you to have some confidence in yourself. The different people are not like other people, but being different is nothing to be ashamed of. Because other people are not such wonderful people. They're one hundred times one thousand. You're one times one! They walk all over the earth. You just stay here. They're common as—weeds, but—you—well, you're—*Blue Roses!*

[IMAGE ON SCREEN: BLUE ROSES. MUSIC CHANGES.]

Laura. But blue is wrong for—roses . . .

Jim. It's right for you!—You're—pretty!

Laura. In what respect am I pretty?

Jim. In all respects—believe me! Your eyes—your hair—are pretty! Your hands are pretty! [*He catches hold of her hand.*]

You think I'm making this up because I'm invited to dinner and have to be nice. Oh, I could do that! I could put on an act for you, Laura, and say lots of things without being very sincere. But this time I am. I'm talking to you sincerely. I happened to notice you had this inferiority complex that keeps you from feeling comfortable with people. Somebody needs to build your confidence up and make you proud instead of shy and turning away and—blushing——

Somebody—ought to——

Ought to—*kiss* you, Laura!

[*His hand slips slowly up her arm to her shoulder.* MUSIC SWELLS TUMULTUOUSLY. *He suddenly turns her about and kisses her on the lips. When he releases her,* LAURA *sinks on the sofa with a bright, dazed look.* JIM *backs away and fishes in his pocket for a cigarette.* LEGEND ON SCREEN: "SOUVENIR."]

Stumble-john!

[*He lights the cigarette, avoiding her look. There is a peal of girlish laughter from* AMANDA *in the kitchen.* LAURA *slowly raises and opens her hand. It still contains the little broken glass animal. She looks at it with a tender, bewildered expression.*]

Stumble-john!

I shouldn't have done that—— That was way off the beam.

You don't smoke, do you?

[*She looks up, smiling, not hearing the question. He sits beside her a little gingerly. She looks at him speechlessly—waiting. He coughs decorously and moves a little farther aside as he considers the situation and senses her feelings, dimly, with perturbation. Gently.*]

Would you—care for a—mint?

[*She doesn't seem to hear him but her look grows brighter even.*]

Peppermint—Life-Saver?

My pocket's a regular drug store—wherever I go . . .

[*He pops a mint in his mouth. Then gulps and decides to make a clean breast of it. He speaks slowly and gingerly.*]

Laura, you know, if I had a sister like you, I'd do the same thing as Tom. I'd bring out fellows and—introduce her to them. The right type of boys of a type to—appreciate her.

Only—well—he made a mistake about me.

Maybe I've got no call to be saying this. That may not have been the idea in having me over. But what if it was?

There's nothing wrong about that. The only trouble is that in my case—I'm not in a situation to—do the right thing.

I can't take down your number and say I'll phone.

I can't call up next week and—ask for a date.

I thought I had better explain the situation in case you—misunderstood it and—hurt your feelings. . . .

[*Pause. Slowly, very slowly,* LAURA'S *look changes, her eyes returning slowly from his to the ornament in her palm.* AMANDA *utters another gay laugh in the kitchen.*]

Laura. [*Faintly.*] You—won't—call again?

Jim. No, Laura, I can't.

[*He rises from the sofa.*]

As I was just explaining, I've—got strings on me.

Laura, I've—been going steady!

I go out all of the time with a girl named Betty. She's a home-girl like you, and Catholic, and Irish, and in a great many ways we—get along fine.

I met her last summer on a moonlight boat trip up the river to Alton, on the *Majestic.*

Well—right away from the start it was—love!

[LEGEND: LOVE! LAURA *sways slightly forward and grips the arm of the sofa. He fails to notice, now enrapt in his own comfortable being.*]

Being in love has made a new man of me!

[*Leaning stiffly forward, clutching the*

arm of the sofa, LAURA *struggles visibly with her storm. But* JIM *is oblivious; she is a long way off.*]

The power of love is really pretty tremendous!

Love is something that—changes the whole world, Laura!

[*The storm abates a little and* LAURA *leans back. He notices her again.*]

It happened that Betty's aunt took sick; she got a wire and had to go to Centralia. So Tom—when he asked me to dinner—I naturally just accepted the invitation, not knowing that you—that he—that I——

[*He stops awkwardly.*]

Huh—I'm a stumble-john!

[*He flops back on the sofa. The holy candles in the altar of* LAURA'S *face have been snuffed out. There is a look of almost infinite desolation.* JIM *glances at her uneasily.*]

I wish that you would—say something. [*She bites her lip which was trembling and then bravely smiles. She opens her hand again on the broken glass ornament. Then she gently takes his hand and raises it level with her own. She carefully places the unicorn in the palm of his hand, then pushes his fingers closed upon it.*] What are you—doing that for? You want me to have him? —Laura? [*She nods.*] What for?

Laura. A—souvenir . . .

[*She rises unsteadily and crouches beside the victrola to wind it up.* LEGEND ON SCREEN: "THINGS HAVE A WAY OF TURNING OUT SO BADLY!" OR IMAGE: "GENTLEMAN CALLER WAVING GOOD-BYE! —GAILY." *At this moment* AMANDA *rushes brightly back in the front room. She bears a pitcher of fruit punch in an old-fashioned cut-glass pitcher and a plate of macaroons. The plate has a gold border and poppies painted on it.*]

Amanda. Well, well, well! Isn't the air delightful after the shower?

I've made you children a little liquid refreshment.

[*Turns gaily to the gentleman caller.*]

Jim, do you know that song about lemonade?

"Lemonade, lemonade
Made in the shade and stirred with a spade——
Good enough for any old maid!"

Jim. [*Uneasily.*] Ha-ha! No—I never heard it.

Amanda. Why, Laura! You look so serious!

Jim. We were having a serious conversation.

Amanda. Good! Now you're better acquainted!

Jim. [*Uncertainly.*] Ha-ha! Yes.

Amanda. You modern young people are much more serious-minded than my generation. I was so gay as a girl!

Jim. You haven't changed, Mrs. Wingfield.

Amanda. Tonight I'm rejuvenated! The gaiety of the occasion, Mr. O'Connor!

[*She tosses her head with a pearl of laughter. Spills lemonade.*]

Oooo! I'm baptizing myself!

Jim. Here—let me——

Amanda. [*Setting the pitcher down.*] There now. I discovered we had some maraschino cherries. I dumped them in, juice and all!

Jim. You shouldn't have gone to that trouble, Mrs. Wingfield.

Amanda. Trouble, trouble? Why, it was loads of fun!

Didn't you hear me cutting up in the kitchen? I bet your ears were burning! I told Tom how outdone with him I was for keeping you to himself so long a time! He should have brought you over much, much sooner! Well, now that you've found your way, I want you to be a very frequent caller! Not just occasional but all the time.

Oh, we're going to have a lot of gay times together! I see them coming!

Mmm, just breathe that air! So fresh, and the moon's so pretty!

I'll skip back out—I know where my place is when young folks are having a—serious conversation!

Jim. Oh, don't go out, Mrs. Wingfield. The fact of the matter is I've got to be going.

Amanda. Going, now? You're joking! Why, it's only the shank of the evening, Mr. O'Connor!

Jim. Well, you know how it is.

Amanda. You mean you're a young workingman and have to keep workingmen's hours. We'll let you off early tonight. But only on the condition that next time you stay later.

What's the best night for you? Isn't Saturday night the best night for you workingmen?

Jim. I have a couple of time-clocks to punch, Mrs. Wingfield. One at morning, another one at night!

Amanda. My, but you *are* ambitious! You work at night, too?

Jim. No, Ma'am, not work but—Betty!

[*He crosses deliberately to pick up his hat. The band at the Paradise Dance Hall goes into a tender waltz.*]

Amanda. Betty? Betty? Who's—Betty?

[*There is an ominous cracking sound in the sky.*]

Jim. Oh, just a girl. The girl I go steady with!

[*He smiles charmingly. The sky falls.* LEGEND: "THE SKY FALLS."]

Amanda. [*A long-drawn exhalation.*] Ohhhh . . . Is it a serious romance, Mr. O'Connor?

Jim. We're going to be married the second Sunday in June.

Amanda. Ohhhh—how nice!

Tom didn't mention that you were engaged to be married.

Jim. The cat's not out of the bag at the warehouse yet.

You know how they are. They call you Romeo and stuff like that.

[*He stops at the oval mirror to put on his hat. He carefully shapes the brim and the crown to give a discreetly dashing effect.*]

It's been a wonderful evening, Mrs. Wingfield. I guess this is what they mean by Southern hospitality.

Amanda. It really wasn't anything at all.

Jim. I hope it don't seem like I'm rushing off. But I promised Betty I'd pick her up at the Wabash depot, an' by the time I get my jalopy down there her train'll be in. Some women are pretty upset if you keep 'em waiting.

Amanda. Yes, I know—— The tyranny of women! [*Extends her hand.*]

Good-bye, Mr. O'Connor.

I wish you luck—and happiness—and success! All three of them, and so does Laura! —Don't you, Laura?

Laura. Yes!

Jim. [*Taking her hand.*] Good-bye, Laura. I'm certainly going to treasure that souvenir. And don't you forget the good advice I gave you.

[*Raises his voice to a cheery shout.*]

So long, Shakespeare!

Thanks again, ladies—— Good night!

[*He grins and ducks jauntily out. Still bravely grimacing,* AMANDA *closes the door on the gentleman caller. Then she turns back to the room with a puzzled expression. She and* LAURA *don't dare to face each other.* LAURA *crouches beside the victrola to wind it.*]

Amanda. [*Faintly.*] Things have a way of turning out so badly.

I don't believe that I would play the victrola.

Well, well—well——

Our gentleman caller was engaged to be married!

Tom!

Tom. [*From back.*] Yes, Mother?

Amanda. Come in here a minute. I want to tell you something awfully funny.

Tom. [*Enters with macaroon and a glass of the lemonade.*] Has the gentleman caller gotten away already?

Amanda. The gentleman caller has made an early departure.

What a wonderful joke you played on us!

Tom. How do you mean?

Amanda. You didn't mention that he was engaged to be married.

Tom. Jim? Engaged?

Amanda. That's what he just informed us.

Tom. I'll be jiggered! I didn't know about that.

Amanda. That seems very peculiar.

Tom. What's peculiar about it?

Amanda. Didn't you call him your best friend down at the warehouse?

Tom. He is, but how did I know?

Amanda. It seems extremely peculiar that you wouldn't know your best friend was going to be married!

Tom. The warehouse is where I work, not where I know things about people!

Amanda. You don't know things anywhere! You live in a dream; you manufacture illusions! [*He crosses to the door.*]

Where are you going?

Tom. I'm going to the movies.

Amanda. That's right, now that you've had us make such fools of ourselves. The effort, the preparations, all the expense! The new floor lamp, the rug, the clothes for Laura! All for what? To entertain some other girl's fiancé!

Go to the movies, go! Don't think about us, a mother deserted, an unmarried sister who's crippled and has no job! Don't let anything interfere with your selfish pleasure!

Just go, go, go—to the movies!

Tom. All right, I will! The more you shout about my selfishness to me the quicker I'll go, and I won't go to the movies!

Amanda. Go, then! Then go to the moon —you selfish dreamer!

[TOM *smashes his glass on the floor. He plunges out on the fire-escape, slamming the door.* LAURA *screams—cut off by door. Dance-hall music up.* TOM *goes to the rail and grips it desperately, lifting his face in the chill white moonlight penetrating the narrow abyss of the alley.* LEGEND ON SCREEN: "AND SO GOOD-BYE . . ." TOM'S *closing speech is timed with the interior pantomime. The interior scene is played as though viewed through soundproof glass.* AMANDA *appears to be making a comforting speech to* LAURA *who is huddled upon the sofa. Now that we cannot hear the mother's speech, her silliness is gone and she has dignity and tragic beauty.* LAURA'S *dark hair hides her face until at the end of the speech she lifts it to smile at her mother.* AMANDA'S *gestures are slow and graceful, almost dancelike, as she comforts the daughter. At the end of her speech she glances a moment at the father's picture—then withdraws through the portieres. At close of* TOM'S *speech,* LAURA *blows out the candles, ending the play.*]

Tom. I didn't go to the moon, I went much further—for time is the longest distance between two places——

Not long after that I was fired for writing a poem on the lid of a shoe-box.

I left Saint Louis. I descended the steps of this fire-escape for the last time and followed, from then on, in my father's footsteps, attempting to find in motion what was lost in space——

I traveled around a great deal. The cities swept about me like dead leaves, leaves that were brightly colored but torn away from the branches.

I would have stopped, but I was pursued by something.

It always came upon me unawares, taking me altogether by surprise. Perhaps it was a familiar bit of music. Perhaps it was only a piece of transparent glass——

Perhaps I am walking along a street at night, in some strange city, before I have found companions. I pass the lighted window of a shop where perfume is sold. The window is filled with pieces of colored glass, tiny transparent bottles in delicate colors, like bits of a shattered rainbow.

Then all at once my sister touches my shoulder. I turn around and look into her eyes . . .

Oh, Laura, Laura, I tried to leave you behind me, but I am more faithful than I intended to be!

I reach for a cigarette, I cross the street, I run into the movies or a bar, I buy a drink, I speak to the nearest stranger—anything that can blow your candles out!

[LAURA *bends over the candles.*]

—for nowadays the world is lit by lightning! Blow out your candles, Laura—and so good-bye. . . .

[*She blows the candles out.*]

THE SCENE DISSOLVES

THE MADWOMAN OF CHAILLOT*

(*La Folle de Chaillot*)

By

JEAN GIRAUDOUX

Adapted by MAURICE VALENCY

At the beginning of the modern period of dramatic creativity, about 1870, France was the theatrical center of the world. From France came the theory and first successful practice of naturalism, unquestionably the dominant dramatic mode since then, and in Paris arose the first fruitful reform of theatrical organization, The Free Theatre, under Antoine. But after the anti-naturalism of Rostand and Maeterlinck had spent its force, French drama seemed to fall into barrenness. Leadership in theatrical and dramatic innovation passed to other nations: to Scandinavia with Ibsen and Strindberg, to Britain with Shaw, to Russia with Stanislavsky, to Germany with Reinhardt. Early in the twentieth century France had no dramatic or theatrical genius to rank with these. But new forces began slowly to appear. Paul Claudel's first play, produced in New York in 1923 as *The Tidings Brought to Mary,* was played in Paris in 1912, and marked the revival of religious drama, so notable a phenomenon in the twentieth-century theatre. The next year Jacques Copeau founded *Le Théâtre du Vieux Colombier,* a group at first of actors, which gradually attracted to itself an audience for its wide repertoire of classic and foreign plays, and then French writers to enrich that repertoire with contemporary drama of distinction. Such writers were André Gide, Roger Martin du Gard, Charles Vildrac. But the *Vieux Colombier* made its most profound impression through Copeau's disciples who left him to carry on his principles independently. Two of these, the most distinguished as actor-managers, were Charles Dullin and Louis Jouvet. Under their leadership French drama came to renewed fire and charm until in the middle of the twentieth century French dramatists such as Sartre, Anouilh, Salacrou, Montherlant, were among the most impressive in the Western World. Jean Giraudoux was not least among these, and he was brought into the theatre by Louis Jouvet.

Giraudoux had won a reputation as a novelist and was already 46 years old in 1928 when Jouvet produced his *Siegfried,* dramatized from a novel Giraudoux had published six years before. Evidently Giraudoux liked the dramatic form, for in the next year Jouvet produced his *Amphitryon 38.* This play, according to Giraudoux the thirty-eighth use of the Amphitryon plot, united the themes of love and war, two themes which were to reappear in Giraudoux's work. *Siegfried* had dealt with post-war reconciliation between France and Germany. *La guerre de Troie n'aura pas lieu* was to show that nations in confrontation could scracely avoid war—destiny wills their conflict. And *Judith* showed the helplessness of love when God willed to destroy Holophernes.

The choice of such themes, though they are not his only themes, shows that Giraudoux belongs to the ranks of philosophic dramatists. Yet to define Giraudoux's philosophy is extremely difficult. Though summaries might seem to emphasize determinism in his thinking, and certainly determinism is present, it is not final and conclusive, as *The Madwoman of Chaillot* shows. For the Madwoman saves civilization by an act of will, and surely we are not meant to feel when the play is finished that Giraudoux has mocked at our real helplessness. The Madwoman may be mad, but she inspires us to be like her, not in her madness but in her sanity. And mad or sane, her company is delightful.

Delight, in fact, Giraudoux tries to give

us in the theatre, but delight from ideas and language, from the brilliant perception shiningly set forth, and from the remarkable characters of his women. Giraudoux's gallery of women is truly extraordinary: Alcmene in *Amphitryon 38;* Judith; Isabelle in *Intermezzo* (known on the English-speaking stage as *The Enchanted*); Ondine; the Madwomen; Electra and Clytemnestra in *Électre;* Helen and Andromache in *La guerre de Troie;* they are every one different, yet every one memorable. Giraudoux's men are not so striking; they clearly interested him less; they tend to be feebler in will, to have less insight than the women.

Giraudoux's plays somewhat lack movement, and this static quality has kept many of them from the English-speaking stage. Jouvet's style of acting was static; he thought of the theatre as a place for listening; so does Giraudoux. But listening to Giraudoux can be a rich experience. He seizes the imagination whether his work is read or seen; his own liveliness and fertility of mind stimulates liveliness and fertility in the audience's mind and emotion even without startling theatricality. France may indeed point to him as evidence of her renewed distinction in drama.

JEAN GIRAUDOUX

Born 1882, Bellac, France.

Educated at L'École Normale, Paris.

1906–1907, Assistant in French at Harvard University.

1907–1910, Journalism in Paris.

1910, Entered the French diplomatic service.

1914, As sergeant in the French Army, wounded at the Aisne.

1915, Restored to duty, and wounded again at the Dardanelles. Cited in Army orders, promoted to lieutenant, and awarded the Legion of Honor.

1916, Military instructor in Portugal.

1917, Military instructor at Harvard University.

1918, Returned to France. Married. Resumed diplomatic career.

1928, First play, *Siegfried.* Earlier he had published some fifteen volumes of novels, essays, and political comment.

1936, Declined offered directorship of the Comédie Française.

1939, War declared. Commissioner of Information in the French government.

1940, Fall of France. Retired to unoccupied France.

1942, Returned to Paris; devoted himself to writing about the war, the defeat, and the political future, and also to writing for motion pictures.

1944, Died suddenly, January 31.

PLAYS

1928 *Siegfried* (translated). With new last act, *Fin de Siegfried,* 1934. 1929 *Amphitryon 38* (translated). 1931 *Judith* (translated). 1933 *Intermezzo* (translated as *The Enchanted*). 1934 *Tessa* (adapted from Margaret Kennedy's *The Constant Nymph*). 1935 *La Guerre de Troie n'aura pas lieu* (translated as *Tiger at the Gates*). 1935 *Supplément au voyage de Cook* (adapted for television as *Virtuous Island*). 1937 *Électre* (translated). 1937 *L'Impromptu de Paris* (translated). 1938 *Cantique des Cantiques.* 1939 *Ondine* (translated). 1942 *L'Appolon de Bellac* (also called *L'Appolon de Marsac*). 1943 *Sodome et Gomorrhe.* 1945 *La Folle de Chaillot* (translated as *The Madwoman of Chaillot*). 1953 *Pour Lucrèce.*

SCREENWRITING

1942 *La Duchesse de Langeais* (from Balzac). 1944 *Béthanie* (*Les Anges du Péché*).

WRITINGS ON DRAMA

In *Littérature,* 1941: "Racine," "Discours sur le théâtre," "L'auteur au théâtre," "Un duo," "Le metteur en scène," "Bellac et la tragédie." *L'Impromptu de Paris,* 1937, discusses in play form dramatic criticisms, dramatists, actors, and the theatre. *Visitations,* 1947, comments on the theatre and acting with illustrative scenes from the author's plays.

THE MADWOMAN OF CHAILLOT

Characters

THE WAITER.
THE LITTLE MAN.
THE PROSPECTOR.
THE PRESIDENT.
THE BARON.
THERESE.
THE STREET SINGER.
THE FLOWER GIRL.
THE RAGPICKER.
PAULETTE.
THE DEAF-MUTE.
IRMA.
THE SHOE-LACE PEDDLER.
THE BROKER.
THE STREET JUGGLER.
DR. JADIN.
COUNTESS AURELIA, *Madwoman of Chaillot.*
THE DOORMAN.
THE POLICEMAN.
PIERRE.
THE SERGEANT.
THE SEWER-MAN.
MME. CONSTANCE, *Madwoman of Passy.*
MLLE. GABRIELLE, *Madwoman of St. Sulpice.*
MME. JOSEPHINE, *Madwoman of La Concorde.*
THE PRESIDENTS.
THE PROSPECTORS.
THE PRESS AGENTS.
THE LADIES.
THE ADOLPHE BERTAUTS.

SCENES

ACT ONE: *The Café Terrace of* Chez Francis.
ACT TWO: *The Countess' Cellar—21 Rue de Chaillot.*

ACT ONE

SCENE: *The café terrace at* Chez Francis, *on the Place de l'Alma in Paris. The Alma is in the stately quarter of Paris known as Chaillot, between the Champs Élysées and the Seine, across the river from the Eiffel Tower.*

Chez Francis *has several rows of tables set out under its awning, and, as it is lunch time, a good many of them are occupied. At a table, downstage, a somewhat obvious* BLONDE *with ravishing legs is sipping a vermouth-cassis and trying hard to engage the attention of* THE PROSPECTOR, *who sits at an adjacent table taking little sips of water and rolling them over his tongue with the air of a connoisseur. Downstage right, in front of the tables on the sidewalk, is the usual Paris bench, a stout and uncomfortable affair provided by the municipality for the benefit of those who prefer to sit without drinking. A* POLICEMAN *lounges about, keeping the peace without unnecessary exertion.*

TIME: *It is a little before noon in the Spring of next year.*

AT RISE: THE PRESIDENT *and* THE BARON *enter with importance, and are ushered to a front table by* THE WAITER.

The President. Baron, sit down. This is a historic occasion. It must be properly celebrated. The waiter is going to bring out my special port.

The Baron. Splendid.

The President. [*Offers his cigar case.*] Cigar? My private brand.

The Baron. Thank you. You know, this all gives me the feeling of one of those enchanted mornings in the *Arabian Nights* when thieves foregather in the market place. Thieves—pashas . . .

[*He sniffs the cigar judiciously, and begins lighting it.*]

The President. [*Chuckles.*] Tell me about yourself.

The Baron. Well, where shall I begin?

[THE STREET SINGER *enters. He takes off a battered black felt with a flourish and begins singing an ancient mazurka.*]

The Street Singer. [*Sings.*]

"Do you hear, Mademoiselle,
Those musicians of hell?"

The President. Waiter! Get rid of that man.

The Waiter. He is singing *La Belle Polonaise.*

The President. I didn't ask for the program. I asked you to get rid of him. [THE WAITER *doesn't budge.* THE SINGER *goes by himself.*] As you were saying, Baron . . . ?

The Baron. Well, until I was fifty . . . [THE FLOWER GIRL *enters through the café door, center.*] my life was relatively uncomplicated. It consisted of selling off one by one the various estates left me by my father. Three years ago, I parted with my last farm. Two years ago, I lost my last mistress. And now—all that is left me is . . .

The Flower Girl. [*To* THE BARON.] Violets, sir?

The President. Run along.

[THE FLOWER GIRL *moves on.*]

The Baron. [*Staring after her.*] So that, in short, all I have left now is my name.

The President. Your name is precisely the name we need on our board of directors.

The Baron. [*With an inclination of his head.*] Very flattering.

The President. You will understand when I tell you that mine has been a very different experience. I came up from the bottom. My mother spent most of her life bent over a washtub in order to send me to school. I'm eternally grateful to her, of course, but I must confess that I no longer remember her face. It was no doubt beautiful—but when I try to recall it, I see only the part she invariably showed me—her rear.

The Baron. Very touching.

The President. When I was thrown out of school for the fifth and last time, I decided to find out for myself what makes the world go round. I ran errands for an editor, a movie star, a financier. . . . I began to understand a little what life is. Then, one day, in the subway, I saw a face. . . . My rise in life dates from that day.

The Baron. Really?

The President. One look at that face, and I knew. One look at mine, and he knew. And so I made my first thousand—passing a boxful of counterfeit notes. A year later, I saw another such face. It got me a nice berth in the narcotics business. Since then, all I do is to look out for such faces. And now here I am—president of eleven corporations, director of fifty-two companies, and, beginning today, chairman of the board of the international combine in which you have been so good as to accept a post. [THE RAGPICKER *passes, sees something under* THE PRESIDENT'S *table, and stoops to pick it up.*] Looking for something?

The Ragpicker. Did you drop this?

The President. I never drop anything.

The Ragpicker. Then this hundred-franc note isn't yours?

The President. Give it here.

[THE RAGPICKER *gives him the note, and goes out.*]

The Baron. Are you sure it's yours?

The President. All hundred-franc notes, Baron, are mine.

The Baron. Mr. President, there's something I've been wanting to ask you. What exactly is the purpose of our new company? Or is that an indiscreet question . . . ?

The President. Indiscreet? Not a bit. Merely unusual. As far as I know, you're the first member of a board of directors ever to ask such a question.

The Baron. Do we plan to exploit a commodity? A utility?

The President. My dear sir, I haven't the faintest idea.

The Baron. But if you don't know—who does?

The President. Nobody. And at the moment, it's becoming just a trifle embarrassing. Yes, my dear Baron, since we are now close business associates, I must confess that for the time being we're in a little trouble.

The Baron. I was afraid of that. The stock issue isn't going well?

The President. No, no—on the contrary. The stock issue is going beautifully. Yesterday morning at ten o'clock we offered 500,000 shares to the general public. By 10:05 they were all snapped up at par. By 10:20, when the police finally arrived, our offices were a shambles. . . . Windows smashed—doors torn off their hinges—you never saw anything so beautiful in your life! And this morning our stock is being quoted over the counter at 124 with no sellers, and the orders are still pouring in.

The Baron. But in that case—what is the trouble?

The President. The trouble is we have a tremendous capital, and not the slightest idea of what to do with it.

The Baron. You mean all those people are fighting to buy stock in a company that has no object?

The President. My dear Baron, do you imagine that when a subscriber buys a share of stock, he has any idea of getting behind a counter or digging a ditch? A stock certificate is not a tool, like a shovel, or a commodity, like a pound of cheese. What we sell a customer is not a share in a business, but a view of the Elysian Fields. A financier is a creative artist. Our function is to stimulate the imagination. We are poets!

The Baron. But in order to stimulate the imagination, don't you need some field of activity?

The President. Not at all. What you need for that is a name. A name that will stir the pulse like a trumpet call, set the brain awhirl like a movie star, inspire reverence like a cathedral. *United General International Consolidated!* Of course that's been used. That's what a corporation needs.

The Baron. And do we have such a name?

The President. So far we have only a blank space. In that blank space a name must be printed. This name must be a masterpiece. And if I seem a little nervous today, it's because—somehow—I've racked my brains, but it hasn't come to me. Oho! Look at that! Just like the answer to a prayer . . . ! [THE BARON *turns and stares in the direction of* THE PROSPECTOR.] You see? There's one. And what a beauty!

The Baron. You mean that girl?

The President. No, no, not the girl. That face. You see . . . ? The one that's drinking water.

The Baron. You call that a face? That's a tombstone.

The President. It's a milestone. It's a signpost. But is it pointing the way to steel, or wheat, or phosphates? That's what we have to find out. Ah! He sees me. He understands. He will be over.

The Baron. And when he comes . . . ?

The President. He will tell me what to do.

The Baron. You mean business is done this way? You mean, you would trust a stranger with a matter of this importance?

The President. Baron, I trust neither my wife, nor my daughter, nor my closest friend. My confidential secretary has no idea where I live. But a face like that I would trust with my inmost secrets. Though we have never laid eyes on each other before, that man and I know each other to the depths of our souls. He's no stranger—he's my brother, he's myself. You'll see. He'll be over in a minute. [THE DEAF-MUTE *enters and passes slowly among the tables, placing a small envelope before each customer. He comes to* THE PRESIDENT'S *table.*] What is this anyway? A conspiracy? We don't want your envelopes. Take them away. [THE DEAF-MUTE *makes a short but pointed speech in sign language.*] Waiter, what the devil's he saying?

The Waiter. Only Irma understands him.

The President. Irma? Who's Irma?

The Waiter. [*Calls.*] Irma! It's the waitress inside, sir. Irma!

[IRMA *comes out. She is twenty. She has the face and figure of an angel.*]

Irma. Yes?

The Waiter. These gentlemen would . . .

The President. Tell this fellow to get out of here, for God's sake! [THE DEAF-MUTE *makes another manual oration.*] What's he trying to say, anyway?

Irma. He says it's an exceptionally beautiful morning, sir. . . .

The President. Who asked him?

Irma. But, he says, it was nicer before the gentleman stuck his face in it.

The President. Call the manager!

[IRMA *shrugs. She goes back into the restaurant.* THE DEAF-MUTE *walks off, left. Meanwhile a* SHOELACE PEDDLER *has arrived.*]

Peddler. Shoelaces? Postcards?

The Baron. I think I could use a shoelace.

The President. No, no . . .

Peddler. Black? Tan?

The Baron. [*Showing his shoes.*] What would you recommend?

Peddler. Anybody's guess.

The Baron. Well, give me one of each.

The President. [*Putting a hand on* THE BARON'S *arm.*] Baron, although I am your chairman, I have no authority over your personal life—none, that is, except to fix the amount of your director's fees, and eventually to assign a motor car for your use. Therefore, I am asking you, as a personal favor to me, not to purchase anything from this fellow.

The Baron. How can I resist so gracious a request? [THE PEDDLER *shrugs, and passes on.*] But I really don't understand. . . . What difference would it make?

The President. Look here, Baron. Now that you're with us, you must understand that between this irresponsible riff-raff and us there is an impenetrable barrier. *We* have no dealings whatever with *them.*

The Baron. But without us, the poor devil will starve.

The President. No, he won't. He expects nothing from us. He has a clientele of his own. He sells shoelaces exclusively to those who have no shoes. Just as the necktie peddler sells only to those who wear no shirts. And that's why these street hawkers can afford to be insolent, disrespectful, and independent. They don't need us. They have a world of their own. Ah! My broker. Splendid. He's beaming.

[THE BROKER *walks up and grasps* THE PRESIDENT'S *hand with enthusiasm.*]

The Broker. Mr. President! My heartiest congratulations! What a day! What a day!

[THE STREET JUGGLER *appears, right. He removes his coat, folds it carefully, and puts it on the bench. Then he opens a suitcase, from which he extracts a number of colored clubs.*]

The President. [*Presenting* THE BROKER.] Baron Tommard, of our Board of Directors. My broker. [THE BROKER *bows. So does* THE JUGGLER. THE BROKER *sits down and signals for a drink.* THE JUGGLER *prepares to juggle.*] What's happened?

The Broker. Listen to this. Ten o'clock this morning. The market opens. [*As he speaks,* THE JUGGLER *provides a visual counterpart to* THE BROKER'S *lines, his clubs rising and falling in rhythm to* THE BROKER'S *words.*] Half million shares issued at par, par value a hundred, quoted on the curb at 124 and we start buying at 126, 127, 129—and it's going up—up—up— [THE JUGGLER'S *clubs rise higher and higher.*] —132—133—138—141—141—141—141 . . .

The Baron. May I ask . . . ?

The President. No, no—any explanation would only confuse you.

The Broker. Ten forty-five we start selling short on rumors of a Communist plot; market bearish. . . . 141—138—133—132—and it's down—down—down—102—and we start buying back at 93. Eleven o'clock, rumors denied—95—98—101—106—124—141—and by 11:30 we've got it all back—net profit three and a half million francs.

The President. Classical. Pure. [THE JUGGLER *bows again. A* LITTLE MAN *leans over from a near-by table, listening intently, and trembling with excitement.*] And how many shares do we reserve to each member of the board?

The Broker. Fifty, as agreed.

The President. Bit stingy, don't you think?

The Broker. All right—three thousand.

The President. That's a little better. [*To* THE BARON.] You get the idea?

The Baron. I'm beginning to get it.

The Broker. And now we come to the exciting part . . . [THE JUGGLER *prepares to juggle with balls of fire.*] Listen carefully: With 35 percent of our funded capital under Section 32 I buy 50,000 United at 36 which I immediately reconvert into 32,000 National Amalgamated two's preferred which I set up as collateral on 150,000 General Consols which I deposit against a credit of fifteen billion to buy Eastern Hennequin which I immediately turn into Argentine wheat realizing 136 percent of the original investment which naturally accrues as capital gain and not as corporate income thus saving twelve millions in taxes, and at once convert the 25 percent cotton reserve into lignite, and as our people swing into action in London and New York, I beat up the price on greige goods from 26 to 92—114—203—306 —— [THE JUGGLER *by now is juggling his fireballs in the sky. The balls no longer return to his hands.*] 404 . . .

[THE LITTLE MAN *can stand no more. He rushes over and dumps a sackful of money on the table.*]

The Little Man. Here—take it—please, take it!

The Broker. [*Frigidly.*] Who is this man? What is this money?

The Little Man. It's my life's savings. Every cent. I put it all in your hands.

The Broker. Can't you see we're busy?

The Little Man. But I beg you . . . It's my only chance . . . Please don't turn me away.

The Broker. Oh, all right. [*He sweeps the money into his pocket.*] Well?

The Little Man. I thought—perhaps you'd give me a little receipt. . . .

The President. My dear man, people like us don't give receipts for money. We take them.

The Little Man. Oh, pardon. Of course. I was confused. Here it is. [*Scribbles a receipt.*] Thank you—thank you—thank you.

[*He rushes off joyfully.* THE STREET SINGER *reappears.*]

The Street Singer. [*Sings.*]

"Do you hear, Mademoiselle,
Those musicians of hell?"

The President. What, again? Why does he keep repeating those two lines like a parrot?

The Waiter. What else can he do? He doesn't know any more and the song's been out of print for years.

The Baron. Couldn't he sing a song he knows?

The Waiter. He likes this one. He hopes if he keeps singing the beginning someone will turn up to teach him the end.

The President. Tell him to move on. We don't know the song.

[THE PROFESSOR *strolls by, swinging his cane. He overhears.*]

The Professor. [*Stops and addresses* THE PRESIDENT *politely.*] Nor do I, my dear sir. Nor do I. And yet, I'm in exactly the same predicament. I remember just two lines of my favorite song, as a child. A mazurka also, in case you're interested. . . .

The President. I'm not.

The Professor. Why is it, I wonder, that one always forgets the words of a mazurka?

I suppose they just get lost in that damnable rhythm. All I remember is: [*He sings.*]

"From England to Spain
I have drunk, it was bliss . . ."

The Street Singer. [*Walks over, and picks up the tune.*]

"Red wine and champagne
And many a kiss."

The Professor. Oh, God! It all comes back to me . . . ! [*He sings.*]

"Red lips and white hands I have known
Where the nightingales dwell. . . ."

The President. [*Holding his hands to his ears.*] Please—please . . .

The Street Singer.

"And to each one I've whispered, 'My own,'
And to each one, I've murmured: 'Farewell.'"

The President. Farewell. Farewell.

The Street Singer.
The Professor. } [*Duo.*]

"But there's one I shall never forget. . . ."

The President. This isn't a café. It's a circus!

[*The two go off, still singing:* "There is one that's engraved in my heart." THE PROSPECTOR *gets up slowly and walks toward* THE PRESIDENT'S *table. He looks down without a word. There is a tense silence.*]

The Prospector. Well?

The President. I need a name.

The Prospector. [*Nods, with complete comprehension.*] I need fifty thousand.

The President. For a corporation.

The Prospector. For a woman.

The President. Immediately.

The Prospector. Before evening.

The President. Something . . .

The Prospector. Unusual?

The President. Something . . .

The Prospector. Provocative?

The President. Something . . .

The Prospector. Practical.

The President. Yes.

The Prospector. Fifty thousand. Cash.

The President. I'm listening.

The Prospector. *International Substrate of Paris, Inc.*

The President. [*Snaps his fingers.*] That's it! [*To* THE BROKER.] Pay him off. [THE BROKER *pays with* THE LITTLE MAN'S *money.*] Now—what does it mean?

The Prospector. It means what it says. I'm a prospector.

The President. [*Rises.*] A prospector! Allow me to shake your hand. Baron. You are in the presence of one of nature's noblemen. Shake his hand. This is Baron Tommard. [*They shake hands.*] It is this man, my dear Baron, who smells out in the bowels of the earth those deposits of metal or liquid on which can be founded the only social unit of which our age is capable—the corporation. Sit down, please. [*They all sit.*] And now that we have a name . . .

The Prospector. You need a property.

The President. Precisely.

The Prospector. I have one.

The President. A claim?

The Prospector. Terrific.

The President. Foreign?

The Prospector. French.

The Baron. In Indo-China?

The Broker. Morocco?

The President. In France?

The Prospector. [*Matter of fact.*] In Paris.

The President. In Paris? You've been prospecting in Paris?

The Baron. For women, no doubt.

The President. For art?

The Broker. For gold?

The Prospector. Oil.

The Broker. He's crazy.

The President. Sh! He's inspired.

The Prospector. You think I'm crazy. Well, they thought Columbus was crazy.

The Baron. Oil in Paris?

The Broker. But how is it possible?

The Prospector. It's not only possible. It's certain.

The President. Tell us.

The Prospector. You don't know, my dear sir, what treasures Paris conceals. Paris is the least prospected place in the world. We've gone over the rest of the planet with a fine-tooth comb. But has anyone ever thought of looking for oil in Paris? Nobody. Before me, that is.

The President. Genius!

The Prospector. No. Just a practical man. I use my head.

The Baron. But why has nobody ever thought of this before?

The Prospector. The treasures of the earth, my dear sir, are not easy to find nor to get at. They are invariably guarded by dragons. Doubtless there is some reason for this. For once we've dug out and consumed the internal ballast of the planet, the chances are it will shoot off on some irresponsible tangent and smash itself up in the sky. Well, that's the risk we take. Anyway, that's not my business. A prospector has enough to worry about.

The Baron. I know—snakes—tarantulas—fleas . . .

The Prospector. Worse than that, sir. Civilization.

The President. Does that annoy you?

The Prospector. Civilization gets in our way all the time. In the first place, it covers the earth with cities and towns which are damned awkward to dig up when you want to see what's underneath. It's not only the real-estate people—you can always do business with them—it's human sentimentality. How do you do business with that?

The President. I see what you mean.

The Prospector. They say that where we pass, nothing ever grows again. What of it? Is a park any better than a coal mine? What's a mountain got that a slag pile hasn't? What would you rather have in your garden—an almond tree or an oil well?

The President. Well . . .

The Prospector. Exactly. But what's the use of arguing with these fools? Imagine the choicest place you ever saw for an excavation, and what do they put there? A playground for children! Civilization!

The President. Just show us the point where you want to start digging. We'll do the rest. Even if it's in the middle of the Louvre. Where's the oil?

The Prospector. Perhaps you think it's easy to make an accurate fix in an area like Paris where everything conspires to put you off the scent? Women—perfume—flowers—history. You can talk all you like about geology, but an oil deposit, gentlemen, has to be smelled out. I have a good nose. I go further. I have a phenomenal nose. But the minute I get the right whiff—the minute I'm on the scent—a fragrance rises from what I take to be the spiritual deposits of the past —and I'm completely at sea. Now take this very point, for example, this very spot.

The Baron. You mean—right here in Chaillot?

The Prospector. Right under here.

The President. Good heavens!

[*He looks under his chair.*]

The Prospector. It's taken me months to locate this spot.

The Baron. But what in the world makes you think . . . ?

The Prospector. Do you know this place, Baron?

The Baron. Well, I've been sitting here for thirty years.

The Prospector. Did you ever taste the water?

The Baron. The water? Good God, no!

The Prospector. It's plain to see that you are no prospector! A prospector, Baron, is addicted to water as a drunkard to wine. Water, gentlemen, is the one substance from which the earth can conceal nothing. It sucks out its innermost secrets and brings them to our very lips. Well—beginning at Notre Dame, where I first caught the scent of oil three months ago, I worked my way across Paris, glassful by glassful, sampling the water, until at last I came to this café. And here—just two days ago—I took a sip. My heart began to thump. Was it possible that I was deceived? I took another, a third, a fourth, a fifth. I was trembling like a leaf. But there was no mistake. Each time that I drank, my taste-buds thrilled to the most exquisite flavor known to a prospector—the flavor of— [*With utmost lyricism.*] petroleum!

The President. Waiter! Some water and four glasses. Hurry. This round, gentlemen, is on me. And as a toast—I shall propose International Substrate of Paris, Incorporated. [THE WAITER *brings a decanter and the glasses.* THE PRESIDENT *pours out the water amid profound silence. They taste it with the air of connoisseurs savoring something that has never before passed human lips. Then they look at each other doubtfully.* THE PROSPECTOR *pours himself a second glass and drinks it off.*] Well . . .

The Broker. Ye-es . . .

The Baron. Mm . . .

The Prospector. Get it?

The Baron. Tastes queer.

The Prospector. That's it. To the unpracticed palate it tastes queer. But to the tastebuds of the expert—ah!

The Baron. Still, there's one thing I don't quite understand . . .

The Prospector. Yes?

The Baron. This café doesn't have its own well, does it?

The Prospector. Of course not. This is Paris water.

The Broker. Then why should it taste different here than anywhere else?

The Prospector. Because, my dear sir, the pipes that carry this water pass deep through the earth, and the earth just here is soaked with oil, and this oil permeates the pores of the iron and flavors the water it carries. Ever so little, yes—but quite enough to betray its presence to the sensitive tongue of the specialist.

The Baron. I see.

The Prospector. I don't say everyone is capable of tasting it. No. But I—I can detect the presence of oil in water that has passed within fifteen miles of a deposit. Under special circumstances, twenty.

The President. Phenomenal!

The Prospector. And so here I am with the greatest discovery of the age on my hands—but the blasted authorities won't let me drill a single well unless I show them the oil! Now how can I show them the oil unless they let me dig? Completely stymied! Eh?

The President. What? A man like you?

The Prospector. That's what they think. That's what they want. Have you noticed the strange glamor of the women this morning? And the quality of the sunshine? And this extraordinary convocation of vagabonds buzzing about protectively like bees around a hive? Do you know why it is? Because they know. It's a plot to distract us, to turn us from our purpose. Well, let them try. I know there's oil here. And I'm going to dig it up, even if I . . . [*He smiles.*] Shall I tell you my little plan?

The President. By all means.

The Prospector. Well . . . For heaven's sake, what's that?

[*At this point, the* MADWOMAN *enters. She is dressed in the grand fashion of 1885, a taffeta skirt with an immense train—which she has gathered up by means of a clothespin—ancient button shoes, and a hat in the style of Marie Antoinette. She wears a lorgnette on a chain, and an enormous cameo pin at her throat. In her hand she carries a small basket. She walks in with great dignity, extracts a dinner bell from the bosom of her dress, and rings it sharply.* IRMA *appears.*]

Countess. Are my bones ready, Irma?

Irma There won't be much today, Countess. We had broilers. Can you wait? While the gentleman inside finishes eating?

Countess. And my gizzard?

Irma. I'll try to get it away from him.

Countess. If he eats my gizzard, save me the giblets. They will do for the tomcat that lives under the bridge. He likes a few giblets now and again.

Irma. Yes, Countess.

[IRMA *goes back into the café. The* COUNTESS *takes a few steps and stops in front of* THE PRESIDENT'S *table. She examines him with undisguised disapproval.*]

The President. Waiter. Ask that woman to move on.

The Waiter. Sorry, sir. This is her café.

The President. Is she the manager of the café?

The Waiter. She's the Madwoman of Chaillot.

The President. A Madwoman? She's mad?

The Waiter. Who says she's mad?

The President. You just said so yourself.

The Waiter. Look, sir. You asked me who she was. And I told you. What's mad about her? She's the Madwoman of Chaillot.

The President. Call a policeman.

[*The* COUNTESS *whistles through her fingers. At once,* THE DOORMAN *runs out of the café. He has three scarves in his hands.*]

Countess. Have you found it? My feather boa?

The Doorman. Not yet, Countess. Three scarves. But no boa.

Countess. It's five years since I lost it. Surely you've had time to find it.

The Doorman. Take one of these, Countess. Nobody's claimed them.

Countess. A boa like that doesn't vanish, you know. A feather boa nine feet long!

The Doorman. How about this blue one?

Countess. With my pink ruffle and my green veil? You're joking! Let me see the yellow. [*She tries it on.*] How does it look?

The Doorman. Terrific.

[*With a magnificent gesture, she flings the scarf about her, upsetting* THE PRESIDENT'S *glass and drenching his trousers with water. She stalks off without a glance at him.*]

The President. Waiter! I'm making a complaint.

The Waiter. Against whom?

The President. Against her! Against you! The whole gang of you! That singer! That shoelace peddler! That female lunatic! Or whatever you call her!

The Baron. Calm yourself, Mr. President. . . .

The President. I'll do nothing of the sort! Baron, the first thing we have to do is to get rid of these people! Good heavens, look at them! Every size, shape, color, and period of history imaginable. It's utter anarchy! I tell you, sir, the only safeguard of order and discipline in the modern world is a standardized worker with interchangeable parts. That would solve the entire problem of management. Here, the manager . . . And there—one composite drudge grunting and sweating all over the world. Just we two. Ah, how beautiful! How easy on the eyes! How restful for the conscience!

The Baron. Yes, yes—of course.

The President. Order. Symmetry. Balance. But instead of that, what? Here in Chaillot, the very citadel of management, these insolent phantoms of the past come to beard us with their raffish individualism—with the right of the voiceless to sing, of the dumb to make speeches, of trousers to have no seats and bosoms to have dinner bells!

The Baron. But, after all, do these people matter?

The President. My dear sir, wherever the poor are happy, and the servants are proud, and the mad are respected, our power is at an end. Look at that! That waiter! That madwoman! That flower girl! Do I get that sort of service? And suppose that I—president of twelve corporations and ten times a millionaire—were to stick a gladiolus in my buttonhole and start yelling— [*He tinkles his spoon in a glass violently, yelling.*] Are my bones ready, Irma?

The Baron. [*Reprovingly.*] Mr. President . . .

[*People at the adjoining tables turn and stare with raised eyebrows.* THE WAITER *starts to come over.*]

The President. You see? Now.

The Prospector. We were discussing my plan.

The President. Ah yes, your plan. [*He glances in the direction of the* MADWOMAN'S *table.*] Careful—she's looking at us.

The Prospector. Do you know what a bomb is?

The President. I'm told they explode.

The Prospector. Exactly. You see that white building across the river. Do you happen to know what that is?

The President. I do not.

The Prospector. That's the office of the City Architect. That man has stubbornly refused to give me a permit to drill for oil anywhere within the limits of the city of Paris. I've tried everything with him—influence, bribes, threats. He says I'm crazy. And now . . .

The President. Oh, my God! What is this one trying to sell us?

[*A little* OLD MAN *enters left, and doffs his hat politely. He is somewhat ostentatiously respectable—gloved, pomaded, and carefully dressed, with a white handkerchief peeping out of his breast pocket.*]

Dr. Jadin. Nothing but health, sir. Or rather the health of the feet. But remember —as the foot goes, so goes the man. May I present myself . . . ? Dr. Gaspard Jadin, French Navy, retired. Former specialist in the extraction of ticks and chiggers. At present specializing in the extraction of bunions and corns. In case of sudden emergency, Martial the waiter will furnish my home address. My office is here, second row, third table, week days, twelve to five. Thank you very much. [*He sits at his table.*]

The Waiter. Your vermouth, Doctor?

Dr. Jadin. My vermouth. My vermouths. How are your gallstones today, Martial?

The Waiter. Fine. Fine. They rattle like anything.

Dr. Jadin. Splendid. [*He spies the* COUNTESS.] Good morning, Countess. How's the floating kidney? Still afloat? [*She nods graciously.*] Splendid. Splendid. So long as it floats, it can't sink.

The President. This is impossible! Let's go somewhere else.

The Prospector. No. It's nearly noon.

The President. Yes. It is. Five to twelve.

The Prospector. In five minutes' time you're going to see that City Architect blown up, building and all—boom!

The Broker. Are you serious?

The Prospector. That imbecile has no one to blame but himself. Yesterday noon, he got my ultimatum—he's had twenty-four hours to think it over. No permit? All right. Within two minutes my agent is going to drop a little package in his coal bin. And three minutes after that, precisely at noon . . .

The Baron. You prospectors certainly use modern methods.

The Prospector. The method may be modern. But the idea is old. To get at the treasure, it has always been necessary to slay the dragon. I guarantee that after this, the City Architect will be more reasonable. The new one, I mean.

The President. Don't you think we're sitting a little close for comfort?

The Prospector. Oh no, no. Don't worry. And, above all, don't stare. We may be watched. [*A clock strikes.*] Why, that's noon. Something's wrong! Good God! What's this? [*A* POLICEMAN *staggers in bearing a lifeless body on his shoulders in the manner prescribed as "The Fireman's Lift."*] It's Pierre! My agent! [*He walks over with affected nonchalance.*] I say, Officer, what's that you've got?

The Policeman. Drowned man.

[*He puts him down on the bench.*]

The Waiter. He's not drowned. His clothes are dry. He's been slugged.

The Policeman. Slugged is also correct. He was just jumping off the bridge when I came along and pulled him back. I slugged him, naturally, so he wouldn't drag me under. Life Saving Manual, Rule 5: "In cases where there is danger of being dragged under, it is necessary to render the subject unconscious by means of a sharp blow." He's had that.

[*He loosens the clothes and begins applying artificial respiration.*]

The Prospector. The stupid idiot! What the devil did he do with the bomb? That's what comes of employing amateurs!

The President. You don't think he'll give you away?

The Prospector. Don't worry. [*He walks over to* THE POLICEMAN.] Say, what do you think you're doing?

The Policeman. Lifesaving. Artificial respiration. First aid to the drowning.

The Prospector. But he's not drowning.

The Policeman. But he thinks he is.

The Prospector. You'll never bring him round that way, my friend. That's meant for people who drown in water. It's no good at all for those who drown without water.

The Policeman. What am I supposed to do? I've just been sworn in. It's my first day on the beat. I can't afford to get in trouble. I've got to go by the book.

The Prospector. Perfectly simple. Take him back to the bridge where you found him and throw him in. Then you can save his life and you'll get a medal. This way, you'll only get fined for slugging an innocent man.

The Policeman. What do you mean, innocent? He was just going to jump when I grabbed him.

The Prospector. Have you any proof of that?

The Policeman. Well, I saw him.

The Prospector. Written proof? Witnesses?

The Policeman. No, but . . .

The Prospector. Then don't waste time arguing. You're in trouble. Quick—before anybody notices—throw him in and dive after him. It's the only way out.

The Policeman. But I don't swim.

The President. You'll learn how on the way down. Before you were born, did you know how to breathe?

The Policeman. [*Convinced.*] All right. Here we go. [*He starts lifting the body.*]

Dr. Jadin. One moment, please. I don't like to interfere, but it's my professional duty to point out that medical science has definitely established the fact of intra-uterine respiration. Consequently, this policeman, even before he was born, knew not only how to breathe but also how to cough, hiccup, and belch.

The President. Suppose he did—how does it concern you?

Dr. Jadin. On the other hand, medical science has never established the fact of intra-uterine swimming or diving. Under the circumstances, we are forced to the opinion, Officer, that if you dive in you will probably drown.

The Policeman. You think so?

The Prospector. Who asked you for an opinion?

The President. Pay no attention to that quack, Officer.

Dr. Jadin. Quack, sir?

The Prospector. This is not a medical matter. It's a legal problem. The officer has made a grave error. He's new. We're trying to help him.

The Broker. He's probably afraid of the water.

The Policeman. Nothing of the sort. Officially, I'm afraid of nothing. But I always follow doctor's orders.

Dr. Jadin. You see, Officer, when a child is born . . .

The Prospector. Now, what does he care about when a child is born? He's got a dying man on his hands. . . . Officer, if you want my advice . . .

The Policeman. It so happens, I care a lot about when a child is born. It's part of my duty to aid and assist any woman in childbirth or labor.

The President. Can you imagine!

The Policeman. Is it true, Doctor, what they say, that when you have twins, the first born is considered to be the youngest?

Dr. Jadin. Quite correct. And what's more, if the twins happen to be born at midnight on December 31st, the older is a whole year younger. He does his military service a year later. That's why you have to keep your eyes open. And that's the reason why a queen always gives birth before witnesses. . . .

The Policeman. God! The things a policeman is supposed to know! Doctor, what does it mean if, when I get up in the morning sometimes . . .

The Prospector. [*Nudging* THE PRESIDENT *meaningfully.*] The old woman . . .

The Broker. Come on, Baron.

The President. I think we'd better all run along.

The Prospector. Leave him to me.

The President. I'll see you later.

[THE PRESIDENT *steals off with* THE BROKER *and* THE BARON.]

The Policeman. [*Still in conference with* DR. JADIN.] But what's really worrying me, Doctor, is this—don't you think it's a bit risky for a man to marry after forty-five?

[THE BROKER *runs in breathlessly.*]

The Broker. Officer! Officer!

The Policeman. What's the trouble?

The Broker. Quick! Two women are calling for help—on the sidewalk—Avenue Wilson!

The Policeman. Two women at once? Standing up or lying down?

The Broker. You'd better go and see. Quick!

The Prospector. You'd better take the Doctor with you.

The Policeman. Come along, Doctor, come along. . . . [*Pointing to* PIERRE.] Tell him to wait till I get back. Come along, Doctor.

[*He runs out,* THE DOCTOR *following.* THE PROSPECTOR *moves over toward* PIERRE, *but* IRMA *crosses in front of him and takes the boy's hand.*]

Irma. How beautiful he is! Is he dead, Martial?

The Waiter. [*Handing her a pocket mirror.*] Hold this mirror to his mouth. If it clouds over . . .

Irma. It clouds over.

The Waiter. He's alive.

[*He holds out his hand for the mirror.*]

Irma. Just a sec—— [*She rubs it clean and looks at herself intently. Before handing it back, she fixes her hair and applies her lipstick. Meanwhile* THE PROSPECTOR *tries to get around the other side, but the* COUNTESS' *eagle eye drives him off. He shrugs his shoulders and exits with* THE BARON.] Oh, look—he's opening his eyes!

[PIERRE *opens his eyes, stares intently at* IRMA *and closes them again with the expression of a man who is among the angels.*]

Pierre. [*Murmurs.*] Oh! How beautiful!

Voice. [*From within the café.*] Irma!

Irma. Coming. Coming.

[*She goes in, not without a certain reluctance. The* COUNTESS *at once takes her place on the bench, and also the young man's hand.* PIERRE *sits up suddenly, and finds himself staring, not at* IRMA, *but into the very peculiar face of the* COUNTESS. *His expression changes.*]

Countess. You're looking at my iris? Isn't it beautiful?

Pierre. Very.

[*He drops back, exhausted.*]

Countess. The Sergeant was good enough to say it becomes me. But I no longer trust his taste. Yesterday, the flower girl gave me a lily, and he said it didn't suit me.

Pierre. [*Weakly.*] It's beautiful.

Countess. He'll be very happy to know that you agree with him. He's really quite sensitive. [*She calls.*] Sergeant!

Pierre. No, please—don't call the police.

Countess. But I must. I think I hurt his feelings.

Pierre. Let me go, Madame.

Countess. No, no. Stay where you are. Sergeant!

[PIERRE *struggles weakly to get up.*]

Pierre. Please let me go.

Countess. I'll do nothing of the sort. When you let someone go, you never see him again. I let Charlotte Mazumet go. I never saw her again.

Pierre. Oh, my head.

Countess. I let Adolphe Bertaut go. And I was holding him. And I never saw him again.

Pierre. Oh, God!

Countess. Except once. Thirty years later. In the market. He had changed a great deal —he didn't know me. He sneaked a melon from right under my nose, the only good one of the year. Ah, here we are. Sergeant!

[THE POLICE SERGEANT *comes in with importance.*]

The Sergeant. I'm in a hurry, Countess.

Countess. With regard to the iris. This young man agrees with you. He says it suits me.

The Sergeant. [*Going.*] There's a man drowning in the Seine.

Countess. He's not drowning in the Seine. He's drowning here. Because I'm holding him tight—as I should have held Adolphe Bertaut. But if I let him go, I'm sure he will go and drown in the Seine. He's a lot better looking than Adolphe Bertaut, wouldn't you say? [PIERRE *sighs deeply.*]

The Sergeant. How would I know?

Countess. I've shown you his photograph. The one with the bicycle.

The Sergeant. Oh, yes. The one with the harelip.

Countess. I've told you a hundred times! Adolphe Bertaut had no harelip. That was a scratch in the negative. [THE SERGEANT *takes out his notebook and pencil.*] What are you doing?

The Sergeant. I am taking down the drowned man's name, given name, and date of birth.

Countess. You think that's going to stop him from jumping in the river? Don't be silly, Sergeant. Put that book away and try to console him.

The Sergeant. I should try and console him?

Countess. When people want to die, it is your job as a guardian of the state to speak out in praise of life. Not mine.

The Sergeant. I should speak out in praise of life?

Countess. I assume you have some motive for interfering with people's attempts to kill each other, and rob each other, and run each other over? If you believe that life has some value, tell him what it is. Go on.

The Sergeant. Well, all right. Now look, young man . . .

Countess. His name is Roderick.

Pierre. My name is not Roderick.

Countess. Yes, it is. It's noon. At noon all men become Roderick.

The Sergeant. Except Adolphe Bertaut.

Countess. In the days of Adolphe Bertaut, we were forced to change the men when we got tired of their names. Nowadays, we're more practical—each hour on the hour all names are automatically changed. The men remain the same. But you're not here to discuss Adolphe Bertaut, Sergeant. You're here to convince the young man that life is worth living.

Pierre. It isn't.

The Sergeant. Quiet. Now then—what was the idea of jumping off the bridge, anyway?

Countess. The idea was to land in the river. Roderick doesn't seem to be at all confused about that.

The Sergeant. Now how can I convince anybody that life is worth living if you keep interrupting all the time?

Countess. I'll be quiet.

The Sergeant. First of all, Mr. Roderick, you have to realize that suicide is a crime against the state. And why is it a crime against the state? Because every time anybody commits suicide, that means one soldier less for the army, one taxpayer less for the . . .

Countess. Sergeant, isn't there something about life that you really enjoy?

The Sergeant. That I enjoy?

Countess. Well, surely in all these years, you must have found something worth living for. Some secret pleasure, or passion. Don't blush. Tell him about it.

The Sergeant. Who's blushing? Well, naturally, yes—I have my passions—like everybody else. The fact is, since you ask me—I love—to play—casino. And if the gentleman would like to join me, by and by when I go off duty, we can sit down to a nice little game in the back room with a nice cold glass of beer. If he wants to kill an hour, that is.

Countess. He doesn't want to kill an hour. He wants to kill himself. Well? Is that all the police force has to offer by way of earthly bliss?

The Sergeant. Huh? You mean—— [*He jerks a thumb in the direction of the pretty* BLONDE, *who has just been joined by a* BRUNETTE *of the same stamp.*] Paulette?

[*The young man groans.*]

Countess. You're not earning your salary, Sergeant. I defy anybody to stop dying on your account.

The Sergeant. Go ahead, if you can do any better. But you won't find it easy.

Countess. Oh, this is not a desperate case at all. A young man who has just fallen in love with someone who has fallen in love with him!

Pierre. She hasn't. How could she?

Countess. Oh, yes, she has. She was holding your hand, just as I'm holding it, when all of a sudden . . . Did you ever know Marshal Canrobert's niece?

The Sergeant. How could he know Marshal Canrobert's niece?

Countess. Lots of people knew her—when she was alive. [PIERRE *begins to struggle energetically.*] No, no, Roderick—stop—stop!

The Sergeant. You see? You won't do any better than I did.

Countess. No? Let's bet. I'll bet my iris against one of your gold buttons. Right? —Roderick, I know very well why you tried to drown yourself in the river.

Pierre. You don't at all.

Countess. It's because that Prospector wanted you to commit a horrible crime.

Pierre. How did you know that?

Countess. He stole my boa, and now he wants you to kill me.

Pierre. Not exactly.

Countess. It wouldn't be the first time they've tried it. But I'm not so easy to get rid of, my boy, oh, no . . . Because . . .

[THE DOORMAN *rides in on his bicycle. He winks at* THE SERGEANT, *who has now seated himself while* THE WAITER *serves him a beer.*]

The Doorman. Take it easy, Sergeant.

The Sergeant. I'm busy saving a drowning man.

Countess. They can't kill me because—I have no desire to die.

Pierre. You're fortunate.

Countess. To be alive is to be fortunate, Roderick. Of course, in the morning, when you first awake, it does not always seem so very gay. When you take your hair out of the drawer, and your teeth out of the glass, you are apt to feel a little out of place in this world. Especially if you've just been dreaming that you're a little girl on a pony looking for strawberries in the woods. But all you need to feel the call of life once more is a letter in your mail giving you your schedule for the day—your mending, your shopping, that letter to your grandmother that you never seem to get around to. And so, when you've washed your face in rosewater, and powdered it—not with this awful rice-powder they sell nowadays, which does nothing for the skin, but with a cake of pure white starch—and put on your pins, your rings, your brooches, bracelets, earrings, and pearls—in short, when you are dressed for your morning coffee—and have had a good look at yourself—not in the glass, naturally—it lies—but in the side of the brass gong that once belonged to Admiral Courbet—then, Roderick, then you're armed, you're strong, you're ready—you can begin again.

[PIERRE *is listening now intently. There are tears in his eyes.*]

Pierre. Oh, Madame . . . ! Oh, Madame . . . !

Countess. After that, everything is pure delight. First the morning paper. Not, of course, these current sheets full of lies and vulgarity. I always read the *Gaulois,* the issue of March 22, 1903. It's by far the best. It has some delightful scandal, some excellent fashion notes, and, of course, the last-minute bulletin on the death of Leonide Leblanc. She used to live next door, poor woman, and when I learn of her death every morning, it gives me quite a shock. I'd gladly lend you my copy, but it's in tatters.

The Sergeant. Couldn't we find him a copy in some library?

Countess. I doubt it. And so, when you've taken your fruit salts—not in water, naturally—no matter what they say, it's water that gives you gas—but with a bit of spiced cake—then in sunlight or rain, Chaillot calls. It is time to dress for your morning walk. This takes much longer, of course—without a maid, impossible to do it under an hour, what with your corset, corset-cover, and drawers, all of which lace or button in the back. I asked Madame Lanvin, a while ago, to fit the drawers with zippers. She was quite charming, but she declined. She thought it would spoil the style.

[THE DEAF-MUTE *comes in.*]

The Waiter. I know a place where they put zippers on anything.

[THE RAGPICKER *enters.*]

Countess. I think Lanvin knows best. But I really manage very well, Martial. What I do now is, I lace them up in front, then twist them around to the back. It's quite simple, really. Then you choose a lorgnette, and then the usual fruitless search for the feather boa that the prospector stole—I know it was he: he didn't dare look me in the eye—and then all you need is a rubber band to slip around your parasol—I lost the catch the day I struck the cat that was stalking the pigeon—it was worth it—ah, that day I earned my wages!

The Ragpicker. Countess, if you can use it, I found a nice umbrella catch the other day with a cat's eye in it.

Countess. Thank you, Ragpicker. They say those eyes sometimes come to life and fill with tears. I'd be afraid . . .

Pierre. Go on, Madame, go on . . .

Countess. Ah! So life is beginning to interest you, is it? You see how beautiful it is?

Pierre. What a fool I've been!

Countess. Then, Roderick, I begin my rounds. I have my cats to feed, my dogs to pet, my plants to water. I have to see what the evil ones are up to in the district—those who hate people, those who hate plants, those who hate animals. I watch them sneaking off in the morning to put on their disguises—to the baths, to the beauty parlors, to the barbers. But they can't deceive me. And when they come out again with blonde hair and false whiskers, to pull up my flowers and poison my dogs, I'm there, and I'm ready. All you have to do to break their power is to cut across their path from the left. That isn't always easy. Vice moves swiftly. But I have a good long stride and I generally manage. . . . Right, my friends? [THE WAITER *and* THE RAGPICKER *nod their heads with evident approval.*] Yes, the flowers have been marvelous this year. And the butcher's dog on the Rue Bizet, in spite of that wretch that tried to poison him, is friskier than ever. . . .

The Sergeant. That dog had better look out. He has no license.

Countess. He doesn't seem to feel the need for one.

The Ragpicker. The Duchess de la Rochefoucauld's whippet is getting awfully thin. . . .

Countess. What can I do? She bought that dog full grown from a kennel where they didn't know his right name. A dog without his right name is bound to get thin.

The Ragpicker. I've got a friend who knows a lot about dogs—an Arab . . .

Countess. Ask him to call on the Duchess. She receives Thursdays, five to seven. You see, then, Roderick. That's life. Does it appeal to you now!

Pierre. It seems marvelous.

Countess. Ah! Sergeant. My button. [THE SERGEANT *gives her his button and goes off. At this point* THE PROSPECTOR *enters.*] That's only the morning. Wait till I tell you about the afternoon!

The Prospector. All right, Pierre. Come along now.

Pierre. I'm perfectly all right here.

The Prospector. I said, come along now.

Pierre. [*To the* COUNTESS.] I'd better go, Madame.

Countess. No.

Pierre. It's no use. Please let go my hand.

The Prospector. Madame, will you oblige me by letting my friend go?

Countess. I will not oblige you in any way.

The Prospector. All right. Then I'll oblige you . . . !

[*He tries to push her away. She catches up a soda-water siphon and squirts it in his face.*]

Pierre. Countess . . .

Countess. Stay where you are. This man isn't going to take you away. In the first place, I shall need you in a few minutes to take me home. I'm all alone here and I'm very easily frightened.

[THE PROSPECTOR *makes a second attempt to drag* PIERRE *away. The* COUNTESS *cracks him over the skull with the siphon. They join battle. The* COUNTESS *whistles.* THE DOORMAN *comes, then the other* VAGABONDS, *and lastly* THE POLICE SERGEANT.]

The Prospector. Officer! Arrest this woman!

The Sergeant. What's the trouble here?

The Prospector. She refuses to let this man go.

The Sergeant. Why should she?

The Prospector. It's against the law for a woman to detain a man on the street.

Irma. Suppose it's her son whom she's found again after twenty years?

The Ragpicker. [*Gallantly.*] Or her long-lost brother? The Countess is not so old.

The Prospector. Officer, this is a clear case of disorderly conduct.

[THE DEAF-MUTE *interrupts with frantic signals.*]

Countess. Irma, what is the Deaf-Mute saying?

Irma. [*Interpreting.*] The young man is in danger of his life. He mustn't go with him.

The Prospector. What does he know?

Irma. He knows everything.

The Prospector. Officer, I'll have to take your number.

Countess. Take his number. It's 2133. It adds up to nine. It will bring you luck.

The Sergeant. Countess, between ourselves, what are you holding him for, anyway?

Countess. I'm holding him because it's very pleasant to hold him. I've never really held anybody before, and I'm making the most of it. And because so long as *I* hold him, he's free.

The Prospector. Pierre, I'm giving you fair warning. . . .

Countess. And I'm holding him because Irma wants me to hold him. Because if I let him go, it will break her heart.

Irma. Oh, Countess!

The Sergeant. [*To* THE PROSPECTOR.] All right, you—move on. Nobody's holding you. You're blocking traffic. Move on.

The Prospector. [*Menacingly.*] I have your number. [*And murderously, to* PIERRE.] You'll regret this, Pierre.

[*Exit* PROSPECTOR.]

Pierre. Thank you, Countess.

Countess. They're blackmailing you, are they? [PIERRE *nods.*] What have you done? Murdered somebody?

Pierre. No.

Countess. Stolen something?

Pierre. No.

Countess. What then?

Pierre. I forged a signature.

Countess. Whose signature?

Pierre. My father's. To a note.

Countess. And this man has the paper, I suppose?

Pierre. He promised to tear it up, if I did what he wanted. But I couldn't do it.

Countess. But the man is mad! Does he really want to destroy the whole neighborhood?

Pierre. He wants to destroy the whole city.

Countess. [*Laughs.*] Fantastic.

Pierre. It's not funny, Countess. He can do it. He's mad, but he's powerful, and he has friends. Their machines are already drawn up and waiting. In three months' time you may see the city covered by a forest of derricks and drills.

Countess. But what are they looking for? Have they lost something?

Pierre. They're looking for oil. They're convinced that Paris is sitting on a lake of oil.

Countess. Suppose it is. What harm does it do?

Pierre. They want to bring the oil to the surface, Countess.

Countess. [*Laughs.*] How silly! Is that a reason to destroy a city? What do they want with this oil?

Pierre. They want to make war, Countess.

Countess. Oh, dear, let's forget about these horrible men. The world is beautiful. It's happy. That's how God made it. No man can change it.

The Waiter. Ah, Countess, if you only knew . . .

Countess. If I only knew what?

The Waiter. Shall we tell her now? Shall we tell her?

Countess. What is it you are hiding from me?

The Ragpicker. Nothing, Countess. It's you who are hiding.

The Waiter. You tell her. You've been a pitchman. You can talk.

All. Tell her. Tell her. Tell her.

Countess. You're frightening me, my friends. Go on. I'm listening.

The Ragpicker. Countess, there was a time when old clothes were as good as new —in fact, they were better. Because when people wore clothes, they gave something to them. You may not believe it, but right this minute, the highest-priced shops in Paris are selling clothes that were thrown away thirty years ago. They're selling them for new. That's how good they were.

Countess. Well?

The Ragpicker. Countess, there was a time when garbage was a pleasure. A garbage can was not what it is now. If it smelled a little strange, it was because it was a little confused—there was everything there—sardines, cologne, iodine, roses. An amateur might jump to a wrong conclusion. But to a professional—it was the smell of God's plenty.

Countess. Well?

The Ragpicker. Countess, the world has changed.

Countess. Nonsense. How could it change? People are the same, I hope.

The Ragpicker. No, Countess. The people are not the same. The people are different. There's been an invasion. An infiltration. From another planet. The world is not beautiful any more. It's not happy.

Countess. Not happy? Is that true? Why didn't you tell me this before?

The Ragpicker. Because you live in a dream, Countess. And we don't like to disturb you.

Countess. But how could it have happened?

The Ragpicker. Countess, there was a time when you could walk around Paris, and all the people you met were just like yourself. A little cleaner, maybe, or dirtier, perhaps, or angry, or smiling—but you knew them. They were you. Well, Countess, twenty years ago, one day, on the street, I saw a face in the crowd. A face, you might say, without a face. The eyes—empty. The expression—not human. Not a human face. It saw me staring, and when it looked back at me with its gelatine eyes, I shuddered. Because I knew that to make room for this one, one of us must have left the earth. A while after, I saw another. And another. And since then, I've seen hundreds come in —yes—thousands.

Countess. Describe them to me.

The Ragpicker. You've seen them yourself, Countess. Their clothes don't wrinkle. Their hats don't come off. When they talk, they don't look at you. They don't perspire.

Countess. Have they wives? Have they children?

The Ragpicker. They buy the models out of shop windows, furs and all. They animate them by a secret process. Then they marry them. Naturally, they don't have children.

Countess. What work do they do?

The Ragpicker. They don't do any work. Whenever they meet, they whisper, and then they pass each other thousand-franc notes. You see them standing on the corner by the Stock Exchange. You see them at auctions—in the back. They never raise a finger—they just stand there. In theater lobbies, by the box office—they never go inside. They don't do anything, but wherever you see them, things are not the same. I remember well the time when a cabbage could sell itself just by being a cabbage. Nowadays it's no good being a cabbage—unless you have an agent and pay him a commission. Nothing is free any more to sell itself or give itself away. These days, Countess, every cabbage has its pimp.

Countess. I can't believe that.

The Ragpicker. Countess, little by little, the pimps have taken over the world. They don't do anything, they don't make anything —they just stand there and take their cut. It makes a difference. Look at the shop-keepers. Do you ever see one smiling at a customer any more? Certainly not. Their smiles are strictly for the pimps. The butcher has to smile at the meat-pimp, the florist at the rose-pimp, the grocer at the fresh-fruit-and-vegetable pimp. It's all organized down to the slightest detail. A pimp for birdseed. A pimp for fishfood. That's why the cost of living keeps going up all the time. You buy a glass of beer—it costs twice as much as it used to. Why? 10 per cent for the glass-pimp, 10 per cent for the beer-pimp,

20 per cent for the glass-of-beer-pimp—that's where our money goes. Personally, I prefer the old-fashioned type. Some of those men at least were loved by the women they sold. But what feelings can a pimp arouse in a leg of lamb? Pardon my language, Irma.

Countess. It's all right. She doesn't understand it.

The Ragpicker. So now you know, Countess, why the world is no longer happy. We are the last of the free people of the earth. You saw them looking us over today. Tomorrow, the street-singer will start paying the song-pimp, and the garbage-pimp will be after me. I tell you, Countess, we're finished. It's the end of free enterprise in this world!

Countess. Is this true, Roderick?

Pierre. I'm afraid it's true.

Countess. Did you know about this, Irma?

Irma. All I know is the doorman says that faith is dead.

The Doorman. I've stopped taking bets over the phone.

The Juggler. The very air is different, Countess. You can't trust it any more. If I throw my torches up too high, they go out.

The Ragpicker. The sky-pimp puts them out.

The Flower Girl. My flowers don't last over night now. They wilt.

The Juggler. Have you noticed, the pigeons don't fly any more?

The Ragpicker. They can't afford to. They walk.

Countess. They're a lot of fools and so are you! You should have told me at once! How can you bear to live in a world where there is unhappiness? Where a man is not his own master? Are you cowards? All we have to do is to get rid of these men.

Pierre. How can we get rid of them? They're too strong.

[THE SERGEANT *walks up again.*]

Countess. [*Smiling.*] The Sergeant will help us.

The Sergeant. Who? Me?

Irma. There are a great many of them, Countess. The Deaf-Mute knows them all. They employed him once, years ago, because he was deaf. [THE DEAF-MUTE *wigwags a short speech.*] They fired him because he wasn't blind. [*Another flash of sign language.*] They're all connected like the parts of a machine.

Countess. So much the better. We shall drive the whole machine into a ditch.

The Sergeant. It's not that easy, Countess. You never catch these birds napping. They change before your very eyes. I remember when I was in the detectives. . . . You catch a president; pfft! he turns into a trustee. You catch him as trustee, and pfft! he's not a trustee—he's an honorary vice-chairman. You catch a Senator dead to rights: he becomes Minister of Justice. You get after the Minister of Justice—he is Chief of Police. And there you are—no longer in the detectives.

Pierre. He's right, Countess. They have all the power. And all the money. And they're greedy for more.

Countess. They're greedy? Ah, then, my friends, they're lost. If they're greedy, they're stupid. If they're greedy—don't worry, I know exactly what to do. Roderick, by tonight you will be an honest man. And, Juggler, your torches will stay lit. And your beer will flow freely again, Martial. And the world will be saved. Let's get to work.

The Ragpicker. What are you going to do?

Countess. Have you any kerosene in the house, Irma?

Irma. Yes. Would you like some?

Countess. I want just a little. In a dirty bottle. With a little mud. And some mange-cure, if you have it. [*To* THE DEAF-MUTE.] Deaf-Mute! Take a letter. [IRMA *interprets in sign language. To* THE SINGER.] Singer, go and find Madame Constance.

[IRMA *and* THE WAITER *go into the café.*]

The Street Singer. Yes, Countess.

Countess. Ask her to be at my house by two o'clock. I'll be waiting for her in the cellar. You may tell her we have to discuss the future of humanity. That's sure to bring her.

The Street Singer. Yes, Countess.

Countess. And ask her to bring Mademoiselle Gabrielle and Madame Josephine with her. Do you know how to get in to speak to Madame Constance? You ring twice, and then meow three times like a cat. Do you know how to meow?

The Street Singer. I'm better at barking.

Countess. Better practise meowing on the way. Incidentally, I think Madame Constance knows all the verses of your mazurka. Remind me to ask her.

The Street Singer. Yes, Countess. [*Exit.*]

[IRMA *comes in. She is shaking the oily concoction in a little perfume vial, which she now hands the* COUNTESS.]

Irma. Here you are, Countess.

Countess. Thanks, Irma. [*She assumes a presidential manner.*] Deaf-Mute! Ready?

[IRMA *interprets in sign language.* THE WAITER *has brought out a portfolio of letter paper and placed it on a table.* THE DEAF-MUTE *sits down before it, and prepares to write.*]

Irma. [*Speaking for* THE DEAF-MUTE.] I'm ready.

Countess. My dear Mr.—— What's his name?

[IRMA *wigwags the question to* THE DEAF-MUTE, *who answers in the same manner. It is all done so deftly that it is as if* THE DEAF-MUTE *were actually speaking.*]

Irma. They are all called Mr. President.

Countess. My dear Mr. President: I have personally verified the existence of a spontaneous outcrop of oil in the cellar of Number 21 Rue de Chaillot, which is at present occupied by a dignified person of unstable mentality. [*The* COUNTESS *grins knowingly.*] This explains why, fortunately for us, the discovery has so long been kept secret. If you should wish to verify the existence of this outcrop for yourself, you may call at the above address at three P.M. today. I am herewith enclosing a sample so that you may judge the quality and consistency of the crude. Yours very truly. Roderick, can you sign the prospector's name?

Pierre. You wish me to?

Countess. One forgery wipes out the other.

[PIERRE *signs the letter.* THE DEAF-MUTE *types the address on an envelope.*]

Irma. Who is to deliver this?

Countess. The Doorman, of course. On his bicycle. And as soon as you have delivered it, run over to the Prospector's office. Leave word that the President expects to see him at my house at three.

The Doorman. Yes, Countess.

Countess. I shall leave you now. I have many pressing things to do. Among others, I must press my red gown.

The Ragpicker. But this only takes care of two of them, Countess.

Countess. Didn't the Deaf-Mute say they are all connected like the works of a machine?

Irma. Yes.

Countess. Then, if one comes, the rest will follow. And we shall have them all. My boa, please.

The Doorman. The one that's stolen, Countess?

Countess. Naturally. The one the Prospector stole.

The Doorman. It hasn't turned up yet, Countess. But someone has left an ermine collar.

Countess. Real ermine?

The Doorman. Looks like it.

Countess. Ermine and iris were made for each other. Let me see it.

The Doorman. Yes, Countess.

[*Exit* DOORMAN.]

Countess. Roderick, you shall escort me. You still look pale. I have some old Chartreuse at home. I always take a glass each year. Last year I forgot. You shall have it.

Pierre. If there is anything I can do, Countess . . . ?

Countess. There is a great deal you can do. There are all the things that need to be done in a room that no man has been in for twenty years. You can untwist the cord on the blind and let in a little sunshine for a change. You can take the mirror off the wardrobe door, and deliver me once and for all from the old harpy that lives in the mirror. You can let the mouse out of the trap. I'm tired of feeding it. [*To her friends.*] Each man to his post. See you later, my friends. [THE DOORMAN *puts the ermine collar around her shoulders.*] Thank you, my boy. It's rabbit. [*One o'clock strikes.*] Your arm, Valentine.

Pierre. Valentine?

Countess. It's just struck one. At one, all men become Valentine.

Pierre. [*He offers his arm.*] Permit me.

Countess. Or Valentino. It's obviously far from the same, isn't it, Irma? But they have that much choice.

[*She sweeps out majestically with* PIERRE. *The others disperse. All but* IRMA.]

Irma. [*Clearing off the table.*] I hate ugliness. I love beauty. I hate meanness. I adore kindness. It may not seem so grand to some to be a waitress in Paris. I love it. A waitress meets all sorts of people. She observes life. I hate to be alone. I love people. But I have never said I love you to a man. Men try to make me say it. They put their arms around me—I pretend I don't see it. They pinch me—I pretend I don't feel it. They kiss me—I pretend I don't know it. They take me out in the evening and make me drink—but I'm careful, I never say it. If they don't like it, they can leave me alone. Because when I say I love you to Him, He will know just by looking in my eyes that many have held me and pinched me and kissed me, but I have never said I love you to anyone in the world before. Never. No. [*Looking off in the direction in which* PIERRE *has gone, she whispers softly:*] I love you.

Voice. [*From within the café.*] Irma!

Irma. Coming. [*Exits.*]

CURTAIN

ACT TWO

SCENE: *The cellar of the* COUNTESS' *house. An ancient vault set deep in the ground, with walls of solid masonry, part brick and part great ashlars, mossy and sweating. A staircase of medieval pattern is built into the thickness of the wall, and leads up to the street level from a landing halfway down. In the corners of the cellar are piled casks, packing cases, bird cages, and other odds and ends—the accumulation of centuries—the whole effect utterly fantastic.*

In the center of the vast underground room, some furniture has been arranged to give an impression of a sitting-room of the 1890's. There is a venerable chaise-longue piled with cushions that once were gay, three armchairs, a table with an oil lamp and a bowl of flowers, a shaggy rug. It is two P.M., *the same day.*

AT RISE: *The* COUNTESS *is sitting over a bit of mending, in one of the armchairs.* IRMA *appears on the landing and calls down.*

Irma. Countess! The Sewer-Man is here.

Countess. Thank goodness, Irma. Send him down. [THE SEWER-MAN *enters. He carries his hip-boots in his hand.*] How do you do, Mr. Sewer-Man? [THE SEWER-MAN *bows.*] But why do you have your boots in your hand instead of on your feet?

The Sewer-Man. Etiquette, Countess. Etiquette.

Countess. How very American! I'm told that Americans nowadays apologize for their gloves if they happen to take one's hand. As if the skin of a human were nicer to touch than the skin of a sheep! And particularly if they have sweaty hands . . . !

The Sewer-Man. My feet never sweat, Countess.

Countess. How very nice! But please don't stand on ceremony here. Put your boots on. Put them on.

The Sewer-Man. [*Complying.*] Thanks very much, Countess.

Countess. [*While he draws on his boots.*] I'm sure you must have a very poor opinion of the upper world, from what you see of it. The way people throw their filth into your territory is absolutely scandalous! I burn all my refuse, and I scatter the ashes. All I ever throw in the drain is flowers. Did you happen to see a lily float by this morning? Mine. But perhaps you didn't notice?

The Sewer-Man. We notice a lot more down there, Countess, than you might think. You'd be surprised the things we notice. There's lots of things come along that were obviously intended for us—little gifts, you might call them—sometimes a brand-new shaving brush—sometimes, *The Brothers Karamazov.* . . . Thanks for the lily, Countess. A very sweet thought.

Countess. Tomorrow you shall have this iris. But now, let's come to the point. I have two questions to ask you.

The Sewer-Man. Yes, Countess?

Countess. First—and this has nothing to do with our problem—it's just something that has been troubling me. . . . Tell me, is it true that the sewer-men of Paris have a king?

The Sewer-Man. Oh, now, Countess, that's another of those fairy tales out of the Sunday supplements. It just seems those writers can't keep their minds off the sewers! It fascinates them. They keep thinking of us moving around in our underground canals like gondoliers in Venice, and it sends them into a fever of romance! The things they say about us! They say we have a race of girls down there who never see the light of day! It's completely fantastic! The girls naturally come out—every Christmas and Easter. And orgies by torchlight with gondolas and guitars! With troops of rats that dance as they follow the piper! What nonsense! The rats are not allowed to dance. No, no, no. Of course we have no king. Down in the sewers, you'll find nothing but good Republicans.

Countess. And no queen?

The Sewer-Man. No. We may run a beauty contest down there once in a while. Or crown a mermaid Queen of the May. But no queen what you'd call a queen. And, as for these swimming races they talk so much about . . . possibly once in a while—in the summer—in the dog days . . .

Countess. I believe you. I believe you. And now tell me. Do you remember that night I found you here in my cellar—looking very pale and strange—you were half-dead as a matter of fact—and I gave you some brandy. . . .

The Sewer-Man. Yes, Countess.

Countess. That night you promised if ever I should need it—you would tell me the secret of this room.

The Sewer-Man. The secret of the moving stone?

Countess. I need it now.

The Sewer-Man. Only the King of the Sewer-Men knows this secret.

Countess. I'm sure of it. I know most secrets, of course. As a matter of fact, I have three magic words that will open any door that words can open. I have tried them all—in various tones of voice. They don't seem to work. And this is a matter of life and death.

The Sewer-Man. Look, Countess.

[*He locates a brick in the masonry, and pushes it. A huge block of stone slowly pivots and uncovers a trap from which a circular staircase winds into the bowels of the earth.*]

Countess. Good heavens! Where do those stairs lead?

The Sewer-Man. Nowhere.

Countess. But they must go somewhere.

The Sewer-Man. They just go down.

Countess. Let's go and see.

The Sewer-Man. No, Countess. Never again. That time you found me, I had a pretty close shave. I kept going down and around, and down and around for an hour, a year—I don't know. There's no end to it, Countess. Once you start you can't stop. . . . Your head begins to turn—you're lost. No—once you start down, there's no coming up.

Countess. You came up.

The Sewer-Man. I—I am a special case. Besides, I had my tools, my ropes. And I stopped in time.

Countess. You could have screamed—shouted.

The Sewer-Man. You could fire off a cannon.

Countess. Who could have built a thing like this?

The Sewer-Man. Paris is old, you know. Paris is very old.

Countess. You don't suppose, by any chance, there is oil down there?

The Sewer-Man. There's only death down there.

Countess. I should have preferred a little oil too—or a vein of gold—or emeralds. You're quite sure there is nothing?

The Sewer-Man. Not even rats.

Countess. How does one lower this stone?

The Sewer-Man. Simple. To open, you press here. And to close it, you push there. [*He presses the brick. The stone descends.*] Now there's two of us in the world that know it.

Countess. I won't remember long. Is it all right if I repeat my magic words while I press it?

The Sewer-Man. It's bound to help.

[IRMA *enters.*]

Irma. Countess, Madame Constance and Mademoiselle Gabrielle are here.

Countess. Show them down, Irma. Thank you very much, Mr. Sewer-Man.

The Sewer-Man. Like that story about the steam laundry that's supposed to be running day and night in my sewer . . . I can assure you. . . .

Countess. [*Edging him toward the door.*] Thank you very much.

The Sewer-Man. Pure imagination! They never work nights.

[*He goes off, bowing graciously.* CONSTANCE, *the Madwoman of Passy, and* GABRIELLE, *the Madwoman of St. Sulpice, come down daintily.* CONSTANCE *is all in white. She wears an enormous hat graced with ostrich plumes, and a lavender veil.* GABRIELLE *is costumed with the affected simplicity of the 1880's. She is atrociously made up in a remorseless parody of blushing innocence, and she minces down the stairs with macabre coyness.*]

Constance. Aurelia! Don't tell us they've found your feather boa?

Gabrielle. You don't mean Adolphe Bertaut has proposed at last! I knew he would.

Countess. How are you, Constance? [*She shouts.*] How are you, Gabrielle?

Gabrielle. You needn't shout today, my dear. It's Wednesday. Wednesdays, I hear perfectly.

Constance. It's Thursday.

Gabrielle. Oh, dear. Well, never mind. I'm going to make an exception just this once.

Constance. [*To an imaginary dog who has stopped on the landing.*] Come along, Dickie. Come along. And stop barking. What a racket you're making! Come on, darling—we've come to see the longest boa and the handsomest man in Paris. Come on.

Countess. Constance, it's not a question of my boa today. Nor of poor Adolphe. It's a question of the future of the human race.

Constance. You think it has a future?

Countess. Please don't make silly jokes. Sit down and listen to me. Today we must make a decision which may alter the fate of the world.

Constance. Couldn't we do it tomorrow? I want to wash my slippers. Now, Dickie—please!

Countess. We haven't a moment to waste. Where is Josephine? Well, we'd best have our tea, and the moment Josephine comes . . .

Gabrielle. Josephine is sitting on her bench in front of the palace waiting for President Wilson to come out. She says she's sorry, but she positively must see him today.

Constance. Dickie!

Countess. What a pity! [*She gets the tea things from the side table, pours tea and serves cake and honey.*] I wish she were here to help us. She has a first-class brain.

Constance. Go ahead, dear. We're listening. [*To* DICKIE.] What is it, Dickie? You want to sit in Aunt Aurelia's lap. All right, darling. Go on. Jump, Dickie.

Countess. Constance, we love you, as you know. And we love Dickie. But this is a serious matter. So let's stop being childish for once.

Constance. And what does that mean, if you please?

Countess. It means Dickie. You know perfectly well that we love him and fuss over him just as if he were still alive. He's a sacred memory and we wouldn't hurt his feelings for the world. But please don't plump him in my lap when I'm settling the future of mankind. His basket is in the corner—he knows where it is, and he can just go and sit in it.

Constance. So you're against Dickie too! You too!

Countess. Constance! I'm not in the least against Dickie! I adore Dickie. But you know as well as I that Dickie is only a convention with us. It's a beautiful convention —but it doesn't have to bark all the time. Besides, it's you that spoil him. The time you went to visit your niece and left him with me, we got on marvelously together. He didn't bark, he didn't tear things, he didn't even eat. But when you're with him, one can pay attention to nothing else. I'm not going to take Dickie in my lap at a solemn moment like this, no, not for anything in the world. And that's that!

Gabrielle. [*Very sweetly.*] Constance, dear, I don't mind taking him in my lap. He loves to sit in my lap, don't you, darling?

Constance. Kindly stop putting on angelic airs, Gabrielle. I know you very well. You're much too sweet to be sincere. There's plenty of times that I make believe that Dickie is here, when really I've left him home, and you cuddle and pet him just the same.

Gabrielle. I adore animals.

Constance. If you adore animals, you shouldn't pet them when they're not there. It's a form of hypocrisy.

Countess. Now, Constance, Gabrielle has as much right as you . . .

Constance. Gabrielle has no right to do what she does. Do you know what she does? She invites *people* to come to tea with us. *People* whom we know nothing about. *People* who exist only in her imagination.

Countess. You think that's not an existence?

Gabrielle. I don't invite them at all. They come by themselves. What can I do?

Constance. You might introduce us.

Countess. If you think they're only imaginary, there's no point in your meeting them, is there?

Constance. Of course they're imaginary. But who likes to have imaginary people staring at one? Especially strangers.

Gabrielle. Oh, they're really very nice. . . .

Constance. Tell me just one thing, Gabrielle—are they here now?

Countess. Am I to be allowed to speak? Or is this going to be the same as the argument about inoculating Josephine's cat, when we didn't get to the subject at all?

Constance. Never! Never! Never! I'll never give my consent to that. [*To* DICKIE.] I'd never do a thing like that to you, Dickie sweet. . . . Oh, no! Oh, no!

[*She begins to weep softly.*]

Countess. Good heavens! Now we have her in tears. What an impossible creature! With the fate of humanity hanging in the balance! All right, all right, stop crying. I'll take him in my lap. Come, Dickie, Dickie.

Constance. No. He won't go now. Oh, how can you be so cruel? Don't you suppose I know about Dickie? Don't you think I'd rather have him here alive and woolly and frisking around the way he used to? You have your Adolphe. Gabrielle has her birds. But I have only Dickie. Do you think I'd be so silly about him if it wasn't that it's only by pretending that he's here all the time that I get him to come sometimes, really? Next time I won't bring him!

Countess. Now let's not get ourselves worked up over nothing. Come here, Dickie. . . . Irma is going to take you for a nice walk. [*She rings her bell.*] Irma!

[IRMA *appears on the landing.*]

Constance. No. He doesn't want to go. Besides, I didn't bring him today. So there!

Countess. Very well, then. Irma, make sure the door is locked.

Irma. Yes, Countess. [IRMA *exits.*]

Constance. What do you mean? Why locked? Who's coming?

Countess. If you'd let me get a word in, you'd know by now. A terrible thing has happened. This morning, this very morning, exactly at noon . . .

Constance. [*Thrilled.*] Oh, how exciting!

Countess. Be quiet. This morning, exactly at noon, thanks to a young man who drowned himself in the Seine . . . Oh, yes, while I think of it—do you know a mazurka called *La Belle Polonaise?*

Constance. Yes, Aurelia.

Countess. Could you sing it now? This very minute?

Constance. Yes, Aurelia.

Countess. All of it?

Constance. Yes, Aurelia. But who's interrupting now, Aurelia?

Countess. You're right. Well, this morning, exactly at noon, I discovered a horrible plot. There is a group of men who intend to tear down the whole city!

Constance. Is that all?

Gabrielle. But I don't understand, Aurelia. Why should men want to tear down the city? It was they themselves who put it up.

Countess. You are so innocent, my poor Gabrielle. There are people in the world who want to destroy everything. They have the fever of destruction. Even when they pretend that they're building, it is only in order to destroy. When they put up a new building, they quietly knock down two old ones. They build cities so that they can destroy the countryside. They destroy space with telephones and time with airplanes. Humanity is now dedicated to the task of universal destruction. I am speaking, of course, primarily of the male sex.

Gabrielle. [*Shocked.*] Oh . . . !

Constance. Aurelia! Must you talk sex in front of Gabrielle?

Countess. There *are* two sexes.

Constance. Gabrielle is a virgin, Aurelia!

Countess. Oh, she can't be as innocent as all that. She keeps canaries.

Gabrielle. I think you're being very cruel about men, Aurelia. Men are big and beautiful, and as loyal as dogs. I preferred not to marry, it's true. But I hear excellent reports from friends who have had an opportunity to observe them closely.

Countess. My poor darling! You are still living in a dream. But one day, you will wake up as I have, and then you will see what is happening in the world. The tide has turned, my dear. Men are changing back into beasts. They know it. They no longer try to hide it. There was once such a thing as manners. I remember a time when the hungriest was the one who took the longest to pick up his fork. The one with the broadest grin was the one who needed most to go to the . . . It was such fun to keep them grinning like that for hours. But now they no longer pretend. Just look at them—snuffling their soup like pigs, tearing their meat like tigers, crunching their lettuce like crocodiles! A man doesn't take your hand nowadays. He gives you his paw.

Constance. Would that trouble you so much if they turned into animals? Personally, I think it's a good idea.

Gabrielle. Oh, I'd love to see them like that. They'd be sweet.

Constance. It might be the salvation of the human race.

Countess. [*To* CONSTANCE.] You'd make a fine rabbit, wouldn't you?

Constance. I?

Countess. Naturally. You don't think it's only the men who are changing? You change along with them. Husbands and wives together. We're all one race, you know.

Constance. You think so? And why would my poor husband have to be a rabbit if he were alive?

Countess. Remember his front teeth? When he nibbled his celery?

Constance. I'm happy to say, I remember absolutely nothing about him. All I remember on that subject is the time that Father Lacordaire tried to kiss me in the park.

Countess. Yes, yes, of course.

Constance. And what does that mean, if you please, "Yes, yes, of course"?

Countess. Constance, just this once, look us in the eye and tell us truly—did that really happen or did you read about it in a book?

Constance. Now I'm being insulted!

Countess. We promise you faithfully that we'll believe it all over again afterwards, won't we, Gabrielle? But tell us the truth this once.

Constance. How dare you question my memories? Suppose I said your pearls were false!

Countess. They were.

Constance. I'm not asking what they were. I'm asking what they are. Are they false or are they real?

Countess. Everyone knows that little by little, as one wears pearls, they become real.

Constance. And isn't it exactly the same with memories?

Countess. Now do not let us waste time. I must go on.

Constance. I think Gabrielle is perfectly

right about men. There are still plenty who haven't changed a bit. There's an old Senator who bows to Gabrielle every day when he passes her in front of the palace. And he takes off his hat each time.

Gabrielle. That's perfectly true, Aurelia. He's always pushing an empty baby carriage, and he always stops and bows.

Countess. Don't be taken in, Gabrielle. It's all make-believe. And all we can expect from these make-believe men is itself make-believe. They give us face powder made of stones, sausages made of sawdust, shirts made of glass, stockings made of milk. It's all a vulgar pretense. And if that is the case, imagine what passes, these days, for virtue, sincerity, generosity, and love! I warn you, Gabrielle, don't let this Senator with the empty baby carriage pull the wool over your eyes.

Gabrielle. He's really the soul of courtesy. He seems very correct.

Countess. Those are the worst. Gabrielle, beware! He'll make you put on black riding boots, while he dances the can-can around you, singing God knows what filth at the top of his voice. The very thought makes one's blood run cold!

Gabrielle. You think that's what he has in mind?

Countess. Of course. Men have lost all sense of decency. They are all equally disgusting. Just look at them in the evening, sitting at their tables in the café, working away in unison with their toothpicks, hour after hour, digging up roast beef, veal, onion . . .

Constance. They don't harm anyone that way.

Countess. Then why do you barricade your door, and make your friends meow before you let them come up? Incidentally, we must make an interesting sight, Gabrielle and I, yowling together on your doorstep like a couple of tomcats!

Constance. There's no need at all for you to yowl together. One would be quite enough. And you know perfectly well why I have to do it. It's because there are murderers.

Countess. I don't quite see what prevents murderers from meowing like anybody else. But why are there murderers?

Constance. Why? Because there are thieves.

Countess. And why are there thieves? Why is there almost nothing but thieves?

Constance. Because they worship money. Because money is king.

Countess. Ah—now we've come to it. Because we live in the reign of the Golden Calf. Did you realize that, Gabrielle? Men now publicly worship the Golden Calf!

Gabrielle. How awful! Have the authorities been notified?

Countess. The authorities do it themselves, Gabrielle.

Gabrielle. Oh! Has anyone talked to the bishop?

Countess. Nowadays only money talks to the bishop. And so you see why I asked you to come here today. The world has gone out of its mind. Unless we do something, humanity is doomed! Constance, have you any suggestions?

Constance. I know what I always do in a case like this. . . .

Countess. You write to the Prime Minister.

Constance. He always does what I tell him.

Countess. Does he ever answer your letters?

Constance. He knows I prefer him not to. It might excite gossip. Besides, I don't always write. Sometimes I wire. The time I told him about the Archbishop's frigidaire, it was by wire. And they sent a new one the very next day.

Countess. There was probably a commission in it for someone. And what do you suggest, Gabrielle?

Constance. Now, how can she tell you until she's consulted her voices?

Gabrielle. I could go right home and consult them, and we could meet again after dinner.

Countess. There's no time for that. Besides, your voices are not real voices.

Gabrielle. [*Furious.*] How dare you say a thing like that?

Countess. Where do your voices come from? Still from your sewing-machine?

Gabrielle. Not at all. They've passed into my hot-water bottle. And it's much nicer that way. They don't chatter any more. They gurgle. But they haven't been a bit nice to me lately. Last night they kept telling me to let my canaries out. "Let them out. Let them out. Let them out."

Constance. Did you?

Gabrielle. I opened the cage. They wouldn't go.

Countess. I don't call that *voices*. Objects talk—everyone knows that. It's the principle of the phonograph. But to ask a hot-water bottle for advice is silly. What does a hot-water bottle know? No, all we have to consult here is our own judgment.

Constance. Very well then, tell us what you have decided. Since you're asking our opinion, you've doubtless made up your mind.

Countess. Yes, I've thought the whole thing out. All I really needed to discover was the source of the infection. Today I found it.

Constance. Where?

Countess. You'll see soon enough. I've baited a trap. In just a few minutes, the rats will be here.

Gabrielle. [*In alarm.*] Rats!

Countess. Don't be alarmed. They're still in human form.

Gabrielle. Heavens! What are you going to do with them?

Countess. That's just the question. Suppose I get these wicked men all here at once—in my cellar—have I the right to exterminate them?

Gabrielle. To kill them?

[COUNTESS *nods.*]

Constance. That's not a question for us. You'll have to ask Father Bridet.

Countess. I have asked him. Yes. One day, in confession, I told him frankly that I had a secret desire to destroy all wicked people. He said: "By all means, my child. And when you're ready to go into action, I'll lend you the jawbone of an ass."

Constance. That's just talk. You get him to put that in writing.

Gabrielle. What's your scheme, Aurelia?

Countess. That's a secret.

Constance. It's not so easy to kill them. Let's say you had a tank full of vitriol all ready for them. You could never get them to walk into it. There's nothing so stubborn as a man when you want him to do something.

Countess. Leave that to me.

Constance. But if they're killed, they're bound to be missed, and then we'll be fined. They fine you for every little thing these days.

Countess. They won't be missed.

Gabrielle. I wish Josephine were here. Her sister's husband was a lawyer. She knows all about these things.

Countess. Do you miss a cold when it's gone? Or the germs that caused it? When the world feels well again, do you think it will regret its illness? No, it will stretch itself joyfully, and it will smile—that's all.

Constance. Just a moment! Gabrielle, are they here now? Yes or no?

Countess. What's the matter with you now?

Constance. I'm simply asking Gabrielle if her friends are in the room or not. I have a right to know.

Gabrielle. I'm not allowed to say.

Constance. I know very well they are. I'm sure of it. Otherwise you wouldn't be making faces.

Countess. May I ask what difference it makes to you if her friends are in the room?

Constance. Just this: If they're here, I'm not going to say another word! I'm certainly not going to commit myself in a matter involving the death sentence in the presence of third parties, whether they exist or not.

Gabrielle. That's not being very nice to my guests, is it?

Countess. Constance, you must be mad! Or are you so stupid as to think that just because we're alone, there's nobody with us? Do you consider us so boring or repulsive that of all the millions of beings, imaginary or otherwise, who are prowling about in space, there's not one who might possibly enjoy spending a little time with us? On the contrary, my dear—my house is full of guests always. They know that here they have a place in the universe where they can come when they're lonely and be sure of a welcome. For my part, I'm delighted to have them.

Gabrielle. Thank you, Aurelia.

Constance. You know perfectly well, Aurelia . . .

Countess. I know perfectly well that at this moment the whole universe is listening to us—and that every word we say echoes to the remotest star. To pretend otherwise is the sheerest hypocrisy.

Constance. Then why do you insult me in front of everybody? I'm not mean. I'm shy. I feel timid about giving an opinion in front of such a crowd. Furthermore, if you think I'm so bad and so stupid, why did you invite me, in the first place?

Countess. I'll tell you. And I'll tell you why, disagreeable as you are, I always give you the biggest piece of cake and my best honey. It's because when you come there's always someone with you—and I don't mean Dickie—I mean someone who resembles you like a sister, only she's young and lovely, and she sits modestly to one side and smiles at me tenderly all the time you're bickering and quarreling, and never says a word. That's the Constance to whom I give the cake that you gobble, and it's because of her that you're here today, and it's her vote that I'm asking you to cast in this crucial moment. And not yours, which is of no importance whatever.

Constance. I'm leaving.

Countess. Be so good as to sit down. I can't let her go yet.

Constance. [*Crossing toward the stairs.*] No. This is too much. I'm taking her with me. [IRMA *enters.*]

Irma. Madame Josephine.

Countess. Thank heaven!

Gabrielle. We're saved.

[JOSEPHINE, *the Madwoman of La Concorde, sweeps in majestically in a get-up somewhere between the regal and the priestly.*]

Josephine. My dear friends, today once again, I waited for President Wilson—but he didn't come out.

Countess. You'll have to wait quite a while longer before he does. He's been dead since 1924.

Josephine. I have plenty of time.

Countess. In anyone else, Josephine, these extravagances might seem a little childish. But a person of your judgment doubtless has her reasons for wanting to talk to a man to whom no one would listen when he was alive. We have a legal problem for you. Suppose you had all the world's criminals here in this room. And suppose you had a way of getting rid of them forever. Would you have the right to do it?

Josephine. Why not?

Countess. Exactly my point.

Gabrielle. But, Josephine, so many people!

Josephine. *De minimis non curat lex!* * The more there are, the more legal it is. It's impersonal. It's even military. It's the cardinal principle of battle—you get all your enemies in one place, and you kill them all together at one time. Because if you had to track them down one by one in their houses and offices, you'd get tired, and sooner or later you'd stop. I believe your idea is very practical, Aurelia. I can't imagine why we never thought of it before.

Gabrielle. Well, if you think it's all right to do it. . . .

Josephine. By all means. Your criminals have had a fair trial, I suppose?

Countess. Trial?

Josephine. Certainly. You can't kill anybody without a trial. That's elementary. "No man shall be deprived of his life, liberty, and property without due process of law."

Countess. They deprive us of ours.

Josephine. That's not the point. You're not accused of anything. Every accused—man, woman or child—has the right to defend himself at the bar of justice. Even animals. Before the Deluge, you will recall, the Lord permitted Noah to speak in defense of his fellow mortals. He evidently stuttered. You know the result. On the other hand, Captain Dreyfus was not only innocent—he was defended by a marvelous orator. The result was precisely the same. So you see, in having a trial, you run no risk whatever.

Countess. But if I give them the slightest cause for suspicion—I'll lose them.

Josephine. There's a simple procedure prescribed in such cases. You can summon the defendants by calling them three times—mentally, if you like. If they don't appear, the court may designate an attorney who will represent them. This attorney can then argue their case to the court, *in absentia,* and a judgment can then be rendered, *in contumacio.*

Countess. But I don't know any attorneys. And we have only ten minutes.

Gabrielle. Hurry, Josephine, hurry!

Josephine. In case of emergency, it is permissible for the court to order the first passer-by to act as attorney for the defense. A defense is like a baptism. Absolutely indispensable, but you don't have to know anything to do it. Ask Irma to get you somebody. Anybody.

Countess. The Deaf-Mute?

Josephine. Well—that's getting it down a bit fine. That might be questionable on appeal.

Countess. [*Calls.*] Irma! What about the Police Sergeant?

Josephine. He won't do. He's under oath to the state. [IRMA *appears.*]

Irma. Yes, Countess?

Countess. Who's out there, Irma?

Irma. All our friends, Countess. There's the Ragpicker and . . .

Countess. Send down the Ragpicker.

Constance. Do you think it's wise to have all those millionaires represented by a ragpicker?

Josephine. It's a first-rate choice. Criminals are always represented by their opposites. Murderers, by someone who obviously wouldn't hurt a fly. Rapists, by a member of the League for Decency. Experience shows it's the only way to get an acquittal.

Countess. But we must not have an acquittal. That would mean the end of the world!

Josephine. Justice is justice, my dear.

[THE RAGPICKER *comes down, with a stately air. Behind him, on the landing, appear the other* VAGABONDS.]

The Ragpicker. Greetings, Countess.

* The law ignores trifles.

Greetings, ladies. My most sincere compliments.

Countess. Has Irma told you . . . ?

The Ragpicker. She said something about a trial.

Countess. You have been appointed attorney for the defense.

The Ragpicker. Terribly flattered, I'm sure.

Countess. You realize, don't you, how much depends on the outcome of this trial?

Josephine. Do you know the defendants well enough to undertake the case?

The Ragpicker. I know them to the bottom of their souls. I go through their garbage every day.

Constance. And what do you find there?

The Ragpicker. Mostly flowers.

Gabrielle. It's true, you know, the rich are always surrounded with flowers.

Constance. How beautiful!

Countess. Are you trying to prejudice the court?

The Ragpicker. Oh no, Countess, no.

Countess. We want a completely impartial defense.

The Ragpicker. Of course, Countess, of course. Permit me to make a suggestion.

Countess. Will you preside, Josephine?

The Ragpicker. Instead of speaking as attorney, suppose you let me speak directly as defendant. It will be more convincing, and I can get into it more.

Josephine. Excellent idea. Motion granted.

Countess. We don't want you to be too convincing, remember.

The Ragpicker. Impartial, Countess, impartial.

Josephine. Well? Have you prepared your case?

The Ragpicker. How rich am I?

Josephine. Millions. Billions.

The Ragpicker. How did I get them? Theft? Murder? Embezzlement?

Countess. Most likely.

The Ragpicker. Do I have a wife? A mistress?

Countess. Everything.

The Ragpicker. All right. I'm ready.

Gabrielle. Will you have some tea?

The Ragpicker. Is that good?

Constance. Very good for the voice. The Russians drink nothing but tea. And they talk like anything.

The Ragpicker. All right. Tea.

Josephine. [*To the* VAGABONDS.] Come in. Come in. All of you. You may take places. The trial is public. [*The* VAGABONDS *dispose themselves on the steps and elsewhere.*] Your bell, if you please, Aurelia.

Countess. But what if I should need to ring for Irma?

Josephine. Irma will sit here, next to me. If you need her, she can ring for herself. [*To the* POLICE SERGEANT *and* THE POLICEMAN.] Conduct the accused to the bar. [*The* OFFICERS *conduct* THE RAGPICKER *to a bar improvised with a rocking chair and a packing case marked* "Fragile." THE RAGPICKER *mounts the box. She rings the bell.*] The court is now in session. [*All sit.*] Counsel for the defense, you may take the oath.

The Ragpicker. I swear to tell the truth, the whole truth, and nothing but the truth, so help me God.

Josephine. Nonsense! You're not a witness. You're an attorney. It's your duty to lie, conceal and distort everything, and slander everybody.

The Ragpicker. All right. I swear to lie, conceal and distort everything, and slander everybody. [JOSEPHINE *rings stridently.*]

Josephine. Quiet! Begin.

The Ragpicker. May it please the honorable, august, and elegant Court . . .

Josephine. Flattery will get you nowhere. That will do. The defense has been heard. Cross-examination.

Countess. Mr. President . . .

The Ragpicker. [*Bowing with dignity.*] Madame.

Countess. Do you know what you are charged with?

The Ragpicker. I can't for the life of me imagine. My life is an open book. My ways are known to all. I am a pillar of the church and the sole support of the Opera. My hands are spotless.

Countess. What an atrocious lie! Just look at them!

Constance. You don't have to insult the man. He's only lying to please you.

Countess. Be quiet, Constance! You don't get the idea at all. [*To* THE RAGPICKER.] You are charged with the crime of worshipping money.

The Ragpicker. Worshipping money? Me?

Josephine. Do you plead guilty or not guilty? Which is it?

The Ragpicker. Why, Your Honor . . .

Josephine. Yes or no?

The Ragpicker. Yes or no? No! I don't worship money, Countess. Heavens, no! Money worships me. It adores me. It won't let me alone. It's damned embarrassing, I can tell you.

Josephine. Kindly watch your language.

Countess. Defendant, tell the Court how you came by your money.

The Ragpicker. The first time money came to me, I was a mere boy, a little golden-haired child in the bosom of my dear family. It came to me suddenly in the guise of a gold brick which, in my innocence, I picked out of a garbage can one day while playing. I was horrified, as you can imagine. I immediately tried to get rid of it by swapping it for a little rundown one-track railroad which, to my consternation, at once sold itself for a hundred times its value. In a desperate effort to get rid of this money, I began to buy things. I bought the Northern Refineries, the Galeries Lafayette, and the Schneider-Creusot Munition Works. And now I'm stuck with them. It's a horrible fate—but I'm resigned to it. I don't ask for your sympathy, I don't ask for your pity—all I ask for is a little common human understanding. . . . [*He begins to cry.*]

Countess. I object. This wretch is trying to play on the emotions of the Court.

Josephine. The Court has no emotions.

The Ragpicker. Everyone knows that the poor have no one but themselves to blame for their poverty. It's only just that they should suffer the consequences. But how is it the fault of the rich if they're rich?

Countess. Dry your tears. You're deceiving nobody. If, as you say, you're ashamed of your money, why is it you hold onto it with such a death-grip?

The Ragpicker. Me?

Peddler. You never part with a franc!

The Juggler. You wouldn't even give the poor Deaf-Mute a sou!

The Ragpicker. Me, hold onto money? What slander! What injustice! What a thing to say to me in the presence of this honorable, august and elegant Court! I spend all my time trying to spend my money. If I have tan shoes, I buy black ones. If I have a bicycle, I buy a motor car. If I have a wife, I buy . . .

Josephine. [*Rings.*] Order!

The Ragpicker. I dispatch a plane to Java for a bouquet of flowers. I send a steamer to Egypt for a basket of figs. I send a special representative to New York to fetch me an ice-cream cone. And if it's not just exactly right, back it goes. But no matter what I do, I can't get rid of my money! If I play a hundred to one shot, the horse comes in by twenty lengths. If I throw a diamond in the Seine, it turns up in the trout they serve me for lunch. Ten diamonds—ten trout. Well, now, do you suppose I can get rid of forty millions by giving a sou to a deaf-mute? Is it even worth the effort?

Constance. He's right.

The Ragpicker. Ah! You see, my dear? At last, there is somebody who understands me! Somebody who is not only beautiful, but extraordinarily sensitive and intelligent.

Countess. I object!

Josephine. Overruled!

The Ragpicker. I should be delighted to send you some flowers, Miss—directly I'm acquitted. What flowers do you prefer?

Constance. Roses.

The Ragpicker. You shall have a bale every morning for the next five years. Money means nothing to me.

Constance. And amaryllis.

The Ragpicker. I'll make a note of the name. [*In his best lyrical style.*] The lady understands, ladies and gentlemen. The lady is no fool. She's been around and she knows what's what. If I gave the Deaf-Mute a franc, twenty francs, twenty million francs —I still wouldn't make a dent in the forty times a thousand million francs that I'm afflicted with! Right, little lady?

Constance. Right.

Josephine. Proceed.

The Ragpicker. Like on the Stock Exchange. If *you* buy a stock, it sinks at once like a plummet. But if *I* buy a stock, it turns around and soars like an eagle. If I buy it at 33 . . .

Peddler. It goes up to a thousand.

The Ragpicker. It goes to twenty thousand! That's how I bought my twelve chateaux, my twenty villas, my 234 farms. That's how I endow the Opera and keep my twelve ballerinas.

The Flower Girl. I hope every one of them deceives you every moment of the day!

The Ragpicker. How can they deceive me? Suppose they try to deceive me with the male chorus, the general director, the assistant electrician or the English horn—I own them all, body and soul. It would be like deceiving me with my big toe.

Constance. Don't listen, Gabrielle.

Gabrielle. Listen to what?

The Ragpicker. No. I am incapable of jealousy. I have all the women—or I can have them, which is the same thing. I get the thin ones with caviar—the fat ones with pearls . . .

Countess. So you think there are no women with morals?

The Ragpicker. I mix morals with mink—delicious combination. I drip pearls into protests. I adorn resistance with rubies. My touch is jeweled; my smile, a motor car. What woman can withstand me? I lift my little finger—and do they fall?—Like leaves in autumn—like tin cans from a second-story window.

Constance. That's going a little too far!

Countess. You see where money leads.

The Ragpicker. Of course. When you have no money, nobody trusts you, nobody believes you, nobody likes you. Because to have money is to be virtuous, honest, beautiful, and witty. And to be without is to be ugly and boring and stupid and useless.

Countess. One last question. Suppose you find this oil you're looking for. What do you propose to do with it?

The Ragpicker. I propose to make war! I propose to conquer the world!

Countess. You have heard the defense, such as it is. I demand a verdict of guilty.

The Ragpicker. What are you talking about? Guilty? I? I am never guilty!

Josephine. I order you to keep quiet.

The Ragpicker. I am never quiet!

Josephine. Quiet, in the name of the law!

The Ragpicker. I am the law. When I speak, that is the law. When I present my backside, it is etiquette to smile and to apply the lips respectfully. It is more than etiquette—it is a cherished national privilege, guaranteed by the Constitution.

Josephine. That's contempt of court. The trial is over.

Countess. And the verdict?

All. Guilty!

Josephine. Guilty as charged.

Countess. Then I have full authority to carry out the sentence?

All. Yes!

Countess. I can do what I like with them?

All. Yes!

Countess. I have the right to exterminate them?

All. Yes!

Josephine. Court adjourned!

Countess. [*To* THE RAGPICKER.] Congratulations, Ragpicker. A marvelous defense. Absolutely impartial.

The Ragpicker. Had I known a little before, I could have done better. I could have prepared a little speech, like the time I used to sell the Miracle Spot Remover. . . .

Josephine. No need for that. You did very well, extempore. The likeness was striking and the style reminiscent of Clemenceau. I predict a brilliant future for you. Good-bye, Aurelia. I'll take our little Gabrielle home.

[JOSEPHINE *and* GABRIELLE *start up the stairs.*]

Constance. I'm going to walk along the river. [*To* DICKIE.] Oh! So here you are. And your ear all bloody! Dickie! Have you been fighting again? Oh, dear . . . !

Countess. [*To* THE RAGPICKER.] See that she gets home all right, won't you? She loses everything on the way. And in the queerest places. Her prayer book in the butcher shop. And her corset in church.

The Ragpicker. [*Bowing and offering his arm.*] Permit me, Madame.

The Street Singer. Oh, Countess— my mazurka. Remember?

Countess. Oh, yes. Constance, wait a moment. [*To* THE SINGER.] Well? Begin.

The Street Singer. [*Sings.*]

"Do you hear, Mademoiselle,
Those musicians of hell?"

Constance. Why, of course, it's *La Belle Polonaise.* . . . [*She sings.*]

"From Poland to France
Comes this marvelous dance,
So gracious,
Audacious,
Will you foot it, perchance?"

The Street Singer. I'm saved!

Josephine. [*Reappearing at the head of the stairs.*]

"Now my arm I entwine
Round these contours divine,
So pure, so impassioned,
Which Cupid has fashioned. . . ."

Gabrielle. [*Reappearing also, she sings a quartet with the others.*]

"Come, let's dance the mazurka, that devilish measure,
'Tis a joy that's reserved to the gods for their pleasure—
Let's gallop, let's hop,
With never a stop,
My blonde Polish miss,
Let our heads spin and turn
As the dance-floor we spurn—
There was never such pleasure as this!"

[*All except the* COUNTESS *and* IRMA *exit, dancing.*]

Irma. It's time for your afternoon nap.

Countess. But suppose they come, Irma!

Irma. I'll watch out for them.

Countess. Thank you, Irma. I *am* tired. [*She smiles.*] Did you ever see a trial end more happily in your life?

Irma. Lie down and close your eyes a moment.

[*The* COUNTESS *stretches out on the chaise-longue and shuts her eyes.* IRMA *tiptoes out. In a moment,* PIERRE *comes down softly, the feather boa in his hands. He stands over the chaise-longue, looking tenderly down at the sleeping woman, then kneels beside her and takes her hand.*]

Countess. [*Without opening her eyes.*] Is it you, Adolphe Bertaut?

Pierre. It's only Pierre.

Countess. Don't lie to me, Adolphe Bertaut. These are your hands. Why do you complicate things always? Say that it's you.

Pierre. Yes. It is I.

Countess. Would it cost you so much to call me Aurelia?

Pierre. It's I, Aurelia.

Countess. Why did you leave me, Adolphe Bertaut? Was she so very lovely, this Georgette of yours?

Pierre. No. You are a thousand times lovelier.

Countess. But she was clever.

Pierre. She was stupid.

Countess. It was her soul, then, that drew you? When you looked into her eyes, you saw a vision of heaven, perhaps?

Pierre. I saw nothing.

Countess. That's how it is with men. They love you because you are beautiful and clever and soulful—and at the first opportunity they leave you for someone who is plain and dull and soulless. But why does it have to be like that, Adolphe Bertaut? Why?

Pierre. Why, Aurelia?

Countess. I know very well she wasn't rich. Because when I saw you that time at the grocer's, and you snatched the only good melon from right under my nose, your cuffs, my poor friend, were badly frayed. . . .

Pierre. Yes. She was poor.

Countess. "Was" poor? Is she dead, then? If it's because she's dead that you've come back to me—then, no. Go away. I will not take their leavings from the dead. I refuse to inherit you. . . .

Pierre. She's quite well.

Countess. Your hands are still the same, Adolphe Bertaut. Your touch is young and firm. Because it's the only part of you that has stayed with me. The rest of you is pretty far gone, I'm afraid. I can see why you'd rather not come near me when my eyes are open. It's thoughtful of you.

Pierre. Yes. I've aged.

Countess. Not I. I am young because I haven't had to live down my youth, like you. I have it with me still, as fresh and beautiful as ever. But when you walk now in the park at Colombes with Georgette, I'm sure . . .

Pierre. There is no longer a park at Colombes.

Countess. Is there a park still at St. Cloud? Is there a park at Versailles? I've never gone back to see. But I think, if they could move, those trees would have walked away in disgust the day you went there with Georgette. . . .

Pierre. They did. Not many are left.

Countess. You take her also, I suppose, to hear *Denise?*

Pierre. No one hears *Denise* any more.

Countess. It was on the way home from *Denise,* Adolphe Bertaut, that I first took your arm. Because it was windy and it was late. I have never set foot in that street again. I go the other way round. It's not easy, in the winter, when there's ice. One is quite apt to fall. I often do.

Pierre. Oh, my darling—forgive me.

Countess. No, never. I will never forgive you. It was very bad taste to take her to the very places where we'd been together.

Pierre. All the same, I swear, Aurelia . . .

Countess. Don't swear. I know what you did. You gave her the same flowers. You bought her the same chocolates. But has she any left? No. I have all your flowers still. I have twelve chocolates. No, I will never forgive you as long as I live.

Pierre. I always loved you, Aurelia.

Countess. You "loved" me? Then you too are dead, Adolphe Bertaut?

Pierre. No. I love you. I shall always love you, Aurelia.

Countess. Yes. I know. That much I've always known. I knew it the moment you went away, Adolphe, and I knew that nothing could ever change it. Georgette is in his arms now—yes. But he loves me. Tonight he's taken Georgette to hear *Denise*—yes. But he loves me. . . I know it. You never loved her. Do you think I believed for one moment that absurd story about her running off with the osteopath? Of course not. Since you didn't love her, obviously she stayed with you. And, after that, when she came back, and I heard about her going off with the surveyor—I knew that couldn't be true, either. You'll never get rid of her, Adolphe Bertaut—never. Because you don't love her.

Pierre. I need your pity, Aurelia. I need your love. Don't forget me. . . .

Countess. Farewell, Adolphe Bertaut. Farewell. Let go my hand, and give it to little Pierre. [PIERRE *lets go her hand, and after a moment takes it again. The* COUNTESS *opens her eyes.*] Pierre? Ah, it's you. Has he gone?

Pierre. Yes, Countess.

Countess. I didn't hear him go. Oh, he

knows how to make a quick exit, that one. [*She sees the boa.*] Good heavens! Wherever did you find it?

Pierre. In the wardrobe, Countess. When I took off the mirror.

Countess. Was there a purple felt shopping bag with it?

Pierre. Yes, Countess.

Countess. And a little child's sewing box?

Pierre. No, Countess.

Countess. Oh, they're frightened now. They're trembling for their lives. You see what they're up to? They're quietly putting back all the things they have stolen. I never open that wardrobe, of course, on account of the old woman in the mirror. But I have sharp eyes. I don't need to open it to see what's in it. Up to this morning, that wardrobe was empty. And now—you see? But, dear me, how stupid they are! The one thing I really miss is my little sewing box. It's something they stole from me when I was a child. They haven't put it back? You're quite sure?

Pierre. What was it like?

Countess. Green cardboard with paper lace and gold stamping. I got it for Christmas when I was seven. They stole it the very next day. I cried my eyes out every time I thought of it—until I was eight.

Pierre. It's not there, Countess.

Countess. The thimble was gilt. I swore I'd never use any other. Look at my poor fingers. . . .

Pierre. They've kept the thimble too.

Countess. Splendid! Then I'm under no obligation to be merciful. Put the boa around my neck, Pierre. I want them to see me wearing it. They'll think it's a real boa.

[IRMA *runs in excitedly.*]

Irma. Here they come, Countess! You were right—it's a procession. The street is full of limousines and taxis!

Countess. I will receive them. [*As* PIERRE *hesitates to leave her.*] Don't worry. There's nothing to be frightened of. [PIERRE *goes out.*] Irma, did you remember to stir the kerosene into the water?

Irma. Yes, Countess. Here it is.

Countess. [*Looking critically at the bottle.*] You might as well pour in what's left of the tea. [IRMA *shakes up the liquid.*] Don't forget, I'm supposed to be deaf. I want to hear what they're thinking.

Irma. Yes, Countess.

Countess. [*Putting the finishing touches to her make-up.*] I don't have to be merciful—but, after all, I do want to be just. . . .

[IRMA *goes up to the landing and exits. As soon as she is alone, the* COUNTESS *presses the brick, and the trap door opens. There is a confused sound of auto horns in the street above, and the noise of an approaching crowd.*]

Irma. [*Offstage.*] Yes, Mr. President. Come in, Mr. President. You're expected, Mr. President. This way, Mr. President. [*The* PRESIDENTS *come down, led by* THE PRESIDENT. *They all look alike, are dressed alike, and all have long cigars.*] The Countess is quite deaf, gentlemen. You'll have to shout. [*She announces.*] The presidents of the boards of directors!

The President. I had a premonition, Madame, when I saw you this morning, that we should meet again. [*The* COUNTESS *smiles vaguely. He continues, a tone louder.*] I want to thank you for your trust. You may place yourself in our hands with complete confidence.

Second President. Louder. The old trot can't hear you.

The President. I have a letter here, Madame, in which . . .

Second President. Louder. Louder.

Third President. [*Shouting.*] Is it true that you've located . . . ? [*The* COUNTESS *stares at him blankly. He shouts at the top of his voice.*] Oil? [*The* COUNTESS *nods with a smile, and points down.* THE PRESIDENT *produces a legal paper and a fountain pen.*] Sign here.

Countess. What is it? I haven't my glasses.

The President. Your contract.

[*He offers the pen.*]

Countess. Thank you.

Second President. [*Normal voice.*] What is it?

Third President. Waiver of all rights. [*He takes it back signed.*] Thank you. [*He hands it to the* SECOND PRESIDENT.] Witness. [*The* SECOND PRESIDENT *witnesses it.* THE PRESIDENT *passes it on to the* THIRD PRESIDENT.] Notarize. [*The paper is notarized.* THE PRESIDENT *turns to the* COUNTESS *and shouts.*] My congratulations. And now, Madame—— [*He produces a gold brick wrapped in tissue paper.*] If you'll show us the well, this package is yours.

Countess. What is it?

The President. Pure gold. Twenty-four karat. For you.

Countess. Thank you very much. [*She takes it.*] It's heavy.

Second President. Are you going to give her that?

The President. Don't worry. We'll pick it up again on the way out. [*He shouts at the* COUNTESS, *pointing at the trap door.*] Is this the way?

Countess. That's the way.

[*The* SECOND PRESIDENT *tries to slip in first.* THE PRESIDENT *pulls him back.*]

The President. Just a minute, Mr. President. After me, if you don't mind. And watch those cigars. It's oil, you know.

[*But as he is about to descend, the* COUNTESS *steps forward.*]

Countess. Just one moment . . .

The President. Yes?

Countess. Did any of you happen to bring along a little sewing box?

The President. Sewing box? [*He pulls back another impatient* PRESIDENT.] Take it easy.

Countess. Or a little gold thimble?

The President. Not me.

Presidents. Not us.

Countess. What a pity!

The President. Can we go down now?

Countess. Yes. You may go down now. Watch your step!

[*They hurry down eagerly. When they have quite disappeared,* IRMA *appears on the landing and announces the next echelon.*]

Irma. Countess, the Prospectors.

Countess. Heavens! Are there more than one?

Irma. There's a whole delegation.

Countess. Send them down.

[THE PROSPECTOR *comes in, following his nose.*]

Irma. Come in, please.

The Prospector. [*Sniffing the air like a bloodhound.*] I smell something. . . . Who's that?

Irma. The Countess. She is very deaf.

The Prospector. Good.

[*The* PROSPECTORS *also look alike. Sharp clothes, Western hats, and long noses. They crowd down the stairs after* THE PROSPECTOR, *sniffing in unison.* THE PROSPECTOR *is especially talented. He casts about on the scent until it leads him to the decanter on the table. He pours himself a glass, drinks it off, and belches with much satisfaction. The others join him at once, and follow his example. They all belch in unison.*]

Prospectors. Oil?

The Prospector. Oil!

Countess. Oil.

The Prospector. Traces? Puddles?

Countess. Pools. Gushers.

Second Prospector. Characteristic odor? [*He sniffs.*]

The Prospector. Chanel Number 5. Nectar! Undoubtedly—the finest—rarest! [*He drinks.*] Sixty gravity crude: straight gasoline! [*To the* COUNTESS.] How found? By blast? Drill?

Countess. By finger.

The Prospector. [*Whipping out a document.*] Sign here, please.

Countess. What is it?

The Prospector. Agreement for dividing the profits. . . . [*The* COUNTESS *signs.*]

Second Prospector. [*To* FIRST PROSPECTOR.] What is it?

The Prospector. [*Pocketing the paper.*] Application to enter a lunatic asylum. Down there?

Countess. Down there.

[*The* PROSPECTORS *go down, sniffing.* IRMA *enters.*]

Irma. The gentlemen of the press are here.

Countess. The rest of the machine! Show them in.

Irma. The Public Relations Counsellors! [*They enter, all shapes and sizes, all in blue pin-striped suits and black homburg hats.*] The Countess is very deaf, gentlemen. You'll have to shout!

First Press Agent. You don't say—— Delighted to make the acquaintance of so charming and beautiful a lady. . . .

Second Press Agent. Louder. She can't hear you.

First Press Agent. What a face! [*Shouts.*] Madame, we are the press. You know our power. We fix all values. We set all standards. Your entire future depends on us.

Countess. How do you do?

First Press Agent. What will we charge the old trull? The usual thirty?

Second Press Agent. Forty.

Third Press Agent. Sixty.

First Press Agent. All right—seventy-five. [*He fills in a form and offers it to the* COUNTESS.] Sign here, Countess. This contract really gives you a break.

Countess. That is the entrance.

First Press Agent. Entrance to what?

Countess. The oil well.

First Press Agent. Oh, we don't need to see that, Madame.

Countess. Don't need to see it?

First Press Agent. No, no—we don't have to see it to write about it. We can imagine it. An oil well is an oil well. "That's oil we know on earth, and oil we need to know." [*He bows.*]

Countess. But if you don't see it, how can you be sure the oil is there?

First Press Agent. If it's there, well and good. If it's not, by the time we get through, it will be. You underestimate the creative aspect of our profession, Madame.

[*The* COUNTESS *shakes her head, handing back the papers.*] I warn you, if you insist on rubbing our noses in this oil, it will cost you 10 per cent extra.

Countess. It's worth it.

[*She signs. They cross toward the trap door.*]

Second Press Agent. [*Descending.*] You see, Madame, we of the press can refuse a lady nothing.

Third Press Agent. Especially, such a lady.

[THIRD PRESS AGENT *starts going down.*]

Second Press Agent. [*Going down. Gallantly.*] It's plain to see, Madame, that even fountains of oil have their nymphs. . . . I can use that somewhere. That's copy!

[THE PRESS AGENTS *go down. As he disappears, the* FIRST PRESS AGENT *steals the gold brick and blows a kiss gallantly to the* COUNTESS, *who blows one back. There is a high-pitched chatter offstage, and* IRMA *comes in, trying hard to hold back* THREE WOMEN *who pay no attention to her whatever. These* WOMEN *are tall, slender, and as soulless as if they were molded of wax. They march down the steps, erect and abstracted like animated window models, but chattering incessantly.*]

Irma. But, ladies, please—you have no business here—you are not expected. [*To the* COUNTESS.] There are some strange ladies coming. . . .

Countess. Show them in, Irma. [*The* WOMEN *come down, without taking the slightest interest in their surroundings.*] Who are you?

First Woman. Madame, we are the most powerful pressure group in the world.

Second Woman. We are the ultimate dynamic.

Third Woman. The mainspring of all combinations.

First Woman. Nothing succeeds without our assistance. Is that the well, Madame?

Countess. That is the well.

First Woman. Put out your cigarettes, girls. We don't want any explosions. Not with my brand-new eyelashes.

[*They go down, still chattering. The* COUNTESS *crosses to the wall to close the trap. As she does so, there is a commotion on the landing.*]

Irma. Countess . . .

[*A* MAN *rushes in breathlessly.*]

Man. Just a minute! Just a minute!

[*He rushes for the trap door.*]

Countess. Wait! Who are you?

Man. I'm in a hurry. Excuse me. It's my only chance! [*He rushes down.*]

Countess. But . . . [*But he is gone. She shrugs her shoulders, and presses the brick. The trap closes. She rings the bell for* IRMA.] My gold brick! Why, they've stolen my gold brick! [*She moves toward the trap. It is now closed.*] Well, let them take their god with them.

[IRMA *enters and sees with astonishment that the stage is empty of all but the* COUNTESS. *Little by little, the scene is suffused with light, faint at first, but increasing as if the very walls were glowing with the quiet radiance of universal joy. Only around the closed trap a shadow lingers.*]

Irma. But what's happened? They've gone! They've vanished!

Countess. They've evaporated, Irma. They were wicked. Wickedness evaporates.

[PIERRE *enters. He is followed by the* VAGABONDS, *all of them. The new radiance of the world is now very perceptible. It glows from their faces.*]

Pierre. Oh, Countess . . . !

The Waiter. Countess, everything's changed. Now you can breathe again. Now you can see.

Pierre. The air is pure! The sky is clear!

Irma. Life is beautiful again.

The Ragpicker. [*Rushes in.*] Countess—the pigeons! The pigeons are flying!

The Flower Girl. They don't have to walk any more.

The Ragpicker. They're flying. . . . The air is like crystal. And young grass is sprouting on the pavements.

Countess. Is it possible?

Irma. [*Interpreting for* THE DEAF-MUTE.] Now, Juggler, you can throw your fireballs up as high as you please—they won't go out.

The Sergeant. On the street, utter strangers are shaking hands, they don't know why, and offering each other almond bars!

Countess. Oh, my friends . . .

The Waiter. Countess, we thank you. . . .

[*They go on talking with happy and animated gestures, but we no longer hear them, for their words blend into a strain of unearthly music which seems to thrill from the uttermost confines of the universe. And out of this music comes a voice.*]

First Voice. Countess . . .

[*Only the* COUNTESS *hears it. She turns from the group of* VAGABONDS *in wonder.*]

Second Voice. Countess . . .

Third Voice. Countess . . .

[*As she looks up in rapture, the* FIRST VOICE *speaks again.*]

First Voice. Countess, we thank you. We are the friends of animals.

Second Voice. We are the friends of people.

Third Voice. We are the friends of friendship.

First Voice. You have freed us!

Second Voice. From now on, there will be no hungry cats. . . .

Third Voice. And we shall tell the Duchess her dog's right name!

[*The* VOICES *fade off. And now another group of voices is heard.*]

First Voice. Countess, we thank you. We are the friends of flowers.

Second Voice. From now on, every plant in Paris will be watered. . . .

Third Voice. And the sewers will be fragrant with jasmine!

[*These voices, too, are silent. For an instant, the stage is vibrant with music. Then* THE DEAF-MUTE *speaks, and his voice is the most beautiful of all.*]

The Deaf-Mute. Sadness flies on the wings of the morning, and out of the heart of darkness comes the light.

[*Suddenly a group of figures detaches itself from the shadows. These are exactly similar in face and figure and in dress. They are shabby in the fashion of 1900 and their cuffs are badly frayed. Each bears in his hand a ripe melon.*]

First Adolphe Bertaut. Countess, we thank you. We, too, are freed at last. We are the Adolphe Bertauts of the world.

Second Adolphe Bertaut. We are no longer timid.

Third Adolphe Bertaut. We are no longer weak.

First Adolphe Bertaut. From this day on, we shall hold fast to what we love. For your sake, henceforth, we shall be handsome, and our cuffs forever immaculate and new. Countess, we bring you this melon and with it our hearts . . . ! [*They all kneel.*] Will you do us the honor to be our wife?

Countess. [*Sadly.*] Too late! Too late! [*She waves them aside. They take up their melons sadly and vanish. The voices of the* VAGABONDS *are heard again, and the music dies.*] Too late! Too late!

Pierre. Too late, Countess?

Irma. Too late for what?

Countess. I say that it's too late for them. On the twenty-fourth of May, 1881, the most beautiful Easter in the memory of man, it was not too late. And on the fifth of September, 1887, the day they caught the trout and broiled it on the open fire by the brook at Villeneuve, it was not too late. And it was even not too late for them on the twenty-first of August, 1897, the day the Czar visited Paris with his guard. But they did nothing and they said nothing, and now—kiss each other, you two, this very instant!

Irma. You mean . . . ?

Pierre. You mean . . . ?

Irma. But, Countess . . .

Countess. It's three hours since you've met and known and loved each other. Kiss each other quickly. [PIERRE *hesitates.*] Look at him. He hesitates. He trembles. Happiness frightens him. . . . How like a man! Oh, Irma, kiss him, kiss him! If two people who love each other let a single instant wedge itself between them, it grows—it becomes a month, a year, a century; it becomes too late. Kiss him, Irma, kiss him while there is time, or in a moment his hair will be white and there will be another madwoman in Paris! Oh, make her kiss him, all of you! [*They kiss.*] Bravo! Oh, if only you'd had the courage to do that thirty years ago, how different I would be today! Dear Deaf-Mute, be still—your words dazzle our eyes! And Irma is too busy to translate for you. [*They kiss once more.*] Well, there we are. The world is safe. And you see how simple it all was? Nothing is ever so wrong in this world that a sensible woman can't set it right in the course of an afternoon. Only, the next time, don't wait until things begin to look black. The minute you notice anything, tell me at once.

The Ragpicker. We will, Countess. We will.

Countess. [*Puts on her hat. Her tone becomes businesslike.*] Irma. My bones. My gizzard.

Irma. I have them ready, Countess.

Countess. Good. [*She puts the bones into her basket and starts for the stairs.*] Well, let's get on to more important things. Four o'clock. My poor cats must be starved. What a bore for them if humanity had to be saved every afternoon. They don't think much of it, as it is.

CURTAIN

ANOTHER PART OF THE FOREST*

By

LILLIAN HELLMAN

OF MISS HELLMAN'S SEVEN ORIGINAL plays so far produced (1955), only one has had fewer than 100 performances on Broadway in its first run, and some have had very long runs indeed. This is a record of unusual success, not easily matched among playwrights. And Miss Hellman's work when inspected shows clearly that this success has not been gained by giving audiences pap, or "what the public wants," or by any compromising of Miss Hellman's own ideals for plays and playwriting. The genesis of *Another Part of the Forest* demonstrates clearly Miss Hellman's attitude toward both her work and the public which supports it.

The title is rather oddly taken from Theobald's location of the fifth scene of Act III of *As You Like It,* or so they say. But it really has nothing to do with Phebe and Corin and Rosalind, or anything else in Shakespeare; instead, the forest must be the forest in which the little foxes live, the little foxes who spoil the grapes. *The Little Foxes* had appeared seven years before *Another Part of the Forest.* It showed the Hubbard family in 1900, conniving to make more money, even if that meant that Regina should murder her husband and lose her daughter, even if Oscar's son should become a thief. The Hubbards were thoroughly detestable people, though they made an admirable play. As the years went by, however, Miss Hellman noticed in admirers of *The Little Foxes* a feeling that they were morally superior to the Hubbards, and, as she said in a newspaper interview, "this gave me a jolt." Presumably to correct this audience feeling about the Hubbards Miss Hellman set herself to show the family as it had been in 1880, twenty years before *The Little Foxes. Another Part of the Forest* seems to have been intended to show—or reenforce the point already made—that avarice is endemic in our society and that we are all Hubbards or their victims, and that we share their guilt as long as making money wins approval or is socially permissible. Exploitation in the economic world brings exploitation in the family, Miss Hellman says, and such pitiful human wrecks as Birdie in *The Little Foxes* or Lavinia in *Another Part of the Forest* show where the exploitation leads.

Miss Hellman clearly is among the sternest of moralists, though she bases her morality not on religion but on social science. But social science's morality as compared with religion's lacks compassion, and the two plays have led, not surprisingly, to the judgment: "Miss Hellman doesn't so much hate evil; she just hates people." This judgment, however, is only the extreme response to the doctrinaire in Miss Hellman, an element sufficiently strong, no doubt, but probably not central. Central would seem to be her wish that her writing should be clean and efficient and her dramaturgy tight. As a playmaker, master of technical proficiency, she is perhaps without an equal among living American playwrights. And if she lacks tenderness toward her characters, she displays the same lack toward herself as a workman.

But Miss Hellman's method runs another and different risk. Does she sacrifice her characters to her doctrine? This is the risk which Galsworthy insisted, in his famous *Some Platitudes concerning Drama,* every dramatist who wishes to teach a code must run. But Miss Hellman's immense care to make her characters believable undoubtedly keeps them safe in our day. "In our day" is important, because our day is probably conditioned to believe in almost pure evil because of the many blows mankind's self-esteem has received from all kinds of sources: political, economic, scientific, psychological. Though the Hubbards convince us now, we can easily imagine audiences even very slightly differentiated from us who would find them quite incredible. And one may wonder, even now, why a community so ready to lynch Marcus Hubbard is willing at the same time to support his business enterprises so lavishly. But this question arises in the mind only late. Both characters and plot at the moment of contact satisfy and even fascinate.

Miss Hellman herself directed the play on its first production and the very expressive settings were by Jo Mielziner.

LILLIAN HELLMAN

Born 1905, New Orleans, Louisiana.
Attended New York University and Columbia University.
1924, Went to work for a New York City publisher.
1925, Married Arthur Kober, journalist and playwright, and decided to become a writer herself.
Play reader for theatrical producers and reviewer of books.
1932, Divorced.
1941, Awarded prize of the New York Drama Critics' Circle for *Watch on the Rhine.*

PLAYS

1934 *The Children's Hour.* 1936 *Days to Come.* 1939 *The Little Foxes.* 1941 *Watch on the Rhine.* 1944 *The Searching Wind.* 1946 *Another Part of the Forest.* 1950 *Montserrat,* adapted from the French of Emmanuel Roblès. 1951 *The Autumn Garden.* 1955 *The Lark,* adapted from the French of Jean Anouilh.

SCREENWRITING

1935 *The Dark Angel.* 1936 *These Three.* 1937 *Dead End.* 1940 *The Little Foxes.* 1943 *Watch on the Rhine.* 1943 *The North Star.* 1945 *The Searching Wind.*

WRITINGS ON DRAMA

Preface to *Four Plays of Lillian Hellman,* 1942. Preface to *Selected Letters of Chekhov,* 1955.

ANOTHER PART OF THE FOREST

CAST

(IN ORDER OF THEIR APPEARANCE)

REGINA HUBBARD.
JOHN BAGTRY.
LAVINIA HUBBARD.
CORALEE.
MARCUS HUBBARD.
BENJAMIN HUBBARD.
JACOB.
OSCAR HUBBARD.
SIMON ISHAM.
BIRDIE BAGTRY.
HAROLD PENNIMAN.
GILBERT JUGGER.
LAURETTE SINCEE.

SYNOPSIS OF SCENES

ACT ONE: *A Sunday morning in June, 1880, the Alabama town of Bowden, the side portico of the Hubbard house.*

ACT TWO: *The next evening, the living room of the Hubbard house.*

ACT THREE: *Early the next morning, the side portico of the Hubbard house.*

Throughout the play, in the stage directions, left and right mean audience's left and right.

ACT ONE

SCENE: *The side portico of the Hubbard house, a Sunday morning in the summer of 1880 in the Alabama town of Bowden. The portico leads into the living room by back center French doors. On the right side of the portico is an old wing of the house. An exterior staircase to this wing leads to an upper porch, off which are the bedrooms of the house, and behind the staircase are the back gardens and the kitchen quarters. Under the second-story porch is a door leading to the dining room of the house, and a back door leading to the kitchen. The other side of the portico leads to a lawn which faces the town's main street. The main part of the house, built in the 1850's, is Southern Greek. It is not a great mansion but it is a good house built by a man of taste from whom* MARCUS HUBBARD *bought it after the Civil War. There is not much furniture on the portico: two chairs and a table at one end, one comfortable chair and a table at the other end. Twin heads of Aristotle are on high pedestals. There is something too austere, too pretended Greek about the portico, as if it followed one man's eccentric taste and was not designed to be comfortable for anyone else.*

As the curtain rises, REGINA HUBBARD, *a handsome girl of twenty, is standing looking down at* JOHN BAGTRY. REGINA *has on a pretty negligee thrown over a nightgown. Her hair is pinned high, as if she had pinned it up quickly.* JOHN BAGTRY *is a man of thirty-six with a sad, worn face. He is dressed in shabby riding shirt and Confederate Cavalry pants.*

Regina. [*After a long silence.*] Where were you going?

John. [*He has a soft, easy voice.*] And what you doing awake so early?

Regina. Watching for you. But you tried not to hear me when I called you. I called you three times before you turned.

John. I didn't think this was the place or the hour for us to be meeting together. [*Looks around nervously.*] We'll be waking your folks. You out here in your wrapper! That would make a pretty scandal, honey——

Regina. [*Impatiently.*] Nobody's awake. And I don't care. Why didn't you——

John. [*Quickly, gaily.*] Oh, your Mama's up all right. I saw her and your Coralee going into nigger church. I bowed to her——

Regina. [*Softly.*] Why didn't you meet me last night?

John. [*After a second.*] I couldn't. And I didn't know how to send word.

Regina. Why couldn't you? Plantation folks giving balls again? Or fancy dress parties?

John. [*Smiles.*] I haven't been to a party since I was sixteen years old, Regina. The Bacons gave the last ball I ever remember, to celebrate the opening of the war and say good-bye to us——

Regina. You've told me about it. Why couldn't you come last night?

John. I couldn't leave Aunt Clara and Cousin Birdie. They wanted to sit out and talk after supper, and I couldn't.

Regina. [*Slowly.*] They wanted to talk? And so they made you stay?

John. No, they didn't *make* me. They're lonely, Regina, and I'm not with them much, since you and I——

Regina. Why should you be with them? When I want to meet you, I go and do it.

John. Things are different with us. Everything is bad. This summer is the worst, I guess, in all the years. They are lonely——

Regina. It's not the first time you didn't come. And you think I shouldn't be angry, and take you back the next day. It would be better if you lied to me where you were. This way it's just insulting to me. Better if you lied.

John. Lie? Why would I lie?

Regina. Better if you said you were with another woman. But not meeting me because of those two mummies——

John. [*Softly.*] I like them, Regina. And they don't go around raising their voices in anger on an early Sunday day.

Regina. I don't want you to tell me about the differences in your family and mine.

John. [*Stares at her.*] I've never done that. Never.

Regina. That's what you always mean when you say I'm screaming.

John. [*Sharply.*] I mean no such thing. I said only that I stayed with Aunt Clara and Cousin Birdie last night. And I'll do it again. [*Desperately.*] Look, honey, I didn't mean not to come to meet you. But I've lived on them for fifteen years. They're good to me. They share with me the little they got, and I don't give back anything to them——

Regina. [*Tensely.*] I'm getting sick of them. They've got to know about you and me some day soon. I think I'm going to sashay right up to that sacred plantation grass and tell them the war's over, the old times are finished, and so are they. I'm going to tell them to stay out of my way——

John. [*Sharply.*] They've never mentioned you, Regina.

Regina. That's good breeding: to know about something and not talk about it?

John. I don't know about good breeding.

Regina. [*Turns to him.*] They think they do. Your Cousin Birdie's never done more than say good morning in all these years—when she knows full well who I am and who Papa is. Knows full well he could buy and sell Lionnet on the same morning, its cotton and its women with it——

John. [*Takes her arm, very sharply.*] I would not like to hear anybody talk that way again. No, I wouldn't.

Regina. [*Pleadingly, softly.*] I'm sorry, I'm sorry, I'm sorry. I give you my apology. I'm sorry, darling.

John. We shouldn't be——

Regina. [*Runs to him, takes his arm.*] I'm never going to be mean again, never going to talk mean—— Look, honey, I was mad about last night because I wanted to tell you about my plan. I've been thinking about it for months, and I've got Papa almost ready for it. But I can't tell it to you tonight because Papa makes me read to him every Sunday. But late tomorrow night, after Papa's music—it's over early—please, darling, tomorrow night—tomorrow night— [*She clings to him.*]

John. [*Turns to her.*] Regina, we mustn't. We mustn't any more. It's not right for you, honey, we're a scandal now. I'm no good for you. I'm too old, I'm——

Regina. [*Clinging to him, impatient.*] Why do you say that? A man at thirty-six talking that way? It comes from hanging around this town and your kinfolk.

John. I was only good once—in a war. Some men shouldn't ever come home from a war. You know something? It's the only time I was happy.

Regina. [*Draws away from him, wearily.*] Oh, don't tell me that again. You and your damn war. Wasn't it silly to be happy when you knew you were going to lose?

John. You think it is silly? You think we all were? Of course you do. In this house you couldn't think anything else. [*She draws back.*] And now *I'm* sorry. That was most rude. It's late, honey.

Regina. [*Quickly.*] You haven't even asked me about my plan.

John. I have a plan, too. I have a letter from Cod Carter. He's in Brazil. He's fighting down there, he says——

[LAVINIA HUBBARD *and* CORALEE *appear from around the portico, as if com-*

ing from street. JOHN *stares at them, draws back nervously.* REGINA *watches him, amused.* LAVINIA HUBBARD *is a woman of about fifty-eight, stooped, thin, delicate-looking. She has a sweet, high voice and a distracted, nervous way of speaking.* CORALEE *is a sturdy Negro woman of about forty-five. She is holding a parasol over* LAVINIA. JOHN *steps forward.* CORALEE *folds parasol, stares at* REGINA'S *costume, exits under porch to kitchen.*]

Lavinia. [*As if this were an ordinary morning scene.*] Morning, Captain Bagtry. Been for a nice little stroll?

John. [*Quickly.*] Morning, Mrs. Hubbard. No, ma'am. I was just riding by and glimpsed Miss Regina——

Lavinia. [*Nods.*] That's nice. Coralee and I been to our church. The colored folks said a prayer for me and a little song. It's my birthday.

John. Congratulations, ma'am. I sure give you my good wishes.

Lavinia. Thank you, sir. And later I'm going back to the second service. And I know a secret: they're going to give me a cake. Ain't that lovely of them, and me undeserving? [*Looks up at him.*] I always go to the colored church. I ain't been to a white church in years. Most people don't like my doing it, I'm sure, but I got my good reasons——

Regina. All right, Mama.

Lavinia. There's got to be one little thing you do that you want to do, all by yourself you want to do it.

Regina. [*Sharply.*] All right, Mama.

Lavinia. [*Hurries toward the doors of the living room.*] Oh. Sorry. [*At the door of living room, looks back at* JOHN.] I remember you and your cousins the day you left town for war. I blew you a kiss. Course we were living in our little house then and you didn't know. But I blew you all a kiss.

John. [*Very pleased.*] I'm glad to know it, ma'am. It was a great day. A hot day— You know something, ma'am? It was my birthday, too, that day. I was sixteen, and my cousins not much older. My birthday. Isn't that a coincidence, ma'am?

Regina. Why?

John. [*Lamely.*] Because it's your Mama's birthday today.

Lavinia. And you know something else, Captain Bagtry? Tomorrow's my wedding anniversary day. Your birthday, my birthday, and a wedding anniversary day.

Regina. [*Very sharply.*] All right, Mama.

[MARCUS HUBBARD *opens the door of his bedroom and appears on the upper porch. He is a strong-looking man of sixty-three, with a soft voice of tone and depth. He speaks slowly, as if he put value on the words.*]

Marcus. Who's speaking on the porch?

[*At the sound of his voice* LAVINIA *hurries into the house.* JOHN *draws back into the living-room doors.* REGINA *comes forward.*]

Regina. I'm down here, Papa.

Marcus. Morning, darling. Waiting for me?

Regina. Er. Mama's just been to church.

Marcus. Of course—where else would she go? Wait. Have your first coffee with me.

[*He exits into his room.*]

Regina. [*Amused at* JOHN'S *nervous movements, takes his arm.*] I want you to meet Papa. Not now. But soon.

John. I know your Papa. I'm in and out of your store——

Regina. I want you to come *here.* I guess no Bagtry ever been inside our house. But would your Aunt Clara and your Cousin Birdie allow you to come, do you reckon?

John. Allow me? I didn't think that was the way it was. I thought your Papa didn't want anybody here——

Regina. He doesn't. But I'll find a way. Will you meet me tomorrow night, same place? Darling, darling, please. Please. [*She pulls him toward her. He hesitates for a second. Then he takes her in his arms, kisses her with great feeling. She smiles.*] Meet me?

John. [*Softly.*] I always do. No matter what I say or think, I always do.

[*He kisses her again. Then he runs off. She stands for a minute staring after him. Then, from the street side of the lawn,* BENJAMIN HUBBARD *appears. He is followed by* JACOB *carrying a small valise and three boxes.* JACOB *is a tall, thin Negro of about thirty.* BEN *is thirty-five: a powerful, calm man with a quiet manner.*]

Regina. [*Amused.*] Morning, Ben. Have a good trip?

Ben. Was that Bagtry?

Regina. He said that was his name.

Ben. What you doing having men on the porch, you in your wrapper?

Regina. [*Gaily.*] Isn't it a pretty wrapper? Came from Chicago.

Ben. [*Pointing to boxes.*] And so did these, on the mail train. They got your name on 'em. Belong to you?

Regina. [*Giggling.*] Writing can't lie. Specially writing in ink.

Marcus. [*Reappears on balcony, calls down.*] Coffee ready for me, darling?

Regina. [*Gaily, smiling at* BEN.] Going in to brew it myself, honey.

[*She disappears into house.* MARCUS *comes forward on the porch, sees* BEN *and* JAKE.]

Marcus. [*Stares at* JAKE.] Jake, take the boxes in. [JAKE *starts in.*] And put Mr. Benjamin's valise out of your hand. [JAKE *hesitates, looks puzzled.* BEN *stares up at* MARCUS. *Then* JAKE *puts valise down, exits.*] How was the world of fashion, Benjamin?

Ben. I was only in it for twenty-four hours.

Marcus. Ah. That isn't long enough.

Ben. You ordered me back.

Marcus. What for?

Ben. [*Looks up, smiles.*] The pleasure of it, I think.

Marcus. [*Giggles.*] Certainly. But what did I call the pleasure?

Ben. You said the books needed checking, and I was to be back to do them today.

Marcus. [*Thinks.*] Books? I wouldn't let you touch the books in my library, Benjamin. Certainly you know that.

Ben. [*Annoyed.*] Books for the store. *Store. Bookkeeping. Accounts.*

Marcus. Oh. But why today?

Ben. I don't know, Papa. I'd like to have stayed in Mobile. I had some business——

Marcus. [*Clucks.*] But I brought you back on a Sunday to look at store books. Now why did I do that? I must have had some reason. I'll think of it later. [*He looks down, realizes* BEN *isn't going to answer.*] What business did you have, Ben?

Ben. I wanted to invest two thousand dollars in Birmingham Coal, Incorporated. It will bring fifty thousand some day. There's coal there, and they're sending down men from the North with money for it—— But I couldn't raise it. And you wouldn't lend it to me.

Marcus. That why you went? That foolish old scheme of yours? I had hoped you went to Mobile for a lady.

Ben. No, sir. I have no lady.

Marcus. I believe you. But certainly you went to the concert last night?

Ben. No, I didn't. I told you: I was trying to borrow the two thousand you wouldn't let me have.

Marcus. Well, you must hear a good concert before you die.

[LAVINIA *and* CORALEE *enter from kitchen door.*]

Marcus. [*Starts into his room.*] Carry in your own valise, son. It is not seemly for a man to load his goods on other men, black or white.

[BEN *looks up, half annoyed, half amused. He picks up his valise, starts toward door as* CORALEE *appears, carrying breakfast tray.* LAVINIA *follows her.* BEN *watches them as* CORALEE *puts tray on table.* LAVINIA, *knowing that* MARCUS *is on the balcony, but not knowing whether she should speak to him, helps* CORALEE *by aimlessly fussing about with the tray.*]

Lavinia. [*To* BEN.] Morning, son.

Ben. Morning, Mama.

Lavinia. Pleasant trip?

Ben. No, unsuccessful.

Lavinia. That's good, I'm sure. I mean—— Morning, Marcus.

Marcus. Coralee. I'll be right down. Lavinia, send everybody else to the dining room for breakfast. Go on, Lavinia.

[*He disappears.* LAVINIA *spills coffee.*]

Coralee. [*Quickly.*] All right, Miss Viney. No harm. Go on in and have your breakfast before there's trouble.

Lavinia. I was only trying——

[LAVINIA *goes into living room as* MARCUS *comes downstairs carrying a book. He goes immediately to table.* CORALEE *pours coffee.*]

Marcus. Who is down for breakfast?

Coralee. I don't know.

Lavinia. [*Reappears in living-room doorway.*] Oh, Marcus, Colonel Isham is calling. Can he come out?

Marcus. If he is capable of walking.

[COLONEL ISHAM, *a man of sixty-five, appears in the doorway.*]

Marcus. Colonel Isham.

Isham. You will forgive this too early visit?

Marcus. You're in town for church?

Isham. I've come to see you. I was asked to come to see you.

Marcus. To talk about bad cotton?

Isham. No, sir. I don't mix with a man's Sunday breakfast to talk about cotton. I come to talk about your son Oscar.

Marcus. Then you will need coffee.

Isham. Thank you, no. Two nights ago——

Marcus. People like you don't drink coffee with people like me?

Isham. I've had coffee. Now, Mr. Hubbard——

Marcus. Then come again when you haven't had it.

[*There is a pause. Slowly* ISHAM *comes to the table.* MARCUS *smiles, pours a cup of coffee, hands it to* ISHAM, *who takes it and sits down.*]

Isham. Thank you. I have come here for your sake, Mr. Hubbard. There is dangerous feeling up in my town this morning——

Marcus. Colonel, I hate conversations for my sake. Sunday is my day of study. I don't wish to sound rude but please say quickly what you have come about.

Isham. [*Smiles.*] Mr. Hubbard, I'm too old to frighten.

Marcus. [*Smiles.*] And I should be a daring man to try it. You, one of our great heroes. Commanding the first Alabama troops at——

Isham. [*Sharply.*] I am not interested in talking to you about the War Between the States, or about your personal war on the people of this state—— Now, please listen to me. Two nights ago Sam Taylor in Roseville was badly beaten up. Last night fourteen people identified the night riders as the Cross boys, from over the line, and your son Oscar.

Marcus. [*Shouts into the house.*] Benjamin. Rope Oscar and bring him out here immediately. I told you fifteen years ago you were damn fools to let Klansmen ride around, carrying guns——

Isham. Were you frightened of our riding on you? I came here to tell you to make your son quit. He can thank me he's not swinging from a rope this minute. You have good reason to know there's not a man in this county wouldn't like to swing up anybody called Hubbard. I stopped my friends last night but I may not be able to stop them again. Tell him what patriots do is our business. But he's got no right to be riding down on anybody——

[BEN, *followed by* OSCAR, *appears in the dining-room doorway.* OSCAR *looks frightened, decides to be cute.*]

Oscar. *Rope* me out. I can stand up, Papa. Never felt my Saturday night liquor that bad——

Isham. [*Ignoring* OSCAR, *to* MARCUS.] Taylor is a good man. He's got no money for treatment, got no job now, won't get one again.

Marcus. [*To* OSCAR.] Colonel Isham has just saved you from a lynching party. Should I thank him?

Oscar. [*Terrified.*] Lynching! What did—— Colonel Isham—I——

Isham. I don't want to speak with you.

Marcus. Who does?

Oscar. But what did I——

Marcus. Do I have to tell you that if you ever put on those robes again, or take a gun to any man—— [*Takes roll of bills from his pocket, throws it to* BENJAMIN.] Count out five hundred dollars, Benjamin.

Oscar. [*Very nervous.*] You mean Taylor? I wasn't riding with the Klan boys. No, I wasn't. I was thinking about it, but——

Ben. No, he couldn't have been with them. He took me to the Mobile train, and the train was late, so we sat talking. He couldn't have got up to Roseville.

Isham. You say you're willing to swear to that, Mr. Benjamin? You sure you're willing to go against fourteen people identifying your brother——?

Ben. Oh, Oscar looks like anybody.

Marcus. [*Smiles.*] Give the money to Colonel Isham, Benjamin. Go away, Oscar. [OSCAR *exits through dining-room door.*] Please use the money for Taylor.

Isham. We'll take care of him, Hubbard. Good day, sir.

Marcus. You won't take care of him, because you can't. Learn to be poor, Isham, it has more dignity. Tell Taylor there will be a check each month. Tell him that my other son, Benjamin, wishes to make amends. Ben has a most charitable nature.

[ISHAM *hesitates, decides, takes the money, looks at it.*]

Isham. There is no need for so much. A hundred would be more proper.

Marcus. Good day, Colonel. Don't give me lectures on propriety.

[ISHAM *starts to speak, changes his mind, exits left toward street. There is a pause.* BEN *looks at* MARCUS, *drops the roll of money on* MARCUS's *table.*]

Ben. [*Smiles.*] You didn't like my story about Oscar?

Marcus. Not much. Very loyal of you, however.

Ben. I like it.

Marcus. Good. It's yours. Keep it. You must have one of your usual involved reasons for wanting it.

Ben. Five hundred dollars is a lot of money to a man who allows himself six dollars for a trip to Mobile.

Marcus. Perhaps you're stingy.

Ben. You can't be much else on a salary of twenty dollars a week.

Marcus. Is that all I pay you? Ah, well, you'll be better off when I—if and when I die. But I may not die; did I tell you, Benjamin?

[REGINA, OSCAR, *and* LAVINIA *appear from the living room.* REGINA *hurries to* MARCUS.]

Regina. Forgive me, darling. I forgot your coffee.

[OSCAR *is carrying a cup of coffee and a roll.* LAVINIA, *who never sees anything, bumps into him.* OSCAR *turns on her angrily.*]

Oscar. Goodness' sake, Mama. Watch where you going.

Regina. Oscar's in a bad humor this morning. Oscar's got one of those faces shows everything.

Lavinia. [*To everybody—nobody pays any attention.*] I'm sorry. I'm sure I didn't mean to——

Marcus. Oscar has good reason for being in a bad humor. He owes me five hundred dollars.

[OSCAR's *hand begins to shake on the cup. He rattles the spoon and saucer.*]

Ben. For God's sake sit down and stop rattling that cup.

Oscar. Papa, you can't mean that—— Ben told you where I was. I wasn't even——

Marcus. [*To* REGINA.] You look charming. New?

Regina. No. But I *did* buy a few new dresses.

Marcus. A few? I saw the boxes coming in.

Oscar. Seven dresses. Seven, I counted them.

Regina. Can you count up to seven now? And more coming next week, Papa.

Marcus. What are you going to do with them, honey?

Regina. [*Hesitates, then gaily.*] Could we go for a walk?

Ben. You buying these clothes out of your allowance?

Regina. [*Laughs.*] Aren't you silly? How could I? There's a fur piece and a muff that cost three hundred dollars alone. They're charming, Papa, wait till you see them——

Oscar. [*Delighted at the diversion in the conversation.*] You really gone crazy? Nobody's ever worn furs in this climate since old lady Somers put that bear rug around her and jumped out the porch.

Regina. I won't jump out the porch.

Ben. I will have to O.K. the bills, so would you tell me how much you've spent?

Regina. [*Airily.*] I don't know. I didn't even ask.

Oscar. [*Shrilly.*] Didn't even ask? Didn't even ask? You gone real crazy, acting like Miss Vanderbilt, whatever her name is—rich people up North don't act that way. They watch their money, and their fathers' money.

Regina. Oh, that's not true. Those people in Chicago, just the other day, gave their daughter a hundred-thousand-dollar check for a trousseau——

Ben. [*Looks at her.*] A trousseau? So that's what you're buying? I saw Horace Giddens in Mobile last evening, and he was mighty disappointed you haven't answered his letter about coming up for another visit here.

Oscar. Hey, he wouldn't be bad for you, Regina——

Ben. He's in love with you. That was obvious when he was here. It's good society, that family, and rich. Solid, quiet, rich.

Oscar. And you'd get to like him. A lot of people get married not liking each other. Then, after marriage, they still don't like each other much, I guess——

Ben. [*Sharply.*] Are you still drunk?

Lavinia. [*Comes to life.*] A wedding? That would be nice. I hope you make your plans right quick, Regina, because——

Marcus. [*Very slowly.*] What is all this, Regina?

Lavinia. I didn't say anything. I was twisting my handkerchief——

Regina. It's nothing, Papa, nothing. You know Ben. You know he wants me to marry money for him. I'm not even thinking about Giddens. I don't like him.

Ben. Certainly I want you to marry money. More than that—— [*She wheels around to stare at him.*] You're twenty years old. You ought to be settled down. You been worrying us. [*Pleased at the nervousness* REGINA *is showing.*] Isn't that so, Mama? Hasn't Regina been worrying you?

Lavinia. I really don't know, son. I really couldn't say.

Oscar. Well, I could say she's been worrying me. Many's the time I thought of taking action. Sashaying around as open as——

Regina. [*To* OSCAR.] Oh, shut up. [*To* MARCUS.] Papa. You can't blame me if Ben thinks up one of his plans to annoy you, and Oscar chimes in like he always does. I bought the clothes because I—because I want to take a little trip. That's all, Papa.

Marcus. A trip?

Regina. All right. I'll send back the dresses. I don't know what all this talk's about. [*Comes to him.*] Spoiling your Sunday. Come on, darling. Let's take our lunch and go on a picnic, just you and me. We haven't done that in a long time.

Marcus. No, not for a long time. [*To* BEN.] Something amuses you?

Ben. Yes. You and Regina.

Marcus. [*To* BEN *and* OSCAR.] The two of you have contrived to give me a bad morning. [*To* OSCAR.] And you have cost me five hundred dollars. How much you drawing at the store?

Oscar. [*Nervous but determined.*] I was

going to talk to you about that, Papa. I'm drawing sixteen a week. It ain't enough, Papa, because, well, I'm getting on and I want a little life of my own. I was going to ask you if you couldn't sort of make a little advance against a little raise——

Marcus. You'll get eleven a week hereafter. Five dollars will go to repay me for the five hundred.

Oscar. My God, Papa. You can't—— Eleven a week! My God, Papa—— That wasn't what I meant. You misunderstood me 'cause I wasn't talking clear. I wanted a little *raise,* not a——

Marcus. [*To* BEN, *sharply.*] Put aside your plans for your sister's future. Spend with profit your time today going over the store books. [*Then, amused.*] You'll find we are short of cash. Call in some cotton loans or mortgages. [*Giggles.*] Then go to church.

Lavinia. [*Delighted.*] Want to come with me, Benjamin? I'm going to my church, because they're saying a prayer for my birthday. [*To* MARCUS.] It's my birthday, Marcus.

Marcus. Congratulations, Lavinia.

Lavinia. Thank you. [*Comes to* MARCUS.] We were going to talk today. You promised, Marcus——

Marcus. I promised to talk? Talk about what?

Lavinia. [*Amazed, worried.*] Talk about what? You know, Marcus. You promised last year, on my last birthday. You said you were too busy that day, but this year you said——

Marcus. I'm still busy, my dear. Now you run and tell Belle to make us up a fine picnic basket. [*To* REGINA.] And a good bottle of wine. I'll get it myself.

Lavinia. But, Marcus, I been waiting since last year——

Marcus. Get the lunch now. [*She hesitates, looks frightened, goes toward kitchen door. To* REGINA.] I'll bring my Aristotle. You'll read in English; I'll follow you in Greek. Shall we walk or drive?

Regina. [*Smiling.*] Let's walk. You get the wine and your books. I'll change my clothes—— [*He nods, smiles, goes into house. She stops to look at* BEN, *smiles.*] You never going to learn, Ben. Been living with Papa for thirty-five years, and never going to learn.

Oscar. Regina, you got a few hundred dollars to lend me? Wouldn't take me long to pay it back——

Ben. Learn what, honey?

Oscar. Papa's sure hard on me. It's unnatural. If a stranger came in he'd think Papa didn't like me, his own son.

Regina. [*Turns to* OSCAR.] You want some money? If you had any sense, you'd know how to get it: just tell Papa *Ben* don't want you to have it. You'll get it. [*To* BEN.] You ain't smart for a man who wants to get somewhere. You should have figured out long ago that Papa's going to do just whatever you tell him not to do, unless *I* tell him to do it. [*Pats his shoulder.*] Goodness gracious, that's been working for the whole twenty years I been on earth.

Ben. [*To* REGINA.] You are right, and you're smart. You must give me a full lecture on Papa some day; tell me why he's so good to you, how you manage, and so on.

Regina. [*Laughs.*] I'm busy now, taking him on a picnic.

Ben. Oh, not now. Too hot for lectures. We'll wait for a winter night. Before the fire. I'll sit opposite you and you'll talk and I'll listen. And I'll think many things, like how you used to be a beauty but at fifty years your face got worn and sour. Papa'll still be living, and he'll interrupt us, the way he does even now: he'll call from upstairs to have you come and put him to bed. And you'll get up to go, wondering how the years went by—— [*Sharply.*] Because, as you say, he's most devoted to you, and he's going to keep you right here with him, all his long life.

Regina. [*Angrily.*] He's not going to keep me here. And don't you think he is. I'm going away. I'm going to Chicago—— [BEN *gets up, stares at her.* OSCAR *looks up. She catches herself.*] Oh, well, I guess you'd have to know. But I wanted him to promise before you began any interfering—— I'm going for a trip, and a nice long trip. So you're wrong, honey.

Ben. [*Slowly.*] He's consented to the trip?

Regina. [*Giggles.*] No. But he will by the time the picnic's over.

Oscar. Chicago? You sure got Mama's blood. Little while now, and you're going to be just as crazy as Mama.

Regina. [*To* BEN.] And the trip's going to cost a lot of money. I got books from hotels, and I know. But you'll be working hard in the store and sending it on to me——

Ben. You could always come home occasionally and go on another picnic. [*Comes up to her.*] This time I don't think so. Papa didn't just get mad about you and Horace Giddens. Papa got mad about you and any man, or any place that ain't near him. I wouldn't like to be in the house, for example, the day he ever hears the gossip about you and Bagtry—— [*Sharply.*] Or is Bagtry going to Chicago——

Regina. [*Tensely, softly.*] Be still, Ben.

Oscar. And everybody sure is gossiping. Laurette even heard it up in Roseville. I said there's nothing between you. I wouldn't believe it. But if ever I thought there was I'd ride over to Lionnet, carrying a gun. I sure would——

Regina. [*Carefully.*] And the day you do I'll be right behind you. It'll be your last ride, darling.

Oscar. [*Backing away.*] All right, all right, I was joking. Everybody's talking so wild today——

Regina. [*Turns back to* BEN.] Look, Ben, don't start anything. I'll get you in trouble if you do.

Ben. I believe you.

Regina. Wish me luck. I got a hard day's work ahead.

[*She goes up steps to upper porch and into her room.*]

Oscar. [*Yawns.*] Where she going?

Ben. Try to keep awake. Why did you beat up Sam Taylor?

Oscar. [*After a second, sulkily.*] He's a no-good carpet-bagger.

Ben. [*Wearily.*] All right. Let's try again. Why did you beat up Sam Taylor?

Oscar. He tried to make evening appointments with Laurette. He tried it twice. I told him the first time, and I told her too.

Ben. Is Laurette the little whore you've been courting?

Oscar. [*Slowly, tensely.*] Take that back, Ben. Take back that word. [BEN *laughs.* OSCAR *advances toward him, very angry.*] I don't let any man——

Ben. Now listen to me, you clown. You put away your gun and keep it away. If those fools in your Klan want to beat up niggers and carpetbaggers, you let 'em do it. But you're not going to make this county dangerous to me, or dangerous to the business. We had a hard enough time making them forget Papa made too much money out of the war, and I ain't ever been sure they forgot it.

Oscar. Course they haven't forgot it. Every time anybody has two drinks, or you call up another loan, there's plenty of talk, and plenty of hints I don't understand. [*Rises.*] If I had been old enough to fight in the war, you just bet I'd been right there, and not like you, bought off. I'm a Southerner. And when I see an old carpetbagger or upstart nigger, why, I feel like taking revenge.

Ben. For what? Because Papa got rich on them? [*Very sharply.*] Put away that gun, sonny, and keep it put away, you hear me?

Oscar. [*Frightened.*] All right, all right. I want to thank you. I forgot. For saying that I was talking to you on the train. Thanks, Ben.

Ben. I wasn't lying for you. I was trying to save five hundred dollars.

Oscar. [*Hurt.*] Oh. Guess I should have known. [*Sighs.*] How'm I ever going to pay it back? I'm in a mess. I—Ben, help me, will you? I'm deeply and sincerely in love.

Ben. Go give yourself a cooling sponge bath.

Oscar. I want to marry Laurette. I was going to ask Papa to advance me a little money, so we could ship on down to New Orleans. He's going to leave money when he dies, plenty of it. I just want a little of mine now, and I'll go away——

Ben. He won't leave much. Not at this rate. He's spent forty thousand on nothing in the last six months.

Oscar. My God, forty thousand and us slaving away in the store! And that's the way it's always going to be. I'm telling you: I'm taking Laurette and I'm going. Laurette's a fine girl. Hasn't looked at another man for a year.

Ben. Well, she better take them up again if you're going away. *You* can't earn a living.

[JAKE *appears from the living room.*]

Jake. Mr. Ben, a lady who says she doesn't want to say her name, she would like to speak with you. She's in the front hall, waiting.

Ben. Who? Who is it?

Jake. Miss Birdie Bagtry.

[BEN *and* OSCAR *turn in surprise.*]

Ben. [*After a minute.*] Wants to see *me?* [JAKE *nods vigorously.*] Bring her out.

[JAKE *exits.*]

Oscar. Now what do you think of that? What's she want to come here for? To see *you?* [*Giggles.*] What you been up to, boy?

Ben. Maybe she's come to look at you. Didn't you tell me she once gave you a glass of lemonade?

Oscar. Did she?

Ben. I don't know. I only know that you told me so.

Oscar. Then I guess it happened.

Ben. That doesn't necessarily follow.

Oscar. Well, it was true. I was pushing a lame horse past Lionnet. I was lame myself from something or other——

Ben. Laurette Sincee?

Oscar. I told you once, stop that. I am in love with Laurette, deeply and sincerely.

Ben. Better you'd stayed for the lemonade and fallen in love with Lionnet's cottonfields.

Oscar. Oh, this girl's supposed to be awfully silly. Melty-mush-silly. [*Smiles.*] That's what Laurette calls people like that. Melty-mush-silly.

Ben. She's witty, Laurette, eh? [JAKE *appears in the living-room door followed by a slight, pretty, faded-looking girl of twenty. Her clothes are seedy, her face is worn and frightened.*] Good morning, ma'am.

Oscar. [*With charm.*] Well, hello there, Miss Birdie!

Birdie. [*Bows.*] Mr. Benjamin. And morning to you, Mr. Oscar. [*Nervously*] We haven't seen you in many a long day. You haven't been hunting lately?

Oscar. Oh, my time's been taken up with so many things, haven't had much chance.

Birdie. [*Nods.*] I know, you gentlemen in business. Please, you all, forgive my coming to your house, particularly on this day of privacy. I'll just take a few minutes and——

Oscar. Excuse me, Miss Birdie. Hope you'll come again.

[*He starts toward room.*]

Ben. Wait inside, Oscar. [OSCAR *turns to stare at him, then shrugs, disappears. To* BIRDIE.] Please.

Birdie. [*Sits down.*] Yes, sir. Thank you.

Ben. Can I get you coffee?

Birdie. No, sir. Thank you. You see, I only got a few minutes before Mama begins wondering. I'm sorry to worry you here, but I couldn't come to see you in the store, because then the whole town would know, wouldn't they? And my Mama and Cousin John would just about—— [*Giggles nervously.*] Isn't that so, Mr. Benjamin?

Ben. Isn't what so?

Birdie. [*Very nervous.*] About knowing. I must apologize for disturbing—— Oh, I said that before. It's not good manners to take up all your time saying how sorry I am to take up all your time, now is it? [*Giggles.*] Oh, and I'm doing that again, too. Mama says I say everything in a question. Oh.

Ben. What do you want to talk to me about, Miss Birdie?

Birdie. Yes. [*Rises. Desperately.*] Mr. Benjamin, we're having a mighty bad time. It can't go on. It got so bad that last month Mama didn't want to do it, but she did it, and it was just awful for her.

Ben. [*After a second, politely.*] Did what?

Birdie. Went all the way to Natchez, just to keep from going to our kinfolk in Mobile. Course they're so poor now they couldn't have done anything anyway, but just to keep them from knowing she went all the way to Natchez.

Ben. Really?

Birdie. Yes, sir, all the way by herself. But they said they just couldn't. They said they'd like to, for Papa's dead sake and Grandpapa's, but they just couldn't. Mama said she didn't want it for anybody's sake, not like that, not for those reasons—well, you know Mama, Mr. Benjamin.

Ben. No, I don't.

Birdie. Oh. Well, I don't blame her, although . . . No, when everything else is gone, Mama says you at least got pride left. She did it to save me, Mr. Benjamin, the trip, I mean. I was such a ninny, being born when I did, and growing up in the wrong time. I'm much younger than my brothers. I mean I am younger, if they were living. But it didn't do any good.

Ben. I beg your pardon?

Birdie. The trip to Natchez. It didn't do any good.

Ben. What kind of good didn't it do? [*She looks puzzled.*] Why did your Mama make the trip?

Birdie. To borrow money on the cotton. Or on the land— [*Softly.*] —or even to sell the pictures, or the silver. But they said they couldn't: that everybody was raising cotton that nobody else wanted. I don't understand that. I thought people always wanted cotton.

Ben. They will again in fifty years.

Birdie. [*After a pause.*] Oh. Fifty years. [*Smiles sadly.*] Well, I guess we can't wait that long. The truth is, we can't pay or support our people, Mr. Benjamin, we can't—— Well, it's just killing my Mama. And my Cousin John, he wants to go away.

Ben. Where does he want to go?

Birdie. Away from here. [*Tense, very frightened.*] Forgive me. Would you, I mean your father and you, would you lend money on our cotton, or land, or——

Ben. Your Cousin John, does he want to go to New York or Chicago, perhaps? Has he spoken of going to Chicago?

Birdie. Oh dear, no. There's no war going on in Chicago.

Ben. I beg your pardon?

Birdie. A war. He wants to go back to war. Mama says she can even understand that. She says there isn't any life for our boys any more.

Ben. I see. Where will Captain Bagtry find a war?

Birdie. There's something going on in Brazil, John says. He looked it up in the paper, and he's got a map.

Ben. Brazil. Is there a nice war going on in Brazil?

Birdie. Yes. I think so. [*Eagerly.*] You see, that was one of the things Mama was going to do with the money. Pay all our people and give John the carfare. He can earn a lot in Brazil; he can be a general. [*Pauses, breathes.*] Now about the loan, Mr. Benjamin——

Ben. You will inherit Lionnet?

Birdie. Me? Er. Yes. You mean if Mama were to—— You mustn't believe those old stories. Mama's not so sick that a little good care and—— [*Very embarrassed.*] I'm sorry.

Ben. You don't want your Mama to know you've come here?

Birdie. Oh, no, no. She'd never forgive me, rather die——

Ben. [*Laughs.*] To think you had come to us.

Birdie. I didn't mean that. I am so sorry. I didn't——

Ben. You have not offended me, ma'am. I only ask because as I understand it you don't own Lionnet, your Mama does. But you don't want her to know about the loan. And so who would sign for it?

Birdie. [*Stares at him.*] I would. Oh. You mean you can't sign for what you don't own. Oh! I see. I hadn't thought of that. Oh. That's how much of a ninny I am. Forgive me for bothering you. I shouldn't have. I'm sorry I just ruined your Sunday morning. Good day, sir.

Ben. [*Goes to dining-room door.*] Oscar, Oscar, I know you want to walk Miss Bagtry home.

Birdie. Oh, no. Thank you. I——

Oscar. [*Calling, offstage.*] I have an appointment. I'm late.

Birdie. [*Embarrassed.*] Please, sir——

Ben. [*To* BIRDIE.] How much of a loan were you thinking about?

Birdie. Five thousand dollars. It would take that much to pay our people and buy seed and pay debts and—— But I guess I was as foolish about that as——

Ben. You know, of course, that all loans from our company are made by my father. I only work for him. Yours is good cotton and good land. But you don't own it. That makes it hard. It's very unusual, but perhaps I could think of some way to accommodate you. A promise from you, in a letter——

Birdie. [*Delighted.*] Oh! Oh! Of course, I'd make the promise.

Ben. Why don't you talk to my father yourself? I'll tell him what it's all about, and you come back this afternoon——

Birdie. [*Backing away.*] Oh, no. I couldn't say all that today again. I just couldn't—— [*Softly.*] That's silly. Of course I could. What time will I come?

Ben. I have a pleasanter idea. Come tomorrow evening. Once a month my father has a music evening with musicians from Mobile to play on the violin, and flatter him. He's always in a good humor after his music. Come in then, Miss Birdie, and please invite Captain Bagtry to escort you.

Birdie. You really think there's any chance? Your Papa would—— And my Mama wouldn't ever have to find out?

Ben. [*Bows.*] I will do my best for you before you come.

Birdie. [*After a second, with determination.*] Thank you very much. I will be most pleased to come. Imagine having a concert right in your own house! I just love music. [OSCAR *appears in the door, stares angrily at* BEN.] Thank you for your courtesy in offering to walk me back, Mr. Oscar. And thank you, Mr. Benjamin.

[BIRDIE *smiles happily, moves quickly off.*]

Oscar. [*Comes close to* BEN, *softly, very angry.*] What the hell's the matter with you? Bossing me around, ruining my day?

Ben. [*Softly.*] Be nice to the girl. You hear me?

Oscar. I'm taking her home. That's enough. Damned little ninny.

Ben. I was thinking of trying to do you a favor. I was thinking if something works right for me, I'd lend you the five hundred to pay Papa back.

Oscar. Squee, Ben! If you only could. What would you be doing it for?

Ben. Because I want you to be nice to this girl. Flatter her, talk nice. She's kind of pretty.

Oscar. Pretty? I can't stand 'em like that.

Ben. I know. Virtue in woman offends you. Now go on. Be charming. Five hundred possible dollars' charming.

Oscar. [*Smiles.*] All right.

[*He runs off. After a minute* MARCUS,

carrying three books and a bottle of wine, appears on the porch.]

Marcus. [*Reading.*] "The customary branches of education number four. Reading and writing." You know *those,* Benjamin, I think. "Gymnastic exercise"— [MARCUS *laughs.*] —"and music." Aristotle. *You* don't know any music, Benjamin.

Ben. I've been too busy, Papa.

Marcus. At what?

Ben. Working all my life for you. Doing a lot of dirty jobs. And then watching you have a wild time throwing the money around. But when I ask you to lend me a little . . .

Marcus. You're a free man, Benjamin. A free man. You don't like what I do, you don't stay with me. [*Holding up the book.*] I do wish you would read a little Aristotle, take your mind off money.

[REGINA *comes down the steps, in a new dress, carrying a parasol and a steamer rug.*]

Ben. [*Looks at her.*] Oh. Before I forget. I invited Miss Birdie Bagtry and her cousin to come here tomorrow night.

Marcus. To come here? What do you mean?

Ben. I thought you'd like having the quality folk here. [*Smiles.*] Come here to beg a favor of you.

Marcus. [*Stares at him, giggles.*] You teasing me?

Ben. No. The girl just left here. She wants us to lend money on the cotton. Her Mama didn't know, and mustn't know. But Miss Birdie doesn't own the place——

Marcus. Then what kind of nonsense is that?

Ben. Maybe it's not nonsense. Take a note from her. If she dies before her mother——

Marcus. [*Sharply.*] Who said anything about dying? You're very concerned with people dying, aren't you?

Ben. [*Laughs.*] You hate that word. [*Quickly.*] Her mother could get out of it legally, maybe, but I don't think she would. Anyway, the old lady is sick, and it's worth a chance. Make it a short loan, call it in in a few years. They've wrecked the place and the money won't do 'em much good. I think the time would come when you'd own the plantation for almost nothing—— [*Looks up at* REGINA.] A loan would make them happy, and make us money. Make the Bagtrys grateful to us——

Regina. [*Softly.*] Course I don't know anything about business, Papa, but could I say something, please? I've been kind of lonely here with nobody nice having much to do with us. I'd sort of like to know people of my own age, a girl my own age, I mean——

Marcus. [*To* BEN.] How much does she want?

Ben. [*Hesitates for a minute.*] Ten thousand.

Marcus. On Lionnet? Ten thousand is cheap. She's a fool.

Ben. [*Smiles.*] Yes, I think she's a fool.

Marcus. [*Giggles.*] Well, the one thing I never doubted was your making a good business deal. Kind of cute of you to think of their coming here to get it, too. Bagtrys in this house, begging. Might be amusing for an hour.

Regina. [*Quickly.*] Can't invite 'em for an hour, Papa. And we've got to be nice to them. Otherwise I just wouldn't want to see him come unless we'd be awful nice and polite.

Marcus. They'll think we're nice and polite for ten thousand.

Regina. [*Laughs, in a high good humor.*] I guess. But you be pleasant to them——

Marcus. Why, Regina? Why are you so anxious?

Regina. Papa, I told you. I been a little lonesome. No people my age ever coming here—— I do think people like that sort of want to forgive you, and be nice to us——

Marcus. [*Sharply, angrily.*] Forgive me?

Regina. [*Turns away, little-girl tearful.*] I'm mighty sorry. What have I done? Just said I'd like to have a few people to listen to your old music. Is that so awful to want?

Marcus. [*Quickly, pleadingly.*] Come on, darling. [*Shouts.*] Lavinia, *where* is the basket? Lavinia! Coralee! [*To* REGINA.] Come on now, honey. It's been a long time since you been willing to spend a Sunday with me. If I was sharp, I'm sorry. Don't you worry. I'll be charming to the visiting gentry.

Ben. Miss Birdie got a fear of asking you for the loan and of her cousin, John, knowing about it. Might be better if you just gave your consent, Papa, and didn't make her tell the story all over again. I can do the details.

[LAVINIA *appears with a basket.* MARCUS *takes it from her, peers in it.*]

Marcus. [*To* REGINA.] That's mighty nice-looking. We'll have a good lunch. [*To* BEN.] I don't want to hear the woes of Lionnet and Mistress Birdie. Most certainly you will do the details. Be kind of pleasant owning Lionnet. It's a beautiful house. Very light in motive, very well conceived——

Lavinia. You going now, Marcus? Marcus! You promised you'd talk to me. Today——

Marcus. I'm talking to you, Lavinia.

Lavinia. Last year this morning, you promised me it would be today——

Marcus. [*Gently.*] I'm going out now, Lavinia.

Lavinia. I've fixed you a mighty nice lunch, Marcus, the way you like it. I boiled up some crabs right fast, and——

Marcus. I'm sure. Thank you.

[*He starts to move off.*]

Lavinia. [*Comes running to him.*] Please, Marcus, I won't take up five minutes. Or when you come back? When you come back, Marcus?

Marcus. Another day, my dear.

Lavinia. It can't be another day, Marcus. It was to be on my birthday, this year. When you sat right in that chair, and I brought my Bible and you swore——

Marcus. Another day.

Lavinia. It ought to be today. If you swear to a day, it's got to be that day—— [*Very frightened.*] Tomorrow then. Tomorrow wouldn't hurt so much, because tomorrow is just after today—— I've *got* to go this week, because I had a letter from the Reverend——

Regina. Oh, Mama. Are you talking that way again?

Lavinia. [*Shaking, wildly.*] Tomorrow, Marcus? Tomorrow, tomorrow.

Marcus. [*To Ben.*] Ben, get Coralee.

Lavinia. Tomorrow—— [BEN *exits. She grabs* MARCUS'S *arm.*] Promise me tomorrow, Marcus. Promise me. I'll go get my Bible and you promise me——

Marcus. [*Very sharply.*] Stop that nonsense. Get hold of yourself. I've had enough of that! I want no more.

Lavinia. [*Crying.*] I'm not making any trouble. You know that, Marcus. Just promise me tomorrow.

Marcus. Stop it! I've had enough. Try to act like you're not crazy. Get yourself in hand. [*He exits.*]

Regina. [*As* CORALEE *appears.*] Never mind, Mama. Maybe you'll be coming away with me. Would you like that? There are lots of churches in Chicago——

Coralee. All right, Miss Regina. Don't tease her now.

Regina. [*Gaily, as she goes off.*] I'm not teasing. [*After a pause,* LAVINIA *sits down.*]

Lavinia. Now I'm going to pretend. You ready?

Coralee. [*As if this had happened a thousand times before.*] All right.

Lavinia. He didn't say any of those things. He said he would speak with me sure thing—— [*Her voice rises.*] No man breaks a Bible promise, and you can't tell me they do. You know I got my correspondence with the Reverend. He wants me to come and I got my mission and my carfare. In his last letter, the Reverend said if I was coming I should come, or should write him and say I couldn't ever come. "Couldn't ever come——" Why did he write that?

Coralee. I don't know.

Lavinia. Your people are my people. I got to do a little humble service. I lived in sin these thirty-seven years, Coralee. [*Rocks herself.*] Such sin I couldn't even tell you.

Coralee. You told me.

Lavinia. Now I got to finish with the sin. Now I got to do my mission. And I'll be—— I'll do it nice, you know I will. I'll gather the little black children round, and I'll teach them good things. I'll teach them how to read and write, and sing the music notes and——

Coralee. [*Wearily.*] Oh, Miss Viney. Maybe it's just as well. Maybe they'd be scared of a white teacher coming among them.

Lavinia. [*After a pause.*] Scared of me?

Coralee. [*Turns.*] No, ma'am. You're right. News of you has gone ahead.

Lavinia. Course they could have many a better teacher. I know mighty little, but I'm going to try to remember better. [*Quietly.*] And the first thing I'm going to remember is to speak to Marcus tomorrow. Tomorrow. [*Turns pleading to* CORALEE.] I was silly to speak today. And I did it wrong. Anyway, he didn't say I *couldn't* go, he just said—— [*Stops suddenly.*] My goodness, it's such a little thing to want. Just to go back where you were born and help little colored children to grow up knowing how to read books and—— [*Giggles.*] You'll be proud of me. I'll remember things to teach them. You remember things when you're happy. And I'm going to be happy. You get to be fifty-nine, you don't be happy then, well, you got to find it. I'm going to be very happy, happy, happy, happy—— I'm going, Coralee——

[*She suddenly stops, looks down in her lap.*]

Coralee. Nice and cool in your room. Want to lie down? [LAVINIA *doesn't answer.*] Want to play a little on the piano? Nobody's inside. [*No answer. She waits, then very gently.*] All right, if you don't want to. I tell you what. Come on in the kitchen and rest yourself with us.

[LAVINIA *gets up,* CORALEE *takes her arm, they start out as*

THE CURTAIN FALLS

ACT TWO

SCENE: *The living room of the* HUBBARD *house. This is the room we have seen through the French doors of the first act, and now we are looking at the room as if we were standing in the French doors of the portico. A large bay window is center stage, leading to a porch that faces the first-act portico. Right stage is a door leading to the dining room. Left stage is an open arch leading to the entrance hall and main staircase. The furniture is from the previous owner but* MARCUS *has cleared the room of the ornaments and the ornamented. Right stage is a round table and three chairs. Left stage is a sofa and chair. Right, upstage, is a desk. Left, upstage, is a piano. Right, upstage, is a long table. Center of the room, before the columns of the porch, are a table and chairs. The room is simpler, more severe, than many rooms of the 1880's. A Greek vase, glass-enclosed, stands on a pedestal; a Greek statue sits on the table; Greek battle scenes are hung on the walls.*

[*As the curtain rises,* BEN *and* OSCAR *are sitting at table, stage right. They each have a glass of port and the port decanter is in front of them.* MARCUS, PENNIMAN, *and* JUGGER *are standing at a music stand, looking down at a music score.* PENNIMAN *is a tall, fattish man.* JUGGER *looks like everybody.* PENNIMAN *looks up from the score, hums, drains his glass, looks at the empty glass, and crosses to* BEN *and* OSCAR. MARCUS *is intent on the score.*]

Penniman. [*Meaning the score.*] Very interesting. Harmonically fresh, eh, Mr. Benjamin?

Ben. I know nothing of music.

Jugger. Why do people always sound so proud when they announce they know nothing of music?

Penniman. [*Quickly, as* OSCAR *fills his glass.*] A fine port, and a mighty good supper. I always look forward to our evening here. I tell my wife Mrs. Hubbard is a rare and masterly housekeeper.

Ben. You like good port, Mr. Penniman?

Penniman. Yes, sir, and don't trust the man who don't.

[OSCAR *goes off into gales of laughter. This pleases* MR. PENNIMAN *and he claps* OSCAR *on the shoulder.* MARCUS *looks up, annoyed, taps bow on music stand.* PENNIMAN *and* OSCAR *stop laughing,* PENNIMAN *winks at* OSCAR, *carries his glass back to music stand.* JAKE *comes from the hall entrance carrying two chairs and a lamp; he passes through to porch.* LAVINIA *hurries in from the dining room. Her hair is mussy, her dress spotted. She looks around the room, smiles at everybody. When nobody notices her, she crosses to* MARCUS, *leans over to examine the score, nods at what she reads.*]

Lavinia. Oh, it's nice, Marcus. Just as nice as anybody could have. It's going to be a cold collation. Is that all right?

Marcus. [*Who is in a good humor.*] Yes, certainly. What's that?

Lavinia. A cold collation? That's what you call food when you have guests. A cold collation.

Penniman. [*Looks toward the dining room, delighted.*] More food? After that fine supper——

Lavinia. This is a special night. Guests. Isn't that pleasant? My, we haven't had guests—— I don't think I remember the last time we had guests——

Marcus. [*Looks at her.*] All right, Lavinia.

Lavinia. There'll be a dish of crabs, of course. And a dish of crawfish boiled in white wine, the way Belle does. And a chicken salad, and a fine strong ham we've been saving. [*Stops.*] Oh. I'm worrying you gentlemen——

Penniman. [*Lifting his glass.*] Worrying us? You, the honor of Rose County, and the redeemer of this family——

[JUGGER *and* MARCUS *look up sharply.* BEN *laughs.* MARCUS *reaches over and takes* PENNIMAN'S *glass, carries it to table.*]

Marcus. I am awaiting your opinion.

Penniman. [*Who has the quick dignity of a man with too much port.*] The judgment of music, like the inspiration for it, must come slow and measured, if it comes with truth.

Oscar. [*To* BEN.] Talks like a Christmas tree, don't he?

Lavinia. It's your third composition, isn't it, Marcus? Oh, I'm sure it's lovely. Just lovely.

Marcus. [*Looks at her—softly.*] How would you know, Lavinia?

Lavinia. [*Hurt.*] I can read notes, Marcus. Why, I taught you how to read music. Don't you remember, Marcus? [*She goes toward* BEN *and* OSCAR.] I did. Yes, I did.

Ben. [*Amused.*] Of course you did.

Penniman. [*Hurriedly.*] I would say this: It is done as the Greeks might have imposed the violin upon the lute. [*Hums.*] Right here. Close to Buxtehude—— [*Inspiration.*] Or, the Netherland Contrapuntalists. Excellent.

[OSCAR *pours himself another port;* LAVINIA *has wandered to the piano, mumbling to herself.*]

Marcus. [*Very pleased, to* PENNIMAN.] You like it?

Penniman. I like it very much. And if you would allow us, I would like to introduce it in Mobile during the season. Play it first at the school, say; then, *possibly*——

Marcus. That would make me very happy. And what do you think of it, Mr. Jugger?

Jugger. [*Slowly.*] Penniman speaks for me. He always does.

Penniman. [*Quickly.*] Come. We'll try it for you. I am most anxious to hear it. [*Points to* MARCUS's *violin, coyly.*] I daresay you know the solo part you have written for yourself?

Marcus. Well, I—yes. [*Very pleased.*] I had hoped you would want to try it tonight. I—— [JUGGER *picks up his violin, starts for portico.* MARCUS *turns to him.*] Mr. Jugger. Would *you* like to try it now?

Jugger. [*Turns, looks at* MARCUS, *seems about to say something, changes his mind.*] I would like to try.

Penniman. But where *is* my cello? Goodness God——

Jugger. [*Sharply, at door of portico.*] It's out here. When will you learn that it's hard to mislay a cello?

[PENNIMAN *giggles, trips out to porch.*]

Lavinia. [*Suddenly plays a few notes on the piano.*] See? I told you, Marcus. *That's* it. I told you I could read music just as good as I used to——

Marcus. Is there something disturbing you this evening, Lavinia? More than usual?

[REGINA *enters from the hall. She is dressed up, very handsome. They all turn to stare at her. She smiles, goes to* MARCUS.]

Marcus. [*Softly.*] You're a beautiful girl.

Oscar. Looks like the decorated pig at the county fair.

Regina. [*Wheels around for* MARCUS.] It's my Chicago dress. *One* of my Chicago dresses. [REGINA *notices* LAVINIA.] Oh, Mama, it's late. Do go and get dressed.

Lavinia. I'm dressed, Regina.

Regina. You can't look like that. Put on a nice silk——

Lavinia. I only have what I have——

Regina. Put on your nice dress, Mama. It will do for tonight. We must order you new things. You can't go to Chicago looking like a tired old country lady——

Lavinia. [*Wheels around.*] *Chicago?* I'm not going to Chicago. Where I'm going I don't need clothes or things of the world. I'm going to the poor, and it wouldn't be proper to parade in silk—— Marcus! You tell Regina where I'm going. *Tell her where I'm going.* You tell her right now. You——

Regina. All right, Mama. Now don't you fret. Go upstairs and get dressed up for the high-toned guests. [*She leads* LAVINIA *to the hall.*] Don't you worry now. Go on up, honey. Coralee's waiting for you. [*She comes back into room. To* MARCUS.] Whew! I'm sorry. I should have known. I hope she isn't going to act queer the rest of the evening.

Marcus. There's always that chance.

Regina. Well, don't let's worry. [*Gaily.*] I'll see to everything. I'd better have a look in the kitchen, and more chairs—— Let's have the very good champagne, Papa.

Penniman. [*From portico.*] Mr. Hubbard——

Marcus. [*Takes keys from his pocket, throws them to* BEN.] Wine as good as Regina's dress. And count the bottles used. I don't want to find that Oscar has sold them again.

Ben. [*To* REGINA.] So your picnic was successful? When do you leave for Chicago?

Regina. [*Gaily.*] In ten days, two weeks. [*Comes to him.*] Going to miss me?

Ben. Yes. Very much.

Marcus. What's the matter? What's the matter, Regina?

Regina. [*Gaily, leaving* BEN.] Matter? Nothing. [*Calls into dining room as she exits.*] Two more chairs, Jake.

Oscar. Now just tell me how I'm going to get word to Laurette that I can't meet her till later tonight, just somebody tell me that.

Marcus. [*Very sharply to* BEN.] I told you to get the wine.

[BEN *looks at him, smiles as if he understood why* MARCUS *was angry; exits through dining-room door.* MARCUS *stands staring at him. Then goes to piano, looks through scores.* OSCAR *moves nervously toward* MARCUS.]

Oscar. [*Desperately.*] Papa, I'm in trouble. You see, I had an appointment with a lady from out of town; Roseville, I mean.

Marcus. What were they doing?

Oscar. Who?

Marcus. Regina and Ben when they were standing together——

[*Breaks off, turns sharply away.*]

Oscar. Oh, you know Ben. Always up to something. Yesterday, trying to marry off Regina; tonight trying to press me on the Bagtry girl.

Marcus. [*Looks up.*] Oh, come. Ben's not a fool. You and a Bagtry is a very comic idea.

Oscar. I know, but Ben's figured they're so hard up for money they might even have me. It all fits in with this mortgage you're giving them, or something. He's got his eye on the cotton—— [*Giggles.*] And Ben's eye goes in a lot of directions, mostly around corners. It's true, Papa. He made me take the girl home yesterday——

Marcus. [*Looks at* OSCAR.] The mortgage, and then the girl and you. Interesting man, Benjamin.

Oscar. [*Pleadingly.*] Papa, like I say. I've got a friend who's waiting for me right now. I want you to meet her. You see, I'm deeply and sincerely in love. Deeply and sincerely. She's a fine girl. But *Ben* cries her down. *Ben* don't want me to be happy.

Marcus. Isn't that too bad? Your own brother. It's a shame.

Oscar. Course she's of the lower classes, and that doesn't fit in with Ben's plans for us to marry money for him. But the lower classes don't matter to me; I always say it's not how people were born but what they are——

Marcus. You always say that, eh? Well, some people are democrats by choice, and some by necessity. You, by necessity.

Oscar. Could I go fetch her here— [*Desperately.*] tonight? Could I, Papa?

Marcus. What is this, a night at the circus?

Oscar. [*Slyly, as a last chance.*] I think it would just about finish Mr. Ben to have a member of the lower classes, sort of, mixing with the gentry, here. I thought it would sort of, sort of amuse you; and well, you could meet her at the same time. Be a good joke on Ben, sort of——

Marcus. [*Slowly.*] Is this Laurette that, that little, er—little thing from Roseville you been steaming about?

Oscar. She's not, Papa. Oh, maybe she was a little wild before I met her, but—— She was left an orphan and she didn't know what else to do, starving and cold, friendless.

Marcus. [*Shudders.*] Oh God, shut up. [*Hesitates, then laughs.*] All right, go and get her, if you like. Er. Does she come dressed? I wouldn't like her here, er, unrobed.

Oscar. [*Hurt but happy.*] Aw, she's a fine woman, Papa, don't talk like that. And she loves music. She wants to learn just about everything——

Marcus. Don't bring her as a student, Oscar.

Oscar. Oh, no. No, I wouldn't. She won't say a word. She admires you, Papa——

Marcus. For what?

Oscar. Well, just about—— well, just for everything, I guess—— [MARCUS *makes a dismissive gesture, goes on porch as* REGINA *comes into room.* OSCAR *sees* REGINA, *smiles.*] I'll be back in a few minutes. Going across the square to get Laurette—— bring her here.

Regina. [*Starts toward him, as* BEN *comes in carrying champagne bottles.*] Here? That girl?—What's the matter with you? You're doing nothing of the kind. Come back here. You can't bring that——

Oscar. Can't I? Well, just ask Papa. *He* wants her to meet my folks.

Regina. [*Turns to* BEN.] Ben, stop him. He can't bring her here tonight—— Stop him! [*But* OSCAR *has disappeared.*] Get him, Ben!

Ben. What am I supposed to do, shoot him? I'm too old to run down streets after men in love.

Regina. He *can't* bring her here. You know what John will think. I saw him this afternoon: I had to beg him to come tonight. He doesn't know why Birdie wants him to come, but—— Ben, he'll think we meant to do it, planned to insult them——

Ben. Yes, I'm sure he will.

[*The music on the porch begins.*]

Regina. What's the matter with Papa? Why did he let Oscar——

Ben. [*Smiles.*] *You're* going to learn some day about Papa. It's not as easy as you think, Regina. [*They stand looking out to the porch, listening to the music.*] He gave those clowns five thousand last month for something they call their music school. Now that they are playing his composition he should be good for another five thousand——

Regina. [*Turns. Softly, amazed.*] Did he? Really? [*Shakes her head.*] Well, anyway, he's promised me plenty for——

Ben. To marry Bagtry? Enough to support you the rest of your life, you and your husband? I'm taking a vacation the day he finds out about your marriage plans.

Regina. [*Angrily, nervous.*] I don't know what you're talking about. Marry—— What are you saying? I—— [*Turns to him, tensely.*] Leave me alone, Ben. Leave me alone. Stop making trouble. If you dare say *anything* to Papa about John, I'll——

Ben. [*Very sharply.*] Don't threaten me. I'm sick of threats.

Regina. [*Angry.*] You'll be much sicker of them if you—— [*Then, softly.*] Ben, don't. I'm in love with John.

Ben. [*Softly.*] But he's not in love with you.

[LAVINIA *comes into room, followed by* CORALEE, *who is pulling at her, trying to button her dress.* REGINA *turns away from* BEN.]

Lavinia. Don't bother with the lower buttons. [*Timidly.*] Am I proper now, daughter? [REGINA *doesn't answer her.* LAVINIA *points out to porch, meaning the music.*] You know, I've made myself cheer up. I know you were just teasing about Chicago, Regina, and I know full well I've never been good about teasing. What do people do now, curtsy or shake hands? I guess it's just about the first guests we had since the suspicion on your Papa.

Regina. Now, Mama. Please don't talk about any of that tonight. Don't talk at all about the war, or anything that happened. Please remember, Mama. Do you hear?

Coralee. [*Quickly.*] She won't. You all have been teasing her, and she's tired.

[CORALEE *goes to* BEN, *takes the champagne bottles from the table.* JAKE *comes in from the dining room carrying a tray of glasses and a punch bowl.*]

Lavinia. Could I try the nice punch, Coralee?

Coralee. You certainly can. [JAKE *exits.* BEN *starts to the table. As if such courtesy were unusual,* CORALEE *stares at him.*] Thank you, Mr. Ben.

[CORALEE *exits.* BEN *pours three glasses of punch.*]

Lavinia. Regina, when you don't frown you look like my Grandmama— [*As* BEN *brings her a glass of punch, and moves on to* REGINA.] —the one who taught me to read and write. And 'twas mighty unusual, a lady to know how to read and write, up in the piney woods.

Ben. [*Laughs.*] Now, that's a safer subject, Mama. Tell the Bagtrys about our kinfolk in the piney woods. [*He lifts his glass to* REGINA.] To you, honey.

Regina. [*Smiles.*] And to you, *honey.*

[*On the porch the music comes to an end.* REGINA *who has not, of course, been paying any attention, starts to applaud. She turns to* LAVINIA, *indicates* MARCUS *on porch.*]

Lavinia. But I didn't hear it. I wasn't paying any attention.

[MARCUS *comes into room.*]

Regina. [*Goes to him.*] It's brilliant of you, Papa.

Marcus. I'm glad you liked it. Come along. We're about to start— [*Laughs.*] —the better-known classics.

Ben. Won't you wait for our guests?

Marcus. Certainly not. I resent their thinking they can stroll in late on my music.

Regina. [*Placatingly.*] You're right, darling. *We'll* come out.

[MARCUS *goes to porch.* REGINA *follows.* BEN *follows her.* LAVINIA *puts down her glass, follows* BEN. REGINA *and* BEN *sit down,* LAVINIA *sits down. The musicians tune up.* MARCUS, PENNIMAN, *and* JUGGER *begin to play a divertimento by Leopold Mozart, a trio for violin, viola, and cello. Then the hall door opens and closes. On the porch,* REGINA *and* BEN *both turn, turn back again. After a second,* OSCAR *appears in the living room pulling* LAURETTE SINCEE. LAURETTE *is about twenty, pig-face cute, a little too fashionably dressed. She stands in the door, admiring the room.*]

Laurette. Squee!

Oscar. [*Proud and excited.*] Not bad, eh? [*Looks toward portico.*] We got to talk soft.

Laurette. This *is* nice. You born here, Oskie?

Oscar. No. Like I told you. Right after the war Papa bought— [*Giggles.*] —or something, this house from old man Reed. Like it?

Laurette. Squee. Who wouldn't?

Oscar. Well, maybe, some day——

Laurette. Ah, go on, Oskie. Go on.

Oscar. You just wait and see.

Laurette. [*Points to portico.*] What's that?

Oscar. What?

Laurette. The noise?

Oscar. That's music, honey.

Laurette. Oh.

Oscar. When you speak to Papa, tell him how much you like music. Tell him how fine he plays.

Laurette. What's he playing?

Oscar. The violin.

Laurette. Ain't that a coincidence? I had a beau who said he played the violin. A Frenchman, much older than me. Had to leave his very own country because of the revolution.

Oscar. [*Winces.*] I don't like to hear about him, Laurette, him or any other men. I am deeply and sincerely in love with you.

Laurette. [*Pleasantly, but without too much interest.*] Are you really, Oskie?

Oscar. Laurette, I'm going to ask Papa for a loan. Then we'll go on down to New Orleans. Would you, Laurette——

Laurette. You've asked me the same question for the last year, twenty times. But you never yet asked your Papa for the loan.

Oscar. I've been waiting for the right opportunity. I want you to be my *wife,* honey. I am deeply and——

Laurette. We can't eat on deeply and sincerely.

Oscar. No, I know. But this is the big night, don't you see? [*Laughs happily.*] I never thought he'd let you come here. I mean—I mean a chance like this. And he's in a good humor about something. Now, darling, be very very—well, er. I tell you: you speak with him about what *he* likes. Tell him how much you think of music, not new music, mind you, but—and tell him how you stay awake reading.

Laurette. I've always been a reader. But I can't talk about it. What's there to say?

Oscar. And he's fond of Mozart. Talk about Mozart.

Laurette. I can't do that.

Oscar. Well, just try to please him. So much depends on it. We could have our own little place in New Orleans——

Laurette. What kind of place?

Oscar. I'd find a job. You bet I would, and with you behind me to encourage and love me, with you to fight for, I'd forge ahead.

Laurette. [*Looks at him, puzzled.*] Oh. Well, I'd certainly like to go to New Orleans. I know a girl there. She has an embroidery shop on Royal Street. I'm good at embroidery. It's what I always wanted to do. Did I ever tell you that? Always wanted to do embroidery.

Oscar. Did you?

Laurette. Yep. Instead of whoring. I just wanted to do fancy embroidery.

Oscar. [*Loudly, in a hurt cry.*] Don't, Laurette, don't talk that way! [BEN *and* REGINA, *on the porch, look into room.* REGINA *coughs loudly.*] We better go out now.

Laurette. Why did your papa let me come tonight?

Oscar. Don't let him worry you, honey. Just take it nice and easy. Pretend nobody knows anything about you, pretend you're just as good as them——

Laurette. [*Stares at him.*] *Pretend?* Pretend I'm as good as anybody called Hubbard? Why, my Pa died at Vicksburg. He didn't stay home bleeding the whole state of Alabama with money tricks, and suspected of worse. You think I been worried for that reason?

Oscar. [*Desperately.*] No, no. I—— For God's sake don't talk like that——

Laurette. You may be the rich of this county, but everybody knows how. Why, the Frenchman, I used to eat dinner with, and his sister, the Countess. What you mean, boy, your folks—?

Oscar. I didn't mean anything bad. Haven't I just said I wanted to *marry* you? I think you're better than anybody.

Laurette. I'm not better than anybody, but I'm as good as piney wood crooks.

Oscar. [*Puts his hand over her mouth, looks toward porch.*] Stop, *please.* We've got to go outside. *Please*——

Laurette. [*Good-natured again.*] Sometimes you bring out the worst in my nature, Oskie, and make me talk foolish. Squee, it's the truth—I am a little twitchy about coming here and meeting your folks. That's why I'm talking so brave. I ain't been in a place like this before. [. . . *Pats him.*] All right, I'll be very good and nice. I would like to go to New Orleans.

[OSCAR *takes her in his arms. The front bell rings, but they don't hear it.*]

Oscar. Course you would, with me. You love me, honey? [*He leans down to kiss her.*] Tell me you love me.

Laurette. Now, Oskie, you know this ain't the place or the time for mush——

[BEN *rises at the sound of the bell. As* BEN *comes from the porch,* JAKE *brings in the* BAGTRYS. *As they enter,* OSCAR *is kissing* LAURETTE, *she is giggling, trying to push him away. The* BAGTRYS *stop in the doorway as they see the scene.* BEN *comes to meet them, crosses stage. As he passes* OSCAR *and* LAURETTE, *he shoves* OSCAR.]

Ben. Excuse me. [*As* LAURETTE *jumps away,* REGINA *comes in from porch, tapping* LAVINIA *on the arm as she comes.* BEN *speaks to* BIRDIE.] My apologies. We don't always arrange this scene for our guests.

[BIRDIE *smiles nervously.* JOHN *stares at* LAURETTE.]

Oscar. We were just, I was, we were——

Regina. [*Sharply.*] All right. [*Goes quickly to* BIRDIE.] I am happy to have you here, Miss Birdie.

[BIRDIE *curtsies, puts out her hand, smiles warmly.* LAVINIA *enters room.*]

John. [*Bows to* REGINA, BEN, OSCAR, *then speaks to* LAURETTE.] Hello, Laurette.

Laurette. Hello, John.

John. [*Turns to* BIRDIE.] Birdie, this is Miss Sincee.

Laurette. Finely, thank you.

[BIRDIE *bows.*]

Lavinia. [*Hears* LAURETTE *speak and so hurries to her.*] An honor to have you here, Miss Birdie——

Regina. [*Sharply.*] *This* is Miss Birdie, Mama.

Lavinia. [*Who is shaking hands with* LAURETTE, *looks bewildered.*] Oh. Sorry. I——

[OSCAR *bumps into* LAVINIA, *who is coming toward* BIRDIE.]

Birdie. I'm sorry we're late. I just couldn't seem to get dressed——

Regina. Do come out now for the music.

[*They move out together.* LAVINIA *speaks to* BIRDIE.]

Lavinia. Come, ma'am. And you, Miss—— [*Brightly, to* BIRDIE.] Is the other lady your sister?

Laurette. [*Annoyed, shoves* OSCAR.] What's the matter with you?

Oscar. Oh. Mama, this is Miss Laurette Sincee. She's a visitor in town.

Lavinia. Who's she visiting?

Ben. Us.

[BEN *reaches the porch door, stands aside to let* LAVINIA *pass him. She looks puzzled, passes on to porch.* LAURETTE, OSCAR, REGINA, JOHN, *are now seated on the porch.* LAVINIA *sits near them.* BIRDIE *and* BEN *stand for a minute listening to the music.*]

Birdie. Nice. To have a special night, just to play music—I've heard your father is a very cultured gentleman. Have you been able—did he, speak of the matter that I——

Ben. Yes. We will make the loan.

Birdie. [*Turns radiant—softly.*] Oh, what fine news! You can't imagine how worried I've been. I am very grateful to you, sir——

Ben. You don't have to be. It is a good loan for Hubbard Company, or my father wouldn't be taking it. We'll meet tomorrow, you and I, and work out the details.

Birdie. Oh, you won't have any trouble with me, Mr. Ben.

Ben. You wanted five thousand dollars, Miss Birdie. I have asked my father to lend you ten thousand.

Birdie. [*Puzzled—worried.*] Oh. Mr. Ben, I don't need——

Ben. [*Quickly.*] You can take five now, but if you should happen to need more, it will be there for you.

Birdie. But I won't need ten thousand dollars. No, indeed I won't. It's very kind of you, but——

Ben. [*Carefully.*] You will only get five. I will keep the rest waiting for you. That's the way these things are done— [*Smiles.*] —sometimes.

Birdie. But it's bad enough to owe five thousand, not less ten——

Ben. You will only owe five. Now don't worry about it. Will you take my advice now about something else? Don't speak to my father about the loan. It is all arranged. And he's a man of such culture, as you say, that talk of money would disturb him on his music night.

Birdie. [*Gently.*] Oh, of course. After all, it's a party, and as worried and pushing as I am, I wouldn't ever have talked business with him at a party.

Ben. [*Smiles down at her.*] Good breeding is very useful. Thank you, Miss Birdie.

Birdie. [*Gently.*] No, sir. It is I who must thank you.

[*He bows, stands aside, indicates porch. She moves to it, sits down.* BEN *stands in the doorway. The music continues. After a minute we see* OSCAR *trying to move into the room. He leans over, bends down, moves rapidly into room, passes* BEN. LAURETTE *turns and* OSCAR *beckons to her to come into room.*]

Oscar. Papa going to play all night? [*Crosses to get a drink.*] Laurette's getting restless, sitting there.

Ben. She's not accustomed to a sitting

position? Have another drink. I got a feeling you're going to need it.

Laurette. [*Enters the room from the porch.*] Squee. I don't like this punch. It don't mean anything.

Ben. Can I put in a little brandy? I think that would make it mean more.

[MARCUS *appears on the porch, comes up the aisle of chairs. He bows to* BIRDIE *and to* JOHN, *comes into room.* OSCAR *rushes to get him a drink of punch.*]

Oscar. Papa, this is Miss Sincee.

Marcus. [*Finishes drink, hands glass to* OSCAR.] How do you do?

Laurette. Finely, thank you. [MARCUS *stares at her. She becomes very nervous.*] I love music, Mr. Hubbard. I had an uncle who played. *He* taught me to love music.

Oscar. [*Too brightly.*] Did he play the violin, like Papa?

Laurette. Er. Er. No. He had a little drum.

Oscar. [*Very fast.*] He liked Mozart. You told me, remember?

Laurette. Yeah. Sure did.

[REGINA *and* BIRDIE, *followed by* JOHN *and* LAVINIA, *come in from the porch.*]

Marcus. Miss Sincee pleases me. Her uncle played Mozart on a little drum. Have you ever heard of that, Miss Bagtry?

Birdie. Oh. Well, *I* haven't, but I'm sure there must be such an arrangement.

Marcus. [*Looks at her with interest.*] That's very kind of you, to be so sure. Do you play any instrument, Miss Bagtry? Not the little drum?

Birdie. Yes, sir. Not well. The piano.

Marcus. Then you would oblige me— [*She smiles, moves toward the piano, quickly.*] —some other night, very soon.

Birdie. [*Very flustered.*] Yes. Yes, sir.

Oscar. It's a coincidence, ain't it, that Laurette's Papa liked Mozart?

Regina. [*To* LAURETTE.] I thought it was your uncle? Was your Papa the same as your uncle?

Laurette. What do you mean? Do you mean mon père was on one side of my family, and mon oncle on the other? I can understand *that.*

Ben. [*Fills her glass from the brandy decanter.*] Your family were French?

Laurette. No. I learned that from a French gentleman who came from France. I don't know where is is now. I liked him.

Ben. Perhaps we could locate him for you.

Laurette. No. He married money.

Regina. Oh, dear. All foreigners do, I guess. Light wines and light money.

Laurette. I never blamed him. I figured, well—— [*Looks at* REGINA.] You've had some bad experiences with Frenchmen?

[REGINA, BEN, *and* MARCUS *laugh.*]

Birdie. [*To* MARCUS—*making conversation.*] John's been to Europe, you know.

Marcus. I didn't know.

Birdie. Yes, he has. Just a few months before the war. Paris, France; London, England; St. Petersburg, Russia; Florence, Italy; Lake Como, Switzerland——

Marcus. Your geography is remarkable.

Birdie. Oh, I only know because John kept a book. Pictures and notes and menus —if the war hadn't come, and my Papa had lived, I would have gone to Europe. It was planned for me to study water color.

Marcus. Water color?

Birdie. Small water color. I like small water color.

Marcus. Is that very different from large water color?

Laurette. [*Belligerently.*] She means she likes small water color. What's the matter with that?

Birdie. [*Smiles at her.*] Yes. [*To* MARCUS.] You've been to Europe, Mr. Hubbard?

Marcus. [*Laughs.*] No, but I'm going. Might even settle down there. Yes, Regina?

Regina. [*Looks at* JOHN, *nervously.*] Maybe some day, Papa. Chicago first.

Marcus. Of course, we'll take our residence in Greece, but some place gayer, for Regina, at first. Perhaps you'd advise us, Captain Bagtry?

John. I'd like to, sir. But I have no memory of Europe.

Marcus. [*Turns elaborately in his chair.*] Something unpleasant took it from your mind?

John. No, sir. I just don't remember. It's as if I had never been there.

Lavinia. I used to have a good memory. [*Quickly.*] I still have. Most of the time.

Marcus. [*Very politely, to* JOHN.] Captain Bagtry, does anything stay in your memory, anything at all?

John. [*Looks at* MARCUS, *but the tone has been polite.*] The war.

Regina. [*Softly.*] Only the war?

Lavinia. [*To* JOHN, *motherly.*] Well, I just bet. That's natural: you rode off so young.

John. [*Turns to her.*] Yes, ma'am. I can't remember the years before, and the years after have just passed like a wasted day. But the morning I rode off, and for three years, three months, and eight days after—well, I guess I remember every soldier, every gun, every meal, even every dream I had at night——

[BEN *is pouring* LAURETTE *another drink.* OSCAR *is trying to keep her from having it. She pushes* OSCAR'S *hand.*]

Laurette. I wouldn't ever name a boy Oscar. It's silly.

Regina. Well?

[MARCUS *and* BEN *laugh. The others look embarrassed.* OSCAR *makes an angry move, decides not to speak.*]

Lavinia. I can't remember why we chose the name. Can you, Marcus?

Marcus. [*To* LAVINIA.] Your father's name was Oscar.

Lavinia. [*Worried, crushed.*] Oh, goodness, yes.

Birdie. [*Embarrassed, speaks quickly.*] John's just wonderful about the war, Mr. Hubbard. Just as good as having a history book. He was everywhere: Vicksburg, Chattanooga, Atlanta.

Marcus. And he remembers it *all?* What now seems to you the most important of your battles, Captain Bagtry?

John. [*Annoyed.*] I don't know. But there's no need for us to talk about the war, sir.

Marcus. Oh, I'm interested. I know more of the Greek wars than I do of our own.

Laurette. Bet you anything there's a good reason for that. There's a good reason for everything in this vale of tears.

[MARCUS *turns to stare at her.*]

Birdie. John, Mr. Hubbard says he's interested. Bet he'd like to hear about Vicksburg, just the way you always tell it to Mama and me.

[JAKE *appears at the door.*]

Jake. Supper's laid out, waiting.

Marcus. [*To* JOHN.] People remember what made them happy, and you were happy in the war, weren't you?

John. Yes, sir. I was happy. I thought we would win.

Marcus. I never did. Never, from the first foolish talk to the last foolish day. [JOHN *sharply turns away.*] I have disturbed you. I'm most sorry. I speak the truth—whenever I can.

Birdie. [*Hastily.*] Oh, John doesn't mind. He means—well, you see, it's hard for us to understand anybody who thought we'd lose——

John. [*Sharply.*] It's still hard for a soldier to understand.

Birdie. [*Quickly.*] John means once a soldier, always a soldier. He wants to go to Brazil right now. Of course you know, Mr. Hubbard, the radical people down there are trying to abolish slavery, and ruin the country. John wants to fight for his ideals.

Marcus. Why don't you choose the other side? Every man needs to win once in his life.

John. [*Angrily.*] I don't like that way of saying it. I don't necessarily fight for slavery, I fight for a way of life.

Marcus. Supper, Captain. [*Turns, calls to the porch.*] Put away the music, gentlemen, and have a little more to eat. [*Turns back to* REGINA.] What is disturbing you, Regina?

[LAVINIA, BIRDIE, OSCAR, *and* LAURETTE *exit to dining room.*]

Regina. [*Sharply.*] Nothing. [BEN *exits.*]

Marcus. [*Looks at* JOHN.] You disapprove of me, Captain?

John. I am in your house, sir, and you forced me into this kind of talk.

[PENNIMAN *and* JUGGER *come through the room, go into the dining room.*]

Marcus. Well, I disapprove of you. Your people deserved to lose their war and their world. It was a backward world, getting in the way of history. Appalling that you still don't realize it. Really, people should read more books.

Regina. [*Angrily.*] Papa, I didn't ask John here to listen to you lecture and be nasty and insulting.

Marcus. *You* asked him here? You asked *John?* [*Sharply.*] Come in to supper, Regina.

Regina. [*Very sharply.*] When I'm ready, Papa. [MARCUS *looks at her, hesitates for a second, then goes into dining room. There is a pause. She goes to* JOHN.] I am so sorry.

John. Why should you be sorry? It's the way you feel, too.

Regina. [*Impatiently.*] All that damn war nonsense—— Don't worry about Papa. I'll take care of him. You didn't give me a chance to tell you about Chicago——

John. You didn't give me a chance to tell you about Brazil.

Regina. Will you stop that foolish joke——

John. It may not be a joke. Birdie has a plan. She won't tell me about it. Anyway, she says there's going to be money to run Lionnet and enough for me to borrow a little. I'll go on down to Brazil right away. Cod Carter says there's no trick in getting a commission with good pay. The planters there are looking for Confederate officers.

I want to be with fighting men again. I'm lonely for them.

Regina. Now you stop frightening me. I'm going to Chicago, and a month later you're coming and we'll get married. When Papa finds out he'll have a fit. Then we'll come on home for a while, and I'll talk him out of his fit——

John. [*Gently, smiles.*] Now you're joking. Don't talk silly, honey.

Regina. [*Softly.*] You don't want to come with me? You don't want to marry me?

John. [*After a second.*] You don't ask that seriously.

Regina. [*Softly.*] Answer me, please.

John. No. I don't. I never said I did. [*Comes to her.*] I don't want to talk this way, but I don't want to lie, either. Honey, I like you so much, but—I shouldn't have let us get like this. You're not in love with me. I'm no good for you——

Regina. I am in love with you. I've never loved before, and I won't love again.

John. My darling child, everybody thinks that, the first time. You're a lonely girl and I'm the first man you've liked. You can have anybody you want——

Regina. John. Come away with me. We'll be alone. And after a while, if you still don't want me, then—— [*Softly.*] I've never pleaded for anything in my life before. I might hold it against you.

John. Oh, Regina, don't speak of pleading. You go away. By the time you come back, you'll be in love with somebody else, and I'll be gone.

Regina. [*Stares at him.*] Where did you say Miss Birdie was getting this money, this money for you to travel with?

John. I don't know where: she won't tell me. But she says we'll have five thousand dollars this week.

Regina. [*After a second.*] Five thousand?

John. [*Nods.*] I'd guess she's arranged something about the Gilbert Stuart or the West. We haven't anything but the portraits——

Regina. Is that what you'd guess? Well, I'd guess different. So she's planning to get you away from me?

John. Nobody's *planning* anything. Oh, look, honey. This isn't any good. We'll go home now——

Regina. [*Quickly, looking toward dining room.*] Papa's coming. Please go into supper now. It will be bad for me if you make any fuss or left now—— [*Softly.*] We'll talk tomorrow. I love you. Go in to supper.

[MARCUS *appears in the dining-room door.*]

John. [*Who has his back to the door.*] I'm sorry, honey, if——

[*He turns, moves across room, passes* MARCUS *in the doorway, disappears into the dining room.* MARCUS *stares at* REGINA; *she does not look at him.*]

Marcus. Who is sillier, who is more dead, the captain or his cousin? [*She doesn't answer him.*] You have a reason for not joining us at supper?

Regina. I wanted to talk to—to Captain Bagtry.

Marcus. Can he talk of anything but war?

Regina. Have you agreed to make Ben's loan on Lionnet?

Marcus. Ben's loan? Of course I'll make it. It is good for me, and bad for them. Got nothing to do with Ben.

Regina. No? Have you asked yourself why Ben wants it so much?

Marcus. I am not interested in Ben's motives. As long as they benefit me, he is welcome to them.

Regina. How much money did he say Miss Birdie had asked for?

Marcus. Ten thousand. [REGINA *smiles.*] Why does this interest you?

Regina. [*Rises.*] Don't make the loan, Papa. I don't like the girl. I think she's come here tonight to make fun of us. She's snubbing all of us, laughing up her sleeve. Why should you pay her to do it?

Marcus. [*Stares at her.*] That's not true and I don't think you think it is. You're lying to me about something. Stop it. It hurts me. Tell me why you were talking to that man, why he called you honey——

Regina. [*Carefully.*] Ben is sometimes smarter than you are, and you are so sure he isn't, that you get careless about him. [*Nods toward dining room.*] Bagtry doesn't know about *your* loan on Lionnet, but the girl told him she was getting five thousand dollars this week. *Five thousand dollars, not ten.* I'd like to bet the extra five is meant for Ben to keep. [*Carefully, as he stares at her.*] You're getting older, Papa, and maybe you're getting tired and don't think as fast. I guess that happens to everybody. You'll have to start watching Ben even more——

Marcus. [*Sharply.*] All right, Regina.

[PENNIMAN *and* JUGGER *come in from the dining room. They stand awkwardly, not knowing what to do.* REGINA *goes into dining room.*]

Penniman. [*Hesitates.*] Shall we—would you like us to continue the music?

Marcus. As soon as you have finished overeating.

[PENNIMAN *coughs, embarrassed.* JUGGER *starts forward angrily, then stops, follows* PENNIMAN *out to the porch.* LAVINIA *comes in from the dining room.*]

Lavinia. I think that Miss Laurette has a touch of heart trouble. I asked the poor child what she was doing for it. She said she was trying to see if good, strong drinks would help. I've never heard that, although Ben says it's a good cure. She's a nice little thing.

Marcus. You've always been a good judge of people, Lavinia, but that's true of all the pure in heart, isn't it?

[LAURETTE, *followed by* OSCAR, *comes into the room. She is steady, but the liquor has blinded her a little, and she bumps into things.* OSCAR *follows her, very nervous, staring at* MARCUS, *who does not turn around.*]

Lavinia. [*Speaks to* LAURETTE *only because she is nervous.*] Hello.

[LAURETTE *now finds herself near the piano. She strikes a note. Pleased, she presses her right hand on the keyboard. Delighted, she presses both hands.* OSCAR *jumps toward her.*]

Laurette. Hello . . . I never had opportunities . . . [OSCAR *grabs both her hands, she pulls them away, pounds again, grins, indicates* MARCUS.] Your Papa likes music, he says.

Marcus. [*To* OSCAR.] Is there any effective way of stopping that?

[LAURETTE *throws off* OSCAR, *comes over to* MARCUS.]

Laurette. Oskie says he wants to marry little old Laurette.

Marcus. Does little old Laurette think that fortunate?

Laurette. [*Laughs—puts her hand through his arm.*] Sometimes yes, sometimes no. We're going on down to New Orleans.

[BEN *and* BIRDIE *come in from the dining room.*]

Marcus. [*Takes* LAURETTE'S *hand from his arm*] This will sound very rude but I have a nervous dislike of being grabbed.

Laurette. Oh, sure. Me, too. Can't stand people pressing me unless I know about it, I mean. [*Glares at* OSCAR.] Don't you ever press me, Oskie, unless I know about it.

Marcus. That reminds me. I'm told you work for a living. That is good: Oscar is not a rich man.

Laurette. [*Laughs.*] Rich? How could he be, on that stinking slave salary you pay him? That's why you're sure to repent and help us, Oskie says. When you die you're going to leave it to him anyway, so why not now, Oskie says.

Marcus. [*Softly.*] Oscar is a liar. Always has been. [BIRDIE *moves toward porch.*] And he steals a little. Nothing much, not enough to be respectable. But you know all that, of course.

Lavinia. Oh, Marcus. [*Turns to* BIRDIE.] My husband makes little jokes. All the time——

Oscar. [*Very loudly, to* MARCUS.] It's not true. It's just not true——

Marcus. [*To* BIRDIE.] Miss Bagtry, don't you find that people always think you're joking when you speak the truth in a soft voice?

Birdie. [*Very embarrassed.*] No, sir. I——

Marcus. [*Back to* LAURETTE.] If you want him, Miss Laurette, do have him.

Oscar. [*With dignity.*] Come on, Laurette. I'll settle this later.

[MARCUS *laughs.*]

Laurette. Well, I'll just about say you will. A Papa talking about his son! No animal would talk about their own son that way. I heard tales about you ever since I was born, but——

Oscar. [*Frantic.*] Come on, Laurette.

Laurette. You old bastard.

[MARCUS *slowly rises.*]

Lavinia. [*To* LAURETTE.] Dear child——

Laurette. [*To* MARCUS.] Everybody in this county knows how you got rich, bringing in salt and making poor, dying people give up everything for it. Right in the middle of the war, men dying for you, and you making their kinfolk give you all their goods and money—and I heard how they suspected you of worse, and you only just got out of a hanging rope. [*Points to* OSCAR.] Why, the first night he slept with me, I didn't even want to speak to him because of you and your doings. My uncle used to tell me about——

Ben. Go on, Oscar. Get out.

[JOHN *and* REGINA *come in from dining room.*]

Marcus. [*To* OSCAR.] Take that girl out of here. Then come back. And come back quickly.

[OSCAR *stares at him, starts to speak, changes his mind. Then he hurries to* LAURETTE, *takes her arm, moves her out.* JOHN *crosses to* BIRDIE.]

Lavinia. [*In an odd tone.*] Why, Marcus.

The girl only told the truth. Salt is just a word, it's in the Bible quite a lot. And that other matter, why, death is also just a word. And——

Marcus. You grow daring, Lavinia. [*Moves toward her.*] Now stop that prattling or go to your room——

Ben. [*Moves in front of him.*] We have guests.

John. [*Takes* BIRDIE's *arm, comes forward.*] Good night and thank you, Mrs. Hubbard. [*Coldly, to others.*] Good night.

Marcus. You came to beg a favor, and you stayed to be amused. Good night.

Birdie. [*Scared.*] Mr. Hubbard, please . . .

John. Came to ask a favor? From you? Who in this county would be so dishonored? If you were not an old man, Mr. Hubbard, I——

Marcus. There is never so great a hero as the man who fought on a losing side.

Birdie. [*Goes to* JOHN—*desperate.*] Stop it, John. Go outside. Wait for me in the carriage.

John. I don't want you here. Come on, Birdie——

Birdie. [*Firmly.*] I want to stay for a few minutes. Please go outside. *Please. Please.*

[*He stares at her, then he turns, moves quickly out of the room.* MARCUS *is watching* REGINA. REGINA *looks at* MARCUS, *then turns and moves quickly after* JOHN. MARCUS *wheels around as if to stop* REGINA.]

Birdie. Mr. Hubbard, I am sorry. John is upset. You know that his twin brother was killed that night in the massacre, and any mention of it——

Marcus. [*Sharply.*] What night do you speak of, Miss Birdie, and what massacre?

Birdie. [*Desperately.*] Oh, I don't know. I—I'm just so sorry it has been unpleasant. I was hoping we could all be nice friends. Your family and mine——

Marcus. [*Smiles.*] Your mother hasn't bowed to me in the forty years I've lived in this town. Does she wish to be my nice friend now?

Birdie. [*Desperate.*] Mama is old-fashioned. I'll speak to her and after a bit—— [*Pauses, looks down.*] Oh. I've said the wrong thing again. I don't know how to—— [*Turns to him, simply.*] I guess I just better say it simple, the way it comes to me. I didn't only come tonight for the loan. I *wanted* to come. I was frightened, of course, but, well, it was a big holiday for me, and I tried to get all dressed up in Mama's old things, and that was why we were late because I haven't had a new dress, and I've never had a party dress since I was four years old, and I had to get the dress without Mama's knowing why or where we were going, and I had to sew——

Marcus. Then it *is* too bad you troubled yourself, because I have bad news for you: I have decided not to make the loan.

[BIRDIE *draws back, turns to* BEN, *starts to speak, puts her hands to her face.*]

Ben. [*Slowly.*] Why? Why? You said yourself——

Birdie. [*Moves toward him.*] Oh, please, Mr. Hubbard. Please. I went around all day telling our people they might be paid and—I'll give more, whatever you want——

Marcus. That is unjust of you. I am not bargaining.

Ben. [*Angrily, to* MARCUS.] I want to know why you have changed your mind.

Marcus. I will tell you, in time. [*Turns to* BIRDIE.] I am sorry to disappoint you. Please come another night, without a motive, just for the music.

Birdie. Yes, I had a motive. Why shouldn't I have? It was why I was asked here—— Oh, I mustn't talk proud. I have no right to. Look, Mr. Hubbard, I'll do anything. I'm sure you like good pictures: we have a Stuart and a West, and a little silver left. Couldn't I give—couldn't I bring them to you——

Marcus. [*Gently, hurt.*] Miss Birdie, Miss Birdie, please spare us both.

Birdie. [*Softly.*] I was going to use the first money to buy molasses and sugar. All that land and cotton and we're starving. It sounds crazy, to need even molasses——

Marcus. Everybody with cotton is starving.

Birdie. [*Angrily.*] That's just a way of using a word. That isn't what I mean. I mean starving. [*She looks up at him, her voice changes, sighs.*] I should have known I couldn't do anything right. I never have. I'm sorry to have told you such things about us. You lose your manners when you're poor. [*Goes to* LAVINIA.] Thank you, ma'am.

Lavinia. [*Smiles gently, takes her hand.*] Good night, child. You ride over and see me, or come down by the river and we'll read together.

Birdie. [*Smiles, crosses to* BEN.] Thank you, Mr. Ben. I know you acted as my good friend.

Marcus. [*Laughs.*] Good night.

[*She nods, runs out.*]

Lavinia. [*After a second.*] Goodness, Marcus. Couldn't you have—it's pig mean.

being poor. Takes away your dignity.

Marcus. That's correct, Lavinia. And a good reason for staying rich.

Penniman's Voice. We're waiting for you, Mr. Hubbard.

Marcus. [*Calling out.*] That will be all for tonight.

[REGINA *appears from the hall.*]

Regina. [*To* MARCUS.] I didn't intend you to insult them and make enemies of them.

Marcus. Why are you so disturbed about the Bagtrys? [BEN *laughs.*] You are amused?

Ben. Yes. I am amused.

Marcus. All right. Enjoy yourself—for a few minutes. [PENNIMAN *and* JUGGER *appear carrying their instruments.* MARCUS *turns to them.*] The Mozart was carelessly performed. The carriage is waiting to take you to the station. Good night.

Jugger. "Carelessly performed." What do you know about music? Nothing, and we're just here to pretend you do. Glad to make a little money once a month—— [*Angrily.*] I won't do it any more, do you hear me?

Marcus. Very well. Good night.

[JUGGER *moves quickly out.* PENNIMAN *comes forward, nervously.*]

Penniman. He didn't mean—Gil is tired —— Why, we're just as happy to come here —— [*No answer. Desperately.*] Well, see you next month, sir. Just as usual. Huh?

[*When* MARCUS *doesn't answer,* PENNIMAN *sighs, exits as* OSCAR *appears from porch.*]

Oscar. [*Rushes toward* BEN.] Trying to ruin my life, are you? Pouring liquor down her. Come on outside and fight it out like a man. I'll beat you up for it, the way you deserve——

Lavinia. [*As if she had come out of a doze.*] Oh, goodness! The blood of brothers. [*To* BEN.] You in trouble, Ben? [*Sees* OSCAR.] Oh, *you're* in trouble, Oscar.

Oscar. Come on——

Ben. Oh, shut up.

[MARCUS *laughs.*]

Oscar. [*Turns on* MARCUS, *angrily.*] You laugh. I told you he had his eye on Birdie and Lionnet, and me getting it for him. So I fool him by bringing Laurette here. And then *he* fools *you:* gets Laurette drunk, and you get mad. That's just what he wanted you to do. And you did it for him. I think the joke's kind of on you.

Regina. You must have told the truth once before in your life, Oscar, but I can't remember it.

Marcus. [*To* BEN.] You're full of tricks these days. Did you get the girl drunk?

Ben. Just as good for Oscar to marry a silly girl who owns cotton, as a silly girl who doesn't even own the mattress on which she——

[OSCAR *springs toward* BEN, *grabs his shoulder.*]

Marcus. [*To* OSCAR.] Will you stop running about and pulling at people? Go outside and shoot a passing nigger if your blood is throwing clots into your head.

Oscar. I'm going to kill Ben if he doesn't stop——

Marcus. Are you denying the girl makes use of a mattress, or do you expect to go through life killing every man who knows she does?

Oscar. [*Screaming.*] Papa, stop it! I am deeply and sincerely in love.

Marcus. In one minute I shall put you out of the room. [*Looks at* BEN.] So that was the way it was supposed to work? Or better than that: the girl was to borrow ten thousand from me and you were to keep five of it, and take your chances on her being a fool, and nobody finding out.

Ben. [*Slowly.*] I understand now. [*Softly to* REGINA.] Bagtry told *you.* Yes?

[REGINA *nods, smiles, sits down.*]

Marcus. Your tricks are getting nasty and they bore me. I don't like to be bored: I've told you that before.

Ben. [*Shrugs.*] I want something for myself. I shouldn't think you were the man to blame me for that.

Marcus. I wouldn't have, if you hadn't always been such a failure at getting it. [*Goes to* BEN.] I'm tired of your games, do you hear me? You're a clerk in my store and that you'll remain. You won't get the chance to try anything like this again. But in case you anger me once more, there won't be the job in the store, and you won't be here. Is that clear?

Ben. [*Slowly.*] Very clear.

Oscar. [*Who has been thinking.*] Papa, you couldn't condemn a woman for a past that was filled with loathing for what society forced upon her; a woman of inner purity made to lead a life of outward shame?

Marcus. What are you talking about?

Regina. He's read a book.

Marcus. [*Softly.*] At nine years old I was carrying water for two bits a week. I took the first dollar I ever had and went to the paying library to buy a card. When I was twelve I was working out in the fields, and that same year I taught myself Latin and French. At fourteen I was driving mules all day and most of the night, but that was the year I learned my Greek, read my classics, taught myself—— Think what I must have wanted for sons. And then think what I got. One unsuccessful trickster, one proud illiterate. No, I don't think Oscar's ever read a book.

Lavinia. He did, Marcus. I used to read my Bible to him.

Marcus. [*To* OSCAR.] If you want to go away with this girl, what's detaining you?

Oscar. [*Eagerly.*] Your permission, sir.

Marcus. Talk sense. Do you mean money?

Oscar. Just a loan. Then we'd ship on down to New Orleans——

Marcus. How much?

Oscar. Could invest in a little business Laurette knows about—— [REGINA *laughs loudly.*] Ten thousand could start me off fine, Papa——

Marcus. There will be a thousand dollars for you, in an envelope, on that table by six in the morning. Get on the early train. Send a Christmas card each year to an aging man who now wishes you to go upstairs.

Oscar. [*Starts to protest, changes his mind.*] Well, thank you. Seems kind of strange to be saying good-bye after twenty-five years——

Regina. [*Gaily.*] Oh, don't think of it that way. We'll be coming to see you some day. You'll have ten children, and five of the leaner ones may be yours.

Lavinia. Good-bye, son. I'm sorry if—— I'm sorry.

Oscar. I'll write you, Mama. [*To* BEN, *sharply.*] You've bullied me since the day I was born. But before I leave— [*Fiercely.*] —you're going to do what I tell you. You're going to be on the station platform tomorrow morning. You're going to be there to apologize to Laurette.

Marcus. Goodness, what a thousand dollars won't do!

Oscar. And if you're not ready on time— [*Takes a pistol from his pocket.*] —I'll get you out of bed with this. And then you won't apologize to her standing up, but on your knees——

Marcus. [*Violently, turning around.*] Put that gun away. How dare you, in this house——

Ben. [*Smiles.*] You've always been frightened of guns, Papa. Ever since that night, wasn't it?

Lavinia. That's true, ever since that night.

Marcus. [*Very angry.*] *Put that gun away. And get upstairs. Immediately.*

Oscar. [*To* BEN.] See you at the station.

[*He crosses room, exits.*]

Ben. [*After a second.*] No need to be so nervous. I could have taken the gun away from him.

Lavinia. And they had hot tar and clubs and ropes that night——

Marcus. *Stop your crazy talk, Lavinia.*

Lavinia. [*Softly.*] I don't like that word, Marcus. No, I don't. I think you use it just to hurt my feelings.

Ben. [*Smiles.*] He's upset, Mama. Old fears come back, strong.

Marcus. [*Slowly, to* BEN.] You're wearing me thin.

Regina. [*Yawns.*] Oh, don't you and Ben start again. [*She pats* BEN *on the arm.*] You know Papa always wins. But maybe you'll have your time some day. Try to get along, both of you. After Mama and I leave you'll be here alone together.

Marcus. I don't know, darling. I'm going to miss you. I think I may join you.

Regina. [*Turns, hesitantly.*] Join me? But——

Ben. That would spoil the plan.

Marcus. [*To* REGINA.] I'll let you and Lavinia go ahead. Then I'll come and get you and we'll take a turn in New York. And then Regina and I will go on to Europe and you'll come back here, Lavinia.

Lavinia. Oh, Marcus, you just can't have been listening to me. I been telling you since yesterday, and for years before *that*——

Marcus. [*Looks at* REGINA.] You want me to come, darling?

Regina. [*Nervously.*] Of course. When were you thinking of coming, Papa? Soon or——

Ben. [*To* REGINA—*laughs.*] I'm dying to see you get out of this one, honey.

Marcus. [*Angrily, to* BEN.] What are you talking about?

Ben. I'm going to be sorry to miss the sight of your face when Regina produces the secret bridegroom. [MARCUS *wheels to stare at* REGINA.] Oh, you know about it. You guessed tonight. Captain Bagtry. I don't think he wants to marry her. I don't think he even wants to sleep with her any more. But he's a weak man and—— [MARCUS *is advancing toward him.*] That won't do any good. I'm going to finish. Yesterday, if you remember, Regina wanted you to make the loan to the girl. Tonight, when she found out John Bagtry wanted to use a little of the money to leave here, and her, she talked you out of it.

Regina. *Ben, be still.* Ben—— [*Goes swiftly to* MARCUS.] Don't listen, Papa. I have seen John, I told you that. I like him, yes. But don't you see what Ben is doing? He wanted to marry me off to money, he's angry——

Ben. [*To* MARCUS.] I'm telling the truth. The whole town's known it for a year.

Lavinia. Don't, Benjamin, don't! Marcus, you look so bad——

Ben. You do look bad. Go up to him, Regina, put your arms around him. Tell him you've never really loved anybody else, and never will. Lie to him, just for tonight. Tell him you'll never get in bed with anybody ever again——

[MARCUS *slaps* BEN *sharply across the face.*]

Lavinia. [*Desperately.*] God help us! Marcus! Ben!

Ben. [*Softly.*] I won't forget that. As long as I live.

Marcus. Lock your door tonight, and be out of here before I am down in the morning. Wherever you decide to go, be sure it's far away. Get yourself a modest job, because wherever you are, I'll see to it that you never get any other.

Ben. I spent twenty years lying and cheating to help make you rich. I was trying to outwait you, Papa, but I guess I couldn't do it. [*He exits.*]

Lavinia. Twenty years, he said. Then it would be my fault, my sin, too—— [*She starts for hall door, calling.*] Benjamin! I want to talk to you, son. You're my first-born, going away——

[*She disappears. There is a long pause.* MARCUS *sits down.*]

Marcus. How could you let him touch you? When did it happen? How could you? —*Answer me.*

Regina. [*Wearily.*] Are they questions that can be answered?

Marcus. A dead man, a foolish man, an empty man from an idiot world. A man who wants nothing but war, any war, just a war. A man who believes in nothing, and never will. A man in space——

Regina. [*Softly—comes to him.*] All right, Papa. That's all true, and I know it. And I'm in love with him, and I want to marry him. [*He puts his hands over his face. She speaks coldly.*] Now don't take on so. It just won't do. You let me go away, as we planned. I'll get married. After a while we'll come home and we'll live right here——

Marcus. Are you crazy? Do you think I'd stay in this house with you and——

Regina. Otherwise, I'll go away. I say I will, and you know I will. I'm not frightened to go. But if I go that way I won't ever see you again. And you don't want that: I don't think you could stand that. My way, we can be together. You'll get used to it, and John won't worry us. There'll always be you and me—— [*Puts her hand on his shoulder.*] You must have known I'd marry some day, Papa. Why, I've never seen you cry before. It'll just be like going for a little visit, and before you know it I'll be home again, and it will all be over. You know? Maybe next year, or the year after, you and I'll make that trip to Greece, just the two of us. [*Smiles.*] Now it's all settled. Kiss me good night, darling.

[*She kisses him; he does not move. Then she moves toward door as* LAVINIA *comes in.*]

Lavinia. Ben won't let me talk to him. He'd feel better if he talked, if he spoke out—— I'm his Mama and I got to take my responsibility for what——

Regina. Mama, I think we'll be leaving for Chicago sooner than we thought. We'll start getting ready tomorrow morning. Good night. [*She exits.*]

Lavinia. [*Softly, after a minute.*] Did you forget to tell her that I can't go with her? Didn't you tell them all where I'm going? I think you better do that, Marcus——

Marcus. [*Softly—very tired.*] I don't feel well. Please stop jabbering, Lavinia.

Lavinia. You tell Regina tomorrow. You tell her how you promised me. [*Desperately.*] Marcus. It's all I've lived for. And it can't wait now. I'm getting old, and I've got to go and do my work.

Marcus. [*Wearily.*] It isn't easy to live with you, Lavinia. It really isn't. Leave me alone.

Lavinia. [*Gently.*] I know. We weren't ever meant to be together. You see, being here gives me—well, I won't use bad words, but it's always made me feel like I sinned. And God wants you to make good your sins before you die. That's why I got to go now.

Marcus. I've stood enough of that. Please don't ever speak of it again.

Lavinia. Ever speak of it? But you swore to me over and over again.

Marcus. Did you ever think I meant that nonsense?

Lavinia. But I'm going!

Marcus. You're never going. Dr. Seckles knows how strange you've been; the whole town knows you're crazy. Now I don't want to listen to any more of that talk ever. I try to leave you alone; try to leave me alone. If you worry me any more with it, I'll have to talk to the doctor and ask him to send you away. [*Softly—crying.*] Please go to bed now, and don't walk around all night again.

Lavinia. [*Stares at him.*] Coralee. . . . Coralee! He never ever meant me to go. He says I can't go. Coralee—— [*She starts to move slowly, then she begins to run.*] Coralee, are you in bed——

CURTAIN

ACT THREE

SCENE: *Same as Act One, early the next morning.*

[*At rise of curtain,* LAVINIA *is moving about in the living room.*]

Lavinia. [*Singing.*]

Got one life, got to hold it bold
Got one life, got to hold it bold
Lord, my year must come.

[*She comes on the porch. She is carrying a small Bible.*]

Got one life, got to hold it bold
Got one life, got to hold it bold
Lord, my year must come.

[BEN, *carrying a valise, comes from the living room.*]

Lavinia. All night I been waiting. You wouldn't let your Mama talk to you.

Ben. I put all my stuff in the ironing room. I'll send for it when I find a place.

Lavinia. [*Softly.*] Take me with you, son. As far as Altaloosa. There I'll get off, and there I'll stay. Benjamin, he couldn't bring me back, or send me, or do, or do. He couldn't, if you'd protect me for a while and——

Ben. I, protect you? [*Smiles.*] Didn't you hear him last night? Don't you know about me?

Lavinia. I don't know. I heard so much. I get mixed. I know you're bad off now. [*She reaches up as if to touch his face.*] You're my first-born, so it must be my fault some way.

Ben. Do you like me, Mama?

Lavinia. [*After a second.*] Well. You've grown away from—— I loved you, Benjamin.

Ben. [*Turns away.*] Once upon a time.

Lavinia. Take me with you. Take me where I can do my little good. The colored people are forgiving people. And they'll help me. You know, I should have gone after that night, but I stayed for you children. I didn't know then that none of you would ever need a Mama. Well, I'm going now. *I tell you I'm going.* [*Her voice rises.*] I spoke with God this night, in prayer. He said I should go no matter. Strait are the gates, He said. Narrow is the way, Lavinia, He said——

Ben. [*Sharply.*] Mama! You're talking loud. [*Turns to her.*] Go to bed now. You've had no sleep. I'm late.

[*Starts to move.*]

Lavinia. Take me, Benjamin!

Ben. [*Sharply.*] Now go in to Coralee before you get yourself in bad shape and trouble.

Lavinia. You've got to take me. Last night he said he'd never ever meant me to go. Last night he said if ever, then he'd have Dr. Seckles, have him, have him—— [*Turns, her fist clenched.*] Take me away from here. For ten years he swore, for ten years he swore a lie to me. I told God about that last night, and God's message said, "Go, Lavinia, even if you have to tell the awful truth. If there is no other way, tell the truth."

Ben. [*Turns slightly.*] The truth about what?

Lavinia. I think, now, I should have told the truth that night. But you don't always know how to do things when they're happening. It's not easy to send your own husband into a hanging rope.

Ben. What do you mean?

Lavinia. All night long I been thinking I should go right up those steps and tell him what I know. Then he'd have to let me leave or—— [*Puts her hands to her face.*] I've always been afraid of him, because once or twice——

Ben. Of course. But you're not afraid of me.

Lavinia. Oh, I been afraid of you, too. I spent a life afraid. And you know that's funny, Benjamin, because way down deep I'm a woman wasn't made to be afraid. What are most people afraid of? Well, like your Papa, they're afraid to die. But I'm not afraid to die because my colored friends going to be right there to pray me in.

Ben. [*Carefully.*] Mama, what were you talking about? Telling the truth, a hanging rope——

Lavinia. And if you're not afraid of dying

then you're not afraid of anything. [*Sniffs the air.*] The river's rising. I can tell by the azalea smell——

Ben. [*Tensely, angrily.*] For God's sake, Mama, try to remember what you were saying, if you were saying anything.

Lavinia. I was saying a lot. I could walk up those steps and tell him I could still send him into a hanging rope unless he lets me go: I could say I saw him that night, and I'll just go and tell everybody I did see him——

Ben. What night?

Lavinia. The night of the massacre, of course.

Ben. [*Tensely, sharply.*] Where did you see him, how——

Lavinia. You being sharp with me now. And I never been sharp with you. Never——

Ben. [*Carefully.*] Mama. Now listen to me. It's late and there isn't much time. I'm in trouble, bad trouble, and you're in bad trouble. Tell me fast what you're talking about. Maybe I can get us both out of trouble. Maybe. But only if you tell me now. *Now.* And tell me quick and straight. You can go away and I——

Lavinia. [*Rises.*] I saw him, like I told you, the night of the massacre, on the well-house roof.

Ben. All right. I understand what you mean. All right. But there's a lot I don't know or understand.

Lavinia. [*As if she hadn't heard him.*] One time last night, I thought of getting his envelope of money, bringing it out here, tearing it up, and watching his face when he saw it at breakfast time. But it's not nice to see people grovel on the ground for money——

Ben. The envelope of money? The little envelope of money or the big envelope?

Lavinia. I could get it, tear it up.

Ben. [*Carefully.*] Why not? Get it now and just tear it up.

Lavinia. And I thought too about giving it to the poor. But it's evil money and not worthy of the poor.

Ben. No, the poor don't want evil money. That's not the way.

Lavinia. [*Turns to him.*] Oh, I am glad to hear you say that, but you can see how I have been tempted when I thought what the money could do for my little school. I want my colored children to have many things.

Ben. [*Desperately.*] You can have everything for them if——

Lavinia. Oh, nobody should have everything. All I want is a nice school place, warm in winter, and a piano, and books and a good meal every day, hot and fattening.

Ben. [*Comes to her, stands in front of her.*] Get up, Mama. Come here. He'll be awake soon. [LAVINIA *rises, he takes her by the arms.*] Papa will be awake soon.

Lavinia. [*Looks at him, nods.*] First part of the war I was so ill I thought it was brave of your Papa to run the blockade, even though I knew he was dealing with the enemy to do it. People were dying for salt and I thought it was good to bring it to them. I didn't know he was getting eight dollars a bag for it, Benjamin, a little bag. Imagine taking money for other people's misery.

Ben. [*Softly.*] Yes, I know all that, Mama. Everybody does now.

Lavinia. [*Puzzled.*] But I can't tell what you know, Benjamin. You were away in New Orleans in school and it's hard for me to put in place what you know and—— [BEN *moves impatiently.*] So—well, there was the camp where our boys were being mobilized. It was up the river, across the swamp fork, back behind the old delta fields.

Ben. Yes, I know where it was. And I know that Union troops crossed the river and killed the twenty-seven boys who were training there. And I know that Papa was on one of his salt-running trips that day and that every man in the county figured Union troops couldn't have found the camp unless they were led through to it, and I know they figured Papa was the man who did the leading.

Lavinia. He didn't lead them to the camp. Not on purpose. No, Benjamin, I am sure of that.

Ben. I agree with you. It wouldn't have paid him enough, and he doesn't like danger. So he didn't do it. And he proved to them he wasn't here so he couldn't have done it. [*Turns to her.*] So now where are we?

Lavinia. They were murder mad the night they found the poor dead boys. They came with hot tar and guns to find your Papa.

Ben. [*Softly.*] But they didn't find him.

Lavinia. But I found him. [*She opens the Bible, holds it up, peers at it.* BEN *comes toward her.*] At four-thirty o'clock Coralee and I saw him and heard him, on the well-house roof. We knew he kept money and papers there, and so we guessed right away where to look, and there he was.

Ben. [*Looks at her, smiles, softly.*] And there he was.

Lavinia. So you see I hadn't told a lie, Benjamin. He wasn't ever in the *house.*

But maybe half a lie is worse than a real lie.

Ben. [*Quickly.*] Yes, yes. Now how did he get away, and how did he prove to them——

Lavinia. Coralee and I sat on the wet ground, watching him. Oh, it was a terrible thing for me. It was a wet night and Coralee caught cold. I had to nurse her for days afterward, with——

Ben. [*Looks up at balcony.*] Mama! It's got to be quick now. Shall I tell you why? I've got to go unless—— Now tell me how did he get away, and how did he prove to them that all the time he had been down Mobile road?

Lavinia. [*Opens her Bible.*] Twenty minutes to six he climbed down from the roof, unlocked the well-house door, got some money from the envelope, and went on down through the back pines. Coralee and I ran back to the house, shivering and frightened. I didn't know what was going to happen, so we locked all the doors and all the windows and Coralee coughed, and sneezed, and ran a fever.

Ben. [*Angrily.*] I don't give a damn about Coralee's health.

Lavinia. [*Gently.*] That's the trouble with you, Benjamin. You don't ever care about other folks.

[*There is the sound of a door closing inside the house.*]

Ben. [*Quietly.*] *There is not much time left now. Try, Mama, try hard.* Tell me how he managed.

Lavinia. [*Looks down at the Bible.*] Well, three days later, no, two days later, the morning of April 5, 1864, at exactly ten-five——

Ben. [*Sharply.*] What are you reading?

Lavinia. He rode back into town, coming up Mobile road. They were waiting for him and they roped him and searched him. But he had two passes proving he had ridden through Confederate lines the day before the massacre, and didn't leave till after it. The passes were signed by— [*Looks at Bible.*] —Captain Virgil E. McMullen of the 5th Tennessee from Memphis. They were stamped passes, they were good passes, and they had to let him go. But he had no money when he came home. So Coralee and I just knew he paid Captain Virgil E. McMullen to write those passes. [*Looks down at book.*] Virgil E. McMullen, Captain in the 5th Tennessee——

Ben. [*Tensely—points to Bible.*] It's written down there?

Lavinia. Coralee and I were half wild with what was the right thing to do and the wrong. So we wrote it all down here in my Bible and we each put our hand on the Book and swore to it. That made us feel better——

Ben. I'm sure of it. Give me the Bible, Mama——

Lavinia. I think there's one in your room, at least there used to be——

Ben. Oh, Mama. For God's sake. I need it. It's the only proof we've got, and even then he'll——

Lavinia. You don't need half this proof. That's the trouble with your kind of thinking, Benjamin. My, I could just walk down the street, tell the story to the first people I met. They'd believe me, and they'd believe Coralee. We're religious women and everybody knows it. [*Smiles.*] And then they'd want to believe us; nothing would give them so much pleasure as, as, as, well, calling on your Papa. I think people always believe what they want to believe, don't you? I don't think I'd have any trouble, if you stood behind me, and gave me courage to do the right talking.

Ben. [*Laughs.*] I'll be behind you. But I'd like the Bible behind me. Come, Mama, give it to me now. I need it for us. [*Slowly she hands the Bible to him.*] All right. Now I'd like to have that envelope.

Lavinia. But what has the money got to do with—I don't understand why the envelope—I'm trying hard to understand everything, but I can't see what it has——

Ben. I can't either. So let's put it this way: it would make me feel better to have it. There's nothing makes you feel better at this hour of the morning than an envelope of money.

Lavinia. [*Thinks.*] Oh. Well. [*Points into the living room.*] It's in the small upper left-hand drawer of your Papa's desk. But I don't know where he keeps the key.

Ben. [*Laughs.*] That's very negligent of you. We won't need the key. [*Takes her hand, takes her under balcony.*] Now call Papa. I'll be back in a minute.

Lavinia. Oh, I couldn't do that. I never have——

Ben. [*Softly.*] You're going to do a lot of things you've never done before. Now I want you to do what I tell you, and trust me from now on, will you?

Lavinia. I'm going to do what you tell me.

Ben. [*Goes into living room.*] All right. Now go ahead.

[JAKE *appears. He is carrying a mop and a pail.*]

Jake. You all up specially early; or me, am I late?

Lavinia. [*Calling.*] Marcus. Marcus. [*To* JAKE.] What do you think of that, Jake?

Jake. [*Takes a nervous step toward her —softly.*] I don't think well of it. Please, Miss Viney, don't be doing——

Lavinia. Marcus! Marcus! I want—we want to speak to you. [*To* JAKE.] Hear what I did? [*Nervously.*] Everything's different—Marcus!

[MARCUS *appears on the porch. He has been dressing; he is now in shirt-sleeves. He peers down at* LAVINIA.]

Marcus. Are you shouting at me? What's the matter with you now, Lavinia?

Lavinia. Well, I just——

Marcus. You are up early to give your blessings to your departing sons?

Lavinia. I haven't seen Oscar.

Marcus. Benjamin has gone?

Lavinia. [*Looks into drawing room.*] No, Marcus. He hasn't gone. He's inside knocking off the locks on your desk. My, he's doing it with a pistol. The other end of the pistol, I mean.

[*During her speech, we hear three rapid, powerful blows.* MARCUS *grips the rail of the porch.* BEN *comes onto the porch, the pistol in one hand, a large envelope in the other. He looks up at* MARCUS. *There is a long pause.*]

Marcus. Put the gun on the table. Bring me that envelope.

Lavinia. Same old envelope. Like I said, I used to dream about tearing up that money. You could do it, Benjamin, right now. Make you feel better and cleaner, too.

Ben. I feel fine. [*To* MARCUS.] I like you better up there. So stay there. *Stay there.* [BEN *turns to* JAKE, *takes another envelope from his pocket, puts in money from first envelope.*] Take this over to Lionnet. Ask for Miss Birdie Bagtry and talk to nobody else. Give her this and ask her to forget about last night.

Marcus. Take that envelope from him, Lavinia, and bring it to me quickly.

Lavinia. I can't walk as fast as I used to, Marcus, I'm getting old——

Ben. [*To* JAKE.] Tell Miss Birdie I'll call on her in the next few days and we'll attend to the details then. Go on, be quick——

Marcus. [*To* JAKE.] Come back here! [*To* BEN.] How dare you touch——

Ben. Well, come and get it from me. [*Turns again to* JAKE.] And tell her I wish Captain Bagtry good luck. And stop at the wharf and buy two tickets on the sugar boat.

Lavinia. Thank you, son. [*There is a long pause. She is puzzled by it.*] Well. Why doesn't somebody say something?

Ben. We're thinking.

Marcus. Yes. Shall I tell you what I'm thinking? That I'm going to be sorry for the scandal of a son in jail.

Ben. What would you put me in jail for?

Marcus. For stealing forty thousand dollars.

Ben. [*Looking at the envelope, smiles.*] That much? I haven't had time to count it. I always said there wasn't a Southerner, born before the war, who ever had sense enough to trust a bank. Now do you want to know what *I'm* thinking?

Marcus. Yes, I'm puzzled. This piece of insanity isn't like you. In the years to come, when I do think about you, I would like to know why you walked yourself into a jail cell.

Ben. In the years to come, when you think about me, do it this way. [*Sharply.*] You had been buying salt from the Union garrison across the river. On the morning of April 2nd you rode over to get it. Early evening of April 3rd you started back with it——

Marcus. Are you writing a book about me? I would not have chosen you as my recorder.

Ben. You were followed back—which is exactly what Union officers had been waiting for—at eleven o'clock that night——

Lavinia. Marcus didn't *mean* to lead them back. I explained that to you, Benjamin——

Marcus. [*Sharply.*] *You* explained it to him? What——

Ben. Eleven o'clock that night twenty-seven boys in the swamp camp were killed. The news reached here, and you, about an hour later.

Lavinia. More than that. About two hours later. Or maybe more, Benjamin.

Marcus. What the hell is this? Lavinia, I want——

Ben. And the town, guessing right, and hating you anyway, began to look for you. They didn't find you. Because you were on the well-house roof.

Lavinia. Yes you were, Marcus, that's just where you were. I saw you.

Marcus. [*Softly.*] I don't know why I'm standing here listening to this foolishness, and I won't be for long. Bring me the envelope, and you will still have plenty of time to catch the train. You come up here, Lavinia——

Ben. I'll tell you why you're standing there: you are very, very, very—as Mama would say—afraid.

Marcus. [*Carefully.*] What should I be afraid of, Benjamin? [*Sharply.*] A bungler who leaves broken locks on a desk to prove he's stolen, and gives away money to make sure I have further proof? Or a crazy woman, who dreams she saw something sixteen years ago?

Lavinia. Marcus, I must ask you to stop using that awful word and——

Marcus. And I must ask you to get used to it because within an hour you'll be where they use no other word—

Ben. [*As* LAVINIA *makes frightened motion.*] Mama, stop it. [*To* MARCUS.] And you stop interrupting me. Mama saw you on the well-house roof. Coralee saw you. They saw you take money from an envelope——

Lavinia. The same one. My, it wore well, didn't it?

Ben. To buy the passes that saved you from a hanging. You bought them from——

Marcus. [*Tensely.*] Get out of here. I——

Ben. From a Captain Virgil E. McMullen. Now I'd figure it this way: by the grace of Captain McMullen you got sixteen free years. So if they swing you tonight, tell yourself sixteen years is a long time, and lynching is as good a way to die as any other.

Lavinia. Benjamin, don't talk like that, don't, son——

Marcus. [*In a different voice.*] Walk yourself down to the sheriff's office now. I'll catch up with you. If you're fool enough to believe some invention of your mother's, understand that nobody else will believe it. The whole town knows your mother's been crazy for years, and Dr. Seckles will testify to it——

Ben. Let's put it this way: they think Mama is an eccentric, and that you made her that way. And they know Seckles is a drunken crook. They know Mama is a good woman, they respect her. They'll take her word because, as she told me a little while ago, people believe what they want to believe.

Marcus. [*Carefully.*] Lavinia, you're a religious woman, and religious people don't lie, of course. But I know you are subject to dreams. Now, I wonder why and when you had this one. Remember, will you, that you were ill right after the incident of which you speak so incorrectly, and remember please that we took you— [*Sharply, to* BEN.] —not to that drunken Seckles, but to Dr. Hammanond in Mobile. He told me then that you were—— [LAVINIA *draws back.*] And he is still living to remember it, if you can't.

Lavinia. [*Worried, rattled.*] I was ill after that night. Who wouldn't have been? It had nothing to do with, with my nerves. It was taking part in sin, your sin, that upset me, and not knowing the right and wrong of what to do——

Marcus. She didn't tell you about that illness, did she? You think they'd believe her against Hammanond's word that she was a very sick woman at the time she speaks about? [*Very sharply.*] Now stop this damned nonsense and get out of here or——

Ben. Go change your dress, Mama. Get ready for a walk.

Lavinia. But you told Jake—you said I could go on the sugar boat.

Ben. You can still catch the boat. We won't be walking long. And if you have to stay over a few hours more, I figure you can wear the same costume to a lynching as you can on a boat. We'll walk around to old Isham first, whose youngest son got killed that night. John Bagtry will be mighty happy to remember that his twin brother also died that night. And Mrs. Mercer's oldest son and the two Sylvan boys and—— We won't have to go any further because they'll be glad to fetch their kinfolk and, on their way, all the people who got nothing else to do tonight, or all the people who owe you on cotton or cane or land. Be the biggest, happiest lynching in the history of Roseville County. All right. Go change your clothes——

Marcus. [*Softly, carefully.*] Lavinia. I——

Lavinia. A lynching? *I don't believe in lynching.* If you lynch a white man, it can lead right into lynching a black man. No human being's got a right to take a life, in the sight of God.

Marcus. [*To* BEN.] You're losing your witness. What a clown you turned out to be. Only you would think your mother would go through with this, only you would trust her——

Ben. [*Sharply.*] She won't have to do much. I'm taking her Bible along. [*Opens the book.*] On this page, that night, she wrote it all down. The names, the dates, the hours. Then she and Coralee swore to it. Everybody will like the picture of the two lost innocents and a Bible, and if they don't, sixteen-year-old ink will be much nicer proof than your Mobile doctor. [*Softly.*] Anyway, you won't have time to get him here. Want to finish now?

Lavinia. [*Who has been thinking.*] I never told you I was going to have anything to do with a lynching. No, I didn't.

Marcus. Of course you wouldn't. Of course you wouldn't. Not of your husband——

Lavinia. Not of my husband, not of anybody.

Ben. Mama, go upstairs and let me finish this——

Lavinia. I only said I was going to tell the truth to everybody. And that I'm going to do. [*To* MARCUS.] If there's any nasty talk of lynching, I'm going to plead for your life hard as I can, yes I am.

Ben. [*Laughs.*] Now, that's merciful of you. I'm going to do the same thing. I'm going to plead with them for Papa's life.

Lavinia. That's the least a son can do for his father.

Ben. [*To* MARCUS.] Better than that. I'll come tomorrow morning and cut you down from the tree, and bury you with respect. How did the Greeks bury fathers who were murdered? Tell me, and I'll see to it. You'd like that, wouldn't you?

Lavinia. Benjamin, don't talk that way——

Marcus. You gave him the right to talk that way. You did, Lavinia, and I don't understand anything that's been happening. Do you mean that you actually wrote a lie in your Bible, you who——

Lavinia. [*Very angry.*] Don't you talk like that. Nobody can say there's a lie in my Bible—— You take that back. You take it back right away. I don't tell lies, and then I don't swear to them, and I don't swear on my Bible to a false thing and neither does Coralee. You just apologize to me and then you apologize to Coralee, that's what you do——

Marcus. [*Quickly.*] No, no. I don't mean you knew it was a lie. Of course not, Lavinia. But let me see it, and then tell me——

Lavinia. [*Puts out her hand.*] Let him see it. Of course.

Ben. Tell him to come down and look at it. I'll put it here, under the gun.

Lavinia. Bibles are there for all people. For grown people. I'm not going to have any Bibles in my school. That surprise you all? It's the only book in the world but it's just for grown people, after you know it don't mean what it says. You take Abraham: he sends in his wife, Sarah, to Pharaoh, and he lets Pharaoh think Sarah is his sister. And then Pharaoh, he, he, he— Well, he does, with Sarah. And afterward Abraham gets mad at Pharaoh because of Sarah, even though he's played that trick on Pharaoh. Now if you didn't understand, a little child could get mighty mixed up——

Marcus. [*Gently.*] You want to go to your school, don't you, Lavinia?

Lavinia. Or about Jesus. The poor are always with you. Why, I wouldn't have colored people believe a thing like that: that's what's the matter now. You have to be full grown before you know what Jesus meant. Otherwise you could make it seem like people ought to be poor.

Ben. All right. Go upstairs now and start packing. You're going to be on the sugar boat.

Lavinia. Am I? Isn't that wonderful——

Marcus. Lavinia. [*She turns toward him.*] It would be wrong of me to say ours had been a good marriage. But a marriage it was. And you took vows in church, sacred vows. If you sent me to trouble, you would be breaking your sacred vows——

Ben. Oh, shut up, Papa.

Lavinia. I don't want trouble, for anybody. I've only wanted to go away——

Marcus. [*Slowly, as he comes down from balcony.*] I was wrong in keeping you.

Ben. [*Laughs.*] Yes. That's true.

Marcus. It was wrong, I can see it now, to have denied you your great mission. I should have let you go, helped you build you a little schoolhouse in Altaloosa.

Ben. I built it about ten minutes ago.

Lavinia. What? Oh, about the marriage vows, Marcus. I had a message last night, and it said it was right for me to go now and do my work. Once I get a message, you know.

Marcus. Yes. Yes, you'll want a lot of things for your colored pupils. A schoolhouse isn't enough—you'll need books and——

Lavinia. That's absolutely true. And I want to send for a teacher—— I'm getting old and I'm ignorant—— I want to make a higher learning.

Marcus. Lavinia. I'll get them for you.

Lavinia. Thank you. But of course, it isn't just getting them; I've got to keep up the schoolhouse every year——

Marcus. Certainly. Did your, did your messages suggest any definite figure?

Lavinia. Why, yes, they did.

Marcus. How much was suggested?

Lavinia. To tell you the truth, my message said a thousand dollars a year would make my colored children happy. But I think ten thousand a year would make them happier. Altaloosa's a mighty poor little village and everybody needs help there——

Marcus. Ten thousand wouldn't be enough. I think——

Lavinia. [*Firmly.*] It would be enough. I'd make it enough. Then, of course, I been forgetting about Coralee coming with me. And Coralee supports a mighty lot of kinfolk right here in town. She got a crippled little cousin; her old Mama can't take washing any more——

Marcus. Oh, that's too bad. What could I do for them?

Lavinia. Maybe two hundred dollars a month would take Coralee's mind from worrying.

Marcus. I should think so. They'll be the richest family in the South. But, of course, your friends should have the best.

Lavinia. You're being mighty nice to me, Marcus. I wish it had always been that way.

Marcus. [*Quickly.*] It started out that way, remember? I suppose little things happened, as they do with so many people——

Lavinia. No, I don't really think it started out well. No, I can't say I do.

Marcus. Oh, come now. You're forgetting. All kinds of pleasant things. Remember in the little house? The piano? I saved and bought it for you and——

Lavinia. Bought it for me? No, I don't remember it that way. I always thought you bought it for yourself.

Marcus. But perhaps you never understood why I did anything; perhaps you were a little unforgiving with me.

Ben. [*To* MARCUS.] Aren't you getting ashamed of yourself?

Marcus. For what? For trying to recall to Lavinia's mind that we were married with sacred vows, that together we had children, that she swore in a church to love, to honor——

Ben. If I wasn't in a hurry, I'd be very amused.

Lavinia. [*Thoughtfully.*] I did swear. That's true, I——

Ben. [*Quickly.*] Mama, please go upstairs. Please let me finish here. You won't get on the boat any other way——

Marcus. Indeed you will, Lavinia. And there's no need to take the boat. I'll drive you up. We can stay overnight in Mobile, look at the churches, have a nice dinner, continue on in the morning——

Lavinia. How did you guess? I always dreamed of returning that way. Driving in, nice and slow, seeing everybody on the road, saying hello to people I knew as a little girl, stopping at the river church—church . . . [*To herself.*] Every Sunday here I always saved and put a dollar in the collection box. They're going to miss the dollar. You all know, in my vanity, what I'd like to have when I'm gone to Altaloosa?

Marcus. What, Lavinia? I am most anxious to know.

Lavinia. A mahogany pew, with my name on it, in brass.

Marcus. Brass! It shall be writ in gold——

Lavinia. I don't like gold. Brass. Now, what else did I think about last night?

Marcus. We'll be in constant communication. And if you have more practical messages from God we can take care of them later. Now bring me the envelope and the Bible, and we'll start immediately——

[*She puts her hand on the Bible, as if to pick it up.*]

Ben. [*Quickly takes her hand.*] Do I really have to explain it to you? Do I really have to tell you that unless you go through with it, he's got to take you to the hospital? You don't really think that he's going to leave you free in Altaloosa with what you know, to tell anybody—— Why do you think he took you to Dr. Hammanond in the first place? Because he thought you might have seen him, and because it wouldn't hurt to have a doctor say that you were——

Marcus. [*Very sharply.*] That's a lie.

Ben. Maybe it is. But then you're only sorry you didn't think of it that way.

Marcus. Lavinia——

Lavinia. [*Softly.*] I don't ever want to hear such things again; or one person do or say, to another——

Marcus. Lavinia, you'll get what you want. You know I am not a stingy man or one who——

Ben. You'll get nothing. For the very simple reason that he isn't going to have a nickel to buy it with.

Lavinia. [*Wearily.*] Oh. That isn't what worries me—— It's that Marcus may have been saying things he didn't mean. [*Softly.*] Would you really have told me you would drive me to Mobile and then you would have taken me——

Marcus. *Of course not.* If you listen to

that scoundrel—— You're my wife, aren't you? I also took vows. I also stood up and swore. Would I break a solemn vow——

Lavinia. [*Appalled.*] Oh, now, I don't believe what you're saying. One lie, two lies, that's for all of us: but to pile lie upon lie and sin upon sin, and in the sight of God——

Ben. [*Sharply.*] Write it to him, Mama. Or you'll miss your boat.

Lavinia. Oh, yes. Oh, I wouldn't want to do that.

[*She picks up the Bible, exits.*]

Marcus. You're a very ugly man.

Ben. Are you ready now?

Marcus. For what?

Ben. To write a piece of paper, saying you sell me the store for a dollar.

Marcus. [*Pauses.*] All right. Bring me that envelope. I'll sell you the store for a dollar. Now I have had enough and that will be all.

Ben. You'll write another little slip of paper telling Shannon in Mobile to turn over to me immediately all stocks and bonds, your safe-deposit box, all liens, all mortgages, *all* assets of Marcus Hubbard, Incorporated.

Marcus. I will certainly do no such thing. I will leave you your proper share of things in my will, or perhaps increase it, if you behave——

Ben. [*Angrily.*] You're making fun of me again. A will? That you could change tomorrow? You've made fun of me for enough years. It's dangerous now. One more joke. So stop it now. Stop it.

Marcus. All right. But I would like to give you a little advice—you're so new at this kind of thing. If you get greedy and take everything there's bound to be a lot of suspicion. And you shouldn't want that. Take the store, take half of everything else, half of what's in the envelope. Give me the rest. I'll go on living as I always have, and tell everybody that because you're my oldest son, I wanted you to have——

Ben. You'll tell nobody anything, because you can't, and you'll stop bargaining. You're giving me everything you've got. Is that clear? If I don't have to waste any more time with you, I'll give you enough to live on, here or wherever you want to go. But if I have to talk to you any longer, you won't get that. I mean what I'm saying, and you know I do. And it's the last time I'll say it. [*There is no answer. He smiles.*] All right. Now start writing things down. When you finish, bring them to me. You're waiting for something?

Marcus. [*Softly, as he goes up the porch steps.*] To tell you the truth, I am trying to think of some way out.

Ben. If I told you that it's been a large temptation to see you—to do it the other way, you will believe me, I know; remember the past and don't waste your time, or put yourself in further danger, or tempt me longer. Ever since you started your peculiar way of treating me, many years ago, I have had many ugly dreams. But this is better than I ever dreamed—— Go in and start writing now. I consider you a lucky man: you'll die in bed.

Marcus. You will give me enough for a clean bed?

Ben. Yes, of course.

Marcus. Well, I daresay one could make some small bargains with you still. But I don't like small bargains. You win or you lose——

Ben. And I don't like small talk. [MARCUS *turns, goes into his room.* BEN *waits for a second, then crosses to kitchen door. Calls in.*] Breakfast here, please. [*As* JAKE *comes from street side of porch.*] Yes? Did you find Miss Birdie?

Jake. Yes, sir. She was mighty happy and said to thank you.

Ben. All right. Did you get the tickets?

Jake. Sure. Boat's loading now.

Ben. [*Sits down at* MARCUS's *table.*] Take them up to Miss Lavinia; get the carriage ready. Get me coffee first.

Jake. [*As he goes off.*] Lot of running around this morning.

[*The sound of knocking is heard from the hall of the second floor.*]

Oscar's Voice. [*With the knocking.*] Papa! Papa! It's me. Hey, Papa. Please. Open your door. [*After a second* OSCAR *runs in from the living room, runs up the porch steps, calls into* MARCUS's *room.*] Papa. I'm all ready.

[*Pounds on* MARCUS's *door.*]

Ben. [*Looking up at* OSCAR.] Traveling clothes? You look nice.

Oscar. What you doing there? I told you to get on down to the station to make your apologies. I ain't changed my mind.

Ben. Oh, I never thought you meant that silly talk.

Oscar. You didn't, huh? [*Looks down, sees the gun on the table.*] What's my pistol doing out?

Ben. Waiting for you.

Oscar. You just put it back where you found it—— [*Then as if he remembered.*] Papa. Please. Let me in. *Please.* Papa, I can't find it. Papa—— [REGINA *appears on the balcony. She is arranging her hair. She has on a riding skirt and shirt.*] Regina, go in and tell him, will you? *Please, Regina.* Laurette's waiting for me to fetch her up——

Regina. [*Looks down at* BEN *on the porch. Looks at* OSCAR.] Oh, God. I slept late, hoping you'd both be gone. What's the matter with you, Oscar, what are you carrying on about?

[JAKE *appears with coffee tray, brings cup to* BEN, *puts tray down, and exits.*]

Oscar. [*Desperately.*] The thousand dollars on the table. But it's *not* on the table. You heard him promise last night——

Regina. Go look again. Papa certainly wouldn't stop your going.

Oscar. I tell you it's not there. I been over the whole house. I crawled around under the table——

Ben. Come on down and crawl some more.

Regina. [*Softly.*] You're in Papa's chair, Ben, eating breakfast at Papa's table, on Papa's porch.

Oscar. [*Softly, very puzzled.*] I'm telling you that Ben is a crazy Mama's crazy son.

Ben. [*Looks up at* REGINA.] Come on down and have breakfast with me, darling. I'm lonely for you.

Regina. Papa told you to be out of here.

Ben. [*Smiles.*] Come on down, honey.

Regina. No, I'm going out before the horse-whipping starts.

Ben. Going to look for a man who needs a little persuading?

Regina. That's right.

Oscar. Regina. Help me. It's *not* there. [*Screaming.*] Papa! *Papa!*

Regina. [*Disappears into her room.*] Oh, stop that screaming.

Oscar. Papa, I got to go. The money's not there. Papa, please answer me——

Marcus. [*Comes out from his room.*] You looking for me, son? Speak up.

Oscar. [*Softly.*] It's getting late. The money. You forgot to leave it. [*When he gets no answer, his voice changes to a sudden shriek.*] It just ain't there.

Marcus. A voice injured at your age is possibly never recovered. The money isn't there, Oscar, because I didn't put it there. [*To* BEN.] Would you like to give him a little—some—explanation, or will I, or——

Ben. [*Shakes his head.*] I'm eating.

[OSCAR *stares down at* BEN, *stares at* MARCUS.]

Marcus. [*To* OSCAR.] An unhappy event interfered. I am thus unable to finance your first happy months in the rose-covered brothel about which you have always dreamed. I assure you I am most sorry, for many reasons, none of them having anything to do with you.

Oscar. What the hell does all that mean? That you're *not* giving me the money to leave here——

Ben. [*Nods.*] It means that. And it means that Papa has found a new way of postponing for a few minutes an unpleasant writing job. Go back in, Papa.

[OSCAR *stares at* MARCUS, *stares down at* BEN. *Then he suddenly runs down the steps, off the porch, going toward the street.* BEN *smiles,* MARCUS *smiles.*]

Marcus. Where would you prefer me to have breakfast? A tray in my room, this side of the porch, or the dining room or——

Ben. Any place you like. My house is your house.

Marcus. I eat a large breakfast, as you know. Should that continue?

Ben. Certainly. But before you eat this large breakfast, on this large morning, I want you to finish the papers I'm waiting for.

Marcus. Naturally, I've been inside thinking. Is there any chance I could get out of here and on the train without your interfering with me?

Ben. No, I don't think so. I've thought of that. And if you did, I feel confident I could bring you back.

Marcus. [*Pleasantly.*] Yes. Thank you, Benjamin.

[*He re-enters his room as* REGINA *comes on the porch. She hears his last sentence, stares at* MARCUS. *She comes down the steps, goes to the table, pours herself coffee, takes a biscuit, looks curiously at* BEN *and sits down.*]

Regina. [*After a minute.*] What's the matter with Papa?

Ben. He's changed. You think it's age?

Regina. [*Annoyed.*] Why aren't you getting on the train?

Ben. I'm going to build a new house. I never liked this house; it wasn't meant for people like us. Too delicate, too fancy. Papa's idea of postwar swell.

Regina. [*Stares at him.*] I want to know why you aren't leaving this morning?

Ben. I can't tell you why. [*Laughs.*] My lips are sealed in honor.

Regina. Before there's any more trouble you better go quiet down Mama. She's *packing.* She says she's going to her destiny. You know what that always means. And I'm sick of fights——

Ben. But that's where she is going.

Regina. [*Bewildered.*] Papa said she could go?

Ben. No . . . I said so.

Regina. And who have you become?

Ben. A man who thinks you have handled yourself very badly. It's a shame about you, Regina: beautiful, warm outside, and smart. That should have made a brilliant life. Instead, at twenty, you have to start picking up the pieces, and start mighty fast now.

Regina. [*Gets up, laughs.*] I like the pieces, and I'm off to pick them up.

Ben. To try to persuade the Captain by the deed of darkness to a future legal bed? So early in the morning?

Regina. [*Pleasantly, as she passes him.*] I'm sure something very interesting has happened here. [*Sharply. Turns to him.*] But whatever it is, don't talk that way to me.

Ben. Can I talk this way? You're not going to Chicago. And for a very simple reason. Papa has no money at all—now. No money for you to travel with, or to marry with, or even to go on here with.

Regina. [*Stands staring at him. Then, quietly.*] *What are you talking about? What's happened?* What's he done with his money——

Ben. Given it to me.

Regina. Do you take that new drug I've been reading about? What would make you think he had given it to you?

Ben. You mean what were his reasons? Oh, I don't know. I'm the eldest son: isn't that the way with royalty? Maybe he could find me a Greek title—— Go up and talk to him. I think he's been waiting.

[*Slowly she starts for the staircase. Then the speed of her movements increases, and by the time she is near the door of* MARCUS'S *room she is running. She goes into the room.* BEN *picks up his newspaper. There is low talking from* MARCUS'S *room.* BEN *looks up, smiles. After a moment,* REGINA *comes slowly out of* MARCUS'S *room. She crosses porch, starts downstairs.*]

Regina. [*Slowly.*] He says there is nothing he will tell me. He says there's nothing he can tell me. He's crying. What does all that mean?

Ben. It means there is nothing he can tell you, and that he's crying. Don't you feel sorry for him?

Regina. Why can't he tell me? I'll make him——

Ben. He can't tell you, and I won't tell you. Just take my word: you're, er, you're not well off, shall we say?

Regina. [*Tensely.*] What have you been doing to Papa or——

Ben. A great deal. Whatever you think of me, honey, you know I'm not given to this kind of joke. So take it this way: what is in your room, is yours. Nothing else. And save your time on the talk. No Chicago, honey. No nothing.

Regina. You can't stop my going, and you're not going to stop it——

Ben. Certainly not. What people want to do, they do. You go ahead, your own way. Ride over to your soldier. Stand close and talk soft: he'll marry you. But do it quickly: he was angry last night and I think he wants to get away from you as fast as he can. Catch him quick. Marry him this morning. Then come back here to pack your nice Chicago clothes, and sell your pearls.

Regina. Do you think I'm going to take your word for what's happening, or believe I can't talk Papa out of whatever you've done to him——

Ben. Believe me, you can't. Not because your charms have failed, but because there's nothing to talk him out of. I have it now, and your charms won't work on me. Money from the pearls will be plenty to take you to Brazil, and love and war will feed you. People in love should be poor.

Regina. Ben, tell me what storm happened here this morning. Tell me so that I can—can find out what I think or——

Ben. Or if you don't want to go to the war in Brazil, stay here and starve with them at Lionnet. I'd love to see you in the house with those three ninnies, dying on the vine. Either way, he'd leave you soon enough and you'd find out there's never anybody nastier than a weak man. Hurry —— Or have a cup of coffee.

Regina. [*Softly, tensely.*] I'll find out what's happened, and——

Ben. No you won't.

Regina. And the day I do, I'll pay you back with carnival trimmings.

Ben. Good girl. I won't blame you. But in the meantime, learn to win, and learn to lose. And don't stand here all day losing, because it's my house now, and I don't like loser's talk.

Regina. You've ruined everything I wanted, you've——

Ben. Now, look here. Write *him* a poem, will you? I've ruined nothing. You're not marrying a man who didn't love you. You can't go away, or at least not on my money, and therefore a willful girl can't have a willful way. You're not in love; I don't think anybody in this family can love. You're not a fool; stop talking like one. The sooner you do, the sooner I'll help you.

Regina. You heard me say I'd pay you back for this?

Ben. All right. Be a fool.

[MARCUS *opens his door, comes out on the porch, comes down the steps.* REGINA *turns to look at him.* MARCUS *comes to* BEN, *hands him two pieces of paper.* BEN *takes them, reads them.* MARCUS *puts his hand out to take the newspaper.* BEN *smiles, shakes his head,* MARCUS *quickly takes his hand away.*]

Regina. [*Desperately, to* MARCUS.] You still won't tell me? You're willing to see——

Marcus. [*Softly.*] Regina, honey, I can't. I——

[OSCAR, *dejected and rumpled, appears.*]

Regina. [*To* OSCAR.] Do you know what's happened here? Did you have anything to do with it?

Oscar. What?

[REGINA *turns away from him.* OSCAR *sits down, puts his head in his hands.*]

Regina. [*After a minute.*] Well, what's the matter with you, then? Ben Hubbard trouble?

Oscar. She wouldn't wait. She wouldn't even wait for a few days until Papa could give me the money again.

Ben. Again?

Oscar. That's how much she cared for me. Wouldn't even wait. Said she was going on to New Orleans, anyway. That she'd had enough—— My God, I talked and begged. I even tried to carry her off the train.

Marcus. Oh, how unfortunate.

Ben. I think it's charming. How did you do it, Oscar?

Oscar. [*To nobody.*] You know what she did? She spat in my face and screamed in front of everybody that she was glad I wasn't coming, that she had never cared for me, and had only been doing the best she could. If I didn't have the money, what the hell did she need me for?

Regina. [*Sympathetic.*] Spat in your face! How could she do a thing like that?

Marcus. How does one spit in your face?

Ben. Why, I imagine the way one spits in anybody's face.

Regina. But it's special in a railroad station. How did she do it, Oscar? You can't just up and spit——

Oscar. [*In his sorrow, spits out on the porch.*] Just like that. The way you wouldn't do with a dog. And all the while yelling I was to let her alone, with everybody staring and laughing—— [MARCUS, REGINA, *and* BEN *laugh.* OSCAR *rises.*] So. So, making fun of me, huh?

Regina. Now, really, Oskie, can you blame us? You on a railroad station trying to carry off a spitting—girl? You'd laugh yourself, if you didn't always have indigestion.

Oscar. [*Carefully.*] Your love didn't laugh. Your love, looking like a statue of Robert E. Lee. Dressed up and with his old medals all over him. [REGINA *rises.* MARCUS *rises.*] So you didn't know he was going on the train, huh? I thought not. So you're no better off than me, are you, with all your laughing. Sneaked out on you, did he?

Regina. So you arranged that, too, so that I couldn't——

Ben. All right. That's enough. I'm sick of love. Both of you follow the trash you've set your hearts on, or be still about it from now on. I don't want any more of this.

Oscar. *You* don't want any more. What the——

Ben. [*To* REGINA.] You, early-maturing flower, can go any place you want and find what it's like to be without Papa's money. [*To* OSCAR.] And you, lover, can follow your spitting heart and get yourself a wharf job loading bananas. Or you can stay, keep your job, settle down. I got a girl picked out for you—make yourself useful.

Oscar. [*Completely bewildered, turns to* MARCUS.] What's he talking about, Papa? Since when——

Ben. It's not necessary to explain it to you. [*To* REGINA.] Now, honey, about you, if you're staying. You're a scandal in this town. Papa's the only person didn't know you've been sleeping with the warrior.

Marcus. Benjamin——

Ben. [*Laughs.*] Papa, and Horace Giddens in Mobile. How soon he'll find out about it, I don't know. Before he does, we're taking you up to see him. You'll get engaged to him by next week, or sooner, and you'll get married in the first church we bump into. Giddens isn't bad off, and if you're lucky it'll be years before he hears about you and the Brazilian general. I don't say it's a brilliant future, but I don't say it's bad. You could have done a lot better, but girls who have been despoiled in this part of the country——

Marcus. [*Softly.*] You don't have to marry a man, Regina, just because—— We can go away, you and I——

Oscar. [*Goes toward kitchen door.*] I certainly don't know what's happened here. I certainly don't. I'm hungry. [*Calls in.*] Where's breakfast, you all?

Regina. [*Sharply.*] Order breakfast for me, too, selfish.

Ben. [*Laughs.*] That's my good girl. [*Picks up the newspaper.*] Nothing for anybody to be so unhappy about. You both going to do all right. I'm going to help you. I got ideas. You'll go to Chicago some day, get everything you want—— Then——

Regina. [*Softly.*] When I'm too old to want it.

Marcus. Regina, you didn't hear me. We could go away, you and I—— I could start over again just as I started once before.

Regina. When you did—whatever Ben made you do, did you realize what you were doing to me? Did you care?

Marcus. [*Slowly.*] I cared very much.

Regina. And what good did that do?

Oscar. Sure must have been an earthquake here since last night. You go to bed and Papa's one kind of man, and you wake up——

Ben. [*Reading newspaper.*] They got that ad in again, Oscar. Dr. Melgoyd's "All Cure." Two bits, now, on special sale, for gentlemen only. Sluggish blood, cure for a wild manhood, nothing to be ashamed of, it says——

Regina. He's still got the last bottle.

[JAKE *appears with a large tray. He has on his hat and coat.*]

Oscar. [*Annoyed.*] I never bought that rot. Don't believe in it. Somebody gave it to me.

Regina. [*Laughing.*] That was tactless, wasn't it?

Ben. Big goings on all over the country. Railroads going across, oil, coal. I been telling you, Papa, for ten years. Things are opening up.

Oscar. [*Who has started to eat.*] That don't mean they're opening up in the South.

Ben. But they are. That's what nobody down here sees or understands. Now you take you, Papa. You were smart in your day and figured out what fools you lived among. But ever since the war you been too busy getting cultured, or getting Southern. A few more years and you'd have been just like the rest of them.

Marcus. [*To* JAKE.] Bring my breakfast, Jake.

Jake. Belle will have to do it, Mr. Marcus. Last breakfast I can bring. I got the carriage waiting to take Miss Viney.

[*He exits.*]

Ben. But now we'll do a little quiet investing, nothing big, because unlike Papa I don't believe in going outside your class about anything——

Oscar. [*His mouth full.*] Think we've got a chance to be big rich, Ben?

Ben. I think so. All of us. I'm going to make some for you and Regina and——

[LAVINIA *appears in the living-room door. She is carrying a purse and the Bible.* CORALEE *is standing behind her.*]

Lavinia. Well, I'm off on my appointed path. I brought you each a little something. [*Goes to* REGINA.] This is my pin. [REGINA *gets up,* LAVINIA *kisses her.*] Smile, honey, you're such a pretty girl. [*Goes to* OSCAR.] Here's my prayer book, Oscar. I had it since I was five years old. [OSCAR *kisses her. She goes to* BEN.] I want you to have my Papa's watch, Benjamin.

Ben. Thank you, Mama.

[*He kisses her, she pats his arm.*]

Lavinia. [*Goes to* MARCUS.] I didn't have anything left, Marcus, except my wedding ring.

Marcus. [*Gets up, smiles.*] That's kind, Lavinia.

Lavinia. Well, I guess that's all.

Ben. Mama, could I have your Bible instead of Grandpa's watch? [MARCUS *laughs.*] It would make me happier, and I think——

Marcus. Or perhaps you'd give it to me. I can't tell you how happy it would make me, Lavinia.

Lavinia. Oh, I wouldn't like to give it up. This Bible's been in my Papa's family for a long time. I always keep it next to me, you all know that. But when I die, I'll leave it to you all. Coralee, you hear that? If I die before you, you bring it right back here.

Coralee. Come on, Miss Viney.

Lavinia. I'll be hearing from you, Benjamin?

Ben. You will, Mama. Every month. On time.

Lavinia. Thank you, son. Thank you in the name of my colored children.

Coralee. Miss Viney, it's late.

Lavinia. Well. [*Wistfully.*] Don't be seeing me off, any of you. Coralee and I'll be just fine. I'll be thinking of you, and I'll be praying for you, all of you. Everybody needs somebody to pray for them, and I'm going to pray for you all. [*Turns to* MARCUS.] I hope you feel better, Marcus. We got old, you and me, and—— Well, I guess I just mean it's been a long time. Good-bye.

Marcus. Good-bye, Lavinia.

[LAVINIA *and* CORALEE *exit.* MARCUS *goes to sit by* REGINA.]

Marcus. [*Softly.*] Pour me a cup of coffee, darling.

[REGINA *looks at him, gets up, crosses to table, pours coffee, brings it to him.* MARCUS *pulls forward the chair next to him.* REGINA *ignores the movement, crosses to chair near* BEN, *sits down.* BEN *smiles.*]

CURTAIN

DEATH OF A SALESMAN *

Certain Private Conversations in Two Acts and a Requiem

By

ARTHUR MILLER

This play, following within two years the deep impression upon playgoers and critics made by *All My Sons* with its conventionally realistic pattern, seemed advanced by a half century beyond the "water-tight" dramaturgy of the Ibsen tradition that unmistakably branded the earlier work. It gave impressive evidence that in Arthur Miller the American theatre has not only a new and bold genius capable of captivating the public by serious and significant drama, but one of extraordinary virtuosity and versatility. A dramatist, too, with an unflinching aim: to restore drama to its ancient humanizing function—the purgation of man's soul, and more specifically the American competitive soul blinded to real and lasting values by a spurious show of success. Miller's themes and characters, with little glozing relief, plumb the depths of sham and insincerity that lurk increasingly under the veneer of our vaunted prosperity. They are shocking reminders of democracy's need of unremitting vigilance. It is Miller's unique distinction that while dramatizing such disillusionment with force and cogency rare among our theatrical sophisticates, he at the same time charms and attracts by facile artistry and moments of genuine emotional power and spiritual beauty. Somehow his tragedies grip and hold an audience by the fascination of the abhorrent. Most remarkable and reassuring in their success is the fact that producers and actors of repute have dared to risk the sponsoring of such disturbing plays before a public that moviewise and theatrewise is generally thought to be allergic to the tragic and the elementally emotional unrelieved by the lure of sex—a bait even less conspicuous in Miller's work than in Shaw's.

The present dramatist takes high rank among the now numerous company of our academic playwrights—O'Neill, Paul Green, Elmer Rice, Thornton Wilder, and Sidney Kingsley, for instance,—whose widely varied experimentation has not only paid tribute to the pioneering of such teachers as Baker of Harvard and Yale, Matthews of Columbia, Koch of North Carolina, and Drummond of Cornell; their work may now be viewed in the aggregate as an undeniable enrichment of the American theatre, not only in forms and themes, but more importantly in intellectual integrity and the analytical approach to life itself. Arthur Miller's few Broadway appearances to date give promise that this invaluable contribution to the art of our stage is still to continue strong. They are a reminder, too, that the academic playwright, if he is to succeed, must observe and experience life at first hand, as Miller has done in his own brave struggle to pay his way through a higher education, an experience that gave his observant intellect not only a passionate interest in the sordid realities, but an intimate acquaintance with the culprits and victims that people his plays. His view of life may seem too intense and too narrow, as yet, but of its fidelity to the observed there can be no doubt.

His adroit use of dramatic effect and form evidently stems from a wide knowledge of theatre practice ancient and modern. It would almost seem that he had purposely imagined a setting for *Death of a Salesman*—superbly realized by designer Mielziner—in order to provide every possible device of the "free" stage, blending kaleidoscopically the "orchestra" and apron of the ancients and their varied "levels" with stark realism of interiors and a pervasive expressionism emphasizing domestic littleness and degeneracy against an engulfing progress symbolized by the apartment that looms behind.

Similarly the action calls for almost every variety of expressionistic means to penetrate the minds of the characters and lay bare their inmost hopes, deceits, loves, and aspirations, and, most adroitly of all, what O'Neill liked to call their "behind-life"—all that has made them what they are. Willy Loman's pitiful psychotic illusions, his treasured memories and dreams of parental love that he represses in normal and often uncontrollable anger in his beloved Biff's presence, his futile ambitions and his cankered conscience are laid bare with vividness and pathos by an intricate pattern of alternating flashbacks, muttered monologues, and dream sequences spoken or enacted, often heightened by such symbol characters as Ben with his recurrent: "When I was seventeen I walked into the jungle, and when I was twenty-one I walked out. And by God I was rich." And there is also Charley with his scorching advice to the crestfallen salesman in his desperate groping for love: "The only thing you got in the world is what you can sell." So skilfully are these now familiar devices directed and blended that they never seem to lessen the mounting dramatic force of the father-son conflict that centers the action and ends in a tragic catharsis more poignant than any we can easily recall. They rise in an overpowering climax of thwarted love, hope, and ambition—a phantasmagoria of the mind, but one that is not without its moments of spiritual beauty and compassion. An unmistakable moral significance thus subtly conveyed lifts this remarkable play immeasurably above the wartime hysteria of *All My Sons*.

In a prefatory essay to *Death of a Salesman* published in *Theatre Arts* Miller made clear his driving purpose: to raise the tragedy of the common man to the level of highly conceived drama. Since George Lillo set himself to this ambitious task in the early eighteenth century, few writers have so satisfyingly fulfilled this laudable service to the English-speaking stage as Arthur Miller has in this play.

ARTHUR MILLER

Born 1915, New York City.

1932, Graduated from the Abraham Lincoln High School, Brooklyn.

1938, B.A., University of Michigan, having worked his way and distinguished himself as a student playwright by winning the Avery Hopwood Prize and later the Theatre Guild National Award.

1938, Worked with the Federal Theatre Project; also wrote radio scripts for the Columbia Workshop and Cavalcade of America (NBC).

1944, While serving as 4F because of football injury, assigned to collect data for the Ernie Pyle story of "G.I. Joe."

Also published *Situation Normal*, a non-fictional commentary on the war.

His first play on Broadway, *The Man Who Had All the Luck*, failed.

1945, *Focus*, his first novel, concerning anti-Semitism.

1947, His first Broadway success, *All My Sons*, won the Drama Critics' Circle award, also the Pulitzer Prize.

PLAYS

1936 *The Grass Still Grows* won the Avery Hopwood Prize of $500 at the University of Michigan; later the Theatre Guild National Award of $1250. 1944 *The Man Who Had All the Luck.* 1947 *All My Sons.* 1949 *Death of a Salesman.* 1950 *An Enemy of the People,* an adaptation of Ibsen's play. 1953 *The Crucible.* 1955 *A Memory of Two Mondays* (one-act) and *A View from the Bridge* (one-act).

WRITINGS ON DRAMA

"Tragedy of the Common Man," prefacing the *Theatre Arts'* reprint of *Death of a Salesman,* May 1951, p. 48.

"Picking a Cast," *The New York Times,* Aug. 21, 1955, II.1.1.

"American Theater," *Holiday,* XVII (Jan. 1955), 90 ff.

"A View of One-Acters," *The New York Times,* Sept. 25, 1955, II.1.6.

DEATH OF A SALESMAN

CAST

(in order of appearance)

WILLY LOMAN.
LINDA.
BIFF.
HAPPY.
BERNARD.
THE WOMAN.
CHARLEY.
UNCLE BEN.
HOWARD WAGNER.
JENNY.
STANLEY.
MISS FORSYTHE.
LETTA.

The action takes place in Willy Loman's house and yard and in various places he visits in the New York and Boston of today.

Throughout the play, in the stage directions, left and right mean stage left and stage right.

ACT ONE

A melody is heard, played upon a flute. It is small and fine, telling of grass and trees and the horizon. The curtain rises. Before us is the Salesman's house. We are aware of towering, angular shapes behind it, surrounding it on all sides. Only the blue light of the sky falls upon the house and forestage; the surrounding area shows an angry glow of orange. As more light appears, we see a solid vault of apartment houses around the small, fragile-seeming home. An air of the dream clings to the place, a dream rising out of reality. The kitchen at center seems actual enough, for there is a kitchen table with three chairs, and a refrigerator. But no other fixtures are seen. At the back of the kitchen there is a draped entrance, which leads to the living-room. To the right of the kitchen, on a level raised two feet, is a bedroom furnished only with a brass bedstead and a straight chair. On a shelf over the bed a silver athletic trophy stands. A window opens onto the apartment house at the side. Behind the kitchen, on a level raised six and a half feet, is the boys' bedroom, at present barely visible. Two beds are dimly seen, and at the back of the room a dormer window. (This bedroom is above the unseen living-room.) At the left a stairway curves up to it from the kitchen.

The entire setting is wholly or, in some places, partially transparent. The roof-line of the house is one-dimensional; under and over it we see the apartment buildings. Before the house lies an apron, curving beyond the forestage into the orchestra. This forward area serves as the back yard as well as the locale of all WILLY'S *imaginings and of his city scenes. Whenever the action is in the present the actors observe the imaginary wall-lines, entering the house only through its door at the left. But in the scenes of the past these boundaries are broken, and characters enter or leave a room by stepping "through" a wall onto the forestage.*

[*From the right,* WILLY LOMAN, *the Salesman, enters, carrying two large sample cases. The flute plays on. He hears but is not aware of it. He is past sixty years of age, dressed quietly. Even as he crosses the stage to the doorway of the house, his exhaustion is apparent. He unlocks the door, comes into the kitchen, and thankfully lets his burden down, feeling the soreness of his palms. A word-sigh escapes his lips—it might be "Oh, boy, oh, boy." He closes the door, then carries his cases out into the living-room through the draped kitchen doorway.*

LINDA, *his wife, has stirred in her bed at the right. She gets out and puts on a robe, listening. Most often jovial, she has developed an iron repression of her exceptions to* WILLY's *behavior—she more than loves him, she admires him, as though his mercurial nature, his temper, his massive dreams and little cruelties, served her only as sharp reminders of the turbulent longings which she shares but lacks the temperament to utter and follow to their end.*]

Linda. [*Hearing* WILLY *outside the bedroom, calls with some trepidation.*] Willy!

Willy. It's all right. I came back.

Linda. Why? What happened? [*Slight pause.*] Did something happen, Willy?

Willy. No, nothing happened.

Linda. You didn't smash the car, did you?

Willy. [*With casual irritation.*] I said nothing happened. Didn't you hear me?

Linda. Don't you feel well?

Willy. I'm tired to the death. [*The flute has faded away. He sits on the bed beside her, a little numb.*] I couldn't make it. I just couldn't make it, Linda.

Linda. [*Very carefully, delicately.*] Where were you all day? You look terrible.

Willy. I got as far as a little above Yonkers. I stopped for a cup of coffee. Maybe it was the coffee.

Linda. What?

Willy. [*After a pause.*] I suddenly couldn't drive any more. The car kept going off onto the shoulder, y'know?

Linda. [*Helpfully.*] Oh. Maybe it was the steering again. I don't think Angelo knows the Studebaker.

Willy. No, it's me. Suddenly I realize I'm goin' sixty miles an hour and I don't remember the last five minutes. I'm—I can't seem to—keep my mind to it.

Linda. Maybe it's your glasses. You never went for your new glasses.

Willy. No, I see everything. I came back ten miles an hour. It took me nearly four hours from Yonkers.

Linda. [*Resigned.*] Well, you'll just have to take a rest, Willy, you can't continue this way.

Willy. I just got back from Florida.

Linda. But you didn't rest your mind. Your mind is overactive, and the mind is what counts, dear.

Willy. I'll start out in the morning. Maybe I'll feel better in the morning. [*She is taking off his shoes.*] These goddam arch supports are killing me.

Linda. Take an aspirin. Should I get you an aspirin? It'll soothe you.

Willy. [*With wonder.*] I was driving along, you understand? And I was fine. I was fine. I was even observing the scenery. You can imagine, me looking at scenery, on the road every week of my life. But it's so beautiful up there, Linda, the trees are so thick, and the sun is warm. I opened the windshield and just let the warm air bathe over me. And then all of a sudden I'm goin' off the road! I'm tellin' ya, I absolutely forgot I was driving. If I'd've gone the other way over the white line I might've killed somebody. So I went on again—and five minutes later I'm dreamin' again, and I nearly—— [*He presses two fingers against his eyes.*] I have such thoughts, I have such strange thoughts.

Linda. Willy, dear. Talk to them again. There's no reason why you can't work in New York.

Willy. They don't need me in New York. I'm the New England man. I'm vital in New England.

Linda. But you're sixty years old. They can't expect you to keep traveling every week.

Willy. I'll have to send a wire to Portland. I'm supposed to see Brown and Morrison tomorrow morning at ten o'clock to show the line. Goddammit, I could sell them! [*He starts putting on his jacket.*]

Linda. [*Taking the jacket from him.*] Why don't you go down to the place tomorrow and tell Howard you've simply got to work in New York? You're too accommodating, dear.

Willy. If old man Wagner was alive I'd a been in charge of New York now! That man was a prince, he was a masterful man. But that boy of his, that Howard, he don't appreciate. When I went north the first time, the Wagner Company didn't know where New England was!

Linda. Why don't you tell those things to Howard, dear?

Willy. [*Encouraged.*] I will, I definitely will. Is there any cheese?

Linda. I'll make you a sandwich.

Willy. No, go to sleep. I'll take some milk. I'll be up right away. The boys in?

Linda. They're sleeping. Happy took Biff on a date tonight.

Willy. [*Interested.*] That so?

Linda. It was so nice to see them shaving together, one behind the other, in the bathroom. And going out together. You notice? The whole house smells of shaving lotion.

Willy. Figure it out. Work a lifetime to pay off a house. You finally own it, and there's nobody to live in it.

Linda. Well, dear, life is a casting off. It's always that way.

Willy. No, no, some people—some people accomplish something. Did Biff say anything after I went this morning?

Linda. You shouldn't have criticized him, Willy, especially after he just got off the train. You mustn't lose your temper with him.

Willy. When the hell did I lose my temper? I simply asked him if he was making any money. Is that a criticism?

Linda. But, dear, how could he make any money?

Willy. [*Worried and angered.*] There's such an undercurrent in him. He became a moody man. Did he apologize when I left this morning?

Linda. He was crestfallen, Willy. You know how he admires you. I think if he finds himself, then you'll both be happier and not fight any more.

Willy. How can he find himself on a farm? Is that a life? A farmhand? In the beginning, when he was young, I thought, well, a young man, it's good for him to tramp around, take a lot of different jobs. But it's more than ten years now and he has yet to make thirty-five dollars a week!

Linda. He's finding himself, Willy.

Willy. Not finding yourself at the age of thirty-four is a disgrace!

Linda. Shh!

Willy. The trouble is he's lazy, goddammit!

Linda. Willy, please!

Willy. Biff is a lazy bum!

Linda. They're sleeping. Get something to eat. Go on down.

Willy. Why did he come home? I would like to know what brought him home.

Linda. I don't know. I think he's still lost, Willy. I think he's very lost.

Willy. Biff Loman is lost. In the greatest country in the world a young man with such —personal attractiveness, gets lost. And such a hard worker. There's one thing about Biff—he's not lazy.

Linda. Never.

Willy. [*With pity and resolve.*] I'll see him in the morning; I'll have a nice talk with him. I'll get him a job selling. He could be big in no time. My God! Remember how they used to follow him around in high school? When he smiled at one of them their faces lit up. When he walked down the street . . .

[*He loses himself in reminiscences.*]

Linda. [*Trying to bring him out of it.*] Willy, dear, I got a new kind of American-type cheese today. It's whipped.

Willy. Why do you get American when I like Swiss?

Linda. I just thought you'd like a change——

Willy. I don't want a change! I want Swiss cheese. Why am I always being contradicted?

Linda. [*With a covering laugh.*] I thought it would be a surprise.

Willy. Why don't you open a window in here, for God's sake?

Linda. [*With infinite patience.*] They're all open, dear.

Willy. The way they boxed us in here. Bricks and windows, windows and bricks.

Linda. We should've bought the land next door.

Willy. The street is lined with cars. There's not a breath of fresh air in the neighborhood. The grass don't grow any more, you can't raise a carrot in the back yard. They should've had a law against apartment houses. Remember those two beautiful elm trees out there? When I and Biff hung the swing between them?

Linda. Yeah, like being a million miles from the city.

Willy. They should've arrested the builder for cutting those down. They massacred the neighborhood. [*Lost.*] More and more I think of those days, Linda. This time of year it was lilac and wisteria. And then the peonies would come out, and the daffodils. What fragrance in this room!

Linda. Well, after all, people had to move somewhere.

Willy. No, there's more people now.

Linda. I don't think there's more people. I think——

Willy. There's more people! That's what's ruining this country! Population is getting out of control. The competition is maddening! Smell the stink from that apartment house! And another one on the other side . . . How can they whip cheese?

[*On* WILLY'S *last line,* BIFF *and* HAPPY *raise themselves up in their beds, listening.*]

Linda. Go down, try it. And be quiet.

Willy. [*Turning to* LINDA, *guilty.*] You're not worried about me, are you, sweetheart?

Biff. What's the matter?

Happy. Listen!

Linda. You've got too much on the ball to worry about.

Willy. You're my foundation and my support, Linda.

Linda. Just try to relax, dear. You make mountains out of molehills.

Willy. I won't fight with him any more. If he wants to go back to Texas, let him go.

Linda. He'll find his way.

Willy. Sure. Certain men just don't get started till later in life. Like Thomas Edison, I think. Or B. F. Goodrich. One of them was deaf. [*He starts for the bedroom doorway.*] I'll put my money on Biff.

Linda. And Willy—if it's warm Sunday we'll drive in the country. And we'll open the windshield, and take lunch.

Willy. No, the windshields don't open on the new cars.

Linda. But you opened it today.

Willy. Me? I didn't. [*He stops.*] Now isn't that peculiar! Isn't that a remarkable——

[*He breaks off in amazement and fright as the flute is heard distantly.*]

Linda. What, darling?

Willy. That is the most remarkable thing.

Linda. What, dear?

Willy. I was thinking of the Chevvy. [*Slight pause.*] Nineteen twenty-eight . . . when I had that red Chevvy—— [*Breaks off.*] That funny? I coulda sworn I was driving that Chevvy today.

Linda. Well, that's nothing. Something must've reminded you.

Willy. Remarkable. Ts. Remember those days? The way Biff used to simonize that car? The dealer refused to believe there was eighty thousand miles on it. [*He shakes his head.*] Heh! [*To* LINDA.] Close your eyes, I'll be right up.

[*He walks out of the bedroom.*]

Happy. [*To* BIFF.] Jesus, maybe he smashed up the car again!

Linda. [*Calling after* WILLY.] Be careful on the stairs, dear! The cheese is on the middle shelf!

[*She turns, goes over to the bed, takes his jacket, and goes out of the bedroom. Light has risen on the boys' room. Unseen,* WILLY *is heard talking to himself, "Eighty thousand miles," and a little laugh.* BIFF *gets out of bed, comes downstage a bit, and stands attentively.* BIFF *is two years older than his brother* HAPPY, *well built, but in these days bears a worn air and seems less self-assured. He has succeeded less, and his dreams are stronger and less acceptable than* HAPPY'S. HAPPY *is tall, powerfully made. Sexuality is like a visible color on him, or a scent that many women have discovered. He, like his brother, is lost, but in a different way, for he has never allowed himself to turn his face toward defeat and is thus more confused and hard-skinned, although seemingly more content.*]

Happy. [*Getting out of bed.*] He's going to get his license taken away if he keeps that up. I'm getting nervous about him, y'know, Biff?

Biff. His eyes are going.

Happy. No, I've driven with him. He sees all right. He just doesn't keep his mind on it. I drove into the city with him last week. He stops at a green light and then it turns red and he goes. [*He laughs.*]

Biff. Maybe he's color-blind.

Happy. Pop? Why he's got the finest eye for color in the business. You know that.

Biff. [*Sitting down on his bed.*] I'm going to sleep.

Happy. You're not still sour on Dad, are you, Biff?

Biff. He's all right, I guess.

Willy. [*Underneath them, in the living-room.*] Yes, sir, eighty thousand miles—eighty-two thousand!

Biff. You smoking?

Happy. [*Holding out a pack of cigarettes.*] Want one?

Biff. [*Taking a cigarette.*] I can never sleep when I smell it.

Willy. What a simonizing job, heh!

Happy. [*With deep sentiment.*] Funny, Biff, y'know? Us sleeping in here again? The old beds. [*He pats his bed affectionately.*] All the talk that went across those two beds, huh? Our whole lives.

Biff. Yeah. Lotta dreams and plans.

Happy. [*With a deep and masculine laugh.*] About five hundred women would like to know what was said in this room.

[*They share a soft laugh.*]

Biff. Remember that big Betsy something—what the hell was her name—over on Bushwick Avenue?

Happy. [*Combing his hair.*] With the collie dog!

Biff. That's the one. I got you in there, remember?

Happy. Yeah, that was my first time—I think. Boy, there was a pig! [*They laugh, almost crudely.*] You taught me everything I know about women. Don't forget that.

Biff. I bet you forgot how bashful you used to be. Especially with girls.

Happy. Oh, I still am, Biff.

Biff. Oh, go on.

Happy. I just control it, that's all. I think I got less bashful and you got more so. What happened, Biff? Where's the old humor, the old confidence? [*He shakes* BIFF'S *knee.* BIFF *gets up and moves restlessly about the room.*] What's the matter?

Biff. Why does Dad mock me all the time?

Happy. He's not mocking you, he——

Biff. Everything I say there's a twist of mockery on his face. I can't get near him.

Happy. He just wants you to make good, that's all. I wanted to talk to you about Dad for a long time, Biff. Something's—happening to him. He—talks to himself.

Biff. I noticed that this morning. But he always mumbled.

Happy. But not so noticeable. It got so embarrassing I sent him to Florida. And you know something? Most of the time he's talking to you.

Biff. What's he say about me?

Happy. I can't make it out.

Biff. What's he say about me?

Happy. I think the fact that you're not settled, that you're still kind of up in the air . . .

Biff. There's one or two other things depressing him, Happy.

Happy. What do you mean?

Biff. Never mind. Just don't lay it all to me.

Happy. But I think if you just got started—I mean—is there any future for you out there?

Biff. I tell ya, Hap, I don't know what the future is. I don't know—what I'm supposed to want.

Happy. What do you mean?

Biff. Well, I spent six or seven years after high school trying to work myself up. Shipping clerk, salesman, business of one kind or another. And it's a measly manner of existence. To get on that subway on the hot mornings in summer. To devote your whole life to keeping stock, or making phone calls, or selling or buying. To suffer fifty weeks of the year for the sake of a two-week vacation, when all you really desire is to be outdoors, with your shirt off. And always to have to get ahead of the next fella. And still—that's how you build a future.

Happy. Well, you really enjoy it on a farm? Are you content out there?

Biff. [*With rising agitation.*] Hap, I've had twenty or thirty different kinds of jobs since I left home before the war, and it always turns out the same. I just realized it lately. In Nebraska when I herded cattle, and the Dakotas, and Arizona, and now in Texas. It's why I came home now, I guess, because I realized it. This farm I work on, it's spring there now, see? And they've got about fifteen new colts. There's nothing more inspiring or—beautiful than the sight of a mare and a new colt. And it's cool there now, see? Texas is cool now, and it's spring. And whenever spring comes to where I am, I suddenly get the feeling, my God, I'm not gettin' anywhere! What the hell am I doing, playing around with horses, twenty-eight dollars a week! I'm thirty-four years old, I oughta be makin' my future. That's when I come running home. And now, I get here, and I don't know what to do with myself. [*After a pause.*] I've always made a point of not wasting my life, and everytime I come back here I know that all I've done is to waste my life.

Happy. You're a poet, you know that, Biff? You're a—you're an idealist!

Biff. No, I'm mixed up very bad. Maybe I oughta get married. Maybe I oughta get stuck into something. Maybe that's my trouble. I'm like a boy. I'm not married, I'm not in business, I just—I'm like a boy. Are you content, Hap? You're a success, aren't you? Are you content?

Happy. Hell, no!

Biff. Why? You're making money, aren't you?

Happy. [*Moving about with energy, expressiveness.*] All I can do now is wait for the merchandise manager to die. And suppose I get to be merchandise manager? He's a good friend of mine, and he just built a terrific estate on Long Island. And he lived there about two months and sold it, and now he's building another one. He can't enjoy it once it's finished. And I know that's just what I would do. I don't know what the hell I'm workin' for. Sometimes I sit in my apartment—all alone. And I think of the rent I'm paying. And it's crazy. But then, it's what I always wanted. My own apartment, a car, and plenty of women. And still, goddammit, I'm lonely.

Biff. [*With enthusiasm.*] Listen, why don't you come out West with me?

Happy. You and I, heh?

Biff. Sure, maybe we could buy a ranch. Raise cattle, use our muscles. Men built like we are should be working out in the open.

Happy. [*Avidly.*] The Loman Brothers, heh?

Biff. [*With vast affection.*] Sure, we'd be known all over the counties!

Happy. [*Enthralled.*] That's what I dream about, Biff. Sometimes I want to just rip my clothes off in the middle of the store and outbox that goddam merchandise manager. I mean I can outbox, outrun, and outlift anybody in that store, and I have to take orders from those common, petty sons-of-bitches till I can't stand it any more.

Biff. I'm tellin' you, kid, if you were with me I'd be happy out there.

Happy. [*Enthused.*] See, Biff, everybody around me is so false that I'm constantly lowering my ideals . . .

Biff. Baby, together we'd stand up for one another, we'd have someone to trust.

Happy. If I were around you——

Biff. Hap, the trouble is we weren't brought up to grub for money. I don't know how to do it.

Happy. Neither can I!

Biff. Then let's go!

Happy. The only thing is—what can you make out there?

Biff. But look at your friend. Builds an estate and then hasn't the peace of mind to live in it.

Happy. Yeah, but when he walks into the store the waves part in front of him. That's fifty-two thousand dollars a year coming through the revolving door, and I got more in my pinky finger than he's got in his head.

Biff. Yeah, but you just said——

Happy. I gotta show some of those pompous, self-important executives over there that Hap Loman can make the grade. I want to walk into the store the way he walks in. Then I'll go with you, Biff. We'll be together yet, I swear. But take those two we had tonight. Now weren't they gorgeous creatures?

Biff. Yeah, yeah, most gorgeous I've had in years.

Happy. I get that any time I want, Biff. Whenever I feel disgusted. The only trouble is, it gets like bowling or something. I just keep knockin' them over and it doesn't mean anything. You still run around a lot?

Biff. Naa. I'd like to find a girl—steady, somebody with substance.

Happy. That's what I long for.

Biff. Go on! You'd never come home.

Happy. I would! Somebody with character, with resistance! Like Mom, y'know? You're gonna call me a bastard when I tell you this. That girl Charlotte I was with tonight is engaged to be married in five weeks.

[*He tries on his new hat.*]

Biff. No kiddin'!

Happy. Sure, the guy's in line for the vice-presidency of the store. I don't know what gets into me, maybe I just have an overdeveloped sense of competition or something, but I went and ruined her, and furthermore I can't get rid of her. And he's the third executive I've done that to. Isn't that a crummy characteristic? And to top it all, I go to their weddings! [*Indignantly, but laughing.*] Like I'm not supposed to take bribes. Manufacturers offer me a hundred-dollar bill now and then to throw an order their way. You know how honest I am, but it's like this girl, see. I hate myself for it. Because I don't want the girl, and, still, I take it and—I love it!

Biff. Let's go to sleep.

Happy. I guess we didn't settle anything, heh?

Biff. I just got one idea that I think I'm going to try.

Happy. What's that?

Biff. Remember Bill Oliver?

Happy. Sure, Oliver is very big now. You want to work for him again?

Biff. No, but when I quit he said something to me. He put his arm on my shoulder, and he said, "Biff, if you ever need anything, come to me."

Happy. I remember that. That sounds good.

Biff. I think I'll go to see him. If I could get ten thousand or even seven or eight thousand dollars I could buy a beautiful ranch.

Happy. I bet he'd back you. 'Cause he thought highly of you, Biff. I mean, they all do. You're well liked, Biff. That's why I say to come back here, and we both have the apartment. And I'm tellin' you, Biff, any babe you want . . .

Biff. No, with a ranch I could do the work I like and still be something. I just wonder, though. I wonder if Oliver still thinks I stole that carton of basketballs.

Happy. Oh, he probably forgot that long ago. It's almost ten years. You're too sensitive. Anyway, he didn't really fire you.

Biff. Well, I think he was going to. I think that's why I quit. I was never sure whether he knew or not. I know he thought the world of me, though. I was the only one he'd let lock up the place.

Willy. [*Below.*] You gonna wash the engine, Biff?

Happy. Shh!

[BIFF *looks at* HAPPY, *who is gazing down, listening.* WILLY *is mumbling in the parlor.*]

Happy. You hear that?

[*They listen.* WILLY *laughs warmly.*]

Biff. [*Growing angry.*] Doesn't he know Mom can hear that?

Willy. Don't get your sweater dirty, Biff!

[*A look of pain crosses* BIFF'S *face.*]

Happy. Isn't that terrible? Don't leave again, will you? You'll find a job here. You gotta stick around. I don't know what to do about him, it's getting embarrassing.

Willy. What a simonizing job!

Biff. Mom's hearing that!

Willy. No kiddin', Biff, you got a date? Wonderful!

Happy. Go on to sleep. But talk to him in the morning, will you?

Biff. [*Reluctantly getting into bed.*] With her in the house. Brother!

Happy. [*Getting into bed.*] I wish you'd have a good talk with him.

[*The light on their room begins to fade.*]

Biff. [*To himself in bed.*] That selfish, stupid . . .

Happy. Sh . . . Sleep, Biff.

[*Their light is out. Well before they have finished speaking,* WILLY'S *form is dimly seen below in the darkened kitchen. He opens the refrigerator, searches in there, and takes out a bottle of milk. The apartment houses are fading out, and the entire house and surroundings become covered with leaves. Music insinuates itself as the leaves appear.*]

Willy. Just wanna be careful with those girls, Biff, that's all. Don't make any promises. No promises of any kind. Because a girl, y'know, they always believe what you tell 'em, and you're very young, Biff; you're too young to be talking seriously to girls.

[*Light rises on the kitchen.* WILLY, *talking, shuts the refrigerator door and comes downstage to the kitchen table. He pours milk into a glass. He is totally immersed in himself, smiling faintly.*]

Willy. Too young entirely, Biff. You want to watch your schooling first. Then when you're all set, there'll be plenty of girls for a boy like you. [*He smiles broadly at a kitchen chair.*] That so? The girls pay for you? [*He laughs.*] Boy, you must really be makin' a hit.

[WILLY *is gradually addressing—physically—a point offstage, speaking through the wall of the kitchen, and his voice has been rising in volume to that of a normal conversation.*]

Willy. I been wondering why you polish the car so careful. Ha! Don't leave the hubcaps, boys. Get the chamois to the hubcaps. Happy, use newspaper on the windows, it's the easiest thing. Show him how to do it, Biff! You see, Happy? Pad it up, use it like a pad. That's it, that's it, good work. You're doin' all right, Hap. [*He pauses, then nods in approbation for a few seconds, then looks upward.*] Biff, first thing we gotta do when we get time is clip that big branch over the house. Afraid it's gonna fall in a storm and hit the roof. Tell you what. We get a rope and sling her around, and then we climb up there with a couple of saws and take her down. Soon as you finish the car, boys, I wanna see ya. I got a surprise for you, boys.

Biff. [*Offstage.*] Whatta ya got, Dad?

Willy. No, you finish first. Never leave a job till you're finished—remember that. [*Looking toward the "big trees."*] Biff, up in Albany I saw a beautiful hammock. I think I'll buy it next trip, and we'll hang it right between those two elms. Wouldn't that be something? Just swingin' there under those branches. Boy, that would be . . .

[YOUNG BIFF *and* YOUNG HAPPY *appear from the direction* WILLY *was addressing.* HAPPY *carries rags and a pail of water.* BIFF, *wearing a sweater with a block "S," carries a football.*]

Biff. [*Pointing in the direction of the car offstage.*] How's that, Pop, professional?

Willy. Terrific. Terrific job, boys. Good work, Biff.

Happy. Where's the surprise, Pop?

Willy. In the back seat of the car.

Happy. Boy! [*He runs off.*]

Biff. What is it, Dad? Tell me, what'd you buy?

Willy. [*Laughing, cuffs him.*] Never mind, something I want you to have.

Biff. [*Turns and starts off.*] What is it, Hap?

Happy. [*Offstage.*] It's a punching bag!

Biff. Oh, Pop!

Willy. It's got Gene Tunney's signature on it!

[HAPPY *runs onstage with a punching bag.*]

Biff. Gee, how'd you know we wanted a punching bag?

Willy. Well, it's the finest thing for the timing.

Happy. [*Lies down on his back and pedals with his feet.*] I'm losing weight, you notice, Pop?

Willy. [*To* HAPPY.] Jumping rope is good too.

Biff. Did you see the new football I got?

Willy. [*Examining the ball.*] Where'd you get a new ball?

Biff. The coach told me to practice my passing.

Willy. That so? And he gave you the ball, heh?

Biff. Well, I borrowed it from the locker room. [*He laughs confidentially.*]

Willy. [*Laughing with him at the theft.*] I want you to return that.

Happy. I told you he wouldn't like it!

Biff. [*Angrily.*] Well, I'm bringing it back!

Willy. [*Stopping the incipient argument, to* HAPPY.] Sure, he's gotta practice with a regulation ball, doesn't he? [*To* BIFF.] Coach'll probably congratulate you on your initiative!

Biff. Oh, he keeps congratulating my initiative all the time, Pop.

Willy. That's because he likes you. If somebody else took that ball there'd be an uproar. So what's the report, boys, what's the report?

Biff. Where'd you go this time, Dad? Gee, we were lonesome for you.

Willy. [*Pleased, puts an arm around each boy and they come down to the apron.*] Lonesome, heh?

Biff. Missed you every minute.

Willy. Don't say? Tell you a secret, boys. Don't breathe it to a soul. Someday I'll have my own business, and I'll never have to leave home any more.

Happy. Like Uncle Charley, heh?

Willy. Bigger than Uncle Charley! Because Charley is not—liked. He's liked, but he's not—well liked.

Biff. Where'd you go this time, Dad?

Willy. Well, I got on the road, and I went north to Providence. Met the Mayor.

Biff. The Mayor of Providence!

Willy. He was sitting in the hotel lobby.

Biff. What'd he say?

Willy. He said, "Morning!" And I said, "You got a fine city here, Mayor." And then he had coffee with me. And then I went to Waterbury. Waterbury is a fine city. Big clock city, the famous Waterbury clock. Sold a nice bill there. And then Boston—Boston is the cradle of the Revolution. A fine city. And a couple of other towns in Mass., and on to Portland and Bangor and straight home!

Biff. Gee, I'd love to go with you some time, Dad.

Willy. Soon as summer comes.

Happy. Promise?

Willy. You and Hap and I, and I'll show you all the towns. America is full of beautiful towns and fine, upstanding people. And they know me, boys, they know me up and down New England. The finest people. And when I bring you fellas up, there'll be open sesame for all of us, 'cause one thing, boys: I have friends. I can park my car in any street in New England, and the cops protect it like their own. This summer, heh?

Biff and Happy. [*Together.*] Yeah! You bet!

Willy. We'll take our bathing suits.

Happy. We'll carry your bags, Pop!

Willy. Oh, won't that be something! Me comin' into the Boston stores with you boys carryin' my bags. What a sensation!

[BIFF *is prancing around, practicing passing the ball.*]

Willy. You nervous, Biff, about the game?

Biff. Not if you're gonna be there.

Willy. What do they say about you in school, now that they made you captain?

Happy. There's a crowd of girls behind him everytime the classes change.

Biff. [*Taking* WILLY's *hand.*] This Saturday, Pop, this Saturday—just for you I'm going to break through for a touchdown.

Happy. You're supposed to pass.

Biff. I'm takin' one play for Pop. You watch me, Pop, and when I take off my helmet, that means I'm breakin' out. Then you watch me crash through that line!

Willy. [*Kisses* BIFF.] Oh, wait'll I tell this in Boston!

[BERNARD *enters in knickers. He is younger than* BIFF, *earnest and loyal, a worried boy.*]

Bernard. Biff, where are you? You're supposed to study with me today.

Willy. Hey, looka Bernard. What're you lookin' so anemic about, Bernard?

Bernard. He's gotta study, Uncle Willy. He's got Regents next week.

Happy. [*Tauntingly, spinning* BERNARD *around.*] Let's box, Bernard!

Bernard. Biff! [*He gets away from* HAPPY.] Listen, Biff, I heard Mr. Birnbaum say that if you don't start studyin' math he's gonna flunk you, and you won't graduate. I heard him!

Willy. You better study with him, Biff. Go ahead now.

Bernard. I heard him!

Biff. Oh, Pop, you didn't see my sneakers!

[*He holds up a foot for* WILLY *to look at.*]

Willy. Hey, that's a beautiful job of printing!

Bernard. [*Wiping his glasses.*] Just because he printed University of Virginia on his sneakers doesn't mean they've got to graduate him, Uncle Willy!

Willy. [*Angrily.*] What're you talking about? With scholarships to three universities, they're gonna flunk him?

Bernard. But I heard Mr. Birnbaum say——

Willy. Don't be a pest, Bernard! [*To his boys.*] What an anemic!

Bernard. Okay, I'm waiting for you in my house, Biff.

[BERNARD *goes off. The* LOMANS *laugh.*]

Willy. Bernard is not well liked, is he?

Biff. He's liked, but he's not well liked.

Happy. That's right, Pop.

Willy. That's just what I mean. Bernard can get the best marks in school, y'understand, but when he gets out in the business world, y'understand, you are going to be five times ahead of him. That's why I thank Almighty God you're both built like Adonises. Because the man who makes an appearance in the business world, the man who creates personal interest, is the man who gets ahead. Be liked and you will never want. You take me, for instance. I never have to wait in line to see a buyer. "Willy Loman is here!" That's all they have to know, and I go right through.

Biff. Did you knock them dead, Pop?

Willy. Knocked 'em cold in Providence, slaughtered 'em in Boston.

Happy. [*On his back, pedaling again.*] I'm losing weight; you notice, Pop?

[LINDA *enters, as of old, a ribbon in her hair, carrying a basket of washing.*]

Linda. [*With youthful energy.*] Hello, dear!

Willy. Sweetheart!

Linda. How'd the Chevvy run?

Willy. Chevrolet, Linda, is the greatest car ever built. [*To the boys.*] Since when do you let your mother carry wash up the stairs?

Biff. Grab hold there, boy!

Happy. Where to, Mom?

Linda. Hang them up on the line. And you better go down to your friends, Biff. The cellar is full of boys. They don't know what to do with themselves.

Biff. Ah, when Pop comes home they can wait!

Willy. [*Laughs appreciatively.*] You better go down and tell them what to do, Biff.

Biff. I think I'll have them sweep out the furnace room.

Willy. Good work, Biff.

Biff. [*Goes through wall-line of kitchen to doorway at back and calls down.*] Fellas! Everybody sweep out the furnace room! I'll be right down!

Voices. All right! Okay, Biff.

Biff. George and Sam and Frank, come out back! We're hangin' up the wash! Come on, Hap, on the double!

[*He and* HAPPY *carry out the basket.*]

Linda. The way they obey him!

Willy. Well, that's training, the training. I'm tellin' you, I was sellin' thousands and thousands, but I had to come home.

Linda. Oh, the whole block'll be at that game. Did you sell anything?

Willy. I did five hundred gross in Providence and seven hundred gross in Boston.

Linda. No! Wait a minute, I've got a pencil. [*She pulls pencil and paper out of her apron pocket.*] That makes your commission . . . Two hundred—my God! Two hundred and twelve dollars!

Willy. Well, I didn't figure it yet, but . . .

Linda. How much did you do?

Willy. Well, I—I did—about a hundred and eighty gross in Providence. Well, no —it came to—roughly two hundred gross on the whole trip.

Linda. [*Without hesitation.*] Two hundred gross. That's . . . [*She figures.*]

Willy. The trouble was that three of the stores were half closed for inventory in Boston. Otherwise I woulda broke records.

Linda. Well, it makes seventy dollars and some pennies. That's very good.

Willy. What do we owe?

Linda. Well on the first there's sixteen dollars on the refrigerator——

Willy. Why sixteen?

Linda. Well, the fan belt broke, so it was a dollar eighty.

Willy. But it's brand new.

Linda. Well, the man said that's the way it is. Till they work themselves in, y'know.

[*They move through the wall-line into the kitchen.*]

Willy. I hope we didn't get stuck on that machine.

Linda. They got the biggest ads of any of them!

Willy. I know, it's a fine machine. What else?

Linda. Well, there's nine-sixty for the washing machine. And for the vacuum cleaner there's three and a half due on the fifteenth. Then the roof; you got twenty-one dollars remaining.

Willy. It don't leak, does it?

Linda. No, they did a wonderful job. Then you owe Frank for the carburetor.

Willy. I'm not going to pay that man! That goddam Chevrolet, they ought to prohibit the manufacture of that car!

Linda. Well, you owe him three and a half. And odds and ends, comes to around a hundred and twenty dollars by the fifteenth.

Willy. A hundred and twenty dollars! My God, if business don't pick up I don't know what I'm gonna do!

Linda. Well, next week you'll do better.

Willy. Oh, I'll knock 'em dead next week. I'll go to Hartford. I'm very well liked in Hartford. You know, the trouble is, Linda, people don't seem to take to me.

[*They move onto the forestage.*]

Linda. Oh, don't be foolish.

Willy. I know it when I walk in. They seem to laugh at me.

Linda. Why? Why would they laugh at you? Don't talk that way, Willy.

[WILLY *moves to the edge of the stage.* LINDA *goes into the kitchen and starts to darn stockings.*]

Willy. I don't know the reason for it, but they just pass me by. I'm not noticed.

Linda. But you're doing wonderful, dear. You're making seventy to a hundred dollars a week.

Willy. But I gotta be at it ten, twelve hours a day. Other men—I don't know—they do it easier. I don't know why—I can't stop myself—I talk too much. A man oughta come in with a few words. One thing about Charley. He's a man of few words, and they respect him.

Linda. You don't talk too much, you're just lively.

Willy. [*Smiling.*] Well, I figure, what the hell, life is short, a couple of jokes. [*To himself.*] I joke too much!

[*The smile goes.*]

Linda. Why? You're——

Willy. I'm fat. I'm very—foolish to look at, Linda. I didn't tell you, but Christmas time I happened to be calling on F. H. Stewarts', and a salesman I know, as I was going in to see the buyer I heard him say something about—walrus. And I—I cracked him right across the face. I won't take that. I simply will not take that. But they do laugh at me. I know that.

Linda. Darling . . .

Willy. I gotta overcome it. I know I gotta overcome it. I'm not dressing to advantage, maybe.

Linda. Willy, darling, you're the handsomest man in the world——

Willy. Oh, no, Linda.

Linda. To me you are. [*Slight pause.*] The handsomest.

[*From the darkness is heard the laughter of a woman.* WILLY *doesn't turn to it, but it continues through* LINDA'S *lines.*]

Linda. And the boys, Willy. Few men are idolized by their children the way you are.

[*Music is heard as behind a scrim, to the left of the house,* THE WOMAN, *dimly seen, is dressing.*]

Willy. [*With great feeling.*] You're the best there is, Linda, you're a pal, you know that? On the road—on the road I want to grab you sometimes and just kiss the life outa you.

[*The laughter is loud now, and he moves into a brightening area at the left, where* THE WOMAN *has come from behind the scrim and is standing, putting on her hat, looking into a "mirror" and laughing.*]

Willy. 'Cause I get so lonely—especially when business is bad and there's nobody to talk to. I get the feeling that I'll never sell anything again, that I won't make a living for you, or a business, a business for the boys. [*He talks through* THE WOMAN'S *subsiding laughter;* THE WOMAN *primps at the "mirror."*] There's so much I want to make for——

The Woman. Me? You didn't make me, Willy. I picked you.

Willy. [*Pleased.*] You picked me?

The Woman. [*Who is quite proper-looking,* WILLY'S *age.*] I did. I've been sitting at that desk watching all the salesmen go by, day in, day out. But you've got such a sense of humor, and we do have such a good time together, don't we?

Willy. Sure, sure. [*He takes her in his arms.*] Why do you have to go now?

The Woman. It's two o'clock . . .

Willy. No, come on in! [*He pulls her.*]

The Woman. . . . my sisters'll be scandalized. When'll you be back?

Willy. Oh, two weeks about. Will you come up again?

The Woman. Sure thing. You do make me laugh. It's good for me. [*She squeezes his arm, kisses him.*] And I think you're a wonderful man.

Willy. You picked me, heh?

The Woman. Sure. Because you're so sweet. And such a kidder.

Willy. Well, I'll see you next time I'm in Boston.

The Woman. I'll put you right through to the buyers.

Willy. [*Slapping her bottom.*] Right. Well, bottoms up!

The Woman. [*Slaps him gently and laughs.*] You just kill me, Willy. [*He suddenly grabs her and kisses her roughly.*] You kill me. And thanks for the stockings. I love a lot of stockings. Well, good night.

Willy. Good night. And keep your pores open!

The Woman. Oh, Willy!

[THE WOMAN *bursts out laughing, and* LINDA'S *laughter blends in.* THE WOMAN *disappears into the dark. Now the area at the kitchen table brightens.* LINDA *is sitting where she was at the kitchen table, but now is mending a pair of her silk stockings.*]

Linda. You are, Willy. The handsomest man. You've got no reason to feel that——

Willy. [*Coming out of* THE WOMAN'S *dimming area and going over to* LINDA.] I'll make it all up to you, Linda, I'll——

Linda. There's nothing to make up, dear. You're doing fine, better than——

Willy. [*Noticing her mending.*] What's that?

Linda. Just mending my stockings. They're so expensive——

Willy. [*Angrily, taking them from her.*] I won't have you mending stockings in this house! Now throw them out!

[LINDA *puts the stockings in her pocket.*]

Bernard. [*Entering on the run.*] Where is he? If he doesn't study!

Willy. [*Moving to the forestage, with great agitation.*] You'll give him the answers!

Bernard. I do, but I can't on a Regents! That's a state exam! They're liable to arrest me!

Willy. Where is he? I'll whip him, I'll whip him!

Linda. And he'd better give back that football, Willy, it's not nice.

Willy. Biff! Where is he? Why is he taking everything?

Linda. He's too rough with the girls, Willy. All the mothers are afraid of him!

Willy. I'll whip him!

Bernard. He's driving the car without a license!

[THE WOMAN'S *laugh is heard.*]

Willy. Shut up!

Linda. All the mothers——

Willy. Shut up!

Bernard. [*Backing quietly away and out.*] Mr. Birnbaum says he's stuck up.

Willy. Get outa here!

Bernard. If he doesn't buckle down he'll flunk math! [*He goes off.*]

Linda. He's right, Willy, you've gotta——

Willy. [*Exploding at her.*] There's nothing the matter with him! You want him to be a worm like Bernard? He's got spirit, personality . . .

[*As he speaks,* LINDA, *almost in tears, exits into the living-room.* WILLY *is alone in the kitchen, wilting and staring. The leaves are gone. It is night again, and the apartment houses look down from behind.*]

Willy. Loaded with it. Loaded! What is he stealing? He's giving it back, isn't he? Why is he stealing? What did I tell him? I never in my life told him anything but decent things.

[HAPPY *in pajamas has come down the stairs;* WILLY *suddenly becomes aware of* HAPPY'S *presence.*]

Happy. Let's go now, come on.

Willy. [*Sitting down at the kitchen table.*] Huh! Why did she have to wax the floors herself? Everytime she waxes the floors she keels over. She knows that!

Happy. Shh! Take it easy. What brought you back tonight?

Willy. I got an awful scare. Nearly hit a kid in Yonkers. God! Why didn't I go to Alaska with my brother Ben that time! Ben! That man was a genius, that man was success incarnate! What a mistake! He begged me to go.

Happy. Well, there's no use in——

Willy. You guys! There was a man started with the clothes on his back and ended up with diamond mines!

Happy. Boy, someday I'd like to know how he did it.

Willy. What's the mystery? The man knew what he wanted and went out and got it! Walked into a jungle, and comes out, the age of twenty-one, and he's rich! The world is an oyster, but you don't crack it open on a mattress!

Happy. Pop, I told you I'm gonna retire you for life.

Willy. You'll retire me for life on seventy goddam dollars a week? And your women and your car and your apartment, and you'll retire me for life! Christ's sake, I couldn't get past Yonkers today! Where are you guys, where are you? The woods are burning! I can't drive a car!

[CHARLEY *has appeared in the doorway. He is a large man, slow of speech, laconic, immovable. In all he says, despite what he says, there is pity, and, now, trepidation. He has a robe over pajamas, slippers on his feet. He enters the kitchen.*]

Charley. Everything all right?

Happy. Yeah, Charley, everything's . . .

Willy. What's the matter?

Charley. I heard some noise. I thought something happened. Can't we do something about the walls? You sneeze in here, and in my house hats blow off.

Happy. Let's go to bed, Dad. Come on.

[CHARLEY *signals to* HAPPY *to go.*]

Willy. You go ahead. I'm not tired at the moment.

Happy. [*To* WILLY.] Take it easy, huh?

[*He exits.*]

Willy. What're you doin' up?

Charley. [*Sitting down at the kitchen table opposite* WILLY.] Couldn't sleep good. I had a heartburn.

Willy. Well, you don't know how to eat.

Charley. I eat with my mouth.

Willy. No, you're ignorant. You gotta know about vitamins and things like that.

Charley. Come on, let's shoot. Tire you out a little.

Willy. [*Hesitantly.*] All right. You got cards?

Charley. [*Taking a deck from his pocket.*] Yeah, I got them. Someplace. What is it with those vitamins?

Willy. [*Dealing.*] They build up your bones. Chemistry.

Charley. Yeah, but there's no bones in a heartburn.

Willy. What are you talkin' about? Do you know the first thing about it?

Charley. Don't get insulted.

Willy. Don't talk about something you don't know anything about.

[*They are playing. Pause.*]

Charley. What're you doin' home?

Willy. A little trouble with the car.

Charley. Oh. [*Pause.*] I'd like to take a trip to California.

Willy. Don't say.

Charley. You want a job?

Willy. I got a job; I told you that. [*After a slight pause.*] What the hell are you offering me a job for?

Charley. Don't get insulted.

Willy. Don't insult me.

Charley. I don't see no sense in it. You don't have to go on this way.

Willy. I got a good job. [*Slight pause.*] What do you keep comin' in here for?

Charley. You want me to go?

Willy. [*After a pause, withering.*] I can't understand it. He's going back to Texas again. What the hell is that?

Charley. Let him go.

Willy. I got nothin' to give him, Charley. I'm clean, I'm clean.

Charley. He won't starve. None a them starve. Forget about him.

Willy. Then what have I got to remember?

Charley. You take it too hard. To hell with it. When a deposit bottle is broken you don't get your nickel back.

Willy. That's easy enough for you to say.

Charley. That ain't easy for me to say.

Willy. Did you see the ceiling I put up in the living-room?

Charley. Yeah, that's a piece of work. To put up a ceiling is a mystery to me. How do you do it?

Willy. What's the difference?

Charley. Well, talk about it.

Willy. You gonna put up a ceiling?

Charley. How could I put up a ceiling?

Willy. Then what the hell are you bothering me for?

Charley. You're insulted again.

Willy. A man who can't handle tools is not a man. You're disgusting.

Charley. Don't call me disgusting, Willy.

[UNCLE BEN, *carrying a valise and an umbrella, enters the forestage from around the right corner of the house. He is a stolid man, in his sixties, with a mustache and an authoritative air. He is utterly certain of his destiny, and there is an aura of far places about him. He enters exactly as* WILLY *speaks.*]

Willy. I'm getting awfully tired, Ben.

[BEN'S *music is heard.* BEN *looks around at everything.*]

Charley. Good, keep playing; you'll sleep better. Did you call me Ben?

[BEN *looks at his watch.*]

Willy. That's funny. For a second there you reminded me of my brother Ben.

Ben. I only have a few minutes.

[*He strolls, inspecting the place.* WILLY *and* CHARLEY *continue playing.*]

Charley. You never heard from him again, heh? Since that time?

Willy. Didn't Linda tell you? Couple of weeks ago we got a letter from his wife in Africa. He died.

Charley. That so.

Ben. [*Chuckling.*] So this is Brooklyn, eh?

Charley. Maybe you're in for some of his money.

Willy. Naa, he had seven sons. There's just one opportunity I had with that man . . .

Ben. I must make a train, William. There are several properties I'm looking at in Alaska.

Willy. Sure, sure! If I'd gone with him to Alaska that time, everything would've been totally different.

Charley. Go on, you'd froze to death up there.

Willy. What're you talking about?

Ben. Opportunity is tremendous in Alaska, William. Surprised you're not up there.

Willy. Sure, tremendous.

Charley. Heh?

Willy. There was the only man I ever met who knew the answers.

Charley. Who?

Ben. How are you all?

Willy. [*Taking a pot, smiling.*] Fine, fine.

Charley. Pretty sharp tonight.

Ben. Is Mother living with you?

Willy. No, she died a long time ago.

Charley. Who?

Ben. That's too bad. Fine specimen of a lady, Mother.

Willy. [*To* CHARLEY.] Heh?

Ben. I'd hoped to see the old girl.

Charley. Who died?

Ben. Heard anything from Father, have you?

Willy. [*Unnerved.*] What do you mean, who died?

Charley. [*Taking a pot.*] What're you talkin' about?

Ben. [*Looking at his watch.*] William, it's half-past eight!

Willy. [*As though to dispel his confusion he angrily stops* CHARLEY'S *hand.*] That's my build!

Charley. I put the ace——

Willy. If you don't know how to play the game I'm not gonna throw my money away on you!

Charley. [*Rising.*] It was my ace, for God's sake!

Willy. I'm through, I'm through!

Ben. When did Mother die?

Willy. Long ago. Since the beginning you never knew how to play cards.

Charley. [*Picks up the cards and goes to the door.*] All right! Next time I'll bring a deck with five aces.

Willy. I don't play that kind of game!

Charley. [*Turning to him.*] You ought to be ashamed of yourself!

Willy. Yeah?

Charley. Yeah! [*He goes out.*]

Willy. [*Slamming the door after him.*] Ignoramus!

Ben. [*As* WILLY *comes toward him through the wall-line of the kitchen.*] So you're William.

Willy. [*Shaking* BEN'S *hand.*] Ben! I've been waiting for you so long! What's the answer? How did you do it?

Ben. Oh, there's a story in that.

[LINDA *enters the forestage, as of old, carrying the wash basket.*]

Linda. Is this Ben?

Ben. [*Gallantly.*] How do you do, my dear.

Linda. Where've you been all these years? Willy's always wondered why you——

Willy. [*Pulling* BEN *away from her impatiently.*] Where is Dad? Didn't you follow him? How did you get started?

Ben. Well, I don't know how much you remember.

Willy. Well, I was just a baby, of course, only three or four years old——

Ben. Three years and eleven months.

Willy. What a memory, Ben!

Ben. I have many enterprises, William, and I have never kept books.

Willy. I remember I was sitting under the wagon in—was it Nebraska?

Ben. It was South Dakota, and I gave you a bunch of wild flowers.

Willy. I remember you walking away down some open road.

Ben. [*Laughing.*] I was going to find Father in Alaska.

Willy. Where is he?

Ben. At that age I had a very faulty view of geography, William. I discovered after a few days that I was heading due south; so instead of Alaska, I ended up in Africa.

Linda. Africa!

Willy. The Gold Coast!

Ben. Principally diamond mines.

Linda. Diamond mines!

Ben. Yes, my dear. But I've only a few minutes——

Willy. No! Boys! Boys! [YOUNG BIFF *and* HAPPY *appear.*] Listen to this. This is your Uncle Ben, a great man! Tell my boys, Ben!

Ben. Why, boys, when I was seventeen I walked into the jungle, and when I was twenty-one I walked out. [*He laughs.*] And by God I was rich.

Willy. [*To the boys.*] You see what I been talking about? The greatest things can happen!

Ben. [*Glancing at his watch.*] I have an appointment in Ketchikan Tuesday week.

Willy. No, Ben! Please tell about Dad. I want my boys to hear. I want them to know the kind of stock they spring from. All I remember is a man with a big beard, and I was in Mamma's lap, sitting around a fire, and some kind of high music.

Ben. His flute. He played the flute.

Willy. Sure, the flute, that's right!

[*New music is heard, a high, rollicking tune.*]

Ben. Father was a very great and a very wild-hearted man. We would start in Boston, and he'd toss the whole family into the wagon, and then he'd drive the team right across the country; through Ohio, and Indiana, Michigan, Illinois, and all the Western states. And we'd stop in the towns and sell the flutes that he'd made on the way. Great inventor, Father. With one gadget he made more in a week than a man like you could make in a lifetime.

Willy. That's just the way I'm bringing them up, Ben—rugged, well liked, all-around.

Ben. Yeah? [*To* BIFF.] Hit that, boy —hard as you can.

[*He pounds his stomach.*]

Biff. Oh, no, sir!

Ben. [*Taking boxing stance.*] Come on, get to me! [*He laughs.*]

Willy. Go to it, Biff! Go ahead, show him!

Biff. Okay!

[*He cocks his fists and starts in.*]

Linda. [*To* WILLY.] Why must he fight, dear?

Ben. [*Sparring with* BIFF.] Good boy! Good boy!

Willy. How's that, Ben, heh?

Happy. Give him the left, Biff!

Linda. Why are you fighting?

Ben. Good boy!

[*Suddenly comes in, trips* BIFF, *and stands over him, the point of his umbrella poised over* BIFF'S *eye.*]

Linda. Look out, Biff!

Biff. Gee!

Ben. [*Patting* BIFF'S *knee.*] Never fight fair with a stranger, boy. You'll never get out of the jungle that way. [*Taking* LINDA'S *hand and bowing.*] It was an honor and a pleasure to meet you, Linda.

Linda. [*Withdrawing her hand coldly, frightened.*] Have a nice—trip.

Ben. [*To* WILLY.] And good luck with your—what do you do?

Willy. Selling.

Ben. Yes. Well . . .

[*He raises his hand in farewell to all.*]

Willy. No, Ben, I don't want you to think . . . [*He takes* BEN'S *arm to show him.*] It's Brooklyn, I know, but we hunt too.

Ben. Really, now.

Willy. Oh, sure, there's snakes and rabbits and—that's why I moved out here. Why, Biff can fell any one of these trees in no time! Boys! Go right over to where they're building the apartment house and get some sand. We're gonna rebuild the entire front stoop right now! Watch this, Ben!

Biff. Yes, sir! On the double, Hap!

Happy. [*As he and* BIFF *run off.*] I lost weight, Pop, you notice?

[CHARLEY *enters in knickers, even before the boys are gone.*]

Charley. Listen, if they steal any more from that building the watchman'll put the cops on them!

Linda. [*To* WILLY.] Don't let Biff . . .

[BEN *laughs lustily.*]

Willy. You shoulda seen the lumber they brought home last week. At least a dozen six-by-tens worth all kinds of money.

Charley. Listen, if that watchman——

Willy. I gave them hell, understand. But I got a couple of fearless characters there.

Charley. Willy, the jails are full of fearless characters.

Ben. [*Clapping* WILLY *on the back, with a laugh at* CHARLEY.] And the stock exchange, friend!

Willy. [*Joining in* BEN'S *laughter.*] Where are the rest of your pants?

Charley. My wife bought them.

Willy. Now all you need is a golf club and you can go upstairs and go to sleep. [*To* BEN.] Great athlete! Between him and his son Bernard they can't hammer a nail!

Bernard. [*Rushing in.*] The watchman's chasing Biff!

Willy. [*Angrily.*] Shut up! He's not stealing anything!

Linda. [*Alarmed, hurrying off left.*] Where is he? Biff, dear! [*She exits.*]

Willy. [*Moving toward the left, away from* BEN.] There's nothing wrong. What's the matter with you?

Ben. Nervy boy. Good!

Willy. [*Laughing.*] Oh, nerves of iron, that Biff!

Charley. Don't know what it is. My New England man comes back and he's bleedin', they murdered him up there.

Willy. It's contacts, Charley, I got important contacts!

Charley. [*Sarcastically.*] Glad to hear it, Willy. Come in later; we'll shoot a little casino. I'll take some of your Portland money. [*He laughs at* WILLY *and exits.*]

Willy. [*Turning to* BEN.] Business is bad, it's murderous. But not for me, of course.

Ben. I'll stop by on my way back to Africa.

Willy. [*Longingly.*] Can't you stay a few days? You're just what I need, Ben, because I—I have a fine position here, but

I—well, Dad left when I was such a baby and I never had a chance to talk to him and I still feel—kind of temporary about myself.

Ben. I'll be late for my train.

[*They are at opposite ends of the stage.*]

Willy. Ben, my boys—can't we talk? They'd go into the jaws of hell for me, see, but I——

Ben. William, you're being first-rate with your boys. Outstanding, manly chaps!

Willy. [*Hanging on to his words.*] Oh, Ben, that's good to hear! Because sometimes I'm afraid that I'm not teaching them the right kind of—— Ben, how should I teach them?

Ben. [*Giving great weight to each word, and with a certain vicious audacity.*] William, when I walked into the jungle, I was seventeen. When I walked out I was twenty-one. And, by God, I was rich!

[*He goes off into darkness around the right corner of the house.*]

Willy. . . . was rich! That's just the spirit I want to imbue them with! To walk into a jungle! I was right! I was right! I was right!

[BEN *is gone, but* WILLY *is still speaking to him as* LINDA, *in nightgown and robe, enters the kitchen, glances around for* WILLY, *then goes to the door of the house, looks out and sees him. Comes down to his left. He looks at her.*]

Linda. Willy, dear? Willy?

Willy. I was right!

Linda. Did you have some cheese? [*He can't answer.*] It's very late, darling. Come to bed, heh?

Willy. [*Looking straight up.*] Gotta break your neck to see a star in this yard.

Linda. You coming in?

Willy. Whatever happened to that diamond watch fob? Remember? When Ben came from Africa that time? Didn't he give me a watch fob with a diamond in it?

Linda. You pawned it, dear. Twelve, thirteen years ago. For Biff's radio correspondence course.

Willy. Gee, that was a beautiful thing. I'll take a walk.

Linda. But you're in your slippers.

Willy. [*Starting to go around the house at the left.*] I was right! I was! [*Half to* LINDA, *as he goes, shaking his head.*] What a man! There was a man worth talking to. I was right!

Linda. [*Calling after* WILLY.] But in your slippers, Willy!

[WILLY *is almost gone when* BIFF, *in his pajamas, comes down the stairs and enters the kitchen.*]

Biff. What is he doing out there?

Linda. Sh!

Biff. God Almighty, Mom, how long has he been doing this?

Linda. Don't, he'll hear you.

Biff. What the hell is the matter with him?

Linda. It'll pass by morning.

Biff. Shouldn't we do anything?

Linda. Oh, my dear, you should do a lot of things, but there's nothing to do, so go to sleep.

[HAPPY *comes down the stairs and sits on the steps.*]

Happy. I never heard him so loud, Mom.

Linda. Well, come around more often; you'll hear him.

[*She sits down at the table and mends the lining of* WILLY'S *jacket.*]

Biff. Why didn't you ever write me about this, Mom?

Linda. How would I write to you? For over three months you had no address.

Biff. I was on the move. But you know I thought of you all the time. You know that, don't you, pal?

Linda. I know, dear, I know. But he likes to have a letter. Just to know that there's still a possibility for better things.

Biff. He's not like this all the time, is he?

Linda. It's when you come home he's always the worst.

Biff. When I come home?

Linda. When you write you're coming, he's all smiles, and talks about the future, and—he's just wonderful. And then the closer you seem to come, the more shaky he gets, and then, by the time you get here, he's arguing, and he seems angry at you. I think it's just that maybe he can't bring himself to—to open up to you. Why are you so hateful to each other? Why is that?

Biff. [*Evasively.*] I'm not hateful, Mom.

Linda. But you no sooner come in the door than you're fighting!

Biff. I don't know why. I mean to change. I'm tryin', Mom, you understand?

Linda. Are you home to stay now?

Biff. I don't know. I want to look around, see what's doin'.

Linda. Biff, you can't look around all your life, can you?

Biff. I just can't take hold, Mom. I can't take hold of some kind of a life.

Linda. Biff, a man is not a bird, to come and go with the springtime.

Biff. Your hair . . . [*He touches her hair.*] Your hair got so gray.

Linda. Oh, it's been gray since you were in high school. I just stopped dyeing it, that's all.

Biff. Dye it again, will ya? I don't want my pal looking old. [*He smiles.*]

Linda. You're such a boy! You think you can go away for a year and . . . You've got to get it into your head now that one day you'll knock on this door and there'll be strange people here——

Biff. What are you talking about? You're not even sixty, Mom.

Linda. But what about your father?

Biff. [*Lamely.*] Well, I meant him too.

Happy. He admires Pop.

Linda. Biff, dear, if you don't have any feeling for him, then you can't have any feeling for me.

Biff. Sure I can, Mom.

Linda. No. You can't come just to see me, because I love him. [*With a threat, but only a threat, of tears.*] He's the dearest man in the world to me, and I won't have anyone making him feel unwanted and low and blue. You've got to make up your mind now, darling, there's no leeway any more. Either he's your father and you pay him that respect, or else you're not to come here. I know he's not easy to get along with—nobody knows that better than me—but . . .

Willy. [*From the left, with a laugh.*] Hey, hey, Biffo!

Biff. [*Starting to go out after* WILLY.] What the hell is the matter with him? [HAPPY *stops him.*]

Linda. Don't—don't go near him!

Biff. Stop making excuses for him! He always, always wiped the floor with you. Never had an ounce of respect for you.

Happy. He's always had respect for——

Biff. What the hell do you know about it?

Happy. [*Surlily.*] Just don't call him crazy!

Biff. He's got no character—— Charley wouldn't do this. Not in his own house—spewing out that vomit from his mind.

Happy. Charley never had to cope with what he's got to.

Biff. People are worse off than Willy Loman. Believe me, I've seen them!

Linda. Then make Charley your father, Biff. You can't do that, can you? I don't say he's a great man. Willy Loman never made a lot of money. His name was never in the paper. He's not the finest character that ever lived. But he's a human being, and a terrible thing is happening to him. So attention must be paid. He's not to be allowed to fall into his grave like an old dog. Attention, attention must be finally paid to such a person. You called him crazy——

Biff. I didn't mean——

Linda. No, a lot of people think he's lost his—balance. But you don't have to be very smart to know what his trouble is. The man is exhausted.

Happy. Sure!

Linda. A small man can be just as exhausted as a great man. He works for a company thirty-six years this March, opens up unheard-of territories to their trademark, and now in his old age they take his salary away.

Happy. [*Indignantly.*] I didn't know that, Mom.

Linda. You never asked, my dear! Now that you get your spending money some place else you don't trouble your mind with him.

Happy. But I gave you money last——

Linda. Christmas time, fifty dollars! To fix the hot water it cost ninety-seven fifty! For five weeks he's been on straight commission, like a beginner, an unknown!

Biff. Those ungrateful bastards!

Linda. Are they any worse than his sons? When he brought them business, when he was young, they were glad to see him. But now his old friends, the old buyers that loved him so and always found some order to hand him in a pinch—they're all dead, retired. He used to be able to make six, seven calls a day in Boston. Now he takes his valises out of the car and puts them back and takes them out again and he's exhausted. Instead of walking he talks now. He drives seven hundred miles, and when he gets there no one knows him any more, no one welcomes him. And what goes through a man's mind, driving seven hundred miles home without having earned a cent? Why shouldn't he talk to himself? Why? When he has to go to Charley to borrow fifty dollars a week and pretend to me that it's his pay? How long can that go on? How long? You see what I'm sitting here and waiting for? And you tell me he has no character? The man who never worked a day but for your benefit? When does he get the medal for that? Is this his reward—to turn around at the age of sixty-three and find his sons, who he loved better than his life, one a philandering bum——

Happy. Mom!

Linda. That's all you are, my baby! [*To

BIFF.] And you! What happened to the love you had for him? You were such pals! How you used to talk to him on the phone every night! How lonely he was till he could come home to you!

Biff. All right, Mom. I'll live here in my room, and I'll get a job. I'll keep away from him, that's all.

Linda. No, Biff. You can't stay here and fight all the time.

Biff. He threw me out of this house, remember that.

Linda. Why did he do that? I never knew why.

Biff. Because I know he's a fake and he doesn't like anybody around who knows!

Linda. Why a fake? In what way? What do you mean?

Biff. Just don't lay it all at my feet. It's between me and him—that's all I have to say. I'll chip in from now on. He'll settle for half my pay check. He'll be all right. I'm going to bed.

[*He starts for the stairs.*]

Linda. He won't be all right.

Biff. [*Turning on the stairs, furiously.*] I hate this city and I'll stay here. Now what do you want?

Linda. He's dying, Biff.

[HAPPY *turns quickly to her, shocked.*]

Biff. [*After a pause.*] Why is he dying?

Linda. He's been trying to kill himself.

Biff. [*With great horror.*] How?

Linda. I live from day to day.

Biff. What're you talking about?

Linda. Remember I wrote you that he smashed up the car again? In February?

Biff. Well?

Linda. The insurance inspector came. He said that they have evidence. That all these accidents in the last year—weren't—weren't—accidents.

Happy. How can they tell that? That's a lie.

Linda. It seems there's a woman . . .

[*She takes a breath as*

Biff. [*Sharply but contained.*] What woman . . .

Linda. [*Simultaneously*] . . . and this woman . . .

Linda. What?

Biff. Nothing. Go ahead.

Linda. What did you say?

Biff. Nothing. I just said what woman?

Happy. What about her?

Linda. Well, it seems she was walking down the road and saw his car. She says that he wasn't driving fast at all, and that he didn't skid. She says he came to that little bridge, and then deliberately smashed into the railing, and it was only the shallowness of the water that saved him.

Biff. Oh, no, he probably just fell asleep again.

Linda. I don't think he fell asleep.

Biff. Why not?

Linda. Last month . . . [*With great difficulty.*] Oh, boys, it's so hard to say a thing like this! He's just a big stupid man to you, but I tell you there's more good in him than in many other people. [*She chokes, wipes her eyes.*] I was looking for a fuse. The lights blew out, and I went down the cellar. And behind the fuse box—it happened to fall out—was a length of rubber pipe—just short.

Happy. No kidding?

Linda. There's a little attachment on the end of it. I knew right away. And sure enough, on the bottom of the water heater there's a new little nipple on the gas pipe.

Happy. [*Angrily.*] That—jerk.

Biff. Did you have it taken off?

Linda. I'm—I'm ashamed to. How can I mention it to him? Every day I go down and take away that little rubber pipe. But, when he comes home, I put it back where it was. How can I insult him that way? I don't know what to do. I live from day to day, boys. I tell you, I know every thought in his mind. It sounds so old-fashioned and silly, but I tell you he put his whole life into you and you've turned your backs on him. [*She is bent over in the chair, weeping, her face in her hands.*] Biff, I swear to God! Biff, his life is in your hands!

Happy. [*To* BIFF.] How do you like that damned fool!

Biff. [*Kissing her.*] All right, pal, all right. It's all settled now. I've been remiss. I know that, Mom. But now I'll stay, and I swear to you, I'll apply myself. [*Kneeling in front of her, in a fever of self-reproach.*] It's just—you see, Mom, I don't fit in business. Not that I won't try. I'll try, and I'll make good.

Happy. Sure you will. The trouble with you in business was you never tried to please people.

Biff. I know, I——

Happy. Like when you worked for Harrison's. Bob Harrison said you were tops, and then you go and do some damn fool thing like whistling whole songs in the elevator like a comedian.

Biff. [*Against* HAPPY.] So what? I like to whistle sometimes.

Happy. You don't raise a guy to a responsible job who whistles in the elevator!

Linda. Well, don't argue about it now.

Happy. Like when you'd go off and swim in the middle of the day instead of taking the line around.

Biff. [*His resentment rising.*] Well, don't you run off? You take off sometimes, don't you? On a nice summer day?

Happy. Yeah, but I cover myself!

Linda. Boys!

Happy. If I'm going to take a fade the boss can call any number where I'm supposed to be and they'll swear to him that I just left. I'll tell you something that I hate to say, Biff, but in the business world some of them think you're crazy.

Biff. [*Angered.*] Screw the business world!

Happy. All right, screw it! Great, but cover yourself!

Linda. Hap, Hap!

Biff. I don't care what they think! They've laughed at Dad for years, and you know why? Because we don't belong in this nuthouse of a city! We should be mixing cement on some open plain, or—or carpenters. A carpenter is allowed to whistle!

[WILLY *walks in from the entrance of the house, at left.*]

Willy. Even your grandfather was better than a carpenter. [*Pause. They watch him.*] You never grew up. Bernard does not whistle in the elevator, I assure you.

Biff. [*As though to laugh* WILLY *out of it.*] Yeah, but you do, Pop.

Willy. I never in my life whistled in an elevator! And who in the business world thinks I'm crazy?

Biff. I didn't mean it like that, Pop. Now don't make a whole thing out of it, will ya?

Willy. Go back to the West! Be a carpenter, a cowboy, enjoy yourself!

Linda. Willy, he was just saying——

Willy. I heard what he said!

Happy. [*Trying to quiet* WILLY.] Hey, Pop, come on now . . .

Willy. [*Continuing over* HAPPY'S *line.*] They laugh at me, heh? Go to Filene's, go to the Hub, go to Slattery's, Boston. Call out the name Willy Loman and see what happens! Big shot!

Biff. All right, Pop.

Willy. Big!

Biff. All right!

Willy. Why do you always insult me?

Biff. I didn't say a word. [*To* LINDA.] Did I say a word?

Linda. He didn't say anything, Willy.

Willy. [*Going to the doorway of the living-room.*] All right, good night, good night.

Linda. Willy, dear, he just decided . . .

Willy. [*To* BIFF.] If you get tired hanging around tomorrow, paint the ceiling I put up in the living-room.

Biff. I'm leaving early tomorrow.

Happy. He's going to see Bill Oliver, Pop.

Willy. [*Interestedly.*] Oliver? For what?

Biff. [*With reserve, but trying, trying.*] He always said he'd stake me. I'd like to go into business, so maybe I can take him up on it.

Linda. Isn't that wonderful?

Willy. Don't interrupt. What's wonderful about it? There's fifty men in the City of New York who'd stake him. [*To* BIFF.] Sporting goods?

Biff. I guess so. I know something about it and——

Willy. He knows something about it! You know sporting goods better than Spalding, for God's sake! How much is he giving you?

Biff. I don't know, I didn't even see him yet, but——

Willy. Then what're you talkin' about?

Biff. [*Getting angry.*] Well, all I said was I'm gonna see him, that's all!

Willy. [*Turning away.*] Ah, you're counting your chickens again.

Biff. [*Starting left for the stairs.*] Oh, Jesus, I'm going to sleep!

Willy. [*Calling after him.*] Don't curse in this house!

Biff. [*Turning.*] Since when did you get so clean?

Happy. [*Trying to stop them.*] Wait a . . .

Willy. Don't use that language to me! I won't have it!

Happy. [*Grabbing* BIFF, *shouts.*] Wait a minute! I got an idea. I got a feasible idea. Come here, Biff, let's talk this over now, let's talk some sense here. When I was down in Florida last time, I thought of a great idea to sell sporting goods. It just came back to me. You and I, Biff—we have a line, the Loman Line. We train a couple of weeks, and put on a couple of exhibitions, see?

Willy. That's an idea!

Happy. Wait! We form two basketball teams, see? Two water-polo teams. We play each other. It's a million dollars' worth of publicity. Two brothers, see? The Loman Brothers. Displays in the Royal Palms—all the hotels. And banners over the ring and the basketball court: "Loman Brothers." Baby, we could sell sporting goods!

Willy. That is a one-million-dollar idea!

Linda. Marvelous!

Biff. I'm in great shape as far as that's concerned.

Happy. And the beauty of it is, Biff, it wouldn't be like a business. We'd be out playin' ball again . . .

Biff. [*Enthused.*] Yeah, that's . . .

Willy. Million-dollar . . .

Happy. And you wouldn't get fed up with it, Biff. It'd be the family again. There'd be the old honor, and comradeship, and if you wanted to go off for a swim or somethin'—well, you'd do it! Without some smart cooky gettin' up ahead of you!

Willy. Lick the world! You guys together could absolutely lick the civilized world.

Biff. I'll see Oliver tomorrow. Hap, if we could work that out . . .

Linda. Maybe things are beginning to——

Willy. [*Wildly enthused, to* LINDA.] Stop interrupting! [*To* BIFF.] But don't wear sport jacket and slacks when you see Oliver.

Biff. No, I'll——

Willy. A business suit, and talk as little as possible, and don't crack any jokes.

Biff. He did like me. Always liked me.

Linda. He loved you!

Willy. [*To* LINDA.] Will you stop! [*To* BIFF.] Walk in very serious. You are not applying for a boy's job. Money is to pass. Be quiet, fine, and serious. Everybody likes a kidder, but nobody lends him money.

Happy. I'll try to get some myself, Biff. I'm sure I can.

Willy. I see great things for you kids, I think your troubles are over. But remember, start big and you'll end big. Ask for fifteen. How much you gonna ask for?

Biff. Gee, I don't know——

Willy. And don't say "Gee." "Gee" is a boy's word. A man walking in for fifteen thousand dollars does not say "Gee!"

Biff. Ten, I think, would be top, though.

Willy. Don't be so modest. You always started too low. Walk in with a big laugh. Don't look worried. Start off with a couple of your good stories to lighten things up. It's not what you say, it's how you say it—because personality always wins the day.

Linda. Oliver always thought the highest of him——

Willy. Will you let me talk?

Biff. Don't yell at her, Pop, will ya?

Willy. [*Angrily.*] I was talking, wasn't I?

Biff. I don't like you yelling at her all the time, and I'm tellin' you, that's all.

Willy. What're you, takin' over this house?

Linda. Willy——

Willy. [*Turning on her.*] Don't take his side all the time, goddammit!

Biff. [*Furiously.*] Stop yelling at her!

Willy. [*Suddenly pulling on his cheek, beaten-down, guilt-ridden.*] Give my best to Bill Oliver—he may remember me.

[*He exits through the living-room doorway.*]

Linda. [*Her voice subdued.*] What'd you have to start that for? [BIFF *turns away.*] You see how sweet he was as soon as you talked hopefully? [*She goes over to* BIFF.] Come up and say good night to him. Don't let him go to bed that way.

Happy. Come on, Biff, let's buck him up.

Linda. Please, dear. Just say good night. It takes so little to make him happy. Come. [*She goes through the living-room doorway, calling upstairs from within the living-room.*] Your pajamas are hanging in the bathroom, Willy!

Happy. [*Looking toward where* LINDA *went out.*] What a woman! They broke the mold when they made her. You know that, Biff?

Biff. He's off salary. My God, working on commission!

Happy. Well, let's face it: he's no hot-shot selling man. Except that sometimes, you have to admit, he's a sweet personality.

Biff. [*Deciding.*] Lend me ten bucks, will ya? I want to buy some new ties.

Happy. I'll take you to a place I know. Beautiful stuff. Wear one of my striped shirts tomorrow.

Biff. She got gray. Mom got awful old. Gee, I'm gonna go in to Oliver tomorrow and knock him for a——

Happy. Come on up. Tell that to Dad. Let's give him a whirl. Come on.

Biff. [*Steamed up.*] You know, with ten thousand bucks, boy!

Happy. [*As they go into the living-room.*] That's the talk, Biff, that's the first time I've heard the old confidence out of you! [*From within the living-room, fading off.*] You're gonna live with me, kid, and any babe you want just say the word . . .

[*The last lines are hardly heard. They are mounting the stairs to their parents' bedroom.*]

Linda. [*Entering her bedroom and addressing* WILLY, *who is in the bathroom. She is straightening the bed for him.*] Can you do anything about the shower? It drips.

Willy. [*From the bathroom.*] All of a sudden everything falls to pieces! Goddam plumbing, oughta be sued, those people. I hardly finished putting it in and the thing . . . [*His words rumble off.*]

Linda. I'm just wondering if Oliver will remember him. You think he might?

Willy. [*Coming out of the bathroom in his pajamas.*] Remember him? What's the matter with you, you crazy? If he'd've stayed with Oliver he'd be on top by now! Wait'll Oliver gets a look at him. You don't know the average caliber any more. The average young man today—— [*He is getting into bed.*] is got a caliber of zero. Greatest thing in the world for him was to bum around.

[BIFF *and* HAPPY *enter the bedroom. Slight pause.*]

Willy. [*Stops short, looking at* BIFF.] Glad to hear it, boy.

Happy. He wanted to say good night to you, sport.

Willy. [*To* BIFF.] Yeah. Knock him dead, boy. What'd you want to tell me?

Biff. Just take it easy, Pop. Good night. [*He turns to go.*]

Willy. [*Unable to resist.*] And if anything falls off the desk while you're talking to him—like a package or something—don't you pick it up. They have office boys for that.

Linda. I'll make a big breakfast——

Willy. Will you let me finish? [*To* BIFF.] Tell him you were in the business in the West. Not farm work.

Biff. All right, Dad.

Linda. I think everything——

Willy. [*Going right through her speech.*] And don't undersell yourself. No less than fifteen thousand dollars.

Biff. [*Unable to bear him.*] Okay. Good night, Mom. [*He starts moving.*]

Willy. Because you got a greatness in you, Biff; remember that. You got all kinds a greatness . . .

[*He lies back, exhausted.* BIFF *walks out.*]

Linda. [*Calling after* BIFF.] Sleep well, darling!

Happy. I'm gonna get married, Mom. I wanted to tell you.

Linda. Go to sleep, dear.

Happy. [*Going.*] I just wanted to tell you.

Willy. Keep up the good work. [HAPPY *exits.*] God . . . remember that Ebbets Field game? The championship of the city?

Linda. Just rest. Should I sing to you?

Willy. Yeah. Sing to me. [LINDA *hums a soft lullaby.*] When that team came out —he was the tallest, remember?

Linda. Oh, yes. And in gold.

[BIFF *enters the darkened kitchen, takes a cigarette, and leaves the house. He comes downstage into a golden pool of light. He smokes, staring at the night.*]

Willy. Like a young god. Hercules—something like that. And the sun, the sun all around him. Remember how he waved to me? Right up from the field, with the representatives of three colleges standing by? And the buyers I brought, and the cheers when he came out—Loman, Loman, Loman! God Almighty, he'll be great yet. A star like that, magnificent, can never really fade away!

[*The light on* WILLY *is fading. The gas heater begins to glow through the kitchen wall, near the stairs, a blue flame beneath red coils.*]

Linda. [*Timidly.*] Willy dear, what has he got against you?

Willy. I'm so tired. Don't talk any more.

[BIFF *slowly returns to the kitchen. He stops, stares toward the heater.*]

Linda. Will you ask Howard to let you work in New York?

Willy. First thing in the morning. Everything'll be all right.

[BIFF *reaches behind the heater and draws out a length of rubber tubing. He is horrified and turns his head toward* WILLY'S *room, still dimly lit, from which the strains of* LINDA'S *desperate but monotonous humming rise.*]

Willy. [*Staring through the window into the moonlight.*] Gee, look at the moon moving between the buildings!

[BIFF *wraps the tubing around his hand and quickly goes up the stairs.*]

CURTAIN

ACT TWO

Music is heard, gay and bright. The curtain rises as the music fades away. [WILLY, *in shirt sleeves, is sitting at the kitchen table, sipping coffee, his hat in his lap.* LINDA *is filling his cup when she can.*]

Willy. Wonderful coffee. Meal in itself.

Linda. Can I make you some eggs?

Willy. No. Take a breath.

Linda. You look so rested, dear.

Willy. I slept like a dead one. First time in months. Imagine, sleeping till ten on a Tuesday morning. Boys left nice and early, heh?

Linda. They were out of here by eight o'clock.

Willy. Good work!

Linda. It was so thrilling to see them leaving together. I can't get over the shaving lotion in this house!

Willy. [*Smiling.*] Mmm——

Linda. Biff was very changed this morning. His whole attitude seemed to be hopeful. He couldn't wait to get downtown to see Oliver.

Willy. He's heading for a change. There's no question, there simply are certain men that take longer to get—solidified. How did he dress?

Linda. His blue suit. He's so handsome in that suit. He could be a—anything in that suit!

[WILLY *gets up from the table.* LINDA *holds his jacket for him.*]

Willy. There's no question, no question at all. Gee, on the way home tonight I'd like to buy some seeds.

Linda. [*Laughing.*] That'd be wonderful. But not enough sun gets back there. Nothing'll grow any more.

Willy. You wait, kid, before it's all over we're gonna get a little place out in the country, and I'll raise some vegetables, a couple of chickens . . .

Linda. You'll do it yet, dear.

[WILLY *walks out of his jacket.* LINDA *follows him.*]

Willy. And they'll get married, and come for a weekend. I'd build a little guest house. 'Cause I got so many fine tools, all I'd need would be a little lumber and some peace of mind.

Linda. [*Joyfully.*] I sewed the lining . . .

Willy. I could build two guest houses, so they'd both come. Did he decide how much he's going to ask Oliver for?

Linda. [*Getting him into the jacket.*] He didn't mention it, but I imagine ten or fifteen thousand. You going to talk to Howard today?

Willy. Yeah. I'll put it to him straight and simple. He'll just have to take me off the road.

Linda. And, Willy, don't forget to ask for a little advance, because we've got the insurance premium. It's the grace period now.

Willy. That's a hundred . . . ?

Linda. A hundred and eight, sixty-eight. Because we're a little short again.

Willy. Why are we short?

Linda. Well, you had the motor job on the car . . .

Willy. That goddam Studebaker!

Linda. And you got one more payment on the refrigerator . . .

Willy. But it just broke again!

Linda. Well, it's old, dear.

Willy. I told you we should've bought a well-advertised machine. Charley bought a General Electric and it's twenty years old and it's still good, that son-of-a-bitch.

Linda. But, Willy——

Willy. Whoever heard of a Hastings refrigerator? Once in my life I would like to own something outright before its broken! I'm always in a race with the junkyard! I just finished paying for the car and it's on its last legs. The refrigerator consumes belts like a goddam maniac. They time those things. They time them so when you've finally paid for them, they're used up.

Linda. [*Buttoning up his jacket as he unbuttons it.*] All told, about two hundred dollars would carry us, dear. But that includes the last payment on the mortgage. After this payment, Willy, the house belongs to us.

Willy. It's twenty-five years!

Linda. Biff was nine years old when we bought it.

Willy. Well, that's a great thing. To weather a twenty-five year mortgage is——

Linda. It's an accomplishment.

Willy. All the cement, the lumber, the reconstruction I put in this house! There ain't a crack to be found in it any more.

Linda. Well, it served its purpose.

Willy. What purpose? Some stranger'll come along, move in, and that's that. If only Biff would take this house, and raise a family . . . [*He starts to go.*] Good-by, I'm late.

Linda. [*Suddenly remembering.*] Oh, I forgot! You're supposed to meet them for dinner.

Willy. Me?

Linda. At Frank's Chop House on Forty-eighth near Sixth Avenue.

Willy. Is that so! How about you?

Linda. No, just the three of you. They're gonna blow you to a big meal!

Willy. Don't say! Who thought of that?

Linda. Biff came to me this morning, Willy, and he said, "Tell Dad, we want to blow him to a big meal." Be there six o'clock. You and your two boys are going to have dinner.

Willy. Gee whiz! That's really somethin'. I'm gonna knock Howard for a loop, kid. I'll get an advance, and I'll come home with a New York job. Goddammit, now I'm gonna do it!

Linda. Oh, that's the spirit, Willy!

Willy. I will never get behind a wheel the rest of my life!

Linda. It's changing, Willy, I can feel it changing!

Willy. Beyond a question. G'by, I'm late. [*He starts to go again.*]

Linda. [*Calling after him as she runs to the kitchen table for a handkerchief.*] You got your glasses?

Willy. [*Feels for them, then comes back in.*] Yeah, yeah, got my glasses.

Linda. [*Giving him the handkerchief.*] And a handkerchief.

Willy. Yeah, handkerchief.

Linda. And your saccharine?

Willy. Yeah, my saccharine.

Linda. Be careful on the subway stairs.

[*She kisses him, and a silk stocking is seen hanging from her hand.* WILLY *notices it.*]

Willy. Will you stop mending stockings? At least while I'm in the house. It gets me nervous. I can't tell you. Please.

[LINDA *hides the stocking in her hand as she follows* WILLY *across the forestage in front of the house.*]

Linda. Remember, Frank's Chop House.

Willy. [*Passing the apron.*] Maybe beets would grow out there.

Linda. [*Laughing.*] But you tried so many times.

Willy. Yeah. Well, don't work hard today.

[*He disappears around the right corner of the house.*]

Linda. Be careful!

[*As* WILLY *vanishes,* LINDA *waves to him. Suddenly the phone rings. She runs across the stage and into the kitchen and lifts it.*]

Linda. Hello? Oh, Biff! I'm so glad you called, I just . . . Yes, sure, I just told him. Yes, he'll be there for dinner at six o'clock, I didn't forget. Listen, I was just dying to tell you. You know that little rubber pipe I told you about? That he connected to the gas heater? I finally decided to go down the cellar this morning and take it away and destroy it. But it's gone! Imagine? He took it away himself; it isn't there! [*She listens.*] When? Oh, then you took it. Oh—nothing, it's just that I'd hoped he'd taken it away himself. Oh, I'm not worried, darling, because this morning he left in such high spirits, it was like the old days! I'm not afraid any more. Did Mr. Oliver see you? . . . Well, you wait there then. And make a nice impression on him, darling. Just don't perspire too much before you see him. And have a nice time with Dad. He may have big news too! . . . That's right, a New York job. And be sweet to him tonight, dear. Be loving to him. Because he's only a little boat looking for a harbor. [*She is trembling with sorrow and joy.*] Oh, that's wonderful, Biff, you'll save his life. Thanks, darling. Just put your arm around him when he comes into the restaurant. Give him a smile. That's the boy . . . Good-by, dear. . . . You got your comb? . . . That's fine. Good-by, Biff dear.

[*In the middle of her speech,* HOWARD WAGNER, *thirty-six, wheels on a small typewriter table on which is a wire-recording machine and proceeds to plug it in. This is on the left forestage. Light slowly fades on* LINDA *as it rises on* HOWARD. HOWARD *is intent on threading the machine and only glances over his shoulder as* WILLY *appears.*]

Willy. Pst! Pst!

Howard. Hello, Willy, come in.

Willy. Like to have a little talk with you, Howard.

Howard. Sorry to keep you waiting. I'll be with you in a minute.

Willy. What's that, Howard?

Howard. Didn't you ever see one of these? Wire recorder.

Willy. Oh. Can we talk a minute?

Howard. Records things. Just got delivery yesterday. Been driving me crazy, the most terrific machine I ever saw in my life. I was up all night with it.

Willy. What do you do with it?

Howard. I bought it for dictation, but you can do anything with it. Listen to this. I had it home last night. Listen to what I picked up. The first one is my daughter. Get this. [*He flicks the switch and "Roll out the Barrel" is heard being whistled.*] Listen to that kid whistle.

Willy. That is lifelike, isn't it?

Howard. Seven years old. Get that tone.

Willy. Ts, ts. Like to ask a little favor if you . . .

[*The whistling breaks off, and the voice of* HOWARD'S *daughter is heard.*]

His Daughter. "Now you, Daddy."

Howard. She's crazy for me! [*Again the*

same song is whistled.] That's me! Ha! [*He winks.*]

Willy. You're very good!

[*The whistling breaks off again. The machine runs silent for a moment.*]

Howard. Sh! Get this now, this is my son.

His Son. "The capital of Alabama is Montgomery; the capital of Arizona is Phoenix; the capital of Arkansas is Little Rock; the capital of California is Sacramento . . ." [*And on, and on.*]

Howard. [*Holding up five fingers.*] Five years old, Willy!

Willy. He'll make an announcer some day!

His Son. [*Continuing.*] "The capital . . ."

Howard. Get that—alphabetical order! [*The machine breaks off suddenly.*] Wait a minute. The maid kicked the plug out.

Willy. It certainly is a——

Howard. Sh, for God's sake!

His Son. "It's nine o'clock, Bulova watch time. So I have to go to sleep."

Willy. That really is——

Howard. Wait a minute! The next is my wife. [*They wait.*]

Howard's Voice. "Go on, say something." [*Pause.*] "Well, you gonna talk?"

His Wife. "I can't think of anything."

Howard's Voice. "Well, talk—it's turning."

His Wife. [*Shyly, beaten.*] "Hello." [*Silence.*] "Oh, Howard, I can't talk into this . . ."

Howard. [*Snapping the machine off.*] That was my wife.

Willy. That is a wonderful machine. Can we——

Howard. I tell you, Willy, I'm gonna take my camera, and my bandsaw, and all my hobbies, and out they go. This is the most fascinating relaxation I ever found.

Willy. I think I'll get one myself.

Howard. Sure, they're only a hundred and a half. You can't do without it. Supposing you wanna hear Jack Benny, see? But you can't be at home at that hour. So you tell the maid to turn the radio on when Jack Benny comes on, and this automatically goes on with the radio . . .

Willy. And when you come home you . . .

Howard. You can come home twelve o'clock, one o'clock, any time you like, and you get yourself a Coke and sit yourself down, throw the switch, and there's Jack Benny's program in the middle of the night!

Willy. I'm definitely going to get one. Because lots of time I'm on the road, and I think to myself, what I must be missing on the radio!

Howard. Don't you have a radio in the car?

Willy. Well, yeah, but who ever thinks of turning it on?

Howard. Say, aren't you supposed to be in Boston?

Willy. That's what I want to talk to you about, Howard. You got a minute?

[*He draws a chair in from the wing.*]

Howard. What happened? What're you doing here?

Willy. Well . . .

Howard. You didn't crack up again, did you?

Willy. Oh, no. No . . .

Howard. Geez, you had me worried there for a minute. What's the trouble?

Willy. Well, tell you the truth, Howard. I've come to the decision that I'd rather not travel any more.

Howard. Not travel! Well, what'll you do?

Willy. Remember, Christmas time, when you had the party here? You said you'd try to think of some spot for me here in town.

Howard. With us?

Willy. Well, sure.

Howard. Oh, yeah, yeah. I remember. Well, I couldn't think of anything for you, Willy.

Willy. I tell ya, Howard. The kids are all grown up, y'know. I don't need much any more. If I could take home—well, sixty-five dollars a week, I could swing it.

Howard. Yeah, but Willy, see I——

Willy. I tell ya why, Howard. Speaking frankly and between the two of us, y'know—I'm just a little tired.

Howard. Oh, I could understand that, Willy. But you're a road man, Willy, and we do a road business. We've only got a half-dozen salesmen on the floor here.

Willy. God knows, Howard, I never asked a favor of any man. I was with the firm when your father used to carry you in here in his arms.

Howard. I know that, Willy, but——

Willy. Your father came to me the day you were born and asked me what I thought of the name of Howard, may he rest in peace.

Howard. I appreciate that, Willy, but there just is no spot here for you. If I had a spot I'd slam you right in, but I just don't have a single solitary spot.

[*He looks for his lighter.* WILLY *has*

picked it up and gives it to him. Pause.]

Willy. [*With increasing anger.*] Howard, all I need to set my table is fifty dollars a week.

Howard. But where am I going to put you, kid?

Willy. Look, it isn't a question of whether I can sell merchandise, is it?

Howard. No, but it's a business, kid, and everybody's gotta pull his own weight.

Willy. [*Desperately.*] Just let me tell you a story, Howard——

Howard. 'Cause you gotta admit, business is business.

Willy. [*Angrily.*] Business is definitely business, but just listen for a minute. You don't understand this. When I was a boy—eighteen, nineteen—I was already on the road. And there was a question in my mind as to whether selling had a future for me. Because in those days I had a yearning to go to Alaska. See, there were three gold strikes in one month in Alaska, and I felt like going out. Just for the ride, you might say.

Howard. [*Barely interested.*] Don't say.

Willy. Oh, yeah, my father lived many years in Alaska. He was an adventurous man. We've got quite a little streak of self-reliance in our family. I thought I'd go out with my older brother and try to locate him, and maybe settle in the North with the old man. And I was almost decided to go, when I met a salesman in the Parker House. His name was Dave Singleman. And he was eighty-four years old, and he'd drummed merchandise in thirty-one states. And old Dave, he'd go up to his room, y'understand, put on his green velvet slippers—I'll never forget—and pick up his phone and call the buyers, and without ever leaving his room, at the age of eighty-four, he made his living. And when I saw that, I realized that selling was the greatest career a man could want. 'Cause what could be more satisfying than to be able to go, at the age of eighty-four, into twenty or thirty different cities, and pick up a phone, and be remembered and loved and helped by so many different people? Do you know? when he died—and by the way he died the death of a salesman, in his green velvet slippers in the smoker of the New York, New Haven and Hartford, going into Boston—when he died, hundreds of salesmen and buyers were at his funeral. Things were sad on a lotta trains for months after that. [*He stands up.* HOWARD *has not looked at him.*] In those days there was personality in it, Howard. There was respect, and comradeship, and gratitude in it. Today, it's all cut and dried, and there's no chance for bringing friendship to bear—or personality. You see what I mean? They don't know me any more.

Howard. [*Moving away, to the right.*] That's just the thing, Willy.

Willy. If I had forty dollars a week—that's all I'd need. Forty dollars, Howard.

Howard. Kid, I can't take blood from a stone, I——

Willy. [*Desperation is on him now.*] Howard, the year Al Smith was nominated, your father came to me and——

Howard. [*Starting to go off.*] I've got to see some people, kid.

Willy. [*Stopping him.*] I'm talking about your father! There were promises made across this desk! You mustn't tell me you've got people to see—I put thirty-four years into this firm, Howard, and now I can't pay my insurance! You can't eat the orange and throw the peel away—a man is not a piece of fruit! [*After a pause.*] Now pay attention. Your father—in 1928 I had a big year. I averaged a hundred and seventy dollars a week in commissions.

Howard. [*Impatiently.*] Now, Willy, you never averaged——

Willy. [*Banging his hand on the desk.*] I averaged a hundred and seventy dollars a week in the year of 1928! And your father came to me—or rather, I was in the office here—it was right over this desk—and he put his hand on my shoulder——

Howard. [*Getting up.*] You'll have to excuse me, Willy; I gotta see some people. Pull yourself together. [*Going out.*] I'll be back in a little while.

[*On* HOWARD'S *exit, the light on his chair grows very bright and strange.*]

Willy. Pull myself together! What the hell did I say to him? My God, I was yelling at him! How could I! [WILLY *breaks off, staring at the light, which occupies the chair, animating it. He approaches this chair, standing across the desk from it.*] Frank, Frank, don't you remember what you told me that time? How you put your hand on my shoulder, and Frank . . .

[*He leans on the desk and as he speaks the dead man's name he accidentally switches on the recorder, and instantly.*]

Howard's Son. ". . . of New York is Albany. The capital of Ohio is Cincinnati, the capital of Rhode Island is . . ."

[*The recitation continues.*]

Willy. [*Leaping away with fright, shout-*

ing.] Ha! Howard! Howard! Howard!

Howard. [*Rushing in.*] What happened?

Willy. [*Pointing at the machine, which continues nasally, childishly, with the capital cities.*] Shut it off! Shut it off!

Howard. [*Pulling the plug out.*] Look, Willy . . .

Willy. [*Pressing his hands to his eyes.*] I gotta get myself some coffee. I'll get some coffee . . .

[WILLY *starts to walk out.* HOWARD *stops him.*]

Howard. [*Rolling up the cord.*] Willy, look . . .

Willy. I'll go to Boston.

Howard. Willy, you can't go to Boston for us.

Willy. Why can't I go?

Howard. I don't want you to represent us. I've been meaning to tell you for a long time now.

Willy. Howard, are you firing me?

Howard. I think you need a good long rest, Willy.

Willy. Howard——

Howard. And when you feel better, come back, and we'll see if we can work something out.

Willy. But I gotta earn money, Howard. I'm in no position to——

Howard. Where are your sons? Why don't your sons give you a hand?

Willy. They're working on a very big deal.

Howard. This is no time for false pride, Willy. You go to your sons and you tell them that you're tired. You've got two great boys, haven't you?

Willy. Oh, no question, no question, but in the meantime . . .

Howard. Then that's that, heh?

Willy. All right, I'll go to Boston tomorrow.

Howard. No, no.

Willy. I can't throw myself on my sons. I'm not a cripple!

Howard. Look, kid, I'm busy this morning.

Willy. [*Grasping* HOWARD's *arm.*] Howard, you've got to let me go to Boston!

Howard. [*Hard, keeping himself under control.*] I've got a line of people to see this morning. Sit down, take five minutes, and pull yourself together, and then go home, will ya? I need the office, Willy. [*He starts to go, turns, remembering the recorder, starts to push off the table holding the recorder.*] Oh, yeah. Whenever you can this week, stop by and drop off the samples. You'll feel better, Willy, and then come back and we'll talk. Pull yourself together, kid, there's people outside.

[HOWARD *exits, pushing the table off left.* WILLY *stares into space, exhausted. Now the music is heard—* BEN'S *music—first distantly, then closer, closer. As* WILLY *speaks,* BEN *enters from the right. He carries valise and umbrella.*]

Willy. Oh, Ben, how did you do it? What is the answer? Did you wind up the Alaska deal already?

Ben. Doesn't take much time if you know what you're doing. Just a short business trip. Boarding ship in an hour. Wanted to say good-by.

Willy. Ben, I've got to talk to you.

Ben. [*Glancing at his watch.*] Haven't the time, William.

Willy. [*Crossing the apron to* BEN.] Ben, nothing's working out. I don't know what to do.

Ben. Now, look here, William. I've bought timberland in Alaska and I need a man to look after things for me.

Willy. God, timberland! Me and my boys in those grand outdoors!

Ben. You've a new continent at your doorstep, William. Get out of these cities; they're full of talk and time payments and courts of law. Screw on your fists and you can fight for a fortune up there.

Willy. Yes, yes! Linda, Linda!

[LINDA *enters as of old, with the wash.*]

Linda. Oh, you're back?

Ben. I haven't much time.

Willy. No, wait! Linda, he's got a proposition for me in Alaska.

Linda. But you've got—— [*To* BEN.] He's got a beautiful job here.

Willy. But in Alaska, kid, I could——

Linda. You're doing well enough, Willy!

Ben. [*To* LINDA.] Enough for what, my dear?

Linda. [*Frightened of* BEN *and angry at him.*] Don't say those things to him! Enough to be happy right here, right now. [*To* WILLY, *while* BEN *laughs.*] Why must everybody conquer the world? You're well liked, and the boys love you, and someday—[*To* BEN.]—why, old man Wagner told him just the other day that if he keeps it up he'll be a member of the firm, didn't he, Willy?

Willy. Sure, sure. I am building something with this firm, Ben, and if a man is building something he must be on the right track, mustn't he?

Ben. What are you building? Lay your hand on it. Where is it?

Willy. [*Hesitantly.*] That's true, Linda, there's nothing.

Linda. Why? [*To* BEN.] There's a man eighty-four years old——

Willy. That's right, Ben, that's right. When I look at that man I say, what is there to worry about?

Ben. Bah!

Willy. It's true, Ben. All he has to do is go into any city, pick up the phone, and he's making his living and you know why?

Ben. [*Picking up his valise.*] I've got to go.

Willy. [*Holding* BEN *back.*] Look at this boy!

[BIFF, *in his high school sweater, enters carrying suitcase.* HAPPY *carries* BIFF'S *shoulder guards, gold helmet, and football pants.*]

Willy. Without a penny to his name, three great universities are begging for him, and from there the sky's the limit, because it's not what you do, Ben. It's who you know and the smile on your face! It's contacts, Ben, contacts! The whole wealth of Alaska passes over the lunch table at the Commodore Hotel, and that's the wonder, the wonder of this country, that a man can end with diamonds here on the basis of being liked! [*He turns to* BIFF.] And that's why when you get out on that field today it's important. Because thousands of people will be rooting for you and loving you. [*To* BEN, *who has again begun to leave.*] And Ben! when he walks into a business office his name will sound out like a bell and all the doors will open to him! I've seen it, Ben, I've seen it a thousand times! You can't feel it with your hand like timber, but it's there!

Ben. Good-by, William.

Willy. Ben, am I right? Don't you think I'm right? I value your advice.

Ben. There's a new continent at your doorstep, William. You could walk out rich. Rich! [*He is gone.*]

Willy. We'll do it here, Ben! You hear me? We're gonna do it here!

[YOUNG BERNARD *rushes in. The gay music of the* BOYS *is heard.*]

Bernard. Oh, gee, I was afraid you left already!

Willy. Why? What time is it?

Bernard. It's half-past one!

Willy. Well, come on, everybody! Ebbets Field next stop! Where's the pennants?

[*He rushes through the wall-line of the kitchen and out into the living-room.*]

Linda. [*To* BIFF.] Did you pack fresh underwear?

Biff. [*Who has been limbering up.*] I want to go!

Bernard. Biff, I'm carrying your helmet, ain't I?

Happy. No, I'm carrying the helmet.

Bernard. Oh, Biff, you promised me.

Happy. I'm carrying the helmet.

Bernard. How am I going to get in the locker room?

Linda. Let him carry the shoulder guards.

[*She puts her coat and hat on in the kitchen.*]

Bernard. Can I, Biff? 'Cause I told everybody I'm going to be in the locker room.

Happy. In Ebbets Field it's the clubhouse.

Bernard. I meant the clubhouse. Biff!

Happy. Biff!

Biff. [*Grandly, after a slight pause.*] Let him carry the shoulder guards.

Happy. [*As he gives* BERNARD *the shoulder guards.*] Stay close to us now.

[WILLY *rushes in with the pennants.*]

Willy. [*Handing them out.*] Everybody wave when Biff comes out on the field. [HAPPY *and* BERNARD *run off.*] You set now, boy?

[*The music has died away.*]

Biff. Ready to go, Pop. Every muscle is ready.

Willy. [*At the edge of the apron.*] You realize what this means?

Biff. That's right, Pop.

Willy. [*Feeling* BIFF'S *muscles.*] You're comin' home this afternoon captain of the All-Scholastic Championship Team of the City of New York.

Biff. I got it, Pop. And remember, pal, when I take off my helmet, that touchdown is for you.

Willy. Let's go! [*He is starting out, with his arm around* BIFF, *when* CHARLEY *enters, as of old, in knickers.*] I got no room for you, Charley.

Charley. Room? For what?

Willy. In the car.

Charley. You goin' for a ride? I wanted to shoot some casino.

Willy. [*Furiously.*] Casino! [*Incredulously.*] Don't you realize what today is?

Linda. Oh, he knows, Willy. He's just kidding you.

Willy. That's nothing to kid about!

Charley. No, Linda, what's goin' on?

Linda. He's playing in Ebbets Field.

Charley. Baseball in this weather?

Willy. Don't talk to him. Come on, come on! [*He is pushing them out.*]

Charley. Wait a minute, didn't you hear the news?

Willy. What?

Charley. Don't you listen to the radio? Ebbets Field just blew up.

Willy. You go to hell! [CHARLEY *laughs. Pushing them out.*] Come on, come on! We're late.

Charley. [*As they go.*] Knock a homer, Biff, knock a homer!

Willy. [*The last to leave, turning to* CHARLEY.] I don't think that was funny, Charley. This is the greatest day of his life.

Charley. Willy, when are you going to grow up?

Willy. Yeah, heh? When this game is over, Charley, you'll be laughing out of the other side of your face. They'll be calling him another Red Grange. Twenty-five thousand a year.

Charley. [*Kidding.*] Is that so?

Willy. Yeah, that's so.

Charley. Well, then, I'm sorry, Willy. But tell me something.

Willy. What?

Charley. Who is Red Grange?

Willy. Put up your hands. Goddam you, put up your hands!

[CHARLEY, *chuckling, shakes his head and walks away, around the left corner of the stage.* WILLY *follows him. The music rises to a mocking frenzy.*]

Willy. Who the hell do you think you are, better than everybody else? You don't know everything, you big, ignorant, stupid . . . Put up your hands!

[*Light rises, on the right side of the forestage, on a small table in the reception room of* CHARLEY'S *office. Traffic sounds are heard.* BERNARD, *now mature, sits whistling to himself. A pair of tennis rackets and an overnight bag are on the floor beside him.*]

Willy. [*Offstage.*] What are you walking away for? Don't walk away! If you're going to say something say it to my face! I know you laugh at me behind my back. You'll laugh out of the other side of your goddam face after this game. Touchdown! Touchdown! Eighty thousand people! Touchdown! Right between the goal posts.

[BERNARD *is a quiet, earnest, but self-assured young man.* WILLY'S *voice is coming from right upstage now.* BERNARD *lowers his feet off the table and listens.* JENNY, *his father's secretary, enters.*]

Jenny. [*Distressed.*] Say, Bernard, will you go out in the hall?

Bernard. What is that noise? Who is it?

Jenny. Mr. Loman. He just got off the elevator.

Bernard. [*Getting up.*] Who's he arguing with?

Jenny. Nobody. There's nobody with him. I can't deal with him any more, and your father gets all upset everytime he comes. I've got a lot of typing to do, and your father's waiting to sign it. Will you see him?

Willy. [*Entering.*] Touchdown! Touch—— [*He sees* JENNY.] Jenny, Jenny, good to see you. How're ya? Workin'? Or still honest?

Jenny. Fine. How've you been feeling?

Willy. Not much any more, Jenny. Ha, ha! [*He is surprised to see the rackets.*]

Bernard. Hello, Uncle Willy.

Willy. [*Almost shocked.*] Bernard! Well, look who's here!

[*He comes quickly, guiltily, to* BERNARD *and warmly shakes his hand.*]

Bernard. How are you? Good to see you.

Willy. What are you doing here?

Bernard. Oh, just stopped by to see Pop. Get off my feet till my train leaves. I'm going to Washington in a few minutes.

Willy. Is he in?

Bernard. Yes, he's in his office with the accountant. Sit down.

Willy. [*Sitting down.*] What're you going to do in Washington?

Bernard. Oh, just a case I've got there, Willy.

Willy. That so? [*Indicating the rackets.*] You going to play tennis there?

Bernard. I'm staying with a friend who's got a court.

Willy. Don't say. His own tennis court. Must be fine people, I bet.

Bernard. They are, very nice. Dad tells me Biff's in town.

Willy. [*With a big smile.*] Yeah, Biff's in. Working on a very big deal, Bernard.

Bernard. What's Biff doing?

Willy. Well, he's been doing very big things in the West. But he decided to establish himself here. Very big. We're having dinner. Did I hear your wife had a boy?

Bernard. That's right. Our second.

Willy. Two boys! What do you know!

Bernard. What kind of a deal has Biff got?

Willy. Well, Bill Oliver—very big sporting-goods man—he wants Biff very badly. Called him in from the West. Long distance, carte blanche, special deliveries. Your friends have their own private tennis court?

Bernard. You still with the old firm, Willy?

Willy. [*After a pause.*] I'm—I'm overjoyed to see how you made the grade, Bernard, overjoyed. It's an encouraging thing to see a young man really—really—— Looks very good for Biff—very—— [*He breaks off, then.*] Bernard—— [*He is so full of emotion, he breaks off again.*]

Bernard. What is it, Willy?

Willy. [*Small and alone.*] What—what's the secret?

Bernard. What secret?

Willy. How—how did you? Why didn't he ever catch on?

Bernard. I wouldn't know that, Willy.

Willy. [*Confidentially, desperately.*] You were his friend, his boyhood friend. There's something I don't understand about it. His life ended after that Ebbets Field game. From the age of seventeen nothing good ever happened to him.

Bernard. He never trained himself for anything.

Willy. But he did, he did. After high school he took so many correspondence courses. Radio mechanics; television; God knows what, and never made the slightest mark.

Bernard. [*Taking off his glasses.*] Willy, do you want to talk candidly?

Willy. [*Rising, faces* BERNARD.] I regard you as a very brilliant man, Bernard. I value your advice.

Bernard. Oh, the hell with the advice, Willy. I couldn't advise you. There's just one thing I've always wanted to ask you. When he was supposed to graduate, and the math teacher flunked him——

Willy. Oh, that son-of-a-bitch ruined his life.

Bernard. Yeah, but, Willy, all he had to do was go to summer school and make up that subject.

Willy. That's right, that's right.

Bernard. Did you tell him not to go to summer school?

Willy. Me? I begged him to go. I ordered him to go!

Bernard. Then why wouldn't he go?

Willy. Why? Why! Bernard, that question has been trailing me like a ghost for the last fifteen years. He flunked the subject, and laid down and died like a hammer hit him!

Bernard. Take it easy, kid.

Willy. Let me talk to you—I got nobody to talk to. Bernard, Bernard, was it my fault? Y'see? It keeps going around in my mind, maybe I did something to him. I got nothing to give him.

Bernard. Don't take it so hard.

Willy. Why did he lay down? What is the story there? You were his friend!

Bernard. Willy, I remember, it was June, and our grades came out. And he'd flunked math.

Willy. That son-of-a-bitch!

Bernard. No, it wasn't right then. Biff just got very angry, I remember, and he was ready to enroll in summer school.

Willy. [*Surprised.*] He was?

Bernard. He wasn't beaten by it at all. But then, Willy, he disappeared from the block for almost a month. And I got the idea that he'd gone up to New England to see you. Did he have a talk with you then?

[WILLY *stares in silence.*]

Bernard. Willy?

Willy. [*With a strong edge of resentment in his voice.*] Yeah, he came to Boston. What about it?

Bernard. Well, just that when he came back—I'll never forget this, it always mystifies me. Because I'd thought so well of Biff, even though he'd always taken advantage of me. I loved him, Willy, y'know? And he came back after that month and took his sneakers—remember those sneakers with "University of Virginia" printed on them? He was so proud of those, wore them every day. And he took them down in the cellar, and burned them up in the furnace. We had a fist fight. It lasted at least half an hour. Just the two of us, punching each other down cellar, and crying right through it. I've often thought of how strange it was that I knew he'd given up his life. What happened in Boston, Willy?

[WILLY *looks at him as at an intruder.*]

Bernard. I just bring it up because you asked me.

Willy. [*Angrily.*] Nothing. What do you mean, "What happened?" What's that got to do with anything?

Bernard. Well, don't get sore.

Willy. What are you trying to do, blame it on me? If a boy lays down is that my fault?

Bernard. Now, Willy, don't get——

Willy. Well, don't—don't talk to me that way! What does that mean, "What happened?"

[CHARLEY *enters. He is in his vest, and he carries a bottle of bourbon.*]

Charley. Hey, you're going to miss that train. [*He waves the bottle.*]

Bernard. Yeah, I'm going. [*He takes the bottle.*] Thanks, Pop. [*He picks up his rackets and bag.*] Good-by, Willy, and don't worry about it. You know, "If at first you don't succeed . . ."

Willy. Yes, I believe in that.

Bernard. But sometimes, Willy, it's better for a man just to walk away.

Willy. Walk away?

Bernard. That's right.

Willy. But if you can't walk away?

Bernard. [*After a slight pause.*] I guess that's when it's tough. [*Extending his hand.*] Good-by, Willy.

Willy. [*Shaking* BERNARD'S *hand.*] Good-by, boy.

Charley. [*An arm on* BERNARD'S *shoulder.*] How do you like this kid? Gonna argue a case in front of the Supreme Court.

Bernard. [*Protesting.*] Pop!

Willy. [*Genuinely shocked, pained, and happy.*] No! The Supreme Court!

Bernard. I gotta run. 'By, Dad!

Charley. Knock 'em dead, Bernard!

[BERNARD *goes off.*]

Willy. [*As* CHARLEY *takes out his wallet.*] The Supreme Court! And he didn't even mention it!

Charley. [*Counting out money on the desk.*] He don't have to—he's gonna do it.

Willy. And you never told him what to do, did you? You never took any interest in him.

Charley. My salvation is that I never took any interest in anything. There's some money—fifty dollars. I got an accountant inside.

Willy. Charley, look . . . [*With difficulty.*] I got my insurance to pay. If you can manage it—I need a hundred and ten dollars.

[CHARLEY *doesn't reply for a moment; merely stops moving.*]

Willy. I'd draw it from my bank but Linda would know, and I . . .

Charley. Sit down, Willy.

Willy. [*Moving toward the chair.*] I'm keeping an account of everything, remember. I'll pay every penny back. [*He sits.*]

Charley. Now listen to me, Willy.

Willy. I want you to know I appreciate . . .

Charley. [*Sitting down on the table.*] Willy, what're you doin'? What the hell is goin' on in your head?

Willy. Why? I'm simply . . .

Charley. I offered you a job. You can make fifty dollars a week. And I won't send you on the road.

Willy. I've got a job.

Charley. Without pay? What kind of a job is a job without pay? [*He rises.*] Now, look, kid, enough is enough. I'm no genius but I know when I'm being insulted.

Willy. Insulted!

Charley. Why don't you want to work for me?

Willy. What's the matter with you? I've got a job.

Charley. Then what're you walkin' in here every week for?

Willy. [*Getting up.*] Well, if you don't want me to walk in here——

Charley. I am offering you a job.

Willy. I don't want your goddam job!

Charley. When the hell are you going to grow up?

Willy. [*Furiously.*] You big ignoramus, if you say that to me again I'll rap you one! I don't care how big you are!

[*He's ready to fight. Pause.*]

Charley. [*Kindly, going to him.*] How much do you need, Willy?

Willy. Charley, I'm strapped. I'm strapped. I don't know what to do. I was just fired.

Charley. Howard fired you?

Willy. That snotnose. Imagine that? I named him. I named him Howard.

Charley. Willy, when're you gonna realize that them things don't mean anything? You named him Howard, but you can't sell that. The only thing you got in this world is what you can sell. And the funny thing is that you're a salesman, and you don't know that.

Willy. I've always tried to think otherwise, I guess. I always felt that if a man was impressive, and well liked, that nothing——

Charley. Why must everybody like you? Who liked J. P. Morgan? Was he impressive? In a Turkish bath he'd look like a butcher. But with his pockets on he was very well liked. Now listen, Willy, I know you don't like me, and nobody can say I'm in love with you, but I'll give you a job because—just for the hell of it, put it that way. Now what do you say?

Willy. I—I just can't work for you, Charley.

Charley. What're you, jealous of me?

Willy. I can't work for you, that's all, don't ask me why.

Charley. [*Angered, takes out more bills.*] You been jealous of me all your life, you damned fool! Here, pay your insurance.

[*He puts the money in* WILLY'S *hand.*]

Willy. I'm keeping strict accounts.

Charley. I've got some work to do. Take care of yourself. And pay your insurance.

Willy. [*Moving to the right.*] Funny, y'know? After all the highways, and the trains, and the appointments, and the years, you end up worth more dead than alive.

Charley. Willy, nobody's worth nothin' dead. [*After a slight pause.*] Did you hear what I said?

[WILLY *stands still, dreaming.*]

Charley. Willy!

Willy. Apologize to Bernard for me when you see him. I didn't mean to argue with him. He's a fine boy. They're all fine boys, and they'll end up big—all of them. Someday they'll all play tennis together. Wish me luck, Charley. He saw Bill Oliver today.

Charley. Good luck.

Willy. [*On the verge of tears.*] Charley, you're the only friend I got. Isn't that a remarkable thing? [*He goes out.*]

Charley. Jesus!

[CHARLEY *stares after him a moment and follows. All light blacks out. Suddenly raucous music is heard, and a red glow rises behind the screen at right.* STANLEY, *a young waiter, appears, carrying a table, followed by* HAPPY, *who is carrying two chairs.*]

Stanley. [*Putting the table down.*] That's all right, Mr. Loman, I can handle it myself.

[*He turns and takes the chairs from* HAPPY *and places them at the table.*]

Happy. [*Glancing around.*] Oh, this is better.

Stanley. Sure, in the front there you're in the middle of all kinds a noise. Whenever you got a party, Mr. Loman, you just tell me and I'll put you back here. Y'know, there's a lotta people they don't like it private, because when they go out they like to see a lotta action around them because they're sick and tired to stay in the house by theirself. But I know you, you ain't from Hackensack. You know what I mean?

Happy. [*Sitting down.*] So how's it coming, Stanley?

Stanley. Ah, it's a dog's life. I only wish during the war they'd a took me in the Army. I coulda been dead by now.

Happy. My brother's back, Stanley.

Stanley. Oh, he come back, heh? From the Far West.

Happy. Yeah, big cattle man, my brother, so treat him right. And my father's coming too.

Stanley. Oh, your father too!

Happy. You got a couple of nice lobsters?

Stanley. Hundred per cent, big.

Happy. I want them with the claws.

Stanley. Don't worry, I don't give you no mice. [HAPPY *laughs.*] How about some wine? It'll put a head on the meal.

Happy. No. You remember, Stanley, that recipe I brought you from overseas? With the champagne in it?

Stanley. Oh, yeah, sure. I still got it tacked up yet in the kitchen. But that'll have to cost a buck apiece anyways.

Happy. That's all right.

Stanley. What'd you, hit a number or somethin'?

Happy. No, it's a little celebration. My brother is—I think he pulled off a big deal today. I think we're going into business together.

Stanley. Great! That's the best for you. Because a family business, you know what I mean?—that's the best.

Happy. That's what I think.

Stanley. 'Cause what's the difference? Somebody steals? It's in the family. Know what I mean? [*Sotto voce.*] Like this bartender here. The boss is goin' crazy what kinda leak he's got in the cash register. You put it in but it don't come out.

Happy. [*Raising his head.*] Sh!

Stanley. What?

Happy. You notice I wasn't lookin' right or left, was I?

Stanley. No.

Happy. And my eyes are closed.

Stanley. So what's the——?

Happy. Strudel's comin'.

Stanley. [*Catching on, looks around.*] Ah, no, there's no——

[*He breaks off as a furred, lavishly dressed* GIRL *enters and sits at the next table. Both follow her with their eyes.*]

Stanley. Geez, how'd ya know?

Happy. I got radar or something. [*Staring directly at her profile.*] Oooooooo . . . Stanley.

Stanley. I think that's for you, Mr. Loman.

Happy. Look at that mouth. Oh, God. And the binoculars.

Stanley. Geez, you got a life, Mr. Loman.

Happy. Wait on her.

Stanley. [*Going to the* GIRL'S *table.*] Would you like a menu, ma'am?

Girl. I'm expecting someone, but I'd like a——

Happy. Why don't you bring her—excuse me, miss, do you mind? I sell champagne, and I'd like you to try my brand. Bring her a champagne, Stanley.

Girl. That's awfully nice of you.

Happy. Don't mention it. It's all company money. [*He laughs.*]

Girl. That's a charming product to be selling, isn't it?

Happy. Oh, gets to be like everything else. Selling is selling, y'know.

Girl. I suppose.

Happy. You don't happen to sell, do you?

Girl. No, I don't sell.

Happy. Would you object to a compliment from a stranger? You ought to be on a magazine cover.

Girl. [*Looking at him a little archly.*] I have been.

[STANLEY *comes in with a glass of champagne.*]

Happy. What'd I say before, Stanley? You see? She's a cover girl.

Stanley. Oh, I could see, I could see.

Happy. [*To the* GIRL.] What magazine?

Girl. Oh, a lot of them. [*She takes the drink.*] Thank you.

Happy. You know what they say in France, don't you? "Champagne is the drink of the complexion"—— Hya, Biff!

[BIFF *has entered and sits with* HAPPY.]

Biff. Hello, kid. Sorry I'm late.

Happy. I just got here. Uh, Miss—?

Girl. Forsythe.

Happy. Miss Forsythe, this is my brother.

Biff. Is Dad here?

Happy. His name is Biff. You might've heard of him. Great football player.

Girl. Really? What team?

Happy. Are you familiar with football?

Girl. No, I'm afraid I'm not.

Happy. Biff is quarterback with the New York Giants.

Girl. Well, that is nice, isn't it? [*She drinks.*]

Happy. Good health.

Girl. I'm happy to meet you.

Happy. That's my name: Hap. It's really Harold, but at West Point they called me Happy.

Girl. [*Now really impressed.*] Oh, I see. How do you do? [*She turns her profile.*]

Biff. Isn't Dad coming?

Happy. You want her?

Biff. Oh, I could never make that.

Happy. I remember the time that idea would never come into your head. Where's the old confidence, Biff?

Biff. I just saw Oliver——

Happy. Wait a minute. I've got to see that old confidence again. Do you want her? She's on call.

Biff. Oh, no.

[*He turns to look at the* GIRL.]

Happy. I'm telling you. Watch this. [*Turning to the* GIRL.] Honey? [*She turns to him.*] Are you busy?

Girl. Well, I am . . . but I could make a phone call.

Happy. Do that, will you, honey? And see if you can get a friend. We'll be here for a while. Biff is one of the greatest football players in the country.

Girl. [*Standing up.*] Well, I'm certainly happy to meet you.

Happy. Come back soon.

Girl. I'll try.

Happy. Don't try, honey, try hard.

[*The* GIRL *exits.* STANLEY *follows, shaking his head in bewildered admiration.*]

Happy. Isn't that a shame now? A beautiful girl like that? That's why I can't get married. There's not a good woman in a thousand. New York is loaded with them, kid!

Biff. Hap, look——

Happy. I told you she was on call!

Biff. [*Strangely unnerved.*] Cut it out, will ya? I want to say something to you.

Happy. Did you see Oliver?

Biff. I saw him all right. Now look, I want to tell Dad a couple of things and I want you to help me.

Happy. What? Is he going to back you?

Biff. Are you crazy? You're out of your goddam head, you know that?

Happy. Why? What happened?

Biff. [*Breathlessly.*] I did a terrible thing today, Hap. It's been the strangest day I ever went through. I'm all numb, I swear.

Happy. You mean he wouldn't see you?

Biff. Well, I waited six hours for him, see? All day. Kept sending my name in. Even tried to date his secretary so she'd get me to him, but no soap.

Happy. Because you're not showin' the old confidence, Biff. He remembered you, didn't he?

Biff. [*Stopping* HAPPY *with a gesture.*] Finally, about five o'clock, he comes out. Didn't remember who I was or anything. I felt like such an idiot, Hap.

Happy. Did you tell him my Florida idea?

Biff. He walked away. I saw him for one minute. I got so mad I could've torn the walls down! How the hell did I ever get the idea I was a salesman there? I even believed myself that I'd been a salesman for him! And then he gave me one look and—I realized what a ridiculous lie my whole life has been! We've been talking in a dream for fifteen years. I was a shipping clerk.

Happy. What'd you do?

Biff. [*With great tension and wonder.*] Well, he left, see. And the secretary went out. I was all alone in the waiting-room. I don't know what came over me, Hap. The next thing I know I'm in his office—paneled walls, everything. I can't explain it. I—Hap, I took his fountain pen.

Happy. Geez, did he catch you?

Biff. I ran out. I ran down all eleven flights. I ran and ran and ran.

Happy. That was an awful dumb—what'd you do that for?

Biff. [*Agonized.*] I don't know, I just —wanted to take something, I don't know. You gotta help me, Hap; I'm gonna tell Pop.

Happy. You crazy? What for?

Biff. Hap, he's got to understand that I'm not the man somebody lends that kind of money to. He thinks I've been spiting him all these years and it's eating him up.

Happy. That's just it. You tell him something nice.

Biff. I can't.

Happy. Say you got a lunch date with Oliver tomorrow.

Biff. So what do I do tomorrow?

Happy. You leave the house tomorrow and come back at night and say Oliver is thinking it over. And he thinks it over for a couple of weeks, and gradually it fades away and nobody's the worse.

Biff. But it'll go on forever!

Happy. Dad is never so happy as when he's looking forward to something!

[WILLY *enters.*]

Happy. Hello, scout!

Willy. Gee, I haven't been here in years!

[STANLEY *has followed* WILLY *in and sets a chair for him.* STANLEY *starts off but* HAPPY *stops him.*]

Happy. Stanley!

[STANLEY *stands by, waiting for an order.*]

Biff. [*Going to* WILLY *with guilt, as to an invalid.*] Sit down, Pop. You want a drink?

Willy. Sure, I don't mind.

Biff. Let's get a load on.

Willy. You look worried.

Biff. N-no. [*To* STANLEY.] Scotch all around. Make it doubles.

Stanley. Doubles, right. [*He goes.*]

Willy. You had a couple already, didn't you?

Biff. Just a couple, yeah.

Willy. Well, what happened, boy? [*Nodding affirmatively, with a smile.*] Everything go all right?

Biff. [*Takes a breath, then reaches out and grasps* WILLY'S *hand.*] Pal . . . [*He is smiling bravely, and* WILLY *is smiling too.*] I had an experience today.

Happy. Terrific, Pop.

Willy. That so? What happened?

Biff. [*High, slightly alcoholic, above the earth.*] I'm going to tell you everything from first to last. It's been a strange day. [*Silence. He looks around, composes himself as best he can, but his breath keeps breaking the rhythm of his voice.*] I had to wait quite a while for him, and——

Willy. Oliver?

Biff. Yeah, Oliver. All day, as a matter of cold fact. And a lot of—instances—facts, Pop, facts about my life came back to me. Who was it, Pop? Who ever said I was a salesman with Oliver?

Willy. Well, you were.

Biff. No, Dad, I was a shipping clerk.

Willy. But you were practically——

Biff. [*With determination.*] Dad, I don't know who said it first, but I was never a salesman for Bill Oliver.

Willy. What're you talking about?

Biff. Let's hold on to the facts tonight, Pop. We're not going to get anywhere bullin' around. I was a shipping clerk.

Willy. [*Angrily.*] All right, now listen to me——

Biff. Why don't you let me finish?

Willy. I'm not interested in stories about the past or any crap of that kind because the woods are burning, boys, you understand? There's a big blaze going on all around. I was fired today.

Biff. [*Shocked.*] How could you be?

Willy. I was fired, and I'm looking for a little good news to tell your mother, because the woman has waited and the woman has suffered. The gist of it is that I haven't got a story left in my head, Biff. So don't give me a lecture about facts and aspects. I am not interested. Now what've you got to say to me?

[STANLEY *enters with three drinks. They wait until he leaves.*]

Willy. Did you see Oliver?

Biff. Jesus, Dad!

Willy. You mean you didn't go up there?

Happy. Sure he went up there.

Biff. I did. I—saw him. How could they fire you?

Willy. [*On the edge of his chair*.] What kind of welcome did he give you?

Biff. He won't even let you work on commission?

Willy. I'm out! [*Driving*.] So tell me, he gave you a warm welcome?

Happy. Sure, Pop, sure!

Biff. [*Driven*.] Well, it was kind of——

Willy. I was wondering if he'd remember you. [*To* HAPPY.] Imagine, man doesn't see him for ten, twelve years and gives him that kind of a welcome!

Happy. Damn right!

Biff. [*Trying to return to the offensive*.] Pop, look——

Willy. You know why he remembered you, don't you? Because you impressed him in those days.

Biff. Let's talk quietly and get this down to the facts, huh?

Willy. [*As though* BIFF *had been interrupting*.] Well, what happened? It's great news, Biff. Did he take you into his office or'd you talk in the waiting-room?

Biff. Well, he came in, see, and——

Willy. [*With a big smile*.] What'd he say? Betcha he threw his arm around you.

Biff. Well, he kinda——

Willy. He's a fine man. [*To* HAPPY.] Very hard man to see, y'know.

Happy. [*Agreeing*.] Oh, I know.

Willy. [*To* BIFF.] Is that where you had the drinks?

Biff. Yeah, he gave me a couple of—no, no!

Happy. [*Cutting in*.] He told him my Florida idea.

Willy. Don't interrupt. [*To* BIFF.] How'd he react to the Florida idea?

Biff. Dad, will you give me a minute to explain?

Willy. I've been waiting for you to explain since I sat down here! What happened? He took you into his office and what?

Biff. Well—I talked. And—and he listened, see.

Willy. Famous for the way he listens, y'know. What was his answer?

Biff. His answer was—— [*He breaks off, suddenly angry*.] Dad, you're not letting me tell you what I want to tell you!

Willy. [*Accusing, angered*.] You didn't see him, did you?

Biff. I did see him!

Willy. What'd you insult him or something? You insulted him, didn't you?

Biff. Listen, will you let me out of it, will you just let me out of it!

Happy. What the hell!

Willy. Tell me what happened!

Biff. [*To* HAPPY.] I can't talk to him!

[*A single trumpet note jars the ear. The light of green leaves stains the house, which holds the air of night and a dream.* YOUNG BERNARD *enters and knocks on the door of the house*.]

Young Bernard. [*Frantically*.] Mrs. Loman, Mrs. Loman!

Happy. Tell him what happened!

Biff. [*To* HAPPY.] Shut up and leave me alone!

Willy. No, no! You had to go and flunk math!

Biff. What math? What're you talking about?

Young Bernard. Mrs. Loman, Mrs. Loman!

[LINDA *appears in the house, as of old*.]

Willy. [*Wildly*.] Math, math, math!

Biff. Take it easy, Pop!

Young Bernard. Mrs. Loman!

Willy. [*Furiously*.] If you hadn't flunked you'd've been set by now!

Biff. Now, look, I'm gonna tell you what happened, and you're going to listen to me.

Young Bernard. Mrs. Loman!

Biff. I waited six hours——

Happy. What the hell are you saying?

Biff. I kept sending in my name but he wouldn't see me. So finally he . . .

[*He continues unheard as light fades low on the restaurant*.]

Young Bernard. Biff flunked math!

Linda. No!

Young Bernard. Birnbaum flunked him! They won't graduate him!

Linda. But they have to. He's gotta go to the university. Where is he? Biff! Biff!

Young Bernard. No, he left. He went to Grand Central.

Linda. Grand—— You mean he went to Boston!

Young Bernard. Is Uncle Willy in Boston?

Linda. Oh, maybe Willy can talk to the teacher. Oh, the poor, poor boy!

[*Light on house area snaps out*.]

Biff. [*At the table, now audible, holding up a gold fountain pen*.] . . . so I'm washed up with Oliver, you understand? Are you listening to me?

Willy. [*At a loss*.] Yeah, sure. If you hadn't flunked——

Biff. Flunked what? What're you talking about?

Willy. Don't blame everything on me! I

didn't flunk math—you did! What pen?

Happy. That was awful dumb, Biff, a pen like that is worth——

Willy. [*Seeing the pen for the first time.*] You took Oliver's pen?

Biff. [*Weakening.*] Dad, I just explained it to you.

Willy. You stole Bill Oliver's fountain pen!

Biff. I didn't exactly steal it! That's just what I've been explaining to you!

Happy. He had it in his hand and just then Oliver walked in, so he got nervous and stuck it in his pocket!

Willy. My God, Biff!

Biff. I never intended to do it, Dad!

Operator's Voice. Standish Arms, good evening!

Willy. [*Shouting.*] I'm not in my room!

Biff. [*Frightened.*] Dad, what's the matter? [*He and* HAPPY *stand up.*]

Operator. Ringing Mr. Loman for you!

Willy. I'm not there, stop it!

Biff. [*Horrified, gets down on one knee before* WILLY.] Dad, I'll make good, I'll make good. [WILLY *tries to get to his feet.* BIFF *holds him down.*] Sit down now.

Willy. No, you're no good, you're no good for anything.

Biff. I am, Dad; I'll find something else, you understand? Now don't worry about anything. [*He holds up* WILLY'S *face.*] Talk to me, Dad.

Operator. Mr. Loman does not answer. Shall I page him?

Willy. [*Attempting to stand, as though to rush and silence the* OPERATOR.] No, no, no!

Happy. He'll strike something, Pop.

Willy. No, no . . .

Biff. [*Desperately, standing over* WILLY.] Pop, listen! Listen to me! I'm telling you something good. Oliver talked to his partner about the Florida idea. You listening? He —he talked to his partner, and he came to me . . I'm going to be all right, you hear? Dad, listen to me, he said it was just a question of the amount!

Willy. Then you . . . got it?

Happy. He's gonna be terrific, Pop!

Willy. [*Trying to stand.*] Then you got it, haven't you? You got it! You got it!

Biff. [*Agonized, holds* WILLY *down.*] No, no. Look, Pop. I'm supposed to have lunch with them tomorrow. I'm just telling you this so you'll know that I can still make an impression, Pop. And I'll make good somewhere, but I can't go tomorrow, see?

Willy. Why not? You simply——

Biff. But the pen, Pop!

Willy. You give it to him and tell him it was an oversight!

Happy. Sure, have lunch tomorrow!

Biff. I can't say that——

Willy. You were doing a crossword puzzle and accidentally used his pen!

Biff. Listen, kid, I took those balls years ago, now I walk in with his fountain pen? That clinches it, don't you see? I can't face him like that! I'll try elsewhere.

Page's Voice. Paging Mr. Loman!

Willy. Don't you want to be anything?

Biff. Pop, how can I go back?

Willy. You don't want to be anything, is that what's behind it?

Biff. [*Now angry at* WILLY *for not crediting his sympathy.*] Don't take it that way! You think it was easy walking into that office after what I'd done to him? A team of horses couldn't have dragged me back to Bill Oliver!

Willy. Then why'd you go?

Biff. Why did I go? Why did I go! Look at you! Look at what's become of you!

[*Off left,* THE WOMAN *laughs.*]

Willy. Biff, you're going to go to that lunch tomorrow, or——

Biff. I can't go. I've got no appointment!

Happy. Biff, for . . . !

Willy. Are you spiting me?

Biff. Don't take it that way! Goddammit!

Willy. [*Strikes* BIFF *and falters away from the table.*] You rotten little louse! Are you spiting me?

The Woman. Someone's at the door, Willy!

Biff. I'm no good, can't you see what I am?

Happy. [*Separating them.*] Hey, you're in a restaurant! Now cut it out, both of you! [*The* GIRLS *enter.*] Hello, girls, sit down. [THE WOMAN *laughs, off left.*]

Miss Forsythe. I guess we might as well. This is Letta.

The Woman. Willy, are you going to wake up?

Biff. [*Ignoring* WILLY.] How're ya, miss, sit down. What do you drink?

Miss Forsythe. Letta might not be able to stay long.

Letta. I gotta get up very early tomorrow. I got jury duty. I'm so excited! Were you fellows ever on a jury?

Biff. No, but I been in front of them! [*The* GIRLS *laugh.*] This is my father.

Letta. Isn't he cute? Sit down with us, Pop.

Happy. Sit him down, Biff!

Biff. [*Going to him.*] Come on, slugger, drink us under the table. To hell with it! Come on, sit down, pal.

[*On* BIFF'S *last insistence,* WILLY *is about to sit.*]

The Woman. [*Now urgently.*] Willy, are you going to answer the door!

[THE WOMAN'S *call pulls* WILLY *back. He starts right, befuddled.*]

Biff. Hey, where are you going?

Willy. Open the door.

Biff. The door?

Willy. The washroom . . . the door . . . where's the door?

Biff. [*Leading* WILLY *to the left.*] Just go straight down. [WILLY *moves left.*]

The Woman. Willy, Willy, are you going to get up, get up, get up, get up?

[WILLY *exits left.*]

Letta. I think it's sweet you bring your daddy along.

Miss Forsythe. Oh, he isn't really your father!

Biff. [*At left, turning to her resentfully.*] Miss Forsythe, you've just seen a prince walk by. A fine, troubled prince. A hard-working, unappreciated prince. A pal, you understand? A good companion. Always for his boys.

Letta. That's so sweet.

Happy. Well, girls, what's the program? We're wasting time. Come on, Biff. Gather round. Where would you like to go?

Biff. Why don't you do something for him?

Happy. Me!

Biff. Don't you give a damn for him, Hap?

Happy. What're you talking about? I'm the one who——

Biff. I sense it, you don't give a good goddam about him. [*He takes the rolled-up hose from his pocket and puts it on the table in front of* HAPPY.] Look what I found in the cellar, for Christ's sake. How can you bear to let it go on?

Happy. Me? Who goes away? Who runs off and——

Biff. Yeah, but he doesn't mean anything to you. You could help him—I can't! Don't you understand what I'm talking about? He's going to kill himself, don't you know that?

Happy. Don't I know it! Me!

Biff. Hap, help him! Jesus . . . help him . . . Help me, help me, I can't bear to look at his face!

[*Ready to weep, he hurries out, up right.*]

Happy. [*Starting after him.*] Where are you going?

Miss Forsythe. What's he so mad about?

Happy. Come on, girls, we'll catch up with him.

Miss Forsythe. [*As* HAPPY *pushes her out.*] Say, I don't like that temper of his!

Happy. He's just a little overstrung, he'll be all right!

Willy. [*Off left, as* THE WOMAN *laughs.*] Don't answer! Don't answer!

Letta. Don't you want to tell your father——

Happy. No, that's not my father. He's just a guy. Come on, we'll catch Biff, and, honey, we're going to paint this town! Stanley, where's the check! Hey, Stanley!

[*They exit.* STANLEY *looks toward left.*]

Stanley. [*Calling to* HAPPY *indignantly.*] Mr. Loman! Mr. Loman!

[STANLEY *picks up a chair and follows them off. Knocking is heard off left.* THE WOMAN *enters, laughing.* WILLY *follows her. She is in a black slip; he is buttoning his shirt. Raw, sensuous music accompanies their speech.*]

Willy. Will you stop laughing? Will you stop?

The Woman. Aren't you going to answer the door? He'll wake the whole hotel.

Willy. I'm not expecting anybody.

The Woman. Whyn't you have another drink, honey, and stop being so damn self-centered?

Willy. I'm so lonely.

The Woman. You know you ruined me, Willy? From now on, whenever you come to the office, I'll see that you go right through to the buyers. No waiting at my desk any more, Willy. You ruined me.

Willy. That's nice of you to say that.

The Woman. Gee, you are self-centered! Why so sad? You are the saddest, self-centeredest soul I ever did see-saw. [*She laughs. He kisses her.*] Come on inside, drummer boy. It's silly to be dressing in the middle of the night. [*As knocking is heard.*] Aren't you going to answer the door?

Willy. They're knocking on the wrong door.

The Woman. But I felt the knocking. And he heard us talking in here. Maybe the hotel's on fire!

Willy. [*His terror rising.*] It's a mistake.

The Woman. Then tell him to go away!

Willy. There's nobody there.

The Woman. It's getting on my nerves,

Willy. There's somebody standing out there and it's getting on my nerves!

Willy. [*Pushing her away from him.*] All right, stay in the bathroom here, and don't come out. I think there's a law in Massachusetts about it, so don't come out. It may be that new room clerk. He looked very mean. So don't come out. It's a mistake, there's no fire.

[*The knocking is heard again. He takes a few steps away from her, and she vanishes into the wing. The light follows him, and now he is facing* YOUNG BIFF, *who carries a suitcase.* BIFF *steps toward him. The music is gone.*]

Biff. Why didn't you answer?

Willy. Biff! What are you doing in Boston?

Biff. Why didn't you answer? I've been knocking for five minutes; I called you on the phone——

Willy. I just heard you. I was in the bathroom and had the door shut. Did anything happen home?

Biff. Dad—I let you down.

Willy. What do you mean?

Biff. Dad . . .

Willy. Biffo, what's this about? [*Putting his arm around* BIFF.] Come on, let's go downstairs and get you a malted.

Biff. Dad, I flunked math.

Willy. Not for the term?

Biff. The term. I haven't got enough credits to graduate.

Willy. You mean to say Bernard wouldn't give you the answers?

Biff. He did, he tried, but I only got a sixty-one.

Willy. And they wouldn't give you four points?

Biff. Birnbaum refused absolutely. I begged him, Pop, but he won't give me those points. You gotta talk to him before they close the school. Because if he saw the kind of man you are, and you just talked to him in your way, I'm sure he'd come through for me. The class came right before practice, see, and I didn't go enough. Would you talk to him? He'd like you, Pop. You know the way you could talk.

Willy. You're on. We'll drive right back.

Biff. Oh, Dad, good work! I'm sure he'll change it for you!

Willy. Go downstairs and tell the clerk I'm checkin' out. Go right down.

Biff. Yes, sir! See, the reason he hates me, Pop—one day he was late for class so I got up at the blackboard and imitated him. I crossed my eyes and talked with a lithp.

Willy. [*Laughing.*] You did? The kids like it?

Biff. They nearly died laughing!

Willy. Yeah? What'd you do?

Biff. The thquare root of thixthy twee is . . . [WILLY *bursts out laughing;* BIFF *joins him.*] And in the middle of it he walked in!

[WILLY *laughs and* THE WOMAN *joins in offstage.*]

Willy. [*Without hesitation.*] Hurry downstairs and——

Biff. Somebody in there?

Willy. No, that was next door.

[THE WOMAN *laughs offstage.*]

Biff. Somebody got in your bathroom!

Willy. No, it's the next room, there's a party——

The Woman. [*Enters, laughing. She lisps this.*] Can I come in? There's something in the bathtub, Willy, and it's moving!

[WILLY *looks at* BIFF, *who is staring open-mouthed and horrified at* THE WOMAN.]

Willy. Ah—you better go back to your room. They must be finished painting by now. They're painting her room so I let her take a shower here. Go back, go back . . .

[*He pushes her.*]

The Woman. [*Resisting.*] But I've got to get dressed, Willy, I can't——

Willy. Get out of here! Go back, go back . . . [*Suddenly striving for the ordinary.*] This is Miss Francis, Biff, she's a buyer. They're painting her room. Go back, Miss Francis, go back . . .

The Woman. But my clothes, I can't go out naked in the hall!

Willy. [*Pushing her offstage.*] Get outa here! Go back, go back!

[BIFF *slowly sits down on his suitcase as the argument continues offstage.*]

The Woman. Where's my stockings? You promised me stockings, Willy!

Willy. I have no stockings here!

The Woman. You had two boxes of size nine sheers for me, and I want them!

Willy. Here, for God's sake, will you get outa here!

The Woman. [*Enters holding a box of stockings.*] I just hope there's nobody in the hall. That's all I hope. [*To* BIFF.] Are you football or baseball?

Biff. Football.

The Woman. [*Angry, humiliated.*] That's me too. G'night.

[*She snatches her clothes from* WILLY, *and walks out.*]

Willy. [*After a pause.*] Well, better get going. I want to get to the school first thing in the morning. Get my suits out of the closet. I'll get my valise. [BIFF *doesn't move.*] What's the matter? [BIFF *remains motionless, tears falling.*] She's a buyer. Buys for J. H. Simmons. She lives down the hall—they're painting. You don't imagine—— [*He breaks off. After a pause.*] Now listen, pal, she's just a buyer. She sees merchandise in her room and they have to keep it looking just so . . . [*Pause. Assuming command.*] All right, get my suits. [BIFF *doesn't move.*] Now stop crying and do as I say. I gave you an order. Biff, I gave you an order! Is that what you do when I give you an order? How dare you cry! [*Putting his arm around* BIFF.] Now look, Biff, when you grow up you'll understand about these things. You mustn't—— you mustn't overemphasize a thing like this. I'll see Birnbaum first thing in the morning.

Biff. Never mind.

Willy. [*Getting down beside* BIFF.] Never mind! He's going to give you those points. I'll see to it.

Biff. He wouldn't listen to you.

Willy. He certainly will listen to me. You need those points for the U. of Virginia.

Biff. I'm not going there.

Willy. Heh? If I can't get him to change that mark you'll make it up in summer school. You've got all summer to——

Biff. [*His weeping breaking from him.*] Dad . . .

Willy. [*Infected by it.*] Oh, my boy . . .

Biff. Dad . . .

Willy. She's nothing to me, Biff. I was lonely, I was terribly lonely.

Biff. You—you gave her Mama's stockings!

[*His tears break through and he rises to go.*]

Willy. [*Grabbing for* BIFF.] I gave you an order!

Biff. Don't touch me, you—liar!

Willy. Apologize for that!

Biff. You fake! You phony little fake! You fake!

[*Overcome, he turns quickly and weeping fully goes out with his suitcase.* WILLY *is left on the floor on his knees.*]

Willy I gave you an order! Biff, come back here or I'll beat you! Come back here! I'll whip you!

[STANLEY *comes quickly in from the right and stands in front of* WILLY.]

Willy. [*Shouts at* STANLEY.] I gave you an order . . .

Stanley. Hey, let's pick it up, pick it up, Mr. Loman. [*He helps* WILLY *to his feet.*] Your boys left with the chippies. They said they'll see you home.

[*A second waiter watches some distance away.*]

Willy. But we were supposed to have dinner together.

[*Music is heard,* WILLY'S *theme.*]

Stanley. Can you make it?

Willy. I'll—sure, I can make it. [*Suddenly concerned about his clothes.*] Do I—I look all right?

Stanley. Sure, you look all right.

[*He flicks a speck off* WILLY'S *lapel.*]

Willy. Here—here's a dollar.

Stanley. Oh, your son paid me. It's all right.

Willy. [*Putting it in* STANLEY'S *hand.*] No, take it. You're a good boy.

Stanley. Oh, no, you don't have to . . .

Willy. Here—here's some more, I don't need it any more. [*After a slight pause.*] Tell me—is there a seed store in the neighborhood?

Stanley. Seeds? You mean like to plant?

[*As* WILLY *turns,* STANLEY *slips the money back into his jacket pocket.*]

Willy. Yes. Carrots, peas . . .

Stanley. Well, there's hardware stores on Sixth Avenue, but it may be too late now.

Willy. [*Anxiously.*] Oh, I'd better hurry. I've got to get some seeds. [*He starts off to the right.*] I've got to get some seeds, right away. Nothing's planted. I don't have a thing in the ground.

[WILLY *hurries out as the light goes down.* STANLEY *moves over to the right after him, watches him off. The other waiter has been staring at* WILLY.]

Stanley. [*To the waiter.*] Well, whatta you looking at?

[*The waiter picks up the chairs and moves off right.* STANLEY *takes the table and follows him. The light fades on this area. There is a long pause, the sound of the flute coming over. The light gradually rises on the kitchen, which is empty.* HAPPY *appears at the door of the house, followed by* BIFF. HAPPY *is carrying a large bunch of long-stemmed roses. He enters the kitchen, looks around for* LINDA. *Not seeing her, he turns to* BIFF, *who is just outside the house door, and makes a gesture with his hands, indicating "Not here, I guess." He looks into the living-room and freezes. Inside,* LINDA, *unseen, is seated,* WILLY'S *coat on her lap. She rises ominously and quietly and moves toward* HAPPY, *who backs up into the kitchen, afraid.*]

Happy. Hey, what're you doing up? [LINDA *says nothing but moves toward him implacably.*] Where's Pop? [*He keeps backing to the right, and now* LINDA *is in full view in the doorway to the living-room.*] Is he sleeping?

Linda. Where were you?

Happy. [*Trying to laugh it off.*] We met two girls, Mom, very fine types. Here, we brought you some flowers. [*Offering them to her.*] Put them in your room, Ma.

[*She knocks them to the floor at* BIFF's *feet. He has now come inside and closed the door behind him. She stares at* BIFF, *silent.*]

Happy. Now what'd you do that for? Mom, I want you to have some flowers——

Linda. [*Cutting* HAPPY *off, violently to* BIFF.] Don't you care whether he lives or dies?

Happy. [*Going to the stairs.*] Come upstairs, Biff.

Biff. [*With a flare of disgust, to* HAPPY.] Go away from me! [*To* LINDA.] What do you mean, lives or dies? Nobody's dying around here, pal.

Linda. Get out of my sight! Get out of here!

Biff. I wanna see the boss.

Linda. You're not going near him!

Biff. Where is he?

[*He moves into the living-room and* LINDA *follows.*]

Linda. [*Shouting after* BIFF.] You invite him for dinner. He looks forward to it all day— [BIFF *appears in his parents' bedroom, looks around, and exits.*] —and then you desert him there. There's no stranger you'd do that to!

Happy. Why? He had a swell time with us. Listen, when I— [LINDA *comes back into the kitchen.*] —desert him I hope I don't outlive the day!

Linda. Get out of here!

Happy. Now look, Mom . . .

Linda. Did you have to go to women tonight? You and your lousy rotten whores!

[BIFF *re-enters the kitchen.*]

Happy. Mom, all we did was follow Biff around trying to cheer him up! [*To* BIFF.] Boy, what a night you gave me!

Linda. Get out of here, both of you, and don't come back! I don't want you tormenting him any more. Go on now, get your things together! [*To* BIFF.] You can sleep in his apartment. [*She starts to pick up the flowers and stops herself.*] Pick up this stuff, I'm not your maid any more. Pick it up, you bum, you!

[HAPPY *turns his back to her in refusal.* BIFF *slowly moves over and gets down on his knees, picking up the flowers.*]

Linda. You're a pair of animals! Not one, not another living soul would have had the cruelty to walk out on that man in a restaurant!

Biff. [*Not looking at her.*] Is that what he said?

Linda. He didn't have to say anything. He was so humiliated he nearly limped when he came in.

Happy. But, Mom, he had a great time with us——

Biff. [*Cutting him off violently.*] Shut up!

[*Without another word,* HAPPY *goes upstairs.*]

Linda. You! You didn't even go in to see if he was all right!

Biff. [*Still on the floor in front of* LINDA, *the flowers in his hand; with self-loathing.*] No. Didn't. Didn't do a damned thing. How do you like that, heh? Left him babbling in a toilet.

Linda. You louse. You . . .

Biff. Now you hit it on the nose! [*He gets up, throws the flowers in the wastebasket.*] The scum of the earth, and you're looking at him!

Linda. Get out of here!

Biff. I gotta talk to the boss, Mom. Where is he?

Linda. You're not going near him. Get out of this house!

Biff. [*With absolute assurance, determination.*] No. We're gonna have an abrupt conversation, him and me.

Linda. You're not talking to him!

[*Hammering is heard from outside the house, off right.* BIFF *turns toward the noise.*]

Linda. [*Suddenly pleading.*] Will you please leave him alone?

Biff. What's he doing out there?

Linda. He's planting the garden!

Biff. [*Quietly.*] Now? Oh, my God!

[BIFF *moves outside,* LINDA *following. The light dies down on them and comes up on the center of the apron as* WILLY *walks into it. He is carrying a flashlight, a hoe, and a handful of seed packets. He raps the top of the hoe sharply to fix it firmly, and then moves to the left, measuring off the distance with his foot. He holds the flashlight to look at the seed packets, reading off the instructions. He is in the blue of night.*]

Willy. Carrots . . . quarter-inch apart.

Rows . . . one-foot rows. [*He measures it off.*] One foot. [*He puts down a package and measures off.*] Beets. [*He puts down another package and measures again.*] Lettuce. [*He reads the package, puts it down.*] One foot—— *He breaks off as* BEN *appears at the right and moves slowly down to him.*] What a proposition, ts, ts. Terrific, terrific. 'Cause she's suffered, Ben, the woman has suffered. You understand me? A man can't go out the way he came in, Ben, a man has got to add up to something. You can't, you can't—— [BEN *moves toward him as though to interrupt.*] You gotta consider, now. Don't answer so quick. Remember, it's a guaranteed twenty-thousand-dollar proposition. Now look, Ben, I want you to go through the ins and outs of this thing with me. I've got nobody to talk to, Ben, and the woman has suffered, you hear me?

Ben. [*Standing still, considering.*] What's the proposition?

Willy. It's twenty thousand dollars on the barrelhead. Guaranteed, gilt-edged, you understand?

Ben. You don't want to make a fool of yourself. They might not honor the policy.

Willy. How can they dare refuse? Didn't I work like a coolie to meet every premium on the nose? And now they don't pay off? Impossible!

Ben. It's called a cowardly thing, William.

Willy. Why? Does it take more guts to stand here the rest of my life ringing up a zero?

Ben. [*Yielding.*] That's a point, William. [*He moves, thinking, turns.*] And twenty thousand—that *is* something one can feel with the hand, it is there.

Willy. [*Now assured, with rising power.*] Oh, Ben, that's the whole beauty of it! I see it like a diamond, shining in the dark, hard and rough, that I can pick up and touch in my hand. Not like—like an appointment! This would not be another damned-fool appointment, Ben, and it changes all the aspects. Because he thinks I'm nothing, see, and so he spites me. But the funeral—— [*Straightening up.*] Ben, that funeral will be massive! They'll come from Maine, Massachusetts, Vermont, New Hampshire! All the old-timers with the strange license plates—that boy will be thunder-struck, Ben, because he never realized—I am known! Rhode Island, New York, New Jersey—— I am known, Ben, and he'll see it with his eyes once and for all. He'll see what I am, Ben! He's in for a shock, that boy!

Ben. [*Coming down to the edge of the garden.*] He'll call you a coward.

Willy. [*Suddenly fearful.*] No, that would be terrible.

Ben. Yes. And a damned fool.

Willy. No, no, he mustn't; I won't have that! [*He is broken and desperate.*]

Ben. He'll hate you, William.

[*The gay music of the* BOYS *is heard.*]

Willy. Oh, Ben, how do we get back to all the great times? Used to be so full of light, and comradeship, the sleigh-riding in winter, and the ruddiness on his cheeks. And always some kind of good news coming up, always something nice coming up ahead. And never even let me carry the valises in the house, and simonizing, simonizing that little red car! Why, why can't I give him something and not have him hate me?

Ben. Let me think about it. [*He glances at his watch.*] I still have a little time. Remarkable proposition, but you've got to be sure you're not making a fool of yourself.

[BEN *drifts off upstage and goes out of sight.* BIFF *comes down from the left.*]

Willy. [*Suddenly conscious of* BIFF, *turns and looks up at him, then begins picking up the packages of seeds in confusion.*] Where the hell is that seed? [*Indignantly.*] You can't see nothing out here! They boxed in the whole goddam neighborhood!

Biff. There are people all around here. Don't you realize that?

Willy. I'm busy. Don't bother me.

Biff. [*Taking the hoe from* WILLY.] I'm saying good-by to you, Pop. [WILLY *looks at him, silent, unable to move.*] I'm not coming back any more.

Willy. You're not going to see Oliver tomorrow?

Biff. I've got no appointment, Dad.

Willy. He put his arm around you, and you've got no appointment?

Biff. Pop, get this now, will you? Everytime I've left it's been a fight that sent me out of here. Today I realized something about myself and I tried to explain it to you and I—I think I'm just not smart enough to make any sense out of it for you. To hell with whose fault it is or anything like that. [*He takes* WILLY's *arm.*] Let's just wrap it up, heh? Come on in; we'll tell Mom.

[*He gently tries to pull* WILLY *to left.*]

Willy. [*Frozen, immobile, with guilt in his voice.*] No, I don't want to see her.

Biff. Come on!

[*He pulls again, and* WILLY *tries to pull away.*]

Willy. [*Highly nervous.*] No, no, I don't want to see her.

Biff. [*Tries to look into* WILLY'S *face, as if to find the answer there.*] Why don't you want to see her?

Willy. [*More harshly now.*] Don't bother me, will you?

Biff. What do you mean, you don't want to see her? You don't want them calling you yellow, do you? This isn't your fault; it's me, I'm a bum. Now come inside! [WILLY *strains to get away.*] Did you hear what I said to you?

[WILLY *pulls away and quickly goes by himself into the house.* BIFF *follows.*]

Linda. [*To* WILLY.] Did you plant, dear?

Biff. [*At the door, to* LINDA.] All right, we had it out. I'm going and I'm not writing any more.

Linda. [*Going to* WILLY *in the kitchen.*] I think that's the best way, dear. 'Cause there's no use drawing it out; you'll just never get along. [WILLY *doesn't respond.*]

Biff. People ask where I am and what I'm doing, you don't know, and you don't care. That way it'll be off your mind and you can start brightening up again. All right? That clears it, doesn't it? [WILLY *is silent, and* BIFF *goes to him.*] You gonna wish me luck, scout? [*He extends his hand.*] What do you say?

Linda. Shake his hand, Willy.

Willy. [*Turning to her, seething with hurt.*] There's no necessity to mention the pen at all, y'know.

Biff. [*Gently.*] I've got no appointment, Dad.

Willy. [*Erupting fiercely.*] He put his arm around . . . ?

Biff. Dad, you're never going to see what I am, so what's the use of arguing? If I strike oil I'll send you a check. Meantime forget I'm alive.

Willy. [*To* LINDA.] Spite, see?

Biff. Shake hands, Dad.

Willy. Not my hand.

Biff. I was hoping not to go this way.

Willy. Well, this is the way you're going. Good-by.

[BIFF *looks at him a moment, then turns sharply and goes to the stairs.*]

Willy. [*Stops him with.*] May you rot in hell if you leave this house!

Biff. [*Turning.*] Exactly what is it that you want from me?

Willy. I want you to know, on the train, in the mountains, in the valleys, wherever you go, that you cut down your life for spite!

Biff. No, no.

Willy. Spite, spite, is the word of your undoing! And when you're down and out, remember what did it. When you're rotting somewhere beside the railroad tracks, remember, and don't you dare blame it on me!

Biff. I'm not blaming it on you!

Willy. I won't take the rap for this, you hear?

[HAPPY *comes down the stairs and stands on the bottom step, watching.*]

Biff. That's just what I'm telling you!

Willy. [*Sinking into a chair at the table, with full accusation.*] You're trying to put a knife in me—don't think I don't know what you're doing!

Biff. All right, phony! Then let's lay it on the line.

[*He whips the rubber tube out of his pocket and puts it on the table.*]

Happy. You crazy——

Linda. Biff!

[*She moves to grab the hose, but* BIFF *holds it down with his hand.*]

Biff. Leave it there! Don't move it!

Willy. [*Not looking at it.*] What is that?

Biff. You know goddam well what that is.

Willy. [*Caged, wanting to escape.*] I never saw that.

Biff. You saw it. The mice didn't bring it into the cellar! What is this supposed to do, make a hero out of you? This supposed to make me sorry for you?

Willy. Never heard of it.

Biff. There'll be no pity for you, you hear it? No pity!

Willy. [*To* LINDA.] You hear the spite!

Biff. No, you're going to hear the truth —what you are and what I am!

Linda. Stop it!

Willy. Spite!

Happy. [*Coming down toward* BIFF.] You cut it now!

Biff. [*To* HAPPY.] The man don't know who we are! The man is gonna know! [*To* WILLY.] We never told the truth for ten minutes in this house!

Happy. We always told the truth!

Biff. [*Turning on him.*] You big blow, are you the assistant buyer? You're one of the two assistants to the assistant, aren't you?

Happy. Well, I'm practically——

Biff. You're practically full of it! We all are! And I'm through with it. [*To* WILLY.] Now hear this, Willy, this is me.

Willy. I know you!

Biff. You know why I had no address for three months? I stole a suit in Kansas

City and I was in jail. [*To* LINDA, *who is sobbing.*] Stop crying. I'm through with it.

[LINDA *turns away from them, her hands covering her face.*]

Willy. I suppose that's my fault!

Biff. I stole myself out of every good job since high school!

Willy. And whose fault is that?

Biff. And I never got anywhere because you blew me so full of hot air I could never stand taking orders from anybody! That's whose fault it is!

Willy. I hear that!

Linda. Don't, Biff!

Biff. It's goddam time you heard that! I had to be boss big shot in two weeks, and I'm through with it!

Willy. Then hang yourself! For spite, hang yourself!

Biff. No! Nobody's hanging himself, Willy! I ran down eleven flights with a pen in my hand today. And suddenly I stopped, you hear me? And in the middle of that office building, do you hear this? I stopped in the middle of that building and I saw—the sky. I saw the things that I love in this world. The work and the food and time to sit and smoke. And I looked at the pen and said to myself, what the hell am I grabbing this for? Why am I trying to become what I don't want to be? What am I doing in an office, making a contemptuous, begging fool of myself, when all I want is out there, waiting for me the minute I say I know who I am! Why can't I say that, Willy?

[*He tries to make* WILLY *face him, but* WILLY *pulls away and moves to the left.*]

Willy. [*With hatred, threateningly.*] The door of your life is wide open!

Biff. Pop! I'm a dime a dozen, and so are you!

Willy. [*Turning on him now in an uncontrolled outburst.*] I am not a dime a dozen! I am Willy Loman, and you are Biff Loman!

[BIFF *starts for* WILLY, *but is blocked by* HAPPY. *In his fury,* BIFF *seems on the verge of attacking his father.*]

Biff. I am not a leader of men, Willy, and neither are you. You were never anything but a hard-working drummer who landed in the ash can like all the rest of them! I'm one dollar an hour, Willy! I tried seven states and couldn't raise it. A buck an hour! Do you gather my meaning? I'm not bringing home any prizes any more, and you're going to stop waiting for me to bring them home!

Willy. [*Directly to* BIFF.] You vengeful, spiteful mut!

[BIFF *breaks from* HAPPY. WILLY, *in fright, starts up the stairs.* BIFF *grabs him.*]

Biff. [*At the peak of his fury.*] Pop, I'm nothing! I'm nothing, Pop. Can't you understand that? There's no spite in it any more. I'm just what I am, that's all.

[BIFF'S *fury has spent itself, and he breaks down, sobbing, holding on to* WILLY, *who dumbly fumbles for* BIFF'S *face.*]

Willy. [*Astonished.*] What're you doing? What're you doing? [*To* LINDA.] Why is he crying?

Biff. [*Crying, broken.*] Will you let me go, for Christ's sake? Will you take that phony dream and burn it before something happens? [*Struggling to contain himself, he pulls away and moves to the stairs.*] I'll go in the morning. Put him—put him to bed.

[*Exhausted,* BIFF *moves up the stairs to his room.*]

Willy. [*After a long pause, astonished, elevated.*] Isn't that—isn't that remarkable? Biff—he likes me!

Linda. He loves you, Willy!

Happy. [*Deeply moved.*] Always did, Pop.

Willy. Oh, Biff! [*Staring wildly.*] He cried! Cried to me. [*He is choking with his love, and now cries out his promise.*] That boy—that boy is going to be magnificent!

[BEN *appears in the light just outside the kitchen.*]

Ben. Yes, outstanding, with twenty thousand behind him.

Linda. [*Sensing the racing of his mind, fearfully, carefully.*] Now come to bed, Willy. It's all settled now.

Willy. [*Finding it difficult not to rush out of the house.*] Yes, we'll sleep. Come on. Go to sleep, Hap.

Ben. And it does take a great kind of a man to crack the jungle.

[*In accents of dread,* BEN'S *idyllic music starts up.*]

Happy. [*His arm around* LINDA.] I'm getting married, Pop, don't forget it. I'm changing everything. I'm gonna run that department before the year is up. You'll see, Mom. [*He kisses her.*]

Ben. The jungle is dark but full of diamonds, Willy.

[WILLY *turns, moves, listening to* BEN.]

Linda. Be good. You're both good boys, just act that way, that's all.

Happy. 'Night, Pop. [*He goes upstairs.*]

Linda. [*To* WILLY.] Come, dear.

Ben. [*With greater force.*] One must go in to fetch a diamond out.

Willy. [*To* LINDA, *as he moves slowly along the edge of the kitchen, toward the door.*] I just want to get settled down, Linda. Let me sit alone for a little.

Linda. [*Almost uttering her fear.*] I want you upstairs.

Willy. [*Taking her in his arms.*] In a few minutes, Linda. I couldn't sleep right now. Go on, you look awful tired.

[*He kisses her.*]

Ben. Not like an appointment at all. A diamond is rough and hard to the touch.

Willy. Go on now. I'll be right up.

Linda. I think this is the only way, Willy.

Willy. Sure, it's the best thing.

Ben. Best thing!

Willy. The only way. Everything is gonna be—go on, kid, get to bed. You look so tired.

Linda. Come right up.

Willy. Two minutes.

[LINDA *goes into the living-room, then reappears in her bedroom.* WILLY *moves just outside the kitchen door.*]

Willy. Loves me. [*Wonderingly.*] Always loved me. Isn't that a remarkable thing? Ben, he'll worship me for it!

Ben. [*With promise.*] It's dark there, but full of diamonds.

Willy. Can you imagine that magnificence with twenty thousand dollars in his pocket?

Linda. [*Calling from her room.*] Willy! Come up!

Willy. [*Calling into the kitchen.*] Yes! Yes. Coming! It's very smart, you realize that, don't you, sweetheart? Even Ben sees it. I gotta go, baby. 'By! 'By! [*Going over to* BEN, *almost dancing.*] Imagine? When the mail comes he'll be ahead of Bernard again!

Ben. A perfect proposition all around.

Willy. Did you see how he cried to me? Oh, if I could kiss him, Ben!

Ben. Time, William, time!

Willy. Oh, Ben, I always knew one way or another we were gonna make it, Biff and I!

Ben. [*Looking at his watch.*] The boat. We'll be late.

[*He moves slowly off into the darkness.*]

Willy. [*Elegiacally, turning to the house.*] Now when you kick off, boy, I want a seventy-yard boot, and get right down the field under the ball, and when you hit, hit low and hit hard, because it's important, boy. [*He swings around and faces the audience.*] There's all kinds of important people in the stands, and the first thing you know . . . [*Suddenly realizing he is alone.*] Ben! Ben, where do I . . . ? [*He makes a sudden movement of search.*] Ben, how do I . . . ?

Linda. [*Calling.*] Willy, you coming up?

Willy. [*Uttering a gasp of fear, whirling about as if to quiet her.*] Sh! [*He turns around as if to find his way; sounds, faces, voices, seem to be swarming in upon him and he flicks at them, crying.*] Sh! Sh! [*Suddenly music, faint and high, stops him. It rises in intensity, almost to an unbearable scream. He goes up and down on his toes, and rushes off around the house.*] Shhh!

Linda. Willy?

[*There is no answer.* LINDA *waits.* BIFF *gets up off his bed. He is still in his clothes.* HAPPY *sits up.* BIFF *stands listening.*]

Linda. [*With real fear.*] Willy, answer me! Willy!

[*There is the sound of a car starting and moving away at full speed.*]

Linda. No!

Biff. [*Rushing down the stairs.*] Pop!

[*As the car speeds off, the music crashes down in a frenzy of sound, which becomes the soft pulsation of a single cello string.* BIFF *slowly returns to his bedroom. He and* HAPPY *gravely don their jackets.* LINDA *slowly walks out of her room. The music has developed into a dead march. The leaves of day are appearing over everything.* CHARLEY *and* BERNARD, *somberly dressed, appear and knock on the kitchen door.* BIFF *and* HAPPY *slowly descend the stairs to the kitchen as* CHARLEY *and* BERNARD *enter. All stop a moment when* LINDA, *in clothes of mourning, bearing a little bunch of roses, comes through the draped doorway into the kitchen. She goes to* CHARLEY *and takes his arm. Now all move toward the audience, through the wall-line of the kitchen. At the limit of the apron,* LINDA *lays down the flowers, kneels, and sits back on her heels. All stare down at the grave.*]

REQUIEM

Charley. It's getting dark, Linda.

[LINDA *doesn't react. She stares at the grave.*]

Biff. How about it, Mom? Better get some rest, heh? They'll be closing the gate soon. [LINDA *makes no move. Pause.*]

Happy. [*Deeply angered.*] He had no right to do that. There was no necessity for it. We would've helped him.

Charley. [*Grunting.*] Hmmm.

Biff. Come along, Mom.

Linda. Why didn't anybody come?

Charley. It was a very nice funeral.

Linda. But where are all the people he knew? Maybe they blame him.

Charley. Naa. It's a rough world, Linda. They wouldn't blame him.

Linda. I can't understand it. At this time especially. First time in thirty-five years we were just about free and clear. He only needed a little salary. He was even finished with the dentist.

Charley. No man only needs a little salary.

Linda. I can't understand it.

Biff. There were a lot of nice days. When he'd come home from a trip; or on Sundays, making the stoop; finishing the cellar; putting on the new porch; when he built the extra bathroom; and put up the garage. You know something, Charley, there's more of him in that front stoop than in all the sales he ever made.

Charley. Yeah. He was a happy man with a batch of cement.

Linda. He was so wonderful with his hands.

Biff. He had the wrong dreams. All, all, wrong.

Happy. [*Almost ready to fight* BIFF.] Don't say that!

Biff. He never knew who he was.

Charley. [*Stopping* HAPPY'S *movement and reply. To* BIFF.] Nobody dast blame this man. You don't understand: Willy was a salesman. And for a salesman, there is no rock bottom to the life. He don't put a bolt to a nut, he don't tell you the law or give you medicine. He's a man way out there in the blue, riding on a smile and a shoeshine. And when they start not smiling back—that's an earthquake. And then you get yourself a couple of spots on your hat, and you're finished. Nobody dast blame this man. A salesman is got to dream, boy. It comes with the territory.

Biff. Charley, the man didn't know who he was.

Happy. [*Infuriated.*] Don't say that!

Biff. Why don't you come with me, Happy?

Happy. I'm not licked that easily. I'm staying right in this city, and I'm gonna beat this racket! [*He looks at* BIFF, *his chin set.*] The Loman Brothers!

Biff. I know who I am, kid.

Happy. All right, boy. I'm gonna show you and everybody else that Willy Loman did not die in vain. He had a good dream. It's the only dream you can have—to come out number-one man. He fought it out here, and this is where I'm gonna win it for him.

Biff. [*With a hopeless glance at* HAPPY, *bends toward his mother.*] Let's go, Mom.

Linda. I'll be with you in a minute. Go on, Charley. [*He hesitates.*] I want to, just for a minute. I never had a chance to say good-by.

[CHARLEY *moves away, followed by* HAPPY. BIFF *remains a slight distance up and left of* LINDA. *She sits there, summoning herself. The flute begins, not far away, playing behind her speech.*]

Linda. Forgive me, dear. I can't cry. I don't know what it is, but I can't cry. I don't understand it. Why did you ever do that? Help me, Willy, I can't cry. It seems to me that you're just on another trip. I keep expecting you. Willy, dear, I can't cry. Why did you do it? I search and search and I search, and I can't understand it, Willy. I made the last payment on the house today. Today, dear. And there'll be nobody home. [*A sob rises in her throat.*] We're free and clear. [*Sobbing more fully, released.*] We're free. [BIFF *comes slowly toward her.*] We're free . . . We're free . . .

[BIFF *lifts her to her feet and moves out up right with her in his arms.* LINDA *sobs quietly.* BERNARD *and* CHARLEY *come together and follow them, followed by* HAPPY. *Only the music of the flute is left on the darkening stage as over the house the hard towers of the apartment buildings rise into sharp focus, and*

THE CURTAIN FALLS

VENUS OBSERVED*

By

CHRISTOPHER FRY

SKEPTICS REGARDING SHAKESPEARE'S AUthorship, for lack of convincing records of adequate background, training, or experience, should consider the anonymous years of Bernard Shaw and Christopher Fry. Had these dramatists lived under the first Elizabeth, we should now know perhaps less of their immature years than of Shakespeare's. But we have their own revelations and those of their biographers to convince us of their more than adequate self-education, in spite of meager and less than brilliant formal schooling: Shaw, during a decade of obscure reading, abortive writing, and debate, to become an outstanding "intellectual" among world dramatists; Fry, during even more years spent in cultural but unrewarding and little noticed activities, to become a sensationally effective theatre poet.

Along the way, Fry discarded his father's family name of Harris for his mother's ("a matter of euphony"). His father, an unsuccessful architect, but devoted missionary in the Bristol slums, died when Christopher was only three years old. Thanks to the sacrifice of an impoverished mother, Christopher was permitted to complete his not too devoted studies in the Bedford Modern School, his only formal education. Married at the age of nineteen, he somehow provided a scant living for his wife and son while acting in pageants and in repertory companies, as at Bath and Tunbridge Wells. Some of the pageants he wrote and directed himself.

In early childhood he had taken to the piano and by the age of five was already a composer. He was also a juvenile editor, a cartoonist, a script writer for children's radio, a private secretary—to a novelist and later to a tin-pan-alley song writer—a cabaret entertainer, and a collaborator in a verse play never finished. But while still at the Bedford school he completed one wholly his own, *Youth and Peregrines,* that was actually produced a decade later; but from the age of eighteen to twenty-eight, as he confesses, he "didn't write a line."

Only the good luck of a small legacy and two periods of irksome schoolteaching kept his little family from penury. But meanwhile he had become resourceful and competent in the only way that really matters for a dramatist. In 1940, at the age of thirty-three, he was appointed director of the celebrated and creative Oxford Repertory Players, and by 1947 he had become "staff-dramatist" of the highly important Arts Theatre of London. In these responsible offices he had at last found himself as a dramatic poet.

In the following two seasons, when he was past the age of forty, came the harvest for this "unknown dramatist," as *Current Biography* could even then call him: first, *A Phoenix Too Frequent,* a comedy that won favor with the public and the critics; then, *The Lady's Not for Burning,* which, when produced at his Arts Theatre, won the Shaw prize, and, a few months later, when staged professionally, began an enviable career throughout the English-speaking world. The following season, 1949–1950, it was Fry's unprecedented fortune to have four verse plays running at the same time in London: *The Lady's Not for Burning* at the Globe with John Gielgud and Pamela Brown in the cast, the latter a "discovery" of the author's when with the Oxford Repertory; *Venus Observed* at the St. James's, with Laurence Olivier as the Duke; *The Boy and the Cart,* written originally for a village church anniversary; and *Ring Around the Moon,* translated and adapted from the French original, *L'Invitation au Château* by Jean Anouilh.

Clearly the London public had found itself unexpectedly avid for drama in verse; and quite as surely, it was Fry who had created all the enthusiasm by the enchantment of a fresh poetic appeal—the sound of spoken verse of undeniable quality and with no attempt, as in recent theatre verse, to make it sound as much like prose as possible. Although Fry's meaning was often elusive, the verbal beauty, epigram, and haunting symbolism of his dialogue bespoke the advent of a genius of sorts. Here, at last, was a dramatist who was not content to "restore" poetry to the stage in the age-long futile rivalry with Shakespeare on his own grounds of romantic story, meticulous characterization, and faultless iambics. Fry was, in fact, leading the theatre forward into the new experimental realm of contemporary poetry and doing so with facility and mature command.

Nor was this poetic allurement at the cost of theatrical effect, for, as with every really important theatre poet of the past, his was the work of a man whose very life had been the theatre—as actor, producer, technician, and playwright; but one who, like Shakespeare, happened also to be an authentic poet.

Less commendably, perhaps, with apparent unconcern for mere clarity and emotional impact, Fry frankly slights the ancient logic of dramatic action. His dramaturgy seems to have escaped from the rigid cage of forms and probabilities, and to have committed itself to the logic of symbol, with action, far from realistic, sparingly introduced, but excitingly, nevertheless, as might be expected of a man of the theatre. It serves rather as a framework to create suspense and sustain the symbolic patterns than to afford the chief audience interest.

With serious intent, Fry's dramatic poetry has new substance as well as new forms. This substance is not easily definable. It is expressed by metaphor and through the facets of characters like the Duke and Perpetua of the present play and the Countess in *The Dark Is Light Enough,* rather than by formal elaboration. Fry, unlike Sartre, is no systematic philosopher, but he is an informed and purposeful thinker with a strong religious faith shown more clearly in his works for churchly celebrations, like *The Boy with a Cart,* or for enactment in a cathedral, like *A Sleep of Prisoners,* than in his secular comedies. Of these, as of the present play, the purport is a serene confidence in life's beauty and spiritual validity apart from materialistic reality. Derek Sanford in his monograph on Fry calls it "the principle of mystery." With full cognizance of science and its implications, Fry communicates the conviction of enduring spirituality in human existence, even when, as in *Venus Observed,* mankind is shown in its puny microcosm in dramatic contrast to the macrocosm of the heavens, symbolized by the Duke's telescope, which, like the Damoclean sword, overhangs his guests. Fry himself has expressed his intention: "I could see no reason, though writing a comedy, why I should not treat the world as I see it, a world in which we are all poised on the edge of eternity, a world which has deeps and shadows of mystery, in which God is anything but a sleeping partner." Reduced to creeds and tenets, this concept is as old as religion itself; what is fresh in Fry's application of it is its assertion as fact, for so he makes it appear as confidently as the writers of the ancient miracles. In his affirmation he takes a stand like that of the great entomologist Fabre, whose phrase, "The dark is light enough," Fry chose as title for the fourth of these seasonal comedies. When Fabre was once asked if he believed in God, he exclaimed, "I have seen Him!" The God he saw was "the principle of mystery" in the infinitesimal yet infinite existence of insects. Fry as confidently sees Him in the less infinitesimal but far more mysterious reality of man's life and indomitable spirit.

Fry's mysticism that permeates his vivid imagination accounts, no doubt, for his cavalier disregard for the conventions of dramatic realism. In this play, for instance, he leaves the miraculous behavior of Perpetua's revolver for us to account for if we can, and also the still more unaccountable escape of Pebbleman and the Duke down a flaming flight of stairs said to have been consumed, at least in part. These incidents are symbols in a play that makes no pretense to reality, but their theatrical effect is immense, like that of Prospero's magic. Besides, in the spirit of comedy, they playfully add to the pervasive mystery; and the latter action, in the manner of Victorian melodrama, provides an exciting end for the scene.

Fry's poetic nonchalance affords a consistent pattern of its own, as in the stage business of the apples and that of the Temple of the Ancient Virtues. But the immediate appeal to an audience is through the ear—of unmistakably rhythmic verse, more lyric throughout than dramatic, yet fluent and easily spoken, and often expressive of the dramatist's perceptive delight in nature, as when the Duke discourses on man's lonely separateness in creation:

"... if the weed wove its way up river
To breed, and the fish waved green and still,
The water would never wonder: all
Is at one with the rest.
And the trees, when the weather is waking, quicken without
Question, their leaves assemble in perfect faith
Of summer; and so with all the world's life,
Except ours."

Often there is sophisticated humor blended with serious statement:

"Remembering we've been on earth two million years,
Man and boy and Sterkfontein ape."

More strikingly, force without bombast is given to a dramatic moment, as when the incendiary Rosabel, in angry resentment of the Duke's astronomical devotion, cries:

"You'll see, I shall send his Observatory
Where Nero's Rome has gone; I'll blaze a trail
That he can follow towards humanity!"

Fry, in the manner of the classics, imparts to the longer key speeches of his scenes an hypnotic fascination, writing with a purposeful eloquence that betrays a producer's instinct for declamatory values, as in the passages beginning: "We shine. That's a consideration . . . ," "I'm a Roman in a world of Romans . . . ," "Over all the world Men move unhoming . . . ," "But if being alive is a question. . . ."

Some of the longer speeches, however, are baffling upon a first hearing; yet a discerning listener who heard Miss Cornell read the Countess's lines in the still more baffling *The Dark Is Light Enough* must have sensed a depth and a spiritual beauty that are refreshing in this particular decade of theatrical banality.

Venus Observed, Fry informs us, was planned as one of four "seasonal comedies," each cast in the mood of a time of year: *The Lady's Not for Burning* in that of spring; *A Phoenix Too Frequent,* of summer; *Venus Observed,* of autumn; and *The Dark Is Light Enough,* of winter. Beginning with the Duke's declining years, the reader may find it interesting to observe the many ways in which *Venus Observed,* like a musical composition, is keyed to the waning drift of life—the autumnal mood; they vary from direct description ("Only the wind blowing/And the rattle of leaves") to metaphorical suggestion of phrasing ("England's moist and misty devotion"); of character (the goddesses in the sere: Rosabel, Jessie, Hilda; the desiccated Reedbeck); and of whole scenes (like the first in the Temple of the Ancient Virtues). In this connection we may also regard the sun's eclipse and the Duke's description of the title planet:

"The star which, when it's rising, is called Venus,
Setting is Lucifer, the goddess
Graduating into demon, and what good
Is that for a man's immortal spirit?"

Fry is one modern who does not shrink from suggestive alliteration and the clever pun. His dialogue is shot through with double-meanings that one must be alert to detect, as in the passages relating to archery, and the symbolism of that action itself. At times this tendency is carried to excess, exposing Fry to the charge of oversophistication when indulging in such verbal flippancies as "mute as we are mutable," "my equine equability," "supercherify with chousery." His playfulness, at least, helps much to relieve his writing of the dreariness of the beaten path.

He may well be expected to emerge still more impressively from his seclusion, as a home and nature lover, in his farm cottage—that till recently was without electricity,—and to win a more secure place among enduring theatre poets. Already he has demonstrated beyond doubt that sheer poetry can still be potent on the stage, and, more uniquely, he has opened new paths for it to follow.

CHRISTOPHER FRY

Born 1907, Bristol, England; of ardently pious parents named Harris, the mother of Quaker stock, whose name was Fry.

1910, Charles Harris, his father, died; Christopher, then only three, had acquired so strong a reverence for his father's genuine devotion as lay-reader and slum missionary that, together with his mother's Quaker principles, it did much to inspire his writing and way of life.

1925, Completed secondary education at the Bedford Modern School. Taught for a year in the local schools.

1927, Member of the Bath Repertory Company.

1928, Schoolmaster for three years at the Hazelton Preparatory School, Limpfield, Surrey.
The following decade spent in a variety of occupations, entered in *"Who's Who"* as "too complicated for tabulation."

1934, His first completed verse play produced, written ten years earlier while an undergraduate.

1935, *She Shall Have Music,* a musical comedy for which he wrote words and score, produced at the Savoy Theatre, London, for a brief run.

1936, Married journalist Phyllis Hart.

1938, *Thursday's Child,* his third pageant, performed for charity at Albert Hall, London.

1940, Appointed director of the Oxford Repertory Players.
Recruited for four years of military service as noncombatant on account of pacifist scruples.

1944, Returned as director of the Oxford Players.

1947, Appointed staff-dramatist of London's Arts Theatre.

1948, Two years of extraordinary theatre success. In the second, four of his verse plays ran simultaneously; the most notable: *The Lady's Not for Burning,* produced by John Gielgud; *Venus Observed,* produced by Laurence Olivier.

1952, Supplied additional songs and lyrics for the filming of *The Beggar's Opera.*
When not actively engaged in theatre work, Fry lives unpretentiously with his wife and son on his simple farm at Shipton-under-Wychwood, Oxfordshire, devoting his time to farming and writing.

PLAYS

1934 *Youth and Peregrines,* written before 1925. 1935 *She Shall Have Music,* a musical comedy. 1936 *The Open Door,* written to support the Dr. Bernardo Homes. 1938 *The Tower,* a pageant play. 1938 *Thursday's Child,* a charity pageant. 1939 *The Boy with a Cart,* written for a village church, his first play to be published. 1946 *The Firstborn.* 1946 *A Phoenix Too Frequent.* 1948 *The Lady's Not for Burning.* 1948 *Thor, with Angels.* 1950 *Venus Observed.* 1950 *Ring Around the Moon,* translated and adapted from Jean Anouilh's *L'Invitation au château.* 1951 *A Sleep of Prisoners.* 1954 *The Dark Is Light Enough.* 1955 *Tiger at the Gates,* translated from Jean Giraudoux's *La Guerre de Troie n'aura pas lieu.*

VENUS OBSERVED

Characters

(in order of their appearance)

THE DUKE OF ALTAIR.
EDGAR, *his son.*
HERBERT REEDBECK, *his agent.*
DOMINIC, *Reedbeck's son.*
ROSABEL FLEMING.
JESSIE DILL.
CAPTAIN FOX REDDLEMAN, *the Duke's butler.*
BATES, *the Duke's footman.*
HILDA TAYLOR-SNELL.
PERPETUA, *Reedbeck's daughter.*

SCENES

The Observatory Room at Stellmere Park, the Duke's mansion.
The Temple of the Ancient Virtues, Stellmere Park.

ACT ONE

A room at the top of a mansion: once a bedroom, now an observatory.
[When the curtain rises the DUKE OF ALTAIR *is in argument with his son* EDGAR. *Also present is* HERBERT REEDBECK, *the* DUKE'S *agent.]*

Duke. Anyone would think I had made some extraordinary
Suggestion. But in fact how natural it is.
Aren't you my son?
Edgar. Yes, father, of course I am.
Duke. Then it's up to you to choose who shall be your mother.
Does that seem to you improper, Reedbeck?
Reedbeck. No,
Your Grace; it's not, perhaps, always done,
But few parents consider their children as you do.
I don't dislike the plan at all.
Edgar. I sweat
With embarrassment.
Duke. You have been
Too much with the the horses. This, that I ask you to do,
Is an act of poetry, and a compliment
To the freshness of your mind. Why should you sweat?
Here they will be, three handsome women,
All of them at some time implicated
In the joyous routine of my life. (I could scarcely
Put it more delicately.) I wish to marry.
Who am I, in heaven's name, to decide
Which were my vintage years of love?
Good God, to differentiate between
The first bright blow on my sleeping flesh,
The big breasts of mid-morning,
And the high old dance of afternoon—
Value one against the other? Never, not I,
Till the eschatological rain shall lay my dust.
But you, dear boy, with your twenty-five impartial years,
Can perform the judgement of Paris,
Can savour, consider, and award the apple
With a cool hand. You will find an apple
Over there by the spectroscope.
Edgar. But why must you marry?
Or, if that's an impertinence, why do I have to have
A mother? I've been able to grow to a sizable boy
Without one.
Duke. Why? Because I see no end
To the parceling out of heaven in small beauties,
Year after year, flocks of girls, who look
So lately kissed by God
They come out on the world with lips shining,
Flocks and generations, until time
Seems like nothing so much
As a blinding snowstorm of virginity,
And a man, lost in the perpetual scurry of white,
Can only close his eyes
In a resignation of monogamy.
Edgar. Anyway, it would be an impossibly hasty

Judgement. Honour you as I may, I don't
See how I can do it.

Duke. If Paris had no trouble
Choosing between the tide-turning beauty,
Imponderable and sexed with eternity,
Of Aphrodite, Hera, and Athene,
Aren't you ashamed to make heavy weather of a choice
Between Hilda, and Rosabel, and Jessie?
And if you can't make up your mind about a woman
At first meeting, all hope of definition has gone;
Prejudice, delirium, or rage
Will cock their snooks,* and the apple will go bad.
No, boy, no; go and water your horses
And come back and choose your mother.

Edgar. At what time?

Duke. What is it now?

Reedbeck. Five past eleven.

Duke. They should
Be here. At eleven twenty-nine we're to have
The total eclipse of the sun, to which I've invited them.
The mouth of the moon has already begun to munch.
We shall all feel ourselves making a north-west passage
Through the sea of heaven, and darkness will cover
The face of the earth. In that moment
All women will be as one.

Edgar. That's what I was going
To ask you. I don't want to play the heavy son,
But would you say you loved these women equally?

Duke. Equality is a mortuary word. Just choose.
Shall I be happy on Tuesdays, Thursdays, and Saturdays,
Or on Mondays, Wednesdays, and Fridays? Some such difference
Is all that your choice involves.

[*Enter* CAPTAIN FOX REDDLEMAN, *a manservant. He looks like, and was once, a lion tamer.*]

Reddleman. 'Scuse, your Grace:
But a telegram for our little friend Mr. Reedbeck.
A telegram, Mr. Reedbeck. B'Jason, four
Flights I've had to come up to bring it to you.
Please Jenny it's worth it. And the boy's waiting.

Edgar. Well, father, I don't know; with a certain sense
Of preconceiving myself, I may come back.
I shall do what I can for you; I only hope
You'll not live to regret the way my fancy
Takes you. [*Exit* EDGAR.]

Reedbeck. Oh! Would you ever think
Such a joy could happen to me, in the world as we know it?

Reddleman. I have to tell your Grace, in all decency
To the footman Bates, who I religiously despise,
If the fellow comes on duty with a bloody nose
'Tis my doing, and long may it bleed. And h'wot
About the boy below, Mr. Reedbeck? Any answer?

Reedbeck. No, no, Reddleman, only thanksgiving.
Oh, and I suppose a shilling, he'd like a shilling.

Duke. And go gently with Bates, Reddleman, or else
You'll drive him back to his old nervous habits
Of biting his nails and burglary. Remember
You're not a lion tamer now.

Reddleman. And that
Was a hit below—I'm wearing no belt—below
The navel. Thank God I'm severed from my mother
Or she would have felt it severely. I'd remind you
'Twas fighting for king and country I lost me nerve,
And b'Daniel, it's a sad job to be parted
From the lords of the jungle.

Duke. I'm sorry, Reddleman;
I wasn't meaning to hurt you.

Reddleman. Well, go easy,
Go easy with me, your Grace. Now, Mr. Reedbeck:
Thanksgiving and a bob for the boy below:
Very good. [*Exit* REDDLEMAN.]

Reedbeck. A red-letter day for me, your Grace;
Let me see: the twenty-ninth of October?

Duke. Yes;
The leaves transfigured by the thought of death,
The wind south-west, a blue sky buffaloed
By cloud, the sun approaching its eclipse.

Reedbeck. You remember I have a daughter? I've spoken of her

* Thumb their noses.

From time to time; I had the astounding fortune
To beget her, as though I'd been chosen to release
A rose from the world's rock; and then I had
The misery to lose her, when her mother
Left me for America, ten years ago.
Well, now I'm holding in my hand a message
Which says she's returning to me, returning to-day,
No time of arrival, just bare and astonishing
'Am in England hope to kiss you before lunch
Perpetua.' I can hardly believe it could happen,
I can't believe so, not in the world as we know it.

Duke. Go easy, Reedbeck, go easy with yourself.

Reedbeck. If she should come in time for the eclipse——

Duke. Then, of course, she shall join us to see the eclipse.
It will be a change for her after America.
I'm going now, to dress. Subdue yourself, Reedbeck.
Otherwise you'll capsize in disappointment.
Expect the worst. [*Exit the* DUKE.]

Reedbeck. Not at all, oh, no, not at all,
No shadows of that sort.
[*He hums to the telephone.*]
Must warn my housekeeper.
'I galloped, Dirck galloped, we galloped all three . . .'
Oh, Mrs. Lendy, Mr. Reedbeck here; I have to ask you
To prepare a room for my daughter. I'm so glad
To hear you gasp. However, we must keep our heads,
Such as they are. Tell her to join us here
And ask to be shown to the Observatory Room.
There will be refreshment for her, and a total
Eclipse of the sun.
[*Enter* DOMINIC, REEDBECK'S *son.*]

Dominic. I want to speak to you.
How long are we likely to be alone?

Reedbeck. In a moment,
Dominic dear. You'll put her some flowers, Mrs. Lendy.
Are the Helianthus gone? Well, *uliginosum.*
You call them chrysanthemums, I think. And on her bed
The lilac linen sheets. Some time before lunch.
Good-bye. Oh, Dominic, my dear, dear boy,
Your sister's coming home!

Dominic. [*Silent, and then.*] That makes you happy.

Reedbeck. Oh, dear, it's one of your knock-the-bottom-
Out-of-everything mornings. Or do you mean
You've heard, and you know what's bringing her home?
I hope nothing's amiss?

Dominic. Not with her.

Reedbeck. Well, then——

Dominic. Do I say what I have to say *here?* Or do we go back
To the house? It isn't going to be pleasant.

Reedbeck. Of course it is.
There's nothing unpleasant that isn't going to be pleasant.
Perpetua's returning to me; the world
Is no longer depressed at the poles, and everything
Will be pleasant: the east wind, smoking fires,
Revolution, debility——

Dominic. Jail?

Reedbeck. Yes, jail,
Solitary confinement, the cat-o'-nine-tails,
Your Aunt Florence——

Dominic. Can you keep your feet
On sober earth for five difficult minutes
And talk responsibly? Why are we so rich?
I've asked you before; but you, a Duke's bailiff,
An agent: where did our money come from?

Reedbeck. Have you no capacity for delight?
Do for all our sakes be pleasant, dear boy.

Dominic. You said our money came from legacies, you told me
From legacies!

Reedbeck. Just so; we've been very fortunate.
Your Uncle Hector, when he put on immortality
In Tasmania, increased, to a certain extent,
Our freedom from care; and old Lady Bright, my first
Employer, when she passed on, passed on
Herself to heaven and the rest to me; and then——

Dominic. I have to ask for figures. My Uncle Hector
Died, leaving——?

Reedbeck. Don't let's talk of death.
I've a heart this morning as light as a nebula.
But you, you sombre boy, you can't even
Sputter up a few sparks when I tell you
Your sister's coming home!

Dominic. Died, leaving——?

Reedbeck. Really,
How can I be expected to remember?
There was some music, certainly; the piano score
Of *The Quaker Girl;* and I recollect some ninepins;
And a small South American lizard called Faithful
Which died in quarantine. But Lady Bright——

Dominic. You've stolen the money, haven't you: steadily
And consistently? Oh God, why ask? I know
Already. And thieved with so little subtlety
Anyone might know. Raised rents
But entered in your books at the old figure;
Sale of produce and timber, at prices higher
Than you've recorded. I've been ferreting,
Ever since an unmistakable innuendo
From Bates the footman.

Reedbeck. Come now; Bates
Is a common burglar, and sees, of course,
His reflection in all about him. He was caught
Red-handed with the silver, and his Grace,
Being short of staff at the time, asked him to stay
And clean it.

Dominic. Bates is quite a decent fellow.
I've had a long talk to him. He used to suffer
From a pathological lust for climbing ladders
And had to rationalize it when he got
To the top. And now he's determined to be honest,
Even if it makes him ill, he says. But with you
It's unrelieved, wicked cupidity.
Of course I go down from Cambridge. I couldn't stay there
When any morning I might wake up and find
I'd become the son of a convict. We're both in
For misery now, and Perpetua comes home
Just in time to share it.

Reedbeck. I wish I could explain
How very mistaken I'm sure you must be. Especially
On such a cheerful morning. It's really too bad.
We have the dark every twelve hours as it is
Without inventing more.

[*Enter* BATES: *he shows a trace of rough handling. He announces* MISS ROSABEL FLEMING, *and withdraws.*]

Rosabel. I expected to find the Duke here.

Reedbeck. The competitors!
I'd forgotten them. You'll forgive me, madam, I hope;
You find me a little disjunct. His Grace
Will join us shortly. My name is Reedbeck.
This was my son.

Rosabel. Was your son?

Reedbeck. There's no
Other tense for me now except the past,
Miss Belmont. You were Miss Belmont?

Rosabel. Rosabel Fleming.
I am still Rosabel Fleming.

Dominic. Please excuse me.
I'd like to know you, but I can't look anyone
Happily in the eye. I'm pleased to have met you. [*Exit* DOMINIC.]

Rosabel. Is he in trouble?

Reedbeck. The paradoxes of virtue
Have confused him. Won't you sit down, Miss Fleming?

Rosabel. I begin to understand why the theatre
Gives me so little work.
That could scarcely have been called a splendid entrance,
Even by the most loving.

Reedbeck. Go down from Cambridge.
Did you hear him say that? No, you were not here.
It let all the life out of me for a moment.
All the Latin I have myself, you know,
Is horticultural: *muscari comosum*
Monstrosum, and *scrophularia nodosa,*
Et cetera ad infinitum. But how I longed
As a boy for the groves and grooves of Academe.
Give me civilization, Miss Fleming; you can keep
Your progress.

Rosabel. This room, surely, is something new?

Reedbeck. The Observatory Room, giving upon
An uninterrupted sweep of the Surrey heavens;

At night the weeping stars; by day——
[*Enter* MRS. JESSIE DILL.]
Jessie. I'm sorry.
I thought it would be just his Grace. I'll go again.
Reedbeck. No, no, his Grace will be here. By day
The brandishing sun inciting the earth
To revolution and rotation——
Jessie. I'm Mrs. Dill.
It's my own fault the man hasn't announced me.
It seemed to me 'All those stairs, for the poor young chap
Just to say, Here's Jessie.' He went on insisting,
Of course, but when we got to the second landing
He must have thought it was getting a bit undignified
Both of us coming up two steps at a time,
So he slid back down the banisters.
Surely I've met you before, dear?
Rosabel. Rosabel Fleming.
Jessie. I should have remembered. I saw you, once upon a time,
Being very sweet in a play about Ophelia.
And this is a strange thing, too, being up here
In this room together. You'd hardly recognize it.
Well, I don't know, I should say that's a telescope.
Rosabel. I think I must go. I hadn't understood
The Duke would have visitors. . . .
Reedbeck. We were just talking
About this room when you came, Mrs. Dill. My name
Is Reedbeck. This is one of his Grace's
Bedrooms, as perhaps. . . . But now, as you see,
He prefers to regard the skies here, scavenging
Through the night for knowledge. He also uses
The room for experiments.
Jessie. He always did.
Rosabel. I've decided not to stay. I only came in
For a moment, finding myself not far away.
If you'd be kind enough to tell him——
[*Enter the* DUKE.]
Duke. Good morning, Rosabel.
Good morning, Jessie.
Jessie. Here he is, himself.
He's the same boy, God bless him, not a day older,
Even if he does have to use a telescope.
Duke. Flattery, Jessie; for years the frost has lain
On my stubble beard. The swallows and other such
Migratory birds have left me months ago.
Jessie. You must build yourself a nice fire.
Duke. No, Jessie;
I have to consider my years and decline with the sun,
Gracefully but gratefully decline.
I have also to apologize for keeping you waiting.
I was up all night with the universe again
And slept late. Or is that not to be
Forgiven? A silence broods on Rosabel.
Rosabel. I was conscious of it. I was wondering
What note to sound. I'm suddenly very uncertain
Why I'm here.
Duke. For a total eclipse of the sun.
Didn't I mention it to you in my letter?
Rosabel. Is there some tradition that old friends should meet again
During an eclipse? Or what other reason? Your birthday?
No, you're a Sagittarian.* This is only October.
Duke. And the leaves are falling. What shall a robin do then,
Poor thing?
Jessie. Sit in this barn, and keep himself warm,
And tuck himself up alone in the east wing,
Poor thing. [*Enter* EDGAR.]
Duke. My son Edgar, Miss Rosabel Fleming.
I introduce Rosabel first, Jessie, to give you
Time to enjoy your joke. My son Edgar,
Mrs. Dill.
Jessie. How lovely it is to meet you.
I've known your father, you know, ever since
I was ever so slim. Though, of course, properly speaking,
It was my husband who was really his friend.
I hope your father will allow me to say,
His friend.
Duke. I'm delighted to let you say it.
I didn't know he had ever been alive
Or we might have said it before.
Edgar. It's just as well
We understand my father.
Rosabel. And it's just as well
We don't all have to. It's a thing I have no love for,

* Born between Nov. 23 and Dec. 21, the time of Sagittarius, the ninth sign of the Zodiac.

To have to go groping along the corridors
Of someone else's mind, so that I shan't
Be hurt. No one has any right to ask it.

Duke. We're not, I hope, in this mellow October light
Getting ill at ease? We're here this morning to watch
The sun annulled and renewed, and to sit affectionately
Over the year's dilapidation. 'Mellow'
Is the keynote of the hour. We must be mellow,
Remembering we've been on the earth two million years,
Man and boy and Sterkfontein ape.*

Reedbeck. [*Singing abstractedly at the window.*]
You call me old
But I am still
A chippy young chap on Chipperton Hill
And shall be, while
My flesh can cover
The bones of a bona-fide lover.
Heydilly, heydilly, hang me a sheep.

Duke. Happy, happy Reedbeck. He has a daughter
Returning to him.

Jessie. And there he sits and purrs
As though the morning was a saucer of milk.

Reedbeck. I caught myself singing. I do beg your pardon.

Edgar. Sing away, Reedbeck. Bring her in with music.
This is wonderful news.

[Bates *at the door.*]

Reedbeck. Can this be—is it . . . ?

[Bates *announces, and enter,* Mrs. Taylor-Snell.]

Duke. The exact Hilda. Punctuality
Was drawing its last breath. The sun has mooned
Away half its light already.

Hilda. A party, Hereward?
You didn't tell me.

Duke. I scarcely knew. And anyway
We shall all feel quite alone, except, perhaps, Jessie.
Mrs. Dill, Mrs. Taylor-Snell. There will only be
The appearance of people being near to us.
Miss Rosabel Fleming, Mrs. Taylor-Snell.
Reedbeck you know. You've disappointed him.
He hoped you would have been his daughter.

* Earliest form of man, associated with bones found in 1947 at Sterkfontein, South Africa.

Hilda. Did you ever propose it, Reedbeck?

Reedbeck. You see before you
A creaking bough on which, at any moment,
A dear young daughter may alight.

Duke. My extension in time: Edgar.

Edgar. Five feet ten
Of my unlimited father.

Hilda. I have often
Expected to meet you.

Edgar. I suppose so;
But until he's dead I'm really a redundancy.
I make him feel bifurcated.

Jessie. Wherever
Does he learn these terrible words?

Edgar. I spend
Such a lot of my time in the stables.

Duke. [*To* Bates, *who has loitered by the door.*] What is it, Bates?

Bates. There are faces
As can be mauled about wiv, and there are faces
As can't be mauled about wiv. Mine can't
Be mauled about wiv. Memo, guvnor, to be 'anded
On to the proper quarters, and *you* know
What basket I refers to.
Will that be all, guvnor?

Duke. That will be all, Bates.

[*Exit* Bates. Reedbeck *throws open the window and leans out.*]

Hilda. Be careful, Reedbeck! There really is such a thing
As the force of gravity.

Reedbeck. Only the wind blowing
And the rattle of leaves. I hoped it would prove to be
Internal combustion.

Duke. [*Aside to* Edgar.] I should have mentioned to you,
The case of Athene is minutely complicated
By a husband. But don't be deflected. He would still
Have the shooting over the estate. Nothing
Is insurmountable.

Edgar. Except yourself,
I take you to mean. But it's all right,
I'm devoted to you.

Hilda. Why don't you give it up,
Reedbeck? There's no daughter there. How much
This house has aged, Hereward, since I saw it
Last. I was thinking so coming up the stairs.
It looks as though the walls have cried themselves

To sleep for nights on end. And the number of windows
Broken! I don't think you should throw nearly
So many stones. The spiders are larger, the jackdaws
Ruder, the servants more eccentric. You mustn't
Drift into Gothic, when your physique is so
Stubbornly Norman.

Duke. I see no point in trying
To make time look as though it were standing still
By renewing the face of it. I like to watch my own
Deft and reckless plunge into ancient history.
It assuages my lust for speed. Dark glasses for the ladies,
Reedbeck; tell them to look at the sun.

Edgar. And to pray
For all small birds under the eye of the hawk.

Jessie. I can remember, when I was a kid,
Being got out of bed and told I had to look
At something in the sky. I kept on saying
Oh, yes, mum, isn't it lovely, isn't it lovely?
It was a comet or a zeppelin or something,
But all I could see was the usual end
Of the Crystal Palace.

Reedbeck. [*Handing glasses.*] Look at the sun, Mrs. Dill.

Jessie. And now I can't help feeling
As if I'd just been got out of bed again
To look at something I probably shan't see.

Duke. That's the human predicament, in a nutshell.

Rosabel. There's a kind of humour abroad this morning that seems to
Put me outside the party.

Reedbeck. Look at the sun, Miss Fleming.

Rosabel. Thank you.

Edgar. I've such a feeling of pre-natal
Tension, it's more than a boy can bear. Father,
I'm going to make the decision now
And pin the future down for you.

Hilda. But will you
Find that easy? I couldn't help overhearing.
The future has the most uncertain temper.
After all you've said, Hereward, do you teach
Your child to tamper with time?

Duke. He had it to play with
When he was young; but he'll soon see
How it will rag him to death. Meanwhile, the eclipse.
Let me be your guide. Observe how Sol Salome
Almost hidden by the head of the Baptist moon
Dances her last few steps of fire.

Hilda. You're confusing
The sex of the sun.

Duke. It's the act itself: observe
The copulation of Jove, magnificent in
Mid air.

Jessie. The bulk of the moon, creeping on
And on. It makes me feel more solemn than I've ever
Felt before at eleven o'clock in the morning.

Edgar. No nice eclipse for you, Miss Fleming?

Rosabel. Why, yes,
It was what your father invited me to see.
I was far away for the moment.

Edgar. Before you go
To the window, I wonder if you'd mind accepting this apple?

Rosabel. No, thank you. I'll go and see what there is to be seen
Before it's too late.

Edgar. Father, may I have your attention?
There, Miss Fleming, it will come in useful sometime.

Duke. Daylight, you see, is shamming twilight. Nature
Is being made a fool of. Three or four stars there,
You can see them wince, where only a moment earlier
Morning was all serene. The crows, with much
Misgiving, talk themselves into their trees. Even
The usually phlegmatic owls
Care a hoot or two. The bats from the barn
Make one flickering flight, and return to hang
Their heads. All of them tricked and fuddled
By the passing of a small cadaverous planet.

Hilda. Yes, we understand the event perfectly.

Jessie. Let him enjoy it. Space, ever and ever,
On and on. . . . Well, I don't know.

Edgar. Father, I don't know whether you have noticed:
A certain event has occurred.

Duke. Is now occurring.

We're crossing perceptibly into the dark.
Daylight differences are made subordinate
To the general shade.

Edgar. Father, for God's sake, look!
I am giving Miss Fleming an apple.

Rosabel. You've already
Given me an apple.

Duke. I observe you're plying
Rosabel with fruit. *Bis dat qui cito dat.**
We can now turn our attention again to the sun.

Edgar. So a revolutionary change begins
Without raising a hand's turn of the dust.
Ah, well; give me some dark glass.

Hilda. What a shame
If that cloud spoils the climax for us.

Reedbeck. No,
It avoids, you see; it glides mercifully
And dexterously past. I hope and pray
The same will be true of the cloud that hangs over my own
Sunshine: but young men can be so ruthless,
So ruthless; it's terrible to think about.

Duke. What now, Reedbeck?

Reedbeck. Ah, yes; to the cosmos it doesn't
Matter; I suppose I agree.

Jessie. To think
We're in the shadow of old Lunabella.

Duke. To think.

Jessie. When she moves over will she see us
Coming out of her shadow? Are we really
As bright as a moon, from the moon's side of the question?

Duke. We have a borrowed brilliance. At night
Among the knots and clusters and corner boys
Of the sky, among asteroids and cepheids,
With Sirius, Mercury, and Canis Major,
Among nebulae and magellanic cloud,
You shine, Jessie.

Jessie. You're making me self-conscious.

Duke. Here we're as dull as unwashed plates; out there
We shine. That's a consideration. Come
Close to paradise, and where's the lustre?
But still, at some remove, we shine, and truth
We hope is content to keep a distant prospect.
So you, Jessie, and the swamps of the equator,
Shine; the boring overplus of ocean,
The Walworth Road, the Parthenon, and Reedbeck
Shine; the dark tree with the nightingale
At heart, dockyards, the desert, the newly dead,
Minarets, gasometers, and even I
Fall into space in one not unattractive
Beam. To take us separately is to stare
At mud; only together, at long range,
We coalesce in light.

Jessie. I like to think I'm being
A ray of light to some nice young couple out there.
'There's the Great Bear,' they'd say, and 'Look,
There's old Jessie, tilted on her side
Just over the Charing Cross Hotel.'

Hilda. You both
Chatter so. It's a moment for quiet. Who knows
If ever I'll see this again.

Edgar. The end of our lord
The sun.

Rosabel. It's no good. I must get out into the air!
It's impossible to breathe up here!

Duke. What is it,
Rosabel? Claustrophobia on the brink
Of the free heavens? Come now, think of it
As the usual dipping of day's flag. You used
To love this room at night.

Rosabel. How do you know?
How can you tell who loves, or when or why they love,
You without a single beat of heart
Worth measuring? You sit up here all night
Looking at the stars, travelling farther and farther
Away from living people. I hate your telescope!
How can you know, and what, if you knew, can it mean,
What can the darkest bruise on the human mind
Mean, when nothing beats against you heavier
Than a fall of rain? And out you whip
Your impervious umbrella of satisfaction!
How you prink across every puddle, and laugh
To think that other men can drown.
You would never believe there are some affections
Which would rather have decent burial
Than this mocking perpetuation you offer them.
You're a devil, a devil, a devil, a devil!

Duke. Only
On one side of the family, Rosabel,
Please believe that.

Edgar. [*Taking the apple from her hand.*]
I beg your pardon; I think
I've made a mistake.

Rosabel. Now I must go. I've spoilt

*He who gives quickly gives twice.

The eclipse. For that I'm sorry.
Duke. It's frankly impossible
To spoil the eclipse.
Reedbeck. It would be fanciful
No doubt to say that the moon has placed a penny
Not on the dead but on the living eye of the sun.
Edgar. Yes, Reedbeck, it would.
Jessie. Don't you be put down.
It's nice that anyone can say anything at all.
Duke. So Rosabel believes when the cold spell comes
And we're compelled to enter this draughty time
And shuffle about in the slipshod leaves,
Leaves disbanded, leaves at a loose end,
And we know we're in for the drifting of the fall,
We should merely shiver and be silent: never speak
Of the climate of Eden, or the really magnificent
Foliage of the tree of knowledge,
Or the unforgettable hushed emerald
Of the coiling and fettering serpent:
Pretend we never knew it, because love
Quite naturally condescended
To the passing of time. But why should we, Rosabel?
Hilda. But if what I gather to be true is true,
Though it's no business of mine,
I must say, Hereward, you certainly seem to have been
Coruscating on thin ice. I think
She has cause to be angry. I do think so.
You've behaved a great deal less than well.
Duke. I've behaved according to my lights of love
Which were excellent and bright and much to be
Remembered. You have all of you been my moments
Of revelation. I wish I understood why
You want to behave like skeletons in my cupboard.
Jessie. Not Jessie, alas; her weight is all against it.
But need we make Miss Fleming cry?
Edgar. I'd like it,
Father, if Mrs. Dill would have this apple.
Jessie. I'd like it, too; though it's prettier on the tree.
Rosabel. Your moments of revelation! I only wonder
What we revealed. Certainly not
What goes on in other hearts than your own.
That's as remote to you as a seaside lodging-house
To a passing whale.
Hilda. Could she put it more fairly?
Jessie. I remember seeing what was thought to be a whale
At somewhere like Tenby; at least, my father said
Look, there's a whale, Jessie; but all I saw
Was the tip of a fin which might have been finnan haddy
Or Father Neptune or an old forgotten
Channel swimmer.
Reedbeck. Can you play with Leviathan
As with a bird? That's really quite the strangest
Of rhetorical questions. And when will my daughter come?
Duke. Rosabel——
Jessie. We might as well never have changed the subject.
Duke. Rosabel, why pick on me to be
The villain? I'm a Roman in a world
Of Romans, and all creation can recognize me
As genus Man. Old men, young men, virgins,
Viragoes, all walk hand in hand with me
In the green enclosure of insensibility.
An individual torment in Indo-China
Makes less noise in your ear than the drop of a fir cone.
So why do I have to be sensible
Of a heart which is fortunate enough to be
Four thousand miles nearer my way; someone,
Moreover, to whom I've already given pleasure
And the refuge of a bed, which I never gave
(Such is my frailty) to the Indo-Chinee?
Don't let's go mad with inconsistency.
Either everything shall be near, or everything
Shall be far. Allow me the wrong end of the telescope;
I like to conform.
Jessie. Mr. Reedbeck will propose
The vote of thanks.
Reedbeck. I really think, a few moments ago,
I heard what could only have been a motor-car.
Rosabel. Where have I got myself now? Into such
An embarrassment, if I could vanish I should vanish,
And even then transparently kick myself.
It was hopelessly stupid.

Hilda. Stupid, and what was called,
In the days when musk had a scent, indelicate.
Duke. I shall plough up the orchard, Edgar;
It was never a great success.
[*The shadow lifts from the sun, and the light falls on* PERPETUA REEDBECK.]
Edgar. God be praised,
The sun again.
Reedbeck. My daughter, it's my daughter, Perpetua,
My dear, my dear!
[PERPETUA *runs to him.*]
Rosabel. Where shall I hide a most
Unhappy head? [*Exit* ROSABEL.]
Reedbeck. O my little sixpenny
Ha'penny daughter, home again, home again,
Home again!
Hilda. [*Thinking of* ROSABEL.]
Can she take care of herself, that woman?
[*She follows* ROSABEL.]
Perpetua. Let me look at you. Every feature where I left it
Ten years ago! I'd forgotten you were so beautiful.
Reedbeck. You mustn't spoil me, not so soon;
I shall puff myself up and explode like a frog.
Perpetua. Perhaps we should sing until we're used to it?
Might that be the wise thing?
Reedbeck. I should stop at every
Note to listen to you. But, my dear,
I must present you to his Grace. I'd forgotten
We were not in heaven. Your Grace—this—
This is——
Duke. Steady, Reedbeck.
Let me dry your eyes. Dear man, these tears are something
Remarkably like champagne.
Reedbeck. No doubt they are.
My dear daughter: his Grace the Duke of Altair.
Duke. You have made your father as happy as if his heart
Were breaking. And isn't it likely you're going to make
Others happy as well? We have only autumn
To offer you, England's moist and misty devotion,
But spring may come in time to reconcile you
If you'll wait so long.
Perpetua. I need no reconciling.
I was born and grew in this green and pleasant aquarium,
And I've spent four days on a wicked October sea
For love of recollected mildew
And my dear frog-father; only I'd scarcely expected
Quite so much impenetrable murk
In the middle of the morning. Surely there must be something
Out of sorts about your daylight?
Duke. Nothing
Which time won't mend. But, first, let me introduce——
Ah, they've left us; Hilda and Rosabel
Have passed away with no last word. They always
Bore themselves with the true brevity of empires.
But here is Mrs. Dill, more universe
Than empire, less conquered but more embracing.
Jessie. I'm very pleased to meet you. Your father loves you
With every word in the language.
Duke. And this, Miss Reedbeck,
Is my first youth, my younger days: The Marquis
Of Charlock.
Edgar. You're a kind of legend with us here,
But the truth is better.
Perpetua. I'll tell you the truth:
I'm very happy this morning; I'm really out
Of prison.
Reedbeck. Of prison, my darling? Why do you say
Of prison?
Perpetua. I mean, of course, the boat was a prison
And the frowning sea was Dartmoor.*
Duke. To refresh you
There's wine in the bottle, cider from the wood,
Biscuits in the barrel; and there you can see
Our English sun, convalescent after passing
Through the valley of the shadow of the moon.
Perpetua. So that was why I had to search my way
Up the stairs in gloom. How far off is the sun?
Duke. The best part of ninety-three million miles.
Perpetua. You would hardly think it could matter.

* Famous English prison.

Edgar. What will you drink,
Miss Reedbeck?
Perpetua. Something of England, the cider, presently.
I'm so at peace, though I still can feel
The lunge of the sea. Your floor isn't meant to sway?
Duke. The floor is battering at your feet like Attila
With a horde of corybantic atoms,
And travelling at eighteen miles a second,
But it cannot be said to sway.
Jessie. That would be much
Too easy.
Duke. Our stability is a matter
For surprise.
Reedbeck. I feel the terrible truth of that.
Even now, for example, when I see my Perpetua
Sitting like a girl on a swing on an Easter Monday
Under a Wedgwood sky, I can feel my heart——
Perpetua. That's just what it's like, a girl on a swing.
Reedbeck. My heart
Knocking most anxiously against the future,
As though afraid to be alone with the present time:
Ready, really, for almost any disaster
Rather than this unsteady tight-rope of joy
I'm walking on now. Are you ill, perhaps? Is that it?
Have you come home for your health?
Perpetua. I've come home to be home.
A pigeon's return—just so simple, Poppadillo.
I wanted to stand where I first grew, and to have
My roots and my branches all in one place together.
And that's no curious thing. Here, swinging
On my swing, with the Atlantic foam still racing
Under my eyelids, I seem at rest already.
And so I sent no word to say I was coming,
Because, in the sense that means the most,
I was here all the time.
Edgar. And so you emerged
Like Venus from the sea.
Perpetua. But sicker.
Reedbeck. What
Shall I do for my returning Mayflower
Suppose she is disappointed in the land
Her roots are in?
Perpetua. You needn't be afraid.
If this is still an island
Enclosed in a druid circle of stony sea,
As misty as it was that chilly Thursday
When I was born to the wilting of plovers
And the smell of a saturation of hops,
Then I'm safely and happily home.
Jessie. Here's to your happiness,
Dear; God save the King, and a mild winter.
Reedbeck. Your happiness, my dear.
Edgar. Happiness, Miss Reedbeck.
Duke. I should like you to offer Miss Reedbeck an apple, Edgar.
Edgar. Anything except an apple, father.
I will offer her
The cloudy peach, the bristling pineapple,
The dropsical pear, the sportive orange,
Apricot, sloe, King William, or a carillon
Of grapes, but not, as God's my judge, an apple.
Duke. Then, as Paris abdicates, I must offer
The sweet round robin fruit myself—
[*He holds an apple up between his fingers.*]
The green sphere the myth of the world began in,
Which Melanion let fall, delaying
Mercurial Atalanta——
[PERPETUA *has whipped a very small pistol from a pig-skin holster at her belt. She shoots and shatters the apple. There is an incredulous, shaken silence.*]
Perpetua. I—I'm terribly sorry. That was thoughtless of me.
Perhaps you wanted to eat it.
Duke. There are others;
Nature is pleased to give us more. And you
Have been very good; you let me keep my fingers.
Reedbeck. Only by the mercy of God! My dear girl,
My dear girl! What in the world possessed you?
You might have been the death of him!
Perpetua. No, it was quite safe.
To please, I always aim. But that, I agree,
Is no excuse. It was dreadful, and shameful of me.
I was thinking of something else, or else
It would never have happened.
[*Enter* ROSABEL, *followed by* HILDA.]
Rosabel. What was it? We heard a sound
Like a shot!
Reedbeck. Good gracious, a *sound* like a shot!
Hilda. Is no one hurt?
Duke. An apple came to grief

As apples must.
Edgar. One pip too many.
Jessie. And nobody
Was more surprised than the Duke.
Reedbeck. Oh, yes, I think so,
I think my surprise can hardly have been bettered
Except, no doubt, by the apple. And I'm still
Anchored in amazement, I have to confess.
Perpetua. I also have to confess; I see I must.
I thought I could come back again to England
And slip into this new beginning, silently.
But now the pistol has gone off; the silence anyway
Is well and truly broken, and so I'll explain,
Though the explanation, I'm afraid, will seem
As wild as the shot.
Reedbeck. What can it be? Be quick
And tell me.
Perpetua. I've lately been in prison. But not
For what we should call a crime.
Reedbeck. They put you in prison
Without rhyme or reason?
Perpetua. There may have been
A little rhyme. I was thought to be unsafe
For democracy, because I broke, or shot,
Or burnt, a good many things, or rather—and this
Is the reason—a bad many things: the unsightly,
The gimcrack, the tedious, the hideous, the spurious,
The harmful. Not I alone, of course;
We were all students, and called ourselves
The Society for the Desecration
Of Ancient and Modern Monumental Errors.
We destroyed, or tried to destroy, whatever we loathed
As bad.
Rosabel. Whatever you loathed you destroyed?
Why, that was admirable, superb, the most
Heavenly daring!
Perpetua. No, I think it was only
Exasperation. And then we went to prison.
And there I knew it was all no use.
The more we destroyed, the worse the bad sprang up.
And I thought and thought, What can I do for the world?
I was wearing the prison drab. My name was a number.
Inside or outside the prison, Perpetua
(I thought), you're no one, you're everybody's colour.
You must make good, before you break the bad,
Perpetua. And so I came home to England
Simply to trace myself, in my own way.
[*She offers the pistol to the* DUKE.]
I'd better surrender this. I only kept it
For a kind of memento. And I apologize
Again for destroying the apple. Still half at sea
As I am, it appeared to be, in a misty way,
Like a threat to my new-come freedom.
Duke. I hope you will think so again, some other time.
Rosabel. [*Taking the pistol.*] May I have it, to remind me of your story,
To know there has been someone in the world
Who dared to do such things! If only I
Could be such a brave one, there might be
Some justification for me.
Duke. [*Taking it from her.*] Caps for you,
Dear Rosabel, not bullets. I'll have it
Filled for your next big scene.
[*A gong booms from below.*]
Edgar. Luncheon! Can we be supposed to eat
On a day when the sun is drowned by the moon,
And apples meet such a strange end?
Duke. I see nothing strange. If we can move and talk
Under the sun at all, we must have accepted
The incredible as commonplace, long ago;
And even the incredible must eat.
Shall we go down?

CURTAIN

ACT TWO

SCENE ONE

The Temple of the Ancient Virtues, beside the ducal lake, in the afternoon. [DOMINIC *and* PERPETUA *are there.*]

Dominic. You haven't spoken for three and a half minutes.

Four minutes. This is the most pregnant pause
Since darkness was on the face of the deep. I suppose
You think I shouldn't have told you.
Perpetua. Oh, yes, you should.
Dominic. It was better than leaving you in a fool's paradise,
You must admit.
Perpetua. I could be twice as silent
For seven times as long.
Dominic. Well, then you shall be.
I know myself how the shock stuns one.
Perpetua. No shock
At all. I was able to believe you at once.
Poppadillo has the most beguiling
Jackdaw look about him. But you think
He wouldn't be happy in prison?
Dominic. He wouldn't, but what
Difference does that make? Would you be able
To look anyone in the face, with a father jailed?
Perpetua. Oh, yes, if he were comfortable. But I think
He might feel shut in. No, Dominic, I'm sure
You're right. If someone has to go to prison,
I must.
Dominic. You? What can you possibly mean?
Perpetua. You said I should have to, and now all I mean
Is Yes, quite so.
Dominic. Quite what is quite so, will you tell me?
Perpetua. I heard you say, perhaps it might have been
Six minutes ago, if I made myself agreeable
The Duke (you said) being much in that mind at the moment
Might, with any luck, be inclined to marry me,
And no gentleman (you added) would incriminate
His father-in-law. And I agree with you,
And I see my carefree hours already numbered,
My freedom of choice and my individual day.
I'm no longer a woman after my own heart.
Broad cupid's arrows * on my wedding veil.
But still, Dominic, for my father's sake,
Not ours, I mean to try.
Dominic. God bless you, then,
And God speed you, and thank God I can breathe again.
And a coronet's no martyrdom, particularly
When it sits on a man whom women find easy to like.
Perpetua. I wonder how many women have stood perplexed
And plagued in this temple, two whole centuries of them,
Looking out this way, on the same view
Of the metal-rusting year. Lemon, amber,
Umber, bronze and brass, oxblood, damson,
Crimson, scalding scarlet, black cedar,
And the willow's yellow fall to grace.
Dominic. Do you have to be so melancholy? Everything
Is better now. Though there is still the anxiety
Whether you can prepossess him before he strikes.
Perpetua. Oh, yes, there is that anxiety still.
Here comes the straying lamb who gave us life.
Dominic. Don't pamper him. We have to make him realize
He's been sinning all this while.
Perpetua. He looks as worried
As though he knew it already.
[*Enter* REEDBECK, *out of breath.*]
Reedbeck. So here—here
You are. I wondered, missed you, but luckily caught
Sight of you going down through the trees. I lost
My hat on the way; it blew (oh, what a gasping old fellow)
Off, blew off; now upside down on the water
Among the *Alisma Plantago-aquatica.*
Didn't think I should have enough breath to say so.
Perpetua. Try only breathing, for a time; that's always
Nice.

---

* In England, broad arrows mark convicts' clothes.

Dominic. What was the hurry? Did you think I was going
To throw her in the water?
Reedbeck. Among the *Alisma Plantago-aquatica.* Has he been talking to you?
He's not as fond of me as either of us
Would like.
Perpetua. I've been hearing unimaginable
Things about you.
Reedbeck. Yes, the imagination
Is a frail craft, soon capsizes, quite understand.
Now this, my dear, called sometimes the Temple
Of the Ancient Virtues, and at other times
The White Temple, both because it is white
And because it was designed by Martin White
In seventeen hundred and ninety-three, was erected
By the third Duke of Altair for his wife Claire
For her use when she played the part of the Delphic Oracle,
A way she had of informing the Duke of her pregnancy,
Which she did on twenty-seven separate occasions.
Perpetua. Tell me why you've been cheating the Duke,
There's a good boy. What made you do it?
Reedbeck. I hope
I've done nothing so monosyllabic as to cheat.
A spade is never so merely a spade as the word
Spade would imply.
Dominic. One's helpless to help him.
Perpetua. Poppadillo, suppose I put it this way:
What made you supercherify with chousery
The Duke?
Reedbeck. That might be said to—that perhaps
Is not an unfair expression. And I say in reply
The reason was the fading charm of the world.
The banquet of civilization is over——
Perpetua. Shall we call it
The groaning board?
Reedbeck. You may call it what you will.
With a little wealth to do it I should like to perform
The grace after the meat, a last, gentlemanly,
Valedictory grace: a grace for departing grace
(Is that not rather good?):
The spacious lawns of life are being
Inevitably ploughed, and we don't know, we really
Don't know, what's going to be sown there.
Dignity has dropped upon all fours.
Indeed there's hardly to be seen
One intense perpendicular
In all the streets of men. Someone, you know,
Someone must keep alive that quality
Of living which separates us from the brutes;
And I have proposed it should be I.
Dominic. It should be me.
Reedbeck. Beloved boy,
It would be delightful if you thought so.
Perpetua. I understand so far; I only wonder
Why the Duke has to be . . . out of pocket.
Reedbeck. I care so much for civilization,
Its patrician charm, its grave nobility;
He cares so little. Therefore certain eccentric
Means have had to be taken for splendid ends.
Church and State, in a way, agree
In justifying such a course of action.
A kind of casual taxation. I hope I explain
Quite clearly. It's true I have overlaid the Law
With a certain transposition; we might
Call this process Reedbequity. But what
A gain to the world.
Dominic. Do you hear that, Perpetua?
He even unblushingly gives our name
To his wicked practices!
Perpetua. Dominic wants us all
To be good. Perhaps if you had gone to the Duke
And explained all this, he would have eased the path
To Reedbequity without the bother of iniquity.
Don't you think he might?
Reedbeck. My dear, I've never believed
In the equal distribution of property.
I only think it can have more beauty
In my hands than in his. But that would have been
A most impertinent thing to say to him.
Perpetua. We must keep you from harm. Heydee,
I'm not to be myself, I see.

I'm sad to see myself go;
But I was only promise, after all,
And the world can't live on that.

Reedbeck. Have you something that worries you? I believe
I've made you discontented with me, on a day
Which should have turned out so glorious, and now
I don't know *where* we are.

Dominic. It's only a step
From where you are, father, to where you will be
If we can't prevent it. You'll discover
Civilization is sadly dwindled when
You make your way to prison. Here's the Duke.
Be cheerful, if you can, Perpetua.

Perpetua. My smile
Will be like the glint of handcuffs, but he's very
Welcome to it. Sing out a joke, Dominic,
In your merry way.

Dominic. Ssh!

Perpetua. That's a most promising
Start to a conversation. There must be a joke
Lying about somewhere, even when the leaves are falling.

Reedbeck. Something about . . . when the leaves in Eden fell . . .

Perpetua. Dear Poppadillo; thank you.

Reedbeck. Was it at all
Serviceable?

Perpetua. It had a kind of ancient virtue,
Proper for this time and temple, yes.

[*Enter the* DUKE, *carrying a bow and quiver.*]

Duke. May your little girl come out and play, Reedbeck?
Daylight is short, and becoming always shorter.
But there's the space for an arrow or two between
Now and the sunset.

Perpetua. I've never handled a bow.
How shall I manage?

Duke. Beautifully.
The light will hang fire to see you; you might
Even hear the flash of the foliage
Where Artemis parts the leaves to patronize
And praise you; but take no notice, and watch what you're doing,
And do what I tell you.

Perpetua. Implicitly.

Duke. Take notice
Of the excellent marksmanship of the year, whose arrow
Singing from the April bow crossed over the width
Of summer straight for the gold, where now, if you look,
You will see it quivering.

Perpetua. The year has a world of experience.
But still, show me; and I'll try not to shame the shades
Of all the arching duchesses and ladies
Who played on these lawns before.

Duke. They'll arch the more,
Adoring what you do, feathering their shafts
And shooting until doomsday's Parthian shot.
Be confident; and, if you miss,
The fashion of the game will be to miss,
Until you change your mind and hit.

[*He begins to instruct her in the use of the bow, holding it with her, and speaking low into her ear, so that* REEDBECK *and* DOMINIC *cannot hear.*]

And then, Perpetua, to-night
If a clear sky inclines you to it, and the heavens
Remain suspended, how would it be
If we trained the telescope on the infinite
And made what we could of what we could see of it?
Are you still as interested as you were
This morning?

Perpetua. Yes. I come from a city. The stars
Are new to me.

Duke. They shall answer you
By numbers. But we'll not tell the world
What we mean to do. There's a little tension to-day
Already, nerves perhaps not ready to accept
The quiet session of scientific study
You and I propose. So let's be as mute
As we're mutable, and avoid misapprehension.

Perpetua. I—if so—if so—yes, very well.

Duke. You can tell the world you need a long night of sleep.

Perpetua. Yes, yes, I can. But here's the good afternoon light
Fading to waste unless we make use of it.

Duke. I know that thought so well. Come on, then,
Let the trial begin.

Perpetua. Watch me, Poppadillo.
Come and judge what a huntress I should make,
What a rival for Artemis, and what chance Actaeon

Would have if I pursued him.

[*Exeunt the* DUKE *and* PERPETUA.]

Reedbeck. She really makes me
Respectful of astrology; it must
Have been the arrangement of stars she was born under.
It couldn't have been all me and her mother. Why,
I couldn't even dream so beautifully,
Let alone propagate. It must have been
The state of the zodiac when she was conceived.
But even so, I was there, and that in itself
Is remarkable. What did you say to her, Dominic;
What did you say to her?

Dominic. I simply told her
You were crooked.

Reedbeck. And then she said?

Dominic. She said
She was not surprised.

Reedbeck. Oh. *I* should have been;
It would have seemed like a thunder clap to *me*.
But you've made her feel differently towards me,
You've sent me off on my own again. And what
Did she mean by 'sad to see herself go,' and 'not
To be herself any more'? What made her say that?
Was something agreed between you?

Dominic. I made a point.

Reedbeck. What point, now what point?

Dominic. I made the suggestion
She might like to marry the Duke, and save you that way.

Reedbeck. You—said—such a—thing? You dared
To consider selling your sister? You,
Sprung from my loins, and so utterly
Unprincipled?

Dominic. That sounds most convincing,
Coming from you!

Reedbeck. Poor little girl, poor
Little girl. But I'll intervene—*inter venio,*
Yes—though I can't relieve her
Of her inhuman brother.

Dominic. Or her dishonest
Father.

Reedbeck. [*Shaking him, in a sudden burst of rage.*] You're a vain, vexing, incomprehensible,
Crimping, constipated duffer. What's your heart?
All plum duff! Why do I have to be
So inarticulate? God give me a few
Lithontriptical words! You grovelling little
Gobemouche!

Dominic. Stop it, father, stop it at once!

Reedbeck. You spigoted, bigoted, operculated prig! [*Enter* JESSIE.]

Jessie. Am I in the way? I came to write a letter.

[REEDBECK *releases* DOMINIC *suddenly, and* DOMINIC *trips and falls sprawling on the floor.*]

Reedbeck. I was having a word with my son.

Jessie. [*To* DOMINIC.] How do you do?
Please don't bother to get up.

Reedbeck. You're very welcome
To write your letter. I don't wish to shake him
Any more. But if you hadn't come in
I think I should have gone on shaking him
Until I couldn't see him.

Jessie. He would still
Have been there, of course. When my mother used to shake me
It always gave me hiccups, and then I was given
Peppermint on sugar to cure them. If only your son
Had hiccups, and you had peppermint and sugar,
Mr. Reedbeck, everything would seem different.

Dominic. I have to leave you. I'm afraid my father
Must be feeling very chastened and confused. [*Exit* DOMINIC.]

Jessie. It was lovely exercise for both of you.

Reedbeck. It did no good; I've only shaken my own
Composure.

Jessie. Sit down, Mr. Reedbeck, and let it settle.
I have to get a few lines off every day
To my father, eighty-seven. He can't read a word
Of my handwriting, and doesn't try, but he likes
The postman.

Reedbeck. Well, I'll leave you, then;
I won't stop and hinder you. I suppose
That action of mine, that sudden accession of rage,
Wasn't in the nicest mood of civilization.
And yet I don't at all feel like apologizing,
I don't feel at all like apologizing. Would you apologize?

Jessie. I'm sorry, I was trying to think how to begin
So that Dad won't mind he can't read it.
Reedbeck. Well, I won't stop and hinder you now,
But I should be very upset if I proved to be
Nothing but a barbarian after all,
A barbarian dreaming of the higher excellences.
But I won't stop and hinder you.
[*Enter* HILDA.]
Mrs. Dill
Is trying to write a letter. We mustn't hinder her. [*Exit* REEDBECK.]
Hilda. I see Hereward has made another backward
Flight into his heyday. It's a handsome thing
To see him so happy, but are we so happy for the girl?
Jessie. Doesn't she like playing at bows and arrows?
Hilda. She does, no doubt, but—May I interrupt you?
Jessie. I'm only
Writing a letter when nothing else occurs to me;
I like to talk.
Hilda. Because of the strange business
Of the eclipse this morning, and what went on,
We've been thrown into each other's confidence
Unexpectedly soon. And for my part
I think I'm thankful. I've always hidden more
Than was good for me, hoping in that way
To make my life seem pleasant to everyone,
But who should care? So I've lost the habit
Of daring to ask myself what I do, or why.
Why did I come here to-day, and what did I expect?
And why did he ever invite us here together?
I know him painstakingly enough
To be sure it was kindly meant; it couldn't have been
To watch our faces fall.
Jessie. I like being here
So much I never even wondered.
Hilda. There
Was still something in me to be hurt,
Which a little surprised me. And then
Reedbeck's daughter came, as though to show
How the years had gone by for us
But not for him, as though the old
Magician in his blood was bound to draw us
Into that revealing circle. But I sigh
For her, as once I sighed for myself; and, if
I knew how, I should tell her how lightly he flies.
Jessie. And then
You must tell her how nicely he alights.
That's important, too.
I should let them be, because they will.
Hilda. When I first met him, I remember, he seemed
At once to give my spirits a holiday,
Though (like a first holiday abroad) almost too unlike
The daily round of the roundabout life I led—
And lead still, O my heavens—which had, and has,
All the appearance of movement without covering
Any ground whatsoever. I know I have
No particular heights or depths myself;
No one who thought me ordinary or dull
Would be far wrong. But even I despair
For Roderic, my husband, who really is
The height of depth, if it doesn't sound unkind
To say so: not deep depth, but a level depth
Of dullness. Once he had worn away the sheen
Of his quite becoming boyhood, which made me fancy him,
There was nothing to be seen in Roderic
For mile after mile after mile, except
A few sheeplike thoughts nibbling through the pages
Of a shiny weekly, any number of dead pheasants,
Partridges, pigeons, jays, and hares,
An occasional signpost of extreme prejudice
Marked 'No thoroughfare,' and the flat horizon
Which is not so much an horizon
As a straight ruled line beyond which one doesn't look.
Jessie. Keep him warm and fed. They bloom
Once in seven years.
Hilda. Not Roderic.
[*Enter* EDGAR, *carrying a bow and quiver.*]
Edgar. Are either of you ladies any good
At taking out a thorn? I took a look

In a mirror for some reason or other, and there it was.
A bramble slashed me when I was out riding yesterday.
I've brought my own needle.
Hilda. Am I hurting you?
Edgar. Yes, but how nice of you. Isn't it strange?
For the first time in my young life
I'm jealous of my father. I thought I'd better
Mention it before I begin to brood.
Hilda. Jealous of him, why?
Edgar. To me he's a man
Once and for all; once, once only,
And certainly for all. And any man
Who has to follow him (me, for instance)
Feels like the lag-last in a cloud of locusts:
By the time I come to a tree it's as bare
As a hat stand. Talent, conversation, wit,
Ease, and friendliness are all swallowed up
In advance. And just at present
I feel depressed about it.
Hilda. Now, take heart.
You have those virtues, too. There's room for both of you.
Edgar. Not, I think, at the moment.
Jessie. Do you mean
Only two can play at bows and arrows?
Hilda. I think at the moment it's greatly important
There *should* be room for both of you. Suppose
You make a bid for it. Why not?
Nothing hinders you except weakness of hope,
And that's ridiculous. We'll go together.
Mrs. Dill wants to write a letter.
Jessie. Never mind;
Everything writes itself in time.
[*Enter* BATES.]
Bates. It's Mrs. Taylor-Snell I'm looking for;
Oh, that's right, lady, you're here. I have
A message to give you, they said; prompto.
On the telephone it come. It's not so nice
As you might like to have it, but it's not so bad.
It seems there's been a bit of a accident,
And they'd be glad if you could make it convenient
To find your way back 'ome.
Hilda. Roderic!
Bates. Whoever it is, missis, you're not to worry.
Your old man has got hisself throwed off his horse,
Hunting little rabbits and uvver breeders.
Now, now, lady, you never know,
It may only be a front toof a bit loose.
Hilda. Didn't they say what the injury was?
Bates. Took a bit of a toss, come a bit of a purler,
What Jack and Jill done; don't you worry, lady.
Hilda. I can't help worrying, dear Bates. [*To* JESSIE.] I'll go
Without saying good-bye to Hereward. There's no reason
Why anyone's afternoon should suffer,
Except mine; and later I'll telephone
And tell you what has happened.
Jessie. It's wretched for you,
It's really wretched for you; I'm awfully sorry.
What would you like me to do?
Hilda. Nothing, except
To forget I laughed at him. I have my car;
I can slip away easily.
Edgar. I'll run on ahead
And get the car started for you.
Hilda. No.
Thank you, but I'd rather go quietly alone.
If you want to do something for me, put your shoulders
To your father, and make yourself your own success.
Good-bye.
Edgar. Good-bye, good luck.
Jessie. I expect you'll find
It's something nice and simple like a collar-bone. [*Exit* HILDA.]
Oh, please God, make it a collar-bone. She turned
So pale and unhappy, poor lamb.
Bates. I wouldn't have anything happen to that one:
It's a pity we can't do something to oblige her.
But there's that uvver one, Fleming she says she's called:
Flaming nuisance, I reply: what about her,
Eh, miss? What's she doing snooping
About the east wing all the afternoon? I tell you,
Miss, I knows an undesirable character
When I see one; I've been one myself for years.
Jessie. And look how we love you. So don't you have
Nasty thoughts about Miss Fleming, who is not
Undesirable at all. And go away

Like a good boy, and let me write my letter.

Bates. I just fought you might like the opinion of a expert.

[*He begins wandering away.*]

But don't let's say anyfing good about
Captain Fussing Reddleman, lord of the kitchens.
He can go and tame his lions on some uvver poor bastard's mug.
I prefers to keep mine natural.

[*Exit* BATES.]

Edgar. I wonder if I should.

Jessie. If you should what?

Edgar. From here I think I could send an arrow right past him
Into the target.

Jessie. If you think you can, then do.

[EDGAR *takes an arrow, fits it in his bow, and shoots. A distant cry of remonstrance from the* DUKE.]

Edgar. Oh, that was very beautiful. I enjoyed that
Extremely.

Jessie. What did you do? Did I encourage you
To be mischievous? I was thinking about my letter.
You might have shot your father.

Edgar. I jolly nearly
Did. But my arrows, I never quite know why,
Have a considerate way of going where
I mean them to go, which was nearer the gold than his.
He's probably shooting not so well
To give Perpetua some encouragement.
When I come to think of it, that shot of mine
Was taking a very easy advantage.

Jessie. I shouldn't say easy, twice the distance off.
And as you didn't kill anybody, I may say
I think it was splendid, and I think perhaps
You should do it more often.

[*Enter the* DUKE.]

Duke. What, by Saint Sebastian's groin,
Do you think you're up to? Edgar, for goodness' sake!

Edgar. I was drawing a bow at a venture, father.

Duke. So
I thought. But remember what damage was done to Sir Lancelot
By an arrow in the buttocks. Did I beget you
To be shot from behind?

Edgar. I'm extremely sorry,
But you took a step to the south.

Duke. Am I never to move?

Edgar. Oh, yes, father, but the other way, or any way
Except between me and where I aim.

Duke. I hope
I'm being patient. I had quite supposed
The contest was between Miss Reedbeck and me.

Edgar. When all the time it was really between you
And your loving son; or so my hackles tell me.

Duke. Ah—! Now I see;
Your days are starting to press upon me,
You who were always so unassuming and easy.
But not this time. No, I'm sorry,
Not this time, Edgar.

Edgar. It is this time.
I'm sorry, too, but it is this time. You've had
A long innings, and a summer of splendid outings,
And now I must ask you, father, not to monopolize
Every heart in the world any longer.

Jessie. Excuse me
Worrying you, but how do you spell epidemic?
Two *p*'s and two *m*'s?

Edgar. I'd forgotten we weren't alone.

Duke. We're alone with Jessie; nothing could be happier.
One *p*, one *m*. If the generations join
In a life-and-death struggle under your feet
Don't let it, Jessie, disturb your spelling.

Jessie. One *p*, one *m*. Quite enough, when you look at it.

Duke. Now listen, Edgar, take nothing for granted,
Not even my flair for breaking into love;
You're apprehensive far too soon. The field,
If not entirely yours, is not entirely mine:
I am as innocently there
As an old warhorse put out to grass:
My equine equability is pastoral to a fault.

Edgar. But when you're grazing you're irresistible;
Buttercups and daisies fall to your fetlocks in swathes;
I've seen it happen. And between this morning's eclipse
And this afternoon you've lost the autumnal look
Which was such a comfort to me; I see you have

The appearance of a very mild March day.
And what does a boy do then?
Duke. Aren't you being
Just a thought parricidal for a fine afternoon?
Edgar. Oh, God, I love you like the rest of them.
I'm only asking you to forgo yourself
This once, to suspend your animation
For a few short months, for my sake.
Duke. Edgar,
I mean to be a good father to you, but
A good father must be a man. And what
Is a man? Edgar, what is a man? O
My man-child, what in the world is a man?
Speaking for myself, I am precisely that question:
I exist to know that I exist
Interrogatively. But what gives birth
To a question? A desire to be answered. A question
Desires, as a man must desire, as I
Desire. That, at least, you'll allow me.
You wouldn't have your father merely rhetorical.
Edgar. Not at all, but——
Duke. But what is the mark of the question?
What is the note of this interrogation?
Loneliness. The note, my son, is loneliness.
Over all the world
Men move unhoming, and eternally
Concerned: a swarm of bees who have lost their queen.
Nothing else is so ill at ease. We know
How patiently the toad suns on the stone,
How the indolent fish waves its tail in time
With the waving weed. If a pulse was in the stone,
And the stone grew moist, and the toad petrified,
Patience would still be as patient in the sun.
Or if the weed wove its way up river
To breed, and the fish waved green and still,
The water would never wonder: all
Is at one with the rest.
And the trees, when the weather is waking, quicken without
Question, their leaves assemble in a perfect faith
Of summer; and so with all the world's life,
Except ours. We can hear the lyric lark
Flaking its limit of heaven from a cloud,
And see the self-assimilated cat,
The adaptable chameleon, and the mole
Rubbing along companionably
With the obliging earth. But where, O Edgar,
Is an element compatible with *us?*
Edgar. Would you mind if I reminded you, father,
What we were talking about when you started talking?
Duke. Thank you, but I know: your wish to remove me.
But if being alive is a question, heaven-bent
For an answer, and the question is a man's
Estrangement in a world
Where everything else conforms, how should I dare
To suspend myself for a day, or even an hour,
When that hour might ravish me
Into a complete, unsolitary life,
Where happiness leaves no room for the restless mind
And I, as unlaborious
As a laburnum tree, hang in caresses of gold?
Edgar. And what do I hang in?
Duke. You hang in abeyance, Edgar.
If I should die, with the great question unanswered,
I leave myself in you to ask it still.
But this is all academic. The field is still open.
Jessie. I always think 'niece' is such a difficult word.
Duke. *I* before *e*, except after *c*. And so, Edgar, let nothing dismay you——
Jessie. Except
In the case of 'neigh,' that humorous noise of a horse.
[*Enter* PERPETUA.]
Perpetua. Is archery all over? I went to the lake
And tried to spear fish with an arrow, but I'm tired
Of that.
Duke. Edgar, I'm nowhere to be seen;
For all the personality I exert
You might never have had a father; advance, advance,
You son of a cipher.
Perpetua. Could we not all shoot together?
Edgar. Miss Reedbeck——
Perpetua. Perpetua.
Edgar. Yes. Perpetua,
This is All Hallowe'en. To-night half England
Will be dancing in memory of a world they don't remember.
The sky will very likely be black with broomsticks.

There's a dance on in the Old Woolmarket
At Mordenbury. Will you come?
Perpetua. [*Glancing towards the* DUKE.] All Hallowe'en.
I should have liked it dearly, but to-night——
Edgar. You've made some other plan.
Perpetua. No, no.
Edgar. Then come. Meet England first among the wisps
Of magic we still possess. Will you, Perpetua?
Perpetua. If I dared to trust my eyes and my feet
To be lively, so long after sunset,
I should say yes willingly. But I must and will
Sleep early. Four days on the see-saw sea,
And then such a wave of homecoming, have left me
Ready to rest. I'm so sorry to refuse.
Edgar. Well, I see you must, though I'm very sad you must.
But if later you should feel revived, or if
You found you could rest before dinner——
Perpetua. It still has to be no, and still I'm sorry.
Edgar. I can well imagine how tired you are. You can let
Your sleep make you a Hallowe'en instead.
Dreams know where to look for deeper and stranger
Shadows than I do. Horses, it always seems
To me, are half a dream, even when
You have them under your hand, and when I *dream* them
They tremble and sweat, the caves of their nostrils blowing
Bright clouds of breath, a foaming sea
Breaks against their mouths, their flanks are smoking
Like Abel's fire to heaven, as though
A dreadful necessity had ridden them hard
Through the miles of my sleep, all the benighted way
From legend into life. And then in the morning
There they are in the stables, waiting to be blessed.
Perpetua. Show me these wonders.
Edgar. Now?
Perpetua. Yes, why not now?
All of us.
Edgar. That goes for you, papa.
Duke. Invisibly I come.
Edgar. [*Glumly.*] Invisibility
Makes you look younger than ever.
[*Exit* PERPETUA *and* EDGAR.]
Duke. Jessie,
Will you make an end of dotting your *i*'s and join us?
Jessie. Thank you, dear,
But I'd like to finish this letter to my father,
Even though he'll never read it.
Duke. Jessie, my love,
If he'll never read it, do you have to write so much?
Jessie. Well, no, but he lives such a long way out of the village
I like to make it worth the postman's while. [*Enter* ROSABEL.]
Duke. Rosabel, where have you been mooning
All the long afternoon? Come with your friends
And look at horses. Edgar is showing Miss Reedbeck
Round the stables.
Rosabel. Yes, yes, I may follow you—
When do you mean to show her how to observe
The stars through your telescope? Is it to-night?
Duke. No, not to-night; sometime, perhaps, or perhaps
Never; who can say?
Rosabel. But *you* will be there, I suppose.
Who is it that's mooning then? And all night long?
And making the world look small and apologetic
And as good as unpopulated? I hate your telescope!
Duke. So you have said. Don't let it obsess you.
Look up, Mrs. Siddons, it's easy enough
To see over the top of a telescope. So try,
Or you'll soon make yourself ill. Anyway
I'm washing my hands of all the sky to-night,
And I'm going early to bed.
[*Exit the* DUKE.]
Rosabel. [*To herself.*] So no one at all
Will be there. Now I know why all day long
Life has been tilting and driving me towards
To-night. I'm not myself any more,
I am only the meaning of what comes after dark,
If I have the courage.
[*She remembers* JESSIE *and turns to her.*]
Obsessed, obsessed.

It's very true. One thought in my head,
Persevering like someone running on a race-track;
When it seems to be going it's coming again.
I wrestle with it, and hold it close,
I can't let it go, nor laugh it away. Is this
How men get driven to send history lurching on
To God knows where? Nothing matters
Except that he should be made to feel. He hurts
Whomever he touches. He has to be touched by fire
To make a human of him, and only a woman
Who loves him can dare to do it.

Jessie. Listen, love,
You'll be sending yourself silly. I always think,
When someone knocks you down, it doesn't improve things
To knock yourself up. The way a thing is, is often
The way you happen to look at it. He's as kind
As anybody living, if you take a running jump.
And if you only had a stamp we could go together
And put this in the box.

Rosabel. I'm over-run
By the most curious thoughts. I believe I was kept
From quite succeeding in anything I set
My heart on, so that now I should give all
My heart to this, to-night. The girl Perpetua
Has the courage that makes a person come true.
Did you hear her say how she went to war on things
She hated? I think she came to show me
What it is I have to do; indeed, I can't do less!
And nothing less will do to open his eyes
On to the distances that separate him
From other people.

Jessie. Look at me: I've put Cumberland
When I mean Northants.

Rosabel. To-night, no one is there.
You'll see, I shall send his Observatory
Where Nero's Rome has gone; I'll blaze a trail
That he can follow towards humanity!

Jessie. Now I wonder who's the most likely person to have a stamp?

THE CURTAIN FALLS

SCENE TWO

The Observatory Room at night. [*The* DUKE *is lying on a day-bed in the dark. Enter* PERPETUA. *The light from the corridor follows her a little way into the room. She stands uncertain. The* DUKE *speaks from the darkness.*]

Duke. And Endymion, when the moon had borne him
Fifty daughters, was rewarded with
An eternal siesta; his breast and belly rose
And fell like the sea; his breath played
All day with the motes of the dust,
While all about him suffered, withered, and crumbled
Into the dust his breath played with; only,
Between the slats of his perfect sleep
Came little slants of sun, and they were muddy
With the hard wading of humanity;
This made him change his position slightly,
And that stirred up the scent of the thyme which made
His unimpassioned bed.

Perpetua. It's rather frightening
When a dark room starts to speak.

Duke. My original
Syntax, like original sin, grows vastier
In the dark. Come in.

Perpetua. What does your legend mean?

Duke. It means, Perpetua, we're all as well
As can be expected. Does anyone know you're here?

Perpetua. No one.

Duke. They would think I meant to love you.
I wonder if I mean any such thing.
We'll make some light. Matches?

Perpetua. No.

Duke. No, here are some.

[*He lights an oil lamp.*]

This was the first
Astonishment of creation; after that
Came the frenzy of which you and I
Are the humble result. An access of starlight
And the fish began to swim; God gave way
To hallucinations; you and I again.
Would you like a drink?

Perpetua. Thank you. Tell me, as one
Hallucination to another, what
Happiness do you get up here with your telescope?

Duke. I can't remember. That's a handsome moth
Come in to die, two petals, two tendrils,
And a flake of snow, meticulous, irrelevant,
Unwise. You came to see my stars. I have them
Here.
Perpetua. I expect you can find your way about them
Even in the dark. Tell me who it is
We're trained on now.
Duke. Senator Saturn, white-
Hot with gravity. His moon, out of love
For his grey steel brow,
Streamed away her life into a circle
Of tormented arms. You see them there,
You see how they circle and never touch.
Saturn is alone, for all their circling round him.
Perpetua. And alone so long. I'm looking at the same star
That shone alone in the wake of Noah's
Drifting ark as soon as the rain was over,
That shone on shining Charlemagne
Far away, and as clear
As the note of Roland's homing horn.
Alone so long, and now casually
Descending to us, on a Thursday midnight:
Saturn, who once glinted in the glass
Of Ariadne's mirror at the moment
When she died and melted out of Naxos.
Duke. Ariadne died in childbirth. One
Life put the other out. It was Edgar's mode
Of entrance. Where in the sky shall we go to now?
Perpetua. Wherever you may like to take me. I'm
A stranger here.
Duke. She died a girl in love,
And I went on in love without her
For longer than was fair. But this is not
Astronomy.
Perpetua. Astrology, then. You can't
Throw someone against the sky and not expect
A certain vapor of magic to condense
In moisture on their lashes. Let me believe
For a little while in man's ordeal by star
And tell me your own. I want to hear it.
Duke. Isn't it a strange love, Perpetua,
That will never, can never, know what it was?
Death chose to interrupt us while we were still
Careening together high above the spires
Of common sense. And so what modulation
Would have come, how soon, how scaling down,
Is never to be known. And I can never tell
Whether a love, which was haled away
While it still was hale, was all and more
Of love than I could expect again: or if
The one twin-hearted permanence
Was waiting somewhere ahead. That has always
Perplexed me. What have I been doing, since
She died? Making do because the best
Was done? Or have I been turning head by head
To find the face which, willingly,
I should never let pass? For a long while now
I've been thinking the first, but to-day
The question seems to have sprung into life again.
Perpetua. With your mind so full of inquiry, I'm surprised
You've had any time for love.
Duke. It takes no time.
It's on us while we walk, or in mid-sentence,
A sudden hoarseness, enough to choke the sense.
Now isn't that so?
Perpetua. Not so with me.
Duke. You must try
To use longer sentences. Then you would certainly feel
The fumbling in the quiver behind every syllable
And so to the arrow string, like a sudden
Swerving parenthesis.
Perpetua. Do you think I should?
Duke. No doubt of it.
Perpetua. There isn't any reason
Why a sentence, I suppose, once it begins,
Once it has risen to the lips at all
And finds itself happily wandering
Through shady vowels and over consonants
Where ink's been spilt like rivers or like blood
Flowing for the cause of some half-truth
Or a dogma now outmoded, shouldn't go
Endlessly moving in grave periphrasis
And phrase in linking phrase, with commas falling
As airily as lime flowers, intermittently,
Uninterrupting, scarcely troubling
The mild and fragile progress of the sense

Which trills trebling like a pebbled stream
Or lowers towards an oath-intoning ocean
Or with a careless and forgetful music
Looping and threading, tuning and entwining,
Flings a babel of bells, a carolling
Of such various vowels the ear can almost feel
The soul of sound when it lay in chaos yearning
For the tongue to be created: such a hymn
If not as lovely, then as interminable,
As restless, and as heartless, as the hymn
Which in the tower of heaven the muted spheres
With every rippling harp and windy horn
Played for incidental harmony
Over the mouldering rafters of the world,
Rafters which seldom care to ring, preferring
The functional death-watch beetle, stark, staccato,
Economical as a knuckle bone,
Strict, correct, but undelighting,
Like a cleric jigging in the saturnalia,
The saturnalia we all must keep,
Green-growing and rash with life,
Our milchy, mortal, auroral, jovial,
Harsh, unedifying world,
Where every circle of grass can show a dragon
And every pool's as populous as Penge,*
Where birds, with taffeta flying, scarf the air
On autumn evenings, and a sentence once
Begun goes on and on, there being no reason
To draw to any conclusion so long as breath
Shall last, except that breath
Can't last much longer.

Duke. Now point me out the comma
Where you loved me.

Perpetua. Not at any.

Duke. Let me see;
Was there a colon somewhere?

Perpetua. Perhaps one;
But if so we passed it without any trouble
Of any sort.

Duke. Never mind. There are sure
To be other sentences. The little god
Is older than he was, and moves more slowly.

Perpetua. Even when he aims at you?

Duke. For me, I'm afraid,
He makes a special effort, shoots
Most generously, and then, poor boy, can't handle
A bow for several weeks.

Perpetua. Why are you so sure
That I must love you? The field is wide,
And everyone's heart is a great eccentric;
Its whole distinction is a madness. Wildly
Away from any mark it goes, making
Anywhere the same gigantic mimicry of sunshine,
No one else knows why. Be sure of nothing.

Duke. Do you know what night this is?

Perpetua. All-Hallows' Eve.

Duke. All-Hallows' Eve. If the earth is ever wise
To magic, this is the night when magic's wisdom
Comes rolling in across our sedate equation.
All the closed hours unlock; the rigorous ground
Grows as soft as the sea, exhaling
The bloom of the dead everywhere. They almost
Live again: as nearly, at least, as we
Can brush on death. And through the night
They trespass agreeably on our time of trespasses,
Molesting the air in a pale, disinterested
Way, until they thankfully notice
The dark is paler, and sigh themselves out again;
Though not before they've planted, as they go,
A seed of chill which grows rapidly
Into a rigid winter where the sun
Can hardly raise himself to make a noon.
But still, that's presently. What's more to our purpose
Is that to-night the gravity of mirrors
Is so potent it can draw the future
Into the glass, and show shadows of husbands
To girls who sit and comb their hair. Suppose
You try it.

Perpetua. I'm two or three centuries
Too late.

Duke. We know nothing yet.
There's the mirror. In your bag no doubt
A comb. And while you comb tradition says
You must eat an apple: though God knows why
Any apple should trust itself between your teeth
After this morning's little episode.
However, here's one intrepid to the core.

Perpetua. How old is this mirror? The glass
Is very loath to let me in.

Duke. Eight duchesses

---

* Suburb of London; pronounced penj.

Have rested there in passing, before the glass
Began to cloud; and after that came three
Peering housekeepers, a chambermaid
Who, what with frequent tears and the ageing mirror,
Never saw her face; and me, who by
Much early study have overcome the need
To try.

Perpetua. And I am the eight duchesses
And the three housekeepers and the chambermaid
Combing their hair. I am any girl: Perpetua
Perpetual, making no gesture I can call
My own, engraving theirs one lifetime deeper.
Midnight, the apple, and Perpetua
Combing her hair, as all the time she was.

[*The* DUKE *quietly crosses the room until his reflection falls into the mirror.* PERPETUA'S *attention is caught; she stares into the glass before she turns suddenly to look at the* DUKE.]

It seemed to be your son.

Duke. Perpetua,
You must play fair.

Perpetua. You must tell that to the mirror.
The reflection seemed to be Edgar.

Duke. Then the mirror
Is very penetrating. It has seen
How young, to all intents, I am.

Perpetua. I suppose so.
You think there's no magic.

Duke. That's as kind
As anything you've said. I think there *is*
Magic: an old dim-sighted mirror
And a shaded lamp for one genial moment
Raised me out of the falling leaves. A pity
The vision has gone. I'll agree to immortality
If immortality is to be always twenty-five
Seen by a man approaching fifty. The thought
Alone sends me begging to Olympus.
And you, being twenty-five, and looked upon
By me, together we make one golden flesh
For which both worlds, this and the next, will try
To outbid each other, and while the bidding mounts
We'll spend our love between them, disregarding
Both, until——

Perpetua. Until, next year,
I am twenty-six.

Duke. Which is twenty-five and one more.
I am the one.

Perpetua. It remains for me to love you.

Duke. It has always been understood to be so easy.
Why ever should you not? Am I, before
God, too old? Consider the rocks
Of Arizona, and then consider me.
How recently the world has had the pleasure
Of pleasing, the opportunity of knowing me.
Age, after all, is only the accumulation
Of extensive childhood: what we were,
Never what we are. Don't deliver me
Up to my grey hairs.

Perpetua. Them I could certainly
Love. No, it's rather that I wonder
Whether you're not almost too young to be lived with.

Duke. When we're married I shall age beside you; forgive me
Loitering now till you draw level.

Perpetua. When we're married?

Duke. Are we to be formal?
Should I have asked you first?

Perpetua. Not if you have
Some other way of knowing the answer. Have you?

Duke. Perhaps I may pass that question back. Have I?

Perpetua. Your Grace——

Duke. Somewhere I have a Christian name.

Perpetua. Do you know anything against my father?

Duke. In my heart, nothing.
He loves me in his way, and that absolves him
From any defect on earth. No doubt
He'll have to stand in a corner of heaven with his face
To a jasper wall, but here let him thrive.

Perpetua. You mean
You know.

Duke. I know he wishes to make honey.
Any bee would tell you, that's impossible
If clover objects to rape.

Perpetua. So this is how
You know I shall marry you: for Poppadillo's sake?

Duke. This is how.

Perpetua. And perhaps it is going to feel
Strange to you at first to know I am not.
No, no, you're mistaken, and I was quite
Mistaken, too! This isn't how I mean
To lose my way, by force of circumstantial
Evidence. When I lose my way I shall lose it

In my own time, and by my own misguided
Sense of direction.

Duke. Planting your own brambles,
Digging your own pitfalls, willing your own
Will-o'-the-wisps, designing
Down to the last detail Perpetua's Folly.

Perpetua. Without respect of persons. But do you mean
You have sat perched up here, for months and years,
Your eyes shrewdly glittering with starlight,
Knowing that my father, fifty feet below,
Was being clever in your clover, and you said
Nothing?

Duke. We were being so happy together.
And if I had mentioned it, he would have felt
Obliged to discontinue, which would have been
Immensely sad. And, what is more,
Swarming stars and solitary Duke
Would have been unvisited to-night.

Perpetua. How happy do you feel to know you tried
For a bride by this conspiracy of silence?

Duke. How happy do you feel to know you were ready
To take a husband to make that silence absolute?

Perpetua. I made no pretence of loving you. I was glad
When Edgar came to the mirror; I don't know why.

Duke. I seem to have come to the end of myself
Sooner than I expected. So there's to be
No climax and adorable close
With ego agonistes crowned and smiling?
The strange charm of being alive breaks off
Abruptly, with nothing determined, nothing solved,
No absolute anything. I thought this time
The ends of the ring would join. But, no,
I'm back among the fragments.

Perpetua. Is this fair?

Duke. How nature loves the incomplete. She knows
If she drew a conclusion it would finish her.
But, O God, for one round Amen!

Perpetua. That only
Comes on judgement day, and so,
As love won't live with judgement, Amen must wait.
Show me one more star and I must go.

Duke. I think they're falling.
While I love you without being loved they're sure
To be restive.

Perpetua. When they fall do they scorch the air
In passing? Is that what I can smell?

Duke. Or is it
The smell of man being born to trouble? Or both
The upward sparks and the downward stars together?

Perpetua. Something *is* on fire. I can hear the flames
Crunching on wood.

Duke. Have my almost mindless gardeners
Been suddenly visited by imagination
And lit us a Hallowe'en bonfire?

Perpetua. Why, look, the garden's
Capering with light. The fire is underneath us——
Look! It's the house, this wing of the house is on fire!

Duke. Merciful heaven,
Wouldn't you think my blood was warm enough
To get us through a night without encouragement?

Perpetua. Shall we be able to get away?

Duke. By all means.
We'll leave the moths to perform whatever
Immolation is necessary. A more
Temperate life is better for us,
And the cooler coast of the garden.

[*He throws open the door and looks on to the stairs.*]

Well, here's a riproaring gantlet to be run
By a couple of God's children.

Perpetua. No! No, no!
Not that way!

Duke. Which other? The only alternative
To downward is upward, and how do you propose
Two such wingless babes as we are——
No, Perpetua; quickly, love, before
The even chance is out of patience with us.

Perpetua. No! There's no chance there. You can see
There's no chance there. It's all in the fire,
Every tread of the stairs. What shall we do?

[*She runs to the window and looks down.*]

So far away, so far away.

Duke. Trust me;
Try this way in my arms, Perpetua. Hope

Is forlorn, but I'm sure very fond of us.
We'll give her the benefit, shall we, and both be brave?

Perpetua. Don't make me. I'd rather jump to the garden, and die
Fair and broken. I'll make my own death
As it suits me.

Duke. That as well? I'm sorry; you can have
Your own way in everything else.

Perpetua. Please,
Please, please, please.

Duke. Well, I see
We've chosen. Hope has got tired of waiting
And taken half the staircase with her. Now,
We'll ring a rescue, and then indulge in the luxury
Of having nothing to do but fold our hands.

[*He holds her beside him while he uses the telephone.*]

Gently, my dear, you White Queen; nothing
Has hurt us yet. A fire at Stellmere Park.
Two people trapped: neither anxious to die.
I suggest you should make remarkable speed.
God bless you. They didn't wait for blessing.

Perpetua. Aren't you desperate, too? Aren't you even afraid?

Duke. Why, yes, yes, I have to be; I love myself,
And I shall be sad to say good-bye to myself;
There's no one like me, though so many better.
Will you kiss the last of a singular man?

Perpetua. Easily, oh, easily.

Duke. There's always a good thing left
Even when the world would seem to be spent out.
Do you think you love me?

Perpetua. Yes, I love you:
Between the giddiness I love you.

Duke. May it also
Be between my arms? I love my love
With a death because it has no alteration
And no end. This concluding grace, Amen.
In the long world we're being shaken from
The star which, when it's rising, is called Venus,
Setting is Lucifer, the goddess
Graduating into demon, and what good
Is that for a man's immortal spirit? But you
And I, pursuing love no farther than this
Pure outcry of recognition,
Possess it most faithfully.

Perpetua. I only know——
Listen to the fire now, listen to it!
It means to let nothing escape. I only know
We go together into pain.

Duke. Out of the world like snow. And so
The phoenix and the turtle did.
Pain took them, too, and welded them
And melted them, and made a union
Of beauty born and beauty reft away,
And, when the air was empty, time was brimming,
And light was beating with one heart.

Perpetua. I'm afraid of the fire, I'm afraid, I am so
Afraid of the fire.

[*The voice of* REDDLEMAN *is heard outside the door.*]

Reddleman. [*Off.*] Your Grace! All right, all right, your Grace!

Duke. The voice of to-morrow morning, after all.
We're not to be allowed perfection, Perpetua.
The kind world intervenes.

[*Enter* REDDLEMAN.]

Reddleman. Ah, you poor sinners. I'm with you now;
Did you think I was never coming?

Perpetua. Never coming,
Never, never coming!

Duke. Quietly yet,
Fly up gently, we've still got far to go.
How do you propose to rescue us, Reddleman?
And how the hell did you get here?

Reddleman. By me flair
For elementary science. I thumbed a lift
On the rising heat. And, by the blistering
Of the blessed St. Laurence and the blessed St. Vincent,
Shadrac, Meshac, Abednego, and all
The sainted salamanders, I've got me nerve again;
For there's the conflagration below, frumping
And grouching like all the golden lads of lions
I ever put me hand into the fire of!
Didn't God make sinners of you and trap you here
For the decent purpose of putting me back
In the way of salvation?

Duke. And us, too, I hope.
Can we go the way you came?

Perpetua. God be kind,
Be kind.

Reddleman. Have you any objection, now,

To dropping from time to time into me arms
From a great way off? 'Twould be to avoid the stairs,
Themselves being gone entirely.
Perpetua. Must it be that way?
Reddleman. In the Captain's keeping,
Via Leo, con brio, the way of the lions!
Duke. He's got himself well up in the god class now,
Perpetua: all we have to do is trust ourselves
To the rope of his nerve, spit on our hands, and go.
[BATES *appears at the window.*]
Bates. Well, *you've* got yourselves in a picklin' walls-up
And no mistake.
Duke. Are we to have all
The guardian angels at a blow?
You spoil us, Bates.
Reddleman. He spoils me night of glory.
Send him about his business, if you love me,
Your Grace, for the love of God, send him
About his business!
Bates. Couldn't the Lord Lieutenant
Even keep his nose out of this little job?
Come on, miss; come and take a butcher's
At the panorama; it's lovely outside 'ere.
Perpetua. Oh, yes, yes!
Reddleman. Monkeys, monkeys, monkeys!
Duke. How do you think we're going to get down, Bates?
Bates. Well, I come up by the ladders, but according
To the rules we have to slip down by the snakes. Still,
Do what your fancy tells you, mate. I'm
Not looking.
Perpetua. And I wish I hadn't looked, and I wish
We were safe on the ground.
Duke. Think of something high
Like Kanchenjunga. That very nearly takes us
Down the ladder before we start.
Reddleman. Your Grace,
You're not so out of your mind as to go
Out of the window? Encouraging robbery
And violence, you are, to set your foot
On a ladder propped up against your property
Without permission, and in the middle of the night
When no decent man would be lashing one ladder
To another, and he in his shirt.
Bates. You save 'em
Wiv your trousers, go on, let's see you; save 'em wiv your trousers.
Duke. Reddleman, by all means love your lions,
But condescend to the snakes. Come on.
Reddleman. Where's a fine soul under heaven?
Duke. Not playing
With fire, wherever else he may be.
Bates. That's right, miss,
Let me take you, miss; fink nuffing of it.
Relax yourself, as though you was mink.
Fink lovely foughts, miss, and you won't weigh nuffing.
Wonder what stretch I'll have to do for abduction?
Duke. [*Climbing through the window after them.*] A beautiful room, Reddleman; worth a fortune
In memories and astronomical equipment.
[*He disappears from view.* REDDLEMAN *leans out.*]
Reddleman. H'wot do you think the dear God gave me back
Me nerve for? To come crawling after heathen
Like spittle down a window? B'Jason,
I've a better opinion of meself.
Anyway, it makes me giddy and it's no position
For any reasonable man to get himself into.
[*He crosses the room, throws open the door, and meets the glare of the fire.*]
Tossing your mighty manes, roaring yellow murder!
The Captain's not afraid!
[*Exit* REDDLEMAN. *The* DUKE *climbs back in at the window calling him, races across the room to the door, calls.*]
Duke. Reddleman, you hell-raking maniac!
[*He picks up the half-eaten apple from the dressing table, calls to* REDDLEMAN.]
Who would have the heart to disappoint you?
[*He puts the apple between his teeth and follows* REDDLEMAN *the way of the stairs.*]

CURTAIN

ACT THREE

The Temple of the Ancient Virtues, an hour or so later. The light from the burning house reflected in the lake. [ROSABEL *is sobbing in the dark. Enter* DOMINIC, *carrying two chairs and a stable lantern. He halts and listens to the sobbing.*]

Dominic. May I interrupt your unhappiness,
Just to bring in one or two things? It's begun
To rain. Everything's going to get wet.
I wonder if you need cry quite so despairingly.
It makes me feel very awkward. I am not good
At comforting people, even when I know
Where to look for them. I'm Dominic Reedbeck . . .
How do you do? And where would you be?
Rosabel. Oh, no,
Don't look for me.
Dominic. I couldn't look for you;
I don't know who you are. Everyone
Is safe, you know; they're all accounted for,
Except Miss Fleming. Do you know where she is?
Rosabel. No. No one must ever see her again.
Dominic. Why not? Is she so badly burned? What is it,
Oh, what *is* it? I wish you'd help me to be helpful;
I find it so difficult.
Rosabel. I'm here. I wish
I were dead.
Dominic. I don't see how you can wish for something
You only know the name of. Now that it's raining
I won't be the only one coming in here. Perhaps
You should try to feel better. If I were you . . .
Rosabel. They wouldn't look for me in hell.
Dominic. Oh, yes, they would.
It's the obvious place to look for anyone,
If you're speaking euphemistically.
Rosabel. I'm grateful to you. So would anyone
In hell be. Your voice is very cold.
I want harshness. I want hatred.
If you would hate me it might help me to bear
To think of myself. You're going to find it easy.
It was I who started the fire. I did it
Deliberately.
Dominic. Perpetua was there.
The Duke was there. They might never have got away.
Rosabel. But you haven't understood. You can't have understood.
It was I who did this unimaginable thing.
Dominic. I was thinking of myself.
My sister was there because I sent her there.
Perhaps you were compelled to be the means
By which I was shown I had fallen into error.
If so, I must thank you. Thank you, Miss Fleming.
Rosabel. You're mad! Do you think I hurled myself away
From all the decent world for your sake?
Hate me, hate me! Oh, why is it
You won't understand?
Dominic. I do understand. I know
Too well our preternatural aptitude
For sin. My father made it quite clear to me.
Rosabel. Oh, what shall I do?
Dominic. There's Sergeant Harry Bullen,
The policeman from Swinford Magna. He's a very
Reasonable chap; I'm sure he'd arrest you
Willingly if you went and asked him.
And he's here, which is very convenient for you.
Rosabel. Yes, where? Where is he?
Dominic. I saw him five minutes ago,
Coming head first down a ladder, to show the Duke
(As he said) that in the ordinary course of living
It makes little difference which way up you are.
He was joking, I think.
Rosabel. I'll find him, and give myself up.
Yes, up, out of this ditch of despair. No one
Need think of me again. I hardly remember
What I was like before to-day, but I think
I was an ordinary woman. No one
Else will remember. 'She was always demented!'
It isn't true: never; until to-day
Struck me like a tornado, God knows from where.
But now I shall give myself up. Do I look

Plain and frightful? It could scarcely matter
Less. But, please God, help me avoid the Duke,
Wherever he may be.

[Enter the DUKE, *carrying things salvaged from the fire and over his shoulders a string of Chinese lanterns.]*

Duke. He's down at the Temple,
I think, putting up some lanterns which he found
In a box. You'll find him there, presumably
Intent on some small ceremony of his own,
Though fairly uncertain whether it's obsequies
Or jubilation; he's in two hearts about it,
And both weigh heavier than the one he had.
God bless you, Rosabel; hold these; for a time
We thought we had lost you.

Rosabel. Did you think so? Lost me?

Dominic. You must tell him now. It will be much easier now;
No postponing. *[Exit* DOMINIC.]

Duke. It's important that we should offset the smacking of the furies
With a little decorous gaiety, with a show
Of holier, if also homelier, flames.
The lanterns, Rosabel. They'll be very pale
Compared with the foment of wild flamboyant rose
We have in the sky to-night; but never mind;
Think what deeds of spring are done
By the glow-worm light of a primrose.

Rosabel. I started the fire.

Duke. How did you come to do that?
A careless flash from your incendiary eyes,
Perhaps.

Rosabel. You must believe me. I fired the wing,
To destroy the observatory, to make you human,
To bring you down to be among the rest of us,
To make you understand the savage sorrows
That go on below you. To-day, this awful day,
The violence of a long unhappiness rocked
And fell, and buried me under itself at last.
How vile it was I know. I know for life.
But I didn't know you were there; believe me, I didn't
Know any living soul was there!

Duke. O,
O, O, O, Rosabel:
If you had only asked me first.
I could have told you no fire would be enough
To burn down heaven, and while it's there
I shall find some wide-eyed place where I can sit
And scrutinize the inscrutable, amazed
That we can live in such a condition of mystery
And not be exasperated out of our flesh,
As we might be, were it not that flesh
Is interesting, too.
Your fire was too small, Rosabel, though enough
To singe my butler into ecstasy,
And smoke tears into eyes unaccustomed to them,
Mine, I mean. So much I delighted in
Is now all of ash, like a dove's breast feathers
Drifting dismally about the garden.

Rosabel. Time and I both know how to bring
Good things to a bad end, all
In the course of love. No wonder
'God be with you' has become 'Good-bye,'
And every day that wishes our welfare says
Farewell. To-night will go past, as a swan
Will pass like a recurring dream
On the light sleep of the lake,
And I shall be smoothed away in the wake of the swan;
But I can never return what I've lost you, or lose
What I gave, though the long steadiness of time
May long to make us well.

Duke. So much I delighted in is all of ash.

[ROSABEL, *giving a moan almost too low to hear, goes out. Her place is taken by* PERPETUA, *but the* DUKE, *now hanging the lanterns, hasn't seen the change.]*

But the lost world of walls and stairs,
Where I could cosset ghosts for their melancholy
Charm, has let the daylight into me
With a straight left of love. So no remorse,
Rosabel. I love my love, and my love loves me.
Everything goes but everything comes.
We fall away into a future, and all
The seven seas, and the milky way
And morning, and evening, and hi-cockalorum are in it.

Nothing is with the past except the past.
So you can make merry with the world, Rosabel.
My grateful thanks.

Perpetua. I have to make you understand.

Duke. I forgive you:
You can mine the lake so that it bursts
In a hundred and one torrential rainbows
Over the roof of the Carpenters' Arms; you can shatter
Conservatories into a deluge of crystal,
And shoot the cowman's nine insufferable
Children: I forgive you in advance.
I've achieved the rare, benevolent place
Where the irk of the lonely human state
Is quite unknown, and the fumbling fury
We call our life—— It wasn't Rosabel
Who spoke then. It was surely Perpetua?

Perpetua. I have to make you understand. You must
Be patient with me.

Duke. God so, it's the little firebird.
Are you rested? Lanterns, you see, to light our love.
I thought we could sit by the cinders
And toast our hearts, if Bates, as he was told to,
Brings the champagne.

Perpetua. You have to give me
Your best and gentlest attention. Be
At your most understanding. I need it, if I don't
Deserve it from you. To-night, when we seemed
Closely, and only us of all the living
World, attended by a dragon breathing out
Almost certain death——

[*Enter* BATES, *with champagne and glasses in a basket, and carrying another lantern.*]

Bates. That Captain Reddleman,
As he likes to demean hisself to call hisself——
Now you're not getting yourselves into anuvver
Critical situation? You can scramble down
Off of that one on your own
Virgin initiative; I'm badgered if I'm going
To throw anuvver expensive rescue party.

Duke. Matches, Perpetua?

Perpetua. No.

Bates. His illuminated
Lordship Reddleman should ought to have
His brain looked into. In and out, in and out,
In and out of the burning building, like
A perishing nigger in and out of a flaming
Woodpile. And what he says about me's
Enough to arrest a cock in the middle of his crow
And bring a blush to his ruddy comb. It isn't
The language I've been brought up to.

Duke. [*Lighting the lanterns.*] The first astonishment
Of creation; after that came the frenzy.

Perpetua. Let me
Talk to you.

Bates. Here's his incandescent majesty
Coming now, wiv his head under the table.

[*Enter* REDDLEMAN, *carrying a table on his head.*]

What's the matter, mate; lost your titfer?

Reddleman. There's no doubt at all Your Grace has noticed
There are some men are born too small in the soul
To do gratifying deeds, and not sprain all decency.
And 'tis the footman Bates
Who's the diminuendo of all small souls.
He's a demi-semi soul, and that's magnanimous.
I have to put on me glasses, and then search
As though I was after looking for a louse
In Molly O'Magan's obster-eperous hair.
Would it be here you were wanting the table set up,
Your Grace?

Duke. Put it where the wind won't blow;
It's blowing cold. And for Christmas' sake
Will you pair of immortals kiss each other
And come off the tiles?

Bates. I'd just like to know who gave him permission
To go measuring my soul? I never done.
I've got it nicely laid away: spotless,
Wiv lavender.

Reddleman. 'Twas a mighty night of miracle,
With Cuchulain at me right hand, and Daniel at me left,
And the smallest soul in the world dashes it from me,
And he naked in his shirt.

Duke. Ah, miracles, Reddleman,
Miracles; don't trust them. How far
Can a man journey on a miracle? It's better
To bounce your behind on any spavined hack
Than to straddle a flash of lightning.
Straighten your laurel wreaths, the couple of you,

And remember one another in your prayers.
It seems I have something else to listen to.

[*Enter* REEDBECK *and* DOMINIC.]

Reedbeck. Ah, here he is. I'm not what you thought me, your Grace.
I must tell you plainly I'm not at all what you thought me.

Duke. No?

Reedbeck. No. If you ask these men to go, your Grace,
I shall be only too grieved to tell you what I am.

Bates. [*To* REDDLEMAN.] Nuffing to stay for, boy. I'll come and see you
Popping yourself in and out of the fire again.

Reddleman. Breakfast, your Grace, at what o'clock?

Duke. The morning
Must wait, Reddleman. I have still
The rest of the night to consider.

[*Exeunt* BATES *and* REDDLEMAN.]

Perpetua. [*To* REEDBECK.] Darling,
Not now. Any day or night of the year,
There's always time, you can go together, and look
At the pigs or the winter wheat, and talk your two
Hearts out; but just this night, and for just
These five minutes of this night, leave me
To talk to him alone.

Reedbeck. I've worked myself up,
I've reached the pitch now; it would never do
To put it—put it off; walked much too fast,
Breath very short, and then heart very heavy,
Imagination—disconcerting—too vivid: I see you
Both up there, no amount of stars
Any use, in dreadful danger, and who but me,
I, whichever it is, responsible?

Dominic. Please blame me for that. Do allow me
To know which sin belongs to whom. We shall only
Get confused, father, unless you keep strictly
To your own wrong turning.

Reedbeck. Extremely difficult
To know where to stop, once you begin to believe
You're not all you should be. Let me see,
There was something worse Dominic said
I had to confess to you.

Perpetua. He knows, he knows.
So now, you poor worried Poppadillo, half
Awash with sleep, you can go back
To bed at once, or else I think I shall cry.

Reedbeck. But I don't quite know what you know he knows,
And I think I'd better——

Duke. Drink, Reedbeck, I think
You'd better drink. We have something to celebrate,
You and I, which lights me more than the most
Tower-toppling blaze that ever lit
A city lane——

Perpetua. Oh, do let me speak to you!

Reedbeck. I've reached the pitch. I've worked myself up
To the point of whatever the point was when I first
Came in. But you're quite right, half awash, suddenly
Woken up in alarm——

Dominic. Now, *think* a minute.

Duke. Master Dominic: pass to your saintly father
This glass of champagne.

Reedbeck. Excuse me. But I know
There's some good reason why I shall have to refuse.
Now that my attention has been drawn
To what must be a myopia in my moral vision——
Must have been suffering from it all my life,
I suppose: and to-night feels very latter-day;
Wrath of God: here we are
Looking such weak vessels and so temporary
Among the four terrible elements
(The rain and the firemen's hose remind me of the fourth)——
What was I going to say? Yes, yes, I think
It wouldn't be correct to drink with you before
I give myself up to Sergeant Bullen.

Duke. Drink up,
And keep your sins for some leisurely angel;
They've nothing to do with me. Dominic,
If what appear to be discrepancies
In your father's books afflict you, let me tell you
Though they seem unusual they're as much in order
As Sergeant Bullen's collar and tie. There exists
A document assigning to your father
All those percentages from rents and sales

Which you seem to have thought are misbegotten.

Dominic. Do you mean you've noticed the discrepancies
And legalized them?

Duke. My dear conscience-nudging,
Parent-pesting, guilt-corroded child,
If I may address you with so much affection,
The arrangement was perfect. It embarrassed
Neither of us. Take a drink to wash
Your conscience down. And one brimming for you,
A pale representation of my heart,
Perpetua.

Perpetua. It's too full, seriously,
Far too full. You've been good to my father.
Please will you put it down? I know my hand
Isn't steady enough to take it.

Duke. Then let me sip
Some away from the western rim
And leave the east for you.

Reedbeck. Made it legal?

Duke. There now. Shall we drink
To the babe born in the fire, the crowning of souls
In extremity? As long as we live, Perpetua,
We shall be able to tell how, at midnight,
We skated over death's high-lit ebony
And heard the dark ring a change of light,
While everywhere else the clocks
Were sounding the depths of a dark, unhappy end.
And then we shall be able to say
How an autumn duke——

Perpetua. —found that fear could seem
Like love to a silly girl, who now knows
It was fear and not love, wishes you to forgive her,
Wishes she could sink away with the night
Where she won't any more trouble you.

Duke. [*After a long pause, raising his glass.*] Then the toast is: Fear.

Perpetua. I had to tell you.

Duke. Do I
Have to drink alone?

Perpetua. No. No.

[*They all drink in silence.*]

Duke. Do you think I can't forgive you? I forgive
Both of us for being born of the flesh,
Which means I forgive all tossing and turning,
All foundering, all not finding,
All irreconcilability,
All the friction of this great orphanage
Where no one knows his origin and no one
Comes to claim him. I forgive even
The unrevealing revelation of love
That lifts a lid purely
To close it, and leaves us knowing that greater things
Are close, but not to be disclosed
Though we die for them. I forgive
Everything, my most dear Perpetua,
Except that I wasn't born something less ambitious,
Such as a Muscovy duck.

Reedbeck. I couldn't think
Of allowing such generosity. Legalized!
No, your Grace, I simply couldn't accept it.

Duke. Reedbeck, my God! For how many years have you
Stood here? You must be very old by now.
I remember you well in happier times.

Perpetua. Poppadillo,
Why do we all have to get between someone else
And the sun? Keep me from doing this again.

Reedbeck. Whatever you say, my dear; though whatever you're saying
I really don't know. I'd like to help, but you're both
Talking in my sleep, evidently.

[*Enter* EDGAR, JESSIE, *and* HILDA.]

Edgar. That was a hideous mile or two of driving!
We saw the fire on the clouds, and guessed
It could only be here.

Hilda. I saw it from home, reflected
In my bedroom window. I tried to telephone
But I couldn't get through.

Duke. I must ask you, if you will,
To remember we've been appreciating this very
Minor act of God for more than two hours.
The earth has moved on roughly a hundred
And thirty thousand miles since then,
And histories have been much altered.
I hope the dance was a great success.

Jessie. Yes, lovely,
But it's doing myself a great kindness to be able
To sit down. Dancing all hours, and a couple of miles
Of apprehension makes All Hallowe'en
Into a marathon if a girl's not quite
As hale and hallow as once she was.
Is everybody safe?

Duke. Safe: I'll not say
'As houses,' considering what goes on,
But as safe and suffering as health can be.
Hilda. It's a fortunate thing that Providence
Was in her friendly mood to-night
And kept you out of Galileo's lap.
Duke. Not she. She saw two souls there, happily occupied
At the narrow end of the telescope,
Two star-loving minutiae, male and female,
Perpetua and my unoffending self:
And instantly shot out a vituperative
Tongue. And we were rescued by two
Heavenly agents, Bates and Reddleman.
Reedbeck. God bless them; I've never liked either of them,
But God bless them.
Hilda. And keep them in the heavenly business.
Jessie. I'll kiss them for it presently. They must
Have got a bit above themselves
To rescue you from there.
Edgar. And so
You meant to meet there, even this afternoon.
And the only comfort I had, all the way home,
Was that Perpetua was safely sleeping
Away in another house.
Perpetua. We meant to meet there,
And this afternoon we were lying to you,
And never was a lie less happy for everyone.
Duke. I hear me whistling down the wind.
Jessie. We wouldn't
Like you to think we're setting up in competition,
But in our own small way we've met
With a catastrophe, too.
Hilda. Both our cars
Swung in at the gates together, and as our attention
Was all on the fire——
Jessie. Our wings aren't what they were,
As Lucifer said after his long day's fall.
Duke. What's the matter with the Fates to-day; fidget, fidget;
Why can't they settle down to some useful spinning?
I forgot to ask you, Hilda (Jessie and Lucifer
Remind me), how is Roderic?
Hilda. Asleep when I left.
Two ribs broken, and a slight concussion,
Nothing worse. But that was enough to show me
How bad it is to see Roderic hurt, but how
Intolerable it would be to see Roderic
Maimed, or dying day by day; and I sat
Beside him and marveled, and wondered how
So much could lie there in a human shell,
The long succession of life that led to him,
Uninterrupted from the time
Of time's aching infancy;
In the beginning was Roderic; and now
Haunting the same shell, were a childhood
And a manhood, half a hundred years
Of sights and sounds which once echoed and shone
And now may only exist in him. And though
He tries to be a copy of all his kind
How can he be? He is Roderic-phenomenon,
Roderic only, and at present Roderic in pain.
I felt I must tell you so. This afternoon
I made a cockshy of him, but this afternoon
I could no more truly see him than he, poor darling,
Can truly see half that there is to see.
I must get back home. I only wanted to be
Quite certain no one was hurt.
Duke. Rosabel
Is hurt.
Edgar. But we saw her with Harry Bullen;
She seemed most vigorous, talking his helmet off;
He was mopping his head with a handkerchief.
Duke. Rosabel,
Why? With Harry Bullen? Why should she be?
Dominic. Because she thought it was necessary
To her peace of mind. She has given herself up.
Duke. And I give you up! How, by hell's grand canyon,
Do you know she has?
Dominic. She was really very unhappy;
I think I helped her to decide.
Jessie. But why?
Given herself up for lost, or what?
Duke. You strapping,
Ice-cold, donkey-witted douche of tasteless water!
I could willingly—Dominic, dear boy,
God would tell me He loves you, but then God
Is wonderfully accomplished, and to me
You seem less lovely, and for this good reason:

You think more of the sin than of the sinner.
Poor Rosabel. Where shall we find her?

Hilda. When
We saw them they were standing by the sundial.
What has she done?

Duke. Loved me beyond her strength.
We go and get her out of the arms of the law,
However attractive Bullen's arms may be.
Dear Rosabel! And after that we must find
Beds for ourselves away from the smell of smouldering
Memory. Bring along some of the lanterns.
Excellent, blessed Rosabel. Ros-a-bel!

[*He goes, calling her.* HILDA *follows him.*]

Reedbeck. [*To* JESSIE.] Beds, yes, yes, beds, quite important.
There's one at least at my house if you'd care to oblige it,
Care to make use of it. No more sleep for me
To-night; it wouldn't be wise; I've only just
Managed to digest the sleep I've had already.
In something of a fuddle.

Jessie. Dear, I'd get
Into anybody's bed to-night, and sleep
Without a murmur, even in the arms of Morpheus
If he'd give up his lute and let me. Where's the step?

[*She goes out,* REEDBECK *holding a lantern for her, and he follows her.*]

Dominic. A fine rain raining still. Aren't you coming,
Perpetua?

Perpetua. I'll stay in the dry and rest.

Dominic. I was hoping to talk to you, to tell you, to say
How responsible I feel for all that fear
And danger, I mean yours to-night. I expect
You think I was very much to blame.

Perpetua. No,
Dominic.

Dominic. They think I'm altogether wrong,
All the time. But I don't know how that can be.
And yet the whole of life is so unconsidering,
Bird, beast, and fish, and everything,
I wonder how the Creator came to be
Mixed up in such company. Do you think I'm wrong?

Perpetua. No, Dominic.

Dominic. [*With a sigh.*] Ethics are very difficult.

[*He goes into the rain, leaving* PERPETUA *and* EDGAR. *They sit in silence for a moment.*]

Edgar. Did you forget I was here?

Perpetua. I didn't forget.
But I wish I could forget, and I wish you had forgotten,
This afternoon's brazen lying.

Edgar. I have forgotten.
Why should we remember this afternoon
When probably no one else does?

Perpetua. But am I sure
I want you to forget as incuriously as that?
I want your father not to be hurt by to-night,
I want you not to be hurt by this afternoon,
I want to be free to make my own way,
But I want to be remembered.

Edgar. My memory
Is for nothing else. But, as it happens,
I hardly need it. Over and over again
I see you for the first time. I round
Some corner of my senses, and there, as though
The air had formed you out of a sudden thought,
I discover you. Any memory I had
Vanishes, to let you in so unannounced
My whole body stammers with surprise.
I imagine I love you. And I don't think
You can fairly object, when all you have to do
Is walk freely through my thoughts and round
My heart. You needn't even turn your head.

Perpetua. Don't say this now. I'm still remembering
I can give pain, and that in itself is loss
Of liberty.

Edgar. No, I just mentioned it in passing.

Perpetua. No one is separate from another; how difficult
That is. I move, and the movement goes from life
To life all round me. And yet I have to be
Myself. And what is *my* freedom becomes
Another person's compulsion. What are we to make
Of this dilemma?

Edgar. I haven't the sense to ask.
Whatever the human mystery may be
I am it.

Perpetua. There's comfort in that.

Edgar. Tell me:

Do I seem to you to be only a sort
Of postscript to my father?
Perpetua. No, Edgar,
Across and across my heart, never at all.
Edgar. I begin to notice myself, too,
I must say. Here the little parents come.
[*Enter the* DUKE *and* REEDBECK.]
So now the house goes with a dragging wing.
Are your spirits very heavy, father?
Duke. They ride;
No, no, they ride well enough.
Reedbeck. [*To* PERPETUA.] Isn't it time
My all night wanderer went to bed?
Duke. She will stay
For a moment's peaceful conversation.
Perpetua. I want to know about Rosabel. When Dominic said——
Duke. I'll keep her story for a rainy day.
Edgar. And for now the rain has blown over. Shall we go
And see how the last of the flames dance down
To sleep among the ruins, Perpetua?
Duke. Our peaceful conversation, Perpetua.
Edgar. Perpetua?
Perpetua. I'll find my way to bed.
Edgar. I shall take the liberty to light you there.
To-morrow, then, father.
Duke. To-morrow to you.
Perpetua. To-morrow to us all, but not too soon.
I need the soft pillows to make my peace
Before I trust myself to another day to-morrow.
[*Exeunt* EDGAR *and* PERPETUA. REEDBECK *is almost asleep in a chair.*]
Duke. Shall I be sorry for myself? In mortality's name
I'll be sorry for myself. Branches and boughs,
Brown hills, the valleys faint with brume,
A burnish on the lake; mile by mile
It's all a unison of ageing,
The landscape's all in tune, in a falling cadence,
All decaying. And nowhere does it have to hear
The quips of spring, or, when so nearing its end,
Have to bear the merry mirth of May.
How fortunate to grow in the crow-footed woods,
Eh, Reedbeck? But I see you're anxious to sleep.
Reedbeck. I? No, no; I'll never go to sleep
Again to-night, much too disturbed.
Don't know what to suggest I make of anything.
I only hope a quiet dignity
Will meet the case. Civilization is simply
(If I had to define it) simply dignity,
Simply simple dignity; but then
Sons and daughters come into it, most lovable,
Most difficult, and unexpected combustion,
And so forth and so forth. Now le Roi Soleil,
How many children did he have? One legitimate,
Several illegitimate . . . le Duc de Maine,
La Duchesse de Chartres. . . .
Duke. Shall I be happy for myself?
In the name of existence I'll be happy for myself.
Why, Reedbeck, how marvelous it is to moulder.
Think how you would have felt when you were lying
Grubbing in your mother's womb,
With only a wall to look at,
If you could have seen in your embryonic eye
The realm of bryony, sloes, rose-hips,
And a hedge's ruin, a golden desuetude,
A countryside like a drowned angel
Lying in shallow water, every thorn
Tendering a tear. Think, Reedbeck,
Think of the wonder of such glimmering woe;
How in a field of milk-white haze the lost
Apollo glows and wanders towards noon;
The wind-blown webs are brighter,
The rolling apples warmer than the sun.
Heavens! you would have cried, the womb
Echoing round you: These are the heavens, and I,
Reedbeck, am stillborn. Would you not?
Reedbeck. [*Waking slightly.*] And la Duchesse de Condé, I think.
Duke. So with ourselves; imagine: to have the sensation
Of nearness of sight, shortness of breath,
Palpitation, creaking in the joints,
Shootings, stabbings, lynching of the limbs,
A sudden illumination of lumbago.
What a rich world of sensation to achieve,
What infinite variety of being.
Is it not?
Reedbeck. Dominic not fond . . .
Perpetua. . . .
Duke. Reedbeck, I have to tell you
I mean to marry. I can still remember,
In my ebbing way, how pleasant it is to love;

An ancient love can blow again, like summer
Visiting St. Martin. A breath will do it,
If the breath comes deep, and deep it has come.
You must give me your felicitations. I marry
Rosabel, when Rosabel
(After six months, I understand)
Is disengaged from custody.

[*Only deep breathing comes from* REEDBECK.]

Thank you, dear fellow. Rosabel
Would thank you, too, if she were here.
She and I, sharing two solitudes,
Will bear our spirits up to where not even
The nightingale can know,
Where the song is quiet, and quiet
Is the song. Tell me, Reedbeck, before
We leave each other in sleep, where would you say
The lonely moment is coaxing us to go?

[REEDBECK *gives a gentle near-whistling snore.*]

Well, yes, yes, quite so, my little one,
It comes to that in the end.

CURTAIN

APPENDIX

GENERAL BIBLIOGRAPHY

BIBLIOGRAPHY OF DRAMATISTS

LIST OF ILLUSTRATIONS TO THE PLAYS

GENERAL BIBLIOGRAPHY

For books published before 1942, see the bibliographies in the earlier volumes of *Contemporary Drama* (37 plays or 9 plays), Scribner's, 1941, 1942.

Albright, H. D., and others, *Principles of Theatre Art.* 1955.

Altman, George, and others, *Theater Pictorial.* 1953.

Atkinson, Brooks, *Broadway Scrapbook.* 1947.

Baker, Blanch M., *Theatre and Allied Arts* (bibliography). 1952.

Bentley, Eric R., *The Playwright as Thinker.* 1946.

——— *In Search of Theater.* 1953.

——— *The Dramatic Event.* 1954.

Blum, Daniel, *A Pictorial History of the American Theatre.* 1950.

——— ed., *Theatre World.* 1944– (annually).

Clark, Barrett H., and Freedley, George, *A History of Modern Drama.* 1947.

Clurman, Harold, *The Fervent Years.* 1945.

Downer, Alan S., *Fifty Years of American Drama.* 1951.

Eliot, T. S., *Poetry and Drama.* 1951.

Ellis-Fermor, Una, *Frontiers of Drama.* 1945.

Fergusson, Francis, *The Idea of the Theatre.* 1949.

Gagey, Edmond M., *Revolution in American Drama.* 1947.

Gassner, John, *The Theatre in Our Times.* 1954.

——— *Masters of the Drama* (rev. ed.). 1954.

Granville-Barker, Harley, *Uses of the Drama.* 1945.

Jones, Robert Edmund, *The Dramatic Imagination.* 1942.

Krutch, Joseph Wood, *"Modernism" in Modern Drama.* 1953.

Lamm, Martin, *Modern Drama,* translated by K. Elliott. 1952.

Langner, Lawrence, *The Magic Curtain.* 1951.

Nicoll, Allardyce, *World Drama.* 1950.

O'Hara, F. H. and Bro, M. H., *Invitation to the Theatre.* 1951.

Peacock, Ronald, *The Poet in the Theatre.* 1946.

Prideaux, Tom, *World Theatre in Pictures.* 1953.

Reynolds, Ernest, *Modern English Drama.* 1949.

Stephens, Frances, ed., *Theatre World Annual.* 1948–.

Thompson, Alan R., *The Anatomy of Drama.* 1942.

——— *The Dry Mock.* 1948.

Trewin, J. C., *Dramatists of Today.* 1953.

——— ed., *Theatre Programme.* 1954.

——— *The Theatre Since 1900.* 1951.

Whiting, Frank M., *An Introduction to the Theatre.* 1954.

Williams, Raymond, *Drama from Ibsen to Eliot.* 1952.

——— *Drama in Performance.* 1954.

Worsley, Thomas C., *The Fugitive Art.* 1952.

BIBLIOGRAPHY OF DRAMATISTS

Jean Anouilh

Hobson, Harold, *The French Theatre of Today.* 1953.

——— *The Theatre Now.* 1953.

Marchant, William, "Pièces Roses," *Theatre Arts,* XXXIV (Nov. 1950), 36–39.

Marsh, Edward Owen, *Jean Anouilh.* 1953.

Perruchot, H., *Le Théâtre rose et noir de Jean Anouilh.* 1950.

Radine, Serge, *Anouilh, Lenormand, Salacrou.* 1951.

Worsley, T. C., *The Fugitive Art.* 1952.

Sample Review: John Mason Brown, in *The Saturday Review of Literature,* XXIX (March 9, 1946), 24–26.

Marc Connelly

Connelly, Marc, "Life of the Theatre," *The Saturday Review of Literature,* XXXVII (Oct. 23, 1954), 13–14.

Downer, Alan S., *Fifty Years of American Drama.* 1951.

Gilder, Rosamond, and others, *Theatre Arts Anthology.* 1951.

Withington, Robert, "Notes on the Corpus Christi Plays and The Green Pastures," *The Shakespeare Association Bulletin,* IX (Oct. 1934), 193–197.

Woollcott, Alexander, "Two-eyed Connelly," *The New Yorker,* VI (April 12, 1930), 29–31.

Young, Stark, *Immortal Shadows.* 1948.

Sample Review: Mark van Doren in *Theatre Guild Magazine,* VII (April 1930), 19–20.

Noël Coward

Agate, James, *First Nights.* 1934.

Brown, John Mason, *Two on the Aisle.* 1938.

Gibbs, Henry, *Theatre Tapestry.* 1949.

Gilder, Rosamond, and others, *Theatre Arts Anthology.* 1951.

Greacen, Robert, *The Art of Noël Coward.* 1953.

Hobson, Harold, *Verdict at Midnight.* 1952.

Noble, Peter, *British Theatre.* 1946.

Short, Ernest, *Theatrical Cavalcade.* 1942.

——— *Introducing the Theatre.* 1949.

——— *60 Years of Theatre.* 1951.

Trewin, J. C., *The Theatre Since 1900.* 1951.

——— *A Play Tonight.* 1952.

Williamson, Audrey, *Theatre of Two Decades.* 1951.

Sample Review: Clifton Fadiman in *Stage,* XIV (March 1937), 41–42.

Christopher Fry

Fry, Christopher, "The Artist Views the Critics," *The Atlantic Monthly*, CXCI (March 1953), 52–55.
Hobson, Harold, "London Hails Mr. Fry, Playwright," *The New York Times Magazine*, March 12, 1950; also "Reply," by I. M. O'Neill and N. Hennebury, April 16, 1950.
Nathan, George Jean, "The Young Man Named Fry," *The American Mercury*, LXXII (Feb. 1951), 220–224.
Redman, Ben Ray, "Christopher Fry, Poet-Dramatist," *English Journal*, XLII (Jan. 1953), 1–7.
Scott-James, R. A., "Fry's Poetic Drama," *The Nation*, CLXXI (Oct. 7, 1950), 315–316.
Stanford, Derek, *Christopher Fry, An Appreciation*. 1951.
——— *Christopher Fry Album*. 1952.
——— *Christopher Fry*. 1954.
Trewin, J. C., *The Theatre Since 1900*. 1951.
——— *Dramatists of Today*. 1953.
——— ed., *Theatre Programme*. 1954.
Worsley, T. C., *The Fugitive Art*. 1952.
Sample Review: Harold Clurman in *The New Republic*, CXXVI (March 3, 1952), 22–23.

Jean Giraudoux

Bentley, Eric R., *In Search of Theater*. 1953.
Clark, Barrett H., and Freedley, George, *A History of Modern Drama*. 1947.
Eustis, Morton, "The Work of Giraudoux," *Theatre Arts*, XXII (Feb. 1938), 127–133.
Jouvet, Louis, "Success," *Theatre Arts*, XX (May 1936), 354–371.
——— *Témoignages sur le théâtre*. 1952.
Mann, Klaus, "Jean Giraudoux," *The Nation*, CXLIX (Dec. 16, 1930), 682–683.
Marker, Christian, ed., *Giraudoux par lui-même*. 1952.
Nicoll, Allardyce, *World Drama*. 1950.
Siepmann, Eric, "The Plays of Giraudoux," *The Nineteenth Century and After*, CXXVII (June 1940), 730–736.
Valency, Maurice, "Bottom! Bless Thee! Thou Art Translated!" *Theatre Arts*, XXXIII (June 1949), 18–20.
Valency, Maurice, "Playwright Who Kept His Rendezvous," *Theatre Arts*, XXXIII (August 1949), 12–16.
Sample Review: John Mason Brown in *The Saturday Review of Literature*, XXXII (Jan. 15, 1949), 32–34.

Lillian Hellman

Clark, Barrett H., "Lillian Hellman," *College English*, VI (Dec. 1944), 127–133.
Downer, Alan S., *Fifty Years of American Drama*. 1951.
Harriman, Margaret Case, "Miss Lily of New Orleans," *The New Yorker*, XVII (Nov. 8, 1941), 22–35.
Isaacs, Edith J. R., "Lillian Hellman, Playwright on the March," *Theatre Arts*, XXVIII (Jan. 1944), 19–24.
Nathan, George Jean, "Playwrights in Petticoats," *American Mercury*, LII (June 1941), 750–752.
Sample Review: Brooks Atkinson in *Broadway Scrapbook*, 255–257. Reply by Miss Hellman: *The New York Times*, Dec. 15, 1946, II, 3, 4.

Arthur Miller

Brown, John Mason, "Seeing Things," *The Saturday Review of Literature*, XXXII (Feb. 26, 1949), 30–32.
Downer, Alan S., *Fifty Years of American Drama*. 1951.
Gassner, John, *The Theatre in Our Times*. 1954.
Kennedy, Sighle, "Who Killed the Salesman?" *Catholic World*, CLXXI (May 1950), 110–116.
Miller, Arthur, "The University of Michigan," *Holiday*, XIV (Dec. 1953), 68–71, 128–143.
Schneider, D. E., "Play of Dreams," *Theatre Arts*, XXXIII (October 1949), 18–21.
Tynan, Kenneth, "American Blues, the Plays of Arthur Miller and Tennessee Williams," *Encounter*, II (May 1954), 13–19.
Sample Review: Joseph Wood Krutch in *The Nation*, CLXVIII (March 5, 1949), 283–284.

William Saroyan

Gagey, Edmond M., *Revolution in American Drama*. 1947.
Hatcher, Harlan, "William Saroyan," *English Journal*, XXVIII (March 1939), 169–177.
Nathan, George Jean, "Saroyan, Whirling Dervish of Fresno," *American Mercury*, LI (Nov. 1940), 303–308.
Rahv, Philip, "William Saroyan, a Minority Report," *American Mercury*, LVII (Sept. 1943), 371–377.
Remenyi, Joseph, "William Saroyan, a Portrait," *College English*, VI (Nov. 1944), 92–100.
Saroyan, William, "How to See," *Theatre Arts*, XXV (Mar. 1941), 203–206.
——— "My Visit with G.B.S." *The New Republic*, CXV (July 22, 1946), 80.
——— "A Formula for the Theatre," *The New York Times Magazine*, Oct. 10, 1948, 12, 32–34.
——— "Time of My Life," *Theatre Arts*, XXXIX (Jan. 1955), 22–24.
Wilson, Edmund, "The Boys in the Back Room: William Saroyan," *The New Republic*, CIII (Nov. 18, 1940), 697–698.
Sample Review: Joseph Wood Krutch in *The Nation*, CLV (Oct. 10, 1942), 357.

George Bernard Shaw

Archer, William, *The Old Drama and the New*. 1923.
Bentley, Eric R., *Bernard Shaw*. 1947.
Campbell, Mrs. Patrick, *My Life and Some Letters*. 1922.
Chesterton, G. K., *George Bernard Shaw*. 1909.
Dent, A., ed., *Bernard Shaw and Mrs. Patrick Campbell: Their Correspondence*. 1952.
Ellehauge, M., *The Position of Bernard Shaw in European Drama*. 1931.

Hamon, A., *The Twentieth-Century Molière: Bernard Shaw*. 1916.
Henderson, Archibald, *Bernard Shaw, Playboy and Prophet*. 1932. (Revision of the earlier *George Bernard Shaw*, 1911; condensed, 1918.)
——— *European Dramatists*. 1916.
——— *Table Talk of G.B.S.* 1925.
Irvine, W., *The Universe of G.B.S.* 1949.
Joad, C. E. M., *Shaw and Society: Anthology and Symposium*. 1953.
Kronenberger, L., *George Bernard Shaw: a Critical Survey*. 1953.
Lewisohn, Ludwig, *The Drama and the Stage*. 1922.
MacCarthy, D., *The Court Theatre*. 1907.
Nethercot, A. H., *Men and Supermen: the Shavian Portrait Gallery*. 1954.
Patch, Blanche E., *Thirty Years With G.B.S.* 1951.
Pearson, Hesketh, *G.B.S., a Full-length Portrait*. 1942.
——— *G.B.S., a Postscript*. 1950.
Priestley, J. B., "Shaw as Social Critic," *The Saturday Review of Literature*, XXIX (July 27, 1946), 5–7. (July 27, 1946.)
St. John, Christopher, ed., *Ellen Terry and Bernard Shaw, a Correspondence*. 1931.
Shaw, G. B., *Advice to a Young Critic*. 1955.
Sample Review: H. W. Massingham in *The Nation* (London), XV (April 18, 1914), 93–94.

THORNTON WILDER

Anon., "An Obliging Man," *Time*, LXI (Jan. 12, 1953), 44–49.
Anon., "The Economic Interpretation of Thornton Wilder," *The New Republic*, LXV (Nov. 26, 1930), 31–32.
Firebaugh, Joseph J., "The Humanism of Thornton Wilder," *Pacific Spectator*, IV (Autumn 1950), 426–438.
Gagey, Edmond M., *Revolution in American Drama*. 1947.
Gold, Michael, "Thornton Wilder, Prophet of the Genteel Christ," *The New Republic*, LXIV (Oct. 22, 1930), 266–267.
Guthrie, Tyrone, "The World of Thornton Wilder," *The New York Times Magazine*, Nov. 27, 1955, 26–27, 64, 66–68.
Isaacs, Edith J. R., "Thornton Wilder in Person," *Theatre Arts*, XXVII (Jan. 1943), 21–30.
Kohler, Dayton, "Thornton Wilder," *The English Journal* (college edition), XXVIII (Jan. 1939), 1–11.
Sample Review: *Theatre World*, XLI (Dec. 1945), 6.

TENNESSEE WILLIAMS

Barnett, Lincoln, "Tennessee Williams," *Life*, XXIV (Feb. 16, 1948), 113ff.
Courtney, Marguerite, *Laurette*. 1955.
Downer, Alan S., *Fifty Years of American Drama*. 1951.
Engle, Paul, "A Locomotive Named Reality," *The New Republic*, CXXXII (Jan. 24, 1955), 26, 27.
Gassner, John, "Tennessee Williams, Dramatist of Frustration," *College English*, X (Oct. 1948), 1–7.
——— *The Theatre in Our Times*. 1954.
Lewis, R. C., "A Playwright Named Tennessee," *The New York Times Magazine*, December 7, 1947, 19, 67, 69, 70.
Moor, Paul, "A Mississippian named Tennessee," *Harper's Magazine*, CXCVII (July 1948), 63–71.
Taylor, Harry, "The Dilemma of Tennessee Williams," *Masses and Mainstream*, I (April 1948), 51–56.
Tynan, Kenneth, "American Blues, the Plays of Arthur Miller and Tennessee Williams," *Encounter*, II (May 1954), 13–19.
Sample Review: Rosamond Gilder in *Theatre Arts*, XXIX (June 1945), 325–329.

LIST OF ILLUSTRATIONS TO THE PLAYS

Illustrations in books are listed first, followed by those in yearbooks and encyclopedias, and then those in periodicals. When illustrations are grouped without page number in a source, a letter is alphabetically assigned following a hyphen and the last numbered page, as, opp. 86-D means the fourth picture-page after page 86.

ABBREVIATIONS

ed(s).—editor(s), edition
front.—frontispiece
n.d.—no date
no.—number
n.s.—new series
opp.—facing
rev.—revised
supp.—supplement
vol.—volume
#—plate number

ANOTHER PART OF THE FOREST

Blum, Daniel, *Great Stars of the American Stage*, #146
——— *A Pictorial History of the American Theatre*, 264.
Hellman, Lillian, *Another Part of the Forest*, front.
Daniel Blum's Theatre World, III (1946–1947), 48, 49, 145.
Mantle, Burns, ed., *The Best Plays of 1946–1947*, opp. 86-D.
Life, XXI (Dec. 9, 1946), 71, 72, 74; XXIV (May 31, 1948), 63, 64, 67.
Newsweek, XXVIII (Dec. 2, 1946), 94; XXXI (May 31, 1948), 73.
The Saturday Review of Literature, XXIX (Dec. 14, 1946), 20.
Theatre Arts, XXXI (Jan. 1947), 14; XXXII (Summer 1948), 42; XXXIV (Jan. 1950), 53.

Time, LI (May 31, 1948), 86.
Vogue, CVIII (Dec. 4, 1946), 204.

ANTIGONE

Barker, Felix, *The Oliviers,* opp. 284.
Blum, Daniel, *A Pictorial History of the American Theatre,* 264, 265.
Five Seasons of the Old Vic Company, 60, 61.
March, Edward Own, *Jean Anouilh,* opp. 113, opp. 128.
Pillement, Georges, *Anthologie du Théâtre Français Contemporain,* I, opp. 433.
Prideaux, Tom, *World Theatre in Pictures,* 34, 35, 36, 37.
Williamson, Audrey, *Theatre of Two Decades,* opp. 192-G.
Worsley, T. C., *The Fugitive Art,* opp. 80.
Daniel Blum's Theatre World, II (1945–1946), 73, 74.
Enciclopedia dello Spettacolo, I, #101, #102.
Mantle, Burns, ed., *The Best Plays of 1945–1946,* opp. 180.
Amerika (Russian title transliterated), no. 11 (n.d.), 53.
Film and Theatre Today, no. 1 (n.d.) 27.
L'Illustration, 102nd année, no. 5268–5269 (Feb. 26, 1944–March 4, 1944), 69, 78.
Life, XX (March 18, 1946), 73, 74.
The Masque, no. 8 (1948), 26.
Newsweek, XXVII (March 4, 1946), 80.
The Saturday Review of Literature, XXIX (March 9, 1946), 24.
Stage Pictorial, III (April 1946), 20.
Theatre Arts, XXX (March 1946), 130; (Dec. 1946), 727; XXXI (Aug. 1947), 28; XXXII (Fall 1948), 69; XXXIII (April 1949), 63; XXXIV (Aug. 1950), 51.
Theatre World, XLV (April 1949), cover, 14–17.
Time, XLVII (March 4, 1946), 54.
World Theatre, III, no. 2 (n.d.), 23; III, no. 3, 43; IV, no. 2, 37.

DEATH OF A SALESMAN

Albright, H. D., and others, *Principles of Theatre Art,* #18.
Altman, George, and others, *Theater Pictorial,* #481, #482.
Blum, Daniel, *A Pictorial History of the American Theatre,* 275.
Cheney, Sheldon, *The Theatre,* rev. ed., #61.
Cinquanta Anni di Teatro in Italia, #63, p. 93.
Gassner, John, ed., *A Treasury of the Theatre,* front.-H.
Morehouse, Ward, *Matinee Tomorrow,* opp. 307.
Prideaux, Tom, *World Theatre in Pictures,* 200, 201.
Samachson, Dorothy and Joseph, *Let's Meet the Theatre,* 19, 90.
Simonson, Lee, *The Art of Scenic Design,* 99.
Worsley, T. C., *The Fugitive Art,* opp. 80-C.
Chapman, John, ed., *The Burns Mantle Best Plays of 1948–1949,* opp. 86.
Daniel Blum's Screen World, IV (1953), 14, 15.
Daniel Blum's Theatre World, V (1948–1949), 90–92; VI (1949–1950), 112, 125; VIII (1951–1952), 151.
Theatre Annual (1954), 71.
Théâtre de France, II, n.d., 134.
Theatre World Annual, I (1949–1950), 58–61.
American Artist, XIII (Nov. 1949), 32, 34.
Drama, n.s., no. 15 (Winter 1949), 9.
France-Illustration, Supplément Théâtral et Littéraire, no. 106 (May 17, 1952), front and back covers.
The Illustrated London News, CCXV (Aug. 27, 1949), 320.
L'Illustrazione Italiana, anno 79, no. 10 (Oct. 1952), 67.
Life, XXVI (Feb. 21, 1949), 115, 117, 118, 121; XXXI (Nov. 19, 1951), 119; XXXII (Jan. 14, 1952), 63, 64, 66.
The New York Times Book Review, May 15, 1949, 4.
The New York Times Magazine, March 16, 1952, 22; Feb. 20, 1955, 22.
Newsweek, XXXIII (Feb. 21, 1949), 78.
The Saturday Review of Literature, XXXII (Feb. 26, 1949), 30.
Theatre Arts, XXXIII (April 1949), 14, 18, 19; (May 1949), 22; (June 1949), 31; (July 1949), cover, 3; (Dec. 1949), 51; XXXV (March 1951), 40, 49; (Sept. 1951), 36; XXXVI (Jan. 1952), 36; XXXIX (May 1955), 27.
Theatre Time, I (Summer 1949), 61; III (Winter 1951), 26.
Theatre World, XLV (April 1949), 31; (Oct. 1949), cover, 11–18.
World Theatre, II, no. 2 (n.d.), 46, 47; no. 4, 17; III, no. 3, 44; IV, no. 3 (Summer 1955), 70.

THE GLASS MENAGERIE

d'Amico, Silvio, ed., *La Regia Teatrale,* #58.
Blank, Earl W., ed., *How They Were Staged,* supp. no. 3, 8, 9.
Blum, Daniel, *A Pictorial History of the American Theatre,* 259.
——— *Great Stars of the American Stage,* #63, #140.
Cinquanta Anni di Teatro in Italia, #62.
Courtney, Marguerite, *Laurette,* opp. 211.
Fordham, Hallam, ed., *John Gielgud,* 105.
Gassner, John, ed., *A Treasury of the Theatre,* rev. ed., front.-H.
Hobson, Harold, *Theatre,* II, opp. 64.
Prideaux, Tom, *World Theatre in Pictures,* 190, 191.
Williams, Tennessee, *The Glass Menagerie* (New Classics ed.), opp. 28, opp. 29, opp. 44, opp. 45.
Williams, Tennessee, *The Glass Menagerie* (Random House ed.), front., opp. 4, opp. 68, opp. 100.
Wilson, A. E., *Post-war Theatre,* 167.
Britannica Book of the Year, 1946 (1945), 731.
Daniel Blum's Screen World, II (1951), 146, 147.
Daniel Blum's Theatre World, I (1944–1945), 86, 87; II (1945–1946), 115.
Mantle, Burns, ed., *The Best Plays of 1944–1945,* opp. 150.
The New International Year Book, 1946 (1945), opp. 608.

Drama, n.s., no. 7 (Winter 1947), 21.
Film and Theatre Today, no. 1 (n.d.), 39.
The Illustrated London News, CCXIII (Aug. 14, 1948), 194.
L'Illustrazione Italiana, anno 74, no. 14 (April 6, 1947), 298.
Life, XVIII (April 30, 1945), 81–83; (June 11, 1945), 12, 13, 14; XXI (July 22, 1946), 7; XXIV (Feb. 16, 1948), 122.
The New York Times Magazine, March 4, 1945, 28, 29.
Newsweek, XXV (April 9, 1945), 86; XXXVI (Oct. 9, 1950), 90.
The Saturday Review of Literature, XXXIII (Oct. 14, 1950), 32.
Stage Pictorial, Spring 1945, 32; Autumn 1945, 19–25.
Teatern (Sweden), XIII (Feb. 1946), 7, 14.
Theatre (Bradford, England), no. 10 (Autumn 1948), 25.
Theatre Arts, XXIX (April 1945), cover, 211; (May 1945), 263; (June 1945), 327; (Oct. 1945), 554; (Dec. 1945), 690; XXXI (Aug. 1947), 38, 39; XXXII (Spring 1948), 96; (Fall 1948), 68; (Oct. 1948), 17; XXXIII (April 1949), 60, 63; (Aug. 1949), 33, 36; XXXIV (Feb. 1950), 35; (Aug. 1950), 44, 59; (Oct. 1950), 54; XXXV (Sept. 1951), 36.
Theatre World, XLI (June 1945), 27; XLIV (Oct. 1948), cover, 13–19.
Time, XLV (April 9, 1945), 86; LVI (Oct. 2, 1950), 76.
World Theatre, II, no. 4, n.d., 15.

The Green Pastures

d'Amico, Silvio, *Storia del Teatro Drammatico*, IV, 171.
Anderson, John, *The American Theatre*, 313.
Blum, Daniel, *A Pictorial History of the American Theatre*, 199.
Connelly, Marc, *The Green Pastures* (Lakeside Press ed.), *passim*.
Davy, Charles, ed., *Footnotes to the Films*, opp. 256.
Dolman, John, Jr., *The Art of Acting*, #21.
Downs, Harold, ed., *Theatre and Stage*, II, 1142, 1143.
Durham, Willard Higley, and Dodds, John W., eds., *British and American Plays*, opp. 596.
Freedley, George, and Reeves, John A., *A History of the Theatre*, #357.
Gassner, John, ed., *A Treasury of the Theatre*, rev. ed., front.-F.
Isaacs, Edith J. R., *The Negro in the American Theatre*, 13, 87.
Prideaux, Tom, *World Theatre in Pictures*, 174, 175.
Rogers, Agnes, *I Remember Distinctly*, 139.
Rotha, Paul, and Manvell, Roger, *Movie Parade*, #313.
Sullivan, Mark, *Our Times*, VI, 409.
Taylor, Deems, *A Pictorial History of the Movies*, 295.
Thrasher, Frederic, *Okay for Sound*, 126.
Daniel Blum's Theatre World, VII (1950–1951), 101.
Mantle, Burns, ed., *The Best Plays of 1929–1930*, front.
The New International Year Book, 1930, 754.
Collier's, LXXXV (May 10, 1930), 23.
Drama, XX (April 1930), 200, 201; XXI (Jan. 1931), 9.
The Graphic, CXXVIII (April 5, 1930), 9.
The Illustrated London News, CLXXXIX (Dec. 12, 1936), 1072.
Ladies' Home Journal, LII (Sept. 1935), 8, 9.
Life, XXX (April 16, 1951), 67–69; XXXI (Nov. 19, 1951), 118.
The Literary Digest, CIV (March 22, 1930), 20–22; CV (June 21, 1930), 22, 23; CXIX (March 9, 1935), 25.
Newsweek, VII (May 30, 1936), 26.
The Saturday Review of Literature, XXXIV (April 7, 1951), 28.
Scenario, II (Dec. 1933), 621.
Stage, X (Dec. 1932), 20; XI (March 1934), 2, 3; XIII (June 1936), 37; (July 1936), 22, 23.
Stage Pictorial, no vol. number, March 1946, 18.
Theatre Arts, XIV (April 1930), 287, 361; (Oct. 1930), 893–896; XVI (April 1932), 299–301; (Dec. 1932), 1019; XIX (Jan. 1935), 37; XXI (Oct. 1937), 810; XXV (Aug. 1941), 598; XXVI (Aug. 1942), 492, 512, 518; XXXIII (Sept. 1949), 25; XXXV (May 1951), 22, 24, 25; XXXIX (April 1955), 30.
Theatre Guild Magazine, VII (April 1930), 20, 22, 23.
Theatre Magazine, LI (April 1930), 16; (May 1930), 32–35; LII (July 1930), 20; (Dec. 1930), 16.
Theatre World, LI (Aug. 1955), 46.
Time, XXV (March 4, 1935), 35; XXVII (June 29, 1936), 38, 39.
Vanity Fair, XXXIV (May 1930), 44, 45.

Happy Journey to Trenton and Camden

Theatre Arts, XXII (July 1938), 474.

Hello Out There

Blum, Daniel, *A Pictorial History of the American Theatre*, 247.

The Madwoman of Chaillot

d'Amico, Silvio, *Storia del Teatro Drammatico*, IV, 113.
Blum, Daniel, *A Pictorial History of the American Theatre*, 271.
Braun, Hanns, *Theater in Germany*, 14.
Derwent, Clarence, *The Derwent Story*, front.-Y, front.-Z.
Giraudoux, Jean, *The Madwoman of Chaillot*, adapted by M. Valency, front., opp. 60, opp. 96.
Giraudoux par lui-même, ed. by Christian Marker, 27, 141.
Lipnitzki, *Images de Louis Jouvet*, #62–#65.
Marker, Christian, ed., *Giraudoux par lui-même*, 27, 141.
Prideaux, Tom, *World Theatre in Pictures*, 118, 119.

Chapman, John, ed., *Burns Mantle's Best Plays of 1948–1949*, opp. 86-C.
Daniel Blum's Theatre World, V (1948–1949), 69, 70, 71; VII (1950–1951), 138.
Enciclopedia dello Spettacolo, II, #52.
Theatre World Annual, II (1950–1951), 14.
America: Revue France-Amérique Latinité, no. 3 (Summer 1946), 81, 82.
France-Illustration, no. 14 (Jan. 5, 1946), 19; no. 307 (Sept. 1, 1951), 198.
The Illustrated London News, CCXVIII (Mar. 3, 1951), 346.
Life, XXVI (Jan. 24, 1949), 64, 67, 68; XXVII (July 18, 1949), 61; XXXVII (Aug. 2, 1954), 74.
Newsweek, XXXIII (Jan. 10, 1949), 72.
Revue d'Histoire du Théâtre, IV (1952), no. 1–2, 113, 141, 142.
The Saturday Review of Literature, XXXII (Jan. 15, 1949), 32.
Theatre Arts, XXX (June 1946), 312, 334; XXXIII (March 1949), 14; (April 1949), 58; (June 1949), cover, 18; (Aug. 1949), 12; (Nov. 1949), 57, 59, 65, 72, 77, 82, 85, 89; XXXV (June 1951), 32; XXXVII (Aug. 1953), 65; XXXVIII (Jan. 1954), 25; (Nov. 1954), 76.
Theatre Time, I (Spring 1949), 25; (Summer 1949), 67.
Theatre World, XLV (March 1949), 33; XLVII (April 1951), 8.
Time, LIII (Jan. 10, 1949), 36.
World Theatre, I, no. 1, n.d., 60; II, no. 4, 36; III, no. 2, 19, 34.

Pygmalion

Balcon, Michael, ed., *Twenty Years of British Film*, 42.
Beerbohm, Max, *Herbert Beerbohm Tree*, opp. 242.
Blank, Earl W., ed., *How They Were Staged*, supp. no. 1, 7.
Blum, Daniel, *A Pictorial History of the American Theatre*, 100, 179, 258.
——— ed., *Great Stars of the American Stage*, #32, #94, #118, #120.
Carrick, Edward, *Art and Design in the British Film*, 72.
Cinquanta Anni di Teatro in Italia, #44.
Eaton, Walter Pritchard, *The Theatre Guild*, opp. 192.
Helvenston, Harold, *Scenery*, 5.
Hume, Samuel J., and Foster, D. M., *Theatre and School*, 78.
Langner, Lawrence, *The Magic Curtain*, opp. 178-D.
McCleery, Albert, and Glick, Carl, *Curtains Going Up*, opp. 308-J.
Mander, Raymond, and Mitchenson, Joe, *Theatrical Companion to the Plays of Bernard Shaw*, 162–166.
Prideaux, Tom, *World Theatre in Pictures*, 150, 151.
Rotha, Paul, and Manvell, Roger, *Movie Parade*, #163.
Rothe, Hans, ed., *Max Reinhardt*, #90, #112.
Shaw, Bernard, *Pygmalion*, illustrated edition, *passim*.
Taylor, Deems, *A Pictorial History of the Movies*, 322.
Trewin, J. C., *The Theatre since 1900*, opp. 113.
Twenty Years of Cinema in Venice, #112.
Williams, Harcourt, ed., *Vic-Wells*, opp. 29.
Williamson, Audrey, *Old Vic Drama*, #17.
Winsten, Stephen, ed., *G.B.S. 90*, opp. 169.
Daniel Blum's Theatre World, II (1945–1946), 51–53; VIII (1951–1952), 165.
Enciclopedia dello Spettacolo, I, 1017.
"The Stage" Year Book, 1915, opp. 9-I; 1926, opp. 87.
Theatre World Annual, V (1953–1954), 81–83.
The Bookman (New York), XL (Dec. 1914), 417.
Collier's, LIV (Jan. 2, 1915), 9.
Current Opinion, LVI (May 1914), 359.
Drama, XII (Jan. 1922), 115; XVII (Jan. 1927), 105.
France–Illustration, no. 420 (March 1955), 76.
The Graphic, LXXXIX (April 18, 1914), 655; CI (March 6, 1920), 364.
The Illustrated London News, CXLIV (April 18, 1914), 627; CXLV (July 11, 1914), 1095; CXCIII (Sept. 17, 1938), 510; (Oct. 15, 1938), 682; CCXXIII (Dec. 5, 1953), 940.
L'Illustration, numéro 5237, 101e année (July 24, 1943), 64.
L'Illustrazione Italiana, anno 41, numero 49 (Dec. 6, 1914), 489.
Life, V (Dec. 12, 1938), 31, 32; XX (Jan. 14, 1946), 67, 68, 70; XXXIII (Oct. 6, 1952), 66.
The Literary Digest, XLVIII (May 16, 1914), 1180, 1181; XLIX (Nov. 14, 1914), 956, 957.
Newsweek, XXVII (Jan. 7, 1946), 82.
Play Pictorial, LXXII (Jan. 1938), 1, 4–6.
The Saturday Review of Literature, XXIX (Jan. 12, 1946), 24.
Scenario, VI (June 1937), 264.
Stage, XIV (Aug. 1937), 76; XVI (Dec. 1938), 20, 21; (Jan. 1939), 48.
Stage Pictorial, no vol. number, March 1946, 24, 25.
The Studio, CXXXVI (Nov. 1948), 154.
Theatre Arts, XI (Jan. 1927), 14; XX (Nov. 1936), 867; XXI (Dec. 1937), 965; XXII (Nov. 1938), 813; XXVII (July 1943), 439; XXIX (July 1945), 404; XXX (Jan. 1946), cover; (Feb. 1946), 69, 70, 71; (March 1946), 136; XXXIII (Aug. 1949), 20; XXXIV (Aug. 1950), 40; XXXV (Nov. 1951), 41; XXXVI (Dec. 1952), 20; XXXIX (June 1955), 74; (Sept. 1955), 25.
Theatre Magazine, XX (Dec. 1914), 262; XLV (Jan. 1927), 29; (Feb. 1927), 17; (March 1927), 20; (April 1927), 35.
Time, XXXII (Dec. 5, 1938), 26; XLVII (Jan. 7, 1946), 70.
Die Woche, XV (Dec. 13, 1913), 2118; XXI (Dec. 13, 1919), 1389; XXXIV (Oct. 1, 1932), 1192; XLVI (April 5, 1944), 18.

Venus Observed

Barker, Felix, *The Oliviers*, opp. 243, opp. 293.
Braun, Hanns, *Theater in Germany*, 13, 22.

Stanford, Derek, *Christopher Fry*, 80.
——— *Christopher Fry Album*, 89, 91, 93, 95, 97, 99.
Trewin, J. C., *Drama 1945–1950*, opp. 24-C.
——— *The Theatre since 1900*, opp. 304.
Chapman, John, ed., *The Best Plays of 1951–1952*, opp. 54-G.
Daniel Blum's Theatre World, VIII (1951–1952), 96, 97.
Theatre World Annual, I (1949–1950), 103–107.
The Year's Work in the Theatre, 1949–1950, opp. 17, opp. 28.
The Illustrated London News, CCXVI (Feb. 11, 1950), 228.
Newsweek, XXXIX (Feb. 25, 1952), 95.
The Saturday Review of Literature, XXXV (March 1, 1952), 20; (May 10, 1952), 26.
Theatre Arts, XXXV (Jan. 1951), 26; XXXVI (April 1952), 19.
Theatre World, XLVI (March 1950), cover, 11–18.
Time, LIX (Feb. 25, 1952), 80.
World Theatre, III, no. 3, n.d., 33, 43.

WAYS AND MEANS

d'Amico, Silvio, *Storia del Teatro Drammatico*, IV, 149.
Daniel Blum's Screen World, 1954, 189.
Daniel Blum's Theatre World, IV (1947–1948), 88.
Life, I (Dec. 7, 1936), 12; XXIII (Dec. 8, 1947), 104.

P9-DCY-9

CONTENTS

RENOIR
A SENSUOUS VISION

Anne Distel

DISCOVERIES
HARRY N. ABRAMS, INC., PUBLISHERS

"I'm like a piece of cork thrown in the water and carried by the current. I let my painting take me where it will!" Renoir's life, unlike that of other artists, is reflected in his paintings and revealed to the public, almost despite himself. "I don't think I've let a single day go by without painting," he noted at the end of his life.

CHAPTER I

ACCEPTED OR REJECTED?

One of Renoir's earliest known paintings is this still life of flowers, dated 1858. Among his last works—in 1919—are more flowers. In between, he never tired of this traditional subject, which he reinterpreted according to his evolving style. This *Vase of Flowers* of 1866 was painted for one of his earliest collectors and patrons, the architect Charles Le Coeur.

Pierre-Auguste Renoir was born in Limoges, France, on 25 February 1841, the next to last of seven children. Two of them died in infancy, the only bit of drama—and a commonplace one for the time—in the history of a poor but hardworking family. His father, Léonard Renoir, was a tailor, his mother, Marguerite Merlet, a dressmaker. The family soon moved to Paris, to the neighborhood of the Louvre, first on the Rue de la Bibliothèque (which vanished when the Rue de Rivoli was rebuilt), then to 23, Rue d'Argenteuil.

When he was still an apprentice porcelain painter—the elaborate vase below is one of the few pieces of his that are known—Renoir roamed his neighborhood and discovered the elegant Fountain of the Innocents, with Jean Goujon's *Nymphs* (1547–9, above).

Apprentice at Thirteen

The young Auguste loved to draw. The example of his brother Henri, ten years older and an engraver of heraldry, encouraged him, as did his brother-in-law Charles Leray, also an engraver. Renoir's parents, unlike those of many of his future colleagues from a more middle-class background, not only did not try to oppose an artistic career but even encouraged it, eager to ensure his ability to earn a living as soon as possible. To this end, they apprenticed him to a porcelain painter when he was thirteen. Until 1860, Renoir experimented with various decorative trades, painting fans, blinds, and armoires. While he proved extremely good at such practical work, it could only have whetted his desire to escape his artisanal toils.

The Ecole des Beaux-Arts

He then set off down the traditional path that all who wished to become painters followed at the time. By

January 1860 he had obtained a pass that enabled him to copy in the Louvre, and on 1 April 1862 he was accepted to the Ecole Impériale et Spéciale des Beaux-Arts. Except for two brief interruptions incurred while fulfilling his military obligations, Renoir attended his classes regularly, earning respectable grades but not even approaching the level of the Prix de Rome, the five-year scholarship to study in Italy that was the ultimate stamp of approval. It is highly unlikely that the official line of teaching, long bogged down in its devotion to antiquity, based on an apprenticeship in drawing, and dependent on the lessons of perspective and anatomy, nourished his ambitions very much.

Below left: A note on the back of this amusing collection of portraits of the students in Gleyre's studio indicates that Sisley's is the third face from the left in the same row as the man with the halo. The clean-shaven man shown in profile just below him would be Renoir, painted by his friend Emile-Henri Laporte, facing Renoir, who painted him in turn.

Above: This 1861 photograph is the only known image of the young Renoir. The artist always remained very reticent about his personal life. "I'm horrified at the thought of the public knowing how I eat my cutlet and that my parents were poor but honest," he wrote. "Painters become very boring with their pathetic stories, and no one gives a damn about it."

Gleyre's Studio

In 1861, Renoir began to work in the private studio of a Swiss painter, Charles Gleyre. Gleyre's relatively liberal and impartial approach to teaching, rather than the quality of his painting itself—grounded as it was in tradition—attracted many students to his studio. Among them was a young man from Montpellier, Frédéric Bazille, who joined near the end of 1862, and one from Le Havre, Claude Monet, as well as Alfred Sisley, the son of a Parisian merchant, all of whom soon became friends of Renoir's. None of them was happy with traditional teaching methods; their tastes were varied, ranging from a master who died in 1863, Eugène Delacroix, to the newly arisen—and still highly controversial—champion of realism, Gustave Courbet. They liked Camille Corot and hated Jean-Léon Gérôme and Alexandre Cabanel, the painters of the moment, but they were not without admiration for Jean-Auguste-Dominique Ingres, who died in 1867. Another young painter, only a few years older than they, provided them with an encouraging example. Edouard Manet defied the forces of conservatism in exhibiting his famous *Déjeuner sur l'Herbe* (1863) at the Salon des Refusés.

As its name ("Salon of the Rejects") implies, that unprecedented venue allowed the public the opportunity to see works that had been rejected from the official Salon. The jury that judged admissions to that official exhibition was largely controlled by a group of powerful conservative academics.

Renoir at the Salon

Acceptance to the Salon, held in Paris every year, conferred a sort of seal of approval on the artists whose works were so honored; they were duly rewarded with medals and with the presentation of their works to prospective buyers at a time when few private galleries existed. The bulk of the public, indoctrinated by this system largely endorsed by the critics, swallowed the

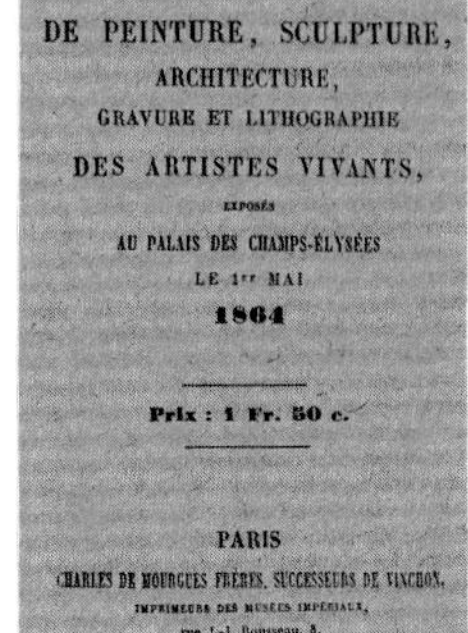

EXPLICATION
DES OUVRAGES
DE PEINTURE, SCULPTURE,
ARCHITECTURE,
GRAVURE ET LITHOGRAPHIE
DES ARTISTES VIVANTS,
EXPOSÉS
AU PALAIS DES CHAMPS-ÉLYSÉES
LE 1er MAI
1864

Prix : 1 Fr. 50 c.

PARIS
CHARLES DE MOURGUES FRÈRES, SUCCESSEURS DE VINCHON,
IMPRIMEURS DES MUSÉES IMPÉRIAUX,
rue J.-J. Rousseau, 8.

Above: The catalogue of the official Salon of 1864 (above) lists the artists in alphabetical order. Renoir's first presentation is number 1618.

Left: For all its apparent simplicity, *Arum and Conservatory Plants*, a large-format still life of 1864, is a complete work that reaches much further than a simple "trying out" of values. Its similarity to comparable works by Courbet demonstrates its creator's early realist tendencies.

"It relaxes my brain to paint flowers. I don't bring to it the same intellectual tension that facing a model calls for. When I paint flowers, I lay down the tones, I boldly try out all the values without worrying about ruining the picture."
Renoir, 1921

Portrait of Mademoiselle Romaine Lacaux of 1864 is one of Renoir's earliest commissioned works. The father of the young girl was a porcelain manufacturer whom Renoir probably knew from the days of his apprenticeship. This painting reveals the young artist's debt to Ingres and Corot, two artists he admired. While honoring the conventions of the genre, Renoir was enough of a master of his medium to express directly the childish freshness of Romaine Lacaux behind the pose of the little bourgeois princess. This sympathy with his young models—conveying both complicity and respect—would show up repeatedly in all his portraits of children, including those of his own.

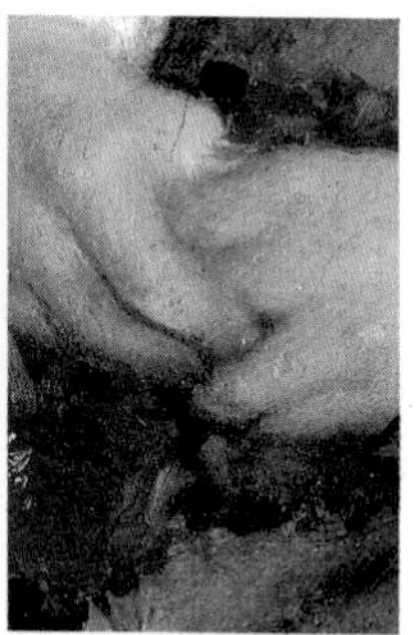

jury's choices wholesale and roused itself only to make fun of any new trends. Then, timidly at first, some journalists, art lovers, and dealers rose to the defense of the protesters, suggesting that the supremacy of an art selected for the public's admiration by the reigning powers could and should be called into question.

In this time of flux, Renoir began his artistic career, exhibiting at the official 1864 Salon a canvas entitled *La Esmeralda*, inspired by Victor Hugo's novel *Notre-Dame-de-Paris* (known as The Hunchback of Notre-Dame). (Renoir claimed to have later destroyed the painting.) In the Salon's catalogue, Renoir named Charles Gleyre as his teacher, following tradition, although he had probably left that artist's studio, which was experiencing financial difficulties, during the course of the year. He also stopped attending the Ecole des Beaux-Arts.

The First Patrons

In 1865 two of Renoir's works were accepted by the Salon, one of them a portrait of Alfred Sisley's father. However, while the two landscapes Monet was exhibiting drew some critical attention, Renoir received no notice whatsoever. That year, the journalists mainly feasted on the scandal created by Manet's *Olympia*. The show of indifference did not seem to discourage Renoir, for he began work on a large painting, *At the Inn of Mother Anthony*, dated 1866. It portrays his closest

Renoir made use of the same dark palette in *Portrait of William Sisley* (1864, above), shown at the Salon of 1865, and *At the Inn of Mother Anthony* (left). In the latter, he depicted two of his painter-friends, Jules Le Coeur (standing) and Alfred Sisley (seated at right). The man with his arms on the table has not been identified.

friends at the time, Sisley and Jules Le Coeur, in an inn at Marlotte, a village on the edge of the forest of Fontainebleau, where artists and writers used to gather outside Paris.

While Sisley became prominent as one of the original group of Impressionists, the painter Jules Le Coeur is mostly known today as one of Renoir's models as well as his first patron, along with his brother Charles Le Coeur.

Mon cher Mr Charles

The Le Coeurs, a well-off Parisian family, were convinced of the young painter's talent early on and commissioned him to paint portraits, still lifes, and even, in 1868, decorations for a town house that Charles had built for Romanian Prince Gheorghe Bibescu.

Marlotte

At the Inn of Mother Anthony apparently was never exhibited at a Salon, yet it figures as a key work in Renoir's early career. This ambitious composition recalls Courbet's large figural canvases. Even if Renoir had not yet had the opportunity to see those works, he had surely heard them discussed. Renoir's painting is a balanced group of realistic portraits in an interior; the subject clearly deals with contemporary life, specifically, the casual, unstudied life of artists. The space is defined simply by the wall of the inn, covered with sketches

Charles Le Coeur, Jules Le Coeur's brother, was among Renoir's earliest patrons. He appears in the photograph above, flanked by his wife, Marie, and their son Joseph. Renoir sketched Marie and Joseph in a letter to Charles (left) proposing a painting, which apparently was never carried out.

"Ask your wife if she would like me to do her portrait standing and holding Jo by the hand.... You would have to pay for the canvas, seeing that I could not possibly ask Carpentier [an artists' supplier], who would turn me down flat."

Renoir to Charles Le Coeur, c. 1866–8

and scrawls by passing daubers, which functions as a backdrop for the figures.

In this same period Monet, who, influenced by his mentor Eugène Boudin, had been painting outdoors for some time, placed the figures for his *Déjeuner sur l'Herbe* under the foliage of the forest of Fontainebleau. In this painting, which is both an homage and a challenge to Manet's painting of the same name, Monet paid special attention to the effects of light.

Renoir was not averse to working outdoors. While in Marlotte, he painted his friend Jules strolling with his dogs in the woods. *Jules Le Coeur in the Forest of Fontainebleau* (1866) closely approaches in its spirit and technique the canvases of one of the most famous of the Barbizon painters, Narcisse Diaz de la Peña. Much later, Renoir recalled having come across Diaz at work in the forest of Fontainebleau. He had helped Renoir out by opening an account for him with his supplier so the young artist could buy materials. In any case, this brilliant and fluent artist clearly counted among Renoir's influences.

"Monsieur Renoir, Poor Fellow, Has Been Rejected"

With this sorrowful statement, Marie Le Coeur, the sister of Jules and Charles, began a narration of the young painter's woes in the spring of 1866. She continued: "On Friday, as no one could tell him if he'd been accepted or rejected, he went to wait for the jury members at the exit to the exhibition, and when he saw Messieurs Corot and [Charles-François] Daubigny (two distinguished landscape painters) come out, he asked them if they knew if the paintings of one of his friends, Renoir, had been accepted. Daubigny recalled the painting and described it, telling him: 'We are greatly upset on your friend's

Jules Le Coeur in the Forest of Fontainebleau (left) is a rare example of Renoir experimenting to learn more about the "business" of painting. He used a palette knife here, a technique favored by Courbet.

Opposite below: To be rejected (*refusé*) by the official Salon, depicted by Honoré Daumier in a caricature in 1855, was the worst setback an artist could suffer. Such was undoubtedly the fate of a painting by Renoir that has since been lost; all that remains of the painting itself is a fragment showing the bust of a seated woman, signed and dated 1866. However, a depiction of it exists, thanks to Bazille, who gave it a prominent spot in his *The Studio of Bazille, Rue de La Condamine* (1870, detail, opposite above), above his own and Monet's works, thus commemorating the many years they worked together. An X ray of Bazille's canvas reveals that he painted over a study of a female nude in the same pose as Renoir's *Diana*, which was rejected by the Salon of 1867. It cannot be determined if Bazille made the study using the same model as his friend or if he painted over a study by Renoir.

behalf but his painting was rejected; we did all we could to prevent it, we asked for its reconsideration ten times, without succeeding at getting it accepted, but what could we do, we were six for it against all the others. Tell your friend not to be discouraged, that his painting shows great qualities; he ought to get up a petition and demand a show of the rejected paintings.' So that, even in his misery, he has the consolation of receiving compliments from two artists he admires."

In the end, the jury offered an olive branch by accepting a small study that Renoir considered only a sketch, though it did reject the one he deemed important. Extremely disappointed, he probably chose not to send anything at all, since his

name does not appear in the Salon's catalogue, while those of his friends Monet, Bazille, and Sisley do. Their works were accepted, but Renoir could console himself by saying that Manet, like he, had been rejected. It is not known whether he followed Daubigny's advice and wrote

to the administration to protest, as did Paul Cézanne, one of the year's notorious rejects. In any case, it is no accident that the newspaper in *At the Inn of Mother Anthony* carries the name *L'Evénement* in capital letters. It was in this daily that Emile Zola, a childhood friend of Cézanne's who was still a budding novelist unknown to the public, published his first pieces of art criticism. In these articles,

Frédéric Bazille's friendship was of great importance to Renoir. When later asked about his early days, Renoir brought up the memory of his friend, killed at twenty-nine in 1870 during the Franco-Prussian War before he had the chance to fulfill his promise. The wealthy Bazille thought it his duty to help out his friends Monet and Renoir, whom he had met at Gleyre's studio. He admired their talent and shared with them the relative luxury of his studios, the first on the Rue Visconti in 1867 (left), then, from 1868 (with Renoir only), at the Rue de La Condamine. He also bought many paintings, especially from Monet.

Bazille painted Renoir (opposite above) and Renoir, Bazille (opposite below). The latter work to many minds symbolizes the period in which Impressionism began: On Bazille's easel is the still life *Heron and Jackdaws*, a subject that Sisley had also painted, while a landscape by Monet hangs on the wall. This portrait was owned by Manet, who lent it to the second Impressionist exhibition in 1876.

which began appearing in April 1866, he fiercely defended Manet and his friends.

"There Is Something New at the Rue Visconti"

Frédéric Bazille, who was never short of money, thanks to a regular stipend from his parents, had rented a spacious studio for several months at 20, Rue Visconti when he wrote to his mother at the beginning of 1867, "Since my last letter there is something new at the Rue Visconti. Monet has fallen from the sky with a collection of magnificent canvases which will be a huge success at the Salon. He will stay here until the end of the month. With Renoir, that makes two needy painters that I'm housing. It's a veritable sanatorium. I'm delighted, I have plenty of space, and both of them are lively sorts." Shortly before this, Bazille had told his father, "I'm putting up one of my friends, a former student of Gleyre's, who hasn't got a studio at the moment. Renoir—that's his name—works very hard, he uses my models and even gives me something to help cover their expense."

At this time, Renoir made a portrait of his friend at work, *Bazille Before His Easel*, which dates to 1867. This painting corresponds to a portrait of the same period by Bazille that shows Renoir perched in an unstable position, in sympathy with the nervous and restless temperament that his friends so often described. His thin face, turned away from the viewer, carries an intense expression. His light brown hair is not yet hidden under what would be an omnipresent head covering, and he sports the mustache and the short, thin beard that he would retain for the rest of his life.

It was probably in the studio on the Rue Visconti that Renoir painted the Roman goddess Diana the hunter. In *Diana*, he managed to combine novelty, in its kinship with Courbet, and convention, in the choice of subject matter, with an eye toward winning the support of the academicians. In this effort he failed: The painting was rejected by the jury of the Salon of 1867, along with works by Monet, Bazille, and Sisley. Renoir signed a petition written by Bazille announcing the formation of a new Salon des Refusés, but nothing came of it. This was the year a world's fair was held in Paris, and the artists were particularly anxious to place their works before the anticipated large and curious crowd. Disgusted to see his paintings rejected by the jury, Manet, like Courbet, decided to mount a show of them at his own expense; it was located at the edge of the grounds of the world's fair.

Lise

It was around this time that a young brunette appeared in Renoir's paintings and personal life. Named Lise Tréhot, she was the model for the canvas titled *Lise* (1867) that was a great success at the Salon of 1868. It was caricatured and discussed, despite the fact that it had been consigned, as Jules-Antoine Castagnary, well-known champion of the new painters, put it, "with the dregs, in the rafters next to Bazille's *Family Reunion* and not far from Monet's large *Boats*." (*Boats* is now lost.)

Young Boy with a Cat (1868) remains a mystery. The model is probably a professional who others would have placed in a Roman pose. Renoir preferred to capture him in a casual moment as he caresses a cat in front of a panel of luxurious flowered cloth, in keeping with the artist's desire to give his paintings a rich appearance.

Renoir's companion Lise Tréhot (below) posed for a painting exhibited at the Salon of 1868 (left). The caricaturist Gill mocked it, comparing her to

"a nice semisoft cheese out for a stroll" (above). More encouraging commentators said of *Lise*, "Realist protest, [showing] a great deal of shining talent and promise."

Numerous critics pointed out Renoir's debt to Manet, although one of them also compared the work to a painting by the American James Abbott McNeill Whistler, *Symphony in White, No. 1: The White Girl,* which had created a stir at the Salon des Refusés of 1863.

Emile Zola perceptively demonstrated the close relationship between the works of Renoir and Monet: "This *Lise* looks to me like the sister of Claude Monet's *Camille* [*Woman in a Green Dress*].... She is one of our wives, or rather, one of our mistresses, painted with great honesty and a successful application of the modern style."

While the painting did not elicit much other commentary, from here on Renoir was inextricably linked with his friends. This is verified by his appearance in two paintings clearly of the new school: *The Studio of Bazille, Rue de La Condamine* by Bazille and *A Studio in the Batignolles* by Henri Fantin-Latour, both of 1870. Renoir and Bazille remained close friends, together moving to 9, Rue de la Paix aux Batignolles (renamed Rue de La Condamine at the end of 1868) at the beginning of 1868, where Renoir lived until the beginning of 1870. Their new neighbor Manet paid them a visit, which served as the pretext for Bazille's painting.

This new studio was close to the well-known Café Guerbois.

Exhibited at the Salon of 1866, Monet's *Woman in a Green Dress* (opposite) received much attention in the press. One of the commentators, Zola, tactlessly pointed out that it was a portrait of the painter's companion, Camille, which he also mentioned in the case of Renoir's *Lise*. Remarkably, Zola remembered Monet's painting well enough two years later to discern its relationship with Renoir's. This offers proof, if any is needed, of his familiarity with the painters of the Café Guerbois, shown above in an 1869 drawing by Manet.

Café Guerbois

A group of artists, writers, and critics followed Manet, who began to frequent the café at 11, Grande Rue des Batignolles (today the Avenue de Clichy). Besides Manet, the most faithful were Emile Zola and the critics

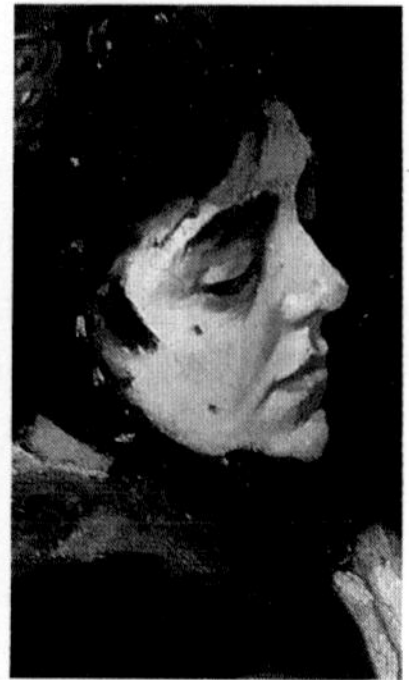

There is no doubt that the model for *Summer* (overleaf right), cautiously subtitled "study" in the catalogue of the Salon of 1869 to explain its boldly "unfinished" look, was again Lise Tréhot. Yet the identity of the woman in *Alfred Sisley and His Wife* (also c. 1868, overleaf left) remains uncertain. The man gallantly offering his arm to the young woman in a striped dress is definitely Alfred Sisley. At the time, he was living with a young florist named Eugénie, whom he later married; no portrait of her is known. The young wife in the painted "couple," however, greatly resembles Lise. Renoir himself alluded in a letter to a work he called *Lise and Sisley*, which could well refer to this painting.

Zacharie Astruc, Edmond Duranty, and Théodore Duret. Among the artists, the engravers Marcellin Desboutin and Félix Bracquemond and Bazille, Renoir, Fantin-Latour, and Degas came often. When they were in Paris, Cézanne, Monet, and Camille Pissarro showed up. Convivial, polemical, impassioned, the group at the Café Guerbois seemed to symbolize the avant-garde just before the Franco-Prussian War of 1870; some malicious critics of the time quickly dubbed the group the Batignolles Group.

Renoir

Official Success

Lise served as the model for *Summer*, a study exhibited at the Salon of 1869, and for the two works Renoir showed at the Salon of 1870—a *Bather* in the spirit of Courbet and *Woman of Algiers*, an homage to Delacroix. These works display a preference for a firm and fluid style, a deliberate choice of clearly modern subjects, and a predilection for the figure. The same qualities can be discerned in the portraits from which Renoir received the most income, such as *Alfred Sisley and His Wife* and *The*

Renoir painted this large portrait, *The Clown,* at the request of the owner of the café at the Cirque d'Hiver (Winter Circus). The monumental image, detailed with care, in contrast to the sketchy treatment of the spectators, bears witness to painters' fascination with the circus, from Edgar Degas to Henri de Toulouse-Lautrec and Georges Seurat to Pablo Picasso.

Clown of 1868. The artist's palette employs lively tones, emphasizing color contrasts.

Renoir and Monet

The bond between Renoir and Monet grew stronger. In 1869 Renoir saved money by living modestly with his parents in Voisins-Louveciennes, a small town just west of Paris. This placed him near Monet, who was living near Bougival. Monet was struggling with constant financial problems, made worse by the birth of a child. Even so, Renoir wrote Bazille, "We don't eat every day, but all the same I'm happy, because Monet is a good painting companion." He added with regret, "I'm doing very little because I have very few paints."

He was undoubtedly thinking of these difficult years, which were just beginning,

Woman of Algiers, shown at the Salon of 1870 (with Lise as the model), was mocked by the caricaturist Cham.

when at the end of his life Renoir told a young friend, painter Albert André, "I never had a fighter's temperament and I would have given up many times over had not my good friend Monet, who had it himself—a fighter's temperament—bucked me up."

"The huge raft covered by a tarpaulin held up by wooden columns was connected to the charming island of Croissy by two gangplanks, one of which entered the center of the aquatic establishment, while the other…reached the ground next to the office of the baths."

Guy de Maupassant
La Femme de Paul, 1881

La Grenouillère

Renoir and Monet painted together at La Grenouillère, a bathing establishment with a restaurant on the Seine at Croissy. The choice of this eminently modern subject suited both artists and shows their nonconformist bent. La Grenouillère was a popular spot, described by

different witnesses as a hangout favored by high-life types and the rowdy rendezvous of the lower classes. Author Guy de Maupassant evoked it several years later in *La Femme de Paul* (Paul's Mistress) and *Yvette*. Artists working for the illustrated newspapers sketched it often.

Guy de Maupassant described perfectly this "floating café" on the Seine that was called La Grenouillère (a 1902 illustration, opposite). In 1869 Renoir and Monet made twin depictions of the scene (top, Renoir; above, Monet).

To make it the subject of a painting intended for the Salon—as Monet dreamed of doing, on his own terms—seemed a losing proposition. For his part, Renoir apparently had no thought of deriving a large and important composition from the small ones that he had made on the theme. However, painting outdoors next to a friend and colleague already experienced in the practice doubtlessly altered his working habits, helped to brighten his palette, and enlivened his stroke by breaking it up into smaller units. A point-by-point comparison of the twin canvases of the two painters reveals their differences as well. Monet organized space more structurally, his brushstroke was firmer, and his format was generally more simplified. Renoir was more expansive with the tip of his brush, the detail of the figures, and the play of colors.

In contrast to these canvases bursting with spontaneity, the works that Renoir sent to the 1870 Salon are, as we have seen, much more conservative. They were accepted; Monet's were rejected. The decade thus ended on an encouraging note for Renoir. The serious young man watching Manet at work in *A Studio in the Batignolles* was, according to Fantin-Latour himself, "a painter who will get himself talked about."

Taille : 1 mètre 69 c **mil.**
visage Ovale
front ordinaire
yeux bruns
nez long
bouche grande
menton rond
cheveux ch
sourcils blonds.

The War of 1870

In July 1870 war was declared between France and Germany. On 26 August Renoir was drafted into the battalion of the Tenth Cavalry Regiment. Sent to Libourne, near Bordeaux, he escaped the hardships of the siege of Paris but fell ill, the victim of severe depression as well as dysentery. After his discharge he returned to Paris, where he paid little attention to politics and went right back to work. Many changes had occurred in the interim: Bazille was dead, killed in battle; Monet was in England, where he had taken refuge; and Sisley, whose house had been ransacked, found himself in desperate financial straits.

Rejected Again

Renoir's first attempt to renew his ties with the official artistic life of Paris met with a rebuff. His large painting *The Harem (Parisian Women Dressed as Algerians)*, an obvious offspring of *Woman of Algiers*, was rejected by the Salon of 1872. This was the last painting for which Lise would pose; in April 1872 she married the architect Georges Brière de l'Isle. A petition that Renoir signed,

---

Renoir's military record (left) gives a physical description of the young man approaching the age of thirty. While he saw little fighting, he heartily resented the war, as his letters make clear.

"For four months I've been unhappy, feeling deprived of letters from Paris. I've been gripped by utter boredom; can't eat or sleep. Finally I got dysentery as my payoff and I almost died.... Looking at my buddies when they came to see me, I realized how far gone I was—they were flabbergasted, they saw me as already dead."

Renoir to Charles Le Coeur, 1 March 1871

along with such artists as Manet, Fantin-Latour, Pissarro, and Cézanne, asking for the creation of a Salon des Refusés, went unanswered. He suffered another rejection the following year with an unidentified portrait and a very large painting titled *A Morning Ride in the Bois de Boulogne* depicting Mme. Henriette Darras, a friend of the Le Coeurs, on a horse, accompanied by Charles Le Coeur's son Joseph on a pony.

These works were displayed at the Salon des Refusés of 1873 in a defiant gesture that showed that Renoir was distancing himself from the official art world. Convinced that the jury was deliberately pushing him away, he decided he would never again send another painting to the Salon.

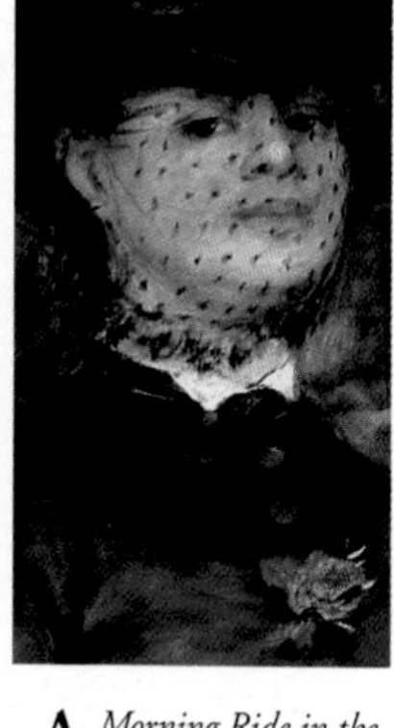

A Morning Ride in the Bois de Boulogne, a large-format painting, was executed in 1873 in the public room of the Ecole Militaire (Military Academy), or so Renoir told Vollard. The arrangements were made by Captain Paul Darras, an amateur painter and friend of the Le Coeurs, whose wife posed as the horsewoman, accompanied by Charles Le Coeur's son. The elegant woman's dotted veil fascinated the painter, who also did a study of her head. This major painting demonstrates Renoir's ambition to rival the elaborate works on important subjects created by the official painters with a large realist composition such as those Courbet was producing—which probably explains why the jury rejected it. This is the last painting with ties to the Le Coeur family, with whom he had a falling-out.

Renoir

“Renoir is above all a painter of human beings. His keynote is a limpid scale of tones modulating from one to the next in a wonderful harmony. You feel that you are seeing Rubens illuminated by the fiery sun of Velázquez.”

Emile Zola
“Deux Expositions d’Art en Mai”
(Two Art Shows in May)
Le Messager de l’Europe
Saint Petersburg, June 1876

CHAPTER II
RENOIR, IMPRESSIONIST

The novelist Zola called to mind Renoir’s *The Swing* (1876) when describing his heroine of *Une Page d’Amour* (A Love Affair, 1878): “Standing on the plank, her arms opened wide holding onto the ropes…she wore a gray dress decorated with light purple bows.” Meanwhile, her daughter was entranced by “round spots, of a lovely golden yellow, that danced on her shawl. It was easy to imagine them as creatures.”

With Claude Monet at Argenteuil

When Monet moved to Argenteuil (just north of Paris) at the end of 1871, after a trip to Holland that followed his voluntary exile in England during the war in 1870, Renoir visited him often. The portraits Renoir made of his friend and his wife, Camille, provide the most visible proof, although there are also the many paintings by the two artists that share a subject, such as *The Seine at Argenteuil.* Here, as elsewhere, the influence of Monet seems to have been predominant, if only because Monet induced his friend to set up his easel in the open air again, as he had at La Grenouillère.

Monet had many other visitors at Argenteuil: Pissarro, Sisley, who remained one of Renoir's closest friends, and somewhat later Manet, who had no hesitation about learning from his

Claude Monet (above left) and Alfred Sisley (above right) remained Renoir's familiar models and close friends over the years. At Argenteuil Monet often painted racing sailboats, which led Renoir to try his hand at the same theme (*The Seine at Argenteuil,* 1874, below).

young friends, all came to see him. The group had never been more tightly bound together.

Renoir made numerous portraits of Claude Monet's wife, Camille, around 1872. One of the best shows her reading a newspaper, stretched out among the fat cushions of a sofa (above). In this small canvas, painted at one sitting, Renoir demonstrated his facility for depicting shimmering textiles with an astonishing economy of means and without disturbing the composition's mood of gracious and spontaneous intimacy, punctuated by the pretty black of the young woman's two small feet.

1874: The First Exhibition of the "Impressionists"

The artists' conversations often turned to the Salon. These "refusés," or rejects, felt compelled to organize exhibitions of their works in order to survive. They realized there was no point in endlessly petitioning the administration for a "Salon des Refusés." It was up to the artists themselves to take the initiative, which would give them control over who would be allowed to show with them. This was not a new idea; in his letters to his parents, Bazille had alluded several times since 1867 to projects for artists' associations, all of which were abandoned due to lack of funds.

In comparison, the Société Anonyme, a cooperative of painters, sculptors, engravers, and other artists, founded on 27 December 1873 with Renoir a member, succeeded in mounting its first exhibition in the

RENOIR, Pierre-Auguste

40 — 35, rue St-Georges

41. *Danseuse.* ——— 3000

42. *L'avant-scène* ——— 2500

43. *Parisienne.* ——— 3500

44. *Moissonneurs.* ——— 1000 vendu par la toile à M. Hartmann.

45. *Fleurs.*

46. *Croquis* (Pastel). —— n'a pas été envoyé à l'Exposition

The annotations in a catalogue of the first Impressionist exhibition (1874, left) reveal the identity of one of the first buyers, the music publisher Hartmann, and the relatively high prices that Renoir set, especially for his large painting *The Parisienne* (1874, below). He later sold this painting to Henri Rouart.

spring of 1874 in Paris. Held in a space rented for the occasion at 35, Boulevard des Capucines, the exhibition included the work of Degas, Pissarro, Sisley, Berthe Morisot, Cézanne, and Armand Guillaumin, as well as Renoir and Monet. Manet decided to show at the Salon instead.

Making fun of the group, a critic called it "impressionist," playing on the title of a painting shown by Monet, *Impression, Sunrise.* The name stuck.

Critical Reaction in 1874

Renoir was represented in the exhibition by an important selection of recent canvases that he put before the public for the first time: *The Dancer, The Box* (more commonly known today as *La Loge*), *The Parisienne, Harvesters,* and two unidentified works called *Flowers* and *Head of a Woman.* It could be said that Renoir was remaining true to his old themes, giving pride of place to the "modern figure." One critic, Jean Prouvaire, saw in the three female subjects of *The Dancer, The Box (La Loge),* and *The Parisienne* "the three stages through which all young ladies of Paris pass," from the adolescent to the "flirt," which indicates that Renoir's contemporaries looked on his work as genre painting.

The critics treated Renoir's work much more gently than they did that of his friends, concentrating more on subject matter than on style. Favorable reviews came from friendly journalists: "M. Renoir is audacious," said Castagnary. "M. Renoir has a

Tradition insists that the models for *The Box (La Loge)* of 1874 were Edmond Renoir, journalist and brother of the artist, and Nini, a model whose nickname Gueule-de-Raie ("Fish Mouth") contrasts cruelly with the elegance of her Watteau-like finery. Contemporary critics were quick to label the woman as a "cocotte," one of those women with "cheeks powdered to a pearl-like sheen, their eyes lit by a banal passion …engaging, empty, delightful, and stupid."

The photographer Nadar had already moved out of 35, Boulevard des Capucines (below) by the time Renoir and his friends held the first exhibition of their group there in 1874.

great future.… He delights in his rainbow effects, his light, pearly tones like Turner's. However, his drawing is much more solid," asserted Philippe Burty. While the exhibition did not pass unnoticed, it was not a commercial success, even though some works were sold.

Impressionism at Auction

The group did not organize an exhibition in 1875, the Société Anonyme having been dissolved due to its large debts. To raise money, Renoir, Monet, Sisley, and Berthe Morisot delivered several works to the auction house at the Hôtel Drouot in Paris on 24 March. The viewing of the pieces was turbulent—the crowd openly jeered the artists of the group—and the financial results proved disastrous for Renoir: little more than 2000 francs for twenty canvases, two of which the artist bought back. This is clearly a negligible sum when seen in comparison with the fact that the government, parsimonious as it was, rarely paid less than 3000 francs for a painting bought from the Salon, and a painting by Jean-Louis-Ernest Meissonier (known for his high prices) could fetch as much as 200,000 francs. Among the buyers were two artists who had exhibited with the group in 1874, the Swiss Auguste de Molins and Henri Rouart, a friend of Degas who was also a distinguished collector; two author-critics, Arsène Houssaye, publisher of the prestigious periodical *L'Artiste*, which was popular in the worldly and literary circles of Paris, and Emile

Blémont; Monet's brother Léon; Morisot's cousin Gabriel Thomas, who later became a promoter for the Eiffel Tower and for Auguste Perret's Théâtre des Champs-Elysées; manufacturer Jean Dollfus; and publisher Georges Charpentier, who would become one of Renoir's strongest supporters.

The artists' disappointment was equaled only by that of the auction's appraiser, the Parisian dealer Paul Durand-Ruel. He did what he could to keep the prices up, including making the high bid himself on several paintings.

A photograph and a self-portrait (opposite center and above) show the artist around 1875. His thin, drawn face seems to reflect his financial difficulties. For example, *The Pont Neuf, Paris* (1872, above) drew a bid of only 300 francs at the Hôtel Drouot, the Paris auction house (illustrated opposite below), where the Impressionists, having lost money in their first exhibition, organized a sale of their works in the spring of 1875.

Durand-Ruel

Soon after the war of 1870, Durand-Ruel had bought paintings from Manet, Monet, and Pissarro, whom he knew from London during the war, and from Degas, Sisley, and finally Renoir. His first Renoir was probably *The Pont des Arts, Paris,* acquired on 16 March 1872 for 200 francs.

Durand-Ruel was the son of a dealer who had supported Delacroix and the school of 1830, Théodore Rousseau, and the painters of the Barbizon school before they became commercially successful. He grasped the mechanisms of the nascent art market very early and knew the value for the dealer of "discovering" new talents before anyone else. At the beginning of the 1860s, Durand-Ruel was practically the only one to champion Manet and his friends, as he had Courbet before them. It would be several years before he began buying Renoir's works in quantity, but the two men stood by each other throughout their relationship, in times both good and bad.

Marcellin Desboutin portrayed Paul Durand-Ruel in 1882 (left). Renoir's *Mother and Children* (opposite) and *Nude in Sunlight* (1875, bottom).

LE PEINTRE IMPRESSIONNISTE.

— Madame, pour votre portrait il manque quelques tons sur votre figure. Ne pourriez-vous avant passer quelques jours au fond d'une rivière?

1876: The Second Exhibition of the Impressionists

According to Théodore Duret and Edmond Maître, two of his friends, in 1875 Renoir was considering sending to the official Salon works that had been rejected the previous year, but no confirmation of this exists. In any case, Renoir again allied himself with the Impressionists when in 1876 they repeated the experiment of an independent exhibition. It had become all the rage for the critics to deride them. Although he came in for slightly less chaff than his fellows—including Degas, Monet, Morisot, Pissarro, Sisley, and a newcomer, Gustave Caillebotte, who were accused of creating works "that would make a horse rear"—

Renoir was still a target of their sarcasm. Arthur Baignières wrote of his 1874 *Mother and Children*, "From afar we see a bluish haze, from which six chocolate drops forcefully emerge. Whatever could it be? We come closer; the candies are the eyes of three people and the haze a mother and her daughters." This comment is characteristic of the overall objection to the Impressionists: that they offered to the public caricaturish unfinished paintings that lacked drawing skills.

Some Patrons in 1876

For the first time, the exhibition catalogue mentioned the owners of some of the exhibited works, which indicates that the Impressionists had indeed been able to attract attention without benefit of the official Salon. Unfortunately, the supporters were precious few in number. Those who championed Renoir were Manet, Victor Chocquet, Jean Dollfus, Alphonse Legrand, and Victor Poupin.

Manet, who was rather more than simply a patron, had nonetheless discreetly purchased from time to time a canvas from one of his young friends in financial straits. He lent to the show the 1867 portrait of Frédéric Bazille in memory of a comrade taken too early. It was on this occasion that he made a trade with Bazille's father, who wanted to possess this memento of his son killed in battle; Manet received a Monet in exchange.

One critic described *Nude in Sunlight* as "a mass of decomposing flesh with green and purplish spots, indicating the state of total putrefaction in a cadaver," an idea cartoonists took up with glee. The caption to the cartoon opposite reads, "Madame, your face lacks certain flesh tones I need for your portrait. Could you not return after spending several days at the bottom of a river?"

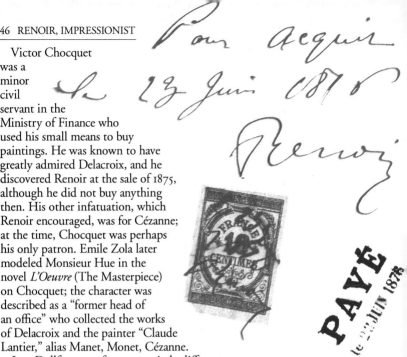

Victor Chocquet was a minor civil servant in the Ministry of Finance who used his small means to buy paintings. He was known to have greatly admired Delacroix, and he discovered Renoir at the sale of 1875, although he did not buy anything then. His other infatuation, which Renoir encouraged, was for Cézanne; at the time, Chocquet was perhaps his only patron. Emile Zola later modeled Monsieur Hue in the novel *L'Oeuvre* (The Masterpiece) on Chocquet; the character was described as a "former head of an office" who collected the works of Delacroix and the painter "Claude Lantier," alias Manet, Monet, Cézanne.

Jean Dollfus came from an entirely different world, the textile and industrial dynasty Dollfus Mieg, and enjoyed a substantial income. This connoisseur of old masters, Corot, Delacroix (Renoir copied Delacroix's *Jewish Wedding in Morocco* for him at the Louvre), and Far Eastern art owned only a few pieces by Renoir. Unusual for his time, Dollfus frequently attended sales at the Hôtel Drouot and daringly bid for and bought a Renoir painting at the sale of 1875. He kept it to the end of his life.

Alphonse Legrand, who lent a portrait of his daughter Delphine, and Victor Poupin were two dealers connected with Durand-Ruel, whose gallery at 11, Rue Le Peletier housed the exhibition.

Two names will complete this modest list. The first, Georges de Bellio, a "Romanian gentleman" and homeopathic physician, would retain a lifelong connection with Renoir. In 1876 he bought his first Renoir from Durand-Ruel; his claim to fame is the purchase, somewhat later, of Monet's notorious *Impression, Sunrise*, the center of a collection that constituted the first group of Impressionist paintings of the Musée Marmottan in Paris (bequeathed by his daughter).

Gustave Caillebotte, Impressionist and Patron

Although his name appeared as an artist rather than a patron, it is appropriate to introduce Gustave Caillebotte on the occasion of the exhibition of 1876.

A rich youth who painted, he saw his *The Floor Scrapers*

On 23 June 1876 Renoir signed a receipt for the modest sum of 300 francs (opposite above) Jean Dollfus paid for two paintings. One was *Head of a Woman*, the other *Portrait of Claude Monet* (1875, opposite below), some of whose works the collector also owned. Dollfus lent both of the Renoirs to the exhibition of the Impressionist group in 1876.

According to Albert André, Renoir and a friend were going through an exhibition and, in front of his

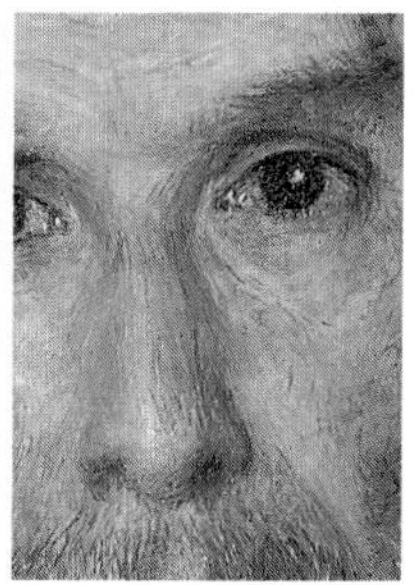

Portrait of Victor Chocquet (1875, left), the painter commented, "Portrait of a nut…by a nut.… What a charming crackpot! He hadn't [inherited] his fortune at that time and he scraped up the means to buy paintings from his salary at the ministry and never gave a thought to whether or not the art would appreciate in value."

rejected by the Salon of 1875, and in February 1876 he accepted the invitation by Renoir and Rouart to show with their group.

He began to buy pieces by his Impressionist colleagues. On 3 November 1876, deeply affected by the death of his older brother René, at the age of twenty-eight Gustave Caillebotte wrote a will that directed that a considerable sum of money be allocated to organize an exhibition of the "painters called the Intransigents or the Impressionists" in 1878. He already envisaged leaving to the State his collection of paintings, naming Renoir and his brother Martial Caillebotte as executors. Fate saw him alive and well in 1877, able to contribute not only extravagant sums of money but also his own works as well as his talents as organizer and conciliator. Symbolically, Caillebotte took over the role Bazille had filled among his friends. Suffice it to say that the circle of Renoir's supporters remained small but did not lack for enthusiasm.

Despite the second exhibition's poor showing,

To do a self-portrait in about 1879, Gustave Caillebotte (above) used a mirror that also reflected a painting hung on the wall of his studio, which he accordingly painted in reverse. It is *Dancing at the Moulin de la Galette*, by his friend Renoir. He probably purchased it soon after the exhibition of 1877, or so an 1879 article in *L'Artiste* implied: "This charming painting ...one of Renoir's best works, was bought by M. Caillebotte, who had no desire to trade it for the *Venus* by Bouguereau," a fashionable painter of the time whose art the Impressionists united in despising.

The Artist's Studio, Rue Saint-Georges (1876–7, left), a small canvas painted in about 1876 with nervous and rapid strokes, shows Renoir's studio and friends, from left to right, painter Pierre Franc-Lamy; Georges Rivière, the artist's biographer; Camille Pissarro, the doyen of the Impressionists (his profile can just be made out); and musician François Cabaner, one of the most striking personalities of that intellectual bohemian circle. Before he died in poverty at the age of forty-eight in 1881, he had been linked with Manet and Cézanne; he invented a system of "colored hearing," and he dedicated his *Sonnet des Sept Nombres* (Sonnet of the Seven Numbers) to poet Arthur Rimbaud. The figure seen from the back in the foreground is Pierre-Eugène Lestringuez, a civil servant and friend of the composer Emmanuel Chabrier. According to the memoirs of Jean Renoir, the painter's filmmaker son, he was also a devotee of the occult sciences. Franc-Lamy, Rivière, and Lestringuez also posed for *Dancing at the Moulin de la Galette.*

Renoir went right back to work, undertaking his most ambitious composition of the decade, *Dancing at the Moulin de la Galette.*

Dancing in Montmartre

While continuing to live at 35, Rue Saint-Georges, where he had moved in 1873 and which remained his address for close to ten years, Renoir rented a studio on the Rue Cortot in Montmartre, which was then still a suburb of the city, sprinkled with gardens and windmills. Several paintings evoke the garden of the Rue Cortot studio, notably *The Swing.* On the other hand, *Dancing at the Moulin de la Galette* (1876) was painted in large part on the site of the pleasure garden of the same name. Today, nothing remains of the

establishment but traces of the windmill; the bright green buildings and the garden where people danced beneath the stunted trees had vanished by the turn of the century.

Georges Rivière, friend and biographer of the artist, emphasized that the painting had been executed "entirely on location," a masterpiece of plein-air painting. However, it should be noted that many sketches of both details and the whole composition do exist.

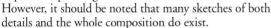

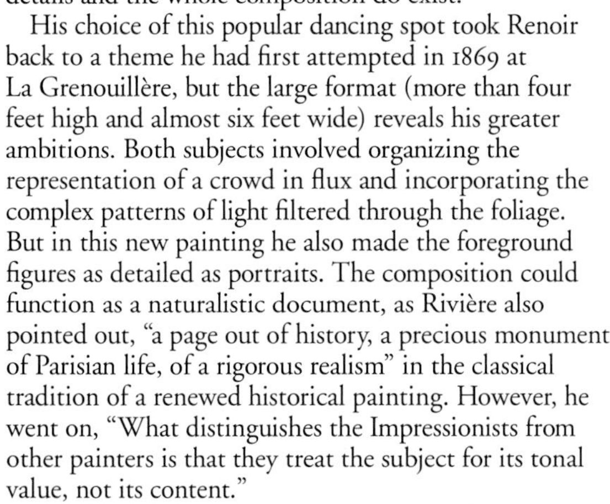

His choice of this popular dancing spot took Renoir back to a theme he had first attempted in 1869 at La Grenouillère, but the large format (more than four feet high and almost six feet wide) reveals his greater ambitions. Both subjects involved organizing the representation of a crowd in flux and incorporating the complex patterns of light filtered through the foliage. But in this new painting he also made the foreground figures as detailed as portraits. The composition could function as a naturalistic document, as Rivière also pointed out, "a page out of history, a precious monument of Parisian life, of a rigorous realism" in the classical tradition of a renewed historical painting. However, he went on, "What distinguishes the Impressionists from other painters is that they treat the subject for its tonal value, not its content."

Renoir clearly was working out a series of experiments that began with much smaller works, especially in the use of a fluid, allusive technique that models forms through color, without depending on outlines; even the shadows are colored.

This aspect of his work came in for attack by the critics of the Impressionists. They were startled to see, for example, "people dancing on a floor that looks like the purplish blue clouds that darken the sky on a stormy day" and defying all the known laws of perspective, while his friends saw "the brilliant reflections of a rainbow."

1877: The Third Exhibition of the Impressionists

Dancing at the Moulin de la Galette was shown at the third Impressionist exhibition in 1877 along with twenty more paintings by Renoir, including *The Swing*, lent by Gustave Caillebotte, who quickly

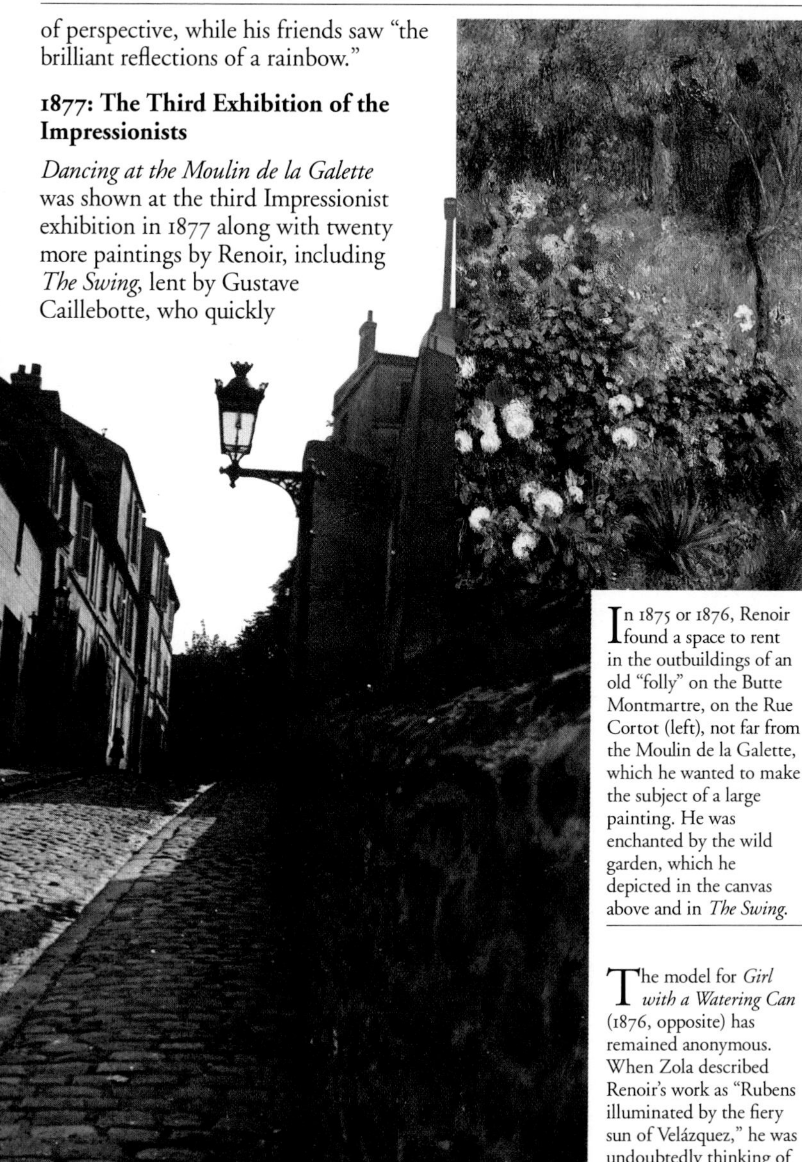

In 1875 or 1876, Renoir found a space to rent in the outbuildings of an old "folly" on the Butte Montmartre, on the Rue Cortot (left), not far from the Moulin de la Galette, which he wanted to make the subject of a large painting. He was enchanted by the wild garden, which he depicted in the canvas above and in *The Swing*.

The model for *Girl with a Watering Can* (1876, opposite) has remained anonymous. When Zola described Renoir's work as "Rubens illuminated by the fiery sun of Velázquez," he was undoubtedly thinking of paintings like this one.

Renoir populated his *Dancing at the Moulin de la Galette* not with professional models but with friends and some working-class women of Montmartre—Jeanne, Estelle, Margot—who were regulars there. Georges Rivière, depicted at the table at right with the painters Norbert Goeneutte and Franc-Lamy, listed the others: painters Gervex, Frédéric Cordey, and a Cuban, Pedro Vidal de Solares y Cardenas, whose painting has nothing in common with Renoir's; and friends Lestringuez and Paul Lhôte, a journalist and aspiring novelist. Lhôte clearly made a tractable model, as he reappeared several years later in the series of *Dances.*

added *Moulin de la Galette* to his collection as well.

Other much-discussed works, since they involved well-known personalities of the day, were portraits of Eugène Spuller, a republican deputy and friend of statesman Léon Gambetta, and the actress Jeanne Samary. Similarly, portraits of the wives of writer Alphonse Daudet and publisher Georges Charpentier were recognized. Charpentier already owned several canvases by Renoir and was on his way to becoming a full-fledged patron. His support, which continued to

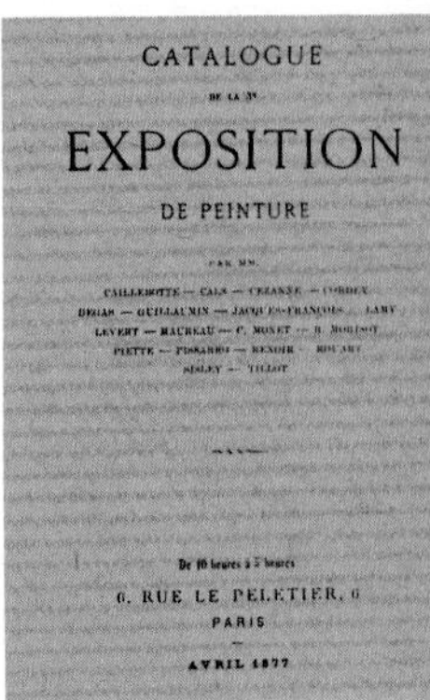

CATALOGUE

DE LA 3e

EXPOSITION

DE PEINTURE

PAR MM.

CAILLEBOTTE — CALS — CÉZANNE — CORDEY

DEGAS — GUILLAUMIN — JACQUES-FRANÇOIS — LAMY

LEVERT — MAUREAU — C. MONET — B. MORISOT

PIETTE — PISSARRO — RENOIR — ROUART

SISLEY — TILLOT

De 10 heures à 5 heures

6, RUE LE PELETIER, 6

PARIS

AVRIL 1877

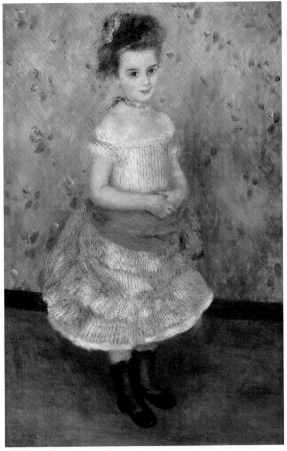

In 1877, the third exhibition of the Impressionist group, like all the others, produced a catalogue (above). Unfortunately, it did not include any reproductions, which has made the identification of the works shown very difficult, the evidence consisting only of descriptions made by critics and the rare confirmation of eyewitnesses.

Jeanne Durand-Ruel, first painted by Renoir in 1876 (left), was one of the five children of Paul Durand-Ruel, Renoir's dealer.

grow, would have a greater impact on Renoir than that of the Le Coeurs, with whom Renoir had a falling-out before 1875.

At the time of the 1877 exhibition, Renoir suggested to Georges Rivière that he publish a periodical called *L'Impressionniste* (The Impressionist). Four issues came out in April. The issue of 14 April included a letter from Renoir signed "A painter," and that of 28 April carried an article he wrote that was called "Decorative and Contemporary Art." In the latter, he set out deeply felt ideas concerning the interdependence of the arts and the decadence of the modern period, victim of mechanization, that he maintained throughout his life. Unfortunately, the periodical never spread beyond the circle of its originators, so it hardly helped in the effort to enlist serious patrons.

Portrait of Delphine Legrand (1875, below) was shown at the second Impressionist exhibition in 1876. Her father, an art dealer, did business with Durand-Ruel, but his association with the Impressionists proved a commercial disaster. He paid for the rental of the exhibition rooms on the Rue Le Peletier in 1876, served as appraiser for the 1877 sale, and with Caillebotte tried unsuccessfully to organize a new exhibition of the group in 1878.

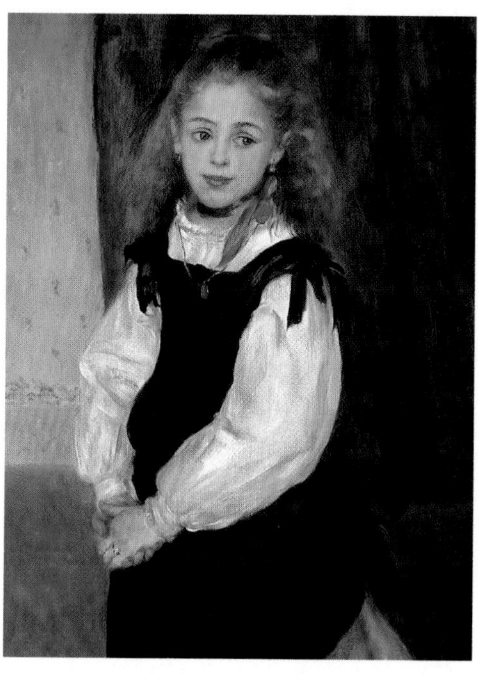

In Search of New Patrons

Another public auction of the works of Renoir, Caillebotte, Pissarro, and Sisley, among others, was held at the Hôtel Drouot on 24 May 1877, and it proved just as disastrous as the first. Fortunately, Renoir had enough portrait commissions to get by. Several of these commissions came from an eccentric character who nevertheless has earned himself a place among the pantheon of the earliest Impressionist patrons.

Under the pseudonym of Murer, Eugène Meunier wrote many eminently forgettable literary works. The real vocation of this self-taught man was running a small but prosperous bakery in Paris. One of his childhood friends, Armand Guillaumin, had introduced him to Cézanne, Pissarro, Sisley, Renoir, and Monet. He bought paintings from all of them (although at low prices, since times were hard and the painters willing to make sacrifices), invited them to dinner, organized local raffles with a painting by Pissarro as first prize. From Renoir, whom he most liked and who responded to him with the greatest warmth, he bought as many as thirty paintings, including such important works as *The Arbor (Sous la Tonnelle)* (about 1876). The collection was subsequently scattered during the collector's lifetime.

Eugène Murer was painted by numerous artists, notably Pissarro and, in 1877, Renoir (above). His friend Dr. Paul Gachet was drawn by illustrator Charles-Lucien Léandre (below).

One of Murer's relatives was an old friend of Pissarro's and Cézanne's, Dr. Paul Gachet, who practiced in Paris. At the beginning of 1879, Renoir appealed to Dr. Gachet and Georges de Bellio to save Anna Leboeuf, a seriously ill young woman who had modeled for him and perhaps played a role in his personal life as well. The doctors could do nothing for her, and she died. As a memento, Renoir offered Dr. Gachet a portrait of another young woman, which joined a collection (later bequeathed by his son to the French national museums) that included many works by Cézanne, Pissarro, and Guillaumin. (It was also to Dr. Gachet that Vincent van Gogh turned after his discharge from the asylum in May 1890. Dr. Gachet could not help him either; Vincent killed himself. The image of the doctor-friend of artists painted by Van Gogh, however, passed to posterity.)

Another of Renoir's patrons of the period is famous in his own right: the composer Emmanuel Chabrier. A friend of Manet's and, especially, Monet's, he was introduced to Renoir by his colleague Pierre-Eugène Lestringuez, who also worked at the Ministry of the Interior and had posed for Renoir's *Dancing at the Moulin de la Galette*. He bought several important works from Renoir to augment his collection of Impressionist paintings, which, unfortunately, was dispersed after his death.

1878: "The Impressionist Painters"

Among the small group of critics favorably disposed toward the Impressionists, one of the most fervent supporters of Renoir was undoubtedly Théodore Duret. A zealous republican who had renounced a political career, he lived off the income from the family cognac

When the composer Emmanuel Chabrier (humorously depicted at the piano by the very serious military painter Edouard Detaille, below left) bought Renoir's *Nude* (1876, below), traditionally known as *Anna*, the presumed model, he was taken aback by his wife's reaction to its frank sensuality. She accepted it, though, as she accepted her husband's passion for the most controversial painting of the time. In many respects, Chabrier's music, which was slow to be appreciated, held a position comparable to that of Impressionism in its time.

business. Closely tied to Emile Zola, he also became a critic and friend of Manet's.

He bought his first Renoir painting in 1873, on his return from a trip around the world that brought him to Japan accompanied by the financier Henri Cernuschi; *Summer* had been shown at the Salon of 1869. This purchase made Duret one of the earliest of Renoir's supporters. He wrote a pamphlet that is now a significant document in the history of the movement, *Les Peintres Impressionnistes* (The Impressionist Painters) of 1878, and

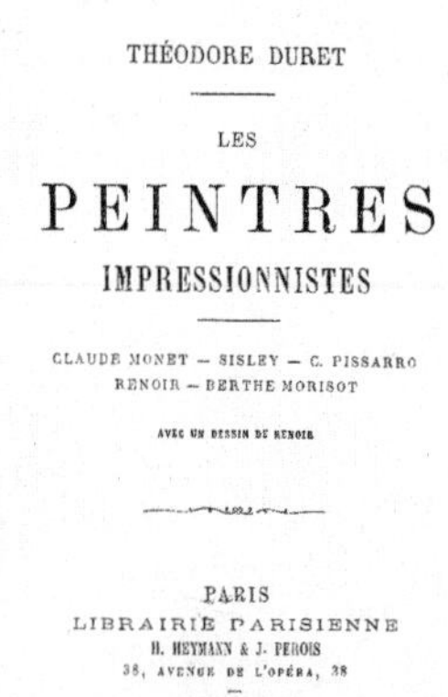

THÉODORE DURET

LES

PEINTRES

IMPRESSIONNISTES

CLAUDE MONET — SISLEY — C. PISSARRO
RENOIR — BERTHE MORISOT

AVEC UN DESSIN DE RENOIR

PARIS
LIBRAIRIE PARISIENNE
H. HEYMANN & J. PEROIS
38, AVENUE DE L'OPÉRA, 38

Mai 1878

he chose a drawing by Renoir to illustrate it. The drawing was done after the painting *Lise*, which Duret owned.

Renoir himself was not particularly happy to be classed among the "Impressionists" or "Intransigents": "I never wanted to play the martyr, and if my paintings had not been rejected by the Salon I would certainly have continued sending them.... I have always believed, and continue to believe, that I am only doing what others, and betters, before me have done," he later said.

In 1878, encouraged by Duret and his new patrons, notably the Charpentiers, he returned to the Salon, again modestly labeling himself a student of Gleyre, with the painting *The Café*. In 1879 he sent four portraits to the Salon and, like Cézanne, Morisot, and Sisley, contributed nothing to the fourth Impressionist

Théodore Duret was portrayed by Manet, Whistler, and Edouard Vuillard—which in itself demonstrates the breadth of his artistic relationships. He may be the only critic who supported Manet and the Impressionist painters early on (witness the frontispiece of his 1878 brochure with a reproduction of Renoir's *Lise*) and who also recognized the genius of Cézanne, Vincent van Gogh, Paul Gauguin, and Toulouse-Lautrec.

Referring to the works by Renoir in his possession, Duret wrote in 1878, "I doubt that any other painter has ever interpreted the woman in as seductive a manner. Renoir's light and rapid brush lends her grace, suppleness, ease, renders her skin transparent, colors her cheeks and lips with a rosy luster. Renoir's women are enchantresses." Happily for other artists, Duret's literary enthusiasm translated into purchases of their works as well, although at friendly prices (or even paid in cognac, the source of the family fortune), and Renoir, like the others, knew where to write for help in a pinch, as illustrated by the envelope reproduced opposite.

Curiously, a little more than a decade after portraying *The Clown*, Renoir painted another circus scene (*Two Little Circus Girls*, 1879, left) using a similar composition. While it was not listed in the catalogue, it was shown at the seventh Impressionist exhibition. Angelina and Francisca Wartenberg, the two young jugglers pictured here, performed at the Cirque Fernando on the Boulevard Rochechouart in Paris, not far from Renoir's studio. The same circus (which became the Cirque Medrano before it vanished) inspired Degas's *Mlle. La La at the Cirque Fernando*, Seurat's *The Circus*, and several works by Toulouse-Lautrec.

exhibition, as no one who had paintings at the Salon was allowed to show there. This strategy brought him luck and marked the beginning of a new phase in the artist's career.

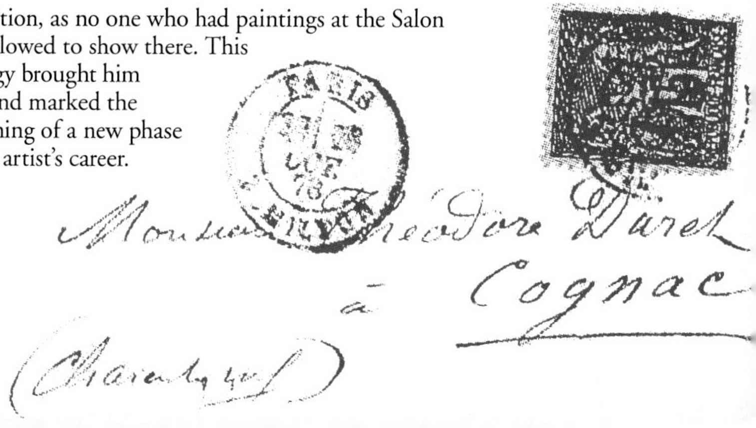

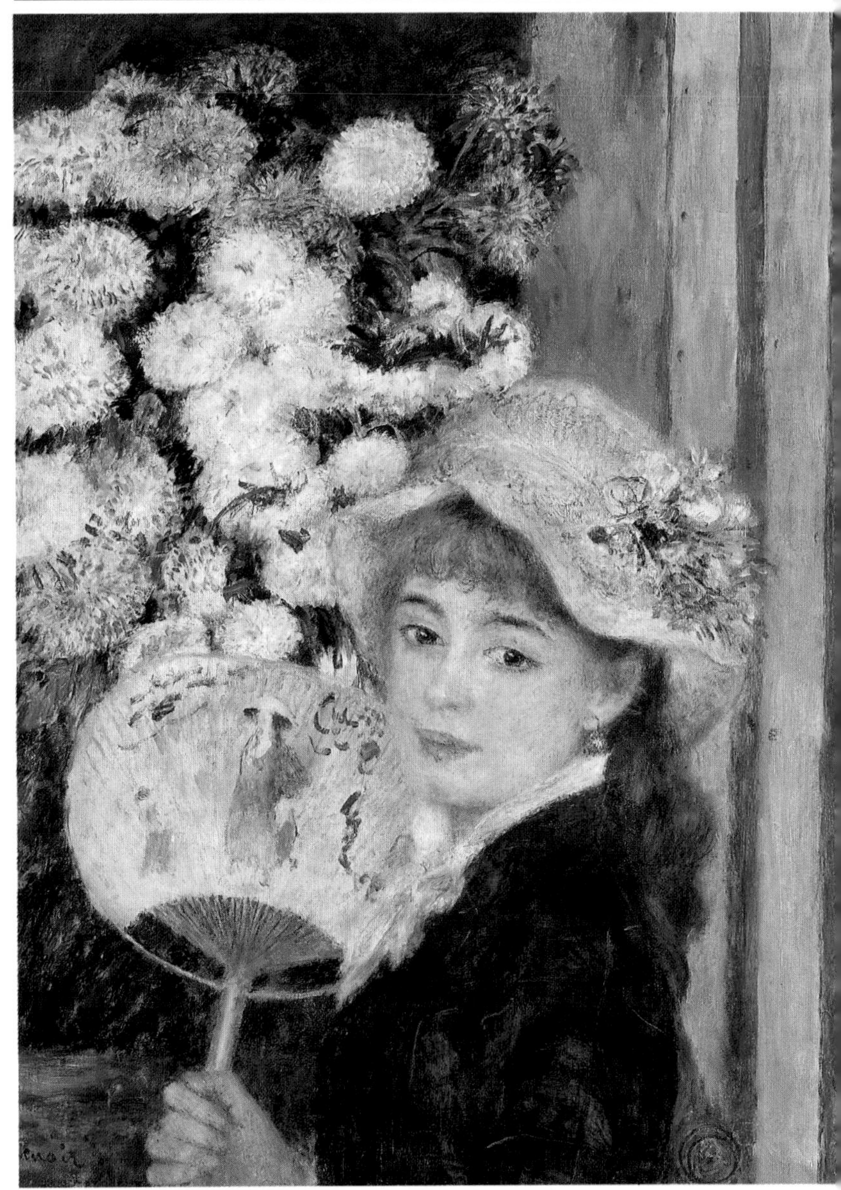

"Renoir has had a great success at the Salon. Good for him, I think he's made it, poverty is so difficult!"

Letter from Camille Pissarro
to Eugène Murer
27 May 1879

CHAPTER III

SUCCESS AND MATURITY

Of all the Impressionists, Renoir was the least affected by the craze for things Japanese that so strongly marked this generation of artists. Nevertheless, by placing a cheap Japanese fan in the hands of his young model (probably the actress Jeanne Samary) in 1881, for once he gave in to the fashion, painting a "Japanese Parisian."

In around 1876 or 1877, Renoir made his first *Portrait of Madame Georges Charpentier* (above), which she placed above the mantel in her drawing room (left). For one of her many dinner parties, which brought together the cream of Paris's intellectual, political, and artistic elite, she had Renoir draw a menu (below).

"The Most Devoted of Painters-in-Waiting"

Renoir owed his success at the Salon of 1879 chiefly to one person, Mme. Charpentier, whose portrait he showed there. Marguerite Charpentier was married to Georges Charpentier, publisher of Gustave Flaubert, Daudet, Zola, the Goncourt brothers, Maupassant, and Joris-Karl Huysmans. She was the offspring of a solid bourgeois family, her father having been jeweler to the imperial court before he was ruined in the fall of the Second Empire.

In her dwelling on the Rue de Grenelle, Mme.

Charpentier held a salon of a decidedly republican cast. However, its main theme was literary, as it united all the authors that her husband published. While it was a high-toned gathering, it was not stuffy, and its habitués found it entertaining. It brought together actresses of the moment, like Jeanne Samary, as well as personalities like Yvette Guilbert, a café-concert singer immortalized by Degas and Toulouse-Lautrec, or the composer Jules Massenet. Numerous artists were welcomed, ranging from Jean-Jacques Henner, whom no one could accuse of avant-garde tendencies, to Manet, a great admirer of the hostess's sister, Isabelle, and Monet, Sisley, and, especially, Renoir, who became the "painter-in-waiting" to the Charpentiers.

Both of the Charpentiers contributed to spreading the renown of their protégé, in different ways. Georges first bought paintings by Renoir at the Impressionist auction of 1875 and soon gave him various commissions for portraits and decorations, paying in advance with no hesitation, just as he had with Monet and Sisley. Marguerite used all the advantages of her salon to benefit Renoir. In addition, Renoir painted several portraits of her—the first of which had been exhibited in 1876 (it is now in the Musée d'Orsay in Paris)—and her children, Georgette, born in 1872, and Paul, born 1875. The large work *Portrait of Madame Charpentier and Her Children*,

Marguerite Charpentier was a strong personality. Not content merely to give dinner parties for her publisher husband's authors or well-known republican politicians, she invited such artists, actors, and popular singers as Yvette Guilbert and later Aristide Bruant (whose vocabulary shocked author Edmond de Goncourt, a regular). At her salon, Renoir met the young actress Jeanne Samary, whose career was just beginning to take off. The large standing portrait he made of her in 1878 (left)—which followed a small bust portrait, as he had done with Mme. Charpentier—contributed to Renoir's success at the official Salon of 1879. The many people Mme. Charpentier introduced to Renoir resulted in numerous portrait commissions, which finally gave the painter a measure of financial security. They also gave this son of a tailor the opportunity to create a network of relationships that would have an important impact on his career.

The large *Portrait of Madame Charpentier and Her Children* (1878, left), which created a stir at the Salon of 1879, shows Marguerite with her daughter, Georgette, and her son, Paul (dressed as a girl, as was customary). Paul posed a few months later with his dog for a photograph (above) wearing short hair and bathing garb. In his book *Le Temps Retrouvé* (The Past Recaptured), Proust devoted a long description to this painting, although he disliked Mme. Charpentier. He marveled at this "luscious painting comparable to Titian's most beautiful compositions" and claimed that the work of Renoir, like no other artist's, captured perfectly "the poetry of an elegant home and exquisite attire."

shown at the Salon of 1879, brought Renoir fame.

"He Has Returned to the Bosom of the Church"

It must be emphasized how much that composition broke with the conventions of fashionable portraits of the time. The artist's younger brother, Edmond, who became a journalist and collaborated on *La Vie Moderne*, the periodical started by Charpentier in 1879, made a special point of the fact that this rendition of a young woman and her children had been executed "in her home, without moving the furnishings from their usual places, without doing anything to highlight one part of the painting over another." This was very much the reverse of contemporary official portraits, in which the model was often placed in a fictive setting and given props to bolster his or her image. Here, on the contrary, aside from the subject itself, the viewer's attention is drawn by the expressive richness of the painting surface. The sheen of the children's flesh tones and hair, the luster of the textiles, the texture of the materials are all carefully rendered, but the painter carries the eye to less-detailed areas, to swaths of simplified color, to sections simply sketched in.

The Charpentiers' connections ensured the painting a prominent spot in the Salon, although they could not shield it from the barbs of the critics, who treated the subject with respect while offering their own kind of welcome to the return of the prodigal son. "Let us not pick a quarrel with M. Renoir, he has

Charpentier's publishing house (its offices on the Rue de Grenelle are shown above in a photograph taken at the turn of the century) started out as an outlet for inexpensive books. Georges Charpentier (left), the son of the founder, had the distinction of publishing Flaubert, the Goncourt brothers, Zola, Daudet, and Huysmans before going bankrupt; he earned a reputation as a warm and generous man. Renoir humorously expressed his gratitude to his patron in a sketch he added at the bottom of a letter to Charpentier (opposite above), showing the painter, mad with joy, leaping on the mailman who has arrived with a money order.

returned to the bosom of the Church: Let us welcome him back, ignore his composition, and speak only of the color," benevolently asserted critic Arthur Baignières in the very serious *Gazette des Beaux-Arts*; he had previously derided Renoir. It was generally agreed that Renoir was a gifted colorist and a terrible draftsman.

Charles Ephrussi, Patron

It was no accident that the *Gazette* managed a kind word for Renoir. Its owner, Charles Ephrussi, had gotten to know Renoir through Théodore Duret. The heir of a Jewish banking family originally from Odessa, Ephrussi was an art historian in love with the work of Dürer. Very up-to-date with the Parisian artistic circles of his day, he defended Degas and Monet, bought their works, and used his family and professional ties from Paris to Vienna and Berlin to help attract other buyers.

He extended his patronage to Renoir, who received many portrait commissions through his offices. (Renoir had asked Mme. Charpentier permission to show her portrait to Ephrussi before its publication.) Among

Elisabeth and Alice Cahen d'Anvers (portrait 1881, left) were the daughters of a banker whom Charles Ephrussi had introduced to Renoir. It seems that the fee for the picture was late in coming, and Renoir, letting drop a familiar bit of anti-Semitism, wrote to Deudon, "As to the Cahens' 1500 francs, if I may say so, I find it a bit stingy. Such meanness is unbecoming. I will definitely keep away from Jews from now on." The Cahen family was disappointed with the painting and relegated it to the servants' quarters.

them is Renoir's portrait of the Cahen girls, a "modern" portrait, rivaling the proven, universally admired formulas of a Léon Bonnat and other painters trapped in this mode. Uncomfortable in this role, and unsuited to be a society painter, Renoir's anti-Semitism came to the fore.

On the other hand, the painter formed much more solid relations with a different circle, composed of Protestant financiers. Duret probably brought Renoir together with another collector also linked with Ephrussi, Charles Deudon.

Paul Berard (left, in a portrait by Renoir of 1880) split his time between his Château de Wargemont near Dieppe (below), where Renoir made extended visits, and his town house on the Rue Pigalle in Paris. Like his wife, a friend of Mme. Charpentier's, he greatly admired Renoir's painting and commissioned from him a series of portraits of his many children. On the birth of Berard's daughter Lucie in July 1880, Renoir made a sketch of the new father (opposite above) in a letter and added, "Congratulations on my new model; I was hoping for twins.... After all, painting comes first!"

Renoir at the Château de Wargemont

Charles Deudon, who had inherited mines in Wales, purchased *The Dancer* in 1878. He was a friend of the man who would become one of Renoir's main patrons, Paul Berard. A man of independent means, Berard sampled a diplomatic career and then divided his time between Paris and his property near Dieppe. Renoir enjoyed the hospitality at the Château de Wargemont many times at the beginning of the 1880s, and his warm reception proved favorable to his painting. For Paul Berard, Renoir made a series of family portraits, and he enjoyed decorating the door panels and fireplace surrounds of the 18th-century Berard country house with flora and fowl. The two men corresponded often; Renoir did not hide his problems, and Berard regretted being unable

to do more to make his protégé's painting accepted.

Besides this group of patrons, Renoir found help from his dealer, Durand-Ruel, who began buying his paintings on a regular basis starting in 1881.

Renoir's unaccustomed financial security in this period allowed him the luxury of working on various projects that had no guaranteed buyer—such as large-format paintings that could represent him in the Salon—and of traveling.

While visiting the Normandy coast, he began a painting that would be exhibited in the Salon of 1880, *Mussel Fishers at Berneval*. The large-format composition tended toward realism by virtue of its subject, although Renoir did not exploit the social misery inherent in it. "There are no poor people in painting," he said. His lyrical, poetic rendition of the fisherwoman and her children evokes a folkloric sentimentality highly cherished in official circles. However, Renoir left his mark in the intensity of the colors and the airy and luminous space that bathes the figures.

Renoir's *Mussel Fishers at Berneval* (1879, above) already shows his changing style.

The painter's brother Edmond Renoir, a journalist and author of a book on fishing, may have inspired the drawing below.

The Charm of the Boating Party

After about 1879, the painter went back to the banks of the Seine, at Asnières and Chatou as well as Nogent-sur-Marne, depicting, in a distant echo of the scene at La Grenouillère, men who took to the water in boats and their attractive companions. These visions of summer, with their brilliant blues and oranges,

Oarsmen at Chatou (1879, left), a subject that evokes the novels of Maupassant, became a favorite theme of Renoir from 1879. Working regularly in the open air unleashed the brightness of the artist's palette.

Located on an island in the Seine across from Chatou, the Fournaise restaurant (below) was a central gathering place for boaters. Renoir painted his great *Luncheon of the Boating Party* from its terrace, visible on the left of the building.

signaled a stylistic evolution that would culminate in the painting *Luncheon of the Boating Party* of 1880–1.

It seems likely that this painting, sold in February 1881 to Durand-Ruel, had been begun during the summer of 1880. Renoir portrayed a boating party reveling on the terrace of the Fournaise restaurant, a popular spot on the island of Chiard at Chatou that Maupassant described in *La Femme de Paul* (Paul's Mistress). Renoir frequented the place himself and painted a series of portraits of the owner, Alphonse Fournaise, and his family. In a letter to Paul Berard, Renoir wrote, "I'm at Chatou…and I'm doing a painting of oarsmen that I have been longing to do for ages.

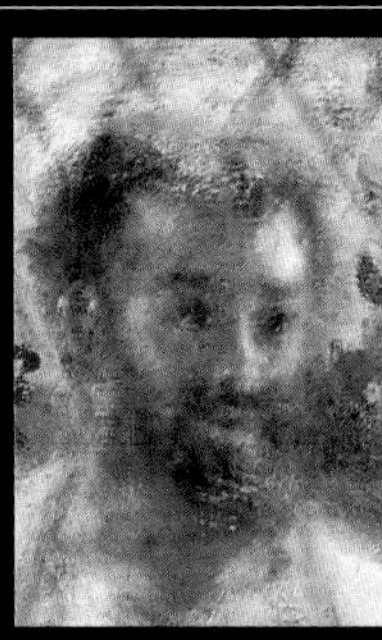

A Modern Genre Scene

The same model, one M. de Lauradour, posed for both *The Luncheon* (c. 1879, left) and *The Rowers' Lunch* (c. 1880, detail above; entire work on title page), depicting oarsmen and their companions, implying that the picture share the same milieu. Here, the intimate scene tempts one to make a "reading" in the naturalis vein of a Maupassant novel. Contemporary critics constantly interpreted paintings in this literary way. Renoir, in contrast, saw himself as reviving the genre scene, made famous by the 17th-century Dutch or the 18th-century French school, firmly fixing it to his own time with the details of the table setting, the attire o the characters, and the ordinary wall decoration.

Luncheon of the Boating Party

Of all Renoir's friends and models who posed for *Luncheon of the Boating Party* (1880–1) only two can be positively identified: the oarsman leaning against the balustrade at left is the son of Alphonse Fournaise, who owned the establishment, and the young woman in front of him playing with the little dog is Aline Charigot, a young dressmaker and Renoir's future wife. What can be said confidently is that in deliberately bringing together a variety of men's hats—cap, straw hat, bowler, top hat—Renoir indicated the social mixture that made up the animated gathering. Contemporary chroniclers let it be understood that the Fournaise restaurant—Maupassant called it the "phalanstery of the oarsmen"—was a noisy and rowdy place. Since painting *At the Inn of Mother Anthony* and *Dancing at the Moulin de la Galette*, Renoir apparently decided to play down the cruder aspects of reality.

"I'm getting somewhat older and I don't want to delay this little feast which I won't be able to afford later on. I don't know if I will finish it, but I've confided my woes to Deudon, who thinks I'm doing the right thing even if the enormous expenditures I'm making prevent me from finishing my painting. It's all a step forward: One must try things beyond one's reach from time to time."

The work went slowly, as he explained to Berard a bit later: "I must have another go at this wretched painting because a high-society dame had the nerve to come to Chatou and want to pose [for it]; that cost me two weeks and, in short, today I scraped her off and… I no longer know where I am with it, just that I'm becoming more and more upset."

A New Style

None of the preparatory drawings remain. Even without them, a close look at the painting itself shows numerous repainted details and leads to the conclusion that Renoir reworked the canvas extensively, altering the poses of the characters or adjusting the tonal values as the work progressed.

Luncheon of the Boating Party has almost exactly the same dimensions as *Dancing at the Moulin de la Galette,*

Renoir added to the note below (to an unknown recipient) a list of colors—flake white, chrome yellow, Naples yellow, yellow ocher, burnt sienna, vermilion, madder lake, Veronese green, emerald green, cobalt blue, and ultramarine—that corresponds to his palette in the 1880s, from which black is missing. The flat brushes are meant for oil painting; the sable brushes (which Renoir characteristically misspelled, labeling them "pinceaux de Marthe" instead of "pinceau de martre") used for watercolors eventually were also employed for very fine details.

l'ocre jaune le jaune de Naples
et la terre de Sienne ne sont
que des tons intermédiaires. donc
on peut les passer puisque vous
pouvez les faire avec les autres couleurs,

Pinceaux de Marthe

Brosses, plates en soie.

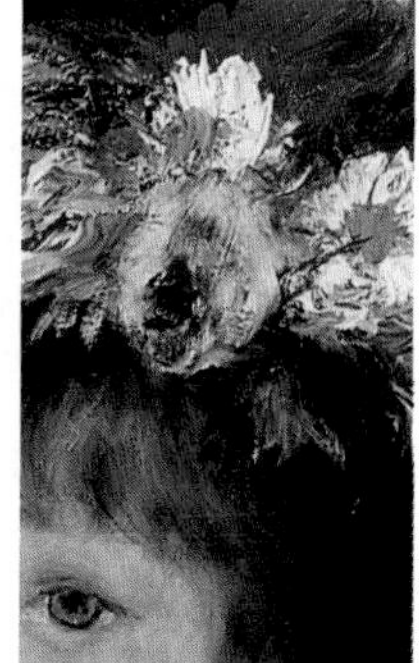

which underlines both the similarity of their subjects—a crowd outdoors—and the remarkable difference in their styles, even though they are separated by only about five years. In the later painting, the palette is lighter and the composition more assured, the artist having simplified the perspective and, especially, used color contrasts to define the figures' clearly individualized features. The pains Renoir took to clarify the outlines seem to be in response to criticism leveled against all of the Impressionists for leaving their objects fuzzy and sketchy. At the same time, Renoir had been heavily engaged in painting portraits, which forced him to look for individuality in his figures.

It was not this magnificent painting that represented

"'The two sisters,' says the catalogue. 'And your sister [sucks eggs]!,' says the public"—this is all one critic could find to say about the painting above, which has since become one of the best known and best loved by Renoir. The models are sitting on the terrace of the Fournaise restaurant, and the work is now known more by the site than by the sisters: *On the Terrace* (1881).

Renoir at the Salon of 1881 but two portraits (not definitely identified) that Renoir, about to go traveling, left to Ephrussi to pick out. Like Monet and Sisley, he again declined to show with the Impressionists. He explained to Durand-Ruel that the decision was based solely on commercial considerations: "There are in Paris," he wrote, "barely fifteen collectors capable of appreciating a painter unless he has exhibited at the Salon."

The Light of Northern Africa

Renoir's first trip abroad took him to Algeria. Exhausted after working all winter and finishing the double portrait of the Cahen girls, Renoir left Paris at the end of February 1881 in search of sun and exoticism, as had one of his favorite artists, Delacroix. The letters he

Starting in 1880, Paul Durand-Ruel began to buy pictures from Renoir on a regular basis, even though the two had never made up a contract. The dealer's account book (below), which recorded the day-to-day operations of the business, gives the status of items bought from Renoir in May 1882 on his return from a long journey that took him through Italy, to L'Estaque, and finally to Algeria, where he convalesced from a severe case of pneumonia. The titles of his paintings give an idea of his itinerary; the prices are coded, following the custom of the day.

1882

23 Mai

Remis à Mr Eual p. être vendu Salle 8 (Vente du 26 Mai)

1193 vendus à Mr Lapointe

1 tableau de Lépine No 3589
1 " " 3590
1 " Maincent 3591
1 " Chintreuil 3592
1 " Lefèbvre 3593
1 " Beaumetz 3594
1 " Desbrosses 3595

acheté à Mr Renoir

× 1 tableau Campagne en Calabre No 2397 tss
1 " l'Estaque près Marseille No 2398 tss
1 " oliviers à l'Estaque No 2399 tss
1 " Marine à Capri No 2400 nss
1 " Jeune Kabyle No 2401 ass
1 " Italienne (tête de profil) No 2402 nss
1 " Jeune fille à l'orange No 2403 tss
1 algérienne assise No 2404 tss

Ensemble nsss

Algerian Landscape: The Ravine of the Wild Woman (1881, above). To his great regret, Renoir was able only to sketch some typical faces (below).

wrote to his friends and patrons demonstrate his love of the country.

In the outskirts of Algiers, where he stayed, he found picturesque motifs and wonderful vegetation, "a mixture of prickly pear and aloes." The vegetation forms the subject of *Algerian Landscape: The Ravine of the Wild Woman*, named for a café-restaurant on the spot where Renoir painted, outside of Algiers. Its deep ultramarine blues suggest shadows that contrast with the bursts of red, orange, and emerald green. Renoir was, however, disappointed that he could not paint as many figures as he wished because the models would back away at the last moment. It was not until his second trip, in the spring of 1882, that he managed to draw several figures.

That summer, back in France, Renoir spent most of his time on the coast of Normandy, where he experienced the opposite of the Berards' warm welcome at the home of Mme. Emile Blanche, wife of the

Although today the painting at left is known as *Mother and Child*, Renoir never called it that, and the young woman holding the child seems a bit young to be the mother. It is certain that it was painted in Naples, probably in November 1881. By this stage on his Italian journey, after having visited Venice and Rome, Renoir was totally captivated by the country. His son Jean recorded his reactions: "I became weary of the skillfulness displayed by the Michelangelos and the Berninis: too much cloth, too many folds, too much muscle! I like painting that has an air of the eternal about it…but, it goes without saying, an eternity of all the days lived on the next street corner.… The Italians don't deserve any praise for creating great painting. They have only to look around them. The Italian streets are chock-full of pagan gods and biblical figures. Every woman who nurses a baby is one of Raphael's Madonnas." Renoir's work could well be taken for a modern version of that Italian master's madonnas.

famous psychiatrist. He had been invited to Dieppe to work with her son, the painter Jacques-Emile Blanche, but in the stiff, reserved household, the artist's rough manners and nervous tics were badly received.

A Trip to Italy

At the end of October 1881, Renoir was off again, this time for Italy: "I've suddenly become a traveler, overtaken by the desire to see the Raphaels.… I've done the North, and I'm going to go down the entire boot."

The first of November found him at Venice, where he left for Rome, probably by way of Padua and Florence. In Rome, he marveled at Raphael's frescoes. "They are full of knowledge and wisdom" were his exact words. From the end of November he stayed in Naples, making many trips to the museum, where the paintings from Pompeii particularly attracted him.

He ended the year at Capri. There, he learned that Manet had been named a chevalier of the Legion of Honor—his first sign of official recognition—and he hastened to offer congratulations.

Parisian friends who, like Renoir, admired Richard Wagner sent the painter to Palermo, where Wagner was working on *Parsifal.* The maestro finally granted him an interview on 14 January 1882 and a sitting of thirty-five minutes the following day. This historic meeting, of which Renoir gave a comical account (see pages 134–7), produced a portrait that the illustrious subject thought resembled "a Protestant minister," as, in fact, it does.

In Italy Renoir acted the well-behaved tourist-painter, and he laughed at himself when he found himself in Venice painting the Doges' palace: "That had never been done before, I think. We were at least six in single file." In Naples, he painted Mount Vesuvius (below), but he could not keep from associating that symbol of antiquity with the most obvious signs of modernity, the carriages that ran next to the sea, which was dotted with traditionally rigged boats.

Renoir and Cézanne

Soon afterward, Renoir returned to France via Naples and Marseilles, ending at L'Estaque, where he worked

Since it was never finished, it is difficult to date the *Nude* (left) that the sculptor Auguste Rodin bought after seeing it at a collector's home; no doubt he was seduced by the free and simplified lines that call to mind his own watercolors. The importance given to line and the range of tones used seem to place it with the work of the early 1880s.

Seated Bather (opposite left) has often been dated to 1885, but the brushwork seems freer than that of work known to be from that period. The rocks in the background and the blue-green sea recall the canvases painted in Guernsey in 1883 that Renoir planned to use for future compositions. It may be the case that this bather was painted shortly after the artist's return from the Channel Islands. Here, Renoir was taking up in a different setting the theme of bathers by the sea that he had begun with *Blonde Bather* under the Mediterranean sun during his trip to Italy.

beside Cézanne. It would be hard to imagine two more different personalities. However, Cézanne, who had always studied and copied the great artists of the past and considered the Louvre "a good book to consult" even while preaching the close observation of nature, had something in common with the man who was "overtaken by the desire to see the Raphaels." Cézanne's influence clearly made Renoir pay more attention to the structure of his compositions and led him to simplify, a direction already suggested by the monumental painting he had seen in Italy.

Renoir fell seriously ill with pneumonia while with Cézanne. His doctor advised him to convalesce in Algeria, and he spent most of March and April there, painting throughout his trip.

The Lesson of Italy

Renoir was represented at the Salon of 1882 by a portrait, passing up the seventh exhibition of the Impressionists. However, he could not prevent Durand-Ruel, who had organized the Impressionist show, from contributing twenty-five canvases from his own collection, including *Luncheon of the Boating Party*.

He spent the summer at Normandy again, where he saw the Berards, the Blanches, and, with Durand-Ruel, Monet, who was working in Pourville. His friends noticed a change in his style when they saw a *Bather* that Renoir said he had painted on a boat to Capri, under the sun. He did not identify the model, but the young woman herself, Aline Charigot, later confided to Julie Manet, Berthe Morisot's daughter, that she had taken a trip to Italy with Renoir. At the time, Renoir did not tell a soul, and he carefully hid all trace of their relationship for many years.

A comparison of this *Bather* and the study *Nude in Sunlight* shown at the second Impressionist exhibition of 1876 reveals the distance the artist had traveled.

Blonde Bather (1881, below) in all likelihood is the painting that Renoir painted in Capri with the very young Aline Charigot as the model. (Can some meaning be read into the gold ring the sitter wears?) Although Renoir and Aline were not married until 1890, the young woman later referred to this trip to Italy as her "honeymoon." This painting is one of the first to signal the artist's return to a classicism inspired by Italian art and the memory of Ingres.

CATALOGUE

DE

L'EXPOSITION DES ŒUVRES

DE

P.-A. RENOIR

Renoir's first solo exhibition (catalogue above) took place in April 1883 at Durand-Ruel's gallery. The owner's sons Charles and Georges (below), as well as Joseph, soon became partners.

Instead of a hazy figure under a dappled light that breaks up the forms, this nude has a generous, monumental presence, set down clearly with a well-defined outline. The transposition has been sensitively achieved; neither boat nor bay of Naples can be seen—there is only a classical theme in an undefined landscape. The canvas seems to correspond to a goal mentioned by the artist in an 1882 letter to Mme. Charpentier: to rediscover "that nobility and simplicity of the ancients."

Variations on the Dance

After his Italian trip, Renoir began three large canvases that he finished in the spring of 1883: *Dance at Bougival* and its two pendants, *Dance in the City* and *Dance in*

the Country, which are related to *Luncheon of the Boating Party* through their theme and style. For *Dance at Bougival* and *Dance in the City* Renoir used a young model named Marie Clémentine Valadon. Encouraged by Degas, she would later become a painter herself, under the name Suzanne Valadon. In December 1883, she gave birth to a boy, Maurice Utrillo, whose father, she sometimes hinted, could have been Renoir. In *Dance in the Country*, the dancer in the arms of Renoir's friend Paul Lhôte is probably Aline Charigot. The two pendant *Dances* were exhibited in a rented space on Boulevard de la Madeleine in April 1883 on the occasion of Renoir's first solo exhibition, organized by Durand-Ruel. The dealer had decided to show "his" painters in succession—Boudin, Monet, Pissarro, Sisley—a new concept.

Dance at Bougival was shown, also by Durand-Ruel but in a London gallery, in a group of ten works by Renoir. This was not Renoir's London debut; his dealer methodically explored all the markets, so that the same year he had paintings by Renoir displayed in Boston and Berlin as well.

In 1883 Renoir created a series of works on the theme of the dance. *Dance at Bougival* (overleaf left), which shows Suzanne Valadon, was reproduced in a small print by Renoir around 1890 (below). To the world of the boaters, evoked once more in *Dance in the Country* (overleaf center), very likely with Aline Charigot, Renoir contrasted his *Dance in the City* (overleaf right), with Suzanne Valadon—a taffeta dress against one of cotton or cretonne.

Jersey, Guernsey, and the Côte d'Azur

Renoir traveled again in 1883. At the end of the summer he went to the Channel Islands, first to Jersey, then to Guernsey, where he stayed for a month, gathering "canvases and documents to make paintings with in Paris…a source of genuine and graceful motifs that I can use," as he told Durand-Ruel.

At the end of the year he accompanied Monet to the Côte d'Azur; together they traveled from Marseilles to Monte Carlo by stages, straying as far as Genoa by way of Bordighera. Although they were gone only two weeks, both artists managed to paint. The "painter of figures," as Renoir described himself, happily made studies of the "pretty landscapes, with distant horizons and the loveliest colors…. Unhappily,

our meager palette wasn't up to it. The beautiful russet tones of the sea came out muddy on the canvas no matter how many pains we took." They next visited Cézanne, who had holed himself up in the south of France.

Renoir went back to Paris in time to see the posthumous exhibition of Manet's work at the Ecole des Beaux-Arts and to celebrate his success, although he regretted being unable to "treat myself to a memento of a lost friend" on sale in Manet's studio.

Guernsey (above) reminded Renoir of a "landscape by Watteau." In a letter to Durand-Ruel (a section is reproduced below), the painter professed himself enchanted by this "source of genuine and graceful motifs."

Renoir with His Family

Around this time, Renoir left his apartment on the Rue Saint-Georges for one closer to Montmartre. He had a studio at 37, Rue de Laval (today Rue Victor-Massé). Aline Charigot gave birth to their first son, Pierre, at 18, Rue Houdon, on 21 March 1885. Gustave Caillebotte, one

rien de plus amusant en
circulant dans ces rochers
que de surprendre des jeunes
filles entrain de s'apprêter
pour le bain, et qui quoique
anglaises ne s'effarouchent
pas autrement. J'espère

of Renoir's few friends to know of Renoir's family, was the child's godfather.

This change in his life—at the age of forty-four—corresponds to a period of questioning and stylistic mutations exemplified by the large painting *The Bathers*, shown in the spring of 1887.

The Umbrellas (opposite) has the peculiarity of having been painted in two styles: the right side around 1881, the left and upper portion in the "dry" style of 1885.

"Around 1883, a crack in my work opened up. I had gone the limit with Impressionism and had come to the realization that I didn't know how to paint or draw. In short, I had reached an impasse."

Renoir to Ambroise Vollard
in *Renoir*, 1920

CHAPTER IV

THE INGRESQUE PERIOD

Among all the nudes of the experimental period that has been called Renoir's "Ingresque period," *Bather Arranging Her Hair* (1885) displays the sharpest outlines. The light tonalities of the painting call to mind the frescoes Renoir had so admired in Italy. However, the artist could not resist animating the landscape around the polished curves of the flesh with nervous brushstrokes.

Raphael or Ingres?

The time described as Renoir's Ingresque, or dry, period culminated in 1887 with the exhibition of his large painting *The Bathers*. It had its origins in the beginning of the 1880s, a time when all the Impressionists were seeking to renew their work. Renoir's style had undergone a profound transformation, which the trip to Italy only confirmed.

Renoir's letters make constant reference, especially after 1883, to the problems he was having in finishing any of his paintings to his satisfaction. He destroyed many of them, all the while resolutely continuing his quest. His questioning also took on a theoretical aspect.

In 1884 Renoir had dreamed of creating a new association of artists, the Société des Irrégularistes (Society of Irregularists), based on his old idea that modern society, with its emphasis on rules, was the source of all decadence. He wanted to publish a *Summary of the Grammar of the Arts*, but it never reached fruition. He thought that modern teaching methods had not managed to replace the old practice of apprenticeship in a master's studio; he felt this lack for himself, repeating over and over again his wish to become a good "worker" of painting, something his artisanal background had given him a glimpse of. This nostalgia for a vanished era was, in fact, common to the period, in progressive as well as reactionary circles, and Renoir did not have a coherent solution to suggest—except, implicitly, in his work.

Pierre, Renoir's first son, was born in March 1885. Throughout the following summer, spent at Essoyes, Renoir made many studies of Aline nursing the child (below). The painting above is also dated 1886.

Children's Afternoon at Wargemont

One of the earliest paintings to display clearly Renoir's new direction is a portrait he made of Paul Berard's daughters in 1884 called *Children's Afternoon at Wargemont*. It used the same format as *Luncheon of the Boating Party* and was only slightly smaller than *Portrait of Madame Charpentier and Her Children*, indicating the work's ambitious nature. The eye is initially struck

by the clear silhouettes of the figures, organized into a strongly decentralized composition, but it is soon diverted by the brilliant tones, few in number and essentially cold. The props are charged with the same intensity as the figures, which are highly simplified. The light is strong but even. The simple decorative rhythms of the composition may be meant to evoke Italy's great tradition of mural painting, from the ancient frescoes of Pompeii to Raphael and Tiepolo, which Renoir had just discovered in his haphazard survey.

His renewed interest in a firm and assured line could also have arisen from the paintings of Ingres in the Louvre, works that Renoir had always admired.

"The Bathers"

Renoir carried out his experiments using the nude, "one of the forms indispensable to art," he asserted to Julie Manet at the time. Around 1885, he began preparing for *The Bathers*. For the first time, an entire series of

Children's Afternoon at Wargemont (1884, above) was the most important commission Renoir received from Paul Berard. Painted at the Château de Wargemont, it portrays Berard's three daughters: Marthe, seated at right, is sewing; Lucie, the youngest, stands in front of Marthe holding her doll; and Marguerite, seated at left, is looking at an album. The painting's modernity derives as much from the simplicity with which the interior, at once elegant and countrified, is represented as from the bold harmonies of the figures and the decor.

drawings and studies for a large composition of Renoir's is known, which indicates that he had changed his work habits as well, placing more importance on his studio work. The composition was taken from a bas-relief, *Nymphs Bathing* (1668–70), by François Girardon that decorated a pool in the park of Versailles. The spirit of François Boucher's *Diana at the Bath* in the Louvre can also be discerned.

Girardon's *Nymphs Bathing* at Versailles (above) was cited in Renoir's day as a source of inspiration for *The Bathers.*

"One must paint according to one's own time. But it's at the museum that we get our feeling for painting, something that nature alone can't give us," said Renoir. The composition is also an homage to Ingres. The smooth surface, with its enameled and exquisitely finished touch, recalls that of the master and has nothing in

Renoir's *The Bathers* (above) attracted considerable criticism when it was exhibited in June 1887 at the gallery of Georges Petit, Durand-Ruel's rival.

common with the surface effects Renoir had sought ten years earlier. *The Bathers* expresses an ideal beauty completely divorced from historical or geographical context; it marks Renoir's independence from a naturalism that had up to this point remained the keynote of his compositions. His interest in decoration and the notion, dear to him, of the interdependence of the arts finally broke through in the subtitle to the work: *Essay in Decorative Painting.* This commentary could also be interpreted as a way to head off the critics (by stating that it was an experimental work) or as a bid for the official plum of which every artist dreams, to be awarded the task of creating a monumental decoration.

"I'm sympathetic to the effort given to experimentation; it is good to wish not to remain fixed in place. But [Renoir] has concerned himself only with line here; the figures stand out from one another clearly with no consideration given to harmonies; as a result, it's incomprehensible."

Pissarro
14 May 1887

Numerous studies for *The Bathers* were made. Some were simple sketches, others, like *Study of Splashing Nude* (above), were more elaborate drawings.

The Ingresque line and porcelain tones of *The Bathers* perplexed Renoir's patrons without winning him new converts from more conservative circles. Durand-Ruel tried to turn him from his new path. The dealer had suffered great losses in the resounding failure of France's major bank, the Union Générale, which almost brought him down with it. Renoir remained faithful to Durand-Ruel, but, like Monet and Pissarro, he tried to escape his domination by participating, beginning in 1886, in the International Exhibition of Painting and Sculpture. This exhibition was organized by a committee of artists and for several years had been held in the galleries of Durand-Ruel's rival, Georges Petit. This was where *The Bathers* was first shown to the public, in 1887.

Summer in the Country

Renoir continued to spend the summer in search of new motifs. In 1885 and 1886 he took his family northwest

During the summer of 1886, Renoir (shown below in a photograph of the period) rented the Maison Perrette at La Chapelle-Saint-Briac in Brittany and painted in the garden, using an extremely detailed technique reminiscent of that used for *The Bathers.* Mme. Renoir, Pierre, and a neighbor were portrayed in the painting at left.

of Paris, near Giverny, where Monet already lived and where he could meet with Cézanne again. In 1886 he made a "tour of northern Brittany" and stayed at La Chapelle-Saint-Briac long enough to do some painting. In 1888 and 1889 (the exact chronology here is unclear) Renoir made several visits to Cézanne in Aix-en-Provence and followed his host's example in painting Mont Sainte-Victoire, evoking "the dryness with the olive tree, which follows the weather, drab in dull weather, lively in the sunshine, silvery in the wind."

Essoyes: Working in the Country, Returning to a Suppler Style

In the autumn of 1885, Renoir visited Essoyes for the first time. Aline Charigot had been born in this village in the Aube, a region southeast of Paris. He returned many times and finally bought a house there. After becoming the head of a family, the bohemian who had "loved the kind of set-up that you could move in a handcart, and which might be left behind altogether" ended up a homeowner. Renoir enjoyed this rustic milieu, whose inhabitants found him surprising, and the house in

Essoyes, where he set up a studio, became a permanent part of his life.

While working at Essoyes, Renoir went back to a more supple style, bringing together line and color. "I have been chatting with Renoir for a long time. He confessed to me that everyone, Durand, old patrons, came complaining to him, deploring his efforts to escape from his romantic period," wrote Pissarro to his son Lucien in October 1888. Soon afterward, Renoir settled in at Essoyes with the aim, he said, of "rustifying [there] to flee the expensive models of Paris [and paint] laundresses, or rather washerwomen, on the banks of the river." He told Durand-Ruel, "I think it will work this time. It's very soft and colored but clear."

The presence of little Pierre in *The Washerwomen* helps date it to about 1888, a time when Renoir, while retaining the clear tones of his Ingresque palette, gradually returned to a softer delineation of volumes and contours, as he explained to Durand-Ruel. Renoir painted this canvas, which evokes a rural, idealized world populated by active women, in Essoyes, where Aline had grown up; Renoir later told his son Jean that he only appreciated women "who do not know how to read." Renoir liked living at Essoyes among the peasants, who first found him startling but were quick to adopt him. Jean Renoir wrote at length about family life at Essoyes. The painter is buried there, in the village cemetery, near his loved ones.

"Women are best off when they kneel to clean the floor, light the fire, or do the washing; these movements benefit their stomachs."

Renoir
in Jean Renoir
Renoir, My Father, 1958

Encounter among three creators: Degas took the photograph at left, his reflection visible in the mirror behind Renoir, seated, and Mallarmé, standing, who posed "fifteen minutes in the light of nine oil lamps," according to poet Paul Valéry. The session took place in 1895 at 40, Rue de Villejust, the home of Julie Manet, whose mother, Berthe Morisot, had just died. Morisot had introduced Renoir and Mallarmé. The painter often confessed that he did not understand much of Mallarmé's poetry, although he greatly enjoyed the man's company. For his part, Mallarmé admired Renoir's painting and made an effort to make it better known. Also, Degas and Renoir often met and conversed at Morisot's apartment and later at her daughter's, but their friendship was not close, as was Renoir's with Monet and Cézanne; the two had little in common besides painting. They had a falling-out at the end of 1898 when Renoir sold a Degas pastel left him by Caillebotte.

The End of Impressionism?

Renoir did not participate in the eighth and last of the Impressionist exhibitions, in 1886. Only a few of the original group, notably Pissarro and Degas, showed paintings at this point, and it was mostly the younger artists, especially Gauguin and Seurat, who drew critical attention. However, in 1884, at Monet's suggestion, the Impressionists took to meeting once a month at the restaurant of the Café Riche. This gathering of the early artists and patrons was a sentimental way to close ranks.

Around 1886 Renoir became a regular at the private soirees that Berthe Morisot, whose painting reveals his influence, began to hold in her Paris apartment on

Renoir painted *Berthe Morisot and Her Daughter, Julie* (left) in 1894. When Morisot died Julie (photograph above) was left an orphan at sixteen. With Monet, Mallarmé, and Degas, Renoir took part in the hanging of a posthumous exhibition of Morisot's work at Durand-Ruel's in 1896. Along with Mallarmé, Julie's tutor, Renoir looked after the girl, often taking her on family vacations to Brittany and giving her painting lessons. Julie spoke of him affectionately in her *Journal* and displayed admiration for his painting whenever she visited his studio.

the Rue de Villejust. That summer, he was her guest at Mézy, a small village near Mantes, just west of Paris. Renoir made several portraits of Julie Manet, including one with her mother in 1894. Berthe Morisot brought Renoir and the poet Stéphane Mallarmé together. Renoir painted a portrait of the poet and illustrated the frontispiece of a volume of *Pages* published in 1891. Mallarmé wrote for Renoir:

> Villa des Arts, near the Avenue
> De Clichy, Monsieur Renoir paints
> In front of a nude shoulder
> Anything but a blue haze.

"I have returned to the old painting, soft and light, for good.... It's nothing new, but it follows the style of 18th-century paintings.... (A lesser Fragonard)."

Renoir to Durand-Ruel
c. 1888

CHAPTER V
OFFICIAL RECOGNITION

Mallarmé convinced the director of the Beaux-Arts, Henri Roujon, to buy this version of *Young Girls at the Piano* (1892, left) for the State in 1892: "It is my feeling, as well as the unanimous opinion of everyone else, that you cannot be sufficiently congratulated on having chosen such a definitive, refreshing, bold work of maturity for a museum," wrote Mallarmé to Roujon.

"Idealist? Naturalist? Whatever You Like.… He Has Created Wonderful Bouquets of Women and Flowers"

At the beginning of the 1890s, Renoir painted peasants carrying out their tasks in the country or young women with the air of the city about them playing the piano, reading, chatting, or picking flowers. Although signs of the time—the end of the 19th century—are in evidence (the piano, hats, and the game of pushing hoops with a stick), Renoir apparently did not want to weigh his figures down with naturalistic details. The bucolic mood and tranquil harmony of these paintings recall both Corot's idyllic countrysides and the well-known outdoor entertainment scenes called "fêtes champêtres" of 18th-century French painting. Renoir himself mentioned the influence of the fêtes, and such references to tradition appear repeatedly throughout the rest of his career.

Renoir managed to work himself out of his "dry" period with these themes, returning to a surface that was suppler, sometimes velvety, more suited to the ideal world he depicted.

In addition, Renoir continued to paint nudes, his favored theme. In 1892, Nabi painter and theorist

The Apple Seller (c. 1890, above left) and *Gathering Flowers (In the Meadow)* (c. 1890, top right and detail above), illustrate perfectly what Renoir meant by a "suite of 18th-century paintings."

Maurice Denis accurately summed up the new spirit of Renoir's painting: "Idealist? Naturalist? Whatever you like. He has shown that he can confine himself to translating his own emotions, presenting all of nature and all of illusion with his own methods: Using the pleasures of his eyes, he has created wonderful bouquets of women and flowers."

New Critics, New Patrons

The admiration expressed by Maurice Denis, who, born in 1870, was just beginning his career, demonstrates that Renoir's work continued to attract the younger generation of artists and critics of the symbolist and decadent schools. Among the critics who wrote about Renoir were Albert Aurier, also one of the first to appreciate Van Gogh; novelists Teodor de Wyzewa, who, like Aurier, was close to symbolist circles, as well as Octave Mirbeau; and Thadée Natanson, one of the founders of *La Revue Blanche.*

Julie Manet was greatly taken with the double portrait of the daughters of painter, collector, and music lover Henri Lerolle, *Yvonne and Christine Lerolle at the Piano* (1897, below), which she saw in Renoir's studio in October 1897. She wrote in her *Journal*, "It's gorgeous. Christine [at right] has a delightful expression; although it's not a good likeness of Yvonne, her white dress is gorgeously painted. The background, with Degas's small dancers in pink with their pigtails and the races, is painted lovingly."

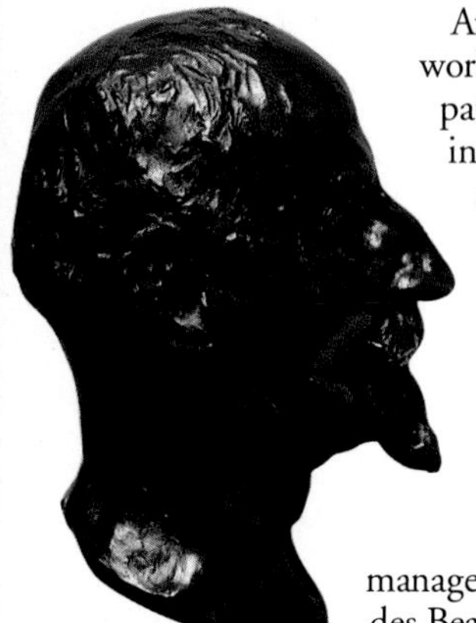

At the same time, Renoir's work was also attracting new patrons, most of whom took an interest in other Impressionist artists as well. They included Georges Viau, a Parisian dentist, and François Depeaux, a businessman from Rouen who owned *Summer* and *Dance at Bougival.* Although Depeaux was forced to sell his collection in 1906, he still managed to leave to Rouen's Musée des Beaux-Arts a select group of Impressionist paintings.

Unlike Renoir's other collectors, Paul Gallimard apparently did not have his portrait done by the artist. He is memorialized instead by a 1916 bust by Léon-Ernest Drivier (left) and a portrait of Eugène Carrière, in that painter's allusive style. In contrast, Renoir made at least two portraits of Mme. Gallimard. The exquisite one shown below dates from 1892.

Among all the collectors, the one with whom Renoir had the closest relationship was Paul Gallimard. Octave Mirbeau described him thus in 1900: "He collected books, paintings, and income." After buying works by Renoir at Durand-Ruel's in 1889, Gallimard soon befriended the artist, even taking him along on a trip to Madrid in 1892. He invited Renoir to his family estate in Bénerville (Normandy) and commissioned him to paint many portraits of his wife. Decorative projects were put in the works, although none would be realized.

The Château des Brouillards

At the end of 1889, Renoir and his family moved to 13, Rue Girardon in Montmartre, in a building surrounded by gardens with the poetic name Château des Brouillards (Foggy Castle). On 14 April 1890 he married Aline Charigot at the administrative office of the ninth arrondissement, making their son Pierre legitimate. Old friends served as witnesses—Franc-Lamy, Lhôte, Lestringuez, and the Italian painter Federico Zandomeneghi.

Even married, Renoir remained discreet about Aline's role in his life, to the amused curiosity of the solidly bourgeois Berthe Morisot. His family did become

Renoir was photographed sitting on the stoop of his studio at the Château des Brouillards in Montmartre (opposite) about 1895 by Martial Caillebotte, Gustave's brother.

the focus of his pictorial world, however, especially after the birth of his second son, Jean (the future filmmaker), on 15 September 1894. Georges Durand-Ruel, son of the dealer, as well as a dealer himself, stepped in as godfather, and Jeanne Baudot, the daughter of a doctor, was the godmother. She had become a student of Renoir's, and she would write a book of memoirs on the artist.

At this time, a cousin of Mme. Renoir's, Gabrielle Renard, came to live with the family to help care for Jean and run the household. She became Renoir's principal model until her marriage in 1914. A third son, Claude, was born at Essoyes on 4 August 1901.

Aside from their many sojourns at Essoyes, the Renoirs left Paris in the summer for Brittany or

Above: *The Artist's Son Jean Drawing,* painted in 1901.

Normandy, where Renoir continued to paint. Julie Manet stayed with the Renoirs many times.

Renoir aged prematurely. His face became partially paralyzed, and he already suffered from the early stages of rheumatism in his legs and his hands; it would become much worse.

Renoir at the Museum

The last decade of the century also brought Renoir official acknowledgment. While public recognition of his work was limited, he was not treated with the fierce ostracism of the early Impressionist days. At the end of 1891 or the beginning of 1892, Mallarmé and the critic Claude

Roger-Marx, who was in the administration of the Beaux-Arts, convinced the director, Henri Roujon, to buy a painting from Renoir on behalf of the State.

This was not the first time that the administration had shown interest in the artist. Roger-Marx had sought him out at the occasion of the Centennale, the retrospective exhibition of French art organized for the Paris World's Fair of 1889. At that time, the artist told him, "I find all my work terrible and it would make me feel infinitely worse to have it shown."

Then, in 1890 Renoir's friends appealed on his behalf to have him decorated by the State; he refused it. Monet wrote to Caillebotte at the time, "I congratulate him.... It would have been helpful to him, it is true, but now he

In 1896, Renoir painted his family (below) in the garden of his house in Montmartre. Mme. Renoir, shown wearing an elaborate hat (perhaps arranged by Renoir himself, who loved to dress his models), stands arm in arm with her son Pierre, who would become an actor. Gabrielle crouches at right with little Jean, who is still wearing a dress in this picture. The figure of a young neighbor (right) balances that of Pierre. Claude (known as Coco) had not yet been born.

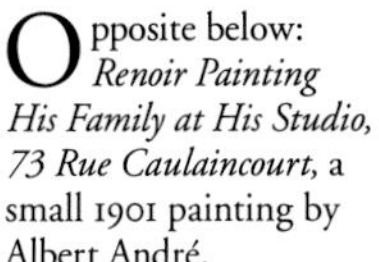

Opposite below: *Renoir Painting His Family at His Studio, 73 Rue Caulaincourt,* a small 1901 painting by Albert André.

Overleaf: Over the years, the nudes that Renoir painted seemed to become more opulent (pages 108–11, in the order mentioned): *Young Girl Bathing* (1892), *Bather* (1895), and even *Sleeping Bather* (1897), according to critic Gustave Geffroy, invoked "small instinctive creatures, simultaneously children and women... sensual without sin." Another critic, Julius Meier-Graefe, called *Bather* (c. 1903) "a transfigured Rubens."

must succeed without it, which is more sporting."

Renoir responded to an informal commission from the administration by painting no fewer than five versions of *Young Girls at the Piano* in oils, plus one in pastels. The purchase was finally made on 2 May 1892 for the sum of 4000 francs. Renoir was only the second living artist from the original Impressionist group from whom the State had bought a painting (the first was Sisley).

In fact, in order to get the State to accept the gift of Manet's *Olympia* in 1890, it took all the perseverance that Monet could muster, as head of the group of private subscribers who had bought the painting from the artist's widow. On that occasion, Monet had asked Renoir for a contribution. Renoir first excused himself due to a lack of funds, but he ended up sending in a small amount.

Woman Playing the Guitar (left), painted about 1896–7 and acquired by the Musée des Beaux-Arts, Lyons, in 1901, indicates Renoir's extravagant propensity for imaginative costumes.

Opposite: Renoir made a self-portrait in 1899 (left). The face shows the marks of age, and the body of the painter, not yet sixty, is already that of an old man whose severe rheumatism has made him dependent on a cane (photographs right).

In 1894, Renoir served as executor of Gustave Caillebotte's estate, with Gustave's brother Martial, whose children he painted in 1895 (below).

The Caillebotte Bequest

Gustave Caillebotte died in February 1894, leaving his collection of works by his friends Cézanne, Degas, Manet, Monet, Pissarro, Renoir, and Sisley, plus two drawings by Jean-François Millet, to the State. This event opened a window on Impressionism's status in the eyes of the public. Renoir was involved on two levels: as artist, since the collection included eight of his paintings—among them *Dancing at the Moulin de la*

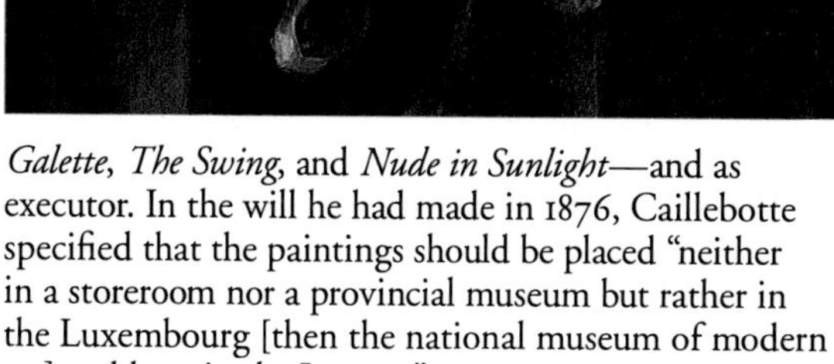

Galette, *The Swing*, and *Nude in Sunlight*—and as executor. In the will he had made in 1876, Caillebotte specified that the paintings should be placed "neither in a storeroom nor a provincial museum but rather in the Luxembourg [then the national museum of modern art] and later in the Louvre."

As Caillebotte had foreseen, the government did not want to display the entire collection of more than sixty paintings. After quite a bit of wrangling (of which Renoir soon wearied), accompanied by a great deal of commentary in the press—both pro and con—forty works were finally selected to be placed before the public in 1897. In spite of official reluctance, Impressionism had penetrated the citadel of the museum.

Caillebotte's bequest contained an unexpected benefit for Renoir, as Caillebotte had stipulated that for his work as executor, Renoir would be permitted to choose for himself a work from the collection. He added, "My heirs insist that he take something important." Renoir selected a pastel by Degas, *Dance Lesson.* Soon after, in need of money, he sold it to Durand-Ruel. Degas found out and never forgave Renoir.

Renoir made numerous portraits of Paul Durand-Ruel's children, but it was not until 1910 that he painted the portrait of the man himself (above), who had discovered Manet and the Impressionists—and had supported Renoir unflinchingly since 1872.

"I Let Myself Be Decorated"

"Whether I've done something stupid or not, I count on your friendship," Renoir wrote to Claude Monet in August 1900. Renoir had been nominated as a chevalier of the Legion of Honor, and his old friend Paul Berard came to deliver the insignia. Author Jules Renard reported Renoir's reaction: "My, my! Yes, you lower your nose, you see the red [ribbon], and, by gum! you hold up your head again."

This honor followed the display of eleven paintings by Renoir at the Centennial Exhibition of French Art, a show officially linked with the Paris World's Fair. Renoir, who continued to distrust the administration, had initially refused to participate, as had Monet and Pissarro, but his friend Roger-Marx, a longtime supporter, persuaded him to change his mind.

Renoir's final offering at the spring Salon was *The Daughters of Catulle Mendès* (1888) in 1890. He no longer needed that forum to present his work. At the same time, he declined to join the ranks of the dissident branch of French artists who created the Salon de la Société Nationale des Beaux-Arts, headed by Pierre Puvis de Chavannes and Jean-Louis-Ernest Meissonier, the same year.

He preferred groups that could be described as avant-garde, like Les XX from Brussels, where he exhibited in 1890, even though he did not share the predilection of the organizer, Octave Maus, for Seurat and his followers. Renoir continued to send works to the successor of

Even if he did business with other dealers Renoir was unquestionably the most faithful of Paul Durand-Ruel's painters, giving him the first look at his works until the end of his career. Renoir seems to have been much less shrewd in his business dealings than Degas or Monet.

Les XX, La Libre Esthétique, in 1894 and 1904, and he also contributed to the Salon d'Automne in 1906, 1910, and 1912.

For the most part, however, Renoir displayed his work in private galleries.

"The Dealers Have Good Qualities, Whatever One May Say About Them, Since the Death of the Medicis..."

"If the wretched painter had to run after the collector before the collector came to him, he would die of hunger." Renoir was thinking above all of Durand-Ruel, his "old friend," in his panegyric to the art dealer. Durand-Ruel clearly had a major influence on the artist's output—not only through his support but through his demands as well—consistently pushing for finished paintings rather than sketches, as Renoir himself acknowledged.

Aided by his son, Paul Durand-Ruel organized several solo exhibitions of Renoir's work, in 1891, 1892 (a major retrospective of 110 paintings), 1896, 1902, and 1908 (at his New York gallery, where he had been active since 1886). Then there were the group shows, notably in New York in 1900 and especially in London in 1905,

When Paul Durand-Ruel took over his father's business as art dealer in 1865, the art trade as it is today barely existed. Durand-Ruel was a pioneer in the field, not only because he was the first to recognize talented artists rejected by popular opinion but also because he set in place all the commercial strategies to support "his" painters: shoring up prices in public auctions, organizing solo exhibitions (like the one at the Grafton Galleries in London in 1905, below), using publications, and perpetually looking for new audiences in France as well as abroad.

at the Grafton Galleries. Unfortunately the London show enjoyed no commercial success, despite the gathering of masterpieces it offered.

In addition to Durand-Ruel, two other dealers had established lasting bonds with Renoir: Ambroise Vollard and the Bernheim-Jeune brothers.

Vollard remembered that his first meeting with Renoir in 1894, soon after he began working as an art dealer, came when he went in asking for information about a painting by Manet. He won the painter's trust, and their relationship lasted until Renoir's death. Vollard liked to have his portrait painted, and the list of artists who portrayed him is long indeed—Cézanne, Picasso, and Bonnard are just a few. Renoir painted him not once but several times, notably in 1908 (above left) with the art dealer holding up a statuette by Aristide Maillol. At Vollard's prodding, Renoir tried his hand at sculpture, assisted by Richard Guino, a young man who had been Maillol's assistant. Renoir created *Venus Victorious* (1914, above) and *Large Washerwoman* (opposite below) in 1917.

Vollard...

Ambroise Vollard gave up his law studies to learn the basics of the trade with a dealer before opening his own shop on the Rue Laffitte, the hub of the Parisian art market. While offering the work of the then-unknown painters Gauguin and Van Gogh, he held the first solo exhibition of Cézanne in 1895. Renoir went to see the latest paintings of his friend there and found in them "an indefinable closeness with Pompeiian art, so unpolished and so wonderful."

Like Manet's widow, Monet, Degas, and Pissarro, Renoir at first gave Vollard only minor works to sell and then, as he got to know the young dealer, developed a more active partnership. Over the following years Vollard's shop, with its dusty display case and its piles of paintings turned toward the walls, became legendary, and its French, German, American, Russian, and Japanese clients began to pay substantial prices for Renoir's work.

Renoir sometimes showed a certain impatience with Vollard's writings on his work. These pieces have remained among the liveliest sources on the artist, even though they should be taken with several grains of salt. Renoir also agreed to the then-new experiment (attempted many times since) of making a catalogue with Vollard, or at least some kind of illustrated documentation of his work in his lifetime.

Yielding to Vollard's urgings, Renoir tried his hand at lithography and sculpture.

Bernheim-Jeune…

At the beginning of the 1890s, Josse and Gaston Bernheim-Jeune had become active in the gallery founded by their father, progressively giving more and more space to the Impressionists and the artists that followed them. The history of their commercial connection with Renoir, beginning with the important show of his work that they organized in 1900, is punctuated by portraits the artist made for the family in 1901 and 1910. Their connection was broken only by Renoir's death. Among their clients were two who had a particular interest in Renoir.

The wife of Josse Bernheim-Jeune and their son Henry (above) came to Les Collettes to be painted by Renoir in 1910.

…And Their Clients

The first, Maurice Gangnat, was an engineer. It seems that he bought his first Renoir painting at the Berard sale in 1905. He got to know the artist through Gallimard, becoming one of his rare intimate friends, and in less than twenty years he bought more than 150 works, which were dispersed at the public sale of his collection after his death.

The second, Louis-Alexandre Berthier, prince of Wagram, was a career soldier, in deference to the family name, and a "young prince

collector of Impressionist painting and driver," as the admiring Marcel Proust described him. Before his premature death in the final battles of World War I, the young man would appreciably reduce his inheritance while pursuing his dual passions: the automobile—paying damages in lawsuits brought against him by the owners of squashed dogs—and, even more expensive, Impressionist painting. In 1905 he started a frantic buying spree, making a tour of all the Paris dealers and expending large sums. He soon decided

Between 1905 and 1910, Renoir represented the rows of roofs of old Cagnes many times, as in *Terrace in Cagnes* (1905, above). This was painted during one of his first visits to the Mediterranean village where he ended up staying for the rest of his life.

he could speculate in painting and first associated himself with the Bernheim gallery and then brought suit against it; the suit was dismissed in the gallery's favor. In 1908 he began selling his collection—which included dozens of very important paintings by Renoir —at a loss.

Thanks to Durand-Ruel, Vollard, Bernheim-Jeune, and their clients of various nationalities, Renoir was known the world over before 1900. While he suffered the gradual loss of his first patrons and friends, the dispersion of their collections only strengthened the commercial appeal of his work, which, like that of Degas and Monet, fetched high prices. Foreign museums also showed an interest; the Metropolitan Museum of Art in New York acquired *Portrait of Madame Charpentier and Her Children* in 1907, while Berlin's Nationalgalerie obtained *Children's Afternoon at Wargemont* in 1906.

Renoir is shown painting at his easel around 1900 (below). This is one of the last photographs taken before illness compelled him to remain seated while working.

The Aging Renoir

While Renoir finally had enough money to live very comfortably, his tastes remained simple, almost austere. During the winter, the rheumatism he suffered led him to seek out the climate of the south of France, where he stayed at Magagnosc, near Grasse. In 1898 he discovered Cagnes-sur-Mer, near Nice, and its mild climate and beautiful landscape, along with his declining health, induced him to buy a property there in 1907, called Les Collettes. He built a house on it, which gradually became his main residence.

"Now that I can no longer count on my arms and legs, I would like to paint large canvases. I dream only of Veronese, of his *Marriage at Cana.* What misery!"

Renoir to Albert André

1919

CHAPTER VI

RENOIR AT LES COLLETTES

There is not a trace of complacency in this image of an old man under his floppy hat that Renoir painted of himself in 1910. Referring to this man of modest appearance, French poet Guillaume Apollinaire wrote in 1913, "Renoir continually grew greater. The most recent paintings are always the most beautiful. They are also the youngest."

"A Place in the French School"

The man who began to spend most of his time at Les Collettes was already an invalid. He traveled little. His last major trip was to Munich in 1910, where he stayed with Frau Franz Thurneyssen, a niece of Berard's, for whom he executed many portraits. Berard himself had died several years earlier.

However, he continued to spend time at Essoyes, and he retained quarters in Paris as well, on the Boulevard Rochechouart. Thus, he was able to accept the invitation of the well-known financier Alfred Edwards and his current wife, Misia (formerly married to Thadée Natanson), to attend one of the earliest performances of the Ballets Russes in Paris in 1911.

In the spring of 1919—three months before his death—Renoir visited the Louvre, which turned out to be his last excursion. He had been invited by Paul Léon, director of the Ecole des Beaux-Arts, to see the small *Portrait of Madame Georges Charpentier* that had recently come into the national collection and was on display. This was not the first work by Renoir to enter the Louvre; the paintings left by Isaac de Camondo had been there since 1914. Renoir thus lived to see one of his most heartfelt wishes realized: "When I view the old masters, it makes me feel like quite a small man, yet I think that out of all my works, enough of them will assure me a place in the French school, that school that I so love, that is so gentle, so clear, such good company…with nothing flashy about it."

Renoir's Influence

In the course of those years, Renoir's work has proved intensely influential. Exhibitions held before World War I in France, at Durand-Ruel and Bernheim-Jeune, as well as in the United States, Germany, Italy, and even Saint

Writer Elie Faure, who knew and admired Renoir in his last years, reported that Picasso called the master "the Pope." The drawing below, which Picasso made after one of Renoir's early paintings, *Alfred Sisley and His Wife*, betokened a form of homage to the old painter. As for Matisse, he affirmed in 1918, "After the work of Cézanne, whose tremendous influence is paramount among artists, Renoir's work saves us from the dryness of pure abstraction."

In June 1907 Renoir bought the estate called Les Collettes in Cagnes-sur-Mer, which had an old farmhouse (left). There he built a modern villa, large and comfortable. Mme. Renoir, ever practical, planted orange trees, mandarin orange trees, and a kitchen garden. Among the hundred-year-old olive trees, Renoir built a large-windowed studio (below), from whose shelter he could continue to paint while having a sense of working outdoors, something he could no longer do because of his poor health. Although the isolation of Les Collettes offered some protection from people coming to seek him out, many pilgrims from as far away as Scandinavia and Japan started to show up, wanting to meet the old master.

After his father's death, Jean Renoir made many films at Les Collettes evoking the painter's world and work. In 1960 Renoir's house was bought by the town of Cagnes-sur-Mer and turned into a museum.

Petersburg, Russia, displayed his most recent work as well as older canvases to a new generation.

The first illustrated monograph on the painter, by German critic Julius Meier-Graefe, was published in German in 1911 and in French the next year.

Many painters expressed their admiration for the old master, whether or not they made the pilgrimage to Les Collettes. Among them were Maurice Denis, Pierre Bonnard, André Derain, Henri Matisse, and Pablo Picasso.

The Barnes Foundation

On the other side of the Atlantic, in the Philadelphia suburb of Merion, Pennsylvania, lived Albert C. Barnes. Barnes had made his fortune with the development and commercialization of a powerful antiseptic, Argyrol. In 1912, he began to collect paintings, advised by his friend American painter William Glackens and a highly informed connoisseur, Leo Stein, who, with his sister Gertrude and their brother Michael, was one of the earliest collectors of Picasso and Matisse. During his trips to Paris, Barnes bought works by Impressionists and Post-Impressionists, notably by Renoir and Cézanne, as well as by Matisse, Picasso, Chaim Soutine, and Amedeo Modigliani.

Fed up with the mockery these choices elicited, he decided to set up a foundation in 1922 to hold his collection, which would be used to educate the public. A sincere democrat, Barnes hoped to make art accessible to everyone, particularly black American workers. At the same time, he limited access to his collections, indulging his resentment toward critics and art historians by excluding every single one of them.

For all of these reasons, until the 1990s—when many pieces from the collection were shown in museums around the world—the Barnes

At the end of his life, Renoir confided to painter Albert André that he had been drawn to sculpture. He also mentioned his admiration for Jean Goujon's reliefs, which seem to be the direct inspiration for *Reclining Nude (La Source)* (1895–7, above); the trompe l'oeil frame surrounding the painting reinforces the allusion.

"I am convinced that I cannot get too many Renoirs," Albert Barnes (left) wrote to Leo Stein in 1913, barely a year after purchasing his first works by the artist.

Foundation and its masterpieces retained a reputation as being mythic and inaccessible. It may be the only place in the world where next to sixty-nine paintings by Cézanne and sixty by Matisse are 180 by Renoir, the earliest among them bought from the living artist. Oddly, Dr. Barnes never actually met the artist he so greatly admired; first the war and then the painter's death intervened.

Behind the portals of the Barnes Foundation (below) is the richest collection of works by Renoir, Cézanne, and Matisse in the world.

The End

Despite his advanced age and his illness, despite the death of his wife in 1915, and despite the war, in which two of his sons were wounded, the last ten years of the artist's life were fruitful.

Imprisoned in his chair and in pain, Renoir stopped walking around 1912 in order to marshal all his strength for painting. The life of the entire household, which his son Jean has evoked with nostalgia, revolved around his painting: The servants posed; easels that would allow him to paint large canvases were improvised, or he simply painted on small pieces of canvas tacked onto a support; brushes were slid into shriveled hands that had been bandaged to avoid irritation. Such resolution impressed his contemporaries and gave rise to the morbid myth of the artist painting with brushes tied to his hands, a false impression that still cannot be dispelled.

It would be best to overlook the quick oil sketches that Renoir made as exercises, like playing scales; the artist's fame and a rising art market have combined to make them more important than they deserve to be. There remain enough finished paintings—portraits and nudes—to demonstrate the astounding scope of the old painter's mastery, deploying an exuberant palette of colors made

Aline Charigot rarely posed for the painter after the 1880s, once she'd become Mme. Renoir. At the time of the portrait with the dog Bob (above), painted in 1910, she had just reached the age of fifty but, like Renoir, she looked older.

The exuberant *The Judgment of Paris* (left), painted about 1913–4, is linked by means of its mythological theme with the Dianas and Venuses of Renoir's early paintings. The painting's origins are in a plaster relief and the sculpture *Venus Victorious*. Renoir's model Gabrielle can be recognized at the extreme right.

deliberately more intense, thinking that the carmine, yellows heightened with green, and deep blues would fade with time.

"I Think I'm Beginning to Understand Something About This"

In working on his favorite themes, Renoir, no doubt inspired by the Mediterranean light, rediscovered classical mythology: Venus, the shepherd Paris, Neptune, nymphs. But too much emphasis can be placed on the subject: The artist said, "The nude woman emerges from the sea or her bed, she is named Venus or Nini. Impossible to make up anything better. Whatever gives me the excuse to group some figures is all I need. Not too much literature, not too many figures to make one think."

Pierre-Auguste Renoir died on 3 December 1919 at Les Collettes. He had taken to his bed with a pulmonary infection. According to his son Jean, a few hours earlier, the painter had asked for his palette and paintbrush in order to paint some flowers. As he handed them back to his nurse, he murmured, "I think I'm beginning to understand something about this."

"Painting was intended, was it not, to decorate walls. Therefore it should be as rich as possible. For me a painting...should be something to cherish, joyous and pretty, yes, pretty!"

Renoir to Albert André
1919

The Bathers (The Great Bathers) (1918–9, below) constitutes Renoir's pictorial legacy. It once again takes up the constant theme of the nude in a landscape: "My landscape is only a prop," Renoir confided to a visitor in 1918. "When I'm painting it I'm trying to fuse it with my figures."

Overleaf: Renoir painting in Cagnes, c. 1903–7.

DOCUMENTS

Letters

Renoir was not highly educated; he wrote in a style that expressed his lively personality and communicated his artistic concerns with humor or feeling. His letters, full of spelling mistakes, accurately reflect the person who wrote them. Those presented here provide a general sense of a career's worth of correspondence.

A letter to Georges Charpentier, 29 January 1882.

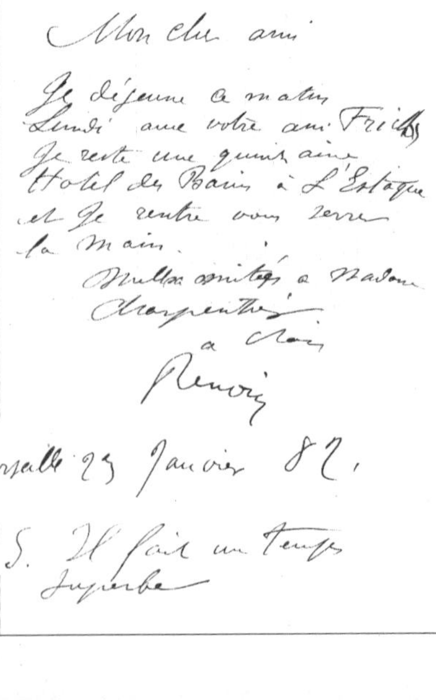

Mon cher ami

Je déjeune ce matin Lundi avec votre ami Fricks Je reste une quinzaine Hotel des Bains à L'Estaque et je rentre vous serrer la main.

Mille amitiés à Madame Charpentier

à vous

Renoir

Marseille 29 Janvier 82.

P.S. Il fait un temps superbe

To Bazille: Household Worries

At the beginning of 1868, Renoir moved in with Bazille at 9, Rue de la Paix aux Batignolles, where they shared a studio. That summer Bazille was in the south of France on vacation at his parents' home, and Renoir wrote to him.

My dear friend, I've just come from Les Batignolles, and I read your letter. Here are the measurements of the windows: four meters high by three meters wide; therefore you need to have four curtains four meters high by two meters wide made up, taking the pleats into account. You'd do well to write to Hardy immediately, to whom I sent the notices of the Salon about a week ago, and I haven't yet seen your paintings in the studio, which makes me worry about the letter that I addressed to 36, Rue du Cherche-Midi. You know I have a small account to settle with him, which makes it impossible for me to write him myself. I can't find the pawn ticket for your watch; tell me exactly where it is. I'm in Ville-d'Avray and rarely come to Les Batignolles, and then only to fetch some things. So that I can do what you want me to do and if you have some money, you'd best send it to me right away, just so you won't use it all up. You don't need to worry about me, seeing as I have neither wife nor child and I'm far from ready to have either one. Drop me a note to let me know if I should see to the carpentry work immediately, which would put me out considerably, since first of all I'm working, plus I don't always have enough to eat in Paris and here I do very well. I'll write a longer letter another time, since I'm hungry and I have a plate of turbot in white sauce in front of me. I'm not putting a stamp on [this letter] since I have only twelve sous in my pocket, and that's for going to Paris when I have to.

in Gaston Poulain,
Bazille et Ses Amis (Bazille and His Friends), 1932

To the Charpentiers: Money and Style

The following two letters were written to the artist's patrons Georges and Marguerite Charpentier in about 1878–80.

My dear friend,

I will ask you, if it's in the realm of possibility, for the sum of three hundred francs before the end of the month, if that's possible, I am very sorry, it is the last time, and I will no longer have to write you anything but banal, completely silly letters without asking you for anything, because you will no longer owe me anything except respect, since I am older than you. I am not sending you my bill because I don't have any.

Now, my dear friend, be kind enough to thank Mme. Charpentier very much on behalf of her most devoted artist, and tell her that I will never forget that if one day I finally make it, I will owe it to her because I certainly am not capable of doing it on my own. I would like to be there already the sooner to express to her all my gratitude.

Friend Renoir
in Barbara Ehrlich White,
Renoir: His Life, Art, and Letters, 1984,
trans. John Shepley with Claude Choquet

Dear Madame

I want to tell you about an idea of Mme. Berard's that in my opinion is not entirely senseless. It is to put the week's fashion on the last page of *La Vie Moderne.*

I would undertake to do the drawings, very accurately, as soon as I get back to Paris. In this way, you will have on your side the whole female staff, who would not always be interested in sketches by [Jean-Louis] Meissonnier [*sic*] or others.

An arrangement could be made with milliners and dressmakers. One week of hats, another of dresses, etc.... I will go to them to do the drawings, from life, from different sides. There's an idea. I'm conveying it to you for what it's worth.

Best regards,
Renoir
trans. in White, *Renoir: His Life, Art, and Letters*, 1984

To Duret: A Thwarted Trip

Critic and collector Théodore Duret made Renoir's acquaintance very early on. This letter was written on Easter Monday, 1881.

My dear Duret,

I'm very embarrassed to tell you why I put off my trip to London. I've just seen Whistler, he was very charming, he came to lunch with me at Chatou, and I am very truly happy to have spent a few moments with this great artist. I tell you all this because were it not for you I would never have dared to speak to him, for I began by mentioning to him your article in the magazine.

Tomorrow I'll lunch with him and I have given him the job of explaining to you the thousand reasons that force me to put off my trip, perhaps to next year. I am struggling with the trees in flower, with women and children, and I have no desire to look at anything else. Still, I'm constantly having regrets. I think of the trouble I caused you for nothing and I ask myself if you will swallow my fickle whims, meanwhile, the whole affair makes me anticipate glimpses of those pretty English women. What a terrible thing it is to be so indecisive, but it's fundamental to my nature and I'm afraid that as I age I will not be able to change. The weather is wonderful and I have models: there, that's my only excuse.

I will have the portraits of the young Cahens at the Salon. I don't know if they will bring the same awful result as my show last year. I hope not.

Whistler told me he left London abruptly and without letting you know[;] he asked me to give you his excuses; he maintains that if he hadn't taken this step, he would not have [been known to have] left, that's true enough.

I will write again soon,

Friend
Renoir.

in Michel Florisoone
"Renoir et la Famille Charpentier"
(Renoir and the Charpentier Family)
L'Amour de l'Art, February 1938

To Durand-Ruel: Why Send Paintings to the Salon?

Renoir left for northern Africa in 1881 after preparing his admissions for the official Salon. He felt it necessary to explain his thinking about the Salon to his dealer Paul Durand-Ruel and sent this letter from Algiers in March.

My dear Monsieur Durand-Ruel,

I shall now try to explain why I am sending to the Salon. There are in Paris barely fifteen collectors capable of appreciating a painter unless he has exhibited at the Salon. There are eighty thousand who will not buy even a nose if a painter is not in the Salon. That is why I send two portraits each year, little though that is. Furthermore, I am not going to fall into the obsessive belief that something is bad just because of where it is. In a word, I don't want to waste my time resenting the Salon. I don't even want to seem to do so. I believe a painter should produce the best painting possible.... That is all. Now if people accused me of neglecting my art, or making sacrifices which go against my own ideas of an idiotic sense of ambition, then I would understand the criticism. But since this is not the case, I cannot be criticized in this way, quite the contrary. All I am concerned with at this moment, as always, is making good things. I want to make you splendid paintings which you will be able to sell for very high prices. I shall soon manage to do this, I hope. I have stayed in the sun, away from all painters, to reflect at length. I think I have reached my aim, and have found what I am looking for. I may be wrong, but it would greatly surprise me. A little more patience and soon I hope to give you the proof that one can send work to the Salon *and* do good paintings.

I therefore beg you to plead my case with my friends. The fact that I am sending work to the Salon is purely a matter of business. In any case, it's like certain medicines. If it does no good, at least it does no harm.

I think I have recovered my health. I shall be able to work solidly and make up for lost time.

Which reminds me, I wish you good health. And a lot of rich collectors. But keep them for my return. I shall be here for another month. I don't want to leave Algiers without bringing back something of this marvelous country. Fondest wishes to our friends and yourself,

Renoir.

in *Renoir: A Retrospective*
ed. Nicholas Wadley, 1987

To Charles Deudon: Goodbye, Venice

Renoir left for Italy in the fall of 1881.

Dear Friend,

Goodbye Veni-i-ce, its lovely gray skies,

Land of promi-i-se, a true pa-ra-dise. I'm off to Rome and next to Naples. I want to see the Raphaels, yessiree, the-Ra, the-pha, the-els. After that, those who won't be satisfied.... I bet they'll say I've been influenced!

I'm sending two awful studies to Paris that will arrive in a fortnight, because I gave them to an art-supply dealer to send when they're dry. I'm sending them to Rue Saint-Georges, you tell me if they remind you of Venice. I've done the Doges' Palace seen from San Giorgio across [the canal], that had never been done before, I think. We were at least six in single file.

Best wishes.

Renoir

in Marcel Schneider, "Lettres de Renoir sur l'Italie," (Letters from Renoir on Italy), *L'Age d'Or*, I, October 1945

To Paul Berard: Italy Forever

It is truly ravishing; the water is wonderful with its reflections of houses. ... I am in love with the sun and its reflections in the water, and to paint them I'd go around the world. But when I'm working on it, I feel my impotence. ... Why bother looking for the sun, since all that I've done doesn't even come close; *he will console himself by going to museums, but* it's nothing next to nature, those great masters come out looking gray and melancholy. It's futile for me to seek out the light, I'll end up like them, black, always black. Sculptors are lucky dogs, their statues stand in the

A letter to Paul Durand-Ruel, July 1885.

sun, and when they are of pure form, they become part of the light, they live in nature like a tree[;] us, we are doomed to interiors or else we fade after a few days, like wilted flowers. Why did I become a painter since I am reduced to admiring without ever imitating, except from such a distance....

Renoir will bring back by way of information a study where I piled chrome yellow on top of bright yellow. You'll see how bad it is. I looked for women, the first day full of enthusiasm, the second day seeing that these [dark women from] Auvergne were horrible. Ah! Paris, with its pretty ladies' hats, with its life. It's a sun that can be represented, why did I leave it?

From sale catalogue of autographs and manuscripts, Drouot-Rive Gauche, Paris, 16 February 1979

To Durand-Ruel: "I'm Still Feverishly Searching"

In Naples Renoir wrote again to his dealer on 21 November 1881.

Dear Monsieur Durand-Ruel,

I've been wanting to write to you for a while but I also wanted to send you a bunch of canvases. But I'm still feverishly searching. I am not satisfied, and I scrape and scrape again. I hope this fever will lift, that's why I'm writing you with my news. I don't think I'll have much to bring back from my trip. But I think I've made progress, which always happens after a long period of searching. We always return to our first loves, but with something extra. Meanwhile, I hope you will forgive me for not having much to show you. But you will see what I will do for you in Paris.

I'm like a schoolboy. The white page should always be neatly written on and boom! a blot. I'm still making blots... and I'm 40 years old. I have seen the Raphaels in Rome. They are very beautiful and I should have seen them before. They are full of knowledge and wisdom. He did not try to do impossible things, like me. But they're beautiful. I prefer Ingres for oil painting. But the frescoes, they are admirable in their simplicity and nobility.

I imagine you are well, and your little family also. But I will see you soon, for Italy is very beautiful. But Paris...Ah! Paris... I am starting on something. I won't tell you what. I would ruin it. I'm superstitious.

in Lionello Venturi
Les Archives de l'Impressionnisme
(The Archives of Impressionism), 1930

At Palermo: An Historic Encounter with Richard Wagner

To an unidentified "Wagnerian friend," Renoir gave an account of his meeting with the composer. The letter is dated 14 January 1882.

My dear friend,

I am very worried about my letter, because after sealing it, I weighed it, uncertain whether to put two stamps. But since I mailed several letters at the same time, I may have put it in another one. Where the hell did it go? Fortunately I have a torn draft of it, so I'm going to try to recopy it as it is, without even asking your indulgence. You know very well that I can't write. That's it, phew!

After having resisted my brother for a long time, he sends me a letter of introduction to Naples, from M. de Brayer. I don't read the letter and above all I don't look at the signature, and there I am on the boat with the prospect of being seasick for at least fifteen hours. It occurs to me to look in my pockets, no letter, I probably forgot it at my hotel, I go through everything on that boat, impossible to lay my hand on it, you see my predicament when I get to Palermo. I find the city sad and I wonder whether I shouldn't take the boat back in the evening. Finally I walk sadly to an omnibus on which is written: Hôtel de France. I go to the post office to find where Wagner is staying; nobody speaks French and nobody knows who Wagner is, but at my hotel, where there are some Germans, I finally learn that he is at the Hôtel des Palmes. I take a carriage and go to visit Monreale where there are fine mosaics, and on the way I abandon myself to a lot of sad thoughts. Before leaving, I send a cable to Naples, without any hope by the way, and I wait; not seeing anything coming, I decide to introduce myself alone, and so there I am, writing a letter in which I ask to pay my respects to the master, my letter ended more or less like this: I will be happy to take news of you back to Paris, especially to M. Lascoux, to Mme. Mendès, I can't put to M. de Brayer, because I hadn't looked at the

Richard Wagner, 1882, resembling a Protestant minister.

signature on my letter of introduction. Here I am at the Hôtel des Palmes; a servant takes my letter, comes back down after a few minutes, telling me in Italian: Non salue [*sic*] il maestro, and he walks away. Next day I receive my letter from Naples, and I present myself again to that same servant, who this time takes my letter from me with obvious scorn. I wait under the carriage entrance, hiding myself as much as possible, not in the mood to be received, because I only brought myself to this second attempt in order to prove to this family that I hadn't come to beg them for 40 sous.

Finally along comes a blond young man whom I take for an Englishman, but he's Russian and his name is Joukovski. He ends up finding me in my corner and takes me into a little room. He says he knows my work very well, that Mme. Wagner is very sorry not to be able to receive me now, and he asks me if I could stay one more day in Palermo, because Wagner is putting the final notes to Parsifal and he is in a state of illness and nerves, and no longer eats, and so on.

I beg him to give my apologies to Mme. Wagner, but I ask only one thing, and that's to leave. We spend some time together and I tell him the purpose of my visit. I see by his smile that it's a failure, then he confesses to me that he is a painter, that he too would like to do a portrait of the master and that for two years he has been following him everywhere in order to fulfill this desire, but he advises me to stay, saying: what he denies me he may grant to you, and anyway you can't go away without seeing Wagner. This Russian man is charming, he ends up consoling me and we make an appointment for the next day at two o'clock. Next day I meet him at the telegraph office. He tells me that yesterday, February [*sic*] 13, Wagner completed his opera, that he is very tired and that I shouldn't come before five o'clock, that he will be there so that I won't be so ill at ease, I accept enthusiastically and go away happy. I'm there at five o'clock sharp, and I run into my servant who greets me with a deep bow, asks me to follow him, and he takes me through a little greenhouse, then into a small adjoining sitting room, sits me down in a huge armchair, and with a gracious smile asks me to wait a moment. I see Mlle. Wagner and a small young man who must be a little Wagner, but no Russian. Mlle. Wagner tells me that her mother is not there, but that her father is coming, and then she takes off. I hear a sound of footsteps muffled by thick carpets. It's the master, in his velvet dressing gown, the wide sleeves lined with black satin. He is very handsome and very courteous, and he shakes my hand, urges me to sit down again, and then the most absurd conversation begins, strewn with uhs and ohs, half French, half German with guttural endings.

I am very gontent. Ach! Oh! and a guttural sound, you are coming from Paris. No, I am coming from Naples, and I tell him about losing my letter, which makes him laugh a lot. We talk about everything. When I say we, I only kept repeating: My dear master, of course, my dear master, and I would get up to leave, and then he would take my hands and put me back in my armchair. Vait a little more, my vife vill be coming, and that goot Lascoux, chow is he? I tell him that I haven't seen him, that I have been in Italy for a long time and he doesn't even know I'm here. Ach! Oh! and a guttural sound in German. We talk about Tannhäuser at the Opéra, in short it goes on for at least three-quarters of an hour, and meanwhile I keep looking to see if the Russian has arrived. Finally he comes in with Mme. Wagner, who asks me if I know M. de Brayer well. I raise my head. M. de Brayer, heavens no, madame, not at all, is he a musician? So then he is not the one who gave you this letter.

Oh, de Brayé, yes, very well, excuse me, we do not pronounce it the same, and I apologize, blushing. But I make up for it with Lascoux, I imitated his voice to show her that I knew him, then she told me to give their regards to their friends when I got back to Paris, and especially to Lascoux, she insisted on it; she repeated it again when I left. We talked about the Impressionists of music. How many foolish things I must have said! I ended up roasting, being completely giddy and red as a rooster. In short, the timid man who plunges in, and goes too far, and yet I know that he was very pleased with me, I don't know why. He detests the German Jews, and among others [the critic Albert] Wolff. He asked me whether we still like [Giacomo Meyerbeer's] Les Diamants de la Couronne in France. I panned Meyerbeer. In the end I had time enough to say all the silly things you can imagine. Then all of a sudden he said to M. Joukovski, if I'm feeling all right at noon, I may let you have a sitting until lunch, you know you'll have to be understanding, but I will do what I can, if it doesn't last very long it won't be my fault. M. Renoir, please ask M. Joukovski if it's all right with him if you do me too, if that doesn't bother him. Joukovski says: But, my dear master, I was just about to ask you, etc., etc.... How would you like to do it? I say, full face. He says to me that's fine, I want to do your back, because I have a composition all ready. Then Wagner says to him, you will do me turning my back on France and M. Renoir will do me from the other side. Ach! Ach! Oh!...

Next day I was there at noon, you know the rest. He was very cheerful, but [I was] very nervous and sorry not to be Ingres. In short, I think my time was well spent, 35 minutes, which is not much, but if I had stopped sooner, it would have been excellent, because my model ended by losing a little of his cheerfulness and getting stiff. I followed these changes too much, anyway you'll see.

At the end Wagner asked to look, and he said Ach! Ach! I look like a Protestant minister—which is true. Anyway I was very glad not to have failed too badly: there is a little souvenir of that splendid head.

Best.

Renoir

I'm not rereading my letter, I would tear it up again and it would be the fifteenth. If there are things I forgot, I will tell them to you.

He repeated several times that the French read the art critics too much. The art critics, Ach! Ach! and a big laugh. The German Jews!, but, M. Renoir, I know that in France there are good guys whom I do not confuse with the German Jews. Unfortunately I'm unable to convey the openness and gaiety of this whole conversation of the master's.

trans. in White, *Renoir: His Life, Art, and Letters*, 1984

To Mme. Charpentier: On the Sun in Painting

On returning from Italy, Renoir made a confession to Marguerite Charpentier toward the end of January or the beginning of February 1882.

Dear Madame,

I got a letter from Deudon at Naples that said that you had spoken of me often which gave me real pleasure, and in addition that you were waiting expectantly for the pastel of your little girl.

I would have had to rush to Paris and I have not done it because I am in the middle of learning a great deal and the

Marguerite Charpentier.

longer I take, the better the portrait will be.... I have constant sun [here] and I can scrape off and begin again as much as I want. That's the only way to learn, and in Paris one must make do with a little [sun]; I've spent a lot of time at the Naples museum, the Pompeian paintings are extremely interesting from all points of view, I also stay in the sun, not to make portraits in the sunshine, but by warming myself and looking around a lot I think I will have arrived at that grandeur and simplicity of the old masters. Raphael who did not work outdoors nevertheless must have studied the sun, as it fills his frescoes. Thus by dint of looking outdoors I got to the point where I see only the larger harmonies without getting lost in the small details that blot out the sun instead of setting it on fire. Therefore I hope on returning to Paris to do something that would show the results of these general studies, and you will benefit from it. I could be deluding myself, as you might well think, but I have done whatever I could to prevent that. Humans were made to fool themselves. Please excuse me.

Best regards, and a firm handshake for Monsieur Charpentier.

Renoir.

in Michel Florisoone, "Renoir et la Famille Charpentier," February 1938

"Independent" Despite Himself

On his return from Italy, Renoir became troubled by Durand-Ruel's plans to enter his paintings in an Impressionist exhibition. He registered his opposition in a letter to his dealer.

L'Estaque, 26 February 1882

My dear Monsieur Durand-Ruel,

...This morning I sent you a telegram as follows: The paintings of mine that you have are your property. I cannot prevent you from disposing of them, but it will not be me who is exhibiting.

These few words express my thought completely.

It is therefore quite clear that I am not having any part of the Pissarro-Gauguin group and that I do not agree to be included in the so-called group of Independents for a single moment.

The first reason is that I am exhibiting at the Salon, which does not fit in with the rest.

Therefore I refuse, and refuse again.

Now you may put in the canvases that you have, without my permission. They are yours, and I do not claim the right to prevent you from disposing of them as you see fit, if it is in your own name. Only let it be clearly agreed and accepted that it is you who, as the owner of canvases signed with my name, are exhibiting them, and not me.

In these conditions the catalog, posters, brochures and other information to the public shall state

Paul Durand-Ruel's large drawing room.

that my canvases are the property of...and exhibited by M. Durand-Ruel.

In this way, I shall not be an "independent" despite myself, if I am not allowed not to be an "independent" at all.

Please do not resent this decision which should scarcely affect you personally, since it is not you who is organizing this exhibition, but M. Gauguin, and believe me your ever devoted and faithful artist. Only, I am protecting our common interest, for I believe that to exhibit there would be to devalue my canvases by 50%. I repeat once more, nothing in my refusal should wound you, for nothing is addressed to you and everything to the gentlemen alongside whom I do not wish to find myself, for my own good, because of my own taste, and in your own interest.

I send you my sincere wishes for your good health and a warm-hearted assurance of my friendship, Renoir.

trans. in *Renoir: A Retrospective*
ed. Nicholas Wadley, 1987

When Hands Can No Longer Write

A poignant late letter from the artist to his dealer and friend.

Cagnes, 27 February 1919

My dear Durand-Ruel,

I was very moved that you took the trouble to write to me yourself, given the pain it costs you. That shows me how much affection you have for me, and please believe that I am very grateful.

Please accept, my dear Durand-Ruel, all my sympathy.

Renoir.

P.S. You were able to write to me, but I cannot respond in kind. That is impossible for me.

in Lionello Venturi, *Les Archives de l'Impressionnisme*, 1930

The Painter in His Own Words

Renoir's contemporaries were entertained by the originality of his language. Some of them collected his sayings and jests, often coloring them with their own personalities. Even so, the tone remains true: It is definitely Renoir speaking. Albert André and Jean Renoir were probably the most faithful transcribers.

Bonnard took this photograph of Auguste Renoir with his son Jean in 1916.

As Told to André

Fascinated by Renoir, painter Albert André was an attentive listener. He made an excellent collection of the painter's offhand comments in the studio.

I made that poor Gleyre crazy way back when, in the studio. He came once a week. He stopped in front of my easel.... It was my first week there. I had set myself to copying the model as best I could.

Gleyre looked at my canvas, assumed a stern air, and said, "No doubt you paint to amuse yourself?"

"But of course," I answered, "and if it didn't amuse me, I assure you I wouldn't do it!"

I am not sure that he understood me.

"The essence of Renoir is revealed in his answer to Gleyre. He painted because it deeply amused him," commented Albert André. "He never believed that by putting pigments on the canvas he was fulfilling a religious mission or, as he laughingly put it, that he was saving the Republic."

Painting was intended, was it not, to decorate walls. Therefore it should be as rich as possible. For me a painting, since we are forced to make easel paintings, should be something to cherish, joyous and pretty, yes, pretty!

There are enough annoying things in life without our creating new ones.

I well know how hard it is to accept that a painting could be a great painting and still be joyous. Because Fragonard laughed, people were quick to say he was a minor painter.

People who laugh are not taken seriously. Art that dresses the part, whether in painting, music, or literature, will always get the attention.

You shouldn't think too much of yourself ...but it's also bad to think yourself worse than everyone else. You should know yourself, know your worth.

When I view the old masters, it makes me feel like quite a small man, yet I think that out of all my works, enough of them will assure me a place in the French school, that school that I so love, that is so gentle, so clear, such good company...with nothing flashy about it.

I have always abandoned myself to fate, I never had a fighter's temperament and I would have given up many times over had not my good friend Monet, who had it himself—a fighter's temperament—bucked me up.

Today, when I look back at my life, I compare it with one of those corks thrown in the water. It spins, then it's taken by an eddy, pops up again behind it, dives, resurfaces, is caught by a weed, makes desperate attempts to free itself and finally disappears, god knows where....

Aphorisms on Art

Jean Renoir found his father's notes, which he transcribed in his book about him. These self-contained thoughts are the elements of the "Grammar of the Arts" that Renoir dreamed of putting in published form for the benefit of young artists.

Everything that I call grammar on primary notions of Art can be summed up in one word: Irregularity.

The earth is not round. An orange is not round. Not one section of it has the same form or weight as another. If you divide it into quarters, you will not find in a single quarter the same number of pips as in any of the other three; nor will any of the pips be exactly alike.

If art is superfluous, why caricature or make a pretense of it?... I only wish to be comfortable? Therefore I have furniture made of rough wood for myself, and a house without ornament or decoration.... I only want what is strictly necessary.... If I could obtain that result I should be a man of taste. But the ideal of simplicity is almost impossible to achieve.

The art lover is the one who should be taught. He is the one to whom medals should be given—and not to the artist, who doesn't care a hang about them.

Go and see what others have produced, but never copy anything except nature. You would be trying to enter into a temperament that is not yours and nothing that you would do would have any character.

Jean Renoir
Renoir, My Father, 1958
trans. Randolph and Dorothy Weaver

Renoir and Albert André in 1906.

In the Studio

Rags on the floor, some white wooden chairs, easels, brushes, oil paints… At first glance, the decor of creation disappointed the uninitiated. But once visitors were admitted into this intimate space of the painter, once they saw him at work among his canvases and his models, they were won over.

A seated nude bather drawn in red chalk.

Renoir Before His Easel

Thanks to painter Albert André, who knew Renoir well toward the end of his life, we can enter his studio at Les Collettes. Before he died, Renoir was able to read the book his young friend wrote about him, published in 1919, and express his gratitude.

His studios, whether in Paris or in the country, are empty of any furniture that might encourage visitors to stay for long. A broken down divan, covered in clothes and old flowered hats for his models; a few chairs that are always cluttered with canvases. But for the eyes there is a riot of color, an Aladdin's cave: finished paintings, waiting to dry, and canvases that are still being worked on. They are all tacked on the wall or lying about the floor, with no thought of presentation. If by chance there is a painting that is framed and hung in a presentable way, it will have been done for, and by, someone else in the Renoir circle.

He wears no special painter's garb. He sits in his armchair, his spindly legs crossed; his poor feet clad in woolen slippers; his body wrapped in shawls; his pale, fine head muffled to the ears in a cap, or a white linen hat according to the season; and in his fingers the ever-present cigarette, which he constantly relights.

He welcomes friends joyfully. But if he suspects that anyone has come to see him out of curiosity, he withdraws into himself, says nothing and becomes totally disagreeable. As soon as he has rid himself of such unwelcome visitors, and is back in front of his easels, he is a man transformed. He whistles, hums the tunes which his models so often sing to him and goes into ecstasies over the beauties which only his eye can find in them.

It is only really in such moments that

he may be persuaded to divulge his theory of art in all its simplicity.

This man, who has put painting above all else in his life, speaks very little of the painting he has done.

"Just look at the light on the olive trees.... It glitters like a diamond. It's pink, it's blue.... And the sky coming through them. It's enough to drive you crazy. And those mountains over there which change with the clouds.... They're like the background in a Watteau."

"Ah! this breast! How very soft and heavy it is! That pretty fold underneath with its golden color.... It's enough to bring you to your knees. If there had never been any breasts, I don't think I should ever have painted figures."

Albert André,
Renoir, 1919, trans. in *Renoir: A Retrospective*, ed. Nicholas Wadley, 1987

From the Sketch to the Finished Painting

When starting on a complicated composition, he doesn't make what you would really call a study. Once his motif is decided on, he does some little paintings in the spirit of the subject. Sometimes it is a single figure, sometimes several. This process is a sort of practice for the definitive work. When it is fixed in his mind, he next draws his composition in sanguine, and traces it on to his canvas.

Drawing with a hard pencil doesn't suit him, even though he has done some admirable studies in that medium. He needs something that is softer than the pencil, and more colorful, in order to realize large masses. His preference is for charcoal or for a brown-red pastel.

He can no longer change brushes while he's working. Once the brush is selected, and strapped between his paralyzed fingers, it travels from the canvas to his pot of turps to be cleaned, back to the palette to be recharged, and then returns to the canvas.

When his hand becomes numb with exhaustion, someone has to retrieve the brush from his fingers, since they cannot open by themselves. He asks for a cigarette, rolls back his wheelchair, screws up an eye, gives a dissatisfied grunt or a modest expression of praise before getting back to work.

"How difficult it is in a picture to find the exact point at which to stop copying nature. The painting must not smell too strongly of the model, but at the same time, you must get the feeling of nature. A painting is not a verbatim record. For myself, I like the sort of painting which makes me want to stroll into it if it's a landscape, or if it's a female figure, to run my hand over a breast or back. Corot has some very coarse ways of describing what I mean."

Albert André,
Renoir, 1919, trans. in *Renoir: A Retrospective*, ed. Nicholas Wadley, 1987

Renoir and His Models

"The model is only there to set me going," he says. "She enables me to dare things that I couldn't invent without her, also to help me back on course if I go too far." So he always likes to have a model in the house, on a permanent basis.

He has a taste for heavy hands and feet. The beautiful, robust girls who have served, almost exclusively, as his models during his last twenty years, have been his youngest children's nurse-maids.

Almost all of his figures reveal this single type of feminine beauty that he favored most. The mouth coming forward as if for a kiss; the bright, joyful eyes; the long torsos with exaggerated hips; the slightly short legs, rounded but not particularly muscular; the feeling of bonelessness. This type becomes more emphatic around 1880; he finds it all around him and imparts it, despite himself, to all of his figures.

A new model disturbs him, holds him back a little. He doesn't feel relaxed enough to work, but often he dares not send her away. Without a word, he gets on with painting a rose in the corner of his canvas, or some clothes draped over a chair, while the girl—quite unaware of her irrelevance—continues to pose.

Albert André,
Renoir, 1919, trans. in *Renoir: A Retrospective*, ed. Nicholas Wadley, 1987

Jean Renoir in the Studio

The second privileged witness is Jean Renoir.

Renoir began by putting incomprehensible little touches on the white background, without even a suggestion of form. At times the paint, diluted with linseed oil and turpentine, was so liquid that it ran down the canvas. Renoir called it "juice." Thanks to the juice, he could, with several brushstrokes, establish the general tonality he was trying for. It covered almost the whole surface of the canvas—or rather, the surface of the eventual picture, for Renoir often left part of the background blank. These open spots represented indispensable values to him. The background had to be very clear and smooth. I often prepared my father's canvases with flake-white mixed with one third linseed oil and two thirds turpentine. It was then left to dry for several days.

But to return to the actual execution of the picture. He would begin with little pink or blue strokes, which would then be intermingled with burnt sienna, all perfectly balanced. As a rule Naples yellow and madder red were applied in the later stages. Ivory black came last of all. He never proceeded by direct or angular strokes. His method was round, so to speak, and in curves, as if he were following the contour of a young breast. "There is no such thing as a straight line in nature." At no time was there any sign of imbalance. From the first brushstroke the canvas remained in perfect equilibrium. Renoir's problem was, perhaps, to penetrate his subject without losing the freshness of the first impact. Finally, out of the mist the body of the model or the outlines of a landscape would emerge, as on a photographic plate immersed in a developing bath. Certain features totally neglected in the beginning took on their proper importance.

He succeeded in taking complete possession of his subject only after a struggle. When painting, he sometimes made you think he was fighting a duel. The painter seemed to be eyeing the movements of his opponent and watching for the last weakness in his defenses. He harassed the subject ceaselessly as a lover harassed the girl who puts up a struggle before yielding. He seemed also be to engaged on a hunt. The anxious rapidity of his brushstrokes, which were urgent, precise, flashing extensions of his piercing vision, made me think of the zigzag flight of a swallow catching insects. I purposely borrow a comparison from ornithology. Renoir's brush was linked to his visual perceptions as directly as the swallow's beak is linked to its eyes.

Jean Renoir
Renoir, My Father, 1958

Auguste Renoir and his model Catherine Hessling in the studio at Les Collettes in 1918.

As Seen by Others

Always indecisive and subject to sudden depressions, Renoir was restless. His nervousness contrasted with the serenity of his painting, which betrayed neither effort nor conflict. The energy that he continued to pour into his painting even after he became old and disabled won his contemporaries' admiration.

Renoir in his studio at Les Collettes.

A Brief Portrait

Edmond Renoir, journalist and brother of the artist, put his pen at the service of the Impressionists. He wrote this portrait for the periodical published by Georges Charpentier.

I promised you a twenty-line portrait: rapt, absorbed, somber, remote, you have seen him rushing across the boulevard dozens of times; forgetful, disorderly, he will come back ten times for the same thing and still forget to do it; always running in the street, always motionless indoors, he will spend hours without moving, without speaking; what is he thinking of? Of the painting he is doing or about to do; he speaks about painting only as little as possible. But if you want to see his face light up, if you want to hear him—oh the wonder of it—humming some gay tune, don't look for him at table, or in places where one normally seeks amusement, but try to catch him unawares while he is working.

Edmond Renoir,
"Cinquième Exposition de la Vie Moderne" (The Fifth Exhibition at La Vie Moderne), *La Vie Moderne*, 19 June 1879, trans. in *Renoir: A Retrospective*, ed. Nicholas Wadley, 1987

A Dinner at the Charpentiers

Once when my father was out painting in the Forest of Marly he suddenly remembered an invitation for that evening to a large dinner party at the Charpentiers'. He was to be introduced to [Premier Léon] Gambetta, who was then at the height of his power. Charpentier wanted to persuade the premier to commission Renoir to do the decoration of a large panel in the new Hôtel de Ville....

The necessity for dressing in formal evening clothes always annoyed him, and once he reached home, instead of changing his shirt, he saved time by putting on a strange combination of starched collar and false shirt front, quite a popular device at that time.

Upon reaching the Charpentiers' house, he solemnly handed his top hat, scarf, gloves and overcoat to the footman, and walked into the drawing room before the astonished footman could stop him. He was welcomed by a burst of laughter, and with good reason —for in his haste he had forgotten to put on his dinner jacket, and was only in his shirt sleeves. Charpentier was highly amused and, to make him feel at ease, took his coat off. All the other men did the same. Gambetta declared that it was very "democratic." And the dinner went on with an extra note of gaiety.

Jean Renoir
Renoir, My Father, 1958

Scandal at Dieppe

While Renoir was graciously welcomed by the Charpentiers and the Berards, some households found his presence jarring. This was the case with the Blanches, as shown in this letter the young painter Jacques-Emile Blanche wrote to his father, the famous psychiatrist Dr. Emile Blanche, from Dieppe in July 1881.

Renoir came to see us yesterday. Mama had invited him, as you know, to come work with me. Not having a room ready, we could not have offered him hospitality, and that's a good thing, as you'll see. Mama asked him to stay for dinner. We remained at the table just under three-quarters of an hour (usually we spend fifteen or twenty minutes). This made Mama so impatient that she said he made it impossible to have dinner with him. After having invited him, Mama sounded off about him, finding him lacking in wit, a dauber, a slow eater with unbearable nervous twitches. So, Mama is going to find a way to uninvite him. And she finds it amazing that I love the solitude of this house!...

Renoir painted a sunset in ten minutes. That exasperated Mama, who told him that he was only "wasting paint"! It was fortunate that this fell on one who never notices anything. As to me, I didn't say a word to Mama, I was so put out.

Jacques-Emile Blanche
in *La Pêche aux Souvenirs*
(Fishing for Memories), 1949

At the Soirees of Mallarmé and of Berthe Morisot

Poet Henri de Régnier wrote an introduction for a book of Renoir reproductions in which he recalled these two gatherings.

It was at Stéphane Mallarmé's that I saw Renoir for the first time.... My first impression was of a thin man with a thin face and an extremely nervous manner. I remember a face ravaged and intelligent, stamped with sensitivity, with observant eyes. Sober in attire and simple in demeanor, Renoir had just made a small portrait of Mallarmé, not a very good likeness, more of a mark of friendship between the painter and the poet than a finished work. Their relationship, if not intimate at least friendly, was most likely formed in Manet's studio, where Mallarmé, a regular, also knew Berthe Morisot, now Madame Eugène Manet.

It was at Berthe Morisot's that I met Renoir again. Mallarmé led me to the Rue de Villejust, and we often went together on Sundays, after the concert. It was a strange place, of a rare distinction. Eugène Manet, Berthe Morisot, and their daughter Julie lived in upper-middle-class style of impeccable taste. Eugène Manet, nervous and earnest, Berthe Morisot, with a haughty and cold courtesy, a remote elegance topped by her white hair, a sharp and sad look, and little Julie, a silent and wild child with innocently colored cheeks who from her beautiful Oriental eye gazed on the greyhound Laertes. They entertained in the living room–studio on the ground floor among the noble Empire furniture. Mallarmé repeated the discourse he had given in Belgium on Villiers de l'Isle-Adam. ... Degas responded to Mallarmé. Teodor de Wyzewa contributed his Slavic subtleties. Renoir tore his bread apart in a gesture at once crude and rustic, with hands that were already deformed....

Henri de Régnier
in *Renoir, Peintre du Nu*
(Renoir, Painter of the Nude), 1923

In Perpetual Motion

Thadée Natanson, founder of La Revue Blanche, *defended the avant-garde circles, literary and artistic.*

A constant agitation hastens Renoir's stride, bows, then straightens his back, sets his twisted fingers moving, ceaselessly propels the frail, restive, irritable frame, lost in loose folds of clothes too large for it. It puckers his skin and makes every facial feature twitch, makes his eyelids flicker, focuses and quickens the nervous gesticulation of the body on the narrow mask: a ravaged face, shrunken, desiccated and drawn, and bristling with gray hairs, where the eyes sparkle, but kindly, above protruding cheekbones.

The nimble fingers constantly pluck and smooth the gray mustache and beard: sparse, rebellious hairs which put the finishing touches to an appearance which is forbidding at first sight, but promptly redeemed by the vivacity of the features and the goodness they express.

He comes and goes, sits down, stands up, has hardly stood up than he decides to sit down again, gets up and goes in search of the latest cigarette forgotten on the stool, no, not on the stool, or on the easel, no, on the table, not there either, and at last he decides to roll another which he may well loose before he has had the time to light it, but which is replaced by a third whose ash may have been cold for a day at least....

His working practice tolerates no audience, even of one, and his volubility is some measure of compensation for the silence his work demands. Once he has finished working, he always finds another means to talk passionately again about painting.

Thadée Natanson,
"Renoir," *La Revue Blanche*, May 1896, trans. in *Renoir: A Retrospective*,
ed. Nicholas Wadley, 1987

A Father Who Did Not Blend In

After Jean Renoir was wounded in World War I, he finally was able to get to know his father. They spent the long hours of his convalescence side by side, talking about the past.

When my father came to see me [at school], he seemed out of place among the other parents. His working jacket, with its buttoned-up collar; his hair, which was a little long under his soft felt hat, contrasted strangely with the starched collars, dark silk cravats, waxed mustaches, and impeccably creased trousers of all the other fathers. Instinctively, they shunned this being from another world. While I was kissing him, I was embarrassed by the astonished looks of my schoolmates.

One Monday, after the first class was over and we were having a break, a boy named Roger came up and spoke to me. His father was head of a big grocery establishment in the section near the Opéra, and owned a villa at Trouville. As the last word in "swank," his mother had had her appendix removed by the great surgeon Doyen. In short, they were people really in the swim. The other boys formed a circle around us. Roger took two sous from his pocket and held them out to me. "Here," he said. "Give this to your father, and tell him to get his hair cut."

I should have taken the money and thanked him for it. My parents had taught me that there was nothing shameful in accepting charity. But it was the first time I had ever heard my father criticized. I felt the blood rush to my head. For a fraction of a second the trees in the court and the faces around me blurred. Then I hurled myself on the blasphemer so fiercely that he was taken by surprise and did not have time to defend himself. He fell to the ground, but I kept on hitting him. I seized him by the throat, and would probably have choked him to death if two or three of the Brothers had not intervened. I was summoned before the Prefect of Studies to explain my behavior. But he could make nothing of my story about my father's hair, so he sent me home for a few days to calm down. At least I got that much out of it. When I returned, I was agreeably surprised to find everyone very considerate towards me. Roger came and shook hands with me. "You should have told me your father was an artist!"

Jean Renoir
Renoir, My Father, 1958

A Snapshot in 1914

Poet Guillaume Apollinaire was also an art critic and an admirer of the old painter.

Yesterday I saw the latest photograph of Renoir, the greatest living painter. He is seated in a caned armchair in his studio; behind him are some canvases, turned around, to his left in the background, a country armoire. With his left hand, Renoir clutches the armchair, the right rests on his left knee. His legs are crossed, the left over the right. He wears black pants, gray jacket, dotted tie, bowler hat. His eyes sparkle, astonishingly expressive, and seem to absorb all the beauty of life.

Guillaume Apollinaire, in *Paris-Journal*, 13 July 1914

Renoir in 1900, when he was fifty-nine years old.

From the Painter's Eyes

His talent and his unaffected personality combined to win Renoir many painter-friends, both fellow Impressionists and younger artists.

Cézanne

The "touchy master of Aix," Paul Cézanne, wrote in a July 1902 letter:

I despise all living painters, except Monet and Renoir.

Degas

Ambroise Vollard reported a presumed dialogue with Edgar Degas, who was critical of the practice of plein-air painting.

[Vollard]: But Renoir, like Claude Monet, didn't he work outdoors?

Degas: Renoir, it's not the same with him; he could do whatever he wanted.

Auguste Renoir with Louis Valtat and Georges d'Espagnat (standing, pouring the absinthe), at Magagnosc, near Grasse, in 1900 or 1901.

You have already seen a cat playing with balls of multicolored yarn.... I will show you a Renoir that I have in my Paris studio; it has a sharpness of tones....

Degas subsided into a reverie: "Renoir," he said, "we don't see each other anymore!"

Ambroise Vollard
En Ecoutant Cézanne, Degas, Renoir
(Listening to Cézanne, Degas, Renoir)
1938

Gauguin

This statement by Paul Gauguin was first cited in 1928, with no source given.

A painter who never knew how to draw but who draws well, that's Renoir.... In his painting...don't look for the line, it doesn't exist; like magic, a pretty spot of color, a caressing light are sufficiently expressive. On the cheeks, as on a peach, a light fuzz ripples, animated by the breeze of love that speaks its music in the ears. One feels drawn to take a bite of the cherry that represents the mouth and, through the pearly laugh, the small, white, sharp child's tooth.

in Adolphe Basler
Pierre-Auguste Renoir, 1928

Monet

In a letter to Gustave Geffroy dated 8 December 1919, Claude Monet gave vent to his grief.

Renoir's death hits me like a painful blow. A part of my life vanishes with him, the battles and the enthusiasms of youth. It's truly hard. And here I am, the only one of the group left.

in Daniel Wildenstein,
Claude Monet, Biographie et Catalogue Raisonné (Claude Monet, Biography and Catalogue Raisonné), 1985

Bonnard

I had just illustrated a small book published by *La Revue Blanche* [in 1898] with several brush drawings when I received a note from Renoir. I did not know him and I had never met him. Renoir wrote me that he liked my drawings. You have a small touch of charm—do not neglect it. You will come across painters much bolder than you, but this gift is precious.... This is what Renoir wrote, more or less, to an unknown beginner.

I knew Renoir when he was still in good health. He had come to lunch with our group, as one of us, in a restaurant in the Place Clichy. Lean in a gray suit, and small hat, he was in a good mood and joked with us. I think he found us a bit too serious.

Later, I saw him at his atelier in the Rue Caulaincourt. Gabrielle was then the usual model, and unhappily, already nurse, as Renoir's hands were beginning to be affected. At noon, the friends who were there went off. Renoir had to go out himself, but lingered to talk. So Gabrielle: "Come on, come and piss...."

When he was living in the Midi, where I spent some months, I would go and see him toward the end of the day, so as not to disturb him at work. I would find him smoking a cigarette while peering at the work in progress....

In his last years, he said to me suddenly one day, "Is it not true, Bonnard, that we must embellish?"

This word could appear troubling to many people who think that to embellish is to introduce foreign formulas and aesthetics into the interpretation of one's vision. But Renoir has made for himself a magnificent universe. He has worked following nature and could project onto a model and a light that might be a bit dull his recollections of more enthusiastic moments.

I thought of Renoir as a somewhat stern father.

Pierre Bonnard,
"Souvenirs sur Renoir" (Memories of Renoir), *Comoedia*, 18 October 1941

Matisse

"Renoir," Henri Matisse said, "was interesting for more than just his painting." Nonetheless, he was a great admirer of the older artist's work. He wrote a text for a catalogue to an Impressionist exhibition in Oslo; an extract follows.

Portraits of Renoir by Bonnard (c. 1916, left) and by Louis Valtat (c. 1904–5, opposite).

Renoir's nature, through his modesty as well as his confidence in life, once the effort was made, allowed him to reveal himself with all the generosity in his being, which remained undiminished by afterthoughts. Viewing his work lets us see an artist who has been blessed with the greatest gifts, who has had the gratitude to respect them.

Henri Matisse,
Catalogue of a French art
exhibition, Oslo, 1918

Denis

Maurice Denis, who made several visits to the master at Cagnes, recounted the subterfuge Renoir used to get a painting by Cézanne into a collector's house. "There is in Cézanne a kind of asceticism which is also to be seen in his art; Renoir did not have such a rigid conception of life or painting," declared Denis.

But Renoir admired Cézanne.... He liked to tell how he had got Chocquet's first Cézanne in that important collection into his home.

Madame Chocquet intensely disliked Cézanne's painting, so discretion was called for. It was agreed that Renoir would look after the picture that Chocquet had just acquired and would keep praising Cézanne in Madame Chocquet's presence. "So, my dear Renoir, you are a great admirer of Cézanne's painting?" "I have a very fine one at home," replied Renoir. "There are a few faults but it is a beautiful thing." "Well bring it tomorrow so we can see it."

Renoir brought it several times only to take it away again. At the foot of the stairs Chocquet would say to him: "No, Renoir, not today, my wife won't want to." At last it was shown, to Mme. Chocquet's great alarm. "But Marie, Marie! it isn't mine. You know perfectly well it belongs to M. Renoir." But Renoir felt that the joke had gone on long enough. He took advantage of Chocquet's absence to tell his wife everything. "Pretend you didn't know, you will make him so happy!" And Cézanne's picture was finally hung in the Chocquets' home.

Maurice Denis
"Renoir," *La Vie*, 1 February 1920
trans. in *Renoir: A Retrospective*
ed. Nicholas Wadley
1987

The Critical Reception

"I detest the critics, who cannot praise one artist without disparaging all the others." In the course of his career, a span of more than a half-century, Renoir was the subject of many articles, some devastating. Still, in his lifetime he saw his work anointed and discussed as a chapter in the history of art.

CATALOGUE

DE

L'EXPOSITION DES ŒUVRES

DE

P.-A. RENOIR

9, BOULEVARD DE LA MADELEINE, 9

Ouverte du 1er au 25 Avril

The following mosaic of texts on Renoir is presented in chronological order.

Lise, the Charming Parisian Girl

Zacharie Astruc was linked with Manet, Bazille, and Zola in the Batignolles group. Therefore, it is not surprising that he was among the first, in 1868, to mention the work of Renoir.

The *Lise* of M. Renoir completes an odd trinity that started with the very strange, powerfully expressive and notorious *Olympia*. In the wake of Manet, Monet was soon to create his *Camille*, the beauty in the green dress, putting on her gloves.... Here now is *Lise*, the most demure of them all. Here we have the charming Parisian girl, in the Bois, alert, mocking and laughing, playing the "grande dame" somewhat gauchely, savoring the shade of the woods for all the agreeable diversions that may be had there: the dancing, the open-air café, the fashionable restaurant, the amusing dining room fashioned from a weird tree....

It is an original image. The painting has great charms: beautifully rendered effects, a delicate scale of tones, a general impression that is unified and clear and well conceived lighting. The art that has gone into this painting seems simple, but in fact it is very unusual and very interesting. Given a subject whose whole charm is its light, it could hardly have been executed with greater clarity. The sunlit whites are delicious. Wherever the eye wanders, it is enchanted by the finest of nuances and very distinctive lightness of touch.

Zacharie Astruc,
"The Grand Style: Renoir," *L'Etendart*, 27 June 1868, trans. in *Renoir: A Retrospective*, ed. Nicholas Wadley, 1987

In 1870 Fantin-Latour painted, in homage to Manet (at the easel), *A Studio in the Batignolles,* which depicted Renoir (standing, with a hat on), along with Monet, Bazille, Zola, Otto Schölderer, Astruc, and Maître.

The Prodigal Child of M. Gleyre

Arsène Houssaye, editor-in-chief of L'Artiste, *was a prolific writer. Administrator of the Comédie-Française and then inspector of the provincial museums, he was also one of the first supporters of Monet and Renoir.*

The two real masters of this school, which is concerned less with art-for-art's sake than nature-for-nature's-sake, are MM. Monet (not to be confused with Manet) and Renoir, two true masters, like Courbet of Ornans, by virtue of the brutal candor of their brush. I am told that the [Salon] jury has rejected Monet, but had the good sense to admit Renoir. This painter, as we see, has a fiery temperament, which bursts upon the scene brilliantly in a *Woman of Algiers* which might have been signed by Delacroix.

His master, Gleyre, might well be surprised at having produced such a prodigal son, who mocks every rule of grammar by daring to do things in his own way. But Gleyre is too great an artist not to recognize art whatever its forms of expression.

So remember the names of M. Renoir and M. Monet. I have in my gallery the *Woman in a Green Dress* of Monet and an early bather of Renoir, which I shall present one day to the Luxembourg Museum, when the Luxembourg

Museum opens its doors to all painting without prejudice.

Arsène Houssaye,
L'Artiste, 1 June 1870, trans. in *Renoir: A Retrospective*, ed. Nicholas Wadley, 1987

"Romantic Impressionist"

Philippe Burty, author and art historian, was among the first to defend the Impressionists.

M. Renoir is certainly an Impressionist, but he would be more accurately characterized as a "romantic Impressionist." Highly sensitive in temperament, he is always afraid of being too assertive. By using the odd touch to emphasize all that is unmoving, in *Dancing at the Moulin de la Galette*, (chairs, benches, tables) he would leave the group of dancers and speakers a true sense of movement, the rays of sunlight their tremulous patches, and would imbue the whole scene with an air of reality which in fact is lacking. The drawing of the features in the portrait of our friend Spuller lacks solidity; but his expression is intense; the eyes think, the flesh is alive. The portraits of Mme. Alphonse Daudet and Mme. Georges Charpentier are true to life. The portrait of Mlle. Samary renders the pretty face of a pert soubrette so well and so aptly evokes the particular stage atmosphere that one has to go back as far as the vivid sketches by Fragonard to find, not points of literal comparison, but similarities in the French temperament as applied to portrait painting.

Philippe Burty
"Exposition des Impressionnistes"
(Exhibition of Impressionists)
La République Française, 25 April 1877
trans. in *Renoir: A Retrospective*
ed. Nicholas Wadley, 1987

An occasional art critic, Renoir contributed to the periodical *La Vie Moderne*. He illustrated the cover of 1879 with a portrait of genre painter Léon Riesener.

Canvases with Rainbow Colors

Writer Joris-Karl Huysmans was also one of the most personal of the art critics in the years 1880–90. L'Art Moderne, *a collection of his critical essays, was published in 1883 by Georges Charpentier.*

Oddly enamored of the reflections of the sun on velvet skin, the play of dancing sunbeams over hair and cloth, M. Renoir has bathed his figures in true sunshine, and it is something to see what adorable nuances, what fine rainbows come to light on the canvas! These paintings are surely among the most tasty of the Salon's offerings.

Joris-Karl Huysmans
"Le Salon Officiel de 1881"
(The Official Salon of 1881)
L'Art Moderne, Paris, 1883

"Visions as Profound as Those of Stendhal"

Octave Mirbeau quickly became the champion of the Impressionists, whom he defended brilliantly in his sarcastic and penetrating articles. A great art collector, he had a very fine collection of works by Monet and Van Gogh.

Whatever woman can evoke of grace, of tenderness, of seduction, of dreams, and of coquetry; whatever she has of mystery and morbidity; the indefinable in her look, as deep as the abyss, and the radiance of her skin, on which "perfume prowls"; the sweetness of her eighteen years, blossoming with chaste desires and hopes; her melancholy moods, when she goes, slowly, her eyes circled with shadows, under the shadows of a park that make the purple shadow of the leaves tremble and trail on her light dresses; her abandon when, her back arched, her breast working, she leans her head, shivering and all blonde, on the shoulder of a waltzer, and lets herself be carried away; her attitudes of knowing research and studied provocation, in the brilliant light of a theater box, her eyes taking in everything while

Washerwomen (c. 1912, above) and a study for *The Bathers* (c. 1886–7, below).

appearing lost in space, her ears hearing all while seeming oblivious to nearby murmurs, and to her bare arm resting on the velvet border, lying delicious and heavy, partly covered by the folds of her glove, and circled at the wrist by a dark gold bracelet; the peals of laughter from her lips lit by pleasure and the emphatic merriment in her bold glances; the pains of disillusionments come too soon; the dream of an ideal that will never be realized; the misery of passion beginning, and the disgust of passion ending; the entire poem of love and cruelty that this cruel and charming creature recites; she who offers herself, who hides herself, who understands, who caresses. All this Renoir has understood, grasped, expressed. He is truly the painter of woman, by turns gracious and emotional, wise and innocent, always elegant, with an exquisite sensitivity in her eyes, caresses of the hand as light as kisses, visions as profound as those of Stendhal. He not only paints deliciously the plastic forms of the body, the delicate patterns, the resplendent tones of the young carnations, he also paints the form of the soul, and that aspect of woman that expresses an internal *musicality* and a captivating mystery. His figures, unlike those by most modern painters, are in no way rooted in layers of paint; they sing, animated and lively, the entire scale of clear tones, all the melodies of color, all the vibrations of light.

Octave Mirbeau
"Renoir," *La France*, 8 December 1884

"The Prettyish Babbling Bauble"

A friend of Gauguin and Emile Bernard and the discoverer of Van Gogh, Albert Aurier was a paragon of the symbolist critic, gone too soon.

In that immense and pretty toy bazaar that for him constituted the universe, it was naturally by the tinted applelike cheeks, by the invariably smiling red lips, by the lovely enameled, intensely blue eyes of dolls, adorable dolls, with pink porcelain flesh and shimmering satin finery, that especially and immediately attracted Renoir.

The woman, he wanted to paint the woman, the exquisite, the prettyish babbling bauble, hopping and skipping, that he adored and whose soul, as he guessed, could not be after all very different from the works of a clock, often not running…and, among all women, among all those sweet automatic amusements, among all those dainty artificial beings, it was those who had the most pronounced artificial character. The most obvious, these most attracted and seduced him.…

Given such ideas, such a vision of the world and of femininity, it might be suspected that Renoir created a work that was merely *pretty* and merely *superficial*. Superficial—it is nothing of the kind; profound, on the contrary, for if, in fact, the artist has almost entirely suppressed the intellectuality of his models, he has compensated by throwing all of his own intellectuality into his paintings, and we shall see how exceptionally curious that intellectuality was. As to the nature of *pretty*, it is, in his work, undeniable, but vastly different from the insupportable *pretty* that most fashionable painters exploit. Renoir's *pretty*, which is *pretty* pushed to the furthest limit of affectation, *pretty* par excellence and even impossible, becomes prodigiously interesting, first of all by its very excess and then because it is, in some way, a philosophical *pretty*, a symbolic *pretty*, symbolic of the soul of the artist, of his ideas, his cosmological beliefs.… Psychically organized as he has shown himself to us, how, in effect, was he able to perceive the things and the beings otherwise than with pretty outsides, since the only goal of the beings and the things seem to him to charm, to be joyful, to amuse his child's soul, his artist's soul?

Albert Aurier
"Renoir," *Le Mercure de France*, August 1891

Painting: The Corollary of Vision

Faithful to Renoir, Octave Mirbeau offered a moving homage to the old painter on the occasion of a retrospective of his work held at the Galerie Bernheim-Jeune in 1913.

In this exhibition and this book containing his complete works year by year we see Renoir as the equal even of those whose glory is firmly rooted in universal acclaim. And yet it is among us that he lives and paints, and lives. His painting is inseparable from the man himself. Other painters have set themselves problems, the great problems. They have given us sonorous meditations on the purpose and limits of life, the relation between art and life and the place of art in life and life in art. Esthetes, critics, philosophers, apostles and pedants all offer us an explanation of the world when they condescend not to save it. They have solved all the problems, as if life were a problem, as if there were some solution to life other than life itself, and as if a picture were something other than the happiness that it wrests from nature and gives to men. Renoir has been painting. And I can imagine the astonishment of the beautiful women and young poets. He has been painting, yes painting, in the true sense. Since when has a painter needed to paint?

Renoir paints as you or I breathe. For him, painting has become the corollary of vision. Other people's eyes cannot resist the temptation to wander. But with Renoir his hand has to set down in space the happiness he has seen with his eyes....

Renoir's work has developed by the year, by the month and by the day, as simply as a flower opens out its petals or a fruit ripens. Renoir has not given a thought of fulfilling his destiny. He has lived and painted. He has done his job. It is perhaps there that his genius lies. Furthermore, his whole life and work are a lesson in happiness. He has painted joyfully, with joy enough not to shout from the rooftops that joy in painting that sad painters proclaim lyrically. He has painted women and children, trees and flowers with the admirable sincerity of a man who believes that nature is at the disposal of his palette as simply as if it had been created from all eternity to be painted....

Renoir is perhaps the only great painter who has never painted a sad picture.

Octave Mirbeau
Renoir (exhibition catalogue), 1913
trans. in *Renoir: A Retrospective*
ed. Nicholas Wadley, 1987

Vollard: "Renoir Did My Portrait"

Noted art dealer Ambroise Vollard is also known for his books about Cézanne, Degas, and Renoir, among others. Georges Besson claimed that Renoir accused Vollard of grabbing witticisms on the fly and "then rushing to his study to note them down." The following text, first published in 1920, conveys his tone. Vollard has proven to be an unreliable witness, but for the historian, his writings remain an important source—to be used with caution.

I had already posed for Renoir several times. He had made a lithograph and three oil studies of me, one of them quite finished, in which I am painted with my elbows resting on a table, holding up a statuette by Maillol (1908).

With that I thought I was satisfied. But this was before Renoir did the portrait of Bernstein (1910), that canvas of such an extraordinary harmony in blue.

From that moment, my strongest wish was to have a portrait of me in the same harmony in blue.

Renoir agreed, but on one condition: "As long as you wear a costume of a blue tone that strikes me; you know, Vollard, that metallic blue with silver glints."

I thus gave myself over to blue; but to each new article of clothing that I found, Renoir told me, "No, it's not right yet."

In 1915, I spent several days at Les Collettes. I had forgotten about the portrait. As I was crossing the meadow of orange trees that line the road to the house, I heard someone calling, "Hey, Vollard!"

It was Renoir, returning from the countryside, carried in an armchair with handles by "Big Louise" and Baptistin, the gardener. The model walked ahead, carrying the canvas.

The two porters stopped.

"Don't go so fast, Madeleine," Renoir called to the model, "I want to look at my painting." To me: "For a good fortnight I couldn't go out, and I had an awful need to freshen my vision.... I only had a few brushstrokes left to give my canvas, and I was counting on beginning something with Madeleine, but they'd forgotten to set up my umbrella. What a magician the sun is! One day, in the Algerian countryside, with my friend [Lhôte], we suddenly noticed a wonderful character astride a donkey. He came near: It was simply a beggar, but in the sun his rags looked like jewels."

The model had placed the painting on the ground, against a tree.

"That's not bad, is it?" Renoir said, with a small wink.... "Unfortunately, in the light of the apartment my canvas will look totally dark, but

when it's 'gone through' the studio, in a short session, I'll restore all the brilliance!"

When we arrived at the studio: "Vollard, call my 'doctoress'!"

And, responding to my bewilderment, "I absolutely cannot get used to the word 'nurse'!... Your hat is striking! I have to do something with you.... Sit down on that chair.... You are in a truly peculiar light, but a good painter can work around every kind of light!...You don't know what to do with your hands; here, take hold of Claude's cardboard tiger or, if you prefer, that cat sleeping in front of the fireplace."

I opted for the cat, and worked hard at winning its favor and was fortunate enough that, after purring a moment, it fell asleep on my knees.

The "doctoress" was preparing the palette. Renoir named the colors, she pressed the tubes.

Once the palette was ready, and just as the nurse was sliding the brush between his fingers, Renoir exclaimed, "And my 'thumb' that you've forgotten!"

Around 1901, on the Bernheim estate at Fontainebleau, Renoir executed outdoors a portrait of Suzanne Adler, who later became Madame Gaston Bernheim.

I could see my portrait being jeopardized; but the "doctoress" found the "thumb" in the pocket of her apron.

Renoir always "attacks" his canvas without seeming to take any thought for setting the scene. All you see are spots and more spots, until suddenly, amid these scrawls, a few strokes of the brush "bring out" the subject. Even with his dead fingers, Renoir can still do a head in a single sitting, as before.

I could not lift my eyes from the hand that was painting. Renoir noticed: "You can see, Vollard, that the hand is not essential for painting! The hand, that's crap!"

Ambroise Vollard
Auguste Renoir, 1920

"The Delight Which He Communicates"

In 1910–2 English painter and critic Roger Fry had two exhibitions of Impressionist paintings in London, which helped increase awareness of modern French art on the other side of the English Channel.

More than any other great modern artist, Renoir trusted implicitly to his own sensibility; he imposed no barrier between his own delight in certain things and the delight which he communicates. He liked passionately the obviously good things of life, the young human animal, sunshine, sky, trees, water, fruit; the things that everyone likes; only he liked them at just the right distance with just enough detachment to replace appetite by emotion. He could rely on this detachment so thoroughly that he could dare, what hardly any other genuine modern has dared, to say how much he liked even a pretty sight. But what gives his art so immediate, so universal an appeal is that his detachment went no

Renoir dedicated this self-portrait "To Vollard, my favorite bore."

further than was just necessary. His sensibility is kept at the exact point where it is transmuted into emotion. And the emotion, through it has of course the generalised aesthetic feeling, keeps something of the fullness and immediacy of the simpler attitude. Not that Renoir was either naive or stupid. When he chose he showed that he was capable of logical construction and vigorous design. But for his own pleasure he would, as he himself said, have been satisfied to make little isolated records of his delight in the detail of a flower or a lock of hair.... Renoir...could trust recklessly his instinctive reaction to life.

Roger Fry
"Renoir," *Vision and Design*, 1920
in *Renoir: A Retrospective*
ed. Nicholas Wadley, 1987

Cézanne, Renoir, Women, and Sensuality

Maurice Denis was a painter, a theoretician, and a great admirer of Renoir, who painted a portrait of his wife. After hearing the funeral oration for Renoir, he wrote a long text, concluding by contrasting the art of Cézanne with that of Renoir in the form of a manifesto, which he took up again in his book Nouvelles Théories *(New Theories) in 1922.*

Whereas Cézanne insists on his cubes, spheres, and cylinders with the severity of a Spanish master, Renoir diverts himself by coaxing out invisible transitions between levels. The one is a great but clumsy decorator and logician; the other is a skillful sensualist who abandons himself to his imagination. "Renoir," Cézanne tells us with a hint of disdain, "Renoir, well, what do you expect? He painted Parisian women!" Cézanne's women, on the other hand, have never existed anywhere but in paintings in museums. The angles overlap, the objects sit upside down, but whether he copies or imagines, it all has a style; the painting is complete and, as Renoir says, he cannot place two dabs on a white canvas without it being *painting!* Both of them age well: their color ripens. Renoir's bold gamut, his combinations of wine and brick red calm down and take on a golden hue. Cézanne takes on solidity, like a wall. Renoir's painting becomes as transparent as a lake, as shimmering as silk....

Art's goal is delight. Since Cézanne, our pleasure has been primarily intellectual. In the old aesthetic, intelligence and the senses were in no way opposed, nor the idea of the painting against the imitation of nature.

Let us hope to return to that fortunate time, and that Renoir's example will offer us the taste for the real and the feeling, for common sense and sanity. In the realm of art,

Là, tout n'est qu'ordre et beauté
Luxe, calme et volupté.

(There, all is but order and beauty,/ Richness, quiet, sensuality.)

I am for order. But I find that by virtue of organizing polyhedrons, pipes, women without heads and faces without noses, by virtue of harmonizing clashing colors that are dirty and muddy, it becomes all too easy to forget the role sensuality plays in painting. And the luxury, the richness of the business! The calm, the continuity in the effort! And, above all, the sensuality. That is what Renoir teaches.

Maurice Denis
"Renoir," 1 February 1920
in *Nouvelles Théories*, 1922

Barnes: Expanding the Boundaries

One of Renoir's greatest patrons, Albert C. Barnes, the American millionaire and art collector, wanted the world to know about the artist's unique abilities.

The vital importance in art of a constantly increasing capital of aesthetic meaning, may be illustrated by a comparison of Monet's work with Renoir's. Because Monet's sensitivity and interest were practically restricted to the field of out-of-door light-and-colour effects, each new impact upon his sense called forth a type of reaction similar to previous reactions; selection and interpretation took place each time according to the monotonous dictates of his fixed set habits and limited background, and correspondingly, failed to enrich the latter by expanding the boundaries of his vision.

Renoir too was interested in the impressionistic interpretation of nature and in Monet's technical method of expressing it; but the impact upon his senses, and his interpretation of what was being done by his contemporaries, instead of limiting his field of vision, quickened his sense of perception and broadened his insight. Thus the impressionistic form itself, in Renoir's hands, acquired a richer meaning because his keener perception and greater freedom of receptivity had discovered in it fuller possibilities than were ever suspected by its originators.

A set of landscapes by Monet offers great variety in subject-matter—especially in their character of illumination at different times of the day; but the essential quality expressive of the interaction of the scene with the man's personality is monotonously alike in all. Monet, in other words, was awake to only certain phases of life, beyond which his specialised vision seldom reached; Renoir, on the other hand, was continuously unfolding in his perception of Nature. He consistently inquired for, discovered, selected, established, organised and expressed new pictorial effects, connections, relationships, values and meanings, all reflecting a wide field of life activities, and a profound assimilation of the great traditions of painting. In contrast to Monet, Renoir could paint the very same spot of landscape a number of times and each version would reveal an essentially different ramification of his spirit and feelings.

Albert C. Barnes and Violette de Mazia
The Art of Renoir, 1935
in *Renoir: A Retrospective*
ed. Nicholas Wadley, 1987

Renoir's painting in the 1904 Salon d'Automne at the Grand Palais.

What Is It About Renoir?

The influential 20th-century American critic Clement Greenberg examines his reactions to Renoir's paintings.

My reactions to Renoir keep changing. One day I find him almost powerful, another day almost weak; one moment brilliant, the next merely flashy; one day quite firm and the next merely soft. The extraordinary sensitivity of his pictures—even, and sometimes especially, the late ones—to the lighting under which they are seen has, I feel sure, something to do with this. Supposedly, the Impressionist aesthetic made lighting

ALAIS — Salon d'automne
Salle Renoir.
Serie spéciale — 8 — A. B.

and distance all-important factors in the viewing of a picture—but only supposedly. None of the Impressionists themselves seems actually to have made any more of a case about viewing conditions than artists usually do, and successful Impressionist pictures will generally declare their success under the same conditions as other successful pictures. That Renoir's should form such an exception would seem to be due to Renoir himself rather than to Impressionism.

I think part of the explanation may lie in the very special way in which he handled light and dark, making their contrasts seem just barely to coincide with contrasts of pure color; it may be for this reason that his contrasts tend to fade under a direct or bright light or when seen too near. But the un-Impressionist variety of Renoir's subject matter may also help to explain the fluctuations in one's response to the quality of his art. Landscape, still life, portrait, figure, group and even anecdote—he went from one to another easily and often, if not always with success. Even the best of his landscapes, which came around 1880, lack a certain finality, and so do the famous group scenes of earlier date. With the single figure, the still life and the flower piece—things he could see with an un-Impressionist closeness—he could at the same time succeed more consistently. On the other hand, some of the best pictures of his old age—and thus some of the very best of all his pictures—are group compositions....

Perhaps we are still too close to Renoir fully to appreciate [his] uniqueness. The current notion of what constitutes paint quality and highly finished painting derives very largely from his art, which in his own time was reproached, like that of the other Impressionists, for crudeness of *facture* and lack of finish; and this notion is a compromising one. At the same time, his method of high-keyed modeling has become a staple of academic modernism.

Clement Greenberg
"Renoir," *Art and Culture*, 1950
in *Renoir: A Retrospective*
ed. Nicholas Wadley, 1987

Museography

All the great museums of the world own some works by Renoir. Among the most notable collections are those of the Musée d'Orsay, Paris; the National Gallery, London; the Pushkin Museum of Fine Arts, Moscow; the Hermitage, Saint Petersburg; the Nationalgalerie, Berlin; the Museum Folkwang, Essen; the Nationalmuseum, Stockholm; the Museu de Arte, São Paulo; the National Gallery, Washington, D.C.; the Art Institute of Chicago; the Boston Museum of Fine Arts; and the Philadelphia Museum of Art.

However, two of the artist's greatest masterpieces are housed in less-famous museums: *The Box (La Loge)* is in the Courtauld Institute Galleries, London, and *Luncheon of the Boating Party* is in the Phillips Collection, Washington, D.C. Finally, two extraordinary collections of Renoir's paintings are found in two lesser-known American museums: the Barnes Foundation in Merion, Pennsylvania, which has 180 works, and the Sterling and Francine Clark Art Institute in Williamstown, Massachusetts, which has more than thirty.

The Barnes Foundation, created in 1922, is more of an educational establishment than a true museum, following the wishes of its founder, Albert C. Barnes. His collection of French painting from the end of the 19th century and the beginning of the 20th, ranging from Manet to Matisse, is exceptional in both quantity and quality. For many years, it was shown only to students approved by the foundation and some visitors chosen by the founder and then by his heirs. Recently, as the buildings were being restored, the authorities who control the foundation for the first time allowed a selection of masterpieces that had never left the confines of the Barnes Foundation since their acquisition (for some of them, more than eighty years) to be exhibited in Washington, D.C., London, Paris, and Tokyo, and other venues.

The Sterling and Francine Clark Art Institute in Williamstown, Massachusetts, was founded in 1955 through the generosity of Sterling Clark, whose fortune is linked with the Singer sewing machine. Like Dr. Barnes, Sterling Clark started forming his collection before World War I and built it around 19th-century French, English, and American art, as well as a selection of ancient art.

Two locations in France preserve the artist's memory.

At Cagnes-sur-Mer, his house Les Collettes, in its original state, surrounded by hundred-year-old olive trees, houses a museum, with several works by the artist. It was created by the town in 1960 with help from the Committee for the Purchase and Artistic Use of the Renoir Estate and from the Alpes-Maritime Department.

At Chatou, on the island known as the Impressionists', the Fournaise restaurant has recently returned to its original function, and one can now lunch on the famous terrace overlooking the Seine, as in Renoir's time. This resurrection was made possible by the Association of the Friends of the Fournaise House and the municipality of Chatou, which set up a museum in the same building.

The island of Chiard at Chatou, on the banks of the Seine.

Further Reading

The following list includes only major works on the subject, all of which include excellent bibliographies.

GENERAL WORK

Rewald, John, *The History of Impressionism,* Museum of Modern Art, New York, 1973, 4th rev. ed.

MONOGRAPHS

André, Albert, *Renoir,* Cahiers d'Aujourd'hui, G. Crès, Paris, 1919

André, Albert, and Marc Elder, *Renoir's Atelier,* Alan Wofsy Fine Arts, San Francisco, 1989

Baudot, Jeanne, *Renoir, Ses Amis, Ses Modèles,* Editions Littéraires de France, Paris, 1949

Daulte, François, *Auguste Renoir, Catalogue Raisonné de l'Oeuvre Peint,* vol. 1: *Figures 1860–1890,* Editions Durand-Ruel, Lausanne, 1971 (future volumes are in the works)

Drucker, Michel, *Renoir,* Pierre Tisné, Paris, 1944

Fezzi, Elda, *L'Opera Completa de Renoir nel Periodo Impressionista, 1869–1883,* Milan, 1972

Haesaerts, Paul, *Renoir: Sculptor,* Reynal & Hitchcock, New York, 1947

House, John, Anne Distel, and Lawrence Gowing, *Renoir,* Harry N. Abrams, 1986

Meier-Graefe, Julius, *Auguste Renoir,* R. Piper, Munich, 1911

Pach, Walter, *Renoir,* Harry N. Abrams, New York, 1950

Renoir, Jean, *Renoir, My Father,* Little, Brown and Company, Boston, 1958

Rivière, Georges, *Renoir et Ses Amis,* H. Floury, Paris, 1921

Vollard, Ambroise, *Tableaux, Pastels, et Dessins de Pierre-Auguste Renoir,* 2 vols., Alan Wofsy Fine Arts, San Francisco, 1989

Wadley, Nicholas, ed., *Renoir: A Retrospective,* Park Lane, New York, 1987

White, Barbara Ehrlich, *Renoir: His Life, Art, and Letters,* Harry N. Abrams, New York, 1984

List of Illustrations

All works are by Pierre-Auguste Renoir unless otherwise indicated.

Key: ***a***=above; ***b***=below; ***c***=center; ***l***=left; ***r***=right; o/c=oil on canvas

wood engraving, 1904–5, 13 x 10". Musée de Bagnols-sur-Cèze
154 Frontispiece of catalogue of 1883 Renoir exhibition at the Durand-Ruel Gallery
155 Henri Fantin-Latour. *A Studio in the Batignolles,* o/c, 1870, 68 1/2 x 82". Musée d'Orsay, Paris
156 Cover of *La Vie Moderne,* no. 2, detail, drawing by Renoir, 1879. Bibliothèque des Arts Décoratifs, Paris
157a *Washerwomen,* o/c, c. 1912, 25 1/2 x 21 1/2". The Metropolitan Museum of Art, New York. Gift of Raymonde Paul in memory of her brother C. Michael Paul
157b *Study of Two Left Nudes,* study for *The Bathers,* red and white chalk on paper, c. 1886–7, 49 1/4 x 55 1/8". Fogg Art Museum, Harvard University, Cambridge, Mass.
160–1 Photographs of Renoir and his model in the garden of the Bernheim estate at Fontainebleau, c. 1901
162 *Self-Portrait,* 1916, in Ambroise Vollard, *La Vie et l'Oeuvre de Pierre-Auguste Renoir* (The Life and Work of Pierre-Auguste Renoir), Paris, 1919. Bibliothèque Nationale, Paris
164–5 Photograph of the Renoir room at the Salon d'Automne, 1905 or 1906. Collection Debuisson, Paris
166 Photograph of Chatou, island of Chiard

Index

Page numbers in italics refer to captions and/or illustrations.